THE ROUTLEDGE COMPANION TO GENDER, SEX AND LATIN AMERICAN CULTURE

The Routledge Companion to Gender, Sex and Latin American Culture is the first comprehensive volume to explore the intersections between gender, sexuality, and the creation, consumption, and interpretation of popular culture in the Américas.

The chapters seek to enrich our understanding of the role of pop culture in the everyday lives of its creators and consumers, primarily in the 20th and 21st centuries. They reveal how popular culture expresses the historical, social, cultural, and political commonalities that have shaped the lives of peoples that make up the Américas, and also highlight how pop culture can conform to and solidify existing social hierarchies, whilst on other occasions contest and resist the status quo. Front and center in this collection are issues of gender and sexuality, making visible the ways in which subjects who inhabit intersectional identities (sex, gender, race, class) are "othered", as well as demonstrating how these same subjects can, and do, use pop cultural phenomena in self-affirmative and progressively transformative ways. Topics covered in this volume include TV, film, pop and performance art, hip-hop, dance, slam poetry, gender-fluid religious ritual, theater, stand-up comedy, graffiti, videogames, photography, graphic arts, sports spectacles, comic books, sci-fi and other genre novels, *lotería* card games, news, web, and digital media.

Frederick Luis Aldama is Arts and Humanities Distinguished Professor of English, University Distinguished Scholar, and University Distinguished Teacher at The Ohio State University, USA. He is an award-winning author, co-author, and editor of over thirty books. He is editor and co-editor of eight academic press book series. He has been honored with the American Association of Hispanics in Higher Education's Outstanding Latino/a Faculty in Higher Education Award and inducted into the Academy of Teaching.

"A sharp observer and scholarly commentator, Aldama gives sex and gender a new twist. He gathers expert analysts who put sex and gender into contemporary but unfamiliar contexts of popular culture. They take us into national (Chile, Mexico, Brazil, Japanese Peru, Puerto Rico, Argentina, Cuba), pre-national (Amerindian), and hemispheric transnational spaces (the U.S.–Mexico border, Budapest–Brazil, Japan–Peru, Cuba–U.S.) of cultural production. An absolutely essential resource for all those interested in the dynamic and varied ways that of sex and gender inform the shaping of pop culture in the Américas"

Marta E. Sánchez, author of Shakin' Up Race and Gender,
Professor of Chicano, US Latino, and Latin American Literature,
Arizona State University, USA

"Aldama's Companion brings together under-explored intersectional identities and cultural riches that provide the keys to understand the intricacies of Latin American culture. The essays shed light on how gender, sexuality, race, and class traverse all facets of our lives. This is a must-have for all Latin American Studies programs"

Consuelo Martinez Reyes, Lecturer in Spanish Studies,
Australian National University, Australia

"More than ever, pop culture permeates every nook and cranny of our increasingly globalized world. It is unavoidable. Through richly varied theoretical approaches and methodologies, covering a broad range of topics from comics to futebol, Aldama's Companion reframes pop culture as a central field of study for understanding the complexities of Latin America"

Eli Lee Carter, author of Reimagining Brazilian Television,
Assistant Professor of Portuguese,
University of Virginia, USA

"In Latin America, as elsewhere, popular culture can enforce systems and structures of oppression as well as provide a space for resistance to them. The redoubtable, versatile Aldama is the perfect impresario for these studies into how various forms of pop throughout the Hispanophonic Western hemisphere shape and are shaped by gender and sexuality"

Steven G. Kellman, author of The Translingual Imagination,
Professor of Comparative Literature,
University of Texas at San Antonio, USA

THE ROUTLEDGE COMPANION TO GENDER, SEX AND LATIN AMERICAN CULTURE

Edited by Frederick Luis Aldama

LONDON AND NEW YORK

First published 2018
by Routledge
2 Park Square, Milton Park, Abingdon, Oxon OX14 4RN

and by Routledge
711 Third Avenue, New York, NY 10017

Routledge is an imprint of the Taylor & Francis Group, an informa business

© 2018 selection and editorial matter, Frederick Luis Aldama; individual chapters, the contributors

The right of Frederick Luis Aldama to be identified as the author of the editorial material, and of the authors for their individual chapters, has been asserted in accordance with sections 77 and 78 of the Copyright, Designs and Patents Act 1988.

All rights reserved. No part of this book may be reprinted or reproduced or utilised in any form or by any electronic, mechanical, or other means, now known or hereafter invented, including photocopying and recording, or in any information storage or retrieval system, without permission in writing from the publishers.

Trademark notice: Product or corporate names may be trademarks or registered trademarks, and are used only for identification and explanation without intent to infringe.

British Library Cataloguing-in-Publication Data
A catalogue record for this book is available from the British Library

Library of Congress Cataloging-in-Publication Data
Names: Aldama, Frederick Luis, 1969- editor.
Title: The Routledge companion to gender, sex and Latin American culture / edited by Frederick Luis Aldama.
Description: Abingdon, Oxon; New York, NY: Routledge, 2018. | Includes bibliographical references and index.
Identifiers: LCCN 2017060230 | ISBN 9781138894952 (hardback : alk. paper) | ISBN 9781315179728 (ebook)
Subjects: LCSH: Popular culture–Latin America. | Mass media and culture–Latin America. | Sex–Latin America. | Sex role–Latin America. | Latin America–Civilization.
Classification: LCC F1408.3 .R6755 2018 | DDC 980–dc23
LC record available at https://lccn.loc.gov/2017060230

ISBN: 978-1-138-89495-2 (hbk)
ISBN: 978-1-315-17972-8 (ebk)

Typeset in Bembo
by Deanta Global Publishing Services, Chennai, India

Printed and bound in Great Britain by
TJ International Ltd, Padstow, Cornwall

CONTENTS

List of figures ix
List of contributors xi

Introduction: Putting gender and sexuality at the center of
all that goes pop in Latin America 1
Frederick Luis Aldama

PART I
Transmedial re-mediations **17**

1 Hybrid mass culture 19
Debra A. Castillo

2 The Latin American *flâneur* in the digital age 31
Osvaldo Cleger

3 Intersections of gender and gaming in Latin America 46
Phillip Penix-Tadsen

4 *La lotería mexicana*: Playing with heteronormativity 57
Stacey Alex

5 Diasporic intersectionality: Colonial history and Puerto Rican hero
narratives in *21: The Story of Roberto Clemente* and *La Borinqueña* 71
Ivonne M. García

6 Drawing up a 'post'-Latin America: The possibilities and limits of
gender imagination in post-apocalyptic, post-human, and post-historical
graphic narrative 83
Mauricio Espinoza

Contents

7 Tito Guízar on Radio Row: Intermediality, Latino identity, and two
early 1930s Vitaphone shorts 91
Nicolas Poppe

PART II
***Bending* genre** **101**

8 Interior design and homoerotic spaces in José Asunción Silva's
De sobremesa 103
Sergio Macías

9 Melodramatic attachments: On Puig's *Boquitas pintadas* 115
Ben. Sifuentes-Jáuregui

10 Sex with aliens: Dramatic irony in Daína Chaviano's
"The Annunciation" 129
Matthew David Goodwin

11 Villain or victim?: Undermining the memory of Japanese Peruvians in
Augusto Higa Oshiro's *Gaijin (Extranjero)* 139
Shigeko Mato

12 Art, literature, and mass media in Pedro Lemebel 152
Juan Poblete

PART III
Re-constructing silver screen imaginaries **167**

13 Neoliberal pigmentocracies: Women and the elite body politic in
neoliberal Mexican cinema 169
Ignacio M. Sánchez Prado

14 Class, gender, race in recent filmic urban Brazilian spaces 177
Samuel Cruz

15 El roc ha muerto, viva el roc: Countercultural heroines in
Sergio García Michel's Super 8mm cinema 187
Iván Eusebio Aguirre Darancou

16 Starring Mexico: Female stardom, age and mass media trajectories
in the 20th century 196
Olivia Cosentino

17 Hemisexualizing the Latin lover: Film and live art interpretations
and provocations 206
Paloma Martinez-Cruz and John Cruz

Contents

18 Transnational queerings and *Sense8* 222
Laura Fernández

19 Good gringos, bad hombres: The postlapsarian films of Mel Gibson 231
Ryan Rashotte

PART IV
Putting the feminist and queer pop in the pictorial arts 243

20 Graffiti in Latin America: Preliminary notes 245
Ilan Stavans

21 Graffiti School *Comunidad*: A feminist arts pedagogy of empowerment 252
Guisela Latorre and Marjorie Peñailillo

22 Contemporary Amerindian imaginaries and the challenge of
intersectional analysis 263
Arij Ouweneel

23 The photography of Thomaz Farkas and the Estádo de Pacaembu:
A theatre of Brazilian male homosociality 273
David William Foster

PART V
Bend it like *Pelé* 285

24 A "friendly" game: Homoaffectivity in *Club de Cuervos* 287
Patrick Thomas Ridge

25 Reading race and gender in *The Black Man in Brazilian Soccer* and beyond 300
Jack A. Draper III

26 Hard punches, vulnerable bodies: Latin American boxing films and the
intersections of gender, class, and nation 310
Mauricio Espinoza and Luis Miguel Estrada Orozco

27 "The Blizzard of Oz": Ozzie Guillén and Latino masculinities as spectacle 323
Jennifer Domino Rudolph

PART VI
Alt-hemispheric sound and body performatics 333

28 Somos Mujeres Somos Hip Hop: Feminism and hip hop
in Latin America 335
Melissa Castillo-Garsow

Contents

29 Weirded soundscapes in contemporary Chilean narrative 347
J. Andrew Brown

30 Dance as medicine: Healing bodies in Nicaragua from the colonial
period to the present 356
John Petrus and Jessica Rutherford

31 Gender performativity and indigenous conceptions of duality
in the Inti Raymi–Jatun Puncha Festivals of Cotacachi, Ecuador 368
Michelle Wibbelsman

PART VII
Staging nuevo hemispheric identities **375**

32 Beside motherhood: Staging women's lives in Latin American
Theatre of the Real 377
Julie Ann Ward

33 Can *saraus* speak to gender and migrant politics in São Paulo? 386
Derek Pardue

34 Transfeminism and fake mustachios: Sayak Valencia's decolonial critique
at the U.S.–Mexico border 398
Ignacio Corona

35 Proud sinvergüenza or foolish maricón?: Manu NNa's challenge to
Mexican homonormativity 410
Doug Bush

36 The Cuban Missile Crisis of white masculinity: Tito Bonito and the
burlesque butt 420
Kristie Soares

Index *431*

viii

FIGURES

2.1	The character of Sergio in *Memorias del Subdesarrollo*, using his telescope to explore a changing Havana under the influence of the Cuba Revolution	34
2.2	Homepage of *Caminando Bogotá*	36
2.3	*Caminando Bogotá*. Screenshot of the José Celestino Mutis Avenue as portrayed in the multimedia	37
2.4	Google Street View of the José Celestino Mutis Avenue in the Chapinero district	38
4.1	"El Sireno." Watercolor and Ink by Félix d'Eon	63
4.2	"La Muxe." Watercolor and Ink by Félix d'Eon	64
4.3	"La Tijera." Watercolor and Ink by Félix d'Eon	65
7.1	Tito Guízar performs "Del Palmero"	96
7.2	Tito Guízar performs "Coplas de marihuana"	97
17.1	Morato, Fernando. Latin Lover Provocations: Performance by John Cruz. 2016	218
17.2	Morato, Fernando. Latin Lover Provocation: Performance by John Cruz. 2016	219
20.1	An example of *grafiterios*	247
20.2	An example of *grafiterios* in Puerto Rico	248
20.3	An example of *grafiterios* in San Juan	249
20.4	An example of Mexican graffiti	251
21.1	Gigi (Marjorie Peñailillo), *Formación* (2016), digital sketch	258
21.2	Tess Pugsley and Guisela Latorre working on outlines for *Formación* (2016). The Ohio State University, United States	259
21.3	Lynaya Elliott, Jackie Stotlar and Tess Pugsley working on *Formación* (2016). The Ohio State University, United States	260

21.4	Gigi (Marjorie Peñailillo), Lynaya Elliott, Guisela Latorre, Tess Pugsley and Jackie Stotlar, *Formación* (2016), graffiti mural, Department of Women's, Gender and Sexuality Studies, The Ohio State University, United States	261
22.1	Laura (Mónica del Carmen), *Año bisiesto* (*Leap Year*, 2011), with the knife	268
24.1	Film still from from *Club de Cuervos* showing players in the shower	293
24.2	Film still from *Club de Cuervos* showing players in the locker room	294
24.3	Film still from *Club de Cuervos* with full-body profile shot of Potro	295
24.4	Film still from *Club de Cuervos* showing former coach and vice-president of los Cuervos scoping out potential prospects on a local beach	296

CONTRIBUTORS

Stacey Alex is a Latin American Cultural and Literary Studies and Latina/o Studies doctoral student at The Ohio State University. With a focus on the Latina/o Midwest, her work analyzes narratives of undocumented Latina/o experiences and their potential to decolonize multicultural approaches that include Latina/o literature in apolitical and celebratory ways.

J. Andrew Brown is Professor of Spanish and Comparative Literature at Washington University in St. Louis, Missouri. He is the author of *Test Tube Envy: Science and Power in Argentine Narrative* and *Cyborgs in Latin America*. He has written extensively on the intersections of popular culture, science fiction, and underground music in Latin America. He is currently finishing a project on the aesthetics of remix, mashups, and sampling in contemporary Latin American narrative.

Doug Bush is Assistant Professor of Spanish at Converse College in Spartanburg, South Carolina. He has published on Mexican and Latinx Literature and culture. He is author of *Capturing Mariposas: Reading Cultural Schema in an Emerging Genre* (2019).

Debra A. Castillo is Stephen H. Weiss Presidential Fellow, Emerson Hinchliff Professor of Hispanic Studies, and Professor of Comparative Literature at Cornell University. She specializes in contemporary narrative from the Spanish-speaking world (including the U.S.), gender studies, comparative border studies, and cultural theory. She is author of numerous books and co-editor of *Cartographies of Affect: Across Borders in South Asia and the Americas* (2011), *Hybrid Storyspaces* (2012), *Mexican Public Intellectuals* (2014), *Despite all Adversities: Spanish American Queer Cinema* (2015), and *Theorizing Fieldwork in the Humanities* (2016).

Melissa Castillo-Garsow is a postdoctoral fellow at the Global American Studies Program at Harvard University's Charles Warren Center for Studies in American History. She is the editor of *¡Manteca!: An Anthology of Afro-Latin@ Poets* (2017), co-editor of *La Verdad: An International Dialogue on Hip Hop Latinidades* (2016), author of the poetry collection *Coatlicue Eats the Apple* (2016), and co-author of the novel *Pure Bronx* (2013). Additionally, her short stories, articles, poetry, and essays have been published in numerous collections as well as scholarly and media publications.

Contributors

Osvaldo Cleger is Associate Professor at Georgia Institute of Technology. He specializes in digital culture, e-literature, and emerging technologies in the Hispanic world. He is author of *Narrar en la era de las blogoficciones: literatura, cultura y sociedad de las redes en el siglo XXI/The Art of Narrating in the Age of Blog-fictions* (2010) as well as co-editor of two volumes: *Redes hipertextuales en el aula, Octaedro* (2015) and *Formación literaria, hipertextos y Web 2.0 en el marco educativo* (2016). He has published numerous articles on visual culture, Hispanic e-literature, hypertext fiction, and video games in such journals as *Revista de Estudios Hispánicos, Caribe, Letras Hispanas, Universidad de la Habana, Digital Culture and Education*, as well as in edited volumes such as *Leer Hipertextos, Poesía y poéticas digitales/electrónicas/tecnos/New-Media en América Latina: Definiciones y exploraciones*, and *The Latino Pop Cultural Studies Reader*.

Ignacio Corona is Associate Professor of Mexican and Latin/o American Cultural and Literary Studies at The Ohio State University. He has published extensively in Latin America, the U.S., and Spain. He is the author of *Después de Tlatelolco: las narrativas políticas en México* and co-editor of *The Contemporary Mexican Chronicle: Theoretical Perspectives on the Liminal Genre*; *Postnational Musical Identities: Production, Marketing, and Consumption in a Globalized Scenario*; and *Gender Violence at the U.S.-Mexico Border: Media Representations and Public Intervention*.

Olivia Cosentino is a PhD student in Latin American Literary and Cultural Studies at The Ohio State University. She has published in *The Velvet Light Trap* and contributed to the volume *The Latin American Road Movie* (2016). Her research interests include youth studies, stardom, feminism, and the intersections of affect and violence in 20th- and 21st-century Mexican film, literature, and culture.

John Cruz is a PhD candidate in Contemporary Latin American Literary and Cultural Studies at The Ohio State University. His main areas of research are visual culture, consumer culture, gender issues, and performance, with emphasis on gender-based violence, male homosexuality, stardom, and media. He brings an interdisciplinary approach to the study of gendered violence in film and visual culture in Latin America. He is also a performer.

Samuel Cruz is Assistant Professor of Spanish, Portuguese and Literatures and Cultures of Latin America at Marietta College. He specializes in Latin American film and cultural studies. His research involves the relationship between film and urban areas, more specifically how contemporary films (1990s–present) represent socio-political, economic, and cultural issues in the region.

Jack A. Draper III is Associate Professor of Portuguese at the University of Missouri and his research focuses on the field of Brazilian cultural studies. He is author of *Saudade in Brazilian Cinema: The History of an Emotion on Film* (2017) and *Forró and Redemptive Regionalism from the Brazilian Northeast: Music in a Culture of Migration* (2010). Currently he is editing and translating to English a critical edition of Mário Filho's *O negro no futebol brasileiro/The Black Man in Brazilian Soccer*.

Mauricio Espinoza is Assistant Professor of Spanish and Latin American Cultural Studies at the University of Cincinnati, Ohio. His research and publications focus on Latin American/Latino comics and film, Central American migration narrative and poetry, and Latin American immigrant communities. He has translated the work of Costa Rican poet Eunice Odio into English.

His book *Respiración de piedras* won the 2015 University of Costa Rica Press Poetry Prize. His poetry also appears in *The Wandering Song: Central American Writing in the United States* (2017).

Luis Miguel Estrada Orozco is Postdoctoral International Fellow at the Cogut Institute for Humanities at Brown University. He currently works on boxers in Mexican literature, cinema, theatre, and the press. His collections of short stories have received several awards in Mexico, where he has also published boxing chronicles. His fiction work has been included in anthologies in Mexico and Spain.

Iván Eusebio Aguirre Darancou is Assistant Professor of Hispanic Studies at University of California, Riverside. His research focuses on countercultural expressions in Mexico and the greater Hispanic world, especially through the presence of hallucinogenic substances in literature and other cultural products as well as the insertion in global cultural flows. He has published articles on authors Augusto Monterroso, Guillermo Cabrera Infante, Parménides García Saldaña and José Agustín in journals such as *Hispanic Review, Tierra adentro,* the *Revista de Literatura Mexicana Contemporánea*, and *Romance Notes*.

Laura Fernández is a PhD student in the Latin American Cultural and Literary Studies Program in the Department of Spanish and Portuguese at The Ohio State University. She has published book chapters and articles on Latinx pop culture, specifically the representations of Latinidad in children's media, and Latinx cultural studies.

David William Foster is Regents' Professor of Spanish, Humanities, and Women's Studies at Arizona State University. His research interests focus on urban culture in Latin America, with emphasis on issues of queer gender construction and sexual identity, as well as Jewish culture. He has written extensively on Argentine narrative and theater. He is author of numerous articles, chapters, and books, including recently *Argentine, Mexican, and Guatemalan Photography: Feminist, Queer, and Post-Masculinist Perspectives* (2014) and *Picturing the Barrio: Ten Chicano Photographers* (2017).

Ivonne M. García is Associate Professor of English at Kenyon College. She served as the first Associate Provost for Diversity, Equity, and Inclusion at Kenyon. She is working on her book manuscript on 19th-century representations of Cuba, and has published scholarship on Sophia Hawthorne, Louisa May Alcott, and the American Gothic.

Matthew David Goodwin is Assistant Professor in the Department of English at the University of Puerto Rico at Cayey. His research is centered on the experience of migration in Latinx literature and he is the editor of *Latin@ Rising: An Anthology of Latin@ Science Fiction and Fantasy* (2017).

Guisela Latorre is Associate Professor in the Department of Women's Gender and Sexuality Studies at The Ohio State University. She specializes in modern and contemporary U.S. Latina/o and Latin American art with a special emphasis on gender and women artists. She is author of numerous chapters and articles as well as the book, *Walls of Empowerment: Chicana/o Indigenist Murals from California* (2008) where she explores the recurrence of indigenist motifs in Chicana/o community murals from the 1970s to the turn of the millennium. She is completing a new book on the graffiti and mural movement in Chile during the post-dictatorship era.

Sergio Macías teaches at the University of Denver where he also obtained his PhD. He specializes in contemporary Latin American literature and culture from a sexuality and gender studies perspective. Sergio is currently conducting research on camp aesthetics and queer culture(s) in Mexico.

Paloma Martinez-Cruz is Associate Professor of Latino/a Cultural and Literary Studies at The Ohio State University. Her research and teaching focus on contemporary hemispheric literature and culture, women of color feminism, performance, and alternative epistemologies. She is the author of *Women and Knowledge in Mesoamerica: From East L.A. to Anahuac* (2011), translator of *Ponciá Vicencio*, the debut novel by Afro-Brazilian author Conceição Evaristo, and the editor of *Rebeldes: A Proyecto Latina Anthology* (2013). Her forthcoming works include *Food Fight: Millennial Mestizaje and the Dilemmas of Ethical Eating* (University of Arizona Press) and *La Pocha Nostra: Handbook for the Rebel Artist in a Post-Democratic Society* with Guillermo Gómez-Peña and Saul Garcia-Lopez (Routledge).

Shigeko Mato is Professor of Spanish and Latin American Literature and Culture at the School of International Liberal Studies, Waseda University, Tokyo. She has published several articles and book chapters on contemporary Japanese Peruvian literature in U.S. and Japanese journals. She is also the author of *Cooptation, Complicity, and Representation: Desire and Limits for Intellectuals in Twentieth-Century Mexican Fiction* (2010).

Arij Ouweneel is Associate Professor at Centre for Latin American Research and Documentation, Amsterdam. He is author of numerous articles, as well as the books *Freudian Fadeout* (2012) and *Resilient Memories. Amerindian Cognitive Schemas in Latin American Art* (2018).

Derek Pardue is Associate Professor and Coordinator of Brazilian Studies at Aarhus University in Denmark. He is currently a Senior Fellow at Hanse-Wissenschaftkolleg (HWK), where he is writing a book that employs urban theory and ethnographic fiction to represent contemporary African migration in São Paulo, Brazil. He is author of numerous articles, chapters, and *Cape Verde Let's Go: Creole Rappers and Citizenship in Portugal* (2015).

Marjorie Peñailillo (Gigi) is a visual artist, a professional graffiti writer, and a master printmaker. She holds degrees in education, art, and printmaking from the School of Fine Arts in Viña del Mar and the University of Viña del Mar in Chile. Additionally, Gigi is cofounder of one of the few all-female graffiti crews in Chile, the Turronas Crew. Gigi is creator of Graffiti School Comunidad the first graffiti and street art project born in Chilean public schools.

Phillip Penix-Tadsen is Associate Professor of Spanish and Latin American Studies at the University of Delaware. He is the author of *Cultural Code: Video Games and Latin America* (2016), which offers a synthetic theorization of the relationship between video games and culture, based on analysis of both in-game cultural representation and the real-life economic, political, and societal effects of games. His research and teaching focus on the intersections between politics, economics, new media, and visual culture in Latin America today.

John Petrus is Assistant Professor of Spanish and Latinx Studies at Grinnell College. His research centers on questions of sexual and racial difference in Latinx and Latin American audio-visual media. He investigates representations of heteronormativity and gender transgression in contemporary Managua via film, television, video production, performance art, and as an active participant/observer. He examines counter-hegemonic resistance to coloniality of power, knowledge, and gender, including representations of sexual and racial difference related to the HIV/AIDS crisis in U.S. Latinx communities, especially in the Central American diaspora.

Juan Poblete, Professor at UC-Santa Cruz. Author of *Hacia una historia de la lectura y la pedagogía literaria en América Latina* (2018), *La Escritura de Pedro Lemebel como proyecto cultural y político* (2018), and *Literatura chilena del siglo XIX* (2003); editor of *New Approaches to Latin American Studies: Culture and Power* (2017); co-editor of *Sports and Nationalism in Latin America* (2015), *Humor in Latin American Cinema* (2015), and four other books.

Nicolas Poppe is Assistant Professor of Spanish at Middlebury College. His work on Latin American cinema and cultural studies has appeared in several edited volumes, as well as peer-reviewed journals. He is the coeditor of *Cosmopolitan Film Cultures in Latin America, 1896–1960* (2017) and coeditor of a special issue of *[in]Transition*.

Ryan Rashotte is Assistant Professor of English and Composition at Lakeland University, Japan. He has a PhD in English from the University of Guelph, Canada, and he is the author of *Narco Cinema: Sex, Drugs, and Banda Music in Mexico's B-Filmography* (2015).

Patrick Thomas Ridge is Assistant Professor of Spanish at Virginia Polytechnic Institute and State University. His current research explores literary and cultural representations of soccer in Latin America. This work focuses primarily on questions of gender, nationalism, power, and violence.

Jennifer Domino Rudolph is Associate Professor of Hispanic and Latin American Studies. Her research and teaching focus on popular culture as a site of negotiation of identity and activism. Her book, *Embodying Latino Masculinities, Producing Masculatinidad*, examines how creators and consumers use popular culture to construct and understand Latino masculinities. She is currently working on a new book, *Baseball as Mediated Latinidad*, that looks at how players, fans, and media workers engage with Latin/o Major League Baseball players to process current politics related to Latino masculinities, immigration, and nativism.

Jessica Rutherford (PhD, The Ohio State University) teaches and researches within the fields of colonial Latin America, cultural studies, and the history of science and medicine. She engages with postcolonial debates on the geopolitics of knowledge and power and works beyond the confines of national borders, and challenges Western-dominated paradigms of science and medicine to highlight the contribution of Amerindian intellectuals.

Ignacio M. Sánchez Prado is Professor of Spanish and Latin American Studies at Washington University in St. Louis, Missouri. He is the author of *El canon y sus formas. La reinvención de Harold Bloom y sus lecturas hispanoamericanas* (2002), *Naciones intelectuales. Las fundaciones de la modernidad literaria mexicana (1917–1959)* (2009), the award-winning *Intermitencias americanistas. Ensayos académicos y literarios (2004–2009)* (2012), *Screening Neoliberalism. Transforming Mexican Cinema 1988–2012* (2014), and *Strategic Occidentalism. "World Literature," Mexican Fiction and the Neoliberalization of the Book Market* (2018). He has edited and co-edited 11 scholarly collections, the most recent of which are *A History of Mexican Literature* (2016). He has published over 80 scholarly articles on Mexican literature, culture, and film, and on Latin American cultural theory.

Ben. Sifuentes-Jáuregui is Professor of American Studies and Comparative Literature at Rutgers–New Brunswick. His research focuses on Latino/a and Latin American literature and culture, gender theory and sexuality studies, and psychoanalysis. He is author of *Transvestism, Masculinity, and Latin American Literature* (2002) and *The Avowal of Difference: Queer Latino American Narratives* (2014). He has published numerous articles on sexuality, queer identities in Latino/a America, and melodrama. He is currently working on a book on melodrama and masochism in a series of Latino American novels, performances, films, and essays.

Kristie Soares is Assistant Professor of Women and Gender Studies at the University of Colorado Boulder and an active performance artist. Both her performance work and her research explore issues of queerness in Caribbean and Latinx communities. Her current book project, *Salsa Epistemology*, examines queer cultural production in the Spanish Caribbean during the last 60 years. Professor Soares has published articles in numerous journals, including *Frontiers, Revista de estudios hispánicos, and Letras Femeninas.*

Ilan Stavans is Lewis-Sebring Professor of Humanities, Latin American, and Latino Cultures at Amherst College, Massachusetts and the publisher of Restless Books. He is the author, most recently, of the graphic novel *Angelitos* and the poem *The Wall* (both 2018), *Latinos in the United States: What Everyone Needs to Know, I Love My Selfie* (both 2017), *Borges, the Jew* and *Oy, Caramba!: An Anthology of Jewish Stories from Latin America* (both 2016), and *Quixote: The Novel and the World* (2015). He is also co-founder of Great Books Summer Program and host of the NPR podcast *In Contrast with Ilan Stavans.*

Julie Ann Ward is Assistant Professor of 20th- and 21st-century Latin American Literature at the University of Oklahoma. Her forthcoming book (University of Pittsburgh Press) is on Mexico City's theatre collective Lagartijas Tiradas al Sol. Her work has appeared in *Theatre Journal, TransModernity, Latin American Theatre Review, Revista de Literatura Mexicana Contemporánea, Paso de Gato,* and *World Literature Today.*

Michelle Wibbelsman is Assistant Professor of South American Indigenous Cultures, Ethnographic Studies, and Ethnomusicology in the Department of Spanish and Portuguese at The Ohio State University. She is the author of *Ritual Encounters: Otavalan Modern and Mythic Community* (2009). Two new book projects that are underway center on musical diversity among Otavalan diaspora communities and on indigenous transnational migration, diaspora, and cosmopolitanism.

INTRODUCTION

Putting gender and sexuality at the center of all that goes pop in Latin America

Frederick Luis Aldama

The Routledge Companion to Gender, Sex and Latin American Culture sets its sights on all variety of pop cultural phenomena from across the Américas as it intersects with issues of gender and sexuality in terms of their creation, consumption, and interpretation. The chapters mostly focus on excavating gender, sexuality, and pop culture in the 20th and 21st centuries, with a few focusing on earlier historical periods. Each of the chapters carves out its own scholarly path and also shares some of the following scholarly positions and impulses:

- To study Latin American pop cultural phenomena within local and regional settings and with a hemispheric purview; thus, to account for idiomatic expression of the historical, social, cultural, and political commonalities that have shaped the lives of peoples that make up the Américas: Hispanophone Caribbean, Central, South, and North America.
- To understand that pop culture is everywhere and, at the same time, to realize that there exist gatekeepers in its circulation and asymmetries of power in its production and consumption that determine what is produced and consumed, and by whom.
- To understand that pop cultural production and consumption are complex, in some instances conforming to and solidifying social hierarchies and in other cases contesting and resisting the status quo.
- To put front and center issues of gender and sexuality in the interpretation of pop culture's presence in the Américas, making visible the ways that certain subjects and experiences are Othered as well as how these same subjects can and do use pop cultural phenomena in self-affirmative and progressively transformative ways.
- To consider that pop cultural creations are transculturative. That is, they are the syncretic combination of any and all cultural phenomena into something new.
- To understand how transculturative phenomena can and do open audiences to new ways of perceiving, thinking, and feeling about issues of gender and sexuality.
- To understand that social, political, and economic forces across the Américas have increasingly led all variety of people to reside in urban centers, creating new networks of contact between all variety of social, ethnoracial, gender, and sexuality groups that grow all variety of new tastes for all sorts of pop cultural phenomena.

- To understand that pop culture educates all of the senses: tastes, smells, touch, sounds, sights, and that with this education of the senses grows a wealth of new appetites for a diverse range of pop cultural phenomena—thus triggering and nurturing new aesthetic wants.
- To understand that the creators and consumers of pop culture are not *passive* recipients; they are active recyclers, inheritors, and transformers of pop cultural phenomena.
- To understand the making, circulating, and consuming of pop culture by and about gender and sexuality as taking place in specifics of time (history) and place (region).
- To show that the interpretation of gender and sexuality in the pop culture of the Américas can and does tell us something about national, regional, communal, and individual worldviews.

★

The Routledge Companion to Gender, Sex and Latin American Culture does not exist in a vacuum. There is a robust corpus of scholarship on the creation, circulation, and consumption of cultural phenomena across the Américas, including on radio, film, music, television, genre fiction, performance, street art, Internet, digital media platforms, and much more. The field has been shaped by important pioneers and newcomers, such as: Diana Taylor, Ericka Beckman, Jesús Martín-Barbero, Renato Ortiz, Fernando Ortiz, Angel Rama, Ricardo Gutiérrez Mouat, Néstor García Canclini, William Rowe, Vivian Schelling, Eva P. Bueno, Terry Caesar, Silvia Bermudez, William H. Beezley, Linda A. Curcio-Nagy, John Beverly, Ileana Rodriguez, Reynaldo González, Inés Cornejo, Rubén Gallo, and Guillermo Mastrini, to name just a few. These scholars and others of Latin American culture have approached directly or indirectly the topic of pop culture, and have done so in a variety of ways. *The Routledge Companion to Gender, Sex and Latin American Culture* builds on the work of these scholars while seeking to understand the way pop culture exists in and shapes our everyday lives—for better and worse.

On the darker side of pop cultural scholarship lives work that seeks to reveal how pop culture is a top-down (usually US imperialist) opiate of the masses; that it sells neoliberal ideals and capitalist (aka US) ideology in its shaping the consciousness of the people. And there are those who carve out interpretive paths between these two positions. For instance, in their introduction to *Latin American Pop Culture*, Geoffrey Kantaris and Rory O'Bryen discuss how pop culture and the explosion of mass technologies of cultural creation and circulation bridge both the national and the global; also, they draw attention to a "climate of technocratic neoliberal economic ideology, financial crises marked by new intensified social problems, boom and bust cycles in commodities and resource-extraction, and the rise of demogogical, mediatic neo-populisms" (2013: 1–2). Within this, however, they also consider how pop culture can and does open eyes to new modes of existing and new forms of "social agency" (16). Indeed, In *The Other Side of the Popular* (2002) Gareth Williams focuses on how pop culture technologies of distribution shape everyday life and contribute to political outcomes in negative (dystopic) ways. Williams analyzes how the Peronist regime used popular aspirations and widespread needs to sustain its demagogic exercise of power. In *Cruel Modernity* (2013), Jean Franco identifies how pop culture—e.g., film, comics, and the visual arts—encourages audiences to vicariously experience and enjoy violence against Latin America's Others: peasants, indigenous African and Indian communities, and women.

On the brighter side of scholarly interpretation of all things pop culture in Latin America, there are those who consider it as a space clearing gesture that democratizes participation in making and co-creating cultural phenomena This scholarly thread seeks to demonstrate how the study of Latin American pop culture can shed light on political issues about class, race, gender, and sexuality. Latin American popular culture exists in resistant opposition to the

Introduction

dominant culture. For instance, William Rowe and Vivian Schelling consider how pop cultural flows across national borders, having "the effect of dismantling old forms of marginalization and domination and making new forms of democratization and cultural multiplicity imaginable" (1). And in "Popular Culture in Latin America," Silvia Bermudez identifies how music and dance, for instance, can identify the Othered African and indigenous Indian syncretic cultural roots (from salsa to santería) that have shaped national cultural phenomena. These and other scholars set their sights on pop culture, and not on highbrow arts and letters, as a significant shaper of national cultural identity. (See, also, Eva P. Bueno and Terry Caesar's edited, *Imagination Beyond Nation*.)

These abovementioned scholars working today build on the foundations of Latin American cultural interpreters. I think of Cuban Fernando Ortiz, who formulated a theory of transculturation in 1940, with the publication of his seminal *Contrapunteo cubano del tabaco y el azúcar* (translated into English in 1995 as *Cuban Counterpoint: Tobacco and Sugar*). Ortiz analyzed how the slave trade and agriculture in the Caribbean led to the mixing and combining of African and Hispanic cultures to form an entirely new cultural product. In 1971, Ariel Dorfman and Armand Mattelart published their book-length essay, *Para leer al Pato Donald*. Here they identify the circulation of Disney cartoons and comic books in Latin American spaces as ideological appendages of US imperialism; they naturalize first world (US) versus third world (Latin America) development teleologies of progress and class mobility. Also, during this period of the 1970s we see the work of Mexican critic and essayist Carlos Monsiváis, who set his sights on cultural phenomena like the popular Golden Age of cinema (1930s–50s) in Mexico. For Monsiváis, the masses of working class filmgoers of this period cinema would encounter narratives that dismantled class, gender, and religious hierarchies, waking audiences to new ideas and ways of existing. And Argentine Nestor García Canclini formulated pop cultural phenomena such as graffiti as appropriated and circulated within global networks of cultural flows that reify the local as authentic, but that also have the power to "irritate" the dominant capitalist discourses. In *Culturas populares en el capitalism* (1981; *Transforming Modernity: Popular Culture in Mexico,* 1993) and especially *Culturas híbridas* (1989; *Hybrid Cultures*, 1995) the local and global flows of pop cultural phenomena make for hybrid objects that reflect the complex ways that humans exist between the local and global. In addition to the scholarly books published during this period, there were other ways that the study of Latin American pop culture was being institutionalized. In 1982, the journal *Studies in Latin American Popular Culture* was established. It has since published interdisciplinary scholarship on mass production, circulation, and consumption of cultural goods in Latin America. (Notably, there were also elitist scholars like Carlos Estevam in Brazil who considered the revolutionary potential in pop culture not to come from the "clumsy" and "coarse" masses, but from the educated elite. See his essay, "For a Popular Revolutionary Art," published in 1962.)

This is but a brief sampling of the growing body of scholarship on Latin American pop culture that in one way or another seeks to enrich our understanding of its presence in the everyday lives of creators and consumers; that asks that we revisit categories like folk and mass culture; and that demands that we reconsider categories like lowbrow and highbrow. One way or another, they show the need for us to consider how pop culture informs different identities, including urban, communal, national, and global.

★

Of course, the scholarship on all things Latin American pop culture also includes important forays into its interface with issues of gender and sexuality. Areas of scholarly investigation have included topics like cosmetic surgery, pornography, sports, telenovelas, music, dance, and film, for example. This is important mainly because women and LGBTQ subjects have been and continue to be a significant presence as creators and consumers of pop cultural phenomena. Scholarship has begun to map how discrimination, exploitation, and oppression as well as the struggles and victories of subjects who inhabit intersectional identities (gender, sexuality, race, and class) importantly inflect, shape, create and co-create (consume) anew pop cultural phenomena.

Beginning in the 1970s, Latin American feminist scholars—e.g., Nelly Richard, Cynthia Steele, Sandra Cypess, Elena Poniatowska, Marisa Belausteguigoitia, Sylvia Molloy, Marta Lamas, Jean Franco, Elena González, Eliana Ortega, Josefina Muriel, Francine Masiello, Mary L. Pratt, Sara Castro-Klarén, and Debra Castillo (included herein)—put gender centrally on the map of Latin American studies. Responding to European and US academics either theorizing Latin American as *absent* in feminist creative and intellectual traditions *and* seeking to formulate theories from within the historical, social, and political contexts that have shaped women in Latin America, these scholars forcefully forged critical, interpretive paths. They variously called for feminist action. For instance, in Sara Castro-Klarén's article, "Teoría del la crítica literaria y la escritora en América Latina," she writes, "the figure of Women and the subsequent problematics implied by its presence should cause a profound re-thinking of the possible history of Latin America and its symbolic systems" (1984: 105). (See, also, Castro-Klarén's edited *Narrativa femenina en América Latina. Prácticas y perspectivas teóricas*, 2003.) Additionally, Debra Castillo rises to the occasion with the publication of her seminal *Talking Back: Toward a Latin American Feminist Literary Criticism* (1992), which systematized and gave scholarly due to the feminist theory and literary practices arising out of the Latin Américas.

Throughout the 1980s and 1990s, important struggles and victories were also won in institutionalizing women's studies in scholarly spaces at universities. These were no easy feats. Recall that this was a time of huge repression of women's voices. Indeed, as Jean Franco writes in "The Gender Wars," the Catholic Church refused to use the word "gender," as it considered that its mere use would "generate a new conception of the human being, subjectivity, marriage, family and society," and would incite a "cultural revolution" (1999: 123). (Today, with the huge drop in prestige of the Catholic Church, along with social activism on the streets, we see the sanctioning of LGTBQ partnering and marriage. For more on this see Aldama and Stavans, *Muy Pop!*) Feminist victories took place both on the streets and within the academy. In Mexico, for instance, in 1983, the Colegio de México created the Interdisciplinary Program for Women's Studies; in 1993, the University Program of Gender Studies was founded at the Universidad Nacional Autónoma de México. And during this period of the early 1990s, also at Universidad Nacional Autónoma de México, Marta Lamas founded the important journal, *Debate feminista*.

Hand in hand with the rise of women's studies departments and the publishing of feminist scholarship as situated within the Latin Americas, appeared LGBTQ activism, scholarship, and venues for disseminating information on LGBTQ issues as well as interpreting the work of LGBTQ creators, like Luis Zapata, Salvador Novo López, Gabriela Mistral, Reinaldo Arenas, Pedro Lemebel, Jesusa Rodríguez, and Liliana Felipe. In Brazil, for instance, emerged the newspaper *Lampião* (1978–1981), which cleared a space for the articulation and interpretation of queer identities and experiences. (See the work of both Robert Howe and Néstor Perlongher.)

These were important foundational moves to put gender and sexuality on the scholarly map. Today we have well established departments that focus on LGBTQ issues: e.g., the Programa Universitario de Estudios de Género at the Universidad Nacional Autónoma de México and the

Introduction

Área Queer NorOeste Argentino. These and other scholarly spaces sought to delink the genital apparatus from gendered identities; they allowed scholars to focus on different Latin American historical contexts of colonization, mestizaje, indigeneity (African and Indian) and the ways in which these spaces unfixed restrictive gendered and sexuality categories.

During this period, too, there was a surge of the Anglophone scholarship focused on gender and sexuality in Latin American cultural studies. In 1991, David William Foster published the seminal *Gay and Lesbian Themes in Latin American Writing*. And while not focused on Latin American queer cultural phenomena, Alexander Doty's publication in 1993 of *Making Things Perfectly Queer: Interpreting Mass Culture* (1993) carved out new scholarly paths by bringing a queer lens to the interpretation of pop culture generally; this work and his analysis of intersectionality (Latino and queer) in the *I Love Lucy Show* proved to be hugely influential on scholars like Foster and others. In 1995, Emilie Bergmann and Paul Julian Smith published their edited volume, *¿Entiendes? Queer Readings, Hispanic Writings*. And in 1997, Daniel Balderston and Donna Guy published their edited volume, *Sex and Sexuality in Latin America*. This same year, David Foster published *Sexual Textualities: Essays on Queer/ing Latin American Writing*. And in 1998, Sylvia Molloy and Robert Irwin published their edited volume, *Hispanisms and Homosexualities*. More recently, scholars such as José Quiroga and Ben Sifuentes-Jáuregui have focused their sights on excavating a queer Latin American aesthetic. In *Tropics of Desire* (2001) Quiroga articulates his concepts of strategic silence and "lateral identifications" (1997), in contradistinction to US Anglo coming out narratives. In *Transvestism, Masculinity and Latin American Literature* (2002), he formulates the concept of "tranvestism" to open up vital new interpretations of the work of Severo Sarduy, Alejo Carpentier, Jose Donoso, and Manuel Puig. And in his *The Avowal of Difference* (2014) he formulates a "queer grammar" of an "episteme-rotics" of the Americas, in contradistinction to a US queer theory (Sedgwick, Bersani, and Butler) that pivots around Anglo privilege. Importantly, he troubles the heteromasculine theories of those from south of the border (Octavio Paz, for instance) that privilege a heterosexist national subject. For instance, in his analysis of Luis Zapata's *El vampire de la Colonia Roma*, he skillfully unpacks how a queer subjectivity creates a new grammar, not just in words present on the page, but also in the deliberately placed blank spaces that function as "failed reflections, spilled semen, racial whiteness, and as moments of sexual practice" (83). These scholars and others cleared a space for queer and feminist interpretations of literature, autobiography, film, television, ethnography, testimonios, theatre, performance, and epistles. And because these books were written in English, scholars in the US were learning about the important contributions of queer and feminist creators within historical and social contexts that have uniquely shaped the Latin Americas.

Dance and music have been particularly rich areas of investigation for Latin American queer cultural studies scholars. I think of José Esteban Muñoz (*Disidentifications*), Celeste Fraser Delgado (*Everynight Life*, coedited with Muñoz), and Lawrence La Fountain Stokes (*Queer Ricans*), who tune their ears to music and their eyes to dance and performance art generally. I think of scholars who focus on technologies of transmission, like the radio and how radio vocalizations not only project certain raced, gendered, and sexualized subjects, but also offer an important early space (1930s–1940s) for *performing* gender and sexuality in ways that bend sound performances and clear spaces for women to vocalize like men and men like women. (See Christine Ehrlick's "Radio Transvestism and the Gendered Soundscape in Buenos Aires, 1930s–1940s.")

The hugely popular comic books (mainstream, alternative, and pornographic) have also been mined by Latin Americanists interested in issues of gender and sexuality. For instance, in *From Mafalda to Los Supermachos* (1989) and the more recent *El Eternauta, Daytripper and Beyond:*

Graphic Narrative in Argentina and Brazil (2016) David William Foster excavates a pop politics of gender in Latin American comic books and comic strips. In another instance, scholar Adriana Premat argues that Quino's 1960s *Mafalda* cartoon strip, which captured the imagination of millions of women in Argentina, functioned as an advocacy platform for women's right to access higher education—and this during a time of great repression in Argentine history. For Premat, Mafalda "challenged dominant gender norms that relegated women in Argentina to the role of dutiful mothers, wives, and homemakers" (2015: 43). Moreover, the storylines championed "the possibility of women being independent political agents within the nation" (43). Other scholars considered how comics have been consumed in ways that challenge masculinist and racist ideologies. I think of the work of Juan Poblete (included in this volume), Héctor L'Hoeste, Enrique García, Bruce Campbell, Ana Merino, Harold Hinds, and Charles Tatum. Indeed, Hinds and Tatum are credited by many as pioneers in creating the field of Latin American pop cultural studies. In each of the authors mentioned we see different approaches to the analysis of comics as social, racial, and gender critique by situating the comics within specific cultural, social, historical contexts that differ from those of the US. For instance, Enrique Garcia analyzes the popular Mexican comic, *Memín Penguín*, less as an example of racist minstrelsy and more as the articulation of a critique of the Latin American *casta* system. (See García's "Coon Imagery" in Will Eisner's *The Spirit*, and Yolanda Vargas Dulché's *Memín Pinguín*," as well as Robert McKee Irwin's "Memín Penguín, Rumba, and Racism.")

Some scholars have chosen to launch from the idea that *género* means gender and genre in Spanish, analyzing the conventions of genre or formula storytelling as sites of both oppression and emancipation of women, for instance. Indeed, mass-consumed genre fiction, such as noir, horror, mystery, and science fiction, have proved to be rich resources for scholars interested in how pop culture frames and reframes sexuality and gender. For instance, in the analysis of sci-fi, scholars have considered the work of such male authors as Horacio Quiroga, Ernesto Sabato, Edmundo Paz Soldán, Manuel Puig, and Ricardo Piglia, along with the more recent Yoss (José Miguel Sánchez Gómez), Daína Chaviano, Jorge Baradit, Martin Felipe Castagnet, and Bef (Bernardo Fernández). There has also been important scholarship on women sci-fi authors, such as Alison Spedding, Samanta Schweblein, Alicia Borinsky, Angélica Gorodischer, and Eugenia Prado, among many others. In scholarship on the women authors working in this genre we see the articulation of how the authors clear a space for affirming a re-gendered, posthuman subject that calls into question gender and sexuality binaries and boundaries. For instance, J. Andrew Brown considers how the sci-fi genre once emancipates otherwise marginalized and surveillanced subjects and critiques the neoliberal systems that contain such subjects. The Latin American cyborg, according to Brown, "helps think through the contradictory realities of local histories and global consumerism in a way that is at once an expression of global popular culture and an autochthonous gesture unique to the various countries in which it appears" (2010: 176). In their analysis of the two-volume sci-fi comic book *Angela Della Morte* (2011, 2014), Edward King and Joanna Page Sanz (2017) analyze the eponymous protagonist's various body exchanges as a critique of how women's bodies are caught up in "social processes" of containment and erasure. In their analysis of Jorge Baradit and Martín Cáceres's comic, *Policía del Karma*, they formulate a Latin American cyberpunk worldview that overturns gendered codifications of orifices. Instead, they offer a Latin American cyborg subject whose orifices "have no meaning beyond their utilization as sockets, plugs and channels that yoke us in specific and material ways to systems of communication and the distribution of biological and spiritual energy" (2017: 127). Notably, the cousin of the comic book, photograph, and film—the *fotonovela*—has also been a site for gender and sexuality scholarship. The *fotonovela rosa* (chaste heroine wins heart of wealthy savior), *fotonovela roja* (stories of social deprivation, prostitution, rape, and drug addiction), and

Introduction

the *fotonovela picaresca* (that focus on the sex adventuring of young male lotharios) have been particularly rich areas of investigation.

Photography and film have also been important sites of exploration. Scholars like Eduardo L. Cadava, Gabriela Nouzeilles, Gisela Cánepa Koch, Ingrid Kummels, and David Foster Williams have variously analyzed how photography as a pop cultural phenomenon moves across history, borders, and mediums. For Foster, while photography has objectified women, it has also provided a space for women photographers like Grete Stern, Annemarie Heinrich, Silvina Frydlewsky, Daniela Rossell, and Graciela Iturbide to use the camera to reverse the patriarchal gaze, making visible Latin American women and LGBTQ subjects and agency. (See Cadava and Nouzeilles's *The Itinerant Languages of Photography*, Foster's *Argentine, Mexican, and Guatemalan photography*, and Gisela Cánepa Koch and Ingrid Kummels's *Photography in Latin America*.)

Latin American television has also proved to be an important area of pop cultural investigation that at once reproduces and shakes up gender and sexuality norms. For instance, I have recently begun to research and analyze issues of gender in *Sesame Street* (*Plaza Sésamo*) *Latin America*. In the 1970s and 1980s, in content and form it was a near one-to-one translation of the US content; the space of the street becomes that of a working-class plaza, Big Bird becomes the giant parrot, Abelardo, Oscar becomes the grouchy parrot, Paco, for instance. However, in the 1990s, there was a shift to create content that was uniquely Mexican. And with this, it became the only show for Mexican children to be exposed to the full diversity of Mexican life: from rural to urban, from farmers to ladrilleros (brickworkers), and that was gender inclusive. Within the space of pop cultural televisual consumption, *Plaza Sésamo* grew to become an important space for opening children's eyes to the rich diversity of Mexican life regionally, socioeconomically, culturally, and in terms of gender roles. Brenda Campos, country director of Mexico Sesame Workshop, discusses how the content for *Plaza Sésamo* continues to be grown by local "experts on thematic areas," "testing content" with Mexican children, and "working with local talent of writers" (Aldama interview July 27, 2017). In this way, the content captures "indigenous, non-indigenous, rural, urban, people with disabilities, different socio-economic backgrounds." And the content aims to appeal to "peri-urban (marginalized communities in urban settings, rural, and urban)" children and communities. Gender is front and center in the Sesame Workshops in Latin America. In the debut of the problem-solving, adventurer Lola in 2005, we see the creation of a smart character who is anchored in her Latina-ness. As Brenda Campos states, she "resembles an intellectually curious and confident Latin American girl who actively promotes math and science for young girls." She and Pancho also educate Latin/o American children on healthy food habits: the "plato del buen comer." And after the introduction to US audiences of Julia (on the autism spectrum) in 2017, Latin American creators of Sesame Workshops generally are turning their sights to issues of being differently abled. Finally, while there are transferable content and shared language among the different Sesame Workshops in Latin America that give it its hemispheric sensibility, we see in each instantiation (Mexico, Bolivia, Colombia, and so on) the building of content that's "relevant to children in the respective region." In each, too, there is attention to different regional sounds: music, dance, and songs.

Arguably, in scholarly analyses of gender and sexuality the telenovela's rags-to-riches formula takes up the lion's share of analyses focused on Latin American TV. We see in the work of scholars like Julie Tate, Ana López, Diana Rios, Mari Castañeda, and María de la Luz Casas Pérez, among others, an examination of sexuality and gender that calls attention to and destabilizes traditional aligning of macho and masculine with straight and the feminine with straight women and gay characters.

Indeed, telenovelas like *Rubí, Sabor a ti* have proved a rich field to mine for critiquing dominant gender discourses that inform narratives of nationalism: the "feminine" as linked to women and gay characters only and the "masculine" only to straight men. And, with the introduction more recently of complex gender roles and character sexualities in telenovelas like *Yo amo a Juan Querendón*, this genre has proved a fertile ground for interpreting it as a space for counter-narratives that destabilize traditional gender binaries and heteronormative sexualities.

Latin American cinema has also proved to be an important space for critical inquiry into issues of gender and sexuality. Scholars like David William Foster, Sergio de la Mora, and Vinodh Venkatesh, among others, turn their queer analytic lens to re-read Latin American cinematic history—and to solidify the presence of a contemporary Latin American queer cinema. In *Queer Issues in Contemporary Latin American Cinema* (2003) Foster formulates a queer lens for analyzing conventionally straight films by Maria Luisa Bemberg and Arturo Ripstein, as well as queer films (and a documentary) by the likes of Tomás Gutierrez Alea and Barbet Schroeder. While Foster focuses on films released between 1979 and 2000, in *Cinemachismo* Sergio de la Mora turns his queer lens to Mexico's Golden Age of cinema: the 1930s–1950s. de la Mora carefully unpacks how Golden Age actors like Ramon Navarro and César Romero performed a hypermasculine, mythic scaled Latin lover identity; de la Mora does gesture toward today's Mexican cinema, identifying, for instance, how today's Gael García Bernal performs at the nexus of the "feminine" and "phallic" (2016: 164). In *New Maricón Cinema* Venkatesh identifies a non-urban queer cinema, with its own localized sets of gender and sexuality concepts and actions that vitally destabilize "heteronormative politics and subjectivities" (2016: 22); he contrasts this localized queer cinema to older and genre (romantic comedy, for instance) queer Latin American movies, that further entrench normative gender and sexuality stereotypes.

In Latin American cinema studies, there are others working at the intersection of gender, class, and consumption within neoliberalism. I think readily of such scholars as Patricia Torres San Martín, Ilana Luna, María de la Cruz Castro Ricalde, Ana López, Laura Podalsky, Ignacio Sánchez Prado, Dianna Niebylski, and Patrick O'Connor, who focus on issues of gender in Latin American cinema. Lupe Vélez, Dolores Del Rio, Salma Hayek, and García Bernal have been analyzed in terms of how the pop cultural media format of film, along with all of its commercial offshoots, like t-shirts, posters, and the like, serve up the Latina and Latino as commodified objects. However, these same Latin American pop cultural icons are also actively metabolized and transformed by Latin American audiences. They are, in the words of Dianna Niebylski and Patrick O'Connor, "mediated, appropriated, and re-contextualized" (*Latin American Icons* [16]). Indeed, for Ignacio Sánchez Prado, while US mainstream audiences readily consume Salma Hayek as a hypersexualized Latina, for Mexicans there is no interest in consuming her Mexicanness as such. Hence, for Sánchez Prado, "Hayek's Mexicanness operates in the realm of exchange value, as a symbolic commodity circulated in the exchange of symbols that accompanied economic trade in post-NAFTA North America, thus allowing her reading not only as 'Mexican' but also as 'Latina and even as a nondescript character'" (2014: 152).

Scholars of Latin American cinema also focus on issues of how horror, *chanchadas*, *ranchera*, melo-drama, and comedy, among other genres, function as means of reinforcing and critiquing neoliberal, sexist, heterophobic, and racist paradigms of power. In my coauthored book with Ilan Stavans (included herein), *Muy Pop!,* we analyze the way hero worship in Mexican *ranchera* films reproduced traditional gender roles as well as those that emancipated women from the domestic. For instance, in my *Mex-Ciné* I identify what I call "refrito," or refried, films. For example, *Ladies' Night* (2003), *Efectos secundarios* (2006), *Casi divas* (2008), and *El tigre de Santa Julia* aim to please adult viewers by offering "formulations of time, place, character, and event typical of soap operas. These are Mexican films, but they are made in ways that put them out of time and place" (86). But I also identify a series of what I call bubblegum films, like *Amar te duele* (2002) and *La hija del caníbal* (2003), that offer radical critiques of class and gender identities. And in *Screening Neoliberalism* Sánchez Prado analyzes

Introduction

how Mexican film industries in the 1980s and 1990s used comedy and romances with neoliberal agendas to sell tickets to middle class audiences; along with this came the construction of classist, ethnocentric, and sexist criteria of beauty (he locates with the star-making of Ana Serradilla, Ana de la Reguera, and Martha Higareda) *and* the dropoff in female directed filmmaking.

★

The chapters that comprise *The Routledge Companion to Gender, Sex and Latin American Culture* continue to deepen and broaden the scholarship on Latin American pop cultural phenomena, especially as it intersects with issues of gender and sexuality. The scholars herein seek to understand how creators make pop cultural objects circulated and consumed within different historical, political, and social contexts of Latin America that reproduce or challenge otherwise restrictive modes of being. They seek to identify the clearing and claiming of new transformative spaces in and through the creating and disseminating of such pop cultural phenomena within local and global networks of consumption. Each chapter, too, aims to analyze all of the above from a perspective outside of the US—from within the Américas. They seek to open eyes to different pop cultural phenomena where gender/sexuality transect, and also to provide rich historical and social contextualizations. They attend to local reconstructions and also to how within the technologies of the popular they lead to hemispheric potentialities: audiences and new creators as part of this audience from around the Américas and beyond.

Put simply, each chapter seeks to provide on-the-ground alternative approaches to so-called high culture and low, or pop culture, and how they work within local Latin American contexts and beyond. Each chapter provides a critical, interpretive look at a given area of Latin American pop cultural studies, with a sharp focus on issues of gender and sexuality, including areas that have received scant attention, for example, pop cultural phenomena that consider androgynous, lesbian, and bisexual identities. Each chapter offers in-depth analyses of specific examples determined by the respective scholar's expertise.

I have chosen to divide the volume into eight main parts. The chapters that make up "Part I: Transmedial re-mediations" focus on different multimedia forms used today that throw light on constructions of gender and sexuality within the Américas. I open this first part with Debra A. Castillo's chapter, "Hybrid mass culture." Castillo firmly plants us in 21st-century digital and Internet technologies that allow for the speedy and widespread bottom-up pop cultural creations throughout the Américas that run counter to the elitist "shiny media concoctions," and that give new expression to gendered, Spanish-language experiences and identities. In her analysis of punk rock, a sci-fi graphic novel, slam poetry, and multimedia digital art Castillo demonstrates how the low-fi, low-budget works in Spanish clear spaces of resistance to the onslaught of top-down, corporate, and elitist mainstream culture that reproduces identity hierarchies. In "The Latin American *flâneur* in the digital age," Osvaldo Cleger also sets his sights on digital intermedial and transmedial pop cultural phenomena in the Américas. Cleger examines the construction of the *virtual flâneur*, the urban wanderer figure in the grassroots created, web-based videogame *Caminando Bogotá*, and the big budget, corporate produced videogame *Assassin's Creed IV: Black Flag*. Cleger's comparison of these two pop cultural phenomena and the male gaze of the *flâneur* allows him to articulate how urban spaces of the Américas are framed for middle class, masculine subjects. Phillip Penix-Tadsen's chapter, "Intersections of gender and gaming in Latin America," also focuses on videogames. Penix-Tadsen examines issues of gender and sexuality at the level of creation, marketing, online playing and presence, including sexual harassment. Against this large backdrop, he analyzes how the Latina playable character, Sombra, appeals to women and LGBTQ gamers. For Penix-Tadsen, no matter how "toxic" the representations are in videogames, in

9

the end he reminds us that women and LGBTQ *"prosumers"* are actively creating new communities of gamers, modders, and developers. Stacey Alex also focuses her analysis on games, but games that are more the old-school analog and that have transmuted into other cultural phenomena. In her chapter, *"La lotería mexicana*: Playing with heteronormativity," Alex examines how the *lotería* card game in the Américas has been actively transformed by contemporary lesbian and socially progressive artists and authors in ways that articulate a social justice message. Alex's analyses of creators like Alma López and Lalo Alcaraz, along with novelist Mario Alberto Zambrano, demonstrate how the *lotería* card game has been expanded to be gender and queer inclusive and that clear a space for articulating a hemispheric social resistance and affirmation of intersectional identities. Ivonne García turns her attention to the always-already transmedial (visual and verbal) comic book. In "Colonial history and Puerto Rican hero narratives in *21: The Story of Roberto Clemente* and *La Borinqueña*," García considers how the meshed, hybrid visual and verbal format of comics is especially suited to the expression of complex Puerto Rican identities and experiences. Indeed, in her analysis of Miranda-Rodríguez's superhero comic, *La Borinqueña,* and Wilfred Santiago's biographical *21: The Story of Roberto Clemente,* García reveals how the superheroic genre of comics allows for the affirmation of complex, "racially gendered" fantasies that express the heroism of Puerto Rican subjects surviving colonization (past and present). In "Drawing Up a 'Post'-Latin America" Mauricio Espinoza turns his sights to science and speculative comic books that imagine a post-Latin America with more complex representations of gender. I end this part with Nicholas Poppe's chapter, "Tito Guízar on Radio Row." Poppe analyzes the intermedial pop cultural phenomena (stage, music recording, and TV broadcasting) built around Mexican singer and actor, Tito Guízar. Poppe reveals how instances of intermedial textual phenomena such as seen (and heard) with the production of the protean music video, *Rambling 'Round Radio Row,* which features Guízar, call attention to the race, ethnic, and gender stereotypes used in packaging Mexican-ness for popular consumption in the US.

"Part II: *Bending* genre" brings together chapters that consider how creators work within and against storytelling conventions found in genres like science fiction, noir, romance, and the as-told-to oral format. Sergio Macías's "Man cave and campy interior design in José Asunción Silva's *De sobremesa*" opens this part. Here Macías takes us on a journey from Aaron Marino's blog, *Alpha M*, to José Asunción Silva's 19th-century novel, *De sobremesa*, in order to explore how storytelling generic conventions are used to both construct and destabilize what he calls a "man-cave" masculinity. Macias uses a queer, camp aesthetic lens to reveal how the décor (ornament and furniture) of spaces in, for instance, *De sobremesa*, breaks down gendered dichotomies, e.g., outside versus inside. Following Macias is Ben. Sifuentes-Jáuregui's chapter, "Melodramatic attachments." He analyzes Manuel Puig's use of the romance novel's melodramatic conventions to make visible "unstable" and "unknowable" desiring subjects that destabilize heteronormativity. Matthew David Goodwin sets his sights on the conventions of science fiction as reconfigured within Cuban, feminist literary spaces. In his chapter, "Sex with aliens," Goodwin analyzes how Daína Chaviano uses the science fiction mold to destabilize the way that religion, science, and mythology have traditionally constrained and controlled women's sexuality. In Shigeko Mato's chapter, "Villain or victim?", she explores the tension between the construction of exclusive (academic) versus inclusive (pop culture) readers of the novel, *Gaijin*—which uses the conventions of the oral storytelling format to affirm the point of view and voice of an ordinary Japanese Peruvian woman. By reading *Gaijin* as a site of "unauthorized popular culture" Mato demonstrates how the novel questions the unified collective memory of Japanese Peruvians constructed by the Japanese Peruvian Oral History Project (JPOHP). She also shows how the novel articulates and affirms the stories, memories, and histories of otherwise marginalized Japanese Peruvian subjects and experience. I end this part with Juan Poblete's chapter, "Art, literature, and

Introduction

mass media in Pedro Lemebel," which analyzes the process of "proltarianization" in the works of gay Chilean Pedro Lemebel's use of pop cultural, massmediated textual and performance art spaces that articulate a revolutionary queer politics.

"Part III: Re-constructing silver screen imaginaries" includes chapters that focus on audio-visual pop cultural formats, such as film and television. I open this part with Ignacio Sánchez Prado's "Neoliberal pigmentocracies," which provides a broad and deep, penetrating analysis of the aesthetic and ideological shifts that have taken place in the production and reception of Mexican cinema since 1988. Sánchez Prado explores how the representation of women (from communal/traditional to elite/cosmopolitan) reveals the shift to a Mexican cinematic construction of a "neoliberal womanhood" that seeks to "preserve the symbolic structures of class inequality without even making the gesture of any kind of pretended democratic inclusion." In "Class, gender, race in filmic urban Brazilian spaces," Samuel Cruz also takes interest in the cosmopolitan, but here setting sights on the construction of urban spaces in contemporary Brazilian cinema. In his analysis of films like *Os Inquilinos* and *Linha de Passe*, Cruz examines how the storytelling devices a director uses can construct the urban in ways that open audience eyes to "class-specific, gendered, and racialized social spaces." In "*El roc ha muerto, viva el roc*," Iván Eusebio Aguirre Darancou excavates how Mexico's Sergio García Michel creates films with Super 8mm cameras in ways that work within the countercultural, mexperimental mode *and* calls attention to how countercultural cinema can itself become coopted by the mainstream. Along with identifying how García Michel's resistant Super 8mm cinema creates new networks of social resistance, Aguirre Darancou identifies how Michel articulates a *mestiza*-generated reassembly of "female sexuality, citizenship and political subjectivity." In "Starring Mexico," Olivia Cosentino focuses on Mexican cinema and the construction of the female star from the 1950s through the 1980s. For Cosentino, the star-making of Mexican actresses within increasingly hemispheric and global circuits of pop culture creation at once reproduces and resists their stereotyping. In "Hemisexualizing the Latin lover," Paloma Martínez-Cruz and John Cruz formulate the concept of "hemisexuality" to demonstrate how actors like Rudolph Valentino, Ricardo Montalban, Eugenio Derbez, Carlos Gardel, Vicente Fernandez, Pedro Infante, and John Cruz (co-author of this chapter) solidify and destabilize the Latino sexuality threat narrative: oversexed, perverted, irrational, and in need of control by Anglo reason. Martínez-Cruz and Cruz formulate how the hemisexual performative embrace of the Latino threat narrative can lead to the release of "unspoken" libidinal possibilities. In her chapter, "Transnational queerings and *Sense8*," Laura Fernández examines how Netflix's series, *Sense8*, applauded for its LGBTQ character creation, slips into conventional forms of representing Mexican masculinity. In her analysis of the closeted gay character, Lito, Fernández demonstrates how the show uncritically reproduces the "stereotyped mold of what counts as 'Mexican'" and the role of masculinity in a Latin American cultural context. Finally, while there is some complexity built into Lito's characterization, Fernández argues that the creators (the Wachowski sisters) slip into too-easy molds that exoticize Latino masculinity for North American consumption. I end this part with Ryan Rashotte's chapter, "Good gringos, bad hombres." Rashotte is also interested in the pop cultural, filmic construction of a Latin/o Américas masculinity for North American consumption. In his scholarly meditation on conservative, pro-Catholic US films starring Mel Gibson (*Get the Gringo, Blood Father*, and *Machete Kills*), Rashotte analyzes the way Latino masculinity is constructed as a "violent, socially destabilizing force to be contained by the Gringo Savior, who, in the process of containment, is able to redeem his own masculine agency (on- and off-screen), and safeguard the cultural authority of white masculinity at large in North America."

"Part IV: Putting the feminist and queer pop in the pictorial arts" includes scholarship focused on issues of gender and sexuality in photography, graffiti, murals, and painting. In "Graffiti in

Latin America," Ilan Stavans invites readers to join his meditative journey through different graffitied spaces of the Américas. While each instance of graffiti relates in unique ways to its respective nation-space, this pop cultural means of communication, linked to pre-Columbian and muralist ideographic forms of expression, offers a venue for *graffiteros* (subjects at the social, racial, gendered margins) to affirm an inclusive and complex cultural heritage and, as well, to contest oppression and exploitation. In "Graffiti School *Comunidad*" Guisela Latorre teams up with Chilean graffiti artist, Marjorie Peñailillo, to throw light on the significance of the creation of the Graffiti School Communidad in Valparaiso, Chile, where artists learn feminist street art techniques and pedagogies as well as develop strategies of resistance and resilience to dominant, patriarchal regimes of power. Arij Ouweneel's chapter, "Contemporary Amerindian imaginaries and the challenge of intersectional analysis," examines how Amerindian arts creation expresses and affirms feminist *indígina* civil rights struggles across the Américas. For instance, artists like Rosmery Mamani Ventura and Claudia Coca use their painterly palettes to make art that invites coalition building in and around decolonization actions. They create a mnemonic painterly art that preserves stories and contests colonial and postcolonial legacies of racism and sexism. I end this part with David William Foster's "The photography of Thomaz Farkas and the Estádo de Pacaembu." Foster's focus on Brazilian photographer Thomas Farkas uncovers how his "homo-socializing" camera lens represents soccer as a popular cultural phenomenon and national pastime that solidifies a hetero-masculine Brazilian nationalism.

"Part V: Bend it like *Pelé*" brings together chapters that focus on issues of gender, sexuality, and race in pop cultural framings of such sports as soccer, boxing, and baseball. I open this part with Patrick Ridge's "A 'friendly' game." Like David William Foster, Ridge is interested in teasing out how soccer participates in the construction of a heterosexist, masculinist (machista) nationalism. In his queer analysis of the comedy series, *Club de Cuervo*, Ridge identifies a subterranean "homoaffectivity" at work in soccer that *troubles* the masculinist narrative of nation. In "Reading race and gender in *The Black Man in Brazilian Soccer* and beyond," Jack A. Draper III analyzes how soccer and its media have erased the presence and participation (as players and fans) of Afrolatinos and women in the construction of a Brazilian nationhood. Moreover, Draper complicates the picture by analyzing how black and mixed-race males' breaking soccer's racist color line further marginalized women. Once women were allowed to enter the hypermasculine-coded world of soccer in the 1970s, being identified as tomboys or lesbians also identified them as going against their "nature" and the masculine/feminine order of things. Finally, Draper explores how the struggle of women mirrors the color-line struggles of Afrolatino players in desegregating the sport—and with this, the push to create a more inclusive Brazilian nationalism. With a chapter coauthored by Mauricio Espinoza and Luis Miguel Estrada Orozco, this part turns to boxing. In "Hard punches, vulnerable bodies," Espinoza and Estrada Orozco explore how two films about boxing—Jonathan Jakubowicz's *Hands of Stone* and Florence Jaugey's *La Yuma*—frame issues of gender, class, and nation in the Américas. Building on the work of Hortensia Moreno on women's boxing and Mexican nationalism, they compare and contrast the way these two films handle gender and nationalism. Moreno's creation of a gender progressive and feminist empowering character, Virginia Roa 'La Yuma', stands in sharp contrast to Jakubowicz's representation of Roberto Durán as a stand-in for a machista, masculinist, Panamanian nationalism. I close this part with Jennifer Rudolph's chapter, "'The Blizzard of Oz,'" that analyzes how the media frame Latin/o Américans sports spectacles like baseball as threat narratives that distract the populace from systemic, structural, social, racial, and gender inequities. Rudolph focuses on how the media have turned Cuban Latino Ozzie Guillén's management of the White Sox into a spectacle of masculine irrationalism. Rudolph locates this spectacle making impulse to Latino deeper histories of colonialism and imperialism

Introduction

and its multimedia ideological appendages that continue to represent Latinos as threatening *bandidos* and drug kingpins.

"Part VI: Alt-hemispheric sound and body performatics" moves the volume in the direction of the aural and corporeal. This part begins with Melissa Castillo-Garsow's chapter, "Somos Mujeres Somos Hip Hop," which explores how a new generation of feminist rappers from across the Américas use hip-hop to wake listeners to gender inequities and intersectional identities. In her analysis of the feminist rap collective that forms Somos Mujeres Somos Hip Hop, Castillo-Garsow considers how their auditory (lyric and sound rhythms) *and* audio-visual (music videos) soundscapes "challenge too narrow conceptualizations of the hip hop subject as Black and male, and ask us to think carefully about how hip hop feminists and scholars based outside the US incorporate the lived experiences of women south of the border." In "Weirded soundscapes" J. Andrew Brown examines how Mike Wilson and Álvaro Bisama use underground music culture to explore the formation of identity in contemporary Chile. With particular attention to Wilson's 2011 Rockabilly and Bisama's 2014 story "Death metal," we see how both writers build systems of musical references in the construction of alternative bodies and subcultures that defy traditional views of Chilean culture. John Petrus and Jessica Rutherford's coauthored chapter "Dance as medicine," explores the long history of popular dance rituals in Nicaragua from the colonial to present periods. They demonstrate how rituals of dance and music at once create alternative, indigenous-grown histories *and* help heal the traumas of colonization and its legacies. Moreover, these rituals clear a space that celebrates indigenous knowledge, aesthetic values, and a more inclusive concept of gender and sexuality than those imposed by the colonial and postcolonial gender system. I end this part with Michelle Wibbelsman's chapter, "Gender performativity and indigenous conceptions of duality in the Inti Raymi-Jatun Puncha Festivals of Cotacachi, Ecuador." Based on her on-the-ground research in the highland city of Cotacachi, Ecuador, Wibbelsman explores how the ancient Incan religious ceremony "Inti Raymi" (Festival of the Sun), which continues to be performed today, articulates an indigenous-anchored, gender-fluid (where male dancers dress as women, for instance) ritual that functions as a "spatial-political counter-conquest." Ultimately, Inti Raymi provides a new stage for creating a "*pluridiversidad* (pluridiversity)" that affirms "social, cultural, and political *convivencia* (communal experience and solidarity)."

I conclude the volume with "Part VII: Staging nuevo hemispheric identities," which brings together scholarship on theatre, performance, open mic rituals, and stand-up comedy. I open this final part with Julie Ann Ward's chapter, "Beside motherhood." Ward focuses her attention on feminist playwrights, such as Vivi Tellas and Lola Arias, as well as the work of the theatre troupe, Lagartijas Tirada al Sol. Ward shows how these feminist productions of a theatre of the real affirm the real, biographical, flesh-and-bloods presence of mothers. Moreover, Ward examines how such a theatre demands that audiences actively engage with what's happening on the stage and in their own lives, especially asking that they interrogate their own roles as daughters of mothers. For Ward, these plays that stage "real" mothers as "beyond maternity" and as subjects stage a progressive feminism that runs counter to a long tradition of masculinist Latin American theatre. With Derek Pardue's chapter, "Can *saraus* speak to gender and migrant politics in São Paulo?', we learn how the Brazilian *sarau* provides a space for African, feminist *émigré* subjects to voice and exchange "ideas, beats and stories" concerning issues of violence and displacement against women and African immigrants. The feminist and politicized space of the sarau participates in an "expressive culture" that includes "spoken word, music and street theater" and ultimately affirms "race, gender and belonging." In "Transfeminism and fake mustachios" Ignacio Corona examines Mexican theorist, poet and performer Sayak Valencia's important contribution to violence studies and the double transfeminist and decolonial perspective that

Valencia casts on the most nefarious effects of neoliberalism in Mexico. For Corona, Valencia provides one of the most systematic analyses of the underlying factors behind the security crisis, the war on drugs, and gender violence. He analyzes her most well-known work to date, *Capitalismo gore*, where Valencia establishes a connection between the economic logic of neoliberalism and the crisis of the nation-State with the legacy of colonialism and the reproduction of a model of a violent masculinity pervasive in the cultural industries and in society. Doug Bush's chapter, "Proud sinvergüenza or foolish maricón?", articulates a queer radicalization of the stage performance. Bush does so by analyzing the queer stand-up comedy of Mexican Manu NNa. For Bush, Manu NNa's *sinvergüenza* "bottom-up" stand-up comedy "pulls back the curtain on a queer discourse increasingly privatized by the homonormative impulse." However, as Bush further analyzes, when Manu NNa loses control over his narrative in the "top-down" corporate produced (Comedy Central Latinoamérica) *Se busca comediante*, he is "recast as foolish maricón—one who is not only dangerous to himself, but also to those who associate with him." I end this part and the volume with Kristie Soares's chapter, "The Cuban Missile Crisis of white masculinity." Soares analyzes the way in which the queer comedic performances of Cuban Latino Tito Bonito inhabit the space of the burlesque in ways that call attention to the construction of restrictive, ethnic, gender, and sexuality stereotypes. Soares points out how Bonito's performing these stereotypes allows him to insert "himself into a historical narrative of burlesque that performs not just gender and sexuality, but also *Cubanidad*, in a way that is both sexy and political."

While each of the chapters differs in approach and method, taken as a whole *The Routledge Companion to Gender, Sex and Latin American Culture* offers up-to-date scholarship on this lively area of research, whose aim is to throw light on the growing of pop culture within and *across* specific regions of Latin America. It continues the deep efforts of Latin American scholars to map out this vital, critical terrain where gender and sex make cultural phenomena *pop*. Finally, it shouts from the rooftops that pop culture created and consumed by women and LGBTQ subjects across the Américas calls for our interpretive recognition, appreciation, and affirmation.

Works cited

Aldama, Frederick Luis. *Mex-Ciné: Mexican Filmmaking, Production, and Consumption in the 21st Century.* Ann Arbor, MI: University of Michigan Press, 2013.

Aldama, Frederick Luis. "Interview with Brenda Campos." July 27, 2017.

Aldama, Frederick Luis and Ilan Stavans. *¡Muy Pop! Conversations on Latino Popular Culture.* Ann Arbor, MI: University of Michigan Press, 2013.

Bermudez, Silvia. "Popular Culture in Latin America." In *Companion to Latin American Studies.* Ed. Philip Swanson. New York; London: Routledge, 2003.

Brown, J. Andrew. *Cyborgs in Latin America.* New York: Palgrave 2010.

Bueno, Eva P. and Terry Caesar. Eds. *Imagination Beyond Nation: Latin American Popular Culture.* Pittsburgh, PA: University of Pittsburgh Press, 1998.

Cadava, Eduardo L. and Gabriela Nouzeilles, et al. Eds. *The Itinerant Languages of Photography.* Princeton, NJ: Princeton University Art Museum, 2013.

Canclini, Néstor García. 1989. *Culturas híbridas: Estrategias para entrar y salir de la modernidad.* Mexico City: Grijalbo.

Cánepa Koch, Gisela and Ingrid Kummels. Eds. *Photography in Latin America: Images and Identities Across Time and Space.* Bielefeld: Verlag, 2016.

Casas Pérez, M. de la L. "Cultural Identity: Between Reality and Fiction: A Transformation of Genre and Roles in Mexican Telenovelas." *Television and New Media* 6, 4 (2005): 407–14.

Castillo, Debra. *Talking Back: Toward a Latin American Feminist Literary Criticism.* Ithaca, NY: Cornell University Press, 1992.

Castro-Klarén, Sara. "Teoría del la crítica literaria y la escritora en América Latina." In *La sartén por el mango.* Eds. Patricia Elena González and Eliana Ortega. San Juan: Ediciones Huracán, 1984.

Castro-Klarén, Sara. Ed. *Narrativa femenina en América Latina: Prácticas y perspectivas teóricas.* Madrid: Iberoamericana, 2003.

de la Mora, Sergio. *Cinemachismo: Masculinities and Sexualities in Mexican Film.* Austin, TX: University of Texas Press, 2006.

Dorfman, Ariel, and Armand Mattelart. *How to Read Donald Duck: Imperialist Ideology in the Disney Comic.* New York: International General. 1984.

Ehrick, Christine. "Radio Transvestism and the Gendered Soundscape in Buenos Aires, 1930s–1940s." In *Media, Sound, and Culture in Latin America and Caribbean.* Eds. Alejandra Bronfman and Andrew Grant Wood. Pittsburgh, PA: University of Pittsburgh Press, 2012. 18–34.

Estevam, Carlos. "For a Popular Revoltuionary Art." In *Brazilian Cinema.* Eds. Randal Johnson and Robert Stam. New York: Columbia University Press, 1995. 58–63.

Foster, David William. *Argentine, Mexican, and Guatemalan Photography: Feminist, Queer, and Post-Masculinist Perspectives.* Austin, TX: University of Texas Press, 2014.

Franco, Jean. "The Gender Wars." In *Critical Passions.* Ed. Jean Franco, Durham, NC: Duke University Press, 1999, 123–30.

Franco, Jean. *Cruel Modernity.* Durham, NC: Duke University Press, 2013.

Kantaris, Geoffrey and Rory O'Bryen. Eds. *Latin American Popular Culture: Politics, Media, Affect.* Suffolk, UK/ Rochester, NY: Tamesis, 2013.

King, Edward and Joanna Page Sanz et al. Eds. *Posthumanism and the Graphic Novel in Latin America.* London: UCL Press, 2017. www.ucl.ac.uk/ucl-press/browse-books/posthumanism-and-the-graphic-novel-in-latin-america

Lamas, Marta. *Cuerpo: Diferencia sexual y género.* Mexico City: Taurus, 2002.

López, Ana. "The Melodrama in Latin America: Films, Telenovelas and the Currency of a Popular Form." *Wide Angle* 7, 3 (1985): 4–13.

López, Ana. "Calling for Intermediality: Latin American Mediascapes," *Cinema Journal* 54, 1 (Fall 2014): 135–141. Companion piece in digital site *In Media Res* http://mediacommons.futureofthebook.org/imr/2014/11/18/intermediality-and-brazilian-telenovelas

Martín-Barbero, Jesús. "Identidad, comunicación, y modernidad en América Latina." In *Posmodernidad en la periferia: Enfoques latinoamericanos de la nueva teoría cultural.* Eds. Herman Herlinghaus and Monika Walter. Berlin: Langer, 1994. 83–110

Molloy, Sylvia. "La flexión del género en el texto cultural latinoamericano." *Revista de Crítica Cultural* 21 (November 2000): 49–59.

Mouat, Ricardo Gutiérrez. "Postmodernity and Postmodernism in Latin America: Carlos Fuentes's *Christopher Unborn.*" In *Critical Theory, Cultural Politics, and Latin American Narrative.* Eds. Steven M. Bell, Albert H. Le May, and Leonard Orr. Notre Dame, IN: University of Notre Dame Press 1993. 153–179.

Niebylski, Dianna and Patrick O'Connor. Eds. *Latin American Icons: Fame Across Borders.* Nashville, TN: Vanderbilt University Press, 2014.

Ortiz, Fernando. *Contrapunteo cubano del tabaco y el azúcar.* Havana: J. Montero. 1940

Ortiz, Fernando. *Cuban Counterpoint: Tobacco and Sugar.* Durham, NC: Duke University Press, 1995.

Prado, Ignacio Sánchez. *Screening Neoliberalism: Transforming Mexican Cinema, 1988–2012.* Nashville, TN: Vanderbilt University Press, 2014.

Premat, Adriana. "Popular Culture, Politics, and Alternative Gender Imaginaries in 1960s and 1970s Argentina." *Studies in Latin American Popular Culture* 33, 1 (2015): 41–56.

Rios, Diana and Mari Castañeda. Eds. *Soap Operas and Telenovelas in the Digital Age Global Industries and New Audiences.* New York: Peter Lang, 2011.

Rowe, William, and Vivian Schelling. *Memory and Modernity: Popular Culture in Latin America.* London: Verso, 1991.

Schelling, Vivian. "Introduction: Reflections on the Experience of Modernity in Latin America." In *Through the Kaleidoscope: The Experience of Modernity in Latin America.* Ed. Vivian Schelling. London; New York: Verso, 2000. 1–33.

Sifuentes-Jáuregui, Ben. *Transvestism, Masculinity and Latin American Literature.* New York: Palgrave, 2002.

Sifuentes-Jáuregui, Ben. *The Avowal of Difference: Queer Latino American Narratives.* Albany, NY: SUNY Press, 2014.

Tate, Julie. "From Girly Men to Manly Men: The Evolving Representation of Male Homosexuality in Twenty-First Century Telenovelas." *Studies in Latin American Popular Culture,* 29 (2011): 103–14

Tate, Julie. "Redefining Mexican Masculinity in Twenty-First Century Telenovelas." *Hispanic Research Journal* 14, 6 (December 2013): 538–52.
William H. Beezley and Linda A. Curcio-Nagy. Eds. *Latin American Popular Culture: An Introduction*. Lanham, MD: Rowman & Littlefield, 2012.

Suggested further reading

Attwood, Feona and Danielle Egan. Eds. *The Routledge Companion to Media, Sex and Sexuality*. London; New York: Routledge, 2016.
Blanco, Richard. *Imagination Beyond Nation: Latin American Popular Culture*. Pittsburgh, PA: University of Pittsburgh Press, 1998.
Brown, Gavin and Kath Browne. Eds. *The Routledge Research Companion to Geographies of Sex and Sexualities*. London; New York: Routledge, 2016.
Caliendo, Stephen M. and Charlton D. McIlwain. Eds. *The Routledge Companion to Race and Ethnicity*. London; New York: Routledge, 2010.
Carter, Cynthia and Linda Steiner. Eds. *The Routledge Companion to Media & Gender*. London; New York: Routledge, 2015.
Cepeda, María. *Musical ImagiNation: U.S.-Colombian Identity and the Latin Music Boom*. New York: New York University Press, 2010.
Fojas, Camilla. *Islands of Empire: Pop Culture and U.S. Power*. Austin, TX: University of Texas Press, 2014.
Foster, David William. *From Mafalda to Los Supermachos: Latin American Graphic Humor as Popular Culture*. Boulder, CO: L. Rienner, 1989.
Foster, David William. *Queer Issues in Contemporary Latin American Cinema*. Austin, TX: University of Texas Press, 2003.
Gutmann, Mathew C. and Felix V. Rodriguez et al. Eds. *Perspectives on Las Américas: A Reader in Culture, History & Representation*. Malden, MA: Blackwell Publishing, 2003.
Miller, Toby. *The Routledge Companion to Global Popular Culture*. London; New York: Routledge, 2016.
Natella, Arthur A. *Latin American Popular Culture*. Jefferson, NC; London: McFarland, 2008.
Nichols, Elizabeth and Timothy Robbin. Eds. *Pop Culture in Latin American and the Caribbean*. Santa Barbara, CA: ABC-CLIO, 2015.
Nixon, Angelique. *Resisting Paradise: Tourism, Diaspora, and Sexuality in Caribbean Culture*. Jackson, MS: University Press of Mississippi, 2009.
Qurioga, José. *Tropics of Desire: Interventions from Queer Latino America*. New York University Press, 2001.
Schelling, Vivian. "Popular Culture in Latin America." In *The Cambridge Companion to Modern Latin American Culture*. Ed. John King. Cambridge University Press, 2004. 171–201.
Sluis, Ageeth. *Deco Body, Deco City: Female Spectacle and Modernity in Mexico City, 1900–1939*. Lincoln, NE: University of Nebraska Press, 2016.
Venkatesh, Vinodh. *New Maricón Cinema: Outing Latin American Film*. Austin, TX: University of Texas Press, 2016.
Williams, Gareth. *The Other Side of the Popular: Neoliberalism and Subalternity in Latin America*. Durham, NC: Duke University Press, 2002.

PART I

Transmedial re-mediations

1

HYBRID MASS CULTURE

Debra A. Castillo

When invited by the editor of this volume to contribute a follow-up to an earlier study of hybrid storyspaces, I was immediately intrigued, since the most familiar shape of hybrid narrative in Latin America—as elsewhere—has been overwhelmingly male and resolutely geeky. The context proposed by this volume's challenge to think about gender, sexuality, and mass culture together with hybrid forms reminded me of the dialectal reasoning associated with medieval scholasticism: How many angels can dance on the head of this particular pin?

By this moment in the third millennium, it has become axiomatic to reference—often in simultaneously celebratory and deprecating ways—how the Internet has created new possibilities for the creation and dissemination of human expression. The opportunity offered by cheap or free Internet access and free websites has sponsored a boom in expression, as writers and artists of varying talent vie to share their work with an audience that is, potentially at least, extraordinarily large. Many of even the most traditional writers now have their own YouTube channels as well as their almost obligatory blogs and websites, where one can hear them read from their works, as well as browse the site for more or less elaborately illustrated and contextualized samples of it. And it is through the Internet that many of them create community, connecting with other artists and with their fans. As one of the most important graphics writers of the continent, PowerPaola, notes: "Internet me abrió un camino que antes hubiera sido muy complicado para mi transitar" (Vañó 2013), not least because it was through a crowdfunding campaign that she was able to publish her *Diario.* If there is no quality control in online publication (a frequent complaint[1]), one sign of mass appeal is exactly this: her project was funded, and her followers have made her work popular.

What do we mean by hybridity in this context? How do we characterize mass culture in the times of Web 2.0? What does gender have to do with it? While print novels have always struggled against the limitations of form—as for example, Laura Esquivel's *La ley del amor*, which includes significant passages in graphic format and an attached CD[2]—for our purposes here the focus will not be on the way print has sometimes incorporated other material forms of culture, but rather on the hybridity found in Internet-based cultural creations, exclusive of ancillary or promotional material. A scholar included in this volume, Osvaldo Cleger, provides a helpful overview and taxonomy of hybrid work in this contemporary context in his article, "La creación ciberliteraria" (2015). In the body of this study, he does precisely what the subtitle promises: to provide a "definición, perfil y carta de navegación para orientarse en un campo emergente." The article includes discussion of cybernetic material of many sorts: digital native, electronic, hypertextual, interactive, or multimedia in form. It includes experiments in exploding traditional genres like poetry,[3] the novel or short story, and the performance text; it curates mashups and remixes. Early experiments in this now far-reaching, and extremely varied, practice include digital poetry (William Gibson's 1992 "Agrippa" is often signaled as one of the inaugural texts in this genre) and chat novels; contemporary forms include the Facebook novel, blog-fiction, Twitter narrative, and new creative forms that take advantage of the possibilities of GPS, Snapchat, virtual reality goggles, and CCTV camera footage. The key shared feature is that all of them are housed on computers (or more recently smartphones) and distributed via the Internet.

For this very reason it is almost impossible to generalize about hybrid production, since the range of work is so vast. The thousands of sites range from a basic reproduction of what might otherwise look like simple printed pages or blog pages with modest decorative elements, to elaborate experiments that involve sophisticated coding, extensive use of multimedia, and integral kinetic features. Hybrid forms may be interactive or not, may include sound (voice, music, or other sounds), static or moving images or video, along with manipulations of font, color, and the use of animation in the text—if indeed text is even used. It can involve constraint of the time of reading/listening by the way words and images are streamed and will almost certainly have an innovative relation to space and spacing that plays with the suggestive relationships of screen and text as opposed to paper as the media of transmission. Hallmarks include use of mashups, visual materials, music, gaming technologies, dance, collaborative writing, and computer-generated text.

Anna Katharina Schaffner's focus on text as the distinguishing feature of the pre-electronic genres, and a more multifarious understanding of "the sign" as a hallmark of the electronic age, underlines a now-familiar debate about the nature of cultural production in our time. Likewise, her succinct outline of some of the qualities that most prominently define hybrid forms (in her case, she is specifically referring to digital poetry as an emergent genre) can helpfully move toward a taxonomy that we can read together with Cleger's descriptions, where the fundamental building blocks are no longer material, no longer just language, but an unstable visual display, backed by code. As Schaffner has argued, signs have a substantially different function than text in the hybrid space:

> Firstly, they can move across the screen, they can be animated and programmed to perform a predetermined routine, and thus also gain a temporal dimension. Secondly, they can explore all dimensions of the sign at the same time simultaneously. Thirdly, they are equipped with a halo of technical meaning, and are, in some cases, both message and code at the same time. Fourthly and fifthly, signs are changeable 'flickering' images rather than fixedly inscribed marks. And lastly, digital signs gain an additional volumetric dimension: relationships of depth, foreground and background, proximity and distance can be simulated.
>
> *(2006: 8)*

One of the significant challenges of studying such hybrid works is what Henry Jenkins, Sam Ford, and Joshua Green call their "spreadability." This term shifts the focus from distribution (in the traditional sense applied to print books) to circulation (which also erodes the old divide between production and consumption), and includes the kinds of productive interactions with materials that would have been condemned as plagiarism or destruction of valuable artistic patrimony when applied to earlier forms of art. Jenkins and his collaborators are invested in thinking about how art moves through a cultural landscape, and how it evolves and changes as it finds its way into new creations. Spreadability, they say, "refers to the potential—both technical and cultural—for audiences to share content for their own purposes, sometimes with the permission of rights holders, sometimes against their wishes" (2013: 2, 27).

In thinking about hybrid media then, we necessarily have to contend with objects that spread virally, or that refuse to spread; materials that evolve as they move; as well as materials that, for technical or other reasons, drop out of the conversation through obsolescence or just the evanescent nature of much Internet-based work. For instance, we've all had the experience of programs that no longer work with new computer operating systems, or don't communicate well between platforms, of webpages that have vanished into "404 error" pages, of content that we have accidentally erased from our personal electronic devices and cannot recover. At the same time, there are some materials that we might think have disappeared, but nonetheless remain available through a set of innovative archival practices. William Gibson's "Agrippa" is an excellent example, always on the edge of disappearance (intentionally so), and always pulled back to life by dedicated followers. Originally created in 1992 and distributed on diskette, "Agrippa" was designed as a self-consuming, one-read-only text. Yet it has become one of the most durably available hybrid texts in Internet history. As it migrated from platform to platform through the efforts of dedicated fans who created simulators to run it, this self-destructing poem is now at the heart of a minor industry where it can, ironically, be read over and over again from its home in a university archive ("The *Agrippa* files").

But what subset of this production can be called mass culture? Does this term mean culture produced *by* the masses (however defined) or *for* the masses? While the Internet is anything but democratic, one of its oft-touted democratizing functions is to give a space to homegrown, low budget projects coming from people left out of the cultural mainstream's limited forms of access and limited repertoire of cultural objects and understandings. At the same time, we know that vast swathes of what we call mass culture are shiny media concoctions developed by elites intended for mass consumption. These mass-intended elite creations can become the building blocks for less privileged creators, due to the ease of creating mashups that allows for elite material (whether created with a mass consumption in mind or not) to become mass-ified, and spreadable.

Here is an immediate problem. Information from the many Latin American countries about information spread is hard to capture or consolidate. We know, according to *Internet World Stats*, that as of 2016, about 67% of Latin Americans have access to the Internet (by way of contrast, North America has 89% penetration), and certainly people at all levels of society are using contemporary technologies as ways to create and share their work. Steven Tepper, looking at cultural participation in the USA, cites Pew statistics to show that 57% of US youth engages in artistic creation, largely through remix for the Internet, and he sees this as a significant mass culture phenomenon, reversing the 20th century trends by way of which the arts became professionalized in the USA and enshrined as elite products (2008: 366, 368).

Argentine slam poet Sagrado Sebakis (Sebastián Kizner), in one of his videos, "De por qué la poesía slam y la alt lit son de los más intenso e incredible," implicitly pokes fun at the entire enterprise of high-sheen, high production value video by posting a shaky, webcam recording of himself and a friend reciting a poem/manifesto on why contemporary performance poetry by ordinary folks like him is a more agile and appropriate form of expression for writers whose lives are consumed by new forms of communication and expression.

We likewise know, of course, that many other Latin American youth are engaging in remix practices, often with great panache and originality, mostly as individuals, but also through group efforts like transcultura reciclada (e.g., Fran Ilich) and other rascuache practices of cultural (re)appropriation and production. Their point, finally—one made in other forms by a wide range of creative writers and thinkers—is that these newer, more agile genres require a new aesthetics, a new set of concepts and paradigms: in short, a new theory of production and a new way of reading. In most of these cases, however, these authors are not so much offering new paradigms themselves, as using the advantages of the Internet to creates remixes of existing cultural material or expand the audience for public readings of their work, with only modest technical effects to support a traditional activity.

From another angle, we might ask of any individual work of art: How many clicks define it as a mass culture product rather than art marked for elite consumption? We know there are qualitatively different kinds of clicks: including, on the one hand, those of elites like us who are researching articles, or on the other hand, a wide range of folks who are web browsing for any number of reasons (who in many cases have far less consistent access to these technologies; though it must be said that in the USA undocumented farmworkers are heavy users). Gender plays a role here too, both in production and perceived reception. Fangirls are overwhelmingly enthusiastic in their online responses to their favored works; male-identified fans are somewhat more reticent. Internet trolls and flamers are overwhelmingly male, and the most virulent attacks are saved for women perceived as overstepping into masculine territory.

Surprisingly frequently, scholars and casual critics alike have found ways to denigrate the kind of culture they don't like by writing it off as somehow associated with the feminine, and this has a direct effect on how we implicitly gender mass culture practices and products. This is a quirk that scholars like Susan Noakes ("Superficiality of Women," 1988), Andreas Huyssen ("Mass Culture as Women," 1986), and even Julio Cortázar with his peroration on the "lector femenino" (1963) have long noted. It remains astonishingly intractable today; that which is devalued will be gendered feminine and associated with women. These contradictory appreciations do not disappear when the platform changes. Depending on the critical angle, high culture is associated with powerful, elite male/masculinist enterprise and mass culture is the lowly province of chick lit. In this respect discussion around the hybrid novel, for instance, mirrors discourses of the avant garde familiar to us from Boom writers and high modernism more generally, where serious, difficult, proleptic works are the province of masculinity, while women engage in the more decorative arts (such as blogging, perhaps).[4] In the alternative version of woman-bashing, high culture has been framed as etoliated and effeminate in contrast with brawny, aggressive mass culture artifacts (one example might be the highly gendered structure of serious gamer circles).

High art likes to think of itself as ahead of its time, in contrast to mass culture, which is imagined to be retrograde. In any case, mass culture seems to be cathected with fleshy bodies, male or female, ethnically marked and racially coded, while high art often attempts to erase the signs of race, and gender, while cleaning up the bodies and putting them in order.[5] In this respect, the hybrid space of the Internet, with its chaotic visual potential, makes erasing the body more challenging than in print-based culture. Nonetheless, still today, surprisingly few of the most recognized cultural narratives from either high or low culture, however defined or deplored, pass the Bechdel test (i.e., whether a work of fiction features at least two women who talk to each other about something other than a man).

Nonetheless, there are marked changes. In contrast with the 19th and 20th centuries, when literary works that combined image and text (comics and historietas, for instance) were seen pejoratively, by and large, hybrid forms celebrate exactly this conjunction. In this respect, one of the most interesting Internet phenomena of recent times in terms of production that bridges high art and mass culture is the meteoric career of R.M. Drake (Robert Macías), who has been propelled into the limelight by viral enthusiasm that largely comes from a popular base of fans. In making his work accessible to his fan base, he ably manages his presence on

Hybrid mass culture

some of the most prominent social media platforms (Twitter, Amazon, Etsy, Instagram) while seeming to intentionally take a radical step back from technologically mediated hybrid art into the realm of artisanal work. The son of Colombian immigrants who moved to Miami, Drake has now made a career out of his short poems. He types them mechanically on varying kinds of paper, using a 1940s Royal typewriter that he bought at an antique shop in Miami, before photographing them and uploading them on Instagram. At the same time, he has created highly sophisticated media around his work, using video and elaborate photoshoots to help attract his audience.

He has more than 1.6 million followers, in large part spurred on by the very public enthusiasm of the Kardashian sisters, as well as popular singers Brandy and Ludacris among others, and has sold more than 160,000 copies of his self-published books in the last three years. To put these sales in context, this is at least ten times more than even the bestselling US literary poets like Jorie Graham, and more than 100 times what most top-notch poets can expect to sell. These sales have allowed him to decline offers from major publishers like Random House in favor of continuing with his Amazon connection. The sales of his books, along with other products like the prints and posters he sells on Etsy and directly from his website, have allowed him to quit his day job and have made him that most unusual creature: a poet able to live entirely off the sales of his work.

Perhaps parallel to Drake in success, but entirely opposite in style, is Chilean Jorge Baradit. Baradit is a former punk rock musician, who in addition to his speculative fiction (*Trinidad, Ygrasil, Policía del Karma*) has written alternative history (*Lluscuma, Kalfukura, Synco*), and has a significant presence in livecast television, podcasts, and a collective blog. I want to briefly highlight his very elaborate online transmedial project *Policía del Karma* (PDK or Karma Police; he borrowed the name from a Radiohead hit) featuring a police force that investigates both current and past life crimes. The production around this concept includes the original graphic novel, various websites, a blog, a videogame; Facebook, YouTube, Twitter, and SoundCloud pages; a soundtrack recording composed by Lluvia Ácida; a mockumentary titled "Reportaje del misterio" available on DVD; a book trailer, and a growing body of fanfiction. Baradit describes his work variously as realist fiction, afterpunk, postpop, retrofuturism, and cybershamanic. With respect to PDK, Baradit writes on his main webpage, inviting participation: "Hay, literalmente, miles de personas inscritas de diferentes maneras en el universo PDK. Algunos con un grado de compromiso secreto importante. Ya se han realizado misiones de diversa índole, no todos han sabido de las misiones del resto."

PDK offers a concentrated glimpse into Baradit's extensive production; it is, furthermore, like many Latin American projects by other creative culture producers, deeply imbedded in his reading of the bitter history of his country. In his collection of occasional essays and creative fragments published under the Amazon imprint with an aggressive English title and more descriptive Spanish subtitle (*Mind Fuck Guerrilla! Relatos, fragmentos, canalizaciones y cibertrash*, 2010), Baradit writes that he grew up in a confluence of contradictory, superimposed, official and unofficial histories that made Chile seem less like a functioning democracy than a low-budget theme park, co-sponsored by unusually mendacious politicians and slippery technocrats. Work like PDK, in this sense, offers a social commentary as well as gaming possibilities in a country so overlaid with an accumulated bricolage of decaying and hypermodern technologies that it becomes a perfect surrealist cyberpunk site.

In contrast, Colombian Santiago Ortiz is—in his own words—"a mathematician, data scientist, information visualization researcher and developer. He uses his background in mathematics and complexity sciences to push the boundaries of information visualization and data based storytelling." Santiago Ortiz's work tends to emphasize an interactive form with a game-based interface; each iteration of it is non-repeatable, and it cannot be experienced other as an artifact on a computer screen. N. Katherine Hayles's comment is apposite:

> These works. . . reflect on the materiality of their production. In digital media, the poem has a distributed existence spread among data files and commands, software that executes the commands, and hardware on which the software runs. These digital characteristics imply that the poem ceases to exist as a self-contained object and instead becomes a *process*, an event brought into existence when the program runs on the appropriate software loaded onto the right hardware. The poem is "eventilized," made more an event and less a discrete, self-contained object with clear boundaries in space and time.
>
> *(2006)*

This kind of work is, she says, a "flickering signifier," more of a temporal process than a durable artistic creation.

Ortiz currently leads Moebio Labs, which he calls "a team of data scientists, interactive data visualization developers and designers [who] develop advanced interactive visualization projects that connect with huge data sets" (n.d.). His work is far more sophisticated technically than that of most people working at the interface of the digital and the poetic; certainly, he is pushing the boundaries of what we understand as the kind of text-based aesthetic we traditionally bring to any literary genre. One of his projects based in Moebio labs, "Bacterias argentinas," uses a dynamic model that simulates bacterial evolution in an ecosystem. For this story, he has programmed the simulation such that the "genetic information" carried by the bacteria consists in bits of narrative that can consume each other and/or be promiscuously combined according to preset rules (of grammar).

The model is constantly moving and changing. The user can chase down and click on any bacteria for a bit of text; clicking on one after another leads to the text that scrolls onto the right hand side of the screen. Thus, the evolving narrative is computer-generated, although ultimately defined by the programmer's choice of text for inclusion, with some interaction from the reader/participant. It is "Argentine," because the voice we hear speaking the fragments is that of Argentine sculptor/actor/storyteller Edgardo Franzetti. In this way, says Ortiz, "las bacterias y su comportamiento constituyen una rica metáfora de la libre circulación de la información," that, given the reach of the Internet, is conceptually global, while at the same time they point to a very local geography of enunciation because they are vocalized by a speaker with a strong and unmistakable Argentine accent. In the background of this project is the suggestion as well that these Argentine bacteria will infect the player/user/reader; there is always a cost to presumably free circulation, whether of people or information.

Another of his projects uses Twitter as a source for creative cultural material. His stunningly beautiful, three-dimensional shifting constellation, "Twitter using Twitter" is based on modeling one week of Twitter company communications. Clicking on any dot causes the constellations to rearrange themselves, revealing the stronger and weaker lines of communication, as well as (if the viewer is interested) all the individual tweets. It is a window into corporate speak, an artwork, and a kind of poem. Both of these works bridge a very high level of technological expertise, with a (perhaps winking) interface with mass culture, mining the latter for the purposes of the former.

In his decision to mine Twitter, Ortiz draws attention both to the material and the technology by which his works have been created. The author essentially posits that the artificial generation of aesthetic texts through coding can convey a poetics detached from semantic

Hybrid mass culture

meaning, eliminating the subjective aspect of cultural production, and shifting the aesthetic interest entirely into the purely computational realm. Says Schaffner: "Perhaps the most important aspect of combinatorial and chance-determined works is the surprise moment: the results of chance productions are unpredictable, they display features which astound even the artists themselves" (2006: 11). This is heady stuff. Yet at the bottom, Ortiz's work is grounded in a mashup from popular culture, turned into an artifact that can be played, like a game, that can be enjoyed as a beautiful moving image, while it is also susceptible to high culture analysis.

The attentive reader of this chapter will notice that so far, all my examples have been from men: Sebakis, Drake, Baradit, Ortiz. This conscious or unconscious deformation is typical in most studies of hybrid creations, which tend to focus on the male cultural producers, and often an implicitly male audience as well. Certainly, we can argue that this is a gendered approach; feminist scholars for the last thirty years have been helping us understand how our concept of "culture" is warped when all the examples (as is true in canonical literary histories) come from mainstream men, where unspoken categories of inclusion presume an educated, straight, white/criollo identity.

To conclude this brief survey, then, let us remind ourselves of work by a few of the many talented women from Latin America. While it would be impossible to make a valid general conclusion about gender in hybrid forms with such a small sample, at least we can say that the women featured here foreground the bodies, voices, and experiences of female characters, and do so in a way that is more nuanced and complex than their male colleagues' approach to analogous characters.

Argentine Marina Zerbarini in some senses makes a great counterpart to Santiago Ortiz. The co-author of a short book on Latin American net.art, she is a professor of multimedia and electronic arts, whose website brings together her interests in art, science, and technology. At the same time, in an essay on her brilliant project, "Eveline: fragmentos de una respuesta," she describes her work as "sujetivo, íntimo y público" (2005), where "public" does not mean quite the same thing as mass culture, but points in that direction. "Eveline" is a hypertext project, inspired by James Joyce and based on two of his stories, as well as a background immersion into the last twenty-five years of Argentine history, and trailing bits from a previous Internet project, no longer available online, called "Azul intenso en un profundo mar." It is also a nostalgic text, in the way that the Internet can be nostalgic about technologies only a few years out of date, borrowing from this earlier project the idea and form of a real-life, online chat session between two lovers.

The project, which remains incomplete, combines approximately four hundred image and text archives, many of which are randomly accessed, that the player/reader is never expected to explore in its entirety. The player of this game/reader of this narrative, accesses several moveable screens, some of them interactive, simulating chat texts, but also including graphs, statistics, videos, and audio files. "Eveline," Zebarini says, proposes itself as "un problema de género, inabarcable en su pluralidad, metáfora visual de lecturas varias" (2005), where her canny use of the concept of "género" is key to understanding her aesthetic project as a commentary on both genre and gender expectations.

Helena Torres is a queer Latin American feminist, activist, performer, and scholar, who describes herself as exiled in Europe and living precariously in these neoliberal times. In a pair of sentences with so many moving parts that it makes us dizzy, she describes her most recent work as a compilation of "criaturas bastardas hijas del *Manifiesto Chthuluceno* de Donna Haraway, que traduje al castellano para la revista *Laboratory Planet*. Una de ellas será un taller de lectura musicalizada que acabará en una performance colectiva, dentro de los *Rencontres Bandits Mages* a realizarse en Emmetrop" (n.d.). A performance took place in November 2016.

25

Among her most important creative works is the series of "Narrativas espaciales," which includes two projects available in both English and Spanish on that website: "Serendipia"/"Serendipity" and "159. Otro sonido posporno es possible"/"159" (Cleger also talks about the first of these works; see 2015: 276). Both of these works are constructed for access on an app designed for Android smartphones (the app is available for download via a QR code on the website), including visual and audio tracks tied to GPS mapping. Thus, one of the delights of the project is the play of voices/accents with recorded versus ambient sound. They ask their reader/listener to follow along with the material as we physically walk through designated spaces, following a GPS map; the wanderings of the participant in the space will determine the shape of the narrative.

While "159" is located in a museum space (she clarifies that "que la imagen, el mapa de sonidos, el texto y las pistas sonoras sólo adquieren sentido con el movimiento por el espacio seleccionado, por tanto estos datos son meramente informativos. Este paseo sonoro se puede realizar en el Centro de arte y creación industrial laboral"), in "Serendipia" the site is the Ceares civil cemetery El Sucu, in Gijón (Asturias). In both cases, as the English text notes: "The historical drift was written as a fragmented rhizomatic telling and localized in a non-linear way, so no identical strolls are possible, though an ending and a start are suggested."

"Serendipia" is a fractured detective story about an 1895 murder related to that cemetery. The Spanish text tells us that the title of the narrative:

> reconoce el rol del azar en la investigación y el hallazgo fortuito de conexiones creativas en los procesos de búsqueda de información. *Serendipia* propone un encuentro entre novela negra, historia, geografía, sociología, política, intervenciones en el espacio público, música, sonido, nuevas tecnologías y códigos libres, reconociendo al arte como problematizador de los signos con los que interpretar la cartografía del mundo con el fin de interferir en las lecturas del espacio.

Thus, while the text surrounding the projects seems scholarly in a familiar way, the material itself is engaging and accessible.

Mexican Cecilia Pego has been inspired by artist Leonora Carrington, among others, in her increasingly surreal graphics narratives. A prolific writer in her native Spanish, during a period of four years that she lived in Australia, Cecilia Pego began to develop *Exilia* (2011), a series of highly poetic graphics texts set in Yucatán, but with the text written in English. "These are my field notes from the imaginal frontier," she says (Dooley 2012). Currently envisioned in seven volumes, *Exilia* highlights the capabilities of e-readers as her primary publication platform: "Personally, I think my *Exilia* originals look better in the e-book version. The light shines through the watercolor and the translucent oil layers of the original art. It is like an illuminated manuscript with real light."

She adds: "I am creating the upcoming books of the *Exilia* saga in this manner not only because I need the freedom to write and illustrate as separate but parallel elements, but also because in the e-readers it is very difficult to read comics layouts of the print versions." While only one book has so far been released, the YouTube trailer gives a hint of what to expect in future volumes, in which she plans to include cinematic sequences, as well as even greater adaptations to take advantage of the possibilities of the e-book format: "I am thinking about creating a fluid content of text and illustrations that would be a better reading experience in, for instance, the Kindle and iPad. Maybe in the future I will do *Exilia* as a scroll, because that is the natural way to read with e-readers."

Fellow Mexican Eve Gil's *Sho Shan y la dama oscura* (2008) inaugurates a style the author calls "realismo mángico" (manga realism), a play on the now-exhausted concept of magic realism, so deeply associated with Boom authors of the mid-20th century. The author is invested in all aspects of Japanese popular culture and is drawn to the manga genre's mixture of tenderness and violence, while also exploring gendered questions related to marginalized women and how they deal with their social context. In a larger sense, at the heart of Gil's work is a questioning of how human beings deal with difference of any sort.

The heavily illustrated *Sho Shan* series is written for adults, for anime viewers and manga readers, or for young people who might have been fans of the later, darker Harry Potter books. The fantasy world of these novels combines events that could take place anywhere, except that it soon becomes clear that the characters have been infected by the narrator's manga-perspective and are at best only half human, so that solutions to terrible situations can involve superpowers of various sorts.

Gil is a tireless blogger. One of her blogs, Murasaki Inku, is dedicated to *Sho Shan*, both the first novel and its pair of sequels—*Tinta violeta* (2011) and *Doncella roja* (2013). This blog includes a first-person video describing *Sho Shan* as an autobiography, as well as links to a range of sites, such as pages referencing Mexican research on autism and Asperger's syndrome. She has multiple blogs, however, and many of them are continuations of her fictions, integral to their fundamental conception. She also maintains Facebook pages for her work, some of which extend into parallel fictions, while others serve to publicize her work.

Valeria Luiselli's background is delightfully complex and multifaceted. She enjoys a long-term collaboration with *Granta*, the prestigious British-based journal, has published in *The New York Times*, is a librettist for the New York City Ballet (her libretto for the British choreographer Christopher Wheeldon was performed in the Lincoln Center), and has lived in Costa Rica, South Africa, India, and Spain, as well as the United States, but is generally considered a Mexican writer. In "Swings of Harlem," Luiselli chooses to write in a colloquial English, unlike her first two print novels, both originally published in Spanish. In this project she documents the trips she takes with her daughter around parks in Harlem by way of Google Maps and Polaroid pictures. The photographs divide fragments of text broadly documenting these excursions. The pictures digitalized on the website have a ghostly, sepia tint, making them seem like products of an earlier period. Many of the images are blurry, unreadable, badly composed, stained, finger-printed, damaged with burns or blown out light.

In the accompanying text, she reproduces other imperfections. She calls attention to the accented sounds not easily reproduced in a written text, and notes the way her different languages sit together, sometimes uneasily, on her tongue. Her near-native English, learned in Capetown, with its intonation and vowel differences from US English, and flavored with Mexican Spanish, contrasts with her daughter's native US English, shaped by Harlem: "I pick her words up, one by one, pronounce them after her. She repeats them after me, patiently correcting or perhaps just re-channeling my jaywalking, short-cutting and rather uncharacteristic pronunciation of the English language–her heavy Harlem accent reverberating." Perhaps, after all, Luiselli is talking about her and her daughter's shared languages as a kind of swing music, an interactive jazz form, where the rhythm often involves playing deliberately behind or ahead of the beat.

In considering works like the ones surveyed here, Rita Raley calls for a new type of reading, a new type of analysis acknowledging the semantic significance of spatial design and taking into account the extension of literary space into the third dimension. She argues that interpretation of those works that integrate the z-axis into their repertoire "requires a fundamental reorientation of spatial perspective," and new critical framework for their analysis—a literal rather than merely figurative "deep reading" (2006). She calls this a "volumetric reading" that takes into account all three axes (x, y, and z), "reading surface to depth and back again." But this "deep reading" sounds suspiciously like the opposite of mass culture, whether we take it as dilettant-ishly feminine or brutishly male. One might well want to make an argument for a reading that keeps us on the flickering, changing surface of the screen.

There is a gesture toward mass culture in all of the cases briefly surveyed here, though not all of them will be equally accessible, or equally popular, and all of them are created by people from educated backgrounds. Likewise, while all the works could be analyzed through a gendered lens, only some of them address gender or sexuality directly. Some of the creators—Ortiz and Zerbarini, for example—come from academic/professional backgrounds, and take advantage of web-based technologies to explore challenging aesthetic problems, while also reaching into social media as the energizing force for their work. Others, like Baradit and Gil, are more directly speaking in a popular register and genre. Some, like Drake, are wildly popular; others, like Sebakis, have local followings. Torres' work sometimes, but not always, foregrounds its creator's queer politics.

Luiselli, Pego, Ortiz, and Torres all make at least some of their work available in English. While in Ortiz's case the use is coincidental, based on his decision to use corporate Twitter logs, in the other cases the choice seems strategic. English serves as a bridge language to reach out to wider publics—this is specifically the case with Pego, who comments on her decision to use English for her graphic novel precisely for this reason. Likewise, there is a widely held perception, no longer accurate, that English is the principal language of the web. While researchers tell us that it is hard to determine how many webpages there are in any given language, statisticians think the number in English is going down rapidly as a percentage of total pages, from a high of 80% in 1996 to about 40% today (it is easier to track the language of Internet users; about 26.3% of them use English). In contrast, estimates show about 5% of pages are in Spanish (7.7% of users) and 2.5% in Portuguese (4.3% of users), reason enough for bilingual creators to consider the feasibility of presenting some of their work in English as well as Spanish or Portuguese.

And what about gender? As Huyssen wrote optimistically back in 1986, "it is primarily the visible and public presence of women artists in *high* art, as well as the emergence of new kinds of women performers and producers in mass culture, which make the old gendering device obsolete" (1986: 57). There are telling contrasts between Pego and Baradit, both invested in a murderous, cyberpunk aesthetic, but very different in their approaches, or the mapping projects of Ortiz and Torres, the first more abstract, the second insistently located and grounded in bodies moving in real, as well as virtual space. Luiselli's delicate mother-daughter exploration of Harlem seems to echo with Torres' Girón project, in its sense of sharing a lived space with strangers encountered by chance during our wanderings At the same time, we could argue that Luiselli also shares a nostalgic sensibility with Drake and Zerbarini, albeit with a voicing that is wholly feminine—in whatever imprecise sense we mean that word.

As Internet penetration increases in Latin America, and the number of webpages in languages other than English continue to grow, we can expect many more exciting developments and cross-cutting dialogues from the continent's writers, poets and artists, who, as always, will astound us and humble us with their creativity.

Notes

1 See, for example, Critchley (2013).
2 One could, of course, reach much further back in these text-based experiments, to Raymond Federman's playful typography in *Double or Nothing* (1999), Ursula LeGuin's text/music project, *Always Coming*

Home (1985), William Burroughs' cut-up and fold-in texts (1960s), or even to Laurence Sterne's *Tristam Shandy* (1759–1767), while also looking forward to Chris Ware's 2012 book in a box, *Building Stories.*

3 Digital poetry is an early adopter, and an extremely fertile subgenre, which I have explored at greater depth in another study, "Fungibility and the Intermedial Poem." Poets and artists had already been generating experimental, computer-based work, without any easy means of distribution, since the 1980s. While much of this is high concept art, Argentines Ana María Uribe and Belén Gache, Brazilians Augusto de Campos and the "Ciber & poemas" group, among many others, show how poetry can bridge high art and mass appeal.

4 In Latin America, for example, some of the most recognized hybrid long narrative forms include the hypertext game formats of work such as Colombian Juan B. Gutiérrez's *Condiciones extremas* and Peruvian Doménico Chiappe's *Tierra de extracción* and *Hotel Minotauro.* In contrast, the Argentine blog, *Weblog de una mujer gorda,* was purportedly written by a provincial housewife; one of the scandals surrounding this highly successful project was the discovery that the author was an Argentine man, Hernán Casciari, writing from Barcelona (see Cleger 2015: 270).

5 Some of the most exciting and innovative work happening in the continent can be found in the many indigenous projects that have creatively used computer platforms to share work, but that is beyond the scope of this modest project.

Works cited

Agrippa Files, University of California, Santa Barbara Transcription Project, http://agrippa.english.ucsb.edu/category/the-book-subcategories/the-poem

Baradit, Jorge. www.baradit.cl/

Baradit, Jorge. *Mind Fuck Guerrilla! Relatos, fragmentos, canalizaciones y ciberthrash* (sic). Amazon Digital Services, 2010.

Baradit, Jorge. *Policía del karma.* Santiago: Ediciones B, 2010. Also: www.policiadelkarma.cl

Campos, Augusto de. *Clip poemas.* www2.uol.com.br/augustodecampos/clippoemas.htm

Cleger, Osvaldo. "La creación ciberliteraria: definición, perfil y carta de navegación para orientarse en un campo emergente." *Letras Hispanas,* 11 (2015): 262–280.

Critchley, Adam. "Breaking Down Barriers for Mexican Graphic Novels." *Publishing Perspectives,* 19 March 2013. http://publishingperspectives.com/2013/03/breaking-down-barriers-for-mexican-graphic-novels/

Cortázar, Julio. *Rayuela.* Buenos Aires: Editorial Sudamericana, 1963.

Dooley, Michael. "The Disturbing, Ethereal Comics of C.S. Pego, a Mexican Artist in Exile." *Print,* 19 October 2012. www.printmag.com/interviews/pego-artist-in-exile/

Drake, R. M. (Robert Macías). instagram.com/rmdrk/

Drake, R. M. "Meet R. M. Drake" (video) http://fusion.net/video/30935/meet-rm-drake-instagrams-most-famous-poet/

Gache, Belén. *Wordtoys.* www.findelmundo.com.ar/wordtoys/

Gil, Eve. *Murasaki Inku.* http://fujinkuroi.blogspot.com/

Gil, Eve. *Sho Shan y la dama oscura.* Mexico: Santillana, 2008.

Gruszinski, Ana Cláudia and Sérgio Capparelli. *Ciber & poemas.* www.ciberpoesia.com.br/

Hayles, N. Katherine. "Digital Poetry: From Object to Event." *New Media Poetics.* Eds. Adalaide Kirby Morris and Thomas Swiss. Cambridge, MA: MIT Press, 2006. www.bth.se/tks/lkdm.nsf/pages/73C68 8385492EBD8C12572190027E382/$FILE/Binder6.pdf

Huyssen, Andreas. "Mass Culture as Woman: Modernism's Other." In Tania Modleski, ed., *Studies in Entertainment.* Bloomington, IN: Indiana University Press, 1986.

Ilich, Fran. *Metro Pop.* Mexico: Gran Angular, 2004.

Internet World Stats. Updated 30 June 2016. www.internetworldstats.com/stats2.htm

Jenkins, Henry, Sam Ford, and Joshua Green. *Spreadable Media.* New York: New York University Press, 2013.

Luiselli, Valeria. "Swings of Harlem." http://where-you-are.com/valeria-luiselli#/m/riverside-park-2

Noakes, Susan. (1988). "On the Superficiality of Women." In Clayton Koelb and Susan Noakes, eds., *The Comparative Perspective on Literature.* Ithaca, NY: Cornell University Press, 1988: 339–355.

Ortiz, Santiago. "Bacterias argentinas." http://moebio.com/santiago/bacterias/

Pego, Cecilia. *Exilia: The Invisible Path.* Amazon. 2011.

Pego, Cecilia. "Entrevista: Cecilia Pego." *Historietologo,* 31 October 2011. http://historietologo.blogspot.com.au/2011/10/entrevista-cecilia-pego.html

Raley, Rita "Editor's Introduction: Writing 3D." *Iowa Review*, 8.3 (2006). http://thestudio.uiowa.edu/tirw/TIRW_Archive/september06/raley/editorsintro.html

Sebakis, Sagrado (Sebastián Kirzner). "De porque la poesía slam y la alt lit son de los más intenso e increíble." www.youtube.com/watch?v=xQU-4_oRuf0

Schaffner, Anna Katherine. "From Concrete to Digital: The Reconceptualisation of Poetic Space." Paper presented at the conference "From Concrete to Digital" at the Georg Brandes School, Copenhagen University, 9–10 November 2006. www.logolalia.com/minimalistconcretepoetry/archives/Anna-Katharina-Schaffner-From-Concrete-To-Digital.pdf

Schaffner, Anna Katherine and Andrew Michael Roberts. "Rhetorics of Surface and Depth in Digital Poetry." *Revue des Littératures de l'Union Européenne/Review of Literatures of the European Union*, 5 (2006). www.rilune.org/mono5/5_schaffner_roberts.pdf

Tepper, Steven J. "The Next Great Transformation: Leveraging Policy and Research to Advance Cultural Vitality." In Steven J. Tepper and Bill Ivey, eds., *Engaging Art: The Next Great Transformation of America's Cultural Life*. New York: Routledge, 2008. pp. 363–385.

Torres, Helena. *Narrativas espaciales.* https://narrativasespaciales.wordpress.com/

Uribe, Ana María. *Anipoemas.* www.vispo.com/uribe/anipoemas.html

Vañó, Valentín. "Cuentos reales y ficticias memorias." Babelia, El País. 20 July 2013. https://valentinvano.wordpress.com/category/babelia-2/

Zerbarini, Marina. "Sujectivo, íntimo y público." *Net.art Review*, 2005. www.netartreview.net/monthly/minima_marina.pdf

Zerbarini, Marina, Alejandro Schianchi, Ignacio Nieto, Diego Dalla Benetta, and Liliana Koselevich. *Radiografía del Net Art latino: Vitalidad creativa en riesgo de extinción.* Buenos Aires: Editorial Dunken, 2014.

2

THE LATIN AMERICAN *FLÂNEUR* IN THE DIGITAL AGE

Osvaldo Cleger

This chapter examines the construction of the image of the *virtual flâneur* as well as the digitally enabled experience of *flânerie* through a comparative analysis of two different examples of this phenomenon: an open-world video game partially set in 18th-century Havana that allows players to explore and roam the colonial city as they see fit (Ubisoft's *Assassin's Creed IV: Black Flag*) and a web-based application that invites users to explore the city of Bogotá in an interactive and two-dimensional way (*Caminando Bogotá*, developed at Universidad Javeriana). Since the late 19th century, the figure of the *flâneur* has played a central role within Latin American cultural traditions, particularly in regard to the articulation of the ideological and cultural mapping of the city space from the perspective of the male gaze.[1] Urban chroniclers such as Manuel de Zequeira y Arango (Havana, Cuba, 1764–1846) and José María Vergara y Vergara (Bogotá, Colombia, 1831–1872) are early examples of the crucial role the figure of the "urban explorer" or "city wanderer" played in terms of the literary appropriation of the city space by the cultural elite of these two countries. During the 20th century, a corpus of urban literature and films further disseminated critical approaches to Latin American urban spaces, relying often on the figure of the *flâneur* and the practice of *flânerie* for such approaches. With the advent of video games and interactive media, digitally enabled forms of *flânerie* have been made possible, in most cases through the design of computer-based models of the city and interactive avatars that allow users to explore these simulated city environments in different ways, and in order to accomplish a variety of gaming goals. The latter includes both multimedia developed in Flash and similar low-end technologies – which are characterized by their bi-dimensionality, low production cost and their evocative and minimalist approach to the cityscape – and sophisticated 3D video game simulations developed by the entertainment industry.

In this chapter I examine two illustrative instances of both previously mentioned tendencies. The first example I will discuss, *Caminando Bogotá*, directed by Carlos Torres and produced by a small team of developers at Universidad Javeriana, falls within what I here define as an "auteur multimedia." This multimedia, in addition to explicitly focusing on the figure of the *flâneur* within the context of the city of Bogotá, serves to illustrate several of the tools that flash aesthetics (as defined by Manovich 2002) offers to small studios and individual authors who lack the resources to produce more realistic, three-dimensional simulations of the city. The minimalist approach to the representation of the city space seen in *Caminando Bogotá* also draws on the language of comic narrative (as defined by Scott McCloud 1994) and digital photography to achieve such effect. This basic toolkit offered the key to circumvent the challenge of producing a more realistic depiction of the city, which would have required the use of sophisticated gaming engines as well as the involvement of expensive teams of programmers and graphic designers that are usually out of the reach of these small start-ups. However, what the "author multimedia" lacks in terms of realism, resolution, sharpness, and overall graphic quality of its visuals is often compensated by its greater conceptual depth and its independence from the monetarist logic that prevails within the video game industry.

The second example I will discuss comes from that industry. *Assassin's Creed IV: Black Flag* is a video game developed by the multinational Ubisoft, whose production cost is estimated at one hundred million dollars (Sun 2014), and which included the involvement of over 900 people working on the project (Makuch 2013). The main story of the game is set in the Caribbean during the Golden Age of Piracy, although this story is framed within a series of events that take place in the early 21st century. The game features a historical simulation of three cities that played a central role in relation to the activity of pirates and buccaneers in the 18th century: Havana, Kingston and Nassau. The game also contains a less realistic – but still highly detailed – recreation of a series of small islands and cities along the Greater and Lesser Antilles, South Florida and the Yucatan Peninsula. For the purpose of this chapter, I will focus on the part of the game set in Havana in the early 18th century, as well as the options that the playable character of Edward Kenway offers to explore the colonial city.

I will further limit my enquiry to the discussion of four key problems. 1) I will begin with an exposition of some of the difficulties scholars encounter when trying to offer a definition of the *flâneur* and its practices, since the nature of such practices will vary considerably depending on the expressive medium that different *flâneur*-authors have used (journalistic chronicles, novels, photographs, documentary, film or computational media). 2) I will then offer an elucidation of what is peculiar or distinctive in *flâneur* art once it has been refashioned or remediated for a computational medium; this will allow me to establish the unique features of digitally enabled forms of *flânerie*. 3) I will further discuss some of the tensions that arise between the descriptive, narrative and ludic purposes of both gaming artifacts I analyze in this chapter, and will define computational *flâneur* art as an expressive form lying at the intersection of a variety of exploratory, aesthetic, narrative and ludic purposes. 4) Finally, I will examine the role the male gaze has played in framing what is perceived as "explorable" or "observable" within the city space – which has been historically defined from the perspective of a male wanderer, that is, a *flâneur* and not a *flâneuse*. This will allow me to expose the penchant of both analog media from the past and digital media from the present for portraying women as a mere attribute of the scenery and a projection of the male desire. The latter, which in the case of 19th century literature and 20th century cinema is due to social conventions and a lack of access by women to both artistic expressions, in the contemporary video game industry is attributable to similar restrictions, as well as prevailing stereotypes that insist on conceptualizing the player as a white, middle-class, male adolescent.[2]

Flânerie: From Paris to Havana

Flânerie, as it has been defined since Baudelaire's early writings on this subject, consists mainly of three processes: first, it is a way of gazing upon reality, and more strictly speaking, the urban ecosystem; secondly, it is a method and style of artistic representation of such reality; and finally, it is a way of capturing the viewing horizon of the audience (whether it be a reader, a spectator, an internet user or a video game player) tapping on the artistic affordances of the *flâneur*-author's medium of choice. In *The Painter of Modern Life* (1863), a foundational essay on the subject

The Latin American flâneur *in the digital age*

dedicated to the illustrator Constantin Guys, Baudelaire already noticed the contiguity that exists between the strolls or wanderings undertaken by the *flâneur*-artist (that is, the moment of the observation) and the practice of recording what has been found during such explorations in an artistic medium:

> Few men are gifted with the *capacity of seeing*; there are fewer still who possess the *power of expression*. So now, at a time when others are asleep, Monsieur G. is bending over his table, *darting on to a sheet of paper the same glance that a moment ago he was directing towards external things*, skirmishing with his pencil, his pen, his brush, splashing his glass of water up to the ceiling, wiping his pen on his shirt, in a ferment of violent activity, *as though afraid that the image might escape him*, cantankerous though alone, elbowing himself on.
>
> *(12)*

In this passage we perceive not only a conceptual but also a stylistic effort to capture the artist's nervousness during the creative process: who fears to lose the reflections and images he has collected just "a moment ago" during his wandering around the city. That *fleeting nervousness of the artist at work* that Baudelaire has tried to freeze in his vignette is equivalent to the *sense of transience of modern urban life* that the artist Constantin Guys has previously endeavored to capture in his graphic work. Thus the fleeting nature of the observed reality is reflected in the transience of the sensations of the artist who observes (as well as the critic who observes the artist). Therefore, the work of the *flâneur* will consist of slowing down the fleeting moment in order to "distill the eternal from the transitory" (12).

However, the communicative situation in *flâneur* art and literature does not simply begin with the idle stroll through the city and observation of the fleeting moment worth retaining to conclude with the nervous recount of the images captured during such wanderings. The viewing horizon of the audience is in charge of reactivating with every new reading the concretizations of these texts/art forms. That is how the consumer of *flâneur* art becomes a *flâneur* himself. Through a mental process of reverse engineering, the viewer/reader must be able to retrace the path that led from the physical stroll to the artistic work, in order to mentally reconstruct the experiential encounter that lies at the origin of all the communicative and artistic process, that is, the *flânerie*. In fact, for the ideal *flâneur*-reader is usually not enough to just read or view the literary or artistic product. The act of reading/viewing is often followed or accompanied by the physical – geolocated – experience of the stroll through those same coordinates and points of interest that the work recreates; which allows the viewer to indulge in the intellectual exercise of contrasting the artistic text with the "urban text." *Flâneur* art, we might conclude, is a pre-computational form of geolocated art, created way before the notion and practices of geolocation (and the GPS and mobile technologies that make it possible) were introduced by the new media revolution.

Now, as I have already stated, the relation between these three moments that inform the communicative situation of *flâneur* art (the exploratory stroll, the execution of the work and its geolocated decoding by the spectator) will be different in nature depending on the artistic medium used by the author. In traditional literature and visual arts, the chronotopic distance mediating between the moment of observation and the moment of creation is extremely critical, since as this distance increases, so does the risk that the perception of the fleeting moment will be lost for the artist before he can render it in an artistic form. Hence the anxiety that Baudelaire attributes to Constantin Guys when he portrays the French engraver feverishly outlining sketches in his workshop. For Guy it is a matter of recording what his senses have perceived while touring the panoramic streets of Paris before such a record vanishes from his vision.

33

On the other hand, with the introduction of photography, as well as other media capable of recording sounds and images directly from reality – such as the phonograph and the cinematograph – the anxiety of the artist stemming from his interest in capturing the transience of everyday life is significantly reduced. Since the lens of the photographic or video camera functions as an "eye" capable of exploring the transience of city life at the same time it leaves a record of its journey. This reduction of the mediations between observation and expression endows the *flâneur*-artist (now turned into a photographer or videographer) with a privileged perspective of his artistic subject matter.

Numerous Latin American photographers, documentalists and filmmakers, from the late 19th century forward, have contributed to enrich the Latin American archive of audiovisual works exploring the urban environment; and while they have benefitted from the inherent advantages of their medium, they have also relied on some of the same topoi and imagery that writers such as Manuel de Zequeira y Arango, José María Vergara y Vergara, José Asunción Silva, Julián del Casal or Manuel Gutiérrez Nájera, to quote a few, had previously established when they were first trying to produce a literary cartography of the city. In the specific case of the two cities that I discuss in this chapter, Havana and Bogotá, photographers such as Henry Duperly and José Gómez de la Carrera, and documentalists and filmmakers such as Tomás Gutiérrez Alea, Fernando Pérez and Sergio Cabrera have played a central role in the elaboration of the photographic and audiovisual imaginary of both cities. And this has been achieved both through the explicit representation of the *flâneur*'s wanderings and reflections – as eloquently portrayed by the character of Sergio in Gutiérrez Alea's *Memorias del Subdesarrollo* (Figure 2.1 – and through films that offer a satirical portrayal of strategies to resist eviction in an increasingly gentrified urban environment (as in Sergio Cabrera's *La estrategia del caracol*).

With the introduction of computer simulations and interactive design, the communicative situation of *flâneur* art is going to undergo a new transformation. In this case, the distance between the observed reality and the artistic representation of such reality is not further reduced. On the contrary, the complex engineering process associated with multimedia production and

Figure 2.1 The character of Sergio in *Memorias del Subdesarrollo*, using his telescope to explore a changing Havana under the influence of the Cuba Revolution. The sense of immediacy of the images displayed in his telescope illustrates the new expressive powers enjoyed by filmmakers when it comes to artistically render an urban environment.

interactive design will again increase this distance. Now what changes radically is the horizon of the receiver, through a transfer of the agency of the *flâneur*-artist to the consumer of the work. In computational media, the consumer of *flâneur* art is reconfigured as a player or user, who, rather than experiencing a finished work produced by a writer, graphic artist or documentalist, will be in charge of executing or performing the strollings and explorations of the *flâneur* inside the rich canvas provided by a simulated city environment.

The latter becomes particularly clear in the two examples I examine in this chapter. In both Carlos Torres' *Caminando Bogotá* and Ubisoft's open-world video game *Assassin's Creed IV: Black Flag*, the strolling and wandering around the city exists only potentially: in the form of a variety of possible routes that the user/player could decide to take or not. While the *flâneur* artist of the analog era – armed with his pen, typewriter, or camera – was expected to make use of his narrative agency to recount, describe and even interpret the impressions and images he collected during his explorations of the city, the *flâneur* artist of the digital age, on the other hand, focuses only on establishing the conditions and processes that should regulate the experience of the stroll, while transferring to the user the role of performing it. From the perspective of the digital designer such explorations exist only as a potential driver of gameplay (or human–computer interaction in the case of non-gaming apps), and not as a reified artistic rendition.

That is how the panoramic streets of Paris (as depicted by Constantin Guys and theorized by Charles Baudelaire and Benjamin Walter), and the emulatable model that they provided to future *flâneur* artists in Europe and Latin America, will lead to the animation loops of Bogotá produced by Universidad Javeriana, as well as Ubisoft's more immersive paradigm for exploring colonial Havana. In the remainder of this chapter, I will detail the distinctive ways in which both digital artifacts take on the task of reconfiguring *flâneur* art for a computational medium, looking at the specificities of each example. I will show how despite their very different ways of representing the city – stemming from very dissimilar aesthetic approaches and a dramatic contrast in terms of their production values – both projects exhibit the same effort to endow users with a greater sense of agency by transferring to them the task of exploring the environment. I will also discuss the different solutions offered in each project to solve the tension between their ludic, descriptive and narrative elements. I will conclude by examining the androcentric views underpinning both projects, which are a result of an ideological displacement of ideas that consolidated in early modern *flâneur* art, and that continue to go unchallenged within the context of contemporary Latin American digital culture.

Caminando Bogotá through pointing and clicking

When users access the home page of *Caminando Bogotá*, the first thing they encounter is an animation loop foreshadowing several of the conditions under which the exploration of the city will be performed (Figure 2.2). In this loop we see the Bogotan *flâneur* as Carlos Torres and his production team at Universidad Javeriana have conceptualized him: as a well-coiffed and elegantly dressed white man, who strolls along one of Bogotá's main avenues – looking at the same time attentive and indifferent – with his hands in the pockets of his dress pants. This is obviously someone with the necessary financial solvency to afford a restful and undisturbed leisure. The use of cartoon aesthetics (McCloud 1994) by Torres and his team, rather than hindering the perception of the *flâneur*'s distinctive features – as a middle-class or upper-class white man, armed with a cool, analytical curiosity to explore his surroundings – helps amplify such an archetype. However, even when users knowledgeable of *flâneur* literature could quickly identify this urban archetype and anticipate some of the possibilities and encounters that might lay

Figure 2.2 Homepage of *Caminando Bogotá*.

ahead, such paths only exist potentially, since it is in the hands of users to execute them through their interactions with the program's interface.

Flash-based games and net art usually rely on a rather limited repertoire of functions to generate interactivity with users, such as "point and click," "drag and drop," "drag and click," "mouse-over" and animation loops that are tasked with simulating some degree of narrative continuity while new screens are loaded and/or the user decides what actions to perform next. *Caminando Bogotá* follows closely this model. At the beginning, the user's option to mouse-over different city elements simulates the *flâneur*'s male gaze while he indulges his curiosity about all things that cross his path: cars, buses, traffic signs, buildings, statues, urban archetypes or their attributes (such as the helmet representing the construction worker) and stray dogs. While the functions of pointing and mousing-over suggest the action of glancing at something, the action of clicking indicates the *flâneur*'s decision to pay closer attention or examine an object and its surroundings in greater detail. The choices he makes by clicking over different icons will lead to a variety of explorations and forms of recreation often designed to satisfy the imagination and desires of a male stroller. In this way the animation rehashes several of the same androcentric stereotypes found in late-19th century *flâneur* literature. The different possible paths range from the option to follow a prostitute to Parque Nacional Enrique Olaya Herrera – where the *flâneur* will decide to lean against a light pole while he examines the other people who are enjoying themselves at the park – to the alternative of working as a DJ in a nightclub; or visiting the neighborhood of Santa Fe to spend some time in the brothel La Piscina, exploring the variety of pleasures and sexual adventures that are in the menu. Other less gendered options include a stroll through Plaza Simón Bolivar, where the *flâneur* will stop for a moment to enjoy the view of the proverbial pigeons hovering over the square; a minigame in which the *flâneur* will have to show his ability to cross an avenue without being run over; and several short animations and video clips he will be able to watch from various screens that are located all over the city.

The points of interests (POIs) the *flâneur* can explore in this multimedia are 12 in total. That is a rather small number considering that one of the premises of *flânerie* is the existence of an inexhaustible built environment, which should allow for countless ways of exploring the city. From this perspective, *Caminando Bogotá* would fail to deliver on the promise implicit in its title, since only a handful of landmarks and neighborhoods are included in the project, and their depiction is rather cartoonish. On the other hand, it is also obvious that Carlos Torres and his team are not trying to create a realistic and all-inclusive representation of Bogotá. Instead they

The Latin American flâneur *in the digital age*

rely on the evocative power of cartoon aesthetics and synecdochical references to rapidly sketch a general view of the city with some of its most outstanding characteristics and points of interests. In fact, one of the virtues of this multimedia lies in its expressive economy, that is, its ability to reference large parts of the city and the most common activities in those areas through the use of simplified drawings and very basic interactions.

To illustrate, let's examine one of the options to explore the city with which users are presented. By clicking on one of the 18 icons included in the first animation loop (I'm referring specifically to the icon represented by a late-middle-aged male stroller), the user is transported to the José Celestino Mutis Avenue in the northern part of the Chapinero district, one of Bogotá's most affluent areas. As we can notice by comparing Figures 2.3 and 2.4 (one showing a screenshot of the multimedia, and the other one showing the Google Street View of the José Celestino Mutis Avenue) the simplified rendition of this part of the city is driven by the necessity to include the minimum elements the user will need to be able to identify the street he is walking on and the direction in which he is going. The mountains in the background and the synecdochical inclusion of the Basílica de Nuestra Señora de Lourdes, one of the most iconic buildings of the Chapinero district, are enough to facilitate the identification of the location.

In terms of interactive design, developers here resort once more to the use of point and click and mouse-over events to simulate the *flâneur*'s shifting male gaze as he strolls along the street. By clicking on the silhouettes of pedestrians crossing the *flâneur*'s path, the user can trigger different pop-up images, showing citizens protesting against Colombia's long history of unpunished crimes committed by right-wing paramilitary groups and drug lords à la Pablo Escobar. Even though this interaction does not provide enough content to avoid ambiguity, the user still has enough context to interpret its meaning. It is evidently a reference to the strong presence the recent history of violence has in the psyche of the average Bogotan citizen. The interaction could either refer to the main topic of a casual conversation the *flâneur* may have started with another person in the street, or it could also suggest what other pedestrians are thinking (or the *flâneur* believes they are) while they walk down this avenue. In either scenario, it becomes clear

Figure 2.3 Caminando Bogotá. Screenshot of the José Celestino Mutis Avenue as portrayed in the multimedia.

Figure 2.4 Google Street View of the José Celestino Mutis Avenue in the Chapinero district.

that the minimalist approach adopted by Carlos Torres and his team is expressive enough to evoke a complex street interaction, geolocated at specific, identifiable coordinates, and involving a difficult topic such as politics.

In addition to remarking upon this clever way of telling stories or sketching brief urban scenes through the use of simple animations and two-dimensional images (and with a significant lack of verbal content), it is important to consider the tension found in this multimedia between its narrative and ludic elements. As I have stated before, computational *flâneur* art is based on a transfer of the writer's or artist's agency to the user or player. This allows developers to focus primarily on establishing the conditions under which city explorations should be performed, while users are tasked with performing such explorations as well as constructing their narrative or poetic significance. While the idea of a user empowered with the agency to narrate his/her own story may seem compelling, we ought to consider also the challenges stemming from this new narrative model.

In literary studies, the notion of a "narrative contract" is often used to refer to the tacit agreement in which writers and readers engage through the production and consumption process of any given narrative work (Kaplan 1996: 58–61). A fictional projection of this contract occurs inside the story itself when the narrator engages in such agreement with the narratee or the implicit reader, a very commonly used narrative device since *One Thousand and One Nights*' Scheherazade to *Moby Dick*'s Ishmael. For this contract to be successful or "symbolically binding," the writer must be able to encode his/her story in a way that can be decoded by the reader. But he/she should be able to accomplish much more than that: he/she must persuade the reader to relinquish his/her agency momentarily (which would include the decision to stop reading or deem the whole story implausible) in order to follow the agency of the characters in the narration and accept the rules governing their world.[3] In computational media, instead (or on top) of a narrative contract we have an "interactive contract," which is also based on the decodable nature of the end product. In this case, it is also vital for the user to know what he/she needs to do or what skills ought to be displayed or developed to navigate successfully the interface of the program. That is why many video games include a training session at the beginning to teach

The Latin American flâneur *in the digital age*

players how to use a controller or joystick in order to make characters run, jump or shoot at enemies. By playing this part of the game users are, so to speak, "reading the contract," before deciding whether they want or feel ready to engage in gameplay. Many experienced gamers skip this part of the game, provided the game allows it, signaling this way that they are familiar with the type of "contract" the game implies. But computational media involves also radically different ways of approaching user's and characters' agency. Since the user is empowered to control the agency of characters, it is essential that he/she has enough incentives and in-game cues to accomplish this task in a way that is both engaging and in synch with the program's established procedures and processes. A very common ludic device used in video games consists of cueing players on how to use their agency effectively through a mission-oriented design, that is, by asking players to accomplish a series of simple tasks such as "gather food," "find an exit" or "avoid being killed," and offering in-game rewards when they do so. The completion of several discrete tasks like those mentioned before usually amounts to the completion of a whole "campaign" or narrative arc in the case of games that include a significant storytelling component.

The challenge in computational *flâneur* art is that the use of ludic devices like the one described above could be counterproductive; since *flânerie* implies a high degree of self-dependence when it comes to deciding where to go or what to explore. The inclusion of missions such as "Visit the Chapinero District," "Explore the park," "Follow the prostitute" or "Look at the pigeons" would critically erode the *flâneur's* autonomy, turning him into an implausible street puppet. *Flânerie* is driven primarily by the *flâneur's* oversized sense of self, which translates into a need to enjoy an unrestricted and unguided use of his own agency. In *Caminando Bogotá*, this challenge is partially overcome by reducing to a minimum the incentives and in-game cues offered to users. It is completely up to users to decide what to explore, in what order, for how long or how to make sense of those explorations. In this way, users are in control of both their own wanderings and the narrative that should emerge from that experience. But this is accomplished at the expense of a gaming structure that could help avoid the sense of disorientation or lack of purpose commonly associated with the use of these emerging media formats. The pitfall, in this case, is that developers risk losing completely the interest of users, as they may feel that they lack any motivation or reason to continue engaged with the multimedia. That is one of the areas in which *Caminando Bogotá* fails to create a more compelling remediation of *flânerie*. The ludic elements of the multimedia fail to engage the user with the underlying narrative.

In sum, *Caminando Bogotá* illustrates both the potential advantages and pitfalls of prioritizing the needs of the narrative structure over the use of gaming devices and principles that could make user–computer interactions more effective. The results are a mixed bag that, while showing the benefits of not succumbing to the temptation of adding a reward system in the project (not many would have liked to see the *flâneur* rewarded with coins for visiting "El Septimazo"), it also shows the disadvantages of lacking a more robust gaming structure that could infuse with deeper procedural meaning the actions the user undertakes.

Strolling and jumping rooftops in colonial Havana

> "So it was like a whole new game kind of an experience, you know…You could roam around, just do nothing in the game and still have fun."
>
> *(Cited in Atkinson and Willis 2007)*

The example I discuss next will serve to illustrate a project that lies at the other end of this equation: where gaming principles and devices drive the whole exploratory experience, often at the expense of a deeper narrative. *Assassin's Creed IV: Black Flag* was developed by Ubisoft as an open-world video game set during the Golden Age of Piracy, designed with the clear goal of offering an engaging simulation of what it would be like to be a pirate. Unlike *Caminando Bogotá*, *AC4* does not include any explicit references to *flânerie* or the *flâneur*. The main playable character that gamers control, Edward Kenway, a Welsh-born British privateer who will become a pirate and assassin during the game, is too mission-oriented to inspire the kind of idleness that is required from a true Baudelairian *flâneur*. Being a British pirate touring a Spanish colonial city, Kenway will need to be alert at all times to avoid being spotted by his multiple enemies. Even when he decides to lower his guard and approach the prostitutes who are standing on a street corner, they are only offered as cover for his missions. By the same token, when he chooses to walk into a tavern to enjoy a pint of ale, this action will only get him involved in a bar brawl, which will draw the attention of the authorities and force Kenway to escape from the situation. As Franz Hessel once wrote: "In order to engage in *flânerie*, one must not have anything too definite in mind." (Frisby 81) The problem with Kenway is that he usually has too much in his mind to become a real *flâneur*.

On the other hand, Ubisoft developers have obviously put a lot of effort in creating a realistic and highly detailed simulation of the city of Havana, paying close attention to its layout, architecture, main attractions, street markets, vegetation, ambient sounds and the languages spoken by non-playable characters (NPCs). Several early missions are geared to make Kenway – and by extension, the player – aware of the fact that there is a whole city with real-life landmarks, intriguing alleys and a complex crowd system open to his curiosity. As soon as Kenway disembarks in Old Havana, one of his first tasks consists of climbing to the top of a church to gain a better view of the city and help his companion Stede Bonnet find the way. Once he is at the top, Kenway will be able to "synchronize" this viewpoint, which will allow him to uncover the multiple opportunities for adventure this part of the city offers, including several treasure chests he will be able to loot and numerous contract killings he will be able to carry out for a fee. Synchronizing viewpoints also facilitates moving from one end to the other of the city, since once all viewpoints have been synchronized the player will be able to move instantaneously between them without having to walk, run or parkour all the way to his destination. In other words, climbing city buildings and jumping rooftops in *Assassin Creed* is primarily driven by the goal of providing instant ludic reward to gamers. But climbing and synchronizing viewpoints also offer players an opportunity to indulge in the purely aesthetic contemplation of the simulation, which will bring them closer to the experience of *flânerie*. The sense of wonder that players are expected to feel when they access a viewpoint is emphasized by the cut-scene this event triggers, in which they can see their avatar standing on top of the city, while a circular dolly shot, and romantic leitmotif help convey a sensation of plenitude. While jumping rooftops and parkouring along its neighborhoods, players gain a unique perspective of Havana – always from a cinematic high angle – which is a very rare way of looking at the city, and precisely the one that Ubisoft developers have turned into this franchise's trademark.

In their article "Charting the Ludodrome: The Mediation of Urban and Simulated Space and Rise of the *Flâneur Electronique*," Atkinson and Willis (2007) argue that free-roaming in highly realistic open-world video games à la *Grand Theft Auto* generates a novel kind of *flânerie electronique*, in which in-game and out-game ways of experiencing the city blend together. Several gamers interviewed by the authors report how satisfying they find the opportunity *GTA 3: Liberty City* offers to "just run around, doing whatever you want" or "roam around, just do nothing in the game and still have fun" (828). Atkinson and Willis observe how "the ability of the game environment to be intrinsically interesting [...] twists the notion of gameplay since gamers remarked that wandering around, taking in certain vistas and urban

The Latin American *flâneur in the digital age*

viewpoints was sometimes a release and of interest in its own right" (828). The authors conclude from these surveys that "the common excitement at the pure spectacle of the city generates a sense of wandering in simulated environments that, to some extent, parallels that of the urban *flâneur*" (828).

Something very similar to what Atkinson and Willis report in relation to *GTA* is also at play in the *Assassin's Creed* series; with the difference that while *GTA* invites players to tour the city by car, *AC* encourages walking and running, that is, movements that are much closer to the pace in which the *flâneur* is expected to enjoy the city's streets. In *GTA* the pace of gameplay is much faster and therefore the likelihood that players will pay attention to very small details of the simulation while roaming around is slimmer. *AC*, on the other hand, puts the emphasis precisely in those small details expecting that players will notice them: the way vines climb up the wall of an old building; the casual dialogue between NPCs on a street corner; the refraction of the light piercing the stained-glass windows of a church. All this, together with the fact that *AC* developers strive to create replicas of real-life cities and not just allegorical representations, enables the possibility for virtual *flânerie* in Ubisoft's Havana.

Virtual *flânerie* in *AC* still emerges as the result of a tension between action-driven gameplay and the need to get some release from that action. After looting the warehouse of San Salvador de la Punta Castle, escaping the persecution of Spanish guards or assassinating a Templar who is trading weapons near the harbor, players will often see the option of strolling around and exploring Havana as a desirable change of pace. Several side missions included in the game, such as finding treasure chests located in different districts, synchronizing viewpoints on top of buildings, or visiting specific streets to obtain the sheet music of a shanty that Kenway wants to teach his crew to sing, are all options that will slow down the pace of gameplay, while giving players the opportunity to pay closer attention to those details of the simulation that have a purely cultural or aesthetic interest. Just as we have seen in *Caminando Bogotá*, *flânerie* in *AC* is only possible through the involvement of the user's agency. If players decide to focus on completing the main campaign and disregard the intrinsic interest of the simulation, very little in the game will try to guide them in such a direction. The game's database includes several entries providing players with additional information about real-life landmarks they have visited, such as the Havana Cathedral, the San Francisco de Asís Square or the Morro Castle. But the information included is mainly of historical content or of touristic interest, which deviates from the *flâneur's* usual focus on revealing the unknown or the little-frequented corners of the city. Even within such limitations, *AC4* still manages to let us perceive what *flânerie* could become in a Latin American city of the digital age through the use of computerized 3D modeling.

★

As we have seen in the case of *Caminando Bogotá*, the city that Carlos Torres and his team have built offers an urban spectacle designed for the pleasures of the male gaze. A growing body of criticism (Elkin 2016, Parsons 2000) has been recently pointing to this highly gendered view of *flânerie* that the classic authorities on the subject (Poe, Baudelaire, Benjamin) helped to consolidate. In the 19th and early 20th century "the opportunities and activities of *flânerie* were predominantly the privilege of the man of means, and it was hence implicit that the 'artist of modern life' was necessarily the bourgeois male" (4), writes Deborah Parsons; to which Lauren Elkin adds: "As if a penis were a requisite walking appendage, like a cane" (19). *Flânerie* in 19th-century Paris or Havana is not only the privilege of the bourgeois male, but is also a practice geared to frame women as mere objects to gaze upon.

And from the several female archetypes that populated most Western cities at the time (working- and middle-class women, "obreras," "señoritas de familia," or suffragettes) none other would come to embody the *flâneur*'s desire and fantasies as well as the prostitute. As Judith Walkowitz argues:

> The prostitute was the quintessential figure of the urban scene… for men as well as women, the prostitute was the central spectacle in a set of urban encounters and fantasies. Repudiated and desired, degraded and threatening, the prostitute attracted the attention of a range of urban male explorers.
>
> *(233)*

Despite being a 21st-century media project, *Caminando Bogotá* does not really move the needle in terms of offering a more nuanced depiction of women in the city. In the opening screen, from the 17 clickable objects that cross the path of the Bogotan *flâneur* only one suggests an encounter with a woman, through the cartoonish depiction of a low-life prostitute who will lead the *flâneur* to Parque Nacional Enrique Olaya Herrera. Out of only three buildings and establishments the *flâneur* can visit, one is a brothel. There are almost as many pop-up images of people marching on José Celestino Mutis Avenue as pictures of prostitutes offering their services at La Piscina. Even the night the *flâneur* can spend working as a DJ at a club suggests the presence of over-sexualized female bodies on the dance floor that the *flâneur* can observe from a privileged vantage point. This Bogotan archetype, who takes pleasure in contemplating the decorative and subordinate nature of the opposite sex, is not free of contradictions: his detached attitude as he walks the streets (at times playing distractedly with a yoyo in his right hand) is contradicted by his apparent interest in political activism; his upper-middle-class status, emphasized by the clothes he wears and his whole demeanor, is conflicted by his interest in graffitiing a city wall assisted by 12 paint spray cans of different colors. But his status as a male stroller, and the masculinity implied in this role, is never contradicted in the multimedia; since in *Caminando Bogotá*, *flânerie* still works as a metaphor "for the gendered scopic hierarchy in observations of urban space" (Parsons 4).

AC4 is not very different in this regard from the Colombian production. In an introduction video to the game, Edward Thatch, alias Blackbeard, is shown sitting at a bar telling a group of pirates about Kenway's impressive backstory as terror of the seas. One part of Blackbeard's tale is illustrated with a scene in which Kenway is walking down a dark alley, approaching a couple from behind. Once he gets close enough to the couple, Kenway kills the man with his assassin's hidden blade and grabs the woman by her waist, who continues to walk next to Kenway with an expression of delight in her face, as if nothing had just happened. This interaction early in the game helps establish the place assigned to women inside the world of *AC4*, while also making explicit the expectations game developers have in terms of how gamers are likely to see gender dynamics. Later in the game, when Kenway arrives to Havana, the first NPCs he is able to interact with are a group of prostitutes standing next to the dock. For "a few dozen reales" Kenway will be able to hire them to use them to distract the Spanish guards and complete his missions without being detected. From all NPCs populating Havana, prostitutes are among the most prominent. Their continuously looping monologues, heard in almost every corner of the city, constantly tease gamers with the promise of untold pleasures: "¿Alguna vez has tenido dos zorras en tu madriguera?" "¿Buscas una forma rápida de llegar al cielo?" "¿Querría un caballero de su categoría acompañarme al callejón más cercano?⁴" Even though Kenway – and by extension the player – cannot succumb to their requests, they can be re-directed toward other enemy NPCs as a way to put them out of combat. The role of prostitutes in *AC4* offers also a high contrast with other female NPCs featured in the city, who are usually silent, repeating less intelligible monologues or just gossiping about their neighbors.

The next generation of computational *flâneur* art?

While I have decided to focus here on what I consider to be two of the most illustrative instances of computational *flâneur* art in Latin America of the early 21st century, there have been several other video games and new media projects that have also featured different explorable urban environments, either through bi-dimensional or tri-dimensional modeling of city spaces. As it was mentioned before, the *Grand Theft Auto* franchise is another example in this regard. Ubisoft itself has perfected a brand of adventure games that allows players to explore historical simulations of numerous real-life cities. It is not only the early 18th-century-Havana of *AC4* that gamers can explore, but also the New York and Boston of the American Revolution (in *AC3*), the Port-au-Prince of the mid 18th century (in *Freedom Cry*), the Paris of the French Revolution (in *AC Unity*) or the London of the Industrial Revolution (in *AC Syndicate*). Beyond what Ubisoft's *Assassin's Creed* and Rockstar's *Grand Theft Auto* have to offer, several other games, platforms and companies have also ventured into the world of 3D modeling in ways that have turned virtual *flânerie* into a possibility. In *Second Life* and *Minecraft*, users can build their own fictional or real-life cities, which can be later explored by themselves or by other visitors of these virtual worlds (Fulton 2017). In the *Language of New Media*, Manovich argues that the work of Russian filmmaker Dziga Vertov "stands halfway between Baudelaire's *flâneur* and today's computer user: No longer just a pedestrian walking down a street, but not yet Gibson's data cowboy who zooms through pure data armed with data-mining algorithms" (275). As Lori Landay elaborates in her essay on *Second Life*, the way the residents of this virtual world experience reality follows closely Manovich's description of Vertov's cinema: residents in *Second Life* often behave as half *flâneur/flâneuse* and half data-mining cowboys.

But even more interesting than mapping what has already been produced in computational *flâneur* art will be to follow the promising developments of the next generation of consumer-ready virtual reality. Virtual reality has the potential to turn virtual *flânerie* into a real alternative to 19th- and 20th- century city wanderings. In 2016, with the release of the consumer versions of the Oculus Rift, the HTC Vive and the PlayStation VR headset, the virtual reality industry signaled that it was ready to enter the world of mainstream gaming. Shortly after that, several virtual reality apps became available, allowing VR users to tour numerous world cities, either through the use of 360° panoramic images and video or through more immersive games. Among the latter it is worth mentioning Ubisoft's early foray into the world of VR gaming with the release of *Eagle Flight* (2016). In this multiplatform title, gamers can experience what it is like to explore Paris from the perspective of a bald eagle. Set sometime in the near future – after the extinction of humanity – the game recreates a Paris that is being reclaimed by nature: birds now nest on top of its iconic buildings; elephants roam across its streets, lush vegetation is growing everywhere. The player, in control of a juvenile eagle, can fly over the city or dive closer to the street level where he/she will have to dodge numerous obstacles among the vegetation and still standing city structures to find a path forward. Even though the game includes a story mode, most of its interest lies in the opportunities that it offers for free roaming and exploring this deserted city. It is not difficult to see how the same principles and technology shown in *Eagle Flight* could be used in the near future to provide VR users with highly immersive ways to experience world cities, and tour their main attractions or explore alternatively their less frequented corners, like a *flâneur*/flâneuse would do. Hopefully, Latin American cities and the valuable contributions of Latinx game developers will be part of these developments and discussions still to come.

Notes

1 For a discussion of the Latin American *flâneur* in Modernist literature see Comfort (2011, 2016), and Grzegorczyk (2005).
2 This misconception regarding who plays video games or what is the typical profile of a gamer has been debunked by most recent statistical analysis, which have consistently shown that about half of the population of gamers are women. See Makuch (2013) and Opam (2015).
3 For a discussion on how agency works differently in literature and video games see Perlin 2004. The following paragraphs are particularly relevant to my discussion of the crucial differences that exist between a narrative and an interactive contract: "So, there is something very particular about the way the novel, in all its many variants, goes about its business. By telling us a story, it asks us to set aside our right to make choices—our agency. Instead, the agency of a protagonist takes over, and we are swept up in observation of his struggle, more or less from his point of view, as though we were some invisible spirit or angel perched upon his shoulder, watching but never interfering. By way of contrast, look at games. A game does not force us to relinquish our agency. In fact, the game depends on it. When you play Tomb Raider you don't actually think of Lara Croft as a person the same way, say, you think of Harry Potter as a person [...]. There is a fictional construct in the backstory to the game. But while you're actually playing the game, the very effectiveness of the experience depends on you becoming Lara Croft. The humanlike figure you see on your computer screen is really a game token, and every choice she makes, whether to shoot, to leap, to run, to change weapons, is your choice" (13–14).
4 "Have you ever had two foxes in your den?" "Are you looking for a fast track to heaven?" "Would a gentleman of your rank accompany me to the nearest alley?"

Works cited

Atkinson, Rowland & Paul Willis. "Charting the Ludodrome: The Mediation of Urban and Simulated Space and Rise of the *Flâneur Electronique.*" *Information, Communication & Society,* 10:6 (2007): 818–45.
Baudelaire, Charles. *The Painter of Modern Life and Other Essays.* London: Phaidon Press, 1995.
Comfort, Kelly. *European Aestheticism and Spanish and Spanish American Modernism: Artist Protagonists and the Philosophy of Art for Art's Sake.* Basingstoke and New York: Palgrave Macmillan, 2011.
Comfort, Kelly "The Flâneur in Paris and Mexico City: Manuel Gutiérrez Nájera's Transnational Search for Modern Beauty." *Decimonónica,* 13 (2016): 32–49.
Elkin, Lauren. *Flâneuse: Women Walk the City in Paris, New York, Tokyo, Venice and London.* New York: Farrar, Straus and Giroux, 2016.
Frisby, David. "The *Flâneur* in Social Theory." *The Flâneur.* Ed. Keith Tester. London and New York: Routledge, 2015.
Fulton, Michael. "Amazingly Built American Cities in Minecraft." *Lifewire,* 19 April 2017. Accessed 22 July 2017.
Grzegorczyk, Marzena. *Private Topographies: Space, Subjectivity, and Political Change in Modern Latin America.* New York: Palgrave Macmillan, 2005.
Kaplan, Carla. *The Erotics of Talk: Women's Writing and Feminist Paradigms.* New York and Oxford: Oxford University Press, 1996.
Landay, Lori. "Virtual KinoEye: Kinetic Camera, Machinima, and Virtual Subjectivity in Second Life." *E-Media Studies,* 2 (2009): 1–33
Makuch, Eddie. "900 People Worked on Assassin's Creed IV: Black Flag, Says Director." *Gamespot* 15 October 2013. Accessed 22 July 2017.
Manovich, Lev. *The Language of New Media.* Cambridge, MA: MIT Press, 2001.
Manovich, Lev. "Generation Flash." 2002. http://manovich.net/index.php/projects/generation-flash
McCloud, Scott. *Understanding Comics: The Invisible Art.* New York: William Morrow, 1994.
Opam, Kwame. "Men Call Themselves Gamers, But Just as Many Women Play Games" *The Verge* 15 December 2015. Accessed 22 July 2017.
Parsons, Deborah. *Streetwalking the Metropolis: Women, the City and Modernity.* Oxford and New York: Oxford University Press, 2000.
Perlin, Ken. "Can There Be a Form between a Game and a Story." *First Person: New Media as Story, Performance, and Game.* Eds. Noah Wardrip-Fruin and Pat Harrigan. Cambridge, MA and London: MIT Press, 2004. 12–18.

The Latin American flâneur *in the digital age*

Sun, Leo. "Assassin's Creed Unity Release Set for Fall 2014 – But Is It Too Much, Too Early?" *The Motley Fool,* 1 April 2014. Accessed 22 July 2017.

Torres, Carlos et al. *Caminando Bogotá.* Bogotá: Universidad Javeriana, 2007.

Ubisoft Montreal. *Assassin's Creed IV: Black Flag.* Ubisoft: Montreuil, France (PS3, PS4, Xbox 360, Xbox One, PC, Wii U), 2013.

Walkowitz, Judith. *City of Dreadful Delight: Narratives of Sexual Danger in Late-Victorian London.* London: Virago, 1992.

3

INTERSECTIONS OF GENDER AND GAMING IN LATIN AMERICA

Phillip Penix-Tadsen

The dynamics of gender and sexual identity impact the production, circulation and signification of video games in myriad ways. In Latin America—and indeed in all regions and contexts—these dynamics are made manifold through their intersections with complex questions of class, race, ethnicity, nationality and cultural identity, among others. Likewise, the numerous approaches to analyzing gender's impact on games from development to reception demonstrate the ways gender remains a key consideration—whether as a stumbling block or a passageway to more meaningful gaming experiences—for all facets of video games' meaning. In contemporary Latin America, for example, gender affects games on the levels of women's underrepresentation in the video game industry workforce; in-game depictions of gender and lesbian/gay/bisexual/trans/queer (LGBTQ) identity; online communication and harassment; the shifting player demographics of the 21st century; marketing strategies calculated to appeal to the gendered desires of imagined gaming audiences; the formation of gender- and sexuality-centered gaming communities on social media; and the effort to close the "gender gap" among eSports (professional competitive gaming) participants. Given the multivalent nature of the topic, this chapter will focus on several key aspects of the relationship between gender and video games in Latin America: first, representation, identification and gender in games; next, gender and player demographics in Latin America; third, the gender dynamics of Latin American game development; and finally, intersections of gender and gameplay in 21st-century Latin America.

Representation, identification and gender in games

Research on character representation in mainstream video games shows that women, minority groups, children and the elderly are grossly underrepresented—and males, whites and adults are vastly overrepresented—relative to their overall percentage of the real-world population, as well as to their percentage of the gaming population (Williams et al. 2009: 828). Furthermore, Latin Americans and Latinxs in video games "typically appear as a non-playable character, obstacle to overcome, or simply part of the backdrop" (Aldama 2013: 241), and female characters, when featured, are frequently relegated to secondary roles or act as "accessories or rewards for the hero," contributing to a cycle in which a male-dominated industry creates products for a presumed masculine gaming audience, which can push female or non-binary gamers away from gaming as well as from the game industry in general (Fernández Vara 2014: 93). Latin masculinity is typically represented in video games through the types of characters analyzed by Frederick Luis Aldama: generically "Latin" fighters, "all-body characters in sports games" or "knife-wielding, ominously dangerous types" in roving gangs (Aldama 2013: 242). While there are exceptions, these stereotypical depictions remain the rule in mainstream games.

Given the underrepresentation of both Hispanic and female characters in the medium overall, it may not be surprising that the history of Latina characters in particular is rather sporadic. There is, nevertheless, a considerable history of female Latin American and Latina characters in games, including playable characters like Annet Myer, the "Peruvian sorceress" protagonist of Japanese developer Wolf Team's platformer games *El Viento* (1991) and *Annet Futatabi* (1993), or Colonel Corazón Santiago, commander of the Spartan Federation in *Sid Meier's Alpha Centauri* (1999), or Sombra, the Latina character recently added to Blizzard's popular first-person shooter series *Overwatch* (2016).

Likewise, it is common to find Latina characters who represent "members of the undocumented class" and/or "hypersexualized bodies" (Aldama 2013: 242) playing secondary roles in relation to a male protagonist—princess/damsel-in-distress, sidekick, family member, love interest—including Catalina in the *Grand Theft Auto* series (2001), Val Cortez in *Far Cry* (2004), Isabela Keyes in *Dead Rising* (2006), Eva Cortes in *Red Dead Redemption* (2010) and El Presidente's daughter in *Guacamelee!* (2013). Japanese binary combat fighting games have perhaps the lengthiest and most sustained history of representing Latina characters, from Angel in SNK's *King of Fighters* series, to a spectrum of scantily clad practitioners of Brazilian Capoeira including Christie Monteiro, who first appeared in *Tekken IV* (2001), Pupa Salgueiro in *Rage of the Dragons* (2002) or the more recent Laura Matsuda of *Street Fighter V* (2016). In many cases, these characters lean on longstanding stereotypes as shorthand to the representation of gender and culture. However, rather than merely appealing to the masculine gaze, recent characters like Sombra represent an attempt to attract gamers seeking more varied options among playable characters, an indication of some of the small steps the industry is taking to appeal to gamers of diverse backgrounds.

Contemporary critics, however, have called into question the primacy of representation as a frame for debates on gender and games, suggesting that we need to move beyond basic critiques of stereotypical representation and simplistic presumptions regarding player-character identification in order to understand how gender truly impacts games. Jenny Sundén and Malin Sveningsson promote the development of "intersectional, queer, feminist studies of online gaming" (2012: 7), a call echoed by Adrienne Shaw and Bonnie Ruberg's advocacy for scholarship that "turn[s] to queerness to challenge a variety of dichotomies that have long structured how scholars and designers alike understand games (e.g., narratology/ ludology, production/reception, control/agency, success/failure)" (2017: ix–x)—Shaw and Ruberg's anthology *Queer Game Studies* ultimately "locates queerness in games beyond representation" (xv). By "queering" the boundaries between long-standing binaries, intersectional critiques of gaming and gender have opened new pathways for understanding the ways games meld with our other lived experiences. In *Gaming at the Edge*, Shaw argues that although "industry-level discussion of representation presumes that a concrete group desire, such as that for representation, can be leveraged in production" (2015: 18), there is reason to question "the assumption that members of marginalized groups are 'naturally' concerned with representation of a group in which they might be classified" and therefore "identity, identification, and representation are much more complicated than this model allows" (22). Ultimately, this line of critique suggests that game studies and media representation studies should "break away from this reification of groups that reemphasizes their marginalization" (215), in order to focus on the real-life practices of female and non-binary players. To truly account for gender's impact on players' gaming experiences, then, we must adopt a phenomenological approach capable of accounting for the specificity and complexity of the cultural intersections at play when gender and video games align. Toward that end, this chapter will now turn to examine some of the real-world gender dynamics reflected in the demographics of gamers and game industry workers in contemporary Latin America.

Gender and player demographics in Latin America

Overall, the demographics of actual gamers in Latin America (and elsewhere) are much more diverse than the characters represented in mainstream games. Market data indicates that in Latin America respondents identifying as female make up 48.1% of the regional internet population age 18 and over ("Women on the Web" 2010: 5), while female respondents spent slightly more time online and a slightly greater proportion of their online time playing games than male respondents (7). Another survey of more than 25,000 respondents from seven Latin American countries estimates that online gameplay is more common overall among male respondents (46.4%) than female respondents (35.4%), with male players more prone to playing on consoles and female players showing a preference for the PC (Arango Forero et al. 2010: 47–53). A study of more than 3,500 Argentines found that 30% played video games, including 35% of the male and 23% of the female respondents, and echoed the gender divide between platform preferences reflected above ("Encuesta" 2013: 23–25). Market data also reflect differences in the gender demographics of gamers in different countries and contexts, a reminder of the importance of other factors such as socioeconomic class and political framework in gamers' experiences. For example, according to one source, 28% of Argentine gamers are female, while in Brazil female gamers account for 40% ("The Latin American Games Market" 2016). These numbers are further broken down when examining sub-segments: for example, the gender distribution of mobile gamers in Argentina is balanced more closely at 43% female and 57% male ("The Argentinean Gamer" 2017) than the distribution of Mexican console gamers, where females make up 39% to males' 61% ("The Mexican Gamer" 2017). Projections suggest that Latin America will soon surpass North America in number of smartphone users ("2017 Global Mobile Market" 2017: 15), expanding access to segments of the populace that were previously out of reach of many gaming technologies.

But lest we get too caught up in marketing segments and attempts to pin down gendered preferences of hardware and software, we must interrogate the assumptions underlying the questions being asked. Surveys based on yes-or-no questions, binary gender options and a market-based search for quantifiable and exploitable consumer preferences yield certain results. But we could also expand our view of gender and game-related practices, following Sinem Siyahhan and Elisabeth Gee, to include "legitimate peripheral participation" (2016: 95) aside from playing games and watching others play games, such as when "women and girls talk about games with other family members, solve problems or play a difficult part for other family members, and visit websites related to games," (101–102) taking on roles that impact the meaning and experience of games for all concerned.

Ultimately, making games that appeal to audiences with different gender identities may be less about making games specific to each sub-set of identity, and more about making games that avoid rigid and outdated gender categorizations. Indeed, all the market-based data and theories about gendered hardware and software preferences seem to fall out the window when we examine real-world player practices. An Argentine report on local female gamers showed a preference for hardcore console titles like *League of Legends*, *Counter Strike*, *Grand Theft Auto V* and *World of Warcraft*, among others (Perazo 2015), rather than the poppy casual games and social media titles the market research would suggest that female gamers prefer. Likewise, a study of 668 Brazilian players aged 18 and older concluded that female players primarily took on roles associated with achievement, planning and exploration, avoiding the socializer role conventionally attributed to the feminine gender (Fortim et al. 2016: 1318). The incompatibility of player practices with market-based predictions of purchasing patterns suggests that the mainstream game industry still has much to learn about gender and gaming. As Shira Chess argues, "the category of 'women players' is neither consistent nor predictable," so "[d]esigners, executives and marketers should ask better questions, reaching out to a multitude of players" rather than limiting "womanhood to white, heterosexual, middle-class women" in ways that unproblematically rely upon "industry divisions between 'hardcore' and 'casual' gamers" that "essentialize play styles and tend to map 'casual' play to women and 'hardcore' play to male audiences," thus "repurposing tired stereotypes repeatedly used in media aimed at women audiences" (2013: 176). It is no longer enough (in fact it never was enough) to create "girl games" as a counter-measure to the overall dominance of hyper-masculine games among players and markets. Gamer preferences are as diverse as gamer demographics, and the data clearly show that the industry has some significant catching up to do in order to create games that are as diverse in their approaches to gender and cultural identity as the audiences they seek to attract. Because diversity and demographics are significant not just in games' reception but also in their production process, this chapter will turn now to an examination of gender's impact on game development in Latin America.

Gender dynamics of Latin American game development

In the computer games industry, as in the information technology (IT) industries overall, women are significantly underrepresented, creating a "worldwide problem" for gender equity in the IT profession (Prescott and Bogg 2010: 140). In 2015, the International Game Developers Association (IGDA) released the results of a survey of nearly 6,000 game developers across the globe, which revealed that only 22% of the global games workforce identified as female, while 75% identified as male, 1.5% as transgender, 1% as other and 6% declined to respond (Edwards 2014: 10). Notably, of the total respondents to the IGDA survey, 4% identified "South America" as their region of work, though the survey offered only this option or "North America" (home to 59% of respondents), making it difficult to determine where responses from Mexico, Central America and the Caribbean might fit in (Edwards 2014: 8). If we dig deeper into data specific to Latin America, the global game industry's 22% female workforce may begin to seem impressive by contrast—women make up only 12% of the workforce in the Chilean games industry (Angulo Cáceres) and only 9% in Argentina ("Estado de la industria independiente" 2016). In light of the severity of this gender divide, the industry has begun to strategize ways of attracting more diverse employees, while critics have focused on highlighting the enduring barriers to women's lasting participation in IT fields.

Considerable research has examined the reasons some women avoid careers in the video games industry and related fields, as well as the reasons that those who have found success in game development have decided to stay. Mia Consalvo's work examines the "marketing disconnects, structural sexism and resistance to change" that drive many women away from the game industry on a global level (2008: 177), arguing that there is a need to move beyond the question of how to attract female workers, since "programs, pipelines, and curricula meant to encourage girls and women to enter this industry will have little long-term impact if women leave the industry in a decade or less, as recent reports have suggested" (178). Consalvo concludes that, while women in game development are driven by a passion for their work, their employers "know this, and can trade on that passion to increase output" (185), leading to increased demands for crunch time (defined as "weekly periods of fifty to one hundred hours" for "periods lasting from two weeks to several months" 182–183), as well as "rapid turnover, retention problems, and a work culture that valorizes youth, passion, and long hours over maturity and experience," often resulting in frustration for women who feel they are being made to "'fit in' to a masculine culture, or worse, feel that they are being 'treated differently' simply because they are women" (188). When this gender divide intersects with the economic divisions of neoliberal capitalism, we see the ways intersectionality transforms and magnifies the marginalization of women working in games in Latin America, particularly in contexts such as the *maquiladora* economy of poorly paid manufacturing work in facilities that line the U.S.-Mexico border. Nick Dyer-Witheford documents the episode that arose in 1995 when Alicia Perez, a young woman working in the Maxi-Switch factory that produced parts for the Nintendo GameBoy, led the charge to unionize; Perez was fired after being punched and knocked down by company thugs, along with three other union leaders (1999: 83). In circumstances such as this, it is evident that for many women working in IT industries in Latin America and other parts of the globe, the obstacles presented by gender imbalance are just the beginning.

While greater diversity and gender inclusivity are stated goals for many in the game industry, top-down attempts at reform have frequently missed the mark, while grassroots organizations are working from the ground up to promote IT and game development careers for women. Chess has argued that in the game industry, "women are welcomed while at the same time they are simultaneously marginalized and their tastes essentialized" in games and work conditions that "reify traditional stereotypes of femininity and narrow definitions of womanhood" (2013: 169). This has led some in Latin America and elsewhere to focus on reframing the narrative surrounding IT careers and entrepreneurship for women, such as the Mexico-based organization Epic Queen, led by Dany González, which runs regular events including code parties for girls ages six to 16, meetups, a club, a camp and an accelerator for supporting projects initiated by members. Young entrepreneurs further along their professional paths receive support from entities like Colombia's Global Game Designers Guild, cofounded by design manager Ivonne Marcela Tovar and dedicated to fostering a professional environment that encourages new talent and supports their entrepreneurship—Tovar herself is also cofounder of Press Start Studios, a developer focused on original mobile games. Just like with representation, if the game industry really wants to diversify, it will require more than superficial changes and questions about "what women want" in their game libraries or their working conditions, built on false binaries and assumptions that preclude their usefulness for answering complex questions. Grassroots organizations that attend to the particular concerns of young women preparing for careers in IT and game development offer a platform for future development.

Perhaps the best answers as to how women and non-binary individuals find triumph in the game industry come from looking at success stories and the values and factors they represent. It should not be surprising that in spite of gender divisions in Latin America as in the rest of the world, women have historically played a significant role in game development and continue to do so, contributing to the myriad processes involved in game creation, distribution and promotion. From the earliest days of homebrew-style game development in Latin America, pioneers like Naomi Marcela Nievas of Argentina, alias "Sharara," programmed original games like *Scrunff* (1985) as some of the few women among a male-dominated programming scene (Esnaola et al. 2015: 37). Other pioneering industry leaders in the region include Sofia Battegazzore of Uruguay, co-founder and co-director of Powerful Robot Games along with Gonzalo Frasca from 2002–2012, and currently a freelance game developer and professor of game studies; or Martina Santoro, president of the Argentine Video Game Developers' Association (ADVA) and founder/CEO of Okam Studio, a Buenos Aires-based developer focused on cross-platform games, applications and interactive content. And new platforms for game development and distribution have made it easier for innovative young creators to get a foot in the door of game development, leading to some truly original projects—examples include Paraguayan Gabriela Galilea's 2014 game *Okima*, designed to help cure the ocular condition known as strabismus (Corredor, n.d.), or *Juatsjinyam/Aprendiendo* (2015), a game designed by 17-year-old Colombian student Ayda Milena España Jamioy to help preserve the language of the camëntsá people in Colombia (Calle 2015). As these standout examples demonstrate, women have played an important leadership role in Latin America's game industry from the start, and advances in gaming technology are creating new possibilities for creative entrepreneurship and game development.

Of course, video games are not just the products of singular visionaries, but rather they are complex collaborations that involve a collective effort on development, distribution, promotion and circulation. And in spite of the male dominance of the overall workforce, women and non-binary individuals contribute to all sectors of the game industry, from animation and sound engineering to motion capture and advertising—or in the case of Mercedes Recinos of El Salvador, costume design for the independent horror-themed adventure game *Enola* (Recinos 2017). Other women from Latin America have carved a career path by working in the game industry abroad—an example is Liliana Pantoja, IT project manager for a British online casino gaming company with a presence in more than 30 countries, who explains that she has had to work hard to be successful in "a male-dominated sector, both in IT and in sports betting; coming into an organization with those characteristics, as a foreign woman from a 'developing' country, and making changes to a business with a 100% British legacy, where many employees have been working for decades, has been my greatest professional challenge up to now" (Oroz 2016). Today, the sub-sectors and segments of the game industry are ever-multiplying, creating new interactions between games and other aspects of social and cultural life. Take for example the phenomenon of eSports, which is creating lucrative opportunities as it entertains millions of spectators—Maricarmen Vargas, cofounder of Electronic Sports Puerto Rico (ESPR), organizes events that have attracted more than half a million remote viewers as well as thousands of live spectators (Román 2016). Clearly, "game development" consists of an ever-increasing variety of components, opening up new possibilities for future trajectories.

Game art—the creation of games as art objects, and the promotion and exhibition of games by art institutions—is another important point of intersection between games and the broader realm of culture. More institutions are embracing video games as at least part of their focus, and many have curated exhibitions and events centered entirely on games and gaming. The Argentine exhibition *Game On! El arte en juego*, curated by María Luján Oulton, is preparing to launch its fourth installation since 2009, during which time it has been warmly received by audiences in a number of cultural institutions and galleries in Buenos Aires, where Luján Oulton has combined a traditional museum exhibit with interactive presentations, artists' performances and group events (Bittanti 2013). For their part, a number of Latinx artists have created games that reconfigure the conventions of well-known analog and digital games in order to produce artistic statements. Some of these pieces are relatively ambiguous or oblique—Argentine media artist Mónica Jacobo's *00:04:44* (2005) modifies the first-person shooter *Half Life 2* (2004) into a scenario in which the player walks across the bridge in the shoes of an avatar and finds a virtual red folding chair exactly like the real one offered to players/interactors in the gallery (Jacobo 2012).

Other Latinx game artists make works that more explicitly "play" with gender and intersectional identity. For example, Coco Fusco and Ricardo Dominguez's *Turista Fronterizo*, a digitized version of *Monopoly* framed within the socio-cultural dynamics of the U.S.-Mexico borderlands, offers the player a chance to explore border life from the perspective of four characters—two from Mexico, two from the United States; two women and two men—in a way that combines Fusco's focus on "the representations of otherness, the classification of troubling bodies, and the treatment of (formerly) colonized peoples" with Dominguez's "overt concern for the structural inequalities facing Mexicans and undocumented immigrants, coupled with a tactics of using digital technologies against the grain" (Taylor 2014: 124). Likewise, Brazilian drag queen Amanda Sparks has produced games such as *Flappy DragQueen* (2015), a trans-themed knockoff of *Flappy Bird* (2013), and *The Shade Forest* (2016), which follows the main character of Amanda herself through a *Mega Man*-style adventure (Duarte 2015).

Transgender Latina game artist Micha Cárdenas tackles some similar issues in *Becoming Dragon*, "a mixed-reality performance that questions the one-year requirement of 'Real Life Experience' that transgender people must fulfill in order to receive Gender Confirmation Surgery, and asks if this could be replaced by one year of '*Second Life* Experience' to lead to Species Reassignment Surgery" (Cárdenas 2010). To create the performance piece, Cárdenas undertook a year of research and development that ran concurrent to her real-life hormone replacement therapy, then "lived for 365 hours immersed in the online 3D environment of *Second Life* with a head mounted display, only seeing the physical world through a video-feed, and used a motion-capture system to map [her] movements into *Second Life*," projecting the performance stereoscopically for the audience (Cárdenas 2010). As Claudia Costa Pederson has argued, artists like Cárdenas, Sparks, Fusco and Dominguez "engage in the appropriation, infiltration, and re-articulation of mass-produced games and videogames as a way to challenge, teach about, or otherwise speak back to power" (2016).

In light of these examples from the worlds of eSports, game art and behind-the-scenes development work, the definition of what constitutes "game development" or the "game industry" is in a process of rapid transformation, in Latin America and across the globe. At the same time, the dynamics of play have shifted rapidly with the advent of interactive online games, generating new issues for understanding how gender impacts the contemporary experience of gameplay, which is the subject of this chapter's final section.

Gender and gameplay in 21st-century Latin America

The first two decades of the 21st century have seen major shifts in the gaming landscape, including a boom in the popularity of "casual" games played on mobile devices and social media platforms (along with subsequent expansions, on one hand, of access to games, and on the other hand, of the possibilities for small, local game producers to reach the global games market), the advent of eSports as a major sub-industry unto itself, the appearance of the first major augmented reality and virtual reality games, the massive expansion of multiplayer online gaming and an increase in crossover between gaming and other spheres of creative production such as literature, music and the visual arts. The overall growth and diversification of the gaming population during this period of time has meant an ever-greater number of female-identifying and non-binary players, even if the industry has in many ways seemed slow to adapt to changing audiences and perspectives. The gender divide in the gaming populace has nearly closed, at least according to the statistics available—women made up 48% of the gaming population in the United States in 2014 (Grundberg and Hansegard 2014), the same year in which female gamers came to outnumber males in the United Kingdom (Stuart 2014). As video games become a part of everyday life in Latin America and worldwide, melding with other aspects of our social and cultural lives, they impact and intertwine with an ever-greater number of individuals, all of whom approach games and game culture from distinct intersections of sexual, socio-economic, racial, ethnic and political identity.

Intersections of gender and gaming in Latin America

The representation and performance of gender online is a significant aspect of the contemporary gaming experience. While online interactions were never truly anonymous and "the raced, gendered, classed body" has always been "'outed' in cyberspace just as soon as commerce and discourse come into play" (Nakamura 2002: 11), this revealing of gender and other aspects of identity has taken on new dimensions with the expansion in massive multiplayer online gaming and the ability to communicate via text, voice and even video chat with other players in real time. For many gamers who identify as female, this can often mean confronting a great deal of hostility. Research on player responses to gender cues found that, under controlled conditions, a female voice received an average of three times as many negative comments as a male voice, many of them hostile, even when both voices were communicating the same message (Kuznekoff and Rose 2013: 551–554). This level of hostility toward female gamers can have a negative impact on both individual experiences of gaming and overall attitudes toward gaming among male and female audiences alike. Research by Jesse Fox and Wai Yen Tang shows that female gamers respond to gender-based harassment in online gaming in a variety of manners, including rumination, organizational responsiveness, withdrawal and the use of coping strategies such as avoidance, denial, self-blame, gender masking and seeking help (2016: 9–11). Fox and Tang also argue that "game companies should be concerned with players' perceptions of organizational response to sexual harassment, as this predicted women's withdrawal from games," and that by "remaining passive and not addressing sexual harassment, gaming companies are sending the implicit message to players that it is acceptable" (14). For this and other reasons, it is urgent that game producers and players focus their efforts on ending harassment and exclusive behaviors in order to create a more welcoming gaming environment for all players.

Online interactions through social media can also have a significant impact on the ways video games intertwine with contemporary culture in Latin America, revealing the role gender plays in the circuits through which games' meaning is created and circulated. Take the case of Mariana Villanueva, alias Haku, a successful Mexican illustrator and visual artist who was enjoying a successful career abroad working with Microsoft until October 2016, when she became the target of public attacks via social media after it was revealed that she had plagiarized the work of another illustrator in her work for *Gears of War 4* (2016). While Villanueva accepted responsibility for her "reinterpretation" of this "reference," she rapidly found herself under attack from social media users who dubbed her #LadyPlagio (#MissPlagiarism) and deployed the type of personal, vindictive and at times violently misogynist discourse associated with the anti-feminist phenomenon known as #GamerGate in the United States (Castillo Cabrera 2016). This type of gender-based harassment and mistreatment of women by the gaming community at large is significant, as many female gamers "perceive the game culture rather than the game mechanics to be the primary deterrent" to participation in gaming (Yee 2008: 84), meaning change will have to take place at the community level in order for gaming to truly become more gender inclusive.

Indeed, grassroots community development is one of the brighter sides of gender's impact on contemporary gaming. Today, new communities constructed around gaming and gender or sexual identity are booming, aimed at nurturing an inclusive environment sensitive to the needs and desires of gamers from different backgrounds. LGBTQ groups such as Gaymers México and Gaymers Brasil, each with over 1,000 members, share social media content related to gaming as well as queer issues. Brazil's female gaming group Garotas Gamers boasts more than 50,000 regular users, while several smaller female gaming groups in Brazil and various Chicas Gamers groups out of Mexico, Argentina, Colombia and other Latin American countries have membership numbers in the thousands on social media. Although the advent of social gaming and an increased capacity for interpersonal communication in real time has brought challenges for gamers of different gender backgrounds, it has also created new opportunities to establish communities based on shared interests, affinities and experiences, making gaming an experience that is approachable to, and shared by, an ever more diverse population of players.

Gaming, gender and intersectionality in contemporary Latin America

Video games and their meaning are impacted by issues related to gender from their production to their reception—and indeed beyond, into their recirculation, reinterpretation and reconfiguration by contemporary *prosumer* audiences. The male dominance among playable characters in mainstream video games is compounded by a lack of Latinx characters, as well as a general lack of well-rounded characters from different socioeconomic classes, racial, ethnic, linguistic and LGBTQ backgrounds. However, intersectional analyses of games and game culture have helped shift our attention beyond representation and facile assumptions about player identification with game characters, pointing out the ways analytical frameworks frequently rest on the same binaries and assumptions that they aim to critique, and reframing our discussions of games' meaning around the real-life practices and experiences of players. A phenomenological shift toward lived experiences allows us to examine the impact of gender beyond the surface level of in-game representation, for example noting the makeup of the real-world game industry's workforce, which is also heavily dominated by young white heterosexual males and their perspectives, due in part to longstanding industry values and expectations (i.e., crunch time, youth and passion over maturity and experience) that conflict with recent efforts to attract more female and non-binary employees. Nevertheless, there are many important examples of women, people of color and LGBTQ individuals producing impactful work in the game industry, past and present. Player demographics are also in a process of rapid diversification, impacted in part by innovations like casual games and social media games, as well as expanded availability of internet-enabled smartphones throughout Latin America and the globe. And while the game industry has been relatively slow on the uptake in terms of producing real changes to the toxic masculinity of online gaming culture and the hyper-gendered stereotypical representations of men and especially women in games, new communities of gamers, modders and developers from diverse backgrounds are paving the way toward a Latin American game industry that more accurately reflects the diverse intersections of gender, race, class and sexual identity of the region and its people.

Works cited

"2017 Global Mobile Market Report." *Newzoo.com*, 2017. http://resources.newzoo.com/hubfs/Reports/Newzoo_2017_Global_Mobile_Market_Report_Free.pdf. Accessed 27 June 2017.

Aldama, Frederick Luis. "Getting Your Mind/Body On: Latinos in Video Games." *Latinos and Narrative Media: Participation and Portrayal*, Springer, 2013, pp. 241–258.

Angulo Cáceres, Gabriel. "Maureen Berho y la estrategia de los videojuegos chilenos para competir en el mundo." *El Mostrador*, 25 April 2017. www.elmostrador.cl/vida-en-linea/2017/04/25/maureen-berho-y-la-estrategia-de-los-desarrolladores-chilenos-de-videojuegos-para-mostrarse-al-mundo/. Accessed 27 June 2017.

Arango Forero, Germán, Xavier Bringué Sala and Charo Sádaba Chalezquer. "La generación interactiva en Colombia: adolescentes frente a la Internet, el celular y los videojuegos." *Anagramas: Rumbos y sentidos de la comunicación*, vol. 9, no. 17, 2010, pp. 45–56.

"The Argentinean Gamer." *Newzoo.com*, 15 June 2017. https://newzoo.com/insights/infographics/the-argentinean-gamer-2017/. Accessed 27 June 2017.

Bittanti, Matteo, "Interview: María Luján Oulton and the Argentinean Game Art Scene." *Gamescenes. Art in the Age of Video Games*, 2 June 2013. www.gamescenes.org/2013/02/interview-with-mar%C3%ADa-luj%C3%A1n-oulton-from-object-a.html. Accessed 28 June 2017.

Calle, David, "Estudiante indígena creó juego para salvar su lengua." *El Tiempo* (Colombia), 10 February 2015. www.eltiempo.com/archivo/documento/CMS-15222716. Accessed 28 June 2017.

Cárdenas, Micha "Becoming Dragon, a Transversal Technology Study." *C-Theory*, 2010. www.ctheory.net/articles.aspx?id=639. Accessed 27 June 2017.

Castillo Cabrera, Abril. "De plagios y machismos ilustrados En defensa de Mariana Villanueva (Haku)," *NoFM*, 17 October 2016. http://nofm-radio.com/2016/10/de-plagios-y-machismos-ilustrados-en-defensa-de-mariana-villanueva-haku/. Accessed 27 June 2017.

Chess, Shira. "Youthful White Male Industry Seeks 'Fun'-Loving Middle-Aged Women for Video Games— No Strings Attached." *The Routledge Companion to Media & Gender*, eds. Cynthia Steiner Carter and Lisa Linda McLaughlin, Routledge, 2013, pp. 168–178.

Consalvo, Mia. "Crunched by Passion: Women Game Developers and Workplace Challenges." *Beyond Barbie and Mortal Kombat: New Perspectives on Gender and Gaming*, ed. Yasmin B. Kafai et al., MIT Press, 2008. pp. 177–191.

Corredor, Maximiliano "Innovadores menores de 35 – Paraguay y Bolivia. Gabriela Galilea, 31." *MIT Technology Review* (Spain). www.technologyreview.es/tr35paraguayybolivia/1695/gabriela-galilea/. Accessed 27 June 2017.

Costa Pederson, Claudia. "Gaming Empire: Play and Change in Latin America and Latina Diaspora." *Media-N*, vol. 12, no. 1, 2016.

Duarte, Fanni, "Amanda Sparks: A drag queen que faz games fofinhos cheios de protesto," *VICE Brasil*, 3 December 2015. www.vice.com/pt_br/article/pgevg7/amanda-sparks-a-drag-queen-que-faz-games-fofinhos-cheios-de-protesto. Accessed 27 June 2017.

Dyer-Witheford, Nick. "The Work in Digital Play: Video Gaming's Transnational and Gendered Division of Labour." *Journal of International Communication*, vol. 6, no. 1, 1999, pp. 69–93.

Edwards Kate, et al. "IGDA Developer Satisfaction Survey 2014. Summary Report." 2014. http://c.ymcdn.com/sites/www.igda.org/resource/collection/CB31CE86-F8EE-4AE3-B46A-148490336605/IGDA_DSS14-15_DiversityReport_Aug2016_Final.pdf. Accessed 28 June 2017.

"Encuesta de consumos culturales y entorno digital. Computadora, internet y videojuegos." Ministry of Culture. Buenos Aires, Argentina: Office of the President of the Nation, 2013. www.sinca.gob.ar/sic/encuestas/archivos/videojuegos-01-a4.pdf. Accessed 27 June 2017.

Esnaola, Graciela et al. "Argentina." *Video Games Around the World*, ed. Mark J. P. Wolf, MIT Press, 2015, pp. 35–55.

"Estado de la industria independiente: Informe Ejecutivo." Buenos Aires: Fundación Argentina de Videojuegos, 2016. http://fundav.com/wp-content/uploads/2017/05/FundAV-Encuesta-2016.pdf. Accessed 27 June 2017.

Fernández Vara, Clara. "La problemática representación de la mujer en los videojuegos y su relación con la industria." *Revista de Estudios de Juventud*, no. 106, 2014, pp. 93–108.

Fortim, Ivelise et al. "A Tipologia das Jogadoras: Um estudo do público feminino gamer brasileiro." *SBGames* 2016, São Paulo, Brazil, 8–10 September 2016, pp. 1312–1319.

Fox, Jesse and Wai Yen Tang. "Women's Experiences with General and Sexual Harassment in Online Video Games: Rumination, Organizational Responsiveness, Withdrawal, and Coping Strategies." *New Media & Society*, 2016, pp. 1–18.

Grundberg, Sven and Jens Hansegard. "Women Now Make Up Almost Half of Gamers: Adult Women Gamers Now More Numerous Than Under-18 Boys." *Wall Street Journal*, 20 August 2014. www.wsj.com/articles/gaming-no-longer-a-mans-world-1408464249. Accessed 12 July 2017.

Jacobo, Mónica. "Videojuegos y arte: Primeras manifestaciones de Game Art en Argentina." *Cuadernos del Centro de Estudios en Diseño y Comunicación. Ensayos*, no. 41, 2012, pp. 99–108.

Kuznekoff, Jeffrey H., and Lindsey M. Rose. "Communication in Multiplayer Gaming: Examining Player Responses to Gender Cues." *New Media & Society*, vol. 15, no. 4, 2013, pp. 541–556.

"The Latin American Games Market: Console Still Stands Strong, but Mobile is Winning." *Newzoo.com*, 31 October 2016. https://newzoo.com/insights/articles/latin-american-games-market/. Accessed 27 June 2017.

"The Mexican Gamer – 2017." *Newzoo.com*, 15 June 2017. https://newzoo.com/insights/infographics/the-mexican-gamer-2017/. Accessed 27 June 2017.

Nakamura, Lisa. *Cybertypes: Race, Ethnicity, and Identity on the Internet*. Routledge, 2002.

Oroz, Martha L. "Liliana Pantoja, una colombiana que brilla en la industria de videojuegos del Reino Unido." *ColombiaNosUne.com*, 18 February 2016. www.colombianosune.com/destacado/liliana-pantoja. Accessed 28 June 2017.

Perazo, Cintia. "Cómo es ser una chica gamer en el mundo de los videojuegos." *La Nación* (Argentina), 22 September 2015. www.lanacion.com.ar/1829908-como-es-ser-una-chica-gamer-en-el-mundo-de-los-videojuegos. Accessed 27 June 2017.

Prescott, Julie and Jan Bogg. "The Computer Games Industry: Women's Experiences of Work Role" *Women in Engineering, Science and Technology: Education and Career Challenges: Education and Career Challenges*, eds. Aileen Cater-Steel and Emily Cater, IGI Global, 2010.

Recinos, Mercedes. "Enola. Costume Design." 18 June 2012. https://mercedesrecinos.wordpress.com/2012/06/18/enola-costume-design/. Accessed 27 June 2017.

Román, Olga. "Maricarmen Vargas se aventura en la industria de los gamers profesionales." *ÍNDICE*, 22 August 2016. www.indicepr.com/noticias/2016/08/22/biz/64027/maricarmen-vargas-se-aventura-en-la-industria-de-los-gamers-profesionales/. Accessed 28 June 2017.

Shaw, Adrienne. *Gaming at the Edge: Sexuality and Gender at the Margins of Gamer Culture*. University of Minnesota Press, 2015.

Shaw, Adrienne and Bonnie Ruberg. "Introduction: Imagining Queer Game Studies." *Queer Game Studies*, eds. Bonnie Ruberg and Adrienne Shaw, University of Minnesota Press, 2017, pp. ix–xxxiii.

Siyahhan, Sinem and Elisabeth Gee. "Understanding Gaming and Gender within the Everyday Lives of Mexican-American Family Homes." *Diversifying Barbie and Mortal Kombat: Intersectional Perspectives and Inclusive Designs in Gaming*, ed. Yasmin B. Kafai et al., ETC Press, 2016, pp. 92–104.

Stuart, Keith. "UK Gamers: More Women Play Games than Men, Report Finds." *The Guardian*, 17 September 2014. www.theguardian.com/technology/2014/sep/17/women-video-games-iab. Accessed 12 July 2017.

Sundén, Jenny and Malin Sveningsson. *Gender and Sexuality in Online Game Cultures*. Routledge, 2012.

Taylor, Claire. *Place and Politics in Latin American Digital Culture: Location and Latin American Net Art*. Routledge, 2014.

Williams, Dmitri et al. "The Virtual Census: Representations of Gender, Race and Age in Video Games." *New Media & Society*, vol. 11, no. 5, 2009, pp. 815–834.

"Women on the Web." *ComScore*, June 2010. http://www.digitalads.org/general%20marketing/comScore_onlinewomen_092010.pdf. Accessed 27 June 2017.

Yee, Nick. "Maps of Digital Desires: Exploring the Topography of Gender and Play in Online Games." *Beyond Barbie and Mortal Kombat: New Perspectives on Gender and Gaming*, ed. Yasmin B. Kafai et al., MIT Press, 2008, pp. 83–96.

4

LA LOTERÍA MEXICANA

Playing with heteronormativity

Stacey Alex

La lotería mexicana is a game beloved throughout Mexico and Mexican-American communities in the U.S. Its popularity has extended to other areas of Latin America, especially Central America, as well as other Latina/o communities in the U.S. Through culturally meaningful images and their oral descriptions, the game both reflects and maintains Latin American and Latina/o identities anchored in traditional Western sociocultural constructions of gender, sexuality, race, and class. However, as it is embedded in Mexico's complex history of Spanish colonization, revolution, and struggle with U.S. imperialism, *la lotería mexicana* is also used as vehicle to contest national promises of equality broken on both sides of the Río Grande. While iconic *lotería* images are often reproduced to celebrate Mexican or Latin American heritage without questioning their conservatism, some artists build their own inclusions and criticisms into the game in response to social injustices. By creating alternative mythologies, these reiterations work to empower those who have the deck stacked against them, either by modifying the cards or by creating new ones. Similar to the way regional Mexican versions of the game honor indigenous and African roots and expand their presence, queer *loterías* work against the heteronormative roadmap of the original. This chapter will provide a brief sociohistorical context of the game and review the role of *lotería* in popular culture; especially contemporary re-imaginings that are instrumental in questioning heteronormativity. Finally, it will examine how *Lotería: A Novel* by Mario Alberto Zambrano performs Latin American immigrant intersectionality. The various queer *lotería* adaptations examined here open up possibilities of resistance against heteronormative expectations and social injustices that limit life chances.

An introduction to *lotería mexicana*, its commercialization and ethnic pride

The rules of the game may be familiar to U.S. Anglo readers. As Chicano artist Lalo Alcaraz quips in his *Juego de votería* (2016), "It's like Bingo, Gringo!" Rather than only numbers, *la lotería mexicana* uses images that are randomly drawn and called out by the *cantor/a* (singer). Played among family and friends, young and old, at home and at fairs, participants must quickly identify and mark the corresponding images on their game board with tokens: beans, corn, buttons, or pieces of paper or wood (Morales Carrillo 2008: 157–158). Players take turns leading the game by taking on the role of the *cantor/a,* who often initiates the game with the phrase, *"¡Se va y se corre con la vieja del pozole!"* (*"It's off and running with the old lady who makes maize stew"*).

This speech act signals heteronormative gender roles from the first moment of play by positioning the female gender as belonging to the domestic realm. Following this opening, the *cantor/a* either calls out the name of each image directly, uses well-known sayings or riddles associated with each pictogram, or improvises her/his own descriptions in a kind of *cancionero* poetry slam (Stavans 2004: 26). The commonly known sayings either incorporate word play that alludes to the corresponding image or includes its name directly, but in either case they are often humorous and sometimes sexual in nature. For example, players know to mark *La Sirena* (the mermaid) when they hear "*mírala que bonita, lástima por la colita*" ("*look how pretty she is, too bad about the tail*"). Here women not only prepare food but also serve as objects of male desire.

With origins in Italy, France, and Spain, the game was popularized in Mexico in the 18th century. Although the designers of the original images are unknown, the commercialized version from Pasatiempos Gallo standardized 54 cards and game boards that include either nine or 16 spaces (Pasatiempos, "Lotería" n.d.). French businessman Don Clemente Jacques mass-produced these sets in 1887 and his company, which was briefly owned by United Fruit Company from 1967–77, later increased its exportation to the U.S., Central America, and Europe. It continues to produce the game as Pasatiempos Gallo in Querétaro, Mexico and as Don Clemente Inc. in the U.S. (Pasatiempos, "Historia" n.d.). A number of other companies produce and sell their own versions such as "Lotería de mi tierra" produced by Impresos Africa in Guadalajara, Mexico.

Iconic *lotería* images are commodified today for all sorts of products. While browsing online, they can be found on pillows, purses, and candy tins. They also adorn the walls of restaurant chains such as Lotería Grill in California and the ceiling of La Cantina de los Remedios in Mexico. It may be surmised that *lotería* is used to attract tourists and exoticize Mexican traditions for outsiders. It also inspires artists interested in Mexican culture such as Iowa native Teresa (Smith) Villegas, who created *Lotería,* a contemporary Mexican pop art version published in book format with riddles written by Latina/o Studies scholar Ilan Stavans. Pasatiempos Gallo also produced a trial run of Villegas' version, which includes new kitsch icons such as "Los Churros" and "La Telenovela" as well as two Mexican feminist icons: writer Sor Juana Inés de la Cruz and revolutionary Josepha Ortiz de la Dominguez (McKasson 2013). Along with this interest from non-Latinx artists, the game also wields the power to instill cultural and ethnic pride through national patrimony and nostalgia for a favorite childhood pastime. For example, *lotería* t-shirts are sold by a Mexican vendor at the Westland Flea Market in Columbus, Ohio. Another example is Veronica Camarillo's *lotería* birthday invitations available for sale on her Etsy page, based in Houston, Texas. The familiar cards call family together to celebrate the next generation and highlight the continuation of a favorite tradition. Etsy also offers a number of *lotería* themed products for weddings and baby showers, fittingly supporting these foundations of heteronormativity and nation.

In addition to consumer goods, the *lotería* theme is used in many dance performances, parades, and artwork across a wide variety of contexts. While it is not possible to describe every reiteration here, the following examples speak to the breadth of meaning behind their use. In 2012, students from the private school Instituto Autlense in Autlán, Mexico dressed as *lotería* figures to dance in a parade celebrating the 102nd anniversary of the beginning of the Mexican Revolution (Martinez 2012). In February of 2017, the dance troupe Cachondos Putla used elaborate *lotería* costumes during Carnaval Putleco, where different indigenous communities celebrate together in Putla Villa de Guerrero in Oaxaca, Mexico (Excelsior 2017). The video, posted by the Facebook Community "Estampas de Mexico" currently has more than 13 million views. While the first example demonstrates the game's hand in didactic nationalism, the second is a recuperation of representation to further indigenous traditions. Cachondos Putla took ownership of national paradigms and racial caricatures in *la lotería mexicana*, discussed later in this chapter, and enfolded them into a complex legacy of indigenous dance and music.

Lotería-inspired artwork is powerful ammunition for re-inscribing the role of Latinas/os in the U.S. as well. Just one example is the 2017 graduation cap of Alexandra Del Sarto, decorated with pupusas, *lotería* cards, and sparkles. A Master of Science graduate from the University of Southern California, Del Sarto explains that her design indexes pride in her heritage, "Coming from an immigrant family, and most especially considering where everything is standing politically right now in terms of race and being Latinx in this day and age, the idea of sticking pupusas on my grad cap was perfect" (Simón 2017). Being part Salvadorean, Ecuadorean, and Guatemalan, this case shows how *lotería*, as an expression of Latinidad, is not only restricted to those with Mexican roots. The two human figure cards she included were *La Dama* (the lady) and *El Borracho* (the drunk), which honor traditional feminine roles but simultaneously work to open up social boundaries which continue to prohibit Latina women from both the bar and higher education.

Lotería as Mexicanidad and its subversive potential

Ilan Stavans describes how the game taught him and millions of other children and young adults how to behave as Mexicans, "the way they eat, drink, think, dream, dance, and have sex" (2004: 26). He explains, "To us the images of *lotería* cards and boards weren't types but prototypes and archetypes in the nation's psyche. To play a single game was to traverse the inner chambers of *la mexicanidad*" (27). Reflecting on the Mexican obsession with games of chance, Stavans asserts that the undemocratic reality of political instability and widespread corruption during his childhood in the 1960s and 1970s relegated any feeling of control over the future to the private sphere. While their lives depended on the whim of incompetent politicians, individual spontaneity seemed to be the key to changing the future of the individual and nation (26–7). This argument may be extended to examine how *lotería mexicana* contributes to a similar sense of private control for Latinas/os in the U.S. facing an increasingly hostile environment of English-only rhetoric and racial profiling. Like other traditions, the game may build a sense of security by strengthening social connections with other Latinas/os. Maintaining a connection with home and heritage may be particularly important for immigrants and their mixed status families waiting 30 years (and counting) for comprehensive immigration reform under the threat of deportation and criminalization to the harrowing tune of "Make America Great Again." What makes *lotería mexicana* unique from other Latin American traditions is that it not only allows participants to preserve culture, but also invites them to creatively contribute clues that are meaningful and identifiable to their particular social group. This malleability and potential agency for place-making and belonging will be explored throughout this chapter, while paying particular attention to modifications of the game that break long-held social rules.

While *lotería* serves as a potential source of ethnic pride for Latin Americans and Latinas/os in the U.S., some may be concerned with its continuation of strict gender norms. Frederick Aldama argues that despairing over problematic Latina/o representations in popular culture ignores the power of human imagination to reappropriate those images for positive identity construction (2013: 22–3). This is made clear by the various examples here, as the game is not a static cultural product but is transformed according to its users' needs. The root of this fluidity may be found in Fausta Gantús' claim that the nationally institutionalized gambling through a lottery in Mexico is limited to numerical markers and economic gain whereas the popular version allows for collective diversion, creativity, and ingenuity (2011: 384–5). She also contrasts two forms of popular *lotería: lotería mexicana* which nourishes the national imaginary through symbols of the Church, State, and Militia, and *lotería Campeche* which combines symbols of the Campeche state of the Yucatán Peninsula with the national ones. This synthesis demonstrates how the "*patria,*" the fatherland and the national, depends upon the "*matria,*" a term used by historian Luis González y González to refer to the motherland and the particularity of the regional (Gantús 2011: 385, 392).

Two other regional Mexican versions are Mexican-Canadian artist Alec Dempster's linoleum and wood cuts in book format: *Lotería jarocha* (2013) and *Lotería huasteca* (2011). In the game version of the latter collection, poet Arturo Castillo Tristan contributes refrains for each image. Both are musicians of *son jarocho* and *son huasteco* respectively, which are rooted in indigenous, African, and Spanish traditions. Therefore, they include many cards related to music and dance such as *El Cuatrillo*, *La Banda de Viento*, and *La Huapangueda*. Other cards include everyday objects, places, and customs that anchor subjectivities in the Huasteca region of Mexico. While labor and social roles are gendered—the harvest and music are male domains—female figures also hold key roles through healing, weaving, and food preparation. The book's bilingual format and Canadian publisher may intend to reach English-speaking audiences, yet, for Castillo Tristan, an elementary school teacher, the book is part of a larger project to promote oral tradition in Citlalteptl, Veracruz (Dempster and Castillo Tristan 2011). In his introduction to Dempster's first collection, Tom Smart explains that *jarocho*, originally a racial slur for people of mixed indigenous and African heritage, was appropriated as a term of ethnic pride and currently refers to both the people and culture of southern Veracruz. Dempster illustrates popular *sones'* musical themes and includes their common refrains, although, like *lotería* they are often "improvised and there is ample room for melodic and rhythmic play within the framework of each son" (Smart 2013: 9). These images are also available in game format, "El Fandanguito" with verses from signer and poet Zenen Zeferino and has been used during events in both Mexico and Canada (Dempster n.d.). These three examples of regional *loterías* represent African and indigenous peoples in ways that move beyond the limited treatment of race and ethnicity with *El Negro*, *El Apache*, and *La Chalupa* of the traditional version.

I argue that the game's built-in space for creativity, improvisation, and transformation by "other" local counterpoints to Mexican state power makes *la lotería* prima materia for subverting Western cultural expectations that traditional versions of the game uphold. Artist Teresa Villegas explains that, because *lotería* cards include the name of the pictured character, they are used to teach reading, writing, history, and social values. For example, a liturgical *lotería* was created in the 1930s by the Catholic Church (Villegas 2017). Other versions teach about professions, body parts, fruits and vegetables, and *el día de los muertos*. Since it is used as an educational tool, the game is also uniquely positioned to challenge mainstream discourses on sexuality and intervene by introducing alternative characters and objects. This includes heteronormative constructions of gender and sexuality, especially as the game crosses national borders. A variety of artists and authors of Mexican heritage incorporate *lotería* in their work to contest the enforcement of heteronormativity as well as gender, racial and class boundaries in U.S. and Mexican contexts.

Heteronormative coding and recoding

Lotería is just one of many games used worldwide socialize children into heteronormative pathways. One example is the Victorian card game "Old Maid" in which the person left with the odd card, a queen, loses. The United States Playing Card Company, makers of the iconic BICYCLE® cards, begins its webpage about this game with, "Don't become the old maid!". Their illustrated version for children changes this tagline to "Don't get caught with the old maid," but the warning to young girls remains unchanged: find a husband to avoid becoming a clownish cat lady. In *la lotería mexicana*, gender norms are drawn by several cards.

While they register different social classes, *La Dama* (the lady) and *El Valiente* (the valiant man) have sayings that model acceptable male and female roles. The first, "*Puliendo el paso, por toda la Calle Real*" (Polishing the way down all of Royal Street) positions the upper-class female to be admired through the male gaze. The verb "pulir" indicates that the lady smooths down the walkway as she strolls, but it also means that she perfects or improves the public space through her beauty. While this may be considered a positive contribution, it is a passive one. In contrast, *El Valiente* is an active figure as a working-class male. His saying, "*¿Por qué le corres cobarde, trayendo buen puñal?*" ("*Why do you run coward, carrying a good knife?*"), situates the male as defender and aggressor by insisting that real men stay and fight while cowards run away from confrontation. While the saying for *La Dama* describes her as passively receiving the male gaze from a distance, the *valiente* saying requires participants to engage directly with the figure through an active interrogative phrase.

These two cards are re-imagined by artists of Mexican heritage in the name of feminist self-empowerment. The first is *La Valiente* (the brave woman) card by Yuyi Morales, an award-winning author and illustrator of children's books. The image was submitted to *RESIST!*, a free political comics and graphics publication created in response to the 2016 U.S. election so that "Women's voices will be heard" (Mouly and Spiegelman 2017). Morales writes that:

> For a long time I have felt a great need to redefine and to debunk the patriarchal narrative of what it means to be brave, but never more so after the election. With La Valiente I want to honor and celebrate we, women, as the true embodiment of the brave, courageous—and often painful—fight for dignity, respect, and justice, which now has become even more urgent than ever.
>
> *(2017)*

La Valiente corrects the knife and zarape of the original light-skinned male version with a dark-skinned female figure. She raises her left (perhaps socialist) fist and holds a snake in her right hand, rejecting Judeo-Christian belief that Eve's, and women's, weakness led to the fall of man. Rather than temptation, the snake comes to symbolize women's power. *La Valiente* does not have to reject all constructs of femininity to be powerful but expands them; she can wear a traditional huipil and long flowing hair along with pants and boots. The yellow object she stands on may be a corn husk, a pillar of Mesoamerican culture, and, as a crossbred plant, a symbol of mestiza strength in *Borderlands/La Frontera* by Gloria Anzaldúa, "Like an ear of corn—a female seed-bearing organ—the mestiza is tenacious, tightly wrapped in the husks of her culture. Like kernels she clings to the cob; with thick stalks and strong brace roots, she holds tight to the earth—she will survive the crossroads" (1999: 103). Bravery no longer requires male violence, but female, mestiza preservation.

Artists Kozmo and Matr collaborated to paint *lotería* images on doors in the Pislen neighborhood of Chicago, highlighting a long history of Latina/o communities' contributions to the city's social fabric. Their pin-up version of *La Dama* at Memo's Hot Dogs may still be the object of the male gaze and includes the text of the traditional saying. However, its chola aesthetics, hair pinned into a high quiff, bandana, and tattoos, demand public space for powerful Latinas (@___Kozmo___, "Finished La Dama"). The Guatemalan, Santa Monica-based artist Mike Alfaro transforms *La Dama* into a new card, *La Feminist* for his 2017 Millenial Lotería. The flowers she typically holds are replaced with a protest sign featuring a pink female gender symbol (Alfaro n.d.). This launches her into an active role and, yet, by preserving the white skin of the original figure and incorporating a 'universal' symbol, it may also index the limitations of feminism continued by the Millennial generation. This includes the failure to recognize more fluid conceptions of gender and the experiences of black and brown women. Alfaro's *El Tinder* card features a manicured hand holding a cell phone that displays the original *El Valiente* male figure. The viewer may imagine his or her own potential to either swipe left and reject or swipe right and accept the persistence of machismo in contemporary dating culture. The image also suggests that the technology that mediates gender and sexuality often advances at a faster pace than improvements to social equality; progress in the former does not inherently result in progress for the latter.

Active female figures in traditional *loterías* are either dangerous or indigenous; *La Sirena* lures men with her tantalizing voice, while the indigenous woman featured in *La Chalupa* cannot attain white standards of femininity and, therefore, works by bringing produce to the market in her canoe. The scene portrayed in *La Chalupa* comes to life in the 1944 Mexican film *María Candelaria*, featuring Dolores Del Río as whitened version of the figure. According to Erica Segre, the film typifies rural Indian life as "timeless" with a long-shot of Del Río paddling her picturesque canoe, which could also be found as collectible figurines of trade and customs as popular curiosities since the 19th century (114). While none of these three cards offer active female roles, this last caricature destines indigenous women to a pre-modern limbo. Kozmo and Matr also painted a Pilsen door with *El Apache* to redefine indigenous heritage. By replacing the traditional bow and arrow with a knife at his hip and shot gun held across his thighs, their *Apache* takes on defensive pose that indexes historical struggle (@___Kozmo___, "It's finished!").

Imagining alternatives: Queer *lotería*

While the traditional images may be limiting, several Latina/o artists use *lotería* as a palimpsest for breaking cultural barriers and imagining social change. The first to be discussed here is Alma López, a Mexican-born, queer, Chicana, feminist artist and activist who made headlines for her highly controversial, skin-bearing Virgen de la Guadalupe in her 1999 digital collage print entitled "Our Lady." In an interview with Enrique Limón, López expressed her surprise at the public outcry toward the piece, as it falls in line with a tradition of re-interpretation of la Virgen as a revolutionary activist by other artists in the women's liberation movement such as Yolanda López and Esther Hernandez. Another piece in the same series, "Lupe & Sirena in Love," reconfigures the iconic *lotería* card *La Sirena* by posing her in a passionate embrace with La Virgen de Guadalupe, a sacred icon of ideal Mexican femininity.

López uses this empowering feminist image of indigenous pride to transgressively counter historical amnesia and draw attention to U.S. imperialism. The bottom left corner of the image incorporates a fragment of a historical text that reads "*Mapa de la guerra de los E.U. con México*" (map of the U.S. war with Mexico). The opposite corner features a brick wall with the year 1848 painted in red over a Virgen de Guadalupe mural, referencing the signing of the Guadalupe Hidalgo treaty and the concession of half of Mexico's territory to the U.S. By removing the imperialistic, male gaze altogether, imagined as sailors gazing at *La Sirena*, Mexican lesbian love works to overcome the erasure of history and indigenous identity, all while symbolically restoring feminine, Mexican power.

The second artist to be considered here is Felix d'Eon, who was born in Guadalajara, grew up in Southern California, and returned to Mexico in 2010. The biography included on the artist's website describes d'Eon's vintage style as a rhetorical strategy that counters the taboo nature of the gay subject. Furthermore, "the illustrative imagery of the past does not cease to be wholesome through the inclusion of gay sex and sensibilities. He simply expands the notion of what wholesome is, erasing shame and celebrating desire" (d'Eon n.d.). His 2016 *Gay Lotería* series, available on Etsy, celebrates multiple sexualities and gender-bending with radical characters such as "El Sireno," "La Muxe," "La Tijera" (see Figures 4.1–3), "La Chichifa," and "Las Jainas," as well as objects such as "El Closet," and "El Estrapon."

While all of the reimagined cards push against dominant norms of gender and sexuality, "La Muxe" is particularly powerful because it may index a variety of transgressive subject positions. In his 2015 article "Meet the Muses" for Fusion online, Rafa Fernandez de Castro writes that *muxe* is a pre-Colombian Zapotec term from the Oaxaca region of Mexico for a "community of gay men who date heterosexual men while dressing as women, sometimes assuming traditional female roles within the family and society." However precise this definition may seem, de Castro illustrates how *muxe* identity is complicated by migration of people and ideas about gender and sexuality between Oaxaca and the U.S. Non-Zapotec Mexican-Americans adopt the term to

Figure 4.1 "El Sireno." Watercolor and Ink by Félix d'Eon.

Stacey Alex

Figure 4.2 "La Muxe." Watercolor and Ink by Félix d'Eon.

self-identify with a third gender alternative outside of standard U.S. Anglo LGBTQ categories, but the *muxe* identity in the Oaxaca region also evolves as the younger generation opts for hormonal therapy and sex change surgery, changing the traditional divide between women and *muxes*. Working in parallel with the *lotería* game in which d'Eon's "La Muxe" is incorporated, both the identity and cultural artifact take on a complex transnational character that opens up new possibilities to express and understand gender and sexuality.

A third recuperation of the game is used for political satire by Lalo Alcaraz in his comic series "Votería" (2016). Creator of "La Cucaracha," the first politically themed Latino daily comic strip to be nationally syndicated in the U.S., the Mexican Mitt Romney fictional Twitter personae, and *Migra Mouse: Political Cartoons on Immigration* as well as many other projects, "Alcaraz has been a quill-armed Quixote against the white overclass for years in Los Angeles" (Romero 2012). In his 2016 Voteria comics, Donald Trump is transformed into "El Donaldito" as a reimagined *El Diablito* (little devil) and Hillary Clinton is portrayed as *La Catrina*.

La lotería mexicana

Figure 4.3 "La Tijera." Watercolor and Ink by Félix d'Eon.

The traditional image referenced in the Clinton satire is *El Catrin*, which pokes fun at a dandy figure of 19th-century origins. While *La Catrina* does exist in other *lotería* versions to represent upper class women, she is typically wearing an elegant dress. Alcaraz (2016) employs gender-bending by drawing Clinton in exactly the same pose and tuxedo as the Don Clemente male *Catrin* figure. For Pantsuit Nation, a private Facebook group of Hillary Clinton supporters founded by Libby Chamberlain, the pantsuit serves as a coat of arms to challenge gender roles (Grinberg), yet the group is widely criticized as a social space limited to white feminism. In contrast, and earlier in the election season than the formation of Pantsuit Nation, Alcaraz dresses Clinton in a tuxedo to critique her elitism and corporate interests. It also points to another serious offense: wielding political and financial power as a woman in a man's world only to perpetuate white privilege and neoliberal power structures.

A final example of reappropriation, although not directed at gender norms, is Chepo Peña's "Space Lotería" that incorporates Star Wars into Mexican iconography (Simón 2015). Claiming this science fiction powerhouse as part of Mexican identity highlights cultural hybridity and counters the erasure and demonization of Latinas/os in Hollywood. Though not played by children, these reimagined *loterías* are tools for adults to question and laugh about social injustices. The availability of these images online allows them to be purchased or shared virtually across Latina/o communities. López and D'Eon's versions are likely to have strong currency among non-heteronormative social groups. In this way, *lotería* wields cultural capital to both maintain traditions and imagine new possibilities. In a similar vein, Zambrano's *Loteria: A Novel* (2013) performs *la lotería* to expose the limitations of heteronormative roles and portray immigrants' perseverance to establish a home in the U.S. despite social injustices.

Lotería: A Novel

The novel's protagonist, 11-year-old Luz Maria Castillo, describes how her family joins the neighbors after mass to play *la lotería* and how, together, they develop inside jokes to identify the *lotería* images. *La Sirena* is referred to as Uncle Fernando's nude because the bare-breasted mermaid is his favorite card. In this way, the novel shows how the game facilitates the creation of affective ties among an immigrant community separated from their blood relatives in Mexico. Although they share no biological relation, Luz refers to their neighbors as family by calling them uncles and aunts and the two immigrant families reciprocally fulfill kinship roles (2013: 32). *La lotería mexicana* is a social ritual that forges connections through shared experiences and created understandings. This bonding resists the alienation of asymmetrical power structures that uproot the family to the U.S. where they are treated as second-class citizens under the constant threat of discrimination.

In addition to scenes in which the family plays *lotería*, the narrative voice itself is structured through beautifully illustrated *lotería* cards designed by Jarrod Taylor. They allow the reader to imagine Luz arranging the *lotería* cards one by one to help her write about a traumatic event that she is unable to talk about during her time as a ward of the state in a children's home: suspecting that her father killed her mother for having an affair with her boss. Furthermore, Luz shot and killed her sister in an attempt to protect her father from the authorities. The reader is invited to play a literary kind of *lotería* by connecting the images with a fragmented narration that moves forward and backward in time. Each vignette serves as a riddle to accompany its *lotería* card since it does not directly state the tragedy but encourages the reader to work toward its recognition by piecing together the rapidly accumulating clues. With each page, the reader gets closer to discovering what Luz is working to express. In his introduction to another contemporary *lotería* inspired collection of art and poetry, *Lotería Cards and Fortune Poems: A Book of Lives*, Rupert García explains that "satire and references to contemporary events and politics are often a part of the wordplay involved, and, depending on the cleverness of the announcer, a strategy for winning can rest of the players' ability to divine the card being alluded to before the announcer actually finishes his poem or names the character" (1999: xv). Rather than popular references, Luz draws on her own experiences to tie together past and present.

In a number of Mesoamerican cultures, the spider was a symbol of female endeavors: spinning, weaving, and childbirth (Headrick 2002: 96). As the first illustration, *La Araña* (spider) card sets the stage for interpreting the events to come. Luz resists the constraints of this female identity by revealing her desire to smash a spider who looks at her "like if I'm her *Virgen de Guadalupe*" (Zambrano 2013: 6). Throughout the story, Luz exhibits *macha*, or tomboy, behavior and identifies strongly with her father. Indexing their shared violence and the reason she is now a ward of the state, spiders represent her dark thoughts as she addresses God throughout the novel: "It's not like You don't know what we're thinking when we lie down at night and look up at the ceiling, or when we crawl in our heads the way these spiders crawl over furniture" (Zambrano 2013: 1). In the conclusion to this vignette, Luz imagines herself following the spider into an underwater world where she dreams that her father did kill her mother. This danger associated with the spider presents her with seemingly limited choices: drowning in femininity like her mother or destroying it like her father.

Gender is tied to both class struggle and race in the novel. For example, racial discrimination may be inferred when Papi, who is dark-skinned like Luz, expects a promotion at work but is inexplicably denied. Economic subordination is also highlighted by the *Sol lotería* image. Papi tells Luz that this card is "la cobija de los pobres" (the blanket of the poor) (Zambrano 2013: 176). Employing this popular saying for *El Sol* card creates a strong tie between class struggle, his character, their family, and their historically Chicano and Mexican immigrant community in the Magnolia Park neighborhood of Houston, Texas. Readers are reminded of a long history of communities countering the lazy Mexican worker stereotype through proletarianization by claiming inclusion and legitimacy through Mexican American masculine identity. Oral historian Monica Perales argues that male Mexican workers working at the American Smelting and Refining Company in El Paso, Texas were able to achieve some social mobility during the 20th century through generational ties, by acquiring skills on the job, and by proving their ability to endure arduous and dangerous work. In contrast with this cultural ideal, Luz's father is unable to move up the ranks of industry, and so her mother accepts a job cleaning for a doctor. This leads to conflict with her husband as she violates traditional gender norms by working outside of the home and he becomes suspicious of her fidelity.

Luz writes in a journal according to the cards she draws in order to confess her own act of violence and find a way to accept the reality of her father's actions. After reflecting on her writing, she concludes that everyone arranges their own *tablas,* (game boards) to tell their stories and that "maybe this was a way for You to listen, which is really like listening to myself. A way for me to go to communion. I have to believe that if I keep playing it will be for something" (Zambrano 2013: 254). A parallel is drawn here between Luz and the disciple Peter. Although the *Gallo* card does not appear as one of the illustrations in the novel, a cultural "insider" would know that its *lotería* riddle references Peter's betrayal: "*El que le cantó a San Pedro, no le volverá a cantar*" (the one that sang to Saint Peter will not sing again). Just as Peter is foretold to deny Jesus Christ three times before the rooster cries, Luz tries to deny her father and their suffering by running away.

For Luz, repeated abuse and loss leads her to abandon the U.S. for Mexico and leave her past behind. She wants to replace the first card of the deck, *El Gallo* (the rooster) with *El Águila* (the eagle) because all the former animal can "do is scream loud and fight," but the latter can fly and represents freedom (Zambrano 2013: 256). The eagle appears on *La Bandera* (Mexican flag) card that announces this vignette because the eagle symbolizes the site where the Mexica people were meant to build Tenochtitlan, present day Mexico City. For Luz, it represents rebuilding a new life. Yet, it is from her liminal vantage point at the border as she and her aunt head for Mexico that Luz is able to recover hope. She decides to remain in the U.S. and claim her right to belong in the North, since the eagle also indexes Mexica's roots in Aztlán, the southwestern states and mythical origin of the Mexica people. Her decision challenges U.S. imperialism that resulted in the loss of half of Mexico's territory. Gloria Anzaldúa calls this borderlands history and aftermath a "1,950 mile-long open wound" (1999: 24).

Just before making this decision to stay, Luz sees a migrant struggling through the desert who seems to be reaching his arms up to God and carrying a crucifix. The figure reminds her of her father, inferring a connection with their struggles as immigrants. She realizes, "I was running away and trying to forget what had happened, but what if I couldn't? What if I couldn't forgive myself? I thought of Papi and how he made me, and how Mom made me" (Zambrano 2013: 259). Jumping out of the car, she runs toward an immigration officer, and cries like a rooster, "Kikirikiki" (261). It is significant that she chooses the Spanish version of the onomatopoeia since she previously expressed insecurity with speaking the language. Although she understands it, she doesn't like going to mass because it is held in Spanish (41–42) and, when a convenience store worker speaks to her in Spanish, she looks to her aunt who then tells her she better start practicing if she's going to live in Mexico (257). When Luz decides to live in the U.S., she will do so as a Mexican-American and a Spanish-speaker. She accepts *El Gallo* as a part of her life, as it represents her family's oppression, the resulting violence, and her people's centuries-long struggle. In Gloria Anzaldúa's terms, Luz will be a crossroads and "*un amasamiento*, I am an act of kneading, of uniting and joining that not only has produced both a creature of darkness and a creature of light, but also a creature that questions the definitions of light and dark and gives them new meanings" (1999: 103). Her multiple oppressions: race, class, gender, sexuality, are not experienced separately but intersect to create a unique and powerful perspective.

The climax of the novel reminds readers of the introduction's explanation about the rules of the game. A player could lose with a winning board and miss his chance to claim the prize if he does not "shout his victory as soon as his winning image is called" before the dealer calls another riddle (Zambrano 2013: vi). The introduction ends with a popular Mexican saying, "*El que es buen gallo, en cualquier gallinero canta*" (vii), meaning that if you are good at something, you can be successful anywhere regardless of difficulties. Meritocracy and the American Dream are confronted in the novel as it is increasingly clear that immigrants do not have equal access. However, the saying also reflects Luz's determination. In a strategic narrative move, Luz simultaneously contradicts and reinforces the very rules set up by the framework of the book. While *El Gallo* represents the recovery of Luz's voice as her winning card, it never materializes as an illustration in the novel because it is missing from her deck. She realizes her need for the absent *Gallo* card because of its relationship with *El Sol* (the Sun), with which she identifies the most strongly because of its connection with her name, Luz (light). Despite this limitation, Luz calls it herself by mimicking its cry and taking fate into her own hands. This act also transgresses gender norms because the only other characters that take on the role of *cantor* in her life are male. Because traditional female social roles and the heteronormative institution of marriage tragically failed her mother, Luz will forge new options and claim active social roles typically reserved for men.

Lotería: A Novel asks the reader to consider what happens when a player is forced to play with an incomplete set of cards. It is impossible to win if your game board includes a character that is denied to you because of dominant conceptions of gender, sexuality, race, or class. The missing *Gallo* card, therefore, stages a confrontation with social inequalities that neither ignores the material conditions of the character's reality nor treats them as helpless. *El Gallo* firmly positions Luz as a social actor and, yet, it is not the final card. Two more cards are drawn before the closing of the book, informing the reader that Luz will continue to live at the children's home, called *La Casa de Esperanza*/the House of Hope, and will wait for her father. The final card that Luz chooses for her game board/journal is *La Rana* (the frog), which is known, in some species, to change its sex. It invokes a memory of playing at having sex with a female cousin in Mexico. It may be inferred that the search for love and a sexual and gendered identity never ends. Although there is a final card and page of the narration, the struggle to make meaning of human experiences and contend with social expectations is continuous. Rather than suggest a victory, Zambrano's (2013) narration and Taylor's illustrations create a sense of cyclical movement through time that becomes a resource for ceaseless reconfigurations of possibilities.

Iconic *lotería* images may be perceived as normative and problematic but they are used productively by the narrative voice to tell her story and contest those limits. By creating her own

La lotería mexicana

Gallo card, Luz is not healed, but finds her voice and direction through a new subjectivity informed by a multiplicity of oppressions. Race, class, gender, and sexuality become entwined across multiple spaces and times, resisting any orderly, linear framework and demanding a more rigorous and flexible model for understanding the complexities of intersectionality. Finally, while room is left for agency and resistance, the reader is urged to reconsider dominant narratives of meritocracy and examine how the cards are often stacked against individuals who face social injustices and the limits of heteronormative roles.

Zambrano's (2013) novel, as well as the other *lotería* re-imaginings examined here, open up a wider discussion about the power to reappropriate seemingly limiting traditions in order to wield cultural agency. Both the game and pop culture reproductions of its iconic images may provide some sense of security and preserve cultural pride in the face of social subordinations, particularly in light of current Latina/o racial struggles in the U.S. However, attention must also be paid to reiterations that twist the conservative trappings of the traditional images as well as their specific strategies for self-empowerment. Through a lesbian *Sirena*, a third gender *Muxe*, a Clinton *Catrina*, and many other new characters, *lotería mexicana* lends itself to transgressive transformations because, from its inception, the game was built upon dominant (trans)national frameworks that depend on local variations to maintain its social meaning and position. For this reason, manifestations of *lotería* from marginalized and minoritized groups contribute to networks of support and belonging. From liminal spaces, trouble-makers can claim the cards as their own, redesign them, and construct defiantly inclusive and critical spaces.

Works cited

Alcaraz, Lalo. "La Cucaracha Presents Voteria 2016: It's like BINGO, gringo!" *Pocho.com*, 9 April 2016, www.pocho.com/la-cucaracha-presents-voteria-2016-its-like-bingo-gringo-toon/.

Aldama, Frederick L. "Multimediated Latinos in the Twenty-First Century: An Introduction." *Latinos and Narrative Media: Participation and Portrayal*, edited by Frederick L. Aldama. New York: Palgrave Macmillan, 2013.

Alfaro, Mike. "Millenial Lotería." *Mikealfaro.com*, n.d., mikealfaro.com/millennial-lotera/

Anzaldúa, Gloria. *Borderlands/La Frontera: The New Mestiza.* San Francisco, CA: Aunt Lute Books, 1999.

Camarillo, Veronica. "Loteria Birthday Invitation." *PhotosAndSweets, Etsy.* www.etsy.com/shop/Photos AndSweets?ref=l2-shop-info-name.

Dempster, Alec. "About the Game." *Alecdempster.net*, n.d., www.alecdempster.net/Loteria_Jarocha/Loteria_ About.html.

Dempster, Alec. *Lotería Huasteca: Woodblock Prints.* The Porcupine's Quill, 2015.

Dempster, Alec. *Lotería Jarocha: Linoleum Prints.* The Porcupine's Quill, 2013.

Dempster, Alec and Arturo Castillo Tristan. "Loteria huasteca." *Gallery*, 2011, http://loteria.elsewhere.org/ huasteca/.

D'Eon, Felix. "Bio." n.d., http://felixdeon.com/bio.

Excelsior. "Tradiciones: Dan vida al juego de la lotería en carnaval oaxaqueño." *Excelsior.com*, 3 March 2017, www.excelsior.cozm.mx/nacional/2017/03/03/1149932#view-5.

Fernandez de Castro, Rafa. "Meet the Muxes: How a remote town in southern Mexico reinvented sex and gender." Fusion Media Network, 2015, http://interactive.fusion.net/meet-the-muxes/.

Gantús, Fausta. "Pequeña pedagogía de la nacionalidad: los cartones para el juego de lotería." *La idea de nuestro patrimonio histórico y cultural, 1810–2010, v. 2*, ed. Pablo, Escalante. Mexico, D.F: Consejo Nacional para la Cultura y las Artes, 2011.

García, Rupert. "Introduction: The New Within Tradition." *Lotería Cards and Fortune Poems: A Book of Lives.* San Francisco, CA: City Lights Books, 1999.

Headrick, Annabeth. "Gardening with the Great Goddess at Teotihuacan." *Heart of Creation: The Mesoamerican World and the Legacy of Linda Schele.* Tuscaloosa, AL: University of Alabama Press, 2002, *Project MUSE*.

@___Kozmo___ "Finished up La Dama." *Instagram*, 6 June 2016, www.instagram.com/p/BGU3W pmhLOY/.

@___Kozmo___ "It's finished!" *Instagram*, 27 May 2016, www.instagram.com/p/BF6dTLlhLHp/.

Limón, Enrique. "Shame As It Ever Was: Twelve Years after 'Our Lady' Controversy, Artist Alma López Looks Back." *Santa Fe Reporter*, 2 July 2013, www.sfreporter.com/santafe/article-7526-shame-as-it-ever-was.html.

López, Alma. "Biography." http://almalopez.net/idxpix/artist.html.

Martinez, Axl. "La loteria mexicana." *YouTube*, 20 Nov. 2012, www.youtube.com/watch?v=7RO2nrd5qxA.

McKasson, Molly. "Gambling with All Her Heart: Teresa Villegas Brings Loteria to Etherton Gallery." *Molly's Desert Journal, Tucson Guide*, 2013, www.teresavillegas.com/wp-content/uploads/2013/01/TucsonGuideEditorial.pdf.

Morales, Yuyi. "This is My Loteria Card, La Valiente, The Brave One." *RESIST!*, eds. Francoise Mouly and Nadja Spieglman, 2017, https://resistsubmission.tumblr.com/post/158395315425/by-yuyi-morales-this-is-my-loteria-card-la.

Morales Carrillo, Alfonso. "Instrucciones." *Lotería fotográfica mexicana: cantada con refranes y coplas de la lírica popular*. Mexico: Petra Ediciones, 2008.

Mouly, Francoise and Nadja Spieglman, "About." RAW Books and Graphics, 2017, www.resistsubmission.com/.

Pasatiempos Gallo. "Historia." *Nosotros*, n.d., www.pasatiemposgallo.com/.

Pasatiempos Gallo. "Lotería." *Productos*, n.d., www.pasatiemposgallo.com/.

Perales, Monica. *Smeltertown: Making and Remembering a Southwest Border Community*. Chapel Hill, NC: University of North Carolina Press, 2010.

Romero, Daniel. "The Story of How Lalo Alcaraz's Cinco De Mayo Cartoon Cost Brentwood Patch Editor Dennis Wilen His Job." *LAWeekly.com*, 12 March 2012, www.laweekly.com/news/the-story-of-how-lalo-alcarazs-cinco-de-mayo-cartoon-cost-brentwood-patch-editor-dennis-wilen-his-job-2395586.

Segre, Erica. *Intersecting Identities: Strategies of Visualization Intersected Identities in Nineteenth and Twentieth-Century Mexican Culture*. New York and Oxford: Berghahn Books, 2007.

Simón, Yara. "This USC Student Put Actual Pupusas on Her Grad Cap And We're Very Here For It." *Culture*, Remezcla LLC, 23 May 2017, http://remezcla.com/culture/pupusa-grad-cap-usc/.

Simón, Yara. "Turns Out We're Still Obsessed with Star Wars Loteri" *Culture*, Remezcla LLC, 21 August 2015, http://remezcla.com/culture/turns-out-were-still-obsessed-with-star-wars-loteria/.

Smart, Tom. "Introduction." *Loteria Jarocha: Linoleum Prints*, by Alec Dempster. Ontario, Canada: The Porcupine's Quill, 2013.

Stavans, Ilan. "Mexico's Ritual of Chance." *Lotería*, by Teresa Villegas and Ilan Stavans. Tucson, AZ: University of Arizona Press, 2004.

The United States Playing Card Company. "Big Box Old Maid Cards." *Bicyclecards.com*, 2017, www.bicyclecards.com/product/big-box-old-maid-cards/#filter.

The United States Playing Card Company. "How to play: Old Maid." *Bicyclecards.com*, 2017, www.bicyclecards.com/how-to-play/old-maid/.

Villegas, Teresa. "History of La Lotería." *Teresavillegas.com*, 2017, www.teresavillegas.com/history-of-la-loteria/.

Zambrano, Mario A. *Lotería: A Novel*. New York: Harper, 2013.

5
DIASPORIC INTERSECTIONALITY
Colonial history and Puerto Rican hero narratives in *21: The Story of Roberto Clemente* and *La Borinqueña*

Ivonne M. García

In 1983, Luis López Nieves published *Seva: Historia de la primera invasión norteamericana de la isla de Puerto Rico ocurrida en mayo de 1898* ("Seva: A History of the First North American Invasion of the Island of Puerto Rico, Having Occurred in May 1898"), and he changed Puerto Rican literary history. The historical fiction, published in a newspaper along with ostensibly corroborating photographs and manuscripts, purported to unearth the buried story of the first U.S. invasion of the island through the coastal town of Seva, whose inhabitants valiantly repelled the U.S. invaders, only to be annihilated and have their town leveled. In explaining why he wrote *Seva*, López Nieves has said that "because I didn't like the history of Puerto Rico that I was sold, I decided to change it. I decided to write it the way I thought it should be" (2012). López Nieves has added that he found the history he was forced to consume about Puerto Ricans to be defeatist and depressing, so he crafted his own heroic figure—the professor who investigates and writes the story but vanishes without a trace. The fictional work became a "cultural happening" in Puerto Rico, with politicians and public figures demanding that the government begin an investigation into the whereabouts of López Nieves' disappeared researcher. To many islanders, *Seva* supplied the brave, self-sacrificing, anti-colonial heroes who are absent from the official history of the U.S. invasion, which tells of how no armed Puerto Ricans repelled the invading troops in July 1898. On the contrary, historical records suggest that many on the island welcomed U.S. forces, relieved that the northern nation that purported to represent freedom and republican government had come to rescue them from a decaying, repressive, and neglectful Spanish empire.

In her incisive critique of López Nieves' story, Frances Negrón-Muntaner has argued that without a violent confrontation against the U.S. invaders, "Puerto Rican national identity became more intensely narrated through tropes of shame," and she points to *Seva* as one of the clearest examples of this literary trend (2004: 34). Further, she finds that while this "'other' (American)" did not actually exterminate Puerto Ricans upon arrival, nationalist authors tend to represent it as having "damaged—racialized and feminized [them] in intangible ways that only writers can properly repair" (35). Thus, she argues that many Puerto Rican writers have understood "the obligation of nation-building fiction" to be the racial re-engendering of "the *Boricua* subject as heroic" (37). Within that literary tradition, Negrón-Muntaner points to *Seva* as a text that "served as a collective dreamwork" in which "*boricua* national identity [is] born not in shame or trauma, but in honor and military might (its reverse)" (39). She further notes how *Seva* was conceived "from another site represented as traumatic by nationalists: migration," especially given that López Nieves has said he crafted the story while living in New York (42). For Negrón-Muntaner, therefore, the Puerto Rican "ethno-nation" on the island and in the diaspora shares "common sites of 'colonial' shame," which has led Puerto Rican authors to invent "a heroic past" that promotes "a racially engendered ideological fantasy," one that privileges masculinity and whiteness (6, 38).

Building on Negrón-Muntaner's analysis of Puerto Rican literary heroes, this chapter examines two twenty-first century Latinx pop culture texts (specifically comic books), which, like *Seva*, are born in the Puerto Rican diaspora and exemplify hero narratives, in both actual and fictional figurations. However, unlike *Seva* and its island-centered contemporaries, these two works deploy what I call a "diasporic intersectionality" that not only acknowledges but actually privileges the Puerto Rican migrant experience. Because they are self-consciously diasporic (as opposed to excluding or occluding the Puerto Rican diaspora), these works avoid many of the representational pitfalls identified by Negrón-Muntaner in their literary predecessors. Instead of reifying masculinity, whiteness, and upper-class culture, these stories rely instead on the intersectional identities of racialized, gendered, and working-class protagonists, thereby contributing a counter-narrative of the Puerto Rican hero figure. In exploring these alternative narratives, I focus on Wilfred Santiago's 2011 graphic novel about Roberto Clemente's life, *21: The Story of Roberto Clemente*, and Edgardo Miranda-Rodríguez's first 2016 comic in a series focused on a female superhero named after the Puerto Rican national anthem, *La Borinqueña*.

Both of these texts were born in the diaspora and both author-artists express similar reasons for their artistic choices: the wish to craft a hero narrative.[1] Santiago, born in Ponce, Puerto Rico, has said that the idea for *21* started percolating while he lived on 21st Street in Long Island City, NY, where every "time I saw the street number, I thought about the idea" (Buckler n.d.). *21*, Santiago says, allowed him to explore "the nature of the island's relationship with the United States," since, as an Afro-Latino, Clemente "lived two political realities at the same time," adding that he saw "certain similarities between baseball and a superhero comic" (Seven 2011). Miranda-Rodríguez, who was born in New Jersey but also lived in Puerto Rico as a child, has noted that the idea for *La Borinqueña* arose after co-writing his first Marvel comic book in 2016. "Puerto Rico was in dire straits, what with the debt crisis and environmental issues affecting the island and I thought, 'What if I gave Puerto Ricans a hero that gives them hope?'" (Blanco 2016). To that end, Miranda-Rodríguez created an Afro-Latina title character, Marisol Rios de la Luz, clad in a magical suit that resembles the Puerto Rican flag. By choosing to tell alternative hero narratives, both Santiago and Miranda-Rodríguez set out to "write back" to Puerto Rico's longstanding colonial context but—unlike the authors studied by Negrón-Muntaner—they also chose to represent diasporic subjectivity as crucial to the Puerto Rican national experience, its notion of *patria* (homeland), and even to the future of the Puerto Rican people.

In theorizing the diasporic worldview, Igor Maver has argued that "living in a diasporic space today essentially signifies the forging of a new identity and a new diasporic, hybrid subjectivity," one that "encompasses not only those people who have migrated and their descendants, but also those who are constructed and represented as indigenous to a geographical location" (2009: ix). In their stories, both Santiago and Miranda-Rodríguez explore hybrid subjectivities in their protagonists and represent the indigenous Taínos as crucial cultural markers of identity formation for Puerto Ricans. For her part, Gabriele Griffin, writing in the British context, underscores "that diaspora occurs along identifiable lines, in chartable and specific directions, and with particular and definable effects" within "historically specific dimensions" (2003: 36–37). To speak of the Puerto Rican diasporic subjectivity, therefore, requires a historicized analysis that pays careful attention to the individualized, as well as the shared, experiences of diaspora.

Indeed, by studying pop culture representations of the Puerto Rican diaspora we can further nuance contemporary theorizations of migrant subjectivity. Jorge Duany has noted how the political relationship of the island to the United States, and the movement of Puerto Ricans to and from the States since the late nineteenth century distinguishes this group's experience from that of most other migrants. In *Puerto Rican Nation on the Move*, Duany identifies Puerto Rico's migratory patterns as distinctive for: (1) the island's "persistent colonial condition," (2) "the sheer magnitude" of its diaspora, and (3) the circular and return patterns of migration in which Puerto Ricans have engaged since the 1940s (2002: 13). Duany points out how, in the twentieth century, Puerto Rican diasporic subjects—often categorized generally as "Nuyoricans"—tended to be "discursively constructed as dangerous, hybrid, and contaminated beings, and in danger of, upon returning to Puerto Rico, contaminating Puerto Ricans" (29). In addition, the island's political and cultural circles have privileged the Spanish language "as the essence of national identity," and represented it as the anti-colonial opposition to English, which was unsuccessfully imposed as the mandatory language of instruction in island public schools between the 1930s and 1940s (29). Back in 2002, when he published his work, Duany had found that "No Puerto Rican writer currently living in the United States and writing in English is now included in the Island's official curriculum at the elementary and high school levels" (30). Though Santiago and Miranda-Rodríguez point to how the self-representation of the Puerto Rican diaspora has changed in the twenty-first century, the diasporic identity is still a contested one on the island.

At the time of Duany's writing, Puerto Ricans living on the island exceeded those living in the States, and thus many islanders felt they had a greater say about what it means to be Puerto Rican. However, in 2014 the Pew Hispanic Research Center reported a dramatic change, noting that more people have left the island since 2010 than during the 1970s, 1980s, and 1990s combined, and in an exodus similar to the "Great Migration" in the 1950s and 1960s (2014: 1). This unprecedented migratory push and pull has resulted in a significantly larger number of Puerto Ricans (4.9 million in 2012) currently living stateside than Puerto Ricans living on the island (3.5 million for the same year).[2] What Santiago and Miranda-Rodríguez's texts suggest is that, as the bulk of the Puerto Rican population has shifted from the island to the States, the definition of Puerto Rico's cultural identity has become even more complex. This makes Duany's findings in his discussion of the literature of migration much more salient today: "Even the binary opposition between Puerto Rican and American, so pervasive in cultural nationalism, becomes problematic" as people "move between and betwixt two cultures" (2002: 34). It is not surprising, then, that Santiago and Miranda-Rodríguez both chose to represent diasporic subjectivity as intersectional: that is, as encompassing multiple and simultaneous vectors of identity, influenced by the different but related geographical locations in which their protagonists act and interact.

In literary study, intersectionality functions as a helpful analytical lens to spotlight how multiple and imbricated inequalities may be deployed to represent the "complex ontology" of characters (Phoenix and Pattynama 2006: 187). A term first coined in the late 1980s by Kimberlé Crenshaw. "as a tool particularly adept at capturing and theorizing the simultaneity of race and gender as social processes," intersectionality sought to articulate the multiplied disempowering effects of race and gender on black women within the U.S. legal context (Nash 2008: 1). Broadly hailed for acknowledging "the simultaneity of multiple oppressions and the complexity of identity," the theory has been critiqued for lacking an evident methodology in its application, for its "trans-historical" focus on and "monolithic" treatment of black women, for failing to clarify whether intersectionality is shared across all identities or "whether only marginalized subjects have an intersectional identity," and for not clearly answering "whether its theory explains or describes the processes and mechanisms by which subjects mobilize (or choose not to mobilize) particular aspects of their identities in particular circumstances" (Nash 2008: 2–5). While it is not within the scope of this chapter to define the boundaries of intersectionality, I propose that we understand intersectionality—here defined as the deployment of multiple and simultaneous identities to represent the experience of marginalized subjects—as a foundational characteristic of diasporic subjectivity in the Puerto Rican context.

Indeed, in both Santiago's and Miranda-Rodríguez's works, the intersection of identities becomes "an epistemic advantage" for its protagonists; and, arguably the source (and resource) of their heroism (Nash 2008: 2). By examining these texts through an heuristics in which diasporic subjectivity and intersectionality are key concepts, we can see the ways in which "multiply marginalized subjects" are represented as contributing specific "vantage points" and strategies that "enable intersectional theorists to draw on the ostensibly unique epistemological position of marginalized subjects to fashion a vision of equality" (Nash 2008: 2). Through this goal—one that seeks to encourage empowerment and agency in reader-viewers—artistic/literary/pop culture representations of minoritized subjects have the potential to become even more broadly inspirational and influential.

21: The making of a hero

The diasporic experience was crucial to Santiago's own development, and to his choice of artistic work and subject matters. Santiago, 47, moved to the States for the first time when he was nine, but then returned to Puerto Rico, a change he describes as "the most miserable I have ever been." He explains that while Puerto Rico "is a beautiful island," he doesn't "belong there" (Buckler 2012). Santiago moved back to the States on his own at 19, ultimately settling in Chicago in 2006 (Keller 2011). In discussing his choice of Clemente from among several options he considered, Santiago mentions Clemente's "reputation as a good-hearted Christian," one that was independent from his baseball career and which made him seem almost "to the level of deity" (Buckler n.d.). Santiago knew he had a hero story to tell and he decided to draw on the superhero genre to tell it: "In order to write Spider-Man, you also need to depict his life as a regular teenager. Peter Parker in costume becomes someone else and so are athletes." With the purpose of revealing how Clemente became "21," Santiago set out to show "the people that surrounded him, the period when he lived, these are things that shape all of us, which are the same things that shaped Clemente as a character. Many times you have to separate the myth from the person and sometimes you have to speculate within parameters." Indeed, Christopher González has most recently argued that Santiago "uses elements of narrative fiction as well as comic book storytelling that yank Clemente ever so slightly from fact-based reality" (2017: 83). By doing this, González adds, Santiago falls within the genre he describes as "biographic," which "can do something, narratively speaking, that biography cannot" (85). Such biographic speculation makes 21, which took Santiago six years to complete, a graphic novel rather than a biography.

To craft his hero's narrative, Santiago curates major incidents in the famous baseball player's life. As David Brothers noted in his 2011 review, Santiago shows us sequences of Clemente's childhood, young adulthood, and baseball career (both highs and lows) in scenes that come in "bursts, lasting but a few short pages" (2011). Santiago's text "isn't concerned with the specifics of Clemente's life so much as giving you the feeling of his life," Brothers adds. Santiago wants the reader-viewer to understand how Clemente achieved his standing as a hero, so he has to create an emotional investment in the audience. That affective involvement is further influenced by a

Diasporic intersectionality

limited color palette. Santiago has explained that he initially chose yellow and a dark blue, and "from these all the rest spawned." He notes:

> The Pittsburgh Pirates' colors (yellow, black and white) comprised the template. With the blue and the yellow, I could get colors as dark as black and sepia, browns, greens and beige, muted blues, etc. All this works great with the organic nature of baseball. You know, leather, dirt, grass, jockstraps: You get the idea. It was a nice coincidence that Pittsburgh's colors offered me a palette that compliments [sic] the story perfectly to the point I didn't need any other.

By connecting Clemente's baseball team's colors with the hues of his life, Santiago gives the reader-viewer a sense of continuity between the panels, despite the fact that some events are represented suddenly and without much narrative explanation. As Brothers points out, the 200-page graphic novel, "tends to leap forward in time with little warning, and sometimes even in the middle of the page," giving the reader-viewer a sense that these incidents in Clemente's life are leading us rapidly to its fated conclusion (2011).

One important element of the diasporic intersectionality shared between Santiago's and Miranda-Rodríguez's representations is the use of English as the main language of the narratives. In discussing Santiago's choice, Brothers notes how "white word balloons are the default" in comics, representing "the 'normal' language' of the represented world (2011). But in *21*, Santiago represents Spanish (translated into English) in white balloons "while the bright orange balloons are English." Brothers suggests that this positions "Spanish-speaking, brown-skinned, Puerto Rican Roberto Clemente as being the default, which is something you don't see too often." By "normalizing" Spanish (in translation) as the "default" language in his graphic novel, Santiago establishes Clemente's worldview—his diasporic intersectionality—as the narrative norm. More importantly, this is an example of what Ilan Stavans has described as translationality, or an original "already written in translation" (2002: 88). This term accurately captures the ways in which diasporic subjects are, by definition, constantly in translation (whether being translated by, translating themselves to, or translating the dominant culture to themselves).

In representational terms, Santiago crafts Clemente's translationality and intersectionality by focusing on his multiply marginalized identities as a diasporic Afro-Latino man from a colonized Spanish-speaking island and from a socio-economically disadvantaged background. While Brothers identifies race as "inextricably tied to Clemente's rise to glory, simply due to the period he lived in," Santiago's highlighting of Clemente's "race" goes well beyond pointing to how he benefitted from changing attitudes toward black players in baseball (2011). In a 2016 interview with Frederick Aldama, Santiago discusses how "some of Clemente's experiences, either back on the island (e.g., the political debates and cultural rituals) or here in the States (e.g., language barriers and opportunities that were present in this country) resonated with my own experiences" (2016: 231). By drawing from his own diasporic context, Santiago breathes narrative life into Clemente's story. In my reading, Santiago repeatedly represents Clemente as dealing with overt and covert racism to show how the protagonist achieved the social-justice consciousness that helped transform him into a hero.

Those moments in the text—such as when we see him after a game in Florida where racial slurs are hurled at him, and we later see him walking the streets with yellow balloons over his head that repeat the same demeaning words—are to be mentally juxtaposed by the reader-viewer to earlier representations of racist attitudes in Puerto Rico. In one scene early in the graphic novel, eight-year-old Roberto (or "Momen," as he was nicknamed because of his penchant for asking "*momentito*," or "just a moment") is reminded by his relatives that his mother had wished for him to be "white" when he was born. Instead, the family jokes that he is "just a little dark," and "dark as ink," signaling that he is different from everyone else because he is what we know today as an Afro-Latino. Through these moments, in Clemente's childhood and later in his life as a baseball player, we see how our protagonist's attitudes about race shift from the seemingly good-natured racist ribbing he is subjected to on his own island to having to deal with the often vitriolic and violent racism he experiences in the United States. Racism is one of the major thematic arcs in Santiago's representation of Clemente's life and one of the most significant in developing a diasporic subjectivity in the Puerto Rican context.

While there is enough material to write a whole chapter about *21*, I want to conclude this section by focusing on Santiago's representation of Puerto Rico's colonial history, migration, and the definition of heroism as factors he uses in fashioning his hero's journey. To give us a sense that this is a hero's story (as opposed to a straightforward biography), Santiago bookends the narrative by starting with the representation of Clemente's greatest professional moment on September 30, 1972, when he is about to reach his 3,000th hit in the Major Leagues, and by ending with the disappearance of the plane in which Clemente was traveling to Managua, Nicaragua, four months later to the day. The initial prologue-type pages, narrated by an unidentified narrator, state that: "This was no ordinary game. It was the last game of the season & Roberto Clemente, number 21, was one hit away from 3,000." By this time, Clemente is already "21," known by many for the jersey number that identified him in the Pirates' lineup, suggesting that he has transcended from an ordinary person into a symbol, a signifier of heroic prowess on the field. The narrator then adds that "The Great One was no ordinary player. He was different. Gripping. Peculiar. There was something odd about him…" and then that part of the narrative stops and we move to the title page. In this way, Santiago sets forth the context of what we are going to read: the development of Clemente into "The Great One," a tragic hero who disappeared (his body was never recovered) into the depths of the ocean on his way to help others.

The tragedy of Clemente's death and disappearance is purposefully contextualized within Puerto Rican culture to suggest that he was somehow divinely chosen. The representation of Clemente as a child, mourning for his dead sister (who died of burns sustained in a house fire), is followed by six pages of drawings and narrative that tell the story of the Three Magi Kings who "a long time ago, traveled very far to the land of Jerusalem where Jesus, the son of God, was born." The retold biblical story ends with a representation of three bright yellow stars on a black panel, the same panel that reoccurs when we return to Momen's conversation with his mother, in which she tells him that: "To be absent from this life is to be in the presence of the Lord." These words foreshadow the end of the graphic novel, when three stars reappear on a black panel, next to the page in which a lone small white airplane, against a black background with light blue swirls at the bottom, represents the moment before Clemente himself loses his life. The presence of the three stars, connected to the Three Magi Kings and to transcendence, suggest that Clemente also sacrificed his earthly presence to become something greater.

In addition to using the Three Kings as a repeated trope, Santiago includes two two-page panels in gray with maps drawn lightly in the background and with longer narratives, both of which interrupt the diegesis. The first such panel, found about a third of the way into the story, narrates a "Taíno Myth (C. 300 BC)," a creation story of the indigenous peoples of the island who, after their land is created, happily come out of the forest "and they named their paradise, Boriken, the land of the brave lord." This example of indigenous orature, given without citation, locates the reader-viewer within the context of a long history for Puerto Rico that predates Christianity and colonialism. The point is also that the history of Puerto Ricans includes the worldview of a people whose

Diasporic intersectionality

cosmogony was non-Western and who were known for their brave leaders. Moreover, Santiago also introduces this historical piece, seemingly out of the blue, to ensure that the reader-viewer understands that Spanish colonial violence did not erase the legacy of indigeneity in the Puerto Rican cultural identity. Therefore, Santiago suggests that the history of the island is racialized as non-white (and non-European), and as always-already racially mixed.

Santiago constantly reminds us of the racialization of the island's history, including a representation of Clemente's high school years in which the panels in which his fair-skinned girlfriend breaks up with him (because her "family never approved of us and father, he would love a grandson") are juxtaposed with a sidebar panel describing "miscegenation" on a school blackboard and a teacher stating that "African slaves were imported to the island to replace [Taíno] labor and for centuries, the economic and social order of the times brought about the merger of these three races, the roots of the Puertorican culture..." In this way, Santiago posits the hypocrisy of a cultural history that presented racial mixture as ontological to the Puerto Rican nationality but ignored the actual practice of racism in social interactions among Puerto Ricans.

Representation of this racialized context is culminated in the second diegetic interruption, two pages placed toward the end of the narrative, also depicted in a palette of grays, yellow, white, and black. This representation includes a long excerpt from the third chapter of *A Recent Campaign in Puerto Rico*, published in 1907 by Karl Stephen Herrman, which purports to describe "The People of Puerto Rico." In the latter part of the quotation, which Santiago's quotes verbatim, Herrman states:

> About one-sixth of the population in this island—the educated class, and chiefly of pure Spanish blood—can be set down as valuable acquisitions to our citizenship and the peer, if not the superior, of most Americans in chivalry, domesticity, fidelity, and culture. Of the rest, perhaps on half can be molded by a firm hand into something approaching decency, but the remaining are going to give us a great deal of trouble. They are ignorant, filthy, untruthful, lazy, treacherous, murderous, brutal, and black.

By this time in Santiago's story of Clemente's life, we have already seen how the baseball star has had to handle U.S. racism in many ways. By inserting this citation from an early observer of Puerto Rico from a U.S. colonial perspective, Santiago ensures that we understand that Clemente's experiences with race in the United States made sense, given the context of Herrman's descriptions of Puerto Ricans, which had changed little since the start of the colonial project. In this way, Santiago's work argues, Clemente's diasporic intersectionality must perforce embody the double-consciousness—as first articulated by W.E.B. Dubois in the African American experience—of not only having to be self-aware but also of having to be aware of how he was perceived by others.

Just like racism is shown in both island and U.S. environments, Santiago contextualizes Clemente's story within the history of government-sponsored migration from Puerto Rico to the United States. Right after Clemente gets ready to leave for the United States to play baseball there for the first time, a radio newscast narrates that: "Tax concessions for foreign investors under the [Operation Bootstrap] program have caused manufacturing jobs to edge ahead of farming as Puerto Rico's major source of income... while the migration to the United States by thousands of job seekers has brought balance to the unemployment rate. In 1953 a record number of 69,000 migrated to the mainland, & similar numbers are expected this year." Presenting this narrative serves to connect Clemente's decision to leave with the tens of thousands who were departing the island in search of better opportunities and reminds the reader-viewer that Clemente was part of a migratory movement larger than himself.

As the graphic novel moves toward its conclusion, after we have seen Clemente develop from a carefree child into a somewhat self-centered and attention-seeking young man, we are brought back again to 1972. By this point in the story, we have seen Clemente praised for his consistency and reliability, and for his demeanor on the playing field, which has been described by sports announcers as regal. Santiago also has shown Clemente saying that his dream is,

> to build a city, a sports city! A place where poor children can come and play! [...] I would build a sports city, bring kids from all the United States so they learn how to live and play with each other. I want it to have three baseball fields, swimming pool, basketball, tennis, a lake for fathers and sons to get together!

In addition to this dream, which his widow Vera would help make true after his death, we see Clemente speak his most famous phrase after he wins the MVP prize in January 1972: "If you have the chance to help others, and fail to do so, you are wasting your time on this Earth." In articulating this sense of mission, of having been placed in this life for the benefit of others, Clemente has reached his apex in the hero narrative Santiago has crafted for us.

As our unnamed narrator tells us, Clemente is admired by the "hundreds of kids who collected his signatures, the sick & the poor, recipients of his compassion, treated with dignity & respect. The Great One to baseball, he gave his all. And to his fans, he gave us pride." The narrator concludes by noting that we should all learn from the "pioneers, who are willing to give their lives for the common good, often our highest definition of a hero." Indeed, the narrator adds: "Looking back, Roberto Clemente was a hero because of the way he lived." That is precisely the crux of Santiago's crafting of Clemente's hero story. 21 argues that despite the island's colonial history, the hurtfulness of racism, and the displacement caused by Clemente's migratory experience, it is the diasporic perspective, the ability (and need) to occupy and deploy several identities at once, that transformed Clemente into an unforgettable hero.

La Borinqueña as Afro-Latina

Diasporic intersectionality is also at the heart of Miranda-Rodríguez's *La Borinqueña* (2016), a roughly 57-page comic book, divided into a main narrative with four chapters, and including a shorter "bonus story," all in full color and with realistic drawings. The main story tells the transformation of Marisol Rios de la Luz, a Brooklyn-born, bicycle-riding, asthmatic Puerto Rican environmental sciences student at Columbia University, who finds her superhero powers while doing environmental research in Puerto Rico for her thesis project. Similar to what Santiago does with Clemente, an actual hero figure in Puerto Rican culture, Miranda-Rodríguez locates his fictional superhero within the history and culture of Puerto Rico, especially its colonial history. At the same time, as a U.S.-born Afro-Latina, Marisol is endowed with the wherewithal to move seamlessly between the United States and Puerto Rico, and to represent both the island and the diasporic communities as one. Unlike Santiago, who chose an actual person as the subject of his hero narrative, Miranda-Rodríguez (like López Nieves before him) decides to invent his, though (unlike López Nieves) he locates her firmly within the long history of anti-colonial resistance in Puerto Rican history, both on the island and in the United States.

Indeed, some of the most important aspects of *La Borinqueña* as comic book art and narrative are the intertextual references to Puerto Rican literary culture of anti-colonial resistance, such as when La Borinqueña quotes Julia de Burgos' poetry (uncited by the artist/author) by noting "Ay, ay, ay, es que yo soy pura grifa y pura negra." The poem, translated by Jack Agüeros, is titled "Ay, Ay, Ay, of the Kinky-Haired Negress," and reads "Ay, ay, ay, that I am kinky haired and pure black."

Also, when the people she rescues sing the La Boriqueña anthem to Marisol, they do not sing the official anthem, which speaks of the island's sea and sun (the composite for Marisol's name). Instead, it is the revolutionary La Borinqueña, which sings about awakening to a time of struggle and resistance. In addition to literary references, the comic also draws on geographical markers that Miranda-Rodríguez uses to situate the Puerto Rican experience both on the island (Julio Enrique Monagas National Park; Cueva del Indio; Cavernas de Camuy; La Cueva del Viento) and in New York City (Loisaida, the Puerto Rican term for the Lower East Side; El Barrio; and Harlem). By including diverse literary allusions and locations as important cultural signposts of Puerto Ricanness, Miranda-Rodríguez suggests that racial mixture, anti-colonial resistance, and cross-locational mobility and adaptability are part and parcel of the Puerto Rican experience.

The connections Miranda-Rodríguez makes are not only geocultural, but are also historical, such as when he draws a shooting star, representing the indigenous "mother goddess" Atabex, who empowers Marisol, cutting across several panels as a "timeless" presence. In one panel with five sections, Atabex shows Marisol the Taíno resistance to Spanish domination; the moment pro-independence activist Mariana Bracetti sewed the flag of Lares, the first symbol of Puerto Rican anti-colonial resistance in the 1868 rebellion against Spain; Puerto Rican solders fighting in the U.S. Army unfurling the Puerto Rican flag while in a trench; Nationalist Party leader Pedro Albizu Campos, convalescing from skin burns that one scholar has found were caused by covert radiation in the 1950s; and the Young Lords marching through the streets of New York City in the 1970s. There are no captions or citations for these scenes, so the author-artist again presupposes that the reader-viewer will have the contextual information necessary to make sense of these representations. Thereby, Miranda-Rodríguez suggests a shared history among his Puerto Rican audience, one that encompasses the different locations of resistance in the Puerto Rican experience.

These representations of island and diasporic anti-colonial resistance are further developed and expanded on as they are illuminated by the star that will give Marisol her superpowers in the subsequent set of pages when Atabex narrates how: "My island has been suffering for hundreds of years and when my island suffers, …my children suffer, they need hope, inspiration, a champion." To show Marisol what she means, Atabex allows her to witness, through a kind of time travel, the Taínos fighting with their war sticks against Spaniards clad with armor, shields, and swords; the community in Orlando, Florida, mourning the killings at the Pulse nightclub; Mariana Bracetti sewing the Lares flag as the rebels are captured; Puerto Rican soldiers in war; and the 1937 Ponce Massacre. In having this indigenous "mother goddess" provide Marisol with a panoramic view of Puerto Rican struggle and suffering, also through different but related geographical locations, Miranda-Rodríguez implies that conflict and strife have been and still are a part of the Puerto Rican identity. Invested with the powers of indigenous spirituality and transformed from a nerdy, bespectacled college student into a magical suit-clad superhero, Marisol, now La Borinqueña, goes on to save the day.

In fashioning his superhero as a representative of diasporic intersectionality, Miranda-Rodríguez, 45, a long-time political activist, has said his character "was created to 'represent the real face of diversity,' adding "that people of color and women are still underrepresented in comics, especially in the mainstream that is usually relied on by Hollywood" (Yuhas 2016). As one critic noted:

> Miranda-Rodriguez puts Afro-Caribbean culture on full display with a brown-skinned heroine (both of Marisol's parents are Puerto Rican, and her father is Afro-Puerto Rican) who takes pride in her roots and is comfortable in her skin. After saving the day, La Borinqueña dances in celebration as an onlooker points out that she's got

Ivonne M. García

"tumbao," an African sexiness and style. The comic's embrace of Puerto Rico's African roots is refreshing.

(Betancourt 2016)

In keeping with the intersectional approach, Miranda-Rodriguez says that he created La Borinqueña as "not oversexualized, respectfully designed, a woman who looks like your sister, your daughter, your wife—someone who looks like you" (Yuhas 2016). While there is no doubt that Marisol, like most comic book female figures, is sexualized by being consistently clad in tight-fitting clothes, whether her bike-riding shorts, her jeans, or her superhero costume, her intersectional representation as a strong, intelligent, educated Afro-Latina woman who fights for social justice and the environment does add complexity to her representation.

Not only is Marisol's representation purposefully differentiated, but Miranda-Rodríguez has said that he also wanted her to have an origin story that contrasted with those of other more famous superheroes. In an interview, Miranda-Rodríguez states how:

Comic book stories always towed from a male perspective [...] where, at the height of their powers, something tragic happens that makes that character become an altruistic hero. But she didn't have to have some tragedy to wake up to her sense of civic responsibility—she just wanted to lead. She's one of many who's always been there, serving and being part of the community.

(Yuhas 2016: 2)

In this way, Marisol is very similar to Clemente, who in Santiago's rendition did not have to undergo a tragedy to become socially conscious, but became so because of his individual and diasporic experiences. Furthermore, Miranda-Rodríguez represents an Afro-Latina who is a scientist, an environmentalist, someone who, both as a regular person and as a superhero, is working to improve the planet. In that way, Miranda-Rodríguez suggests that we do not have to wait for a superhero to help with social problems, but that one individual with commitment can make a difference.

Indeed, Miranda-Rodríguez's text is quite self-conscious about the shifting balance of power among Puerto Ricans, in terms of population growth and geographical location, stating that: "It's actually Puerto Ricans in the diaspora that really need to be the ones to step up and speak out," because they have political power by voting for the U.S. President and Congressional/ Senate representation, while Puerto Ricans on the island cannot (Yuhas 2016). "We're a growing demographic as a voting bloc and as consumers. How much more powerful would we feel if we were consuming products that look like us, pursuing candidates that look like us and speak like us?" Miranda-Rodríguez asks (Yuhas 2016). Miranda-Rodríguez chose the pop culture medium to expose the ongoing economic crisis on the island and said La Borinqueña "is a symbol of patriotism at a time when Puerto Ricans need to be reminded of their superpowers" (Reichard 2016). Miranda-Rodríguez adds: "We don't need to look outside of us for the power—we have it inside. If we come together, we will win" (Reichard 2016). In her own words, Marisol echoes her creator by stating: "Even though I'm still getting used to these powers, I've been received so well by mi gente. As puertorriqueños, we have always had a rich history of fighting for our rights, our culture, and our future. That why they call me La Borinqueña. It's a name, no a title that I carry with great pride and responsibility." In this way, Marisol functions as a counter-narrative to the masculine, white, and dominant-class heroes represented by Puerto Rican writers in the twentieth century: not only is she different in racialized, gendered, and class terms, but she also recognizes that heroism need not be invented. It is already part of the culture.

Diasporic intersectionality

It is on this sense of empowerment, created through the assumed disempowered position (that of a migrant from a colonized location to a colonial metropolis), that I want to conclude this analysis of diasporic intersectionality in these comic books. In this chapter, I have used that term to describe the historically situated colonial experience of Puerto Ricans within (and outside) the United States, represented by both Santiago and Miranda-Rodríguez as marked by the intersection of gender, race, sexuality, and socio-economic class. But while others have read the diasporic subjectivity from a liability perspective (what is lost, what is missing, what is missed), I argue that diasporic intersectionality is represented by both Santiago and Miranda-Rodríguez as a source of (super)power(s). In fact, it is the purposefully highlighted or crafted intersectionality of their title characters—the heroes—of these stories that give them the power to *be* heroic. In that way, Santiago and Miranda-Rodríguez represent intersectional experience and self-consciousness as an important byproduct of diasporic subjectivity, one that balances the losses of the migratory push and pull by building on the gains of experiencing in-betweenness.

Ultimately, the heroes crafted by Santiago and Miranda-Rodríguez show us how Puerto Rico's colonial history haunts both actual and fictional representations of the migratory experience, determining the arc of the hero narratives these authors craft. I argue that, while Santiago and Miranda-Rodríguez both participate in the creation of "racially gendered" fantasies, like the ones critiqued by Negrón-Muntaner, the diasporic experiences of the authors empower them to imagine figurations of "Puertoricanness" in which race, gender, and class intersect to subvert dominant national narratives, both on the island and in the United States. Unlike López Nieves, who had to invent a heroic town to imagine a counter to the U.S. invasion, both Santiago and Miranda-Rodríguez find heroism in Puerto Rico's cultural survival, and in its persistent and continued anti-colonial struggles, starting with the Taínos against the Spaniards and through more than a century of U.S. colonial control and repression. Thus, instead of what Negrón-Muntaner critiques as an invented *boricua* national identity "born not in shame or trauma, but in honor and military might," Santiago and Miranda-Rodríguez acknowledge and represent heroism as part of the Puerto Rican experience, both on the island and in the diaspora. Perhaps Miranda-Rodríguez puts that alternative viewpoint best when he states: "I want all Puerto Ricans to know that being Puerto Rican is in and of itself a superpower" (Reichard 2016).

Notes

1 Following Frederick L. Aldama's lead in *Your Brain on Latino Comics*, I refer to the creators of these two texts as "author-artists" and to the audience as "reader-viewers" (2009: 82).
2 After Hurricane Maria in 2017 the migratory patterns away from the island have increased even more significantly.

Works cited

Agüeros, Jack. *Song of the Simple Truth: The Complete Poems of Julia de Burgos*. Willimantic, CT: Curbstone Press, 1997.
Aldama, Frederick L. *Your Brain on Latino Comics*. Austin, TX: University of Texas Press, 2009.
Aldama, Frederick L. "Wilfred Santiago." *Latinx Comic Book Storytelling: An Odyssey by Interview*. San Diego, CA: Hyberbole Books, 2016. pp. 228–243.
Aldama, Frederick L. *Latinx Superheroes in Mainstream Comics*. Tucson, AZ: University of Arizona Press, 2017.
Betancourt, David. "New Superhero La Borinqueña Shows the Power of Puerto Rican Pride." 22 December 2016. *Washington Post*, www.washingtonpost.com/news/comic-riffs/wp/2016/12/22/new-superhero-la-borinquena-shows-the-power-of-puerto-rican-pride/?utm_term=.ec21aa60c81f. Accessed 15 July 2017.

Blanco, Octavio. "Comic Book Maker Creates a Female Superhero for Puerto Rico." 22 December 2016. *CNN Money*, http://money.cnn.com/2017/01/13/smallbusiness/comic-book-puerto-rico-la-borinquena/index.html. Accessed 14 July 2017.

Brothers, David. "'21: The Story of Roberto Clemente' Blazes Trails and Breaks Hearts." 27 April 2011. *Comics Alliance*, http://comicsalliance.com/roberto-clemente-biography. Accessed 15 July 2017.

Buckler, Eric. *Diaflogue: Wilfred Santiago exclusive Q&A about 21*. http://fantagraphics.com/flog/diaflogue-wilfred-santiago-exclusive-qa-about-21. Accessed 15 July 2017.

Buckler, Eric. "'It's Obvious You Can't Fuck with Cartoons': A Wilfred Santiago Interview." 27 February 2012. *The Comics Journal*, www.tcj.com/its-obvious-you-cant-fuck-with-cartoons-a-wilfred-santiago-interview. Accessed 12 July 2017.

Duany, Jorge. *Puerto Rican Nation on the Move*. Chapel Hill, NC: University of North Carolina Press, 2002.

González, Christopher. "Biographic Challenges: Wilfred Santiago's *21: The Story of Roberto Clemente*." *Latinx Superheroes in Mainstream Comics*, edited by Frederick L. Aldama. Tucson, AZ: University of Arizona Press, 2017. pp. 83–108.

Griffin, Gabriele. *Contemporary Black and Asian Women Playwrights in Britain*. Cambridge, UK: Cambridge University Press, 2003.

Hermann, Karl Stephen, *A Recent Campaign in Puerto Rico by the Independent Regular Brigade under the Command of Brig. General Schwan*, Boston, MA: E. H. Bacon, 1907.

Keller, Julia. "Here's the Pitch from Wilfred Santiago." 1 July 2011. *The Chicago Tribune*, www.chicagotribune.com/lifestyles/books/ct-books-0702-wilfred-santiago-20110701-story.html. Accessed 12 July 2017.

López Nieves, Luis. *Seva: Historia de la primera invasión norteamericana de la isla de Puerto Rico ocurrida en mayo de 1898*. Puerto Rico: Editorial Cordillera, 2003.

"Luis López Nieves: Creador de una historia que nos hace justicia." 11 August 2012. *Primera Hora*, www.primerahora.com/noticias/puerto-rico/nota/luislopeznievescreadordeunahistoriaquenoshacejusticia-682315. Accessed 15 July 2017.

Maver, Igor, ed. *Diasporic Subjectivity and Cultural Brokering in Contemporary Post-Colonial Literatures*. Lanham, MD: Lexington Books, 2009.

Miranda-Rodríguez, Edgardo. *La Borinqueña*. Brooklyn, NY: Somos Arte, 2016.

Nash, Jennifer C. "Rethinking Intersectionality." *Feminist Review*, vol. 89, June 2008, pp. 1–15.

Negrón-Muntaner, Frances. *Boricua Pop: Puerto Ricans and the Latinization of American Culture*. New York University Press, 2004.

Phoenix, Ann and Pamela Pattynama. "Intersectionality." *European Journal of Women's Studies*, vol. 13, no. 3, August 2006, pp. 187–192.

"Puerto Rican Population Declines on Island, Grows on U.S. Mainland." 11 August 2014. *Pew Research Center*, www.pewhispanic.org/2014/08/11/puerto-rican-population-declines-on-island-grows-on-us-mainland. Accessed 14 July 2017.

Reichard, Rachel. "Meet La Borinqueña, a Badass Afro-Puerto Rican Superhero Helping Her Island." 16 May 2016. *Latina*, www.latina.com/lifestyle/news/la-borinquena-superhero-helping-island. Accessed 14 July 2017.

Santiago, Wilfred. *21: The Story of Roberto Clemente*. Gary Groth and Kim Thompson Publishers, 2011.

Seven, John. "History, Identity and Baseball: Wilfred Santiago Tells 'The Story of Roberto Clemente.'" 22 February 2011. *Publishers Weekly*, www.publishersweekly.com/pw/by-topic/industry-news/comics/article/46232-history-identity-and-baseball-wilfred-santiago-tells-the-story-of-roberto-clemente.html. Accessed 15 July 2017.

Stavans, Ilan. *On Borrowed Words: A Memoir of Language*. New York: Penguin Books, 2002.

Yuhas, Alan. "Borinqueña: Puerto Rico's New Superhero Fights crime – and a Political Crisis." 4 July 2016. *The Guardian*, www.theguardian.com/world/2016/jul/04/puerto-rico-superhero-borinquena-edgardo-miranda-rodriguez. Accessed 14 July 2017.

6

DRAWING UP
A 'POST'-LATIN AMERICA

The possibilities and limits of gender imagination in post-apocalyptic, post-human, and post-historical graphic narrative

Mauricio Espinoza

In *Juan Solo*, a comic by legendary Chilean author and filmmaker Alejandro Jodorowsky, a baby born with an animal tail in a garbage dump is raised by a dwarf transvestite prostitute in a dystopian South American city where violence is the most important commodity. Meanwhile, in Salvadoran-American Daniel Parada's graphic novel *Zotz: Serpent and Shield*, an alternative reality in which the Spaniards never conquered Mesoamerica unfolds with different visions of history, alliances, confrontations, and cultural developments. Recent graphic narrative production by Latin American and U.S.-based Latino artists is more diverse and multifaceted than ever before, and the titles mentioned above perfectly illustrate the breadth (and oddities) of this expanding field. Within this increasing and vibrant diversity, comics and graphic novels that explore science and speculative fiction are among the most innovative and visually striking. In fact, as Edward King and Joanna Page point out, "while the graphic novel in Europe and North America is currently dominated by autobiographical and journalistic textual modes, the most prevalent genre in Latin America is science fiction" (2017: 2).

While the works being produced throughout the continent deal with a variety of interests and address a number of preoccupations, there is a common element that pops out when opening the pages of these narratives and immersing ourselves in their universes: the preference for post-apocalyptic, post-human, and post-historical themes that make the reading of these comics particularly rich and insightful. In this chapter, I am interested in teasing out how representative examples of recent Latin American and Latino science and speculative fiction graphic narrative engage with politics and gender; and to what extent the comic book medium and these specific genres either restrict or allow for new and more fluid ways of imagining gender roles and relations in a Latin American narrative tradition long dominated by representations of patriarchy and its multiple tentacles.

The study of science fiction (SF) and speculative fiction in Latin American narrative has received increased attention in the past few years, but it is still a lesser field within the larger scholarship on literature and graphic narrative alike. In their 2012 book *Latin American Science Fiction: Theory and Practice*, J. Andrew Brown and M. Elizabeth Ginway explain that SF and speculative fiction in the region "have often been relegated to a subordinate position when compared with the realist fictions decrying various social and political ills, from the mistreatment of the indigenous to the victims of military dictatorships" (2012: 1). Such relegation and dismissal have been caused by two reasons: science and speculative fiction's "lack of an obvious contemporary social or political referent" and their "alleged inferiority to magical realism, which occupied center stage in the connection between fantastic literature and Latin America by critics in both hemispheres" (Brown and Ginway 2012: 1).

This does not mean that there has been a lack of SF and speculative fiction writing in Latin American's literary tradition, or that Latin American comics have not delved into social or political issues. Canonical authors such as Leopoldo Lugones and Jorge Luis Borges, as well as contemporary writers such as Edmundo Paz Soldán and Carmen Boullosa, have written short stories and novels brimming with fantasy, unsolved mysteries, time travel, zombies, and cyborgs. Additionally, there is a significant history of social and political cartooning in the region by artists such as Joaquín Salvador Lavado "Quino," Eduardo del Río García "Rius," and Lalo Alcaraz; while SF comics such as Edgar Clément's *Operación Bolívar* and *Animal Urbano* (Tato Dabat, Guillermo Grillo, and Edu Molina) have employed the trope of supernatural beings to criticize repressive regimes and U.S. imperialist intervention. As King and Page have indicated, the Latin American graphic novel has emerged from the continent's rich tradition of science fiction and fantasy literature and comics (2017: 2). The works I study here emerged from this tradition, but they have also been influenced by and constantly dialogue with the social and political commentary impulses of many of their cartoon and comic book predecessors.

Brown and Ginway have identified three concepts that they view as crucial for studying Latin American SF and speculative fiction, and which seem applicable to "post-" graphic narrative as understood in this chapter. They are fragmentation ("as seen in the use of the tropes of time warps, alternate histories, and the erosion of the canon"); divergences ("as exemplified by Latin America's brand of sexualized or embodied cyberpunk and apocalyptic violence distinguishing it from Anglo-American forms"); and unlikely combinations ("as found in the mix of social realism with mutants and zombies or the merging of dissonant genres such as SF, humor, and horror") (2012: 2). Instances of fragmentation, divergences, and unlikely combinations are commonly found in post-apocalyptic, post-human, and post-historical comics, thus establishing a clear link between these types of narrative and the larger field of Latin American SF and speculative fiction—both in terms of storytelling techniques and issues explored. I argue that the texts explored in the next few pages employ the three concepts identified by Brown and Ginway for the purpose of problematizing and challenging Latin America's traditional literary cannon (predominantly male-centric and White/mestizo-centric) and its dominant gender representations (patriarchal, fixed, and, again, European American-centric).

Reborn in rubbish and violence: Broken hyper-masculinity after the end of times

Two Latin American comic book series published in the past two decades have put forth their particular visions of what a post-apocalyptic future would be like in the region, also speculating on what the impact of such catastrophic events would be on human subjectivities marked by both an indelible cultural baggage from the past and the new realities of a reconfigured world. The first is *Juan Solo* (also known as *Son of the Gun*), first published in 1995 with stories by Alejandro Jodorowsky and illustrations by his long-time French collaborator Georges Bess. The second is *El Arsenal*, created by writer Salvador Vázquez and artist Daniel Pérez (both Mexican) and first released in 2005. A Western-style comic, *Juan Solo* takes place in an imaginary Latin American town (Huatulco City) besieged by violence, drought, and despair. Unlike *El Arsenal*—where a massive California earthquake destroys parts of the United States and Mexico and reconfigures power relations along the Pacific Rim—*Juan Solo* is not presented as a traditional post-apocalyptic narrative with a clearly defined event that unleashes Armageddon.

Rather, Jodorowsky and Bess create a dystopian post-neoliberal future where armed gangs and militias struggle for turf and resources; the military (represented by El General) attempts to keep a tenuous grip on power through puppet prime ministers; and the general population struggles to survive amid daily violence and decay. The comic's post-apocalyptic setting is reinforced visually through an emphasis on showing destroyed buildings, garbage, desolate streets, and depressing landscapes with few signs of life and greenery. Additionally, Bess employs a lot of black in his panels to depict a generalized sense of gloom and darkness, combined with various tones of red, yellow, and orange that highlight the constant violence and spilling of blood as well as the severe drought that threatens to exterminate the town. In a sort of time-travel play, *Juan Solo* combines the harsh sociopolitical realities of past Latin American dictatorial regimes with impending environmental doom, which is common in dystopian narratives.

In the comic, a dwarf transvestite prostitute named Half-Pint finds a baby boy abandoned in a garbage dump and decides to raise him as her own. Using his physical strength as well as fighting and shooting skills, Juan becomes Huatulco's most fear bodyguard, serving a powerful drug lord. After his meteoric rise, however, Juan ends up in misery as the town drunkard. In what appears to be an attempt at redemption from his sinful past, Juan chooses to be sacrificed to bring rain to Huatulco and save it from certain doom. The comic emphasizes traditional Christian religious attitudes toward those who don't conform to normative gender roles and sexual behavior. When we first meet Half-Pint, she is running along with other citizens toward the church, trying to escape soldiers who intend on killing them. However, she is denied shelter: "You can't come in here! Dirty transvestite! Sodomite!" (Jodorowsky and Bess 2014: 7). After surviving by offering sexual favors to the soldiers, Half-Pint stumbles across Juan amid the rubble. She would have gladly left him for the starving dogs to eat but notices the baby's odd appendage and feels an instant connection to him: "You have a tail! You are a freak... like me" (Jodorowsky and Bess 2014: 12).

The bonding between these two unlikely "relatives" is strikingly presented on the next page's panels, as baby Juan sucks on the barrel of Half-Pint's gun and then drinks milk from her dog, which is raising a litter of puppies (Jodorowsky and Bess 2014: 13). In this manner, *Juan Solo* portrays gender difference as monstrosity, blurring the lines not only between traditional male and female representations but also between human and animal subjectivities—Juan is born with a dog's tail and is raised a) by an actual dog and b) by a "freak" who at times is drawn as possessing animal-like features, such as claws. Juan's transformation into an extremely violent, lustful, selfish, and ruthless gunslinger begins when he is young boy and his two "mothers" die: thieves break into their abandoned building-turned-home looking for money, kill the dog that nursed him, and severely injure Half-Pint. In a final act of defiance, the dwarf loads herself along with dynamite sticks onto a cart and plunges into the church, causing an explosion that burns down the entire edifice. With his only inheritance—Half-Pint's gun—Juan soon learns that bullets and violence (including rape and other forms of sexual violence) are the only way to survive in his world. Because of his deformity and his peculiar past, Juan is constantly addressed by his enemies as a freak and a faggot. He responds by asserting his threatened masculinity in two ways: with extreme, unremorseful violence; and by exposing his tail/extra phallus as a way to express an enhanced sense of sexual potency. When having sex with women, he sometimes utilizes his tail to perform double penetration, further emphasizing his need to mask his monstrous appearance through sexual acts of hyper-masculine affirmation. Juan and Half-Pint are thus depicted as sinful queer bodies that are rejected by and react against normative society, though they also engage in acts of selfless redemption that add complexity to their representations.

In *Juan Solo*, Jodorowsky also dialogues with the Latin American literary cannon, from which arises an interesting conversation regarding the nature of patriarchy, lineage, and masculinity. After all, the boy born with an animal tail can be no other than the last first-born of the Buendía dynasty, the collective protagonist of magical realism's opera magna, Gabriel García Márquez's *One Hundred Years of Solitude*. Even Juan's last name (chosen by the character because he's always been "alone" in this world), further reinforces the intertextual connection with the novel. Given the uneasy relationship between Latin America's newer forms of SF and speculative fiction and magical realism (addressed earlier in this chapter), it is not surprising that Jodorowsky chose to engage in such direct manner with García Márquez's work. While the last of the Buendías is devoured by ants, fulfilling the gypsy Melquíades's final prediction for the family, Juan is rescued from ravenous dogs and ends up crucified as a Christ-like redeemer for the sake of his people. By saving the cursed boy, Jodorowsky rewrites the Buendía story, disrupting the long lineage of hyper-masculine patriarchs with a boy who is raised by a transvestite mother, sucks on phallic symbols, and whose sexuality is defined by the monstrosity that the entire Buendía family tried to keep from ever existing in the first place, to no avail. In other words, *Juan Solo* queers *One Hundred Years of Solitude* and the legacy of magical realism.

El Arsenal—produced in Mexico for the U.S. market and published by Canada's Arcana Studio, which makes it a peculiar product of NAFTA-like transnational cultural flows—is less nuanced that *Juan Solo* when it comes to representations of gender. However, it is precisely this lack of nuance that deserves scrutiny. The comic's storyline takes place in a post-apocalyptic, chaotic future where heavily armed mercenaries settle conflicts between the main power players. *El Arsenal*'s dystopian universe originates with a nuclear accident that activates California's San Andreas fault, triggering a major earthquake that breaks off Mexico's Baja California peninsula from the continent, destroys Mexico City, and almost makes Japan disappear into the Pacific Ocean. As a result of the incident and its aftermath, the United States collapses, Mexico descends into chaos, and the Zapatista rebels create their own country in southern Mexico and Central America. Additionally, Japan invades South America in search of new lands to settle, which leads to civil wars in which drug lords become involved.

In the new world order that ensues, skilled and ruthless mercenaries are hired to do the fighting. These warriors are recruited and controlled by El Sistema, an underground organization that stands as the last remaining global power. Meanwhile, the mercenaries represent a precious commodity, and they are ranked according to their "hitting average." The comic's main character and top mercenary is Mexican Simón Templas Masiorare, a man who enjoys his job as much as he delights in beer and women. Simón is the son of an old Mexican *luchador* named "El Templas," from whom he learned the tricks of *lucha libre* that help him excel at his dangerous job. Just as in *Juan Solo*, the male protagonist in *El Arsenal* is decidedly hyper-masculine, underscored by his extreme use of violence and his lust for women. In the foreword to the series' first issue, Mexican SF comic book artist Bernardo Fernández "Bef" describes Simón as "Snake Plissken and Pedro Infante rolled into one" ("Puras Pinches Chingaderas"). In other words, the protagonist is the hybrid product of two twentieth-century stereotypical constructions of dominant males: the rugged, aggressive American action film hero and the Mexican macho *galán*/Latin lover type.

In keeping with its patriarchal and sexist representations of gender roles and norms, *El Arsenal* mainly depicts women as objects that can be consumed, used, and even "designed" for the enjoyment of men. When a beautiful woman enters the bar where Simón is hanging out, he states: "Look at the nice piece of meat I'm going to have for dinner" (*Vol. 1*). That the woman would easily fall for and want to have sex with Simón is a given in the narrative. In fact, it is literally written in the stars. At the beginning of the series' second volume, several characters are playing *lotería*. In the next panel, Simón and the woman (named Mariana) are shown walking together down the street in the background; while in the foreground we see the El Valiente and La Dama cards, which are captioned in this manner: "El Valiente… fearless and strong. La Dama…wants to be on El Valiente's arms" (*Vol. 2*). We later find out that Mariana is one of 13 genetically engineered "whores" developed by U.S. scientists upon request by Don Jon Jara, a *chilango* (Mexico City native) drug lord. Jara wanted to own hyper-lustful women who could satisfy each of his "13 pleasures" (*Vol. 3*). Each woman has a number tattooed on her chest, being thus effectively rendered as branded property. However, Jara became exceedingly jealous at the thought of other men having access to his special women, went crazy, and tried to kill them all. Four survived and escaped, including Mariana, who is No. 13. The only female character who challenges traditional gender expectations in *El Arsenal* is Zazil Moreno, a rookie mercenary. While she is depicted in a hyper-sexualized fashion, she challenges the supremacy of Simón and other top male mercenaries. Additionally, faced by the sexual advances of a mysterious shaman who wants to impregnate her, Zazil categorically refuses motherhood: "I will never carry no child" (*Vol. 3*). Even with the ample possibilities for disruption afforded by a post-apocalyptic world where societal norms that can reshaped, gender roles and visual representations are largely left unchallenged in *El Arsenal*.

Women as post-humankind: Reading cyborg and Maya-futurist graphic novels

In addition to post-apocalyptic narratives, comics engaging with post-humanism and alternatives histories (what I call here post-historical because they replace and go beyond official, particularly Western, accounts of history), are fertile ground for examination of politics and gender. Post-humanism is commonly found in "Science fiction narratives forged from multiple real and imagined couplings between technology, bodies and subjectivities" (King and Page 2017: 1). Cyborgs, for instance, are popular post-human characters appearing in a number of SF films and graphic novels, often raising questions about embodiment, alternative identities and subjectivities, fluidity, and other issues that closely relate to gender preoccupations. Meanwhile, post-historical narratives can take a variety of shapes, including futurism. Futurism is often used by marginalized, subaltern communities that "seize upon the dominant tropes of mass culture and aggressively recode them to suit their own purposes" (Rieder 2017: 140). This process of reterritorialization has given way, among others, to Afrofuturism and Indigenous futurism, whose main purpose is to claim "a place in the cultural present for groups whose history has been systematically distorted or erased and whose future has been scripted predominantly in terms of the disappearance of their specific cultural identity into that of the dominant, white society" (Rieder 2017: 155). As John Rieder explains, futurism also responds to the prevailing way in which SF has dealt with issues of race and ethnicity—that is, "by positing a postracial future where racial differences had become unimportant or simply disappeared" (2017: 141).

Here, I am interested in dissecting the ways in which the graphic novels *Angela Della Morte* (2011, 2014) and *Zotz: Serpent and Shield* (published independently in the United States since 2011) deal with the representation of women in post-human and futurist scenarios. The work of Argentine comic book artist Salvador Sanz, *Angela della Morte* is based on the premise that the soul can be separated from the body and—once dematerialized—transplanted into other bodies. This technology is controlled by two dueling organizations, which seek world domination and, of course, profit. The Sibelius laboratory employs workers whose consciousness can be inserted into the de-souled bodies of politicians, bankers, and other prominent individuals in order to attain money and resources. Meanwhile, the Fluo government has found a way to extract evil from humans and transform it into a liquid that can be stored in tanks. Angela is one of the members of Sibelius whose soul inhabits other bodies. Because she can be transferred into either males or females with a diversity of identities, Angela is constantly embodying new and unexpected bodies and subjectivities that are gendered in a variety of ways. In entering these new bodies that can be radically different from hers, Angela also (inevitably) creates new hybrid identities and subjectivities—just the way a scion is attached to a rootstock in horticultural grafting to create a plant with characteristics from both components.

However, this hybrid, this graft is innately unstable. Human bodies and souls don't seem to merge as seamlessly and predictably as tree trunks or stems. Angela has a difficult time adjusting to the constant process of swapping bodies and inhabiting other realities. If figuratively putting yourself in someone else's shoes is a tough ordeal, just imagine literally putting yourself inside another human being's body. While the idea of somebody's soul invading someone else's body might at first raise issues related to the nature of human immateriality and consciousness, in *Angela della Morte* the question of existence is always grounded by corporeality. And even in the graphic novel's post-human reality, this corporeality is inevitably impacted by gender. Sometimes, after a body swap, Angela walks into the ladies' restroom not having yet realized that she is now inside a man's body. Questions about the biological and social determinants of gender immediately arise in this scenario: Is Angela now a man because she is suddenly in a male body? Does she continue to be a woman because her gender identity has not changed during the process of transmutation? In this way, the graphic novel is successful at engaging in the conversation regarding the real-life scenarios of transgender or transsexual individuals who have described feeling "trapped in the wrong body," although it does not offer visual alternatives to the traditional male-female body binary.

In other instances, even when installing herself in the body of another female, Angela expresses her annoyance at the fact that the new body is fatter than her "real" one. Sanz draws Angela as having a slender and normatively attractive body that is typical of comic book heroines. From these examples, one might conclude that *Angela della Morte* fails to complicate normative gender expectations and representation of bodies. While the process of body transmutation is swift and seamless, the gendering of those transformed bodies offers little fluidity and possibilities for queering gender. As King and Page indicate, *Angela della Morte*'s narrative "closes […] around a recognition of the biological basis of human experience. The reintroduction of the biological might appear to be a retrograde move in the context of the text's gender politics, undoing the work of many feminist and queer theorists who have emphasized the social construction of gender" (2017: 42). However, one must also point out that the choice of a female protagonist is a positive step in a medium dominated by male (and often hyper-masculine) heroes. Also, there is a powerful sense of disruption in the fact that a woman's consciousness is precisely the one that gets to inhabit a variety of bodies, male and female, and interact with a variety of subjectivities. It is a sort of gender decolonialization: we go from the patriarchal concept of men "owning" women's bodies (present in *El Arsenal*) to a mechanism by which a woman takes over men's bodies. Finally, the powerful religious intertext contained in Angela's name must be considered for its ideological implications. Her name literally means "Angel of Death," which connects the graphic novel with Biblical and other Western cultural representations of angels as males. As a result, there is immediately a queering of the angel motif and a rejection of heavily patriarchal religious symbolism in the narrative.

While *Angela della Morte* appears to offer a possibility for decolonizing traditional gender structures, *Zotz: Serpent and Shield* creates a world that has already been decolonialized. In fact, in the Maya-futurist realm of the graphic novel, there never was such thing as the Spanish colonization of Mesoamerica. Rather, local civilizations were able to fend off attacks by Spanish soldiers and their native allies. This radical change in the course of history, however, does not mean that Indigenous groups can now live in peace and untouched by other cultural influences. In fact, history (although an alternative account of history) goes on, and the region's various civilizations must form new alliances as other non-American actors (such as the Ottoman Empire) arrive in the New World. Nevertheless, the defeat of the Spaniards guarantees the preservation of a worldview that is still dominated by Indigenous culture—including those aspects that pertain to gender and the roles of women. Starting with the cover of the comic's first issue, there is already an attempt by Parada to portray balance and equality in the presence and representation of both males and females. In other parts of the narrative, males and females are displayed as a group without any structured placement that would favor or discriminate one sex over the other. The hypersexualized depictions of men and women that we see in *Juan Solo* and *El Arsenal* give way in *Zotz* to representations in which both men and women are shown with bare chests, with nudity viewed as a natural state that is not meant to elicit lust or the kind of sexist gaze that is predatory on the exotic (especially female) Other.

In terms of narrative, the graphic novel concentrates on the adventures of the twin boys Pakal and Kaan. In this manner, *Zotz* attempts to recreate the fundamental tale of the Mayan creation book, the *Popol Vuh*: the perilous journey of the culture heroes Hunahpu and Ixbalanque, who defeat the lords of Xibalba (the underworld) to make human civilization possible. In Mayan cosmogony, the twins become the sun and the moon, providing equilibrium to the universe. While Parada's choice of two mischievous boys as his graphic novel's protagonists may appear to be contributing to the predominance of male heroes in comic books and other action-filled narratives, an understanding of Mesoamerican culture adds nuance to this depiction—as Hunahpu and Ixbalanque represent complementary forces such as sky and earth, day and night, life and death, and male and female. The importance of female presence is evident in *Zotz*, particularly through the story of Xt'actani, another character that represents the moon. In fact, Issue #1 (Parada 2011) begins with the telling of her legend by Pakal and Kaan's father around a fire. In Issue #2 (Parada 2013), when the twin brothers are alone in the jungle and their lives are in danger, Xt'actani descends from the moon embodied as a woman and heals the ailing Pakal, also reassuring Kaan with a motherly kiss that they will be okay. Thanks to Xt'actani's intercession, the twin brothers are able to escape the enemies who had raided their village and killed their parents.

Representations of females and their societal roles change later on in the story. After the twins escape they meet the Mictlan Raiders, a group of Nahuatl-speaking mercenaries. Upon arriving to their camp, the teenagers are introduced to the *ahuiname*, "pleasure girls that dawn from the House of Joy, the House of Courtesans" (Parada 2013: 51). In an attempt to challenge negative Western views about sex workers, *Zotz* presents the *ahuiname* as empowered women with agency who fulfill crucial roles in warfare: "They accompany the men on campaigns, and even support them from the sidelines in battle. Some even partake on the action directly" (Parada 2013: 51). The comic shows one of the "pleasure girls" dressing up to go to the battle along with the men. Later on, the *ahuiname* are shown taunting the enemy soldiers by making fun of their supposedly small penises in order to enrage them and disrupt their preparedness for battle. This depiction of the *ahuiname* is consistent with research on the role of Mesoamerican courtesans. According to Karen Olsen Bruhns and Karen Stothert, prostitutes do not seem to have been outcasts in Aztec society, served warriors and danced with them in various rituals, and enjoyed a certain degree of status. Europeans, however, disparaged Aztec courtesans because of the negative valuation they gave to bathing, face paint, and colored clothing, although all Aztec women shared in these practices (156). Portraying men and women as equals, emphasizing the role of female deities, and challenging Western views about gender roles and agency are a few of the many ways in which Parada engages in decolonialization in his graphic novel, placing Indigenous iconography and worldviews at the center of (post)history.

Concluding remarks

Latin American and U.S. Latino writers and artists have been responsible for an increasingly rich production of science and speculative fiction graphic narrative in the past two decades. Works that employ post-apocalyptic, post-human, or post-historical storyworlds tend to explore the relationship between politics and gender in a variety of ways, either problematizing traditional gender roles and expectations or reproducing limiting, sexist representations of both men and women. In the process of creating a "post-Latin America" through their futuristic graphic universes, these writers and artists have the opportunity to tackle gender in new and imaginative ways. In *Juan Solo*, Jodorowsky and Bess construct a hyper-masculine, uber-violent anti-hero whose representation is otherwise queered by the fact that he was born with an animal tail. Half-Pint, the dwarf transvestite prostitute who rescues and raises Juan, is an outcast because of her appearance and sexual preferences. However, she fulfills a role of nurturing mother that is largely absent in the comic's dark and unforgiving world, finding a common link with the boy because they both have "deformities" that mark them as different.

In *El Arsenal*, the possibilities of gender imagination are largely dismissed, as the comic favors normative hyper-masculine male heroes and hyper-sexualized representations of women. The role of women serving men's desires (a role imposed by patriarchy) is taken to a new level, as science allows for the development of genetically modified whores with a heightened penchant for lust. Meanwhile, *Angela della Morte* raises questions about the social versus biological basis for gender subjectivities, positing that embodiment and gendering cannot be separated even in a future where the soul and the body can exist independent of each other and female consciousness can freely occupy male bodies. Finally, *Zotz: Serpent and Shield* creates an alternative history where Indigenous concepts of gender prevail and challenge Western-imposed views about the societal roles and the visual representation of women. Taken all together, we can see in these graphic narratives that even an imagined "post-Latin American" future may not be as progressive as desired when it comes to issues of gender—unless the predominantly patriarchal history of the region is rewritten and depicted in radically alternative ways.

Works cited

Brown, J. Andrew and M. Elizabeth Ginway. "Introduction." *Latin American Science Fiction: Theory and Practice*, edited by M. Elizabeth Ginway and J. Andrew Brown. New York: Palgrave MacMillan, 2012, pp. 1–15.

Bruhns, Karen Olsen and Karen Stothert. *Women in Ancient America*. Norman, OK: University of Oklahoma Press, 1999.

Fernández, Bernardo. "Puras Pinches Chingaderas." *El Arsenal: Unknown Enemy No. 1*. Coquitlam, BC: Arcana Comics, 2010.

Jodorowsky, Alejandro and Georges Bess. *Juan Solo. Book 1: Born in the Trash*. Los Angeles, CA: Humanoids, 2014.

King, Edward and Joanna Page. *Posthumanism and the Graphic Novel in Latin America*. London: University College London Press, 2017.

Parada, Daniel. *Zotz: Serpent and Shield*, Issue #1. San Francisco, CA: Daniel Parada & Jorge Parada, 2011.

Parada, Daniel. *Zotz: Serpent and Shield*, Issue #2. Pittsburgh, PA: Ra-Some! Comics, 2013.

Rieder, John. *Science Fiction and the Mass Cultural Genre System*. Middletown, CT: Wesleyan University Press, 2017.

Vázquez, Salvador and Daniel Pérez. *El Arsenal: Unknown Enemy Vol. 1*. Coquitlam, BC: Arcana Comics, 2010.

Vázquez, Salvador and Daniel Pérez. *El Arsenal: Unknown Enemy Vol. 2*. Coquitlam, BC: Arcana Comics, 2010.

Vázquez, Salvador and Daniel Pérez. *El Arsenal: Unknown Enemy Vol. 3*. Coquitlam, BC: Arcana Comics, 2010.

7

TITO GUÍZAR ON RADIO ROW

Intermediality, Latino identity, and two early 1930s Vitaphone shorts

Nicolas Poppe

Spanning over seventy years, Tito Guízar's performing career on stage and set, as well as in recording, broadcasting, and television studios made him familiar with audiences not only in Mexico, but throughout the Americas.[1] Closely tied to his most famous film, Fernando de Fuentes' *Allá en el Rancho Grande* (1936), Guízar's stardom is enmeshed within complex cultural (trans)nationalisms. At least in part due to the film's place in traditional Mexican film historiography—it is considered to be the box office hit that made possible the industrialization of national sound film, which, soon thereafter, led to the so-called *Época de Oro—Allá en el Rancho Grande* is frequently bound by the constraints of the paradigm of National Cinema. Recently, however, its transnational horizons are increasingly coming into question by scholars.[2] Guízar's participation as José Francisco in the film has come to overshadow previous and subsequent work in other media industries, principally in Spanish-language United States and Argentina.[3]

In this chapter, I aim to recover a largely forgotten aspect of Tito Guízar's stardom: a transnational Latino identity expressed in English-language media through intermedial linkages between print journalism, radio, and cinema in the early to mid 1930s.[4] Among a constellation including Dolores Del Rio, Ramon Novarro, and Lupe Vélez—all of whom lived in a sociohistorical moment in which Anglos began rejecting "the present enormous vogue of all things Mexican," leading to mass repatriations to Mexico, including hundreds of thousands of U.S. citizens—Tito Guízar's place within English-language media distances him from others whose stars consisted of different elements ("Topics of the Times" 1933: 12).[5] Through examining intertextually the reception of his work by critics and fans on the stage and on radio in popular press publications like *Variety*, *Radio Mirror*, and *Radio Digest/Radio Fan Fare*, as well as English-language newspapers throughout the United States, I trace often conflicting iterations of Latino identities tied to Guízar that spectators later experienced on screen for the first time in a series of Vitaphone shorts. The focus of this chapter, and his first appearance in the cinema, Guízar's participation the *Rambling 'Round Radio Row* series project complex performances of identity that are embedded in competing and sometimes contradictory cultural (trans)nationalisms. Rather than approaching these shorts as threads of transmedial narratives or audiovisual remediations of Guízar's stage and radio repertoires, I suggest we heed Ana M. López's call for intermediality in approaching Latin American mediascapes and, consequently, I propose that the indexing of multiplex representations of Latino/a identity in Guízar's performances of the songs "Del Palmero" and "Coplas de la marihuana" is best understood as representing fragments of cultural understandings whose meanings

91

existed in spaces (in)between media. Encoded and expressed through different forms of media, and intertextually enmeshed within their representation, these overlapping yet distinct performances traverse media, as well as artistic practices on stage, radio, and screen. In so doing, these performances make visible—partially, temporarily—broader cultural understandings relating to Latino/a identity in the United States in the early 1930s.

Before moving to New York in 1929 at the urging of Emilio Azcárraga Viduarreta, Guízar studied in Mexico City with noted vocal coach José Pierson, who also trained famous tenors such as Pedro Vargas, Alfonso Ortiz Tirado, and José Mojica, as well as the baritone Jorge Negrete (Argente 2000: 57).[6] In New York, he studied with the Italian operatic tenor Tito Schipa, who nudged Guízar toward popular music, and recorded songs by Agustín Lara for Victor Records (Henriques 2011: 104). Soon after his arrival, Guízar began to appear in Spanish-language press throughout the United States in late 1929 and early 1930, principally in advertisements for Victor Records, but also in news about New York's Mexican community.[7] He then seems to arrive to the pages of English-language readers in 1931. In newspapers as wide-ranging as *The Evening Star* (Washington, D.C.), the *Cleveland Plain Dealer*, *The Constitution* (Atlanta), *The New York Times*, the *New Yorker Volkszeitung*, and the *Times-Picayune* (New Orleans), notes about Guízar's radio shows were regularly published, often with brief details on the accompanying band (e.g., Los Charros and Vincent Sorey's Gauchos) and songs he was scheduled to sing (e.g., "Passion [sic] Divina").[8]

National magazines followed a similar pattern. An early note in the July 1931 issue of *Cine-Mundial* reports that "Tito Guizar, cuyas canciones mejicanas por la radio, en Nueva York, están popularizándose enormemente, por lo bien que el joven tenor las interpreta" ("Mundiales" 1931: 535), preceded publications in *Radio Digest* and *Variety*. Though fragmentary, these pieces give us insight into how his performances were received by English-language audiences.[9] In two issues of *Radio Digest*, his programs are listed as: "Tito Guizar. Romantic Spanish tenor, in distinctive music from Cuba and South America" ("Blue Ribbon Chain Features" 1932: 77) and "A colorful musical program presented by Tito Guizar and Chago Rodriguez accompanied on the guitar by Juariz [sic] Garcia. All the music featured is the product of Mexico, the native land of these accomplished musicians who, before coming to the United States had an already established reputation as excellent interpreters of their native melodies" ("Chain and Local Features" 1932: 45).[10] While the first review indicates a kind of cultural levelling in which Guízar is described as Spanish and performs Cuban and South American music, the second is careful to detail his cultural specificity, his Mexicanness. These tendencies—levelling and specifying—mark two expressions of the intermedial reception of Guízar's performance of Latino identity.

Reviews of live performances published in *Variety* demonstrate a similar critical reception. Even in brief notes such as "Tito Guizar's Argentine opener and pop sequel were almost show-stoppers, and he had to beg for his release" ("New Acts" 1933: 47), which was published February 21, 1933, contain (inaccurate) cultural referents placing Guízar within a specific musical and identitary context. As he gained popularity, his performances were given more attention in *Variety*. On June 27, 1933, a review states that "Second spot that breaks the familiar programing is with Tito Guizar, guitarist and singer of Spanish songs from CBS. Middle here Guizar lands easily, although his foreign accent is very pronounced. His voice crashes, no matter what he sings" ("Met., Brooklyn" 1933: 12). Guízar's foreignness is not only addressed through specifying the language of the performance, but also by signaling the alienation ostensibly produced by accent. Another review, published on August 1, 1933, asserts:

> Here is Tito Guizar. He sings in Spanish. Coming from the broadcasting routes to the vaude stages, he employs a guitar to provide perhaps that Spanish angle. On the huge

Roxy stage it doesn't matter whether he plays it or not. He gets the colorful background of 30 girls in costume against a Venetian setting with a play of overhead and side lights. Guizar is in white costume and he is permitted to use a mike that spreads his voice into impressive resonance, unlike anything he has been heard to do before. He's a smash here.

("*Roxy N.Y.*" *1933: 13*)

In his show at the Roxy Theater, a lavish movie palace that was located not far from Times Square and Radio City Music Hall in Midtown Manhattan, Guízar not only sings in Spanish but also performs Spanishness. Even though the specific meaning of "that Spanish angle" is somewhat ambiguous, it seems to appeal to the cultural understanding of the serenade, an intimate song played on guitar and crooned by a romantic tenor, for example. The intimacy of Guízar's performance may be lost to the crowds of showgirls, but technology allows him to connect directly with audience members. Levelled or specific, the Spanish-language becomes the marker of a cultural group that is tangible for the magazine's English-language public. It means something to *Variety* and its readers, something, perhaps, now unrecoverable, and gives texture to what is at once a favorable and an ambivalent review.

Published in *Radio Digest*, the section "Voice of the Listener" gives us further fragmentary insight into Guízar's English-language reception not from the perspective of critics or journalists, notably, but rather radio listeners of the early 1930s. Writing to inquire into their favorite radio stars, letter writers gesture toward broader cultural understandings. This is not to say, however, that they are wholly representative, but rather they call attention to an individual's perception of her positioning within society in relation to others. One such individual is Hazel Rhoades from Chicago, who wrote multiple letters that were published by the magazine. In the Summer 1932 letter entitled "We'll Rope This Gaucho," Rhoades writes:

There has been a great scarcity of information concerning one of my favorite artists— Tito Guizar who sings those beautiful Spanish love songs and who has one of the most gorgeous voices I've ever heard. I have thrilled to the exquisite beauty of his voice on the Gauchos program for a long time, and more recently on the Woodbury program. Please won't you tell us about him and give us pictures?

(33)

Referencing language and program name (*gaucho*, of course, refers to a cowboy of the River Plate), Rhoades focuses primarily on his beauty. She perceives of Guízar, whom she knows through his voice, as an object of desire. More notable than a need for further information—a letter published later that year by Kay W. from Marshalltown, Iowa reiterates the request, "One more request—how about Tito Guizar—that delightful chap who sings Spanish songs over the CBS network? Would like, too, to see an article about him" (October 1932: 27)—is Rhoades' objectification of Guízar.

Less than a year later, in February 1933, *Radio Digest* publishes another letter by Hazel Rhoades.[11] Entitled "¡Muy bien, Gracias!" in (Mock) Spanish, she writes:

I WOULD like to say how pleased I was to find the page devoted to that splendid artist, Tito Guizar in a recent issue of your magazine. It was very nice. There is an artist who deserves some good "breaks" and I hope he gets them. Such a perfectly gorgeous voice cannot help winning many, many admirers, but, besides the voice of exquisite liquid gold, he has a personality that is simply irresistible, and by far the most fascinating foreign accent I have ever heard. If you do not care for tenor voices, tune in just to hear him talk—you will be well repaid. I tune in for both, and I am a regular listener. Thank you to you, Tito, for many, many pleasures—especially your "Aye, aye, aye" and "In a Little Spanish Town".

("¡Muy bien, Gracias!" 1933: 37)

Gratified by the outcome of her initial letter (to which she does not refer), she focuses on the enchanting and otherworldly qualities of Guízar's foreign voice. Without explicitly designating him as such, Rhoades nevertheless appeals to a common Latino stereotype in the 1930s, the Latin Lover.[12] Much like this trope, which for many is closely associated with Rudolph Valentino, Guízar enraptures Rhoades through the singular effects of his masculine charm.

Reflecting his increasing popularity in the pages of both fan and trade publications, Guízar began to appear in profiles.[13] Written to bring fans closer to their favorite stars, they bridge two distinct approaches to radio stardom: the fan's yearning to grow nearer to her favorite performer and the journalist's critical perspective. In her July–August 1933 piece "Tito Guizar Sings as He Lives," published in *Radio Fan-Fare (Combining Radio Digest)*, Hope Hale (Davis) focuses attention on what fans may not know about the singer.[14]

The piece begins with a kind of cultural stereotyping to which few, if any, journalists would admit today: rather than appearing as Hale had expected, "He was the dream of artists looking for a model of American college youth" (1933: 8). Guízar is not what she had presumed, for he was "Unlike other Mexican boys, who were too indolent for active sport" (9) and "[...] no sheik. There is nothing oily nor sleek nor practiced about his charm" (9).[15] He bears little resemblance to the Italian star, as the article "For Whom the Title 'Valentino of the Air'?" concedes, but he has an "undeniably ability to stir his audiences and to engender romance" (5).[16] Permeating various media but expressed distinctly by each, this feeling informs the performance and reception of Guízar's intermedial Latino identity.

In the profile, Guízar is portrayed as being without artifice, natural. His success, which, as Hale notes, he enjoys, is merely an expression of who he is. Guízar states, "When I sing love songs, it is natural that women should be romantic about me. Myself, I am romantic. I believe in romance. I like very much to give more romance to the world these days" (1933: 9). However, much to Hale's surprise, his head is not turned by other women. The assumed promiscuity of the star is intensified by the supposedly inherent promiscuity of the Latin Lover. Guízar is presented as wholly dedicated to his wife, whose intelligence he credits with his success. This is not to say, of course, that Guízar is what Hale would understand to be a modern man. He admits not only that in his marriage, "I am the jealous one" (9), but Guízar's career prospered due to his devotion to his self-sacrificing wife, who abandoned her own performing ambitions to promote those of her husband.[17] Recalling anecdotes told in both contemporary English-language press and, even, homages published in Mexico after his death nearly seventy years later, Guízar tells Hale, "My wife's education is a great help to me. For example, I was lazy in school, cared for nothing but sports, and consequently missed many things I should know. When my wife met me I knew no English, even though I was singing in New York. She did not allow me to continue. She forced me to learn" (9, 41). Adjacent to the cultural stereotype of the lazy Mexican, Guízar argues that his modern woman allows the pair to prosper.[18] While this leaves Hale to ruminate on the nature of marriage in the mid-1930s, she ultimately provides readers with an idealized image of their exquisite radio star (41). Perhaps subverting her depiction of a society in transition, she concludes, "A man must be good to deserve such devotion. And Tito Guizar, ladies and gentleman, *is* good" (41).

From its emergence, radio has been enmeshed with other media and forms of cultural production. Initially tied to his recording and stage careers, Guízar's radio popularity led him to become caught in other mediums, the sound cinema and, later, television.[19] In the early sound period, crossover was common. Published in the June 1932 issue of the film magazine *Silver Screen*, the article "Men of the Mikes" asserts:

> The sister arts of Radio and Pictures have found that they have one audience and only one. The great army of listeners of the radio includes the sixty million fans who support the motion picture industry. Under these circumstances the exchange of artists brings to the radio field the most talented players, and brings in exchange from the microphones and radioland, singers whose glamorous voices will add tremendously to picture entertainment.
>
> *(1932: 48)*

Pointing out the success of various players, but paying special attention to Bing Crosby, the piece argues that dividing lines between these forms of media have already disappeared.[20] In its captions, it asks rhetorically, "The Woodbury presentation features Tito Guizar on the Columbia network. Can Hollywood over-look such a romantic possibility?" (48). Guízar, it seemed, might be different than other Latino/a crossover performers such as José Mojica, who aimed to replace silent era stars who dimmed due to the perceived reactions of audiences to their (accented) voices, but usually worked in Hollywood's *films hispanos* produced by Fox Film and other studios. It would not be long before Guízar was to make his debut on the big screen, and he was to do so as a radio star in the English-language Vitaphone series *Rambling 'Round Radio Row*.[21]

In his September 1932 review of its first installment, James Edwin Reid describes the series' aim: "Bing Crosby crashed in via short comedies, and now he's starring in features. All the movie producers are looking around radio studios for talent. And that's just what you're invited to do yourself, in this amusing and entertaining short" (1932: 98). With varying narrative devices linking together individual performances, *Rambling 'Round Radio Row* functioned as a platform for radio stars to make the transition to the movies. Shot in their studios in New York and marketed as one of Vitaphone's "Pepper Pots," a category of entertaining one-reel shorts, Guízar featured in two episodes: Vitaphone #1474 (1932) and Vitaphone #1632 (1934). In them, Guízar performs Latino identity, fine-tuned on the stage and radio, as screen persona whose vocal and guitar performance is accentuated by acting.

The first episode (#1474) in which Guízar appears of *Rambling 'Round Radio Row* begins with a fade-in revealing a medium shot in which three seated gypsies (all uncredited) look toward a glass orb perched on pedestal as a smartly dressed man approaches their circular table.[22] Cutting to a tighter shot of the four, the man introduces himself as the radio host Ted Pearson and offers to sell them a radio. One of the two women brushes him off, informing Pearson that there is no need, as they already have the crystal. Rather less puzzled than one would imagine, Pearson asks if the crystal ball allows them to listen to radio programs to which the woman replies, "We not only hear them, we see them. Tell me your favorite radio star and I'll show you." After quipping that he'd like to see Gracie Allen's brother, Pearson asks to watch Paul Whiteman's Rhythm Boys.[23] After their jazzy number "How'm I doin'," the scene fades out, then in back to the gypsy camp. A delighted Pearson finds out that anyone can be made to appear, so he asks for Tito Guízar. The gypsy assents, and the camera dollies toward the crystal ball around which the gypsy performs a caressing magic sign with her hands, "Tito Guízar! Why he's one of our favorites. Now watch closely."

Using a similar dissolve (fade out, then in), the scene shifts to Guízar in a smart tuxedo performing (using direct sound) a version of the song "Del Palmero."[24] The medium shot is lit so as to center both on the seated performer and his guitar (Figure 7.1).

Figure 7.1 Tito Guízar performs "Del Palmero."

The cosmopolitan mise-en-scène is expressed through wardrobe and luxurious and culturally unspecific furnishings, which contrast with the shades of local color of the song's lyrics: "Cómo que te vas, cómo que te vas, cómo que te vienes / Pero, vida mía, cómo te entretiene / Cómo que te vienes, cómo que te vienes, cómo que te vas / Pero, vida mía, qué borracho que está." After a yelp, the scene cuts to a close-up of Guízar and his guitar. It emphasizes Guízar's facial expressions and good looks and draws the spectator closer to its lyrics, now notably in English: "From the window to the corner / From the corner to your window / Myyy, sweetheart! / I'm getting lazy, pleeease come ooout! / Or I'll go crazy! / Are you coming out? Are you coming out? Are you coming in? / Tipitiptip tipitin! / Are you coming in? Are you coming in? Are you coming ooout? / Please my daaarling! / Tuputuputupuuuuu... I go!" The scene dissolves back to Ted Pearson, who wonders what happens if radio stars are not broadcasting at the moment. The gypsies then allow spectators to see additional performances by the Pickens Sisters, Ann Leaf, and Frank Hazard.

Guízar's second appearance (#1632) on *Rambling 'Round Radio Row* begins with host Eddie Bruce, who introduces his radio program from his desk.[25] After a few jokes, he introduces Tito Guízar, saying "Before I start to talk I want to say something. Ha, ha. I mean I want to say something about Tito Guízar, the handsome troubadour of radioland. I understand that after one look at him wives go home and hiss their husbands. I'll let you take a look at him now."[26] The romantic tenor, it seems, is a sight for sore eyes. A left slide then translocates the viewer from the radio studio to an apartment where Guízar sings "Coplas de la marihuana" and plays guitar. Using similar sound and, to a lesser extent, lighting techniques in "Del Palmero," there are two notable, albeit slight, pans in this performance. In the first, a slight movement to the right draws attention to Guízar, the center of attention. Later, a slight pan toward the door foreshadows the action to occur. The song's subversive lyrics, presented directly, likely would have been incomprehensible to most spectators in the United States. He sings, "Suni suni, cantaba la rana / Suni suni, debajo del agua / Marihuana tuvo un hijito / y le pusieron San Expedito / como era abogado de los de Santa Anna / por esa sazón para la marihuana. / Ayyy, yaaa / Marihuana, ya no puedo / ni levantar la cabeza / con los ojos retecolorados / y la boca reseca, reseca / Ayyy, yaaa." The indolence expressed explicitly in "Del Palmero" may be invisible in "Coplas de marihuana," but it is nevertheless present.

Like "Del Palmero," the subsequent lyrics in English are limited, but function as a kind of fan service. The frog's "suni suni," left unexplained for non-Spanish speakers, becomes a pretext for pithy amorous expressions: "Suni suni I give you / suni suni a kiss / suni suni my darling / suni suni my dear." As it was in "Del Palmero," the focus remains Guízar's photogenic visage. His expressive performance is accentuated by an occasional furtive glance toward and at the camera, as well as a blown kiss (Figure 7.2).

Another slight pan, this time to the left, announces the arrival of a gentleman in a robe (uncredited), who enters the room speaking English and asks Guízar to give him a break. Guízar answers in English that he was told to go to that address, showing the man a card that reads, "Dear Tito, Will you play and sing for me alone. Rosita Apt. 6." The scenario underlines the all too prevalent representation in U.S. English-language media of Latino/as as romantic, if not overtly sexual and, by extension, immoral. It is not only that Tito sings a sensual love song, but also that he was invited to do so, alone, and by a young woman.[27] The exchange, ultimately, is the result of a misunderstanding, as Tito accidentally went to the wrong apartment because its number (nine) had been turned upside down. The scene ends as the gentleman tells Tito, "I hope you'll pardon me" to which Tito replies, "Pardon me," and bows. The same slide wipe is used (from right, this time) and the spectator is brought back to Eddie Bruce's radio program. He introduces the remaining singers (Shirley Howard and the group Men About Town) and Blubber Bergman (Alan Reed), whose comic sketch ends the episode.

Tito Guízar's performances on *Rambling 'Round Radio Row* are pieces of integrated musical programs, but they are also impartial expressions of an (often latent) Latino identity encoded

Figure 7.2 Tito Guízar performs "Coplas de marihuana."

within complex cultural (trans)nationalisms in the United States, Mexico, and beyond. Located in various forms and permutations in distinct media, this representation of identity exists (in)between media, intertextually and intermedially. Culturally levelled or specific, relying on stereotypes or distancing from them, the representation of Guízar's Latino identity evinces racial understandings and cultural prejudices prevalent in the United States in the early to mid-1930s. And as evidenced in a wide-range of media, these understandings and prejudices remain latent to this day. What is notable in an intermedial approach to Tito Guízar's representation of Latino identity on stage, radio, and screen is that his performances of it are never presented or understood as universal. Unlike contemporary mainstream media strategies, which ostensibly aim to appeal to the broadest audience possible (thus denying women and performers of color most kinds of cultural representation), Guízar's identity is always expressed and interpreted as being culturally Other, whether as specifically Mexican or more broadly Hispanic, but always outside the experience of the targeted Anglo audience. Overlapping, albeit incongruously so, other expressions of Latino/a identities by much bigger stars like Del Rio, Novarro, and Vélez, Guízar's orbit gravitated toward different media industries with similar, but distinct trajectories. Tito Guízar's performance of Latino identity in the early 1930s was softly voiced through his accented, romantic tenor and heard by fans in the U.S. and beyond on records, on the stage, on the radio, and, finally, on the movie screen.

Notes

1 I would like to thank Colin Gunckel and John Koegel for their generous feedback on an earlier version of this chapter.
2 In his monumental *Historia documental del cine mexicano*, Emilio García Riera designates 1936 as "El año de Rancho Grande" and argues (in its first edition) that "*Allá en el Rancho Grande* abrió a México todos los mercados de Latinoamérica y cambió el rumbo de la industria. Mejor dicho, su éxito sentó las bases económicas para que el cine mexicano fuera una verdadera industria" (*Historia documental del cine mexicano. I [1929–1937]*. Mexico City: Ediciones Era, 1969: 112). Scholars such as Maricruz Castro Ricalde and Robert McKee Irwin (*El cine mexicano "se impone": mercados internacionales y penetración cultural en la época dorada*), Desirée J. Garcia (*The Migration of Musical Film: From Ethnic Margins to American Mainstream*), Gunckel (*Mexico on Main Street: Transnational Film Culture in Los Angeles before World War II*), and Donald Henriques ("Mariachi Reimaginings: Encounters with Technology, Aesthetics, and Identity") pull at the film's many transnational threads.
3 Recently, both Gunckel and Lisa Jarvinen (*The Rise of Spanish-Language Filmmaking: Out from Hollywood's Shadow, 1929–1939*) have explored his work in *films hispanos*, Spanish-language shorts and features produced by U.S. studios for transnational audiences.
4 In this chapter, I use "Latino," "Latina," and "Latino/a" rather than a more inclusive "Latinx" so as to more clearly signal the strong gender binary embedded within the media objects studied.
5 This obscure quote from *The New York Times* obituary for Zelia Nuttall, an archeologist specializing in pre-Columbian Mesoamerican cultures, serves as the title of Helen Delpar's cultural history (*The Enormous Vogue of Things Mexican: Cultural Relations between the United States and Mexico, 1920–1935*) exploring the interconnections between Mexico and the U.S. from 1920–1935 ("Topics of the Times. Noted Woman Archaeologist." *The New York Times*. 15 April 1933, p. 12). Also, see Francisco E. Balderrama and Raymond Rodríguez's *Decade of Betrayal: Mexican Repatriation in the 1930s*.
6 Azcárraga Viduarreta distributed radios for The Victor Talking Machine Company. He would later found the radio station XEW in 1930, which was a building block of the family media empire that today is Televisa.
7 Initial references to newspaper sources are intended to be suggestive rather than exhaustive. The complete reconstruction of Guízar's reception by papers in the United States is, of course, impossible. "Advertisement for Victor." *La Prensa* (San Antonio), 1 November 1929, p. 2. Rembao, Alberto. "La Colonia Mexicana De N. York Se Unio Para Celebrar Las Fiestas De La Patria." *La Prensa* (San Antonio), 18 September 1930, p. 4.
8 Some examples: "Today on the Radio." *The Evening Star* (Published as *The Sunday Star*, Washington, D.C.), 25 January 1931, part 4, p. 7. "Gigli and Ruth Etting to Sing This Week." *Cleveland Plain Dealer*,

1 March 1931, "Women's Magazine and Amusement Section" p. 18. "CBS Signs Tito Guizar, Noted Mexican Artist." *The Constitution.* 19 Apr. 1931, p. 9F. "Radio-Programme," *New Yorker Volkszeitung*, 2 March 1931, p. 16. Serving a German-language readership, the *New Yorker Volkszeitung* also published pieces in English. "Serenade from Far Away Siam to Be Heard in Orleans." *The Times-Picayune.* 14 May 1931. p. 24.

9   According to an article published on 19 April 1931, Guízar had "been heard as a guest artist on numerous programs during the past year" ("CBS Signs Tito Guizar, Noted Mexican Artist" p. 9F).

10 An ad in *Variety* echoes this language of Guízar as "The Romantic Tenor." *Variety*, 2 May 1933, p. 31.

11 Underlining fans' connections to their magazines, Rhoades ends her letter by stating, "I don't know what I would do without RADIO DIGEST—it is a friend indeed" (37).

12 The cultural stereotype of the Latin Lover has been sketched in a wide range of works such as Mary Beltrán's *Latino/a Stars in U.S. Eyes* and Charles Ramírez Berg's *Latino Images in Film: Stereotypes, Subversion, Resistance.*

13 Early biographical sketches appear in *Broadcast Weekly* ("Silhouettes." 3–9 April 1932, p. 12), *Radio Index* (*Radex*) ("An Artist from Mexico." May 1932, pp. 17, 72), and *Radio Guide* (Ronnell, Lee. "Meet the Artist. Tito Guízar." 15 October 1932, p. 12). Ronnell's piece employs a derisive Mock Spanish. Guízar is quoted as saying, "I loff, you know, to sit and strum my guitar and sing the romantic loff songs. I am so happee in my work. The beautiful loff song... hm tadee dee da" (12). Ronnell states, "[Guízar] doesn't speak English without accenting and mixing up phrases and clauses and genders in a really delightful manner, and this mixing up, combined with his deep, melodic and mellow voice, is an essential part of his charm" (12).

14 After her briefly successful romance magazine *Love Mirror* folded, Hope Hale (Davis) freelanced for periodicals ranging from *Snappy Stories* to *Radio Fan-Fare* to the *New Yorker*. She was active in both feminist movements and leftist politics. In the 1930s, she was a member of the Ware Group.

15 Hale's description of his athletic physique is recalled in the article "Pagent of the Airwaves" (*Radio Mirror*, March 1935, p. 6). In an earlier issue of *Radio Mirror*, it is even claimed that Guízar was a welterweight fighter before his radio career (April 1934, p. 51).

16 Rather than positioning Guízar among Latino/a movie stars like Del Rio, Novarro, and Vélez, or even José Mojica for that matter, "For Whom the Title 'Valentino of the Air'?" compares Guízar with the radio performers Carlos Molina, Ennio Bolognini, Enric Madriguera, and Francisco Flores (1934: 5).

17 In the July 1934 issue of *Radio Mirror*, Ethel Carey's "Meet the Wife!" touches on this issue (pp. 18–19, 80). She argues, "Whoever your favorite radio king, nine chances out of ten, behind the story of his success is a dramatic tale of the unselfish devotion and hard work of his wife" (1934: 18). According to Carey, Guízar is no exception to the rule. She writes:

> "Do you remember when Tito Guizar, the Mexican Troubadour, first went on the air for the Venida Hair Net people? We were thrilled by his warm, emotional Spanish melodies, so different from our Tin Pan Alley numbers. [...] But in a short time their glamor wore off. We tired of listening to Spanish songs whose words were Greek to us. Couldn't he sing some English tunes? [...] It took his lovely, dark-eyed Carmen, soft-spoken but determined, to straighten matters out."

(18)

A similar story is recounted in Adele Whitely Fletcher's "The Love Story of Tito Guizar" (*Tower Radio.* December 1934, pp. 28, 52, 65) and is reiterated more than sixty years later in Héctor Argente's biographical sketch, "Tierna historia de un ranchero enamorado" (2000: 59).

18 Guízar's claim that he was a lazy student is contradicted by two 1933 profiles, "Album. Tito Guizar studied medicine—for a while" (*Radio Stars.* February 1933, p. 39) and "He Gave Up Medicine to Become a Tenor" (Couper, Donald. *Radio Guide.* 25 June–1 July 1933, p. 4). The anecdote also appears in Mildred Mastin's April 1937 story for *Radio Stars*, "He Swore He'd Be a Doctor" (pp. 52, 74–75). These stories also focus attention on Guízar's family life. Another Hope Hale (Davis) feature explains Tito and Carmen's reaction to the birth of their girl Nena ("Give Us a Lullaby Tito!" *Radio Stars.* October 1933, pp. 24–25, 70–71).

19 Like Libertad Lamarque, Ignacio López Tarso, and other stars in the *Época de Oro* constellation, Guízar finished his career with appearances in Televisa *telenovelas* such as *Marimar* (1994), *La usurpadora* (1998), and *El privilegio de amar* (1998–1999). Interestingly, Hope Hale writes in her 1933 article, "My first thought was that it is too bad that television hasn't caught up with the radio" (9).

20 Incongruously published in the film magazine *Modern Screen*, an advertisement for the magazine *Radio Stars* has quite a different perspective, publicizing the piece "How Hollywood Menaces our Radio Favorites." Written by Adele Whitely Fletcher, the article ran in the October 1933 issue (14–15).

21 Later, other Spanish-speaking stars were included in variety films. Carlos Gardel, for example, was slated to appear in *The Big Broadcast of 1936* (dir. Norman Taurog, 1935) before his untimely death. His scenes were cut in the U.S., but not Latin American, version.

22 Originally announced for a May release in the April 21, 1933 issue, this episode of *Rambling 'Round Radio Row* was reviewed as "Good" in *The Film Daily* on 29 July 1933 ("Reviews of New Short Subjects," p. 4).

23 Pearson refers to a topical running gag. With her husband George Burns, Allen appeared on numerous radio shows in 1932–1933 asking for information about her supposedly lost brother. Very much alive, her brother went into hiding until public interest sufficiently abated.

24 Vicente Mendoza's 1939 study *El romance español y el corrido mexicano: estudio comparativo* states the song "De el Palmero," "Procede de Michoacán, region de Los Reyes" (Mexico City: Ediciones de la Universidad Nacional Autónoma, 1939, p. 557).

25 Its review in *The Film Daily* reads, "Their material is well selected and the various bits are worked in so as to make a short that has both entertainment and fan interest" ("Short Subject Reviews." *The Film Daily*. 8 October 1935: 6).

26 In the February 9, 1932 issue of *Variety*, Guízar's radio show "To the Ladies" (also known as "Lovely Ladies" on the U.S. West Coast) is reviewed in "Radio Reports." It reads (in part), "Men won't hand onto a program of this nature for any length of time. Since this product is strictly for women, the lack of male interest may not worry the advertisers" and "[Guízar] has a pleasant tenor voice with a notable Spanish accent. The sponsor probably figured the accent would be considered romantic" (1932: 52).

27 The use of the diminutive with a cognate name with romantic associations is telling. Curiously, "Rose" ranked in the top thirty names given to female babies in the United States from 1900 to 1931 according to the Social Security Administration's index of popular baby names ("Popularity of name Rose." *Official Social Security Website*, 14 June 2017, www.ssa.gov/cgi-bin/babyname.cgi).

Works cited

Argente, Héctor. "Tierna historia de un ranchero enamorado." *Somos Uno*. No. 201, 2000, p. 61.

"Blue Ribbon Chain Features." *Radio Digest*. January 1932, pp. 76–77.

"Chain and Local Features." *Radio Digest*. May 1932, pp. 42–45.

"For Whom the Title 'Valentino of the Air'?" *Radio Guide*. 17 February 1934, p. 5.

Hale, Hope. "Tito Guizar Sings as He Lives." *Radio Fan-Fare (Combining Radio Digest)*. July–August 1933, pp. 8–9, p. 41.

Henriques, Donald. "Mariachi Reimaginings: Encounters with Technology, Aesthetics, and Identity." In *Transnational Encounters: Music and Performance at the U.S.-Mexico Border*. Ed. Alejandro L. Madrid. Oxford: Oxford University Press, 2011, pp. 85–110.

López, Ana M. "Calling for Intermediality: Latin American Mediascapes." *Cinema Journal*, 54 1, 2014, pp. 135–142.

"Men of the Mikes." *Silver Screen*. June 1932, p. 48.

"Met., Brooklyn." *Variety*. 27 June 1933, p. 12.

"Mundiales." *Cine-Mundial*. July 1931, pp. 531–535.

"New Acts." *Variety*. 21 February 1933, p. 47.

Reid, James Edwin. "Featured Shorts: The Best Big Little Pictures of the Month." *Motion Picture*. September 1932, p. 98.

Rhoades, Hazel. "¡Muy bien, Gracias! *Radio Digest*. February 1933, p. 37.

Rhoades, Hazel. "We'll Rope This Gaucho." *Radio Digest*. Summer 1932, p. 33.

"Roxy, N.Y." *Variety*. 1 August 1933, p. 13.

"Short Subject Reviews." *The Film Daily*. 8 October 1935, p. 6.

W., Kay. "Hall Next Month." *Radio Digest*. November 1932, p. 27.

PART II

Bending genre

8

INTERIOR DESIGN AND HOMOEROTIC SPACES IN JOSÉ ASUNCIÓN SILVA'S *DE SOBREMESA*

Sergio Macías

Interior design is one of the most profitable industries in today's market. This enterprise has an annual revenue of approximately 11.5 billion dollars. It is estimated that net sales will triple in the next five years. Rising demand for home goods makes it affordable for more and more consumers to be part of this growing trend. Besides manufacturing and selling home goods, this industry has created a need. Consumerism has ingeniously managed to convert a simple human necessity, such as having a shelter, into a stylized dream every time we open a magazine and we see a stunning living space. The homes and rooms advertised in magazines such as *Sunset*, *Dwell*, *Better Home & Garden*, and *Architectural Digest* quickly becomes a desire in the reader's mind, one that can be achieved through the consumption of home goods. These powerful images translate as the accessibility of luxurious dreams at an affordable price. Reality TV, with trending shows like *Design Star*, and TV networks such as *HGTV*, played a crucial role in achieving this goal. Interestingly, what was once considered to be a market that targeted only women, has now surpassed the boundaries of gender, race, and even socio-economic class in the majority of developed and developing countries around the globe. Single men, for example, can obtain insight into fashion, fitness, and how to live. *Alpha M*, a blog created by Aaron Marino, is nowadays one of the most popular channels on *YouTube* among men. As of today, Marino's channel has more than ten million subscribers and the number keeps growing. Like Marino, other bloggers with similar channels have not only achieved celebrity status, but they have also become an authority on how men in the twenty-first century should dress and decorate their home. *Alpha M* is a perfect example of what I would call a modern-day cyber consulting business in the branding of masculinity, in terms of fashion and interior design.

As I research this new and fascinating trend for men, there is a concept that is continuously repeated. This concept is the "man cave", which in the world of interior design refers to a stylized living space, usually a room, designated exclusively for men's entertainment; a restricted masculine territory demarked by aesthetic boundaries, penetrated only by men. For interior design, the cave, besides being a trendy concept that designates an exclusive male territory, also symbolizes an origin, one that deserves, I believe, a closer examination to expose its potential contemporary meanings. Buie Harwood, Bridget May and Curt Sherman propose the Paleolithic cave[1] as a starting point—a predecessor—for "interior design's historical narrative" and, also, as the "cradle of creativity" (5). The cave does not represent a "domestic space", or even a "practical shelter", however, the cave, as a geo-natural formation, does allude to the "first transformation of an existing space, a space already shaped by geological forces" (Huppatz 2012: 2). John Pile, after considering a series of Paleolithic caves, such as the caves in Altamira, Lascaux and Chauvet[2], argues that caves were prehistorical natural territories in which Homo sapiens have left an artistic mark (12). The primitive paintings are the first pictorial expressions of human identity left on walls as evidence of the early manifestations of interior design. The marking of any given territory, in this case, in the form of art, dictates the beginning of human civilization and the establishment of what we consider a "shelter"—defined as an "inside space or environment for living everyday life" (Pile 13). This shift in paradigm that conceived caves as a plain rock wall randomly available for primitive drawings is reevaluated, in the present, as a blank artistic canvas that set the ground for what we would later call interiority, and the building ground for interior design.

A man cave, in the modern sense of the word, designates a masculine shelter. It represents according to my reading to a type of homoerotism enacted and articulated through style. Furthermore, I interpret the concept of man cave as: 1) a masculine territory that becomes a metaphor of the male body 2) the materialization of same-sex desire and 3) a tribute to the male body through objects and the relationship one establishes towards them. Fashion and interior design, as the manifestation of one's identity through style, can be implemented, "to make claims about ourselves and others" (Brummett 2011: xxviii). Style is therefore "a complex system of actions, objects, and behaviors used to form messages that announce who we are, who we want to be, and who we want to be considered akin to". In a sense, style is a site where *desire*, "power and advantage are negotiated, distributed, and struggled over in society" (Brummett xxviii). "Camp" is a style known for putting into quotation marks masculine heteronormativity, it is "a mode of seduction –one which employs" aesthetic elements, such as interior design, as "susceptible of double interpretation" (Sontag 1964: 57). Camp also "has an affinity for objects and furniture, all elements of visual décor […] Camp art is often decorative art [used by men] to emphasize texture, sensuous surface, and style" (Sontag 1964: 55).

Through the queer eye of Camp, I examine the concept of "man cave" in Latin America by analyzing the novel *De sobremesa*, written by José Asunción Silva in 1896. I argue that the notion of man cave in interior design is not a recent aesthetic phenomenon. It is one that can be traced back to the late nineteenth century, at least in Latin America. Despite the fact that the phrase "man cave" does not appear explicitly in *De sobremesa*—given that this term was not coined until the last decade—Silva's novel does indeed manifest an exaggerated concern with style and interior design, one which intersects with traditional edifications of masculinity. In a significant number of pages in *De sobremesa*, the reader encounters long and detailed passages describing the decoration of interior spaces that are rooms accessed only by men. What's more, other male characters, who happen to be physicians, representing the science of that time, question the masculinity of the protagonist José Fernández, especially those who happen to be doctors. Fernández's sense of style, with regards to interior design, comes across as excessive and interpreted as possible symptoms of homosexuality. This clinical positivist discourse rationalized homosexuality as "a matter of constitutional degeneracy and supports the belief that homosexual subjects were "a living sign of modern degeneracy who suffered from an underlying nervous disorder that could be manifest in certain kinds of physical stigmata as well as in sexually inverted personality traits", and behavior (Terry and Urla 1995: 131). By examining Fernández's décor of his space, his "man cave" that he himself designed and decorated, I attempt to convey how his campy style problematizes traditional notions of masculinity. First, I provide a brief historical overview of interior design from the perspective of gender. Second, I present the concept of "man cave" in this text as expressed through Fernández's campy style. Subsequently, I examine the intersection between style, gender roles and the medical discourse of the time. As a form of conclusion, I reexamine this controversial concept and establish connections between past and present.

Interior design and homoerotic spaces in José Asunción Silva's De sobremesa

The birth of interior design and the separation of gender roles

Prior to the nineteenth century, interior design was conceptualized as an integrated part of architecture, comprised entirely of structural modifications: "The rooms of the past were both simpler in treatment and freer from embellishments than those of today" (Wilson and Sheldon 2004: xx). Later, in the sixteenth and seventeenth centuries, interior decorating as a practice gained a "somewhat notorious reputation for the very rich and their homes", meanwhile the lower classes remained entirely at the margin from such activity (Wilson and Sheldon 2004: xxi). Other factors that prevented the development of interior design, besides the gap between the rich and the poor, were people's lack of mobility and the limited means of transportation available at the time. All types of furniture were "constructed with the double purpose of being easily carried about and of being useful as a trunk" (Wharton, Codman, and Wilson 2007: 7). The Industrial Revolution marks a paradigm shift for interior design, one that occurred alongside the emergence of the upper-middle class. This change made it possible for "the bourgeois of one generation" to live "more like the aristocrat [class] of a previous generation than like his own predecessors" (Wharton, Codman, and Wilson 2007: 7). The period between 1840 and 1890 outlines the birth of interior design as we know it in postmodern times. This newfound discipline was based on two fundamental principles. First, "rooms may be decorated [...] by a superficial application of ornament totally independent of structure" and second, interiors could be designed "by means of those architectural features which are part of the organism of every house, inside as well as out" (Pahlmann 1968). In today's view, some of the crucial factors considered when designing an interior space are color scheme; ambience, mood or atmosphere; patterns and symmetry; and collections, accessories and furniture. All of these factors constitute what we denominate as taste and style in interior design.

In today's society, the notion of interior design is still seen by mainstream culture as "a female hobby", and for some, it is not even considered a discipline at all, but a "female thing" (McGinn 2012: 1). But it seems like "Guys are spending so much more attention to the aesthetics of their personal products and their home" (McGinn 2012: 1). Proof of this is the emergence of the term "man cave" in interior design. In a contemporary sense, a man cave is characterized by its "simplicity and adherence to a function-is-form vibe", targeting "men 25 to 45 years old who are professionals and first-time homebuyers, but the clientele has proved to be much more diverse" (McGinn 2012: 1–3). When it comes to defining what constitutes a masculine design, Dave McGinn declares: "Think clean, modern lines and an absence of frill or unnecessary ornamentation, with wood, metal, leather and canvas all used as popular materials in pieces that are chosen and arranged according to a functionalist philosophy" (2012: 4). This idea of functionality is apparently a decisive factor that determines the gender of a given interior design style. Michelle Miazga, who specializes in interior design for men, says that "men value function in their homes" (McGinn 2012: 3). Miazga refers to pillows as an example of male versus female clients: "Many women may like to stack throw pillows on their couches for no other reason than they look pretty, men, not so much [...] They look fantastic on a sofa. But a guy needs to be able to put his head on it or lie on it" (McGinn 2012: 3). Miazga adds: "That's something we always think about: What's the function of what we're putting in a room for a guy?" A question that comes to mind when considering interior design and gender roles is at what point did this become such a crucial factor and why?

During the Middle Ages women generally stayed home despite often working alongside men in the fields. Men, on the other hand, spent most of their time outside, working and socializing. The separation of the sexes during the rise of agriculture eventually became the hegemonic basis upon which the myth of "women's inevitable domesticity" was edified

(Glazer-Malbin 1976: 912). It was not until the early nineteenth century that women "became chained to the house. At this time, home and workplace, which had been synonymous, were radically split as industrialization began to change the structure of society (Kron 1983: 117). Men went outside to work, and women stayed inside to take care of home and family. The spread of the popular belief, "Men's house, women's home"; meant that men were primarily property owners and women homemakers. Thus, the binary system outside/inside and male/female became institutionalized as the natural order of gender roles (Glazer-Malbin 1976: 913). The Victorian era is responsible for instituting home as the locus of femininity, while men's roles inside the home were to rest, be fed and repair. Nona Glazer-Malbin suggests that the positionality of the sexes, in relationship to one's home, aligned with the anatomical location of the genitals: the vagina found in the interior and the penis in the exterior (1976: 920). Joan Kron reiterates that in interior design we still make gender distinctions today, distinctions that according to my view continue to reproduce traditional sex roles: "Gender jurisdiction lives in our dens, garages, and basements which are still male territories, and in the kitchen, living room, and dining room which are still predominantly female territories—no matter how many women are bringing home the bacon these days and how many men are frying it" (1983: 48). Hence, the birth of interior design as a discipline overlaps with the gender separation. Such distinction of male and female territories had the house as a point of reference, establishing other binaries as well, like interior/exterior and private /public.

Home, camp and thing theory

Our homes say a lot about us. When we use the word "house" we typically refer to the physical structure, whereas "home" implies much more. In interior design, home is not only considered an ordering principle in space, but "a preferred space and a fix point of reference" (J. Douglas Porteus 1989: 383). For the French philosopher Gaston Bachelard, "Home is our corner of the world [and] our first universe, a real cosmos in every sense of the word" (Bachelard and Jolas 2014: 4). Possessions, relationships, experiences and emotions all exist and become reality in our corresponding living spaces. As D. Geoffrey Hayward notes, home is "a reflection of ideas and values" of those living under the same roof and they manifest in the form of taste (7). Home is simultaneously a physical and an abstract space, one saturated with non-verbal symbols that "constitute a body of images" giving "mankind proofs or illusions of stability" (Bachelard and Jolas 2014: 5). From a phenomenological angle, Bachelard states that homes have identity and desire as prevailing subtexts that shape the way in which "[w]e are always re-imagining" the reality and the fiction of our home (Bachelard and Jolas 2014: 18–19). Homes are physical territories in which decorating takes place: "Decorating is like an art […] it is an expression of the desire for beauty through sanctioned form" (89). For Joan Kron, "The pursuit of beauty" in interior design "resembles religious zeal – styles are sects, and conversions to a certain period or idiom can make connoisseurs feel they have found 'the way'. Each specialist feels his or her stylistic faith is the divine one" (1983: 90). Home becomes a temple, a sacred space to worship desire, a territory that can be molded and transformed, but one that requires regulation and control: who can access our homes and under what conditions is a decisive factor in interior design.

There are a wide variety of strategies to control and define space. Polarity and duality prevail when organizing territory. Space is divided "on a whole range of spatial poles such as front/back, clean/dirty, male/female, and yours/mine, that are, if not a blueprint of the way we live, guidelines we follow" (Kron 1983: 46). Restaurants, airports, offices, and schools are all examples of what we consider secondary territories, public spaces. Home, on the other hand, is a primary territory, it is one's shelter. Home is:

Interior design and homoerotic spaces in José Asunción Silva's De sobremesa

> [a] space where a person or group has exclusive control, and because of its versatility, home is one of the most effective privacy regulating mechanisms ever invented. All its parts—walls, doors, furnishings, possessions—can be used to the owner's advantage. To mark home base, some humans use scents, just as animals do.
>
> *(Kron 1983: 29)*

Privacy constitutes one of the primary functions of a home. As Irwin Altman puts it: "Think of privacy as your right to determine what is communicated to others about you and to control access to yourself, which is the essence of individuality for self-identity and freedom. Privacy allows you to be you" (Altman and Wohlwill 1983: 37). With no defined boundaries and "no secrets, no hiding places, no privacy for bodily functions, you are literally nothing" (Altman and Wohlwill 38). The arrangement of furniture, for example, works to "regulate the social system in a house – direct traffic, keep the peace (and the quiet), and thereby control privacy" (Kron 1983: 45). There is a tendency to present spaces in a stylized fashion. People decorate their interior space as a way of personalizing. By personalizing a living space "we are using territory to assert our individual identity as well as our allegiance to a neighborhood, an ethnic group, a taste culture, or class" (Kron 1983: 29). I would even go as far as to assert that gender and sexuality are also encrypted and read by others in interior spaces. Object such as furniture, art pieces, decorations and other elements are essential when it comes to personalizing a space. Without objects, there is practically no interior design.

A movement that recently gained notorious popularity as a field of study, is what has come to be known as "Thing theory". It most certainly overlaps with interior design given that objects are one of the primary building blocks of interior design. Starting with Bill Brown's seminal work, *A Sense of Things* (2003), critics have paid attention to objects in order to explain the relationship between the "subject and the object in terms other than those of the capitalist market system in order to take account of the complexities of the object as a signifier" (1). Coincidently, as the contemporary concept of interior design begins in the nineteenth century, object consumerism starts to acquire notability at the exact same time. Jenniffer Sattaur focuses on the commodity that objects provide proposing materialism as an "occasion for elaborate fantasies of consumption, sensuous experiences of imagined acquisition", displaying "the material progress of the nation and its capitol" (2012: 3). Along these lines, some scholars have examined literary works of the Victorian era to study a series of novels that bring to light ways in which "fiction, from realism through modernism and into postmodernism, accommodate and respond to the commodity's colonization of the social imagination and its desires" (Atzmon and Boradkar 2014: 145). For Mihaly Csikszentmihalyi, "things are cherished not just because of the material comfort they provide but for the information they convey about the owner and his or her ties to others" (2014: ii). Objects for humans represent a language to communicate with others. Every time we make a decision to include or exclude certain objects, we change the message others read about ourselves. As Kron puts it:

> The furnishings of a home, the style of a house, and its landscape are all part of a system—a system of symbols. And every item in the system has meaning. Some objects have personal meanings, some have social meanings which change over time. People understand this instinctively and they desire things, not from some mindless greed, but because things are necessary to communicate with. They are the vocabulary of a sign language.
>
> *(Kron 1983: 19–20)*

A style that that can be positioned under the theoretical umbrella of Thing theory is Camp. First, "Camp is the love of objects" (Sontag 1964: 54). Second, Camp is a view of the world in terms of "artifice", "exaggeration" and "stylization" (Sontag 1964: 54). Third, "Camp is not a thing. Most broadly it signifies a relationship between things, people, and activities or qualities, and [sometimes] homosexuality" (Newton 1979: 102). Gender, desire and sexuality make up a large part of Camp. These are the type of coded messages articulated through objects and interior design. Camp tends to utilize these objects to articulate juxtapositions and incongruities, such as masculine and feminine. Through the queer eye of Camp, I would like to decipher the coded messages about identity and desire that José Fernández—the protagonist in *De sobremesa*—demonstrates through a fascination for collection and interior design, linked to an overwhelming and almost exaggerated sensibility towards the world that surrounds him.

De sobremesa and its campy interior design

De sobremesa can be described as a series of unfortunate events. The original manuscript was entirely lost in the 1895 shipwreck of L'Amerique, during one of Silva's trips from Venezuela to Colombia. The version that currently exists is a rewrite of the original manuscript that sunk with the ship. A year later, after Silva rewrote what would become his only novel, he committed suicide by shooting a bullet into his heart. Though the reasons for Silva's suicide are uncertain, there is much speculation surrounding his death. Some attribute this fatal act to his bankruptcy, others affirm that Silva's suicide was triggered by a severe depression, caused by his homosexuality. Despite Silva's last wish for *De sobremesa* to be published, his close friends that had read the novel considered the manuscript unworthy of publishing. It was not until 1925 that *De sobremesa*, for unknown reasons, was printed and released. At that time, critics and readers alike poorly received Silva's novel. The fate of *De sobremesa* remained uncertain until the early 1980s, when critics from both the United States and Latin America reread Silva's novel, and found an appreciation for the originality and uniqueness of it. For this reason, *De sobremesa* was somehow legitimized and integrated into the Latin American literary canon.

The plot of Silva's novel can be synthetized as the reading of Fernández's diary. This event can also be read as an act of vulnerability since Fernández shares his most intimate memories and deepest desires with his closest male friends, Óscar Sáenz and Juan Rovira. The reading takes place after the three have enjoyed an exquisite dinner characterized by "dainty morsels, the blond aged sherry, the dry Johannesburg Riesling, the Bordeaux and Burgundies that have slept thirty years down in the depths of the wine-cellar; the chilled Russian-style sherbets, the honey-flavored Tokay" (51). Unlike other Saturday nights of socialization with Sáenz and Rovira, Fernández agrees to read his diary in order to satisfy the petition of his guests. More than a traveler's diary—in which Fernández could recount his passage through many European cities for example[3]—Fernández's memories narrate his pursuit and failed love affair with Elena, the young woman with whom he falls in love immediately after he sees her. This enigmatic female character, unlike the other lovers he brags about, is described as a ghostly character, one that can be referred to as a strictly platonic love.

In *De sobremesa* we can identify two narrative frames. Besides the actual events happening inside the diary—Fernández's own voice—we also experience the many hours in which the reading takes place. The second frame integrates the voices of Fernández, Rovira and Sáenz, as well as that of an omniscient narrator. For the purpose of my study, I examine the second frame since it is here where we find the extensive descriptions of the many rooms that constitute his home. Furthermore, this narrative frame is evidence of Fernández's sensibility and campy style towards interior design. James Duncan, who studies the homes of the wealthy, understands that interior design is not only a symbol of the self, it can also be "a symbol of group membership" or a combination of personality and group membership 'in varying proportions" (Schwartz 1968: 741).

Interior design and homoerotic spaces in José Asunción Silva's De sobremesa

At the turn of the nineteenth century, Camp, as far as object possession and décor, was conceived as a type of membership amongst the wealthy, thus this peculiar style became to be known as "something of a private code, a badge of identity even, among small urban cliques", especially amongst men (Sontag 1964: 53). Fernández is a wealthy individual. We find out that at a very early age he published two volumes of poetry and that in his early twenties, he was a politician. He is also an avid reader, traveler and art collector. Other details that *De sobremesa* provides about Fernández is that he is an attractive twenty-seven-year-old single man. His many love affairs make him a lady's man. Nevertheless, the décor of his home problematizes what would seem a stable masculinity. Fernández takes pride in his home. His house symbolizes a token of social prestige. In it we find a conglomeration of art and vestiges he has collected through his many travels all over the world. His guests perceive Fernández's subjectivity as inseparable from his house, as stated by Sáenz when he says that Fernández "wears a mask [...] of perfect worldly uprightness" (56). In this sense, the house becomes a mask through which Fernández lives "isolated among the treasures of art and the lavish creature comforts of a house like this" (56). Indeed, for Fernández, the microcosms that represent his home he refers to as "real life", that is, a shelter from the shallowness of the outside world that Fernández addresses as an "emotionless bourgeois life" (56). Just like "the relationship between Camp and objects is extremely emotional", (Sontag 1964: 54) Fernández's home is a consolidation of his experiences, the materialization of his memories, a shelter that only a selective group of male friends can access.

As the night progresses and Fernández shares his memories with his two male guests, we notice how they constantly change locations, moving from room to room. Amongst these spaces are Fernández's dining room, living room, entertainment room, study, and halls. These characters seem to follow an emotional trajectory. In other words, the feelings and tone that each diary passage transmits correspond to the atmosphere each room conveys. The result of such movement makes it seem as if the readers receive a walk-through of the house. *De sobremesa* provides plentiful information about Fernández's home. For example, we find out that it is located on the outskirts of Bogotá, thus it is situated in an in-between space—it has undefined boundaries—that can be interpreted as both urban and rural, or neither. The property acquires human-like qualities, as well, since it is named after the young girl he falls in love with: "Villa Helena" (78) or Helena's Towns [my translation]. Both the house and Helena—object and subject—become Fernández's obsession (78). However, despite this fact, Fernández's home is a perfect example of a homosocial space, one in which men not only socialize but one in which certain heteronormative boundaries are blurred. As stated before, only men penetrate Fernández's man cave. All of his explicit heterosexual love affairs take place somewhere else, usually hotel rooms and Fernández's lovers' bedrooms. Women never access the territory that is his home. In this way then, we can see a juxtaposition of male and female qualities regarding Fernández's house: a feminine name attributed to the physical property—Villa Helena—while at the same time it is an exclusively masculine territory designated for "the silence of close friendship" between men (51). Camp "is ironic insofar as an incongruous contrast [that] can be drawn between an individual/thing [like Fernández's property] and its contexts/association. The most common incongruity masculine/feminine" (Babuscio 119), just like we see in the house in *De sobremesa*. We can observe a second juxtaposition in relationship to his home when we find out that the property is an inheritance that has been passed down from generation to generation to all the men on Fernández's father's side, but many of the objects referenced by Fernández belonged to his mother. We know that the objects are his mother's by the encrypted symbols found in objects such as "the dull shine of the old silver dinner service imprinted with the coat of arms" (51). The physical structure of the house represents paternal lineage then, while much of the contents are associated with the maternal lineage.

Sergio Macías

Many of the hobbies and activities that Fernández seem to engage in are seen by Rovira and Sáenz as distractions that pull Fernández's focus "in ten opposing directions" (52), amongst these is "cultivating rare flowers in the greenhouse", a hobby that is strictly related to interior design (53). These flowers, like the exotic orchids and irises grown by Fernández, serve as objects that adorn special territories of the house, like Fernández's study, where he keeps the diary:

> José Fernández, after searching in one of the corners of the room, where in the reddish dark only the whiteness of a bouquet of irises and the outline of a bronze vase were suggested, after diming the lights of the chandelier, sat near the desk, and placing closed book on the velvet tablecloth, remained looking at it [the diary] for a few seconds.
>
> *(64)*

In interior design, flowers are conceived as temporary objects used to fill empty spaces. Like candles, these decorative objects have a short-lasting effect. Flowers die in a matter of days and rooms begin to look naked without them. Fernández seems to be aware of this. As what can be read as an act of exercising control, his greenhouse is a year-round generator of such decorative objects. We also find out that flower production extends to Fernández's "hundred-year-old-park, its hothouse where, as in the poisoned atmosphere of the native forests, grow the most singular species of tropical flora" (58). For Joan Kron, flowers, "like precious jewels, […] shine in the observer's direction, while at the same time setting the owner apart" (1983: 250). Flowers are "representative of one's group", a sign of status "with whose whole significance one is 'adorned'" (Kron 1983: 59). By cultivating flowers and using them as an object of décor, Fernández problematizes heteronormative gender roles. His masculinity is put into question given that flowers are typically associated with femininity. Furthermore, the fact that the flowers are exotic highlights the fact that they are not "normal" in some way; they are "other" in their otherworldliness.

Actually, no object in Fernández's home seems to be ordinary, regardless of size or functionality. As seen with the flowers, even nature possesses a certain extraordinary quality. This fact works with the objects to form a motif and transmit a feeling. For example, Fernández's diary is not just a book, "it was a thick volume with dull gold locks and corners. Over a background of enameled blue, encrusted in the black morocco of the covers, there were three leaves on which fluttered a butterfly with its wings wrought in tiny little diamonds" (64). The narrator provides layers of descriptions throughout the text in which not only colors and textures are described, but mostly the atmosphere that each room conveys. The predominant feeling that prevails is sadness and melancholia. Rovira states, "This half-light you like, Fernández, feeds the silence and is a narcotic" (51). As a matter of fact, dim lamplight and candles are the only sources of lighting. Most of the rooms remain in the shadows and in complete darkness, adding a flair for the mysterious: "In the back, dimmed by diminutive shades of reddish gauze, the light from the candlesticks on the piano did battle with the enveloping half-light, while on the open keyboard the brilliant whiteness of its ivory squared off against the dull black of the ebony" (50). We note that the color scheme of Fernández's house is related to the lighting, such as the contrast of black and white here. As the men move from room to room so does the light, and thus new areas of the house are revealed along with new memories as Fernández reads out loud to his guests. We also find a variety of scents, ranging from the scent of flowers, to the burning wax and oriental incense, to the smoke of cigars, whose descriptions combine color, lighting and smell: "the fiery tips burned in the darkness, curled in tenuous bluish spirals in the circle of lamplight, and the sweet enervating smell of opiate tobacco from Orient mingled with that of the Russian leather in which the household furnishings were covered" (50). The walls in Fernández home

Interior design and homoerotic spaces in José Asunción Silva's De sobremesa

are painted in a tone of redness (50). We begin to see the repetition of red as part of Fernández's color scheme: the walls match the gauze. Some of them are covered with an "opaque woolen tapestry", while on others hang "smooth steel blades of crossed swords in a panoply over a shield" (50). Another unique feature that decorates these walls are the original pieces of art "bordered by the gold Florentine frame[s]", that Fernández collects. Over the cold white marble floor, we find a series of area rugs, some of which produce a "gloomy purple semidarkness" (50).

Descriptions in which the male body, in all its physicality, intimately interacts with the decor of Fernández's house homoerotizes the text through the joining of gender and his space. For example: "A man's hand ran along the velvet tablecloth" (50), suggests a sensual and male caress. Images in *De sobremesa* such as "six *erected* candles" (50; my emphasis), the "*hairy* velvet" curtains (58; my emphasis), and the "*musculature* of the armchair" (143; my emphasis) allude to the male anatomy and convert the inanimate objects into living body parts. *De sobremesa* does not hesitate but is rather clear in communicating the relationship between objects and subjects. Besides an emotional and sentimental relationship, as I stated before, it is also a sensual one, as demonstrated by the emphasized words above. This is extremely important in the homoerotization of the text. If the home is both a material and metaphoric extension of the self, then the home is not only an identity but also a corporality. In other words, the home is an extension of Fernández's body, one that interacts with the male guests who penetrate it, one that reacts to stimuli and that seduces through comfort and beauty. Fernández's desire becomes homoerotic then. When Fernández states, "I live for my house and objects", he is in a way saying that he worships and renders tribute to an ideal male body edified through objects. It is no coincidence then that the omniscient narrator describes a model of ideal male beauty when describing the male characters inhabiting an ideal room or space:

> With the brighter light the group that sat in silence came into view: the fine Arabian profile of José Fernández, accentuated by the dull pallor of his complexion and his curly black hair and beard; the Herculean frame and serene features of Juan Rovira, which were rendered very attractive by the contrast between his large eyes with their childlike expression and the gray hair of his thick mustache set against the darkness of his sun-tanned skin; the lean, serious face of Óscar Sáenz, who, with this head sunken in the cushion of the Turkish divan and his body stretched out on it, twisted his pointed blond beard and seemed lost in endless thought.
>
> *(50)*

We see an intersection between male anatomy and the design of this room. The beauty of the male characters is revealed little by little with the light. These characters are all in a vulnerable position: they are laying down relaxed, enjoying the coziness of the space, delighted. The description of Sáenz is quite interesting. He is not only laying down, but his head is buried in the cushion and his body "stretched out"; the intimate physical contact between subject and object is as if Sáenz were to be making love to Fernández's metaphoric male body.

In the second volume of the *History of Sexuality*, Foucault identifies the emergence of a new discourse about human sexuality that takes place in Western cultures. He identifies "the birth of the homosexual" (1988: 5) right around 1870. According to Foucault, prior to this date, the term "sodomite" was a generic term to designate "a category of forbidden acts whose perpetrator was nothing more than a juridical subject of them". The sodomite, says Foucault, "was only a temporary aberration, not solely pertaining to homosexuality" (1988: 5). After 1870, the term "sodomite" became an exclusive tag to designate male homosexual acts (Foucault 1988: 5). Such designation made homosexuality official, consequently, the homosexual subject "was now a species" (Foucault 1988: 6). Foucault attributes this event to a publication in 1869 titled *Contrary Sexual Sensation* by Karl Friedrich Otto Westphal. This so called medical-psychiatric article marks the beginning of a medical positivist discourse about sexuality which circulated around the notion of hygiene. Male homosexuality thus becomes "a type of life", "a life form", "a case history", in short, "a morphology with indiscreet anatomy and a possibly mysterious psychology" (Foucault 1988: 7–10). This marked the beginning of male homosexuality to be described "less by a type of sexual relation than by a certain type of sensibility" (Foucault 6) resulting in social anxiety. Heterosexual men, in conjunction with positivist science, obsessed over "homosexual signs" in order to identify those subjects that presented an "abnormality". Consequently, homosexuality is rationalized as a disease and the homosexual subject as an embodiment of disease. Furthermore, in *The Birth of the Clinic: An Archeology of Medical Perception*, Foucault stipulates that the body, more than flesh and "far from being a self-evident organic whole, is at best a nominal construct and a phantasmatic space, imagined very differently over time and across various cultural contexts" (1994: 33). The scientific methodology implemented by positivist science to determine homosexuality was purely based in a series of observations and deduction. For such reason, in the nineteenth century, "The glance has simply to exercise its right of origin over truth. (Foucault 1994: 19). Foucault explains that social anxiety manifested in the "monitor[ing]" and "spy[ing]", searching for "possible lesions and symptoms" on the "surface of the skin" (1994: 25–26). Fernández's home, his man cave, awakens suspicion in his guests. Saénz, for example, who happens to be a doctor, contrast his work space with Fernández's home: "I breathe in nauseating stenches of filth, decomposition, and death [...] and I come in here to find the dining room lit a giorno" (50). Sáenz goes on stablish a diagnosis, Fernández's unproductivity in other manly occupations, such as his literary work, is caused by all the aesthetic distractions around him, the "Enervating luxury, the refined comfort of this house" (58). Thus, according to Sáenz, Fernández should avoid "the things that stimulate the body [...] the hydrotherapy salon, the bedchamber and boudoir worthy of a courtesan" (58). On the one hand, we observe in *De sobremesa* Fernández's aspiration to reach an ideal of male beauty through interior design—his house, thus become a metaphor of an ideal male body into which he pours his desire. On the other, Fernández's home, characterized as immaculate and well-decorated, is read by his guests, particularly by Sáenz, as an aesthetic sign that contradicts what a man's home, a cave, should be. The materiality of the interior design of Fernández's home edified with objects, also equates to a homosexual body, a sick body. This double narrative of beauty and disease is what problematizes Fernández's masculinity.

As I have begun to demonstrate, in *De sobremesa* José Fernández's man cave breaks the outside/inside and male/female dichotomy, resulting in his male guests questioning of his masculinity. In the case of Sáenz, given his profession as a doctor, he represents the positivist discourse that mainly relied on visual aesthetic signs to determine pathologies. Fernández man cave, an exclusive male territory, is the basis for which his masculinity is put into question. Despite the progress we have made towards understanding gender and sexuality, interior design reveals that we have a lot still to do. Camp, as a style that favors artificiality and represents the love of objects is a valuable tool to study and decontrol gender and heteronormativity, as seen by examining Fernández's sensibility and passion towards interior design. Perhaps it is time to revalue gender roles once again and reconsider how can we move beyond labels such as masculinity and femininity. When it comes to interior design and gender roles, lines between what are labeled as male and female as division within living spaces do exist, and they are not subtle. Fernández's "man cave" is male territory, but one that is extremely aesthetic, rather than purely practical or functional as is suggested above to be heteronormative male preference in design. Not every ornament or piece of furniture serves a purpose other than serving as pieces of art that are on

Interior design and homoerotic spaces in José Asunción Silva's De sobremesa

exhibit. Instead, memories and identity are perhaps the two most distinctive functions of decor in Fernández's home. *De sobremesa* is essentially a Camp novel, the first of its kind in Latin America, particularly because of its emotional excess. Through the analysis of *De sobremesa* we have seen how traditional gender roles are jeopardized, and even perhaps deconstructed, through the use of style and aesthetics.

Notes

1 The Paleolithic period was roughly 45,000–10,000 years ago and it is also referred as the Stone Age. The caves occupied by the first human inhabitants, the Homo sapiens, are the first manifestations of human civilization. The art expression found in these caves has provided valuable information about the lifestyle of our ancestors. These primitive drawings prove that the first human societies were mostly nomadic hunters.
2 These are Paleolithic caves found in the early twentieth century situated in a territory that extends from northern Spain to France. These caves were named after the geographical location they were found.
3 The European cities José Fernández visits and that are referenced in *De sobremesa* are Paris, London and Berna, to name a few.

Works cited

Abercrombie, Stanley. *A Philosophy of Interior Design*. New York: Harper & Row, 1990.
Altman, Irwin, and Joachim F. Wohlwill. *Behavior and the Natural Environment*. vol. 6., Boston, MA: Springer, 1983.
Atzmon, Leslie, and Prasad Boradkar. "Introduction A Design Encounter with Thing Theory". *Design and Culture*, vol. 6, no. 2, 2014, pp. 141–152.
Babuscio, Jack. "Lo Camp y la sensibilidad homosexual." *Archivos De La Filmoteca*, no. 54, 2006, pp. 170.
Bachelard, Gaston, and M. Jolas. *The Poetics of Space*. New York: Penguin Books, 2014.
Brown, Bill. "Thing Theory". *Critical Inquiry*, vol. 28, no. 1, 2001, pp. 1–22.
Brown, Bill. *A Sense of Things: The Object Matter of American Literature*. Chicago, IL: University of Chicago Press, 2003.
Brown, Julia P. *The Bourgeois Interior*. Charlottesville, VA: University of Virginia Press, 2008.
Brummett, Barry. *The Politics of Style and the Style of Politics*. Lanham, MD: Lexington Books, 2011.
Charry Lara, Fernando. *José Asunción Silva, Vida y Creación*. Bogotá, Colombia: Procultura S.A., 1985.
Cleto, Fabio. *Camp: Queer Aesthetics and the Performing Subject: A Reader*. Edinburgh: Edinburgh University Press, 1999.
Core, Philip. *The Lie that Tells the Truth*. London: Plexus, 1984.
Csikszentmihalyi, Mihaly. *The Systems Model of Creativity: The Collected Works of Mihaly Csikszentmihalyi*. Berlin: Springer, 2014; 2015, DOI:10.1007/978-94-017-9085-7.
Erikson, Erik. "Genital Modes and Spatial Modalities". *Childhood and Society*. New York: Norton, 1963.
Foster, David W. (ed). *Chicano/Latino Homoerotic Identities*. New York: Garland Pub, 1999.
Foucault, Michel. *The History of Sexuality*. New York: Vintage Books, 1988.
Foucault, Michel. *The Birth of the Clinic: An Archaeology of Medical Perception*. New York: Vintage Books, 1994.
Glazer-Malbin, Nona. "House Work". *Signs: Journal of Women in Culture and Society*. University of Chicago, 1976, pp. 905–922.
Harwood, Buie, Bridget May, and Curt Sherman. *Architecture and Interior Design through the 18th Century: An Integrated History*. Upper Saddle River, NJ Prentice Hall, 2002.
Hayward, D. G. *The Psychology and Physiology of Light and Color as an Issue in the Planning and Managing of Environments: A Selected Bibliography*. vol. 288. Monticello, IL: Council of Planning Librarians, 1972.
Huppatz, D. J. "The First Interior? Reconsidering the Cave". *Journal of Interior Design*, vol. 37, no. 4, 2012, pp. 1–8.
Kron, Joan. *Home-Psych: The Social Psychology of Home and Decoration*. New York: Potter, 1983.
McGinn, Dave. "The Man Cave Moves Out of the Basement". Toronto: *Globe & Mail*, 2012.
Newton, Esther. *Mother Camp: Female Impersonators in America*. Chicago, IL: University of Chicago Press, 1979.
Pahlmann, William. *The Pahlmann Book of Interior Design*. New York: Viking Press, 1968.

Pile, John F., and Judith Gura. *A History of Interior Design*. Hoboken, NJ: Wiley, 2014.

Porteus, J. D. "Katharsis: Academic Writing as Self-Therapy". *Area*, vol. 21, no. 1, 1989, pp. 83–85.

Price, Alexander. "Beckett's Bedrooms: On Dirty Things and Thing Theory". *Journal of Beckett Studies*, vol. 23, no. 2, 2014, pp. 155–177.

Sattaur, Jennifer. "Thinking Objectively: An Overview of 'Thing Theory' in Victorian Studies." *Victorian Literature and Culture*, vol. 40, no. 1, 2012, pp. 347–357.

Schwartz, Barry. "The Social Psychology of Privacy". *American Journal of Sociology*, vol. 73, no. 6, 1968, pp. 741–752.

Silva, José A. *After-Dinner Conversation: The Diary of a Decadent*. Translated by R. K. Washbourne, Austin, TX: University of Texas Press, 2005.

Sontag, Susan. "Notes on 'Camp'". *Partisan Review*, vol. 31, no. 4, 1964, pp. 515–530.

Spang, Rebecca. "Thing Theory". *The Financial Times*, 2016, pp. 8.

Terry, Jennifer, and Jacqueline Urla. *Deviant Bodies: Critical Perspectives on Difference in Science and Popular Culture*. Bloomington, IL: Indiana University Press, 1995.

Tognoli, Jerome. "The Flight from Domestic Space". *The Family Coordinator*. San Francisco, CA: American Psychological Association, 1978, pp. 599–607.

Wharton, Edith, Ogden Codman, and Richard G. Wilson. *The Decoration of Houses*. New York: Mount Press, 2007.

Wilson, Richard G., and Noah Sheldon. *The Colonial Revival House*. New York: H. N. Abrams, 2004.

9

MELODRAMATIC ATTACHMENTS

On Puig's *Boquitas pintadas*

Ben. Sifuentes-Jáuregui

In this chapter, I would like to present some ideas on how melodramatic representation and identification plays out in the work of Manuel Puig. I choose Puig because a signature of his *oeuvre* has been the masterfully crafted literary adaptation of cinematic melodrama forms into his narrative.[1] I also focus on his work because his sensibility to questions of sexuality and gender is the most nuanced among Latin American male writers of his generation. I want to see how a melodramatic tendency can be read in Puig's rewriting of the *novela rosa* [the romance novel] in his *Boquitas pintadas* [translated as *Heartbreak Tango*, 1969].[2] I also want to speculate on why melodrama takes on such a central place in Latin American cultures. In particular, I am interested in seeing how melodrama is delivered as a pedagogical practice, one that is always mediated. This requires that I first discuss certain conceptualizations of melodrama, then proceed to engage its Latin American difference.

Exquisite anxiety

Of course, in discussing melodrama, I begin with a scene of desire. This one comes from María Luisa Bombal's brilliant *La amortajada* (*The Shrouded Woman*, 1948; reprinted in 1992),[3] what I consider a feminist rewriting of the Latin American *novela de la tierra* (regional novel).[4] The text presents Ana María, a dead woman, the shrouded woman, who peeks from her casket, and finally speaks to retell and to reorder her life's history, which moves from her father's oppressive world to the depths of a forest where her husband places her "confinada en [un] mundo físico" ("confined in a physical world")(Bombal, 108). Pregnant by her lover Ricardo, Ana María becomes overwhelmed:

> Deseos absurdos y frívolos me asediaban de golpe, sin razón y tan furiosamente, que se trocaban en angustiosa necesidad. [...]
>
> No me gustaban, sin embargo, las [fresas] que el jardinero recogía para mí en el bosque. Yo las quería heladas, muy heladas, muy rojas y que supieran también un poco a frambuesa.
>
> ¿Dónde había comido yo fresas así?
>
> *(1992: 106–107)*

> (Absurd and frivolous desires sieged me all of a sudden, without reason, and so furi-
> ously that they became an anguished necessity. […]
>
> I didn't like, however, the strawberries that the gardener picked for me in the forest.
> I wanted the cold, very cold, very red, and that tasted a bit like raspberries.
>
> Where had I eaten such strawberries?)

From frivolity to anguished necessity, Ana María feels besieged, and in one fell swoop becomes transformed; her appetite for those "very cold" strawberries hints at a need for a thing that unfailingly exceeds all known possibilities. In other words, Ana María's desire for those cold strawberries masks another desire, which cannot possibly be satisfied for it is unconscious. Ana María seeks to find an answer to her question "Where had I eaten such strawberries?" as a way to quell her desire, enact her memory, and enact her feelings.

We learn that the strawberries she is looking for are those from a childhood story. The "very cold, very red" strawberries are recalled in and as an act of reading, which in turn complicates her entire notion of desire. That is, desire never accesses its true object directly, but rather desire and its object(s) are mediated. On the one hand, Ana María wants "real" strawberries, which, thus, antici-pate a Proustian memory; however, these are unlike the narrator's *madeleine,* which evoke his *petite histoire.*[5] In Proust, the object provokes a memory. Otherwise, Ana María seeks an object that could possibly contain her desires. Her memories, feelings, and history need an object where to converge; that object is found *in literature.* I would suggest that Ana María's "strawberries" turn the screw of interpretation of Proust's *madeleine,* and deconstruct the ways in which memory, feeling, and objects are linked. We might juxtapose these scenes, and consider that gender difference provokes a situation whereby men possess objects, which are followed by certain memories, whereas women possess memories in search of an object for symbolization. So, on the other hand, Ana María is looking for "those strawberries" which are a figure for the act of reading and writing.

Ana María's psychic survival depends on particular claim to a memory and attaching it to an object. Ironically, the object splits into a real and an imaginary (literary) one. While the real strawber-ries might satisfy her physical craving, the literary strawberries allow her to identify narratively, to write herself. Thus this entire scene introduces a series of issues that I would like to consider in this chapter: frivolity as a marker of excessive memory and feeling that becomes reified as or attached to an already, impossible object; (masochistic) identification as an act of submission to an idealized object; also, the structure of "desire consuming desire"; finally, the act of reading and identification.

In this scene of desire, we see that surface becomes an exquisite anxiety that quivers through subjectivity, transforming it; in other words, we have a tendency toward a melodramatic imagi-nation. I chose this scene rather deliberately because, shortly after this scene, Ana María decides that she must abort her child because her father would become angry if he discovers that she had lost her virginity. Her "frivolous" desire for strawberries in fact reminds the reader of her "condition," and also provides a context and dramatic contrast, which heighten the difficult choice to have an abortion. Yet, aren't those uncertain questions about the body and sexuality always at the center of melodramatic representation? This scene of desire transforms Ana María's desire for strawberries for an "anguished necessity," the desire compacted in language itself— and, I would argue that a centrifugal articulation of this vicissitude of desires can be seen as a series of melodramatic effects registered on the body and in language. *La amortajada,* after all, is a cruel pun: *la amortajada,* the shrouded and silenced dead woman; as well as *la amor-tajada,* the woman slashed by love, a woman divided. From here, another argument that we can make about this scene is how emblematic it is of a particular form of literary consumption, which could be called melodramatic identification.

Melodrama, tout court

Melodrama has a special role in Latin American cultures. I have argued that it must not be reduced to a form of excess and frivolous discourse, but rather it represents a form of hegemony in the conceptualization of culture. Melodrama traverses literature, film, and the everyday.[6] I return to Peter Brooks's *The Melodramatic Imagination* (1976), in which he gives us a very useful critical template to appreciate the qualities that give melodrama its dazzling range of signifying meanings. With a psychoanalytic undertone, he underscores the ways that narrative voice and its authorial positioning put a metatexual pressure on a text, ultimately, this narrative voice as a *sujet-supposé-savoir* interprets the text for its readers. I quote freely from the beginning of Brooks's seminal work:

> [In melodramatic representation,] we can observe the narrator pressuring the surface of reality (the surface of his text) in order to make it yield the full, true terms of his story.
>
> *(1976: 1–2)*

> [In analyzing melodramatic texts, it is important to look at] the kind of pressure which the narrator has exerted upon the surface of things. We have in fact been witnesses to the creation of drama—an exciting, *excessive, parabolic* story—from the banal stuff of reality. States of being beyond the immediate context of the narrative, and *in excess* of it, have been brought to bear on it, to charge it with *intenser* significances.
>
> *(2, italics mine)*

> [Dramatic representations of human encounters] tend toward *intense, excessive representations* of life which strip the façade of manners to reveal the essential conflicts at work—moments of symbolic confrontation which fully articulate the terms of the drama.
>
> *(3, italics mine)*

> The desire to express all seems a fundamental characteristic of the melodramatic mode. Nothing is spared because nothing is left unsaid; the characters stand on stage and utter the unspeakable, give voice to their deepest feelings, dramatize though their heightened and polarized words and gestures the whole lesson of their relationship.
>
> *(4)*

In other words, rather than reducing melodrama to just a list of qualities, Brooks is pointing to melodrama as a process: the reflexive or self-conscious nature of the melodramatic text. This self-reflexivity echoes much of the ways in which Ana María struggles to articulate a persona and claim a voice. The "slashed" self leads to an unfolding of the narrator, which enable another level of discourse within the text, very similar to what Brooks calls the "moral occult" in his analysis.[7]

I would like to focus on one characteristic of melodramatic representation that springs up again and again in literary criticism: that is, excess. What is interesting here is distinguishing which of these two discourses is "excessive": is the moral occult the "real" text or a supplement? What is the relation between the text *prima facie* and the other moral textual authority that hovers beneath (or looms over) the surface? These questions help us understand the initial structuration of melodramatic narrative, restoring to melodrama a certain complexity, and not just viewing it as a unidimensional and "frivolous" form. Melodrama goes beyond choosing a hierarchy of signifying registers; rather melodramatic discourse is precisely about capturing the very possibility of representational plenitude—that is, saying and having it all.

The effects that melodramatic excess produces in the text are always multiple and on different levels. These excesses could be of at least two orders, content and literary style, or a collapse of these two. Furthermore, these melodramatic excesses might be read or weighed differently in different cultural contexts. This cultural valence is what lies at the core of my analysis.

Puig's *Boquitas pintadas*

The novels of Manuel Puig are exemplary texts where gender and sexual naming—some would argue, sexual stereotyping—are formed, only to be readily destabilized. Puig's textuality is laden with sexual personae whose subject awareness enters into crisis, a crisis of identification and self-realization. These sexual subjects are fundamentally unstable and in motion, always on the verge of becoming (un)knowable. Their identities are situated in that "in-between" domain of opposition between subjectivity and objectivity, in other words, in fantasy.

As with most of Puig's works, *Boquitas pintadas* (1969) plays with narrative form, which makes it difficult to present a linear narrative of the sequence of events. The text shuttles back-and-forth, showing different episodes in the lives of its protagonists; furthermore, the narrative changes from epistolary to newspaper clips to dialogue to police reports, and so on. In other words, the text plays with different narrative styles, discourses, and points of view, thereby complicating the task of reading and situating the reader in the place of author. These different literary gestures are without doubt the culmination of the Latin American "Boom" novel, which sought to decenter the place of the author, and to replace narratives of cause-and-effect with more challenging literary expressions. Also, the subtitle of the novel is "Folletín," which shows the author's categorization of the text as a "serial drama." The text presents multiple storylines with different protagonists occupying the central role at different moments. Without a doubt, the reader holds in his or her hands a melodrama in the most traditional sense of the word. But unlike most melodramas in search of a happy ending, this one opens and closes with death scenes. Allow me to try to give a synopsis of just one storyline.

After reading the obituary of Juan Carlos, the love of her life, Nélida (better known as Nené) decides to contact his mother Doña Leonor to share with her a note of sympathy. This initial contact grows into a logorrhea where Nené eventually confesses her personal misery living in Buenos Aires away from her provincial hometown of Coronel Vallejos, how her marriage is a failure, how her husband Massa is a loser, and her two boys are ugly. She declares that she wishes that she had stayed with Juan Carlos, that she had been more willing to give more of herself, as well as been more forgiving of his ways. Throughout, readers never have access to Doña Leonor's letters to Nené.

The text goes into a flashback ten years earlier in the town where we learn about the lives of Juan Carlos and Nené, as well as other friends, including Pancho and Mabel. Juan Carlos is a white man, lazy playboy, whose family has lost its money, but still tries to keep up appearances by joining the Club Social. Nené is also white from a working class family; she works for a local doctor, Dr. Aschero, as his nurse trainee, but is often sexually harrassed by him. Pancho is Juan Carlos's best friend. He is a dark-skinned man who works as a construction worker, but who wants to become a police officer. Mabel is Nené's closest friend. She is a "morocha" [dark-skinned/haired woman] from a very wealthy merchant family; she is a school teacher, and she sleeps around secretly with Juan Carlos and Pancho. Also we are introduced to Celina, Juan Carlos's sister, who is overprotective of him and hates Nené. And finally there is Raba, who is Dr. Aschero's maid. She falls in love with Pancho, but eventually stabs him to death because he was unwilling to accept the paternity of their child.

Melodramatic attachments

Juan Carlos has tuberculosis, yet he is desired by every woman in town. Pancho, on the other hand, is presented as a healthy, strapping young man, who seeks "woman advice" from his friend. Nené is incredibly virtuous, but her reputation is tainted by Celina who spreads the rumor that Nené sleeps around with many men. Celina started spreading this lie after Nené, a beautiful blonde with blue eyes, won the annual beauty pageant, "Reina de la Primavera 1936," at the Club Social, of which she was not a member, rather just a guest! Celina's venom spews into the scene again when we discover that those letters which Nené had been sending to Doña Leonor after Juan Carlos's death, were in reality being answered secretly by Celina. She then takes those letters where Nené has confessed that her husband is a loser, and sends them to him. After this, Nené has to decide whether to stay in an unhappy marriage or move on to a more fulfilling life…

These notes give some contours of the text's melodramatic intrigue. Despite the highly episodic nature of *Boquitas pintadas*, its fragmentariness attempts representing that all-encompassing and totalizing narrative of melodrama. What is not said, what is simply insinuated has as much a narrative force as the parts of the story we do hear; what is not said functions as a melodramatic unconscious. For example, Doña Leonor's responses to Nené, which are totally absent from the text, carry as much weight as Nené's own words; in their absence, Doña Leonor's letters (really, Celina's) structure the opening of the text, giving it a strong moralistic tone. The imaginary nature of those letters supplies the reader a certain melodramatic tension; in fact, at one point, Nené asks perversely if Celina isn't really the one answering her letters, then she just laughs off this idea as some silly paranoia. It is difficult to survey all the currents and conflicting events of the many storylines and their accompanying literary gaps. Therefore, I shall focus on a few particular scenes or events, which will help us understand questions of melodramatic force, gender attachments, and Latin American cultural practices.

Heterosexual pleasures

In her letters to Doña Leonor, Nené becomes increasingly undone: "Para que contarle las cosas que me pasan por la cabeza. […] Si usted me viera lo mal que ando, no tengo ganas de nada. Ni a mi marido ni a los chicos puedo comentarles nada, así que ni bien terminé de darles de almorzar a los chicos, hoy me acosté así pude por lo menos no andar disimulando" (Puig [1969] 1989: 20). ("Why tell you the things that go through my mind. […] If you could only see how badly I'm doing, I don't have energy to do anything. I can't say anything to my husband or kids; today I wasn't able to finish giving the kids lunch, I went to bed so that I didn't have to go around faking it.") Nené is overburdened with a whole series of conflicting issues running through her mind regarding her past choices and her miserable, present condition. Nené is tired of faking her happiness; she can no longer talk to her family, so she turns to Doña Leonor as a confidante. With her, Nené hopes to find solace and comfort: "[O]scurezco bien la pieza. Entonces puedo hacer de cuenta que estoy con Usted y que vamos a la tumba del pobrecito Juan Carlos y juntas lloramos hasta que nos desahogamos" (21). ("I darken the room well. Then I can pretend that I am with you and that we go to poor little Juan Carlos's grave and that we cry together until all our sorrows are gone [*nos desahogamos*, literally: we undrown ourselves].") Nené is living through an impossible catharsis. Whereas she cannot replace the lost object of affection because it was always a phantasmatic one, I would suggest that she is experiencing an extreme melancholia: at one moment she asks whether there can be another man who could "me dé otra vida"? (32). (translated both as: give her life again?, or give her another life?) Her memory and rewriting of "Juan Carlos" stands as an idealization of the "perfect" man; so what Nené loses upon learning of his death is not the real man, but

119

rather the fiction of his perfection. (Here we can see how, as with Ana María's "cold strawberries," Juan Carlos also becomes a memory-object needed to encapsulate Nené's desires.) This loss is so devastating because it renders visible the flimsiness of her present life with her husband and kids. Nené can no longer stop wondering "what if" things had gone differently. She ends the letter asking "Pero ahora no sé qué me pasa, pienso si Celina no hubiese hablado mal de mí, a lo mejor a estas horas Juan Carlos estaba vivo, y casado con alguna buena chica, o conmigo" (21). ("But now I don't know what's happening with me, I think about if Celina hadn't spoken badly about me, perhaps at this time Juan Carlos was still alive and married with a good girl, or with me.") Once more, Nené is unable to comprehend what is happening to her. Her blindness points again to her melancholic condition: her love object might be replaced, but her "love fiction" can't be interpreted or refunctioned.

Her sixth letter to Doña Leonor ends with a newspaper clipping that announces her having won the "Queen of Spring 1936" Pageant at the Club. The news report documents a *temps perdu* in which Nené and Juan Carlos danced a waltz where they "convincingly showed that 'the strength of love overcomes every obstacle'" (22). After describing the dance, the article's reporter asks rhetorically, "Cabe, aquí, la reflexión filosófica: ¡cuántos, cuántos solemos andar por este histriónico mundo llegando diariamente al final de la etapa sin lograr saber qué papel hemos estado desempeñando en el escenario de la vida!" (22–23). ("It is fitting here to make a philosophical reflection: How many, how many of us tend to go around this histrionic world coming everyday to its final stages without knowing what role we are acting out in the play of life!") This question freezes the situation in which Nené finds herself. She is trapped in a scenario without knowing her role or her lines. Here is the melodramatic predicament: a woman who has lost the love of her life, as well as her lines (her script) to express that loss. It's as if melodrama only teaches its protagonists the language of love and attachment, never the language of loss or the releasement of the love-object. Importantly, the news article's own frivolity and excess describes the life of its readers as a theater and a stage. Nené's fetishistic attachment to the newspaper clipping as a precious object that contains her story and desires informs us of the ways in which she acts (out) and performs her femininity, her class, and other social and cultural desires. This article that reports the *petite histoire* of her waltz with Juan Carlos as an act of love-conquering-all bears the power of History. Thus, she kisses it repeatedly before she slips it into the envelope and holds it dearly against her bosom before sending the letter. Now the question that follows would be, if this text was so valuable, why does she give it away? The easy answer would be that the (il)logic of melodrama would call for such a contradictory action; it can be seen as an act of pain and pleasure, of sublime surrender. I think that another equally important reason behind Nené's giving away the precious document is her need to reenact the *petite histoire* of the pageant and the dance by circulating it, by disseminating the story once again in the melodramatic fantasy of reliving it.

The final letter to Doña Leonor bears all the classic oppositions of a melodrama. Nené informs the other woman that she does not want her to get a bad impression of her life:

> …pero ante todo debo hacerle una aclaración: yo gracias a Dios tengo una familia que ya muchos quisieran, mi marido es una persona intachable, muy apreciado en su ramo, no me deja faltar nada, y mis dos hijos están creciendo preciosos, aunque la madre no debería decirlo, pero ya que estoy en tren de sinceridad tengo que decir las cosas como son.
>
> *(33)*
>
> …but before anything I must make one thing clear: I thank God that I have a family that many would like to have, my husband is a respectable person (*intachable*, literally,

Melodramatic attachments

"unmarked"), very esteemed in his profession, he doesn't leave me wanting anything, and my two sons are growing beautifully, even though a mother shouldn't have to say it, but since I am riding a wave of sincerity, I must state things are they are.

With this final letter, Nené makes an effort to normalize her life with a "happy ending." This letter is a radical departure from the last few, which had crescendoed into a cruel and devastating accusation and invective against Celina, that she was a spinster that no man wanted because she had always been a "whore." Nené's final letter goes on to narrate her life as a young woman in the town of Coronel Vallejos, her family, her education and values, and how she was offended by Juan Carlos for "dating" an older woman. This was the reason why she broke up with him: "Y me quedé con la espina para siempre" (35). ("And I was left with a thorn [in my heart] forever.") Nené conjures up a classic melodramatic trope, the thorn in the heart, which in Hispanic letters goes back to Quevedian masochistic dilemma of wanting the very thing that would hurt the Self most. Interestingly, through all this, Juan Carlos remains unmarked, free from any sense of responsibility.

I would like to contrast this scene of Nené's complete and blind commitment to Juan Carlos with her disillusionment in discovering the "real" Juan Carlos. On a visit to Buenos Aires, Mabel stops by and sees Nené; the occasion for Mabel's visit has to do with her making preparations for her upcoming wedding. Nené was always reluctant to have old friends from Coronel Vallejos stop by to visit: she was embarrassed that her house didn't look elegant enough. Indeed, Mabel's compliments about Nené's apartment do not go unqualified: "Tenés muy linda la casa—la voz de Mabel se escuchaba encrespada por la hipocresía" (196). ("'You have a lovely home,' Mabel's voice was heard roughened up by hypocrisy.") The very middle-class pretensions that Nené lives by come back to haunt her. Changing the topic of conversation, Nené quickly asks to see a picture of Mabel's fiancé: however, both women thought about Juan Carlos's perfect facial features and avoid seeing each other in the eyes for a few moments. This is a crucial scene because for the remainder of the visit, the text embroiders the memory of Juan Carlos into everything that the women say. He becomes the object of discursive exchange and disidentification (woman-woman bonding and rivalry).[8] Both women continue chatting and refer to her husband or fiancé as a "loser" or "runt," implicitly as someone less perfect than Juan Carlos. I would argue further that reflecting on Juan Carlos's face initiates and produces an injured narcissism, which the women will try to heal throughout the chapter. This is inevitable because as we have seen before, Juan Carlos is an impossible narrative of idealized masculinity contained in a tubercular body. Yet, as Mabel asks, "[por qué] las mujeres parece que cuando tienen algo con Juan Carlos ya no lo quieren dejar más" (208). ([why do] women, it seems, when they have something with Juan Carlos, they don't want to let him go anymore.) What is this stubborn attachment that regulates "women's" lives vis-à-vis Juan Carlos's presence?

So the two women begin reminiscing about the past:

[Mabel:] —¿Cuánto tiempo hace que no tomamos un mate juntas?

—Añazos, Mabel. Más o menos de la época que salí Reina de la Primavera, … y estamos en abril del 41…

Ambas callaron.

—Nené, dicen que todo tiempo pasado fue mejor, ¿Y no es la verdad?

Callaron nuevamente. Las dos encontraron para este interrogante una respuesta. La misma: sí, el pasado había sido mejor entonces ambas creían en el amor. Al silencio siguió el silencio.

(197–198)

[Mabel:] "How long has it been since we have had *mate* together?"

"Many years, Mabel. More or less around the time that I was named Queen of Spring, and now it's April of '41…"

Both women remained silent.

"Nené, they say that the past was always better, isn't it the truth?"

Again, they were silent. Both women found an answer to this question. The same answer: yes, the past had been better because then both women believed in love. Silence was followed by silence.

This scene of sharing food (or drink) provokes and stirs memories of a romanticized past. Again, we find Nené clinging to the time when she was elected Queen as a monument to her life's history. It is a point of reference to which she returns because it reminds her of when she still "believed in love," but ironically it is the very moment that marks the undoing of her love affair. Being named "Queen of Spring" is highly melodramatic because sexually it represents a moment of heightened femininity, a celebration of fertility and womanliness, where "love conquers all." This scene gets recalled over and over because it rescues an Edenic scene prior to the end of Nené's affair with Juan Carlos. It is a *tableau vivant* which freezes time and works against it, always delivering the security of femininity, idealized and perfect love, and History. In some important ways the Queen scene becomes a narrative of the moral occult, for it contains all the narratives of normativity by which Nené (like other wannabes) lives for and by. Now, while Nené's silence is easy to read in the above passage, Mabel's is much more difficult to decipher. She too is thinking about Juan Carlos, and how she was forced by her parents not to see him in any social setting because of running the risk of getting infected with tuberculosis. (Mabel's parents had found out about Juan Carlos's condition through his unethical doctor, their family friend.) Mabel's silence (read: discretion) is quite threatening to Nené.

To break that silence and to change the topic of conversation, Mabel asks Nené whether or not she is happy. This question paralyzes Nené: "Nené sintió que un contrincante más astuto la había atacado de sorpresa. No sabía que responder, iba a decir 'no puedo quejarme', o 'siempre hay un pero', o 'sí, tengo estos dos hijitos', mas prefirió encogerse de hombros y sonreír enigamáticamente" (198). ("Nené felt that a more astute opponent had attacked her by surprise. She didn't know what to answer, she was going to say 'I can't complain,' or 'there is always a but,' or 'yes, I have these two little boys,' but instead she prefered to shrug her shoulders and smile enigmatically.) Initially, we might wonder what kind of paranoia would frame such a question—are you happy?—as an attack. Yet, it is within the logic of the melodramatic text where questioning happiness would get construed as a challenge to subjectivity; it would be like asking, "Are you a 'good mother' (in the place of a 'happy' woman)?" or, bluntly, "Do you even exist?" Nené's options seems rather strange: "I can't complain" would suggest "I don't want to protest," opening the door to further inquisition by the "astute opponent"; moreover, the refusal to protest and, instead, to withstand the pitiful and disappointing status of her life signals a masochistic tendency so prevalent in melodramatic textualities. "There is always a but" would signify some form of defeat—and melodrama necessitates a clear moral "yes"; and finally, "yes, I have these two little boys," which would seem the best option given that it satisfies her social accomplishment as a "mother," but which would inadvertently displaces her happiness as a "woman." So rather than the possibility of further entrapment or of reducing her life to being a "mother" (which would cover-up her womanly passion for Juan Carlos), Nené opts for the narrative of silence, sealed with a smile. In the games of melodrama, silence eloquently trumps vulnerability.

Melodramatic attachments

Appropriately enough, Nené and Mabel are listening to a *radionovela* about the love affair between a wounded soldier and a married woman who is caring for him. The woman has a dilemma: to cure him completely and having him rejoin his troops and fight for country, or to hope that his wounds do not heal so that he may stay longer at her side. The women's conversation is sprinkled with such platitudes as "Mabel, no me digas que hay algo más hermoso que estar enamorada" (203). ("Mabel, don't tell me there is something more beautiful than being in love.") The radio melodrama signifies powerfully on the lives of both women, where Juan Carlos is imagined as the wounded soldier, and each woman occupies the place of the nursing woman in the drama.

All of a sudden, the conversation turns back to Juan Carlos, but with brutal honesty on Mabel's part. Mabel's earlier, elliptic comment about why women do not want to leave Juan Carlos is answered by Nené with naiveté: "—Es que él es muy buen mozo, Mabel. Y muy comprador" (Puig 1989: 208). ["It's because he is so handsome, Mabel. And very charming."] Mabel responds: "—Ay, vos no querés entender" (208). ["Oh well, you just don't want to understand.] The *radionovela* continues playing in the background, and minutes later, Nené asks:

—Pero, che Mabel ¿qué es lo que yo no quiero entender que vos decís de Juan Carlos?—Nené seguía jugando con su propia destrucción.

—Que las mujeres no lo querían dejar, …por las cosas que pasan en la cama.

—Pero, Mabel, yo no estoy de acuerdo. Las mujeres se enamoran de él porque es muy buen mozo. Eso de la cama, como decís vos, no. Porque hablando la verdad, una vez que se apaga la luz no se ve si el marido es lindo o no, son todos iguales.

—¿Todos iguales? Nené, vos no sabés entonces que no hay dos iguales. […]

—Mabel, vos qué sabés, una chica soltera…

[…]

—Nené ¿vos no sabés la fama que tenía Juan Carlos?

—¿Qué fama?

Mabel hizo un movimiento soez con sus manos indicando una distancia horizontal de aproximadamente treinta centimetros.

(209)

"But, Mabel, what is it that I don't want to understand that you are saying about Juan Carlos?" Nené continued playing with her own destruction.

"That women didn't want to leave him… because of the things that happen in bed."

"But Mabel, I don't agree. Women fall in love with him because he is handsome. All that about the bed, what you are saying, no. Because speaking the truth, once the lights go out, you can't tell if your husband is handsome or not, they are all the same."

"All the same? Nené, you don't know then that no two men that are the same. […]

"Mabel, what do you know, you are a single girl…"

[…]

"Nené, don't you know about Juan Carlos's reputation?"

"What reputation?"

Mabel made a vulgar gesture with her hands showing a horizontal distance of about twelve inches.

Nené's naiveté shines clearly throughout this exchange. Her question about the source of Juan Carlos's attraction is described as a "[play] with her own destruction." So, in effect, what Nené is doing is "playing dumb" to represent herself as an ingénue or "innocent" in the most traditional sense possible. Her question performs a studied ignorance, an ignorance used to manipulate and effect a very limited identity of a "married woman." She insists upon having a certain authority and knowledge about men by the sheer fact that she is married, and that Mabel is disqualified from "knowing" because she is a "single girl." This labeling promotes the myth of virginity; the only physical knowledge a virgin can have about a man is his handsome or ugly face, which disappears when the lights go out.

Throughout we have seen how Nené performs class and gender conceits; her performance is a claim to normalization as a means of upward mobility, and which allows her access and entrance to a higher social class through a highly aestheticized femininity. In this polarized world of appearances and superficial representations, melodrama would necessarily be the operating form of discourse. Therefore, what happens when Mabel crudely displays the *raison d'être* and enthusiasm for Juan Carlos—his twelve-inch manhood—is only to be expected:

> —¡Mabel! me hacés poner colorada de veras—y Nené sintió todos sus temores violentamente confirmados. Temores que abrigaba desde su noche de bodas, ¡hubiese pagado por olvidar el ruin ademán que acababa de ver!
>
> —Y eso parece que tiene mucha importancia, Nené, para que una mujer sea feliz.
>
> —A mi me dijo mi marido que no.
>
> —A lo mejor te hizo el cuento…
>
> (209–210)

> "Mabel! You are really making me blush." And Nené felt all her fears violently confirmed. Fears that she harbored since her wedding night. She would have paid anything to forget that vile gesture she just saw!
>
> "And it seems that *that* is very important, Nené, for a woman to be happy."
>
> "My husband told me it didn't matter."
>
> "Maybe he took you for a ride…"

Mabel reveals the object motivating every woman's desire for Juan Carlos—even Nené's. Mabel's words and gesture confirm any suspicion about Juan Carlos's playboy lifestyle. More importantly, this specific reference to the size of his penis brings up a body of evidence, which shatters through Nené's melodramatic narrative of "love conquering all." The penis, its very physicality, as an object emerges in the place of the moral occult; the endowed penis becomes a symbol of authority by breaking the superficial and excessive textuality of melodrama, and erecting a monument to itself *as* the moral occult. Hence, conventional heterosexuality with all its clichés lies at the heart of melodramatic discourse—and it regulates all questions of erotics, gender identication, and sexual practices. Essentially, Nené's violent reaction *betrays* her secret and greedy desire for a big virile member "since her wedding night." Her desire seems to be mitigated by her husband's "short story": here, the penis/phallus, not only affirms itself, but can also reverse its claims. Finally, we see that this masculinist and sexist ideology, which relates female pleasure proportionally to penis size, circulates as a doctrine in *Boquitas pintadas*, and in much melodrama. In Latin American literature and culture, it is heavily represented and promoted in such gender constructions as *machismo* and *marianismo*, which on the surface seem oppositional, but really are complementary—each is found in the interiority of the other—and

Melodramatic masculinity and pedagogy

Nené is not only an object (of desire) for Juan Carlos, but also for Pancho. In a bordello, Pancho sees a prostitute with blonde hair but with dark pubic hair, and then,

> Pancho sin saber por qué se imagino a Nené dormida con las piernas entreabiertas, sin vello en el pubis, como una niñita, y a la tienda en verano iba sin medias; Nené no usaba alpargatas: sus pies estaban calzados en zapatos de taco alto; no transpiraba: no tenía que fregar como las sirvientas; Nené no era una india bruta: hablaba como una artista de radio y al final de las palabras debidas no olvidaba de pronunciar las eses.
>
> *(79)*

> Without knowing why, Pancho imagined Nené sleeping with her legs slightly apart, without pubic hair, like a little girl, and who went to the store without stockings in the summer; Nené didn't use espadrilles: her feet wore high-heel shoes; she didn't perspire: she didn't have to clean house like the maids; Nené wasn't a stupid Indian: she spoke like a radio personality and never forgot to pronounce the final *s* at the end of words.

Pancho's gaze moves through Nené's body and infantilizes her. To begin with, her name "Nené" makes her always a little girl, thus it deprives her of maturity and change. She is stuck, like or because of her name, in an infantile idea of gender and culture, that she can never fully escape and be realized as a woman. As a child, she must obey or be disciplined. Pancho's pedophilic gaze rests on her virginity, and fetishistically moves to her well-heeled feet, then to her whiteness, and finally to her speech. This movement narrates unconsciously ("sin saber por qué") and contains Pancho's desire. It is a narrative of upward mobility that links gender, sexuality, and race constructions: truly, gender and sexuality are articulated *through* race. Racial difference is always used to heighten or debase notions of gender (femininity and masculinity) and sexuality (passion). Nené's white body represents for Pancho a cultural fetish and capital. When Pancho seduces Mabel, he is literally turned on by her class status, noting that, even though she is a *morocha* (dark-skinned/haired), she is "a female school teacher"; this would bring him class clout when others in town see them walking together. Also, later, when Mabel is having her liaison with Pancho, her racist remarks are used to heighten the passion of the moment, while comparing him with Juan Carlos. [9] (Another example of this use of race and class vocabulary happens between Raba and Pancho, which I will discuss at the end.) These racial, gender and class subject features intersect throughout the novel, constantly destabilizing the idealized and real subjectivities of the characters.

After leaving the bordello, Pancho meets up with Juan Carlos. They get into a conversation about Juan Carlos's fooling around; Pancho warns him that he is going to get caught. He asks,

> ¿por qué no se conformaba con Nené? Juan Carlos le dijo que ni bien consiguiera lo que ambicionaba, se acabaría Nené, y pidió a Pancho que jurara no contarlo a nadie

[...] Pancho le preguntó si seguiría con Nené en caso de conseguir ese trabajo [prometido por Mabel]. Juan Carlos le contestó que esa pregunta la hacía porque no sabía nada de mujeres. Pancho quería aprender pero fingía burlarse. Juan Carlos dijo que Nené era igual a todas, si la trataban bien se envalentonaba, si la trataba mal marchaba derecha.

(81)

[w]hy he didn't settle for Nené? Juan Carlos told him that as soon as he got what he wanted, Nené would be no more, and asked Pancho to swear not to tell anyone. [...] Pancho asked him if he would continue with Nené in case he got that job [that Mabel promised to help him get]. Juan Carlos answered him that he asked that question because he didn't know anything about women. Pancho wanted to learn but he pretended to make fun of the whole thing. Juan Carlos told him that Nené was like all women: if one treated her well, she became haughty; if one treated her badly, she walked a straight line.

It seems clear that Pancho is surveying his chances to get Nené for himself without violating his friendship with Juan Carlos. It is a classic homosocial exchange. The playboy makes it absolutely clear that Nené isn't more than just another conquest: She is a donjuanesque statistic, therefore, dispensable. Ironically, as we well know, Nené can't be part of his catalog of seductions because she never gives it up to Juan Carlos. She remains virtuous, nevertheless Juan Carlos's scandalous speech acts—like those of his eponymous literary father, Don Juan—mark her body and write her story differently.[10] I would argue that Nené resorts to the conventional and the conservative narratives of heteronormativity out of and because of this scandalous narrative of a "marked woman" that Juan Carlos (as well as Celina) imposes onto her. Additionally, what is striking about this scene is Juan Carlos's matter-of-factly cynicism, with which he performs his masculinity. The arrogance of *machismo* is that much more intolerable precisely because its cynical demands—"swear not to tell anyone." Furthermore, not only does he impose his views onto others, but expects to be emulated willy-nilly. That Pancho "wanted to learn" about "women" meant that he needed to perform masculinity like Juan Carlos; this repetition of the same shows the narcissistic nature of male homosociality. Furthermore, I stress that this narcissism carries the cost of homogenizing of identity, erasing race, class and gender considerations, and thereby ultimately guaranteeing the rise of a masculinist language parallel to melodrama's "so what!" mode as a hegemonic, social and cultural discourse. What is essential to recognize is that Juan Carlos's sexist narrative circulates alongside and intersects the very narratives of abnegation, domesticity and heteronormativity that Nené and other women in the text use. In other words, masculine speech acts and the realm of masculinity looks quite melodramatic, as well a pedagogic.

Pancho will take Juan Carlos's lesson to heart and seduce Raba and then Mabel, all the while secretly desiring Nené. Yet this lesson of "doing whatever a man damn pleases"—or this lesson of "whatever," for short—will lead Pancho to his death. Raba discovers that she is pregnant with Pancho's child. At that time, she also finds out that he is sleeping around with Mabel. One evening while he is leaving Mabel's home, she stabs him to death. The lesson of "whatever" (or "anything goes") fails the ethical test of responsibility to the other. Doing (like saying) "whatever!" aggressively dismisses the other.[11] Such a forceful dismissal leaves the other in solitude, but not without agency. In this case, Raba answered Pancho's dismissal with fatal violence against him. In perfect melodramatic symmetry: he effaces her and she kills him.

Bound lessons

As a way of concluding this chapter, I would like to return at the inherent question of masochism suggested by Nené's willingness to accept her unhappy life rather than follow her passions, or even the masochism that we see in the spectacular masculinities that pop up throughout the text.

I have explained masochism through the following formula: "I" exist because "I" don't; in other words, the Self comes into being through her/his own debasement and de-facement. This logic coincides with melodrama's enterprise of wanting to present all points of view—what I refered to earlier as "representational plenitude." Nené manages this masochistic transformation in being reduced to a script—or rather resigned to living—the life of the "good wife." In accepting their respective gendered scripts, we continue seeing how melodramatic subjects—Nené, Mabel as well as Juan Carlos and Pancho—become bound to melodrama's pedagogical lessons and imperative.

The melodramatic text's expressed desire for a "fuller" expression promoted the pleasure of and in contradiction. As we have seen, this contradictory logic adds a crucial and critical element to the discursive power of melodrama, that is, pedagogy. Melodrama instructs its readers, oftentimes of the most conservative lessons, such as "it is okay to be in an unhappy marriage," "you shouldn't complain for having a life of misery," "not being sexually satisfied is really not a problem," "use and abuse women: they'll like it" and so forth… Melodrama captures these lessons, nevertheless, it also permits the possibility to refunction some of those narratives. In a perverse way, Raba's defense of her "honor" by killing Pancho reflects the prevalence of those lessons, and how they are not always contained within specific gender, race and class categories, but rather permeate and travel across them. This proliferation of melodramatic rules and codes creates a dynamic sense of culture that pushes against some more traditionalist and conservative versions of it. Considering and cultivating this dimension of the melodramatic text might give new life to old objects—it might also offer new forms to old cultural desires.

Notes

1 The culmination of this literary practice is his well-known *El beso de la mujer araña* [*Kiss of the Spider Woman*, 1976], where the protagonist narrates classic Hollywood films to make the time in prison less harsh. His first novel, *La traición de Rita Hayworth* [*Betrayed by Rita Hayworth*, 1968], shows Puig's fascination with film and its relation to literature by framing each chapter with an epigraph from different 40s and 50s Hollywood movies. In most cases, the obsession is with the Hollywood diva.

2 Manuel Puig, *Boquitas pintadas* (Barcelona: Editorial Seix Barral, 1989 [1969]). The English translation of the novel is by Suzanne Jill Levine (New York: Penguin Books, 1973); however, for the purpose of this close reading of the novel, all translations from the text are mine.

3 María Luisa Bombal, *La amortajada*. 4th Edition (Barcelona: Editorial Seix Barral, 1992), 108. All translations are mine.

4 For a discussion of the Spanish American regional novel, in particular the relationship between autochthony and identity, see Carlos Alonso's *The Spanish American Regional Novel: Modernity and Autochthony* (Cambridge: Cambridge University Press, 1990). My choice to characterize Bombal's novel as a *novela de la tierra* has much to do to show how melodramatic discourse inhabits other literary genres, not only romances, erotic writing and so forth.

5 "Et tout d'un coup le souvenir m'est apparu. Ce goût, c'était celui du petit morceau de madeleine que le dimance matin à Combray (parce que ce jour-là je ne sortais pas avant l'heure de la messe), quand j'allais lui dire bonjour dans ma chambre, ma tante Léonie m'offrait après l'avoir trempé dans la son infusion de thé ou de tilleul." Marcel Proust, *À la recherche du temps perdu*, I, (Belgium: Bibliothèque de la Pléiade, 1966), pp. 46–47. The memory appears all of a sudden to the narrator—the madeleine, the object, provokes a memory.

6 See my essay "¡…es tu madre!: Pedro Infante and Melodramatic Masculinity [in *Letras Hispanas*, Vol. 11, 2015, pp. 134–146).

7 Ibid., 5. In Ana María's case we might need to reconsider the meaning of the moral occult. Whereas traditionally the moral occult can be seen as a dichotomous tension between "good" and "evil," the moral occult—emphasis on the occult—may have a different meaning for the female protagonist. For her the moral occult might just be her (new, previously hidden) morality that is finally coming to the light.

8 This scene where both women reflect on Juan Carlos's face could be read as perversion of Eve K. Sedgwick's reformulation of erotic triangulation and homosocial desire; however, it is important to consider the asymmetrical nature of the exchange. [*Between Men: English Literature and Male Homosocial Desire*. (New York: Columbia University Press, 1985), especially. "Introduction" and Chapter 1.] Sedgwick argues that a relation "between men" gets transacted though the body of a woman—following what Gayle Rubin calls the "traffic in women"—as a way to dissipate any homoerotic tension or desire. The woman-in-between normalizes and "heterosexualizes" male-male bonding. In this scene of a man-in-between, however, we encounter not so much woman-woman bonding, but rather woman rivalry and disidentification. This rivalry presents a social and political challenge to Adrienne Rich's notion of the lesbian continuum.

9 The seduction scene, which uses eating figs as a not-so-subtle metaphor for cunnilingus (*Boquitas pintadas*, 163–167), is laden with racial and racist metaphors used by Pancho to heighten sexual desire as well as by Mabel to challenge tacitly Pancho's sexual prowess. I would argue that Pancho as a protagonist in this novel, which takes place in Argentina (the "whitest" nation of the hemisphere and with very few blacks), almost makes it seem that racial polarization that Puig sets up is a deliberately exaggerated narrative presence in the text; it is a melodramatic casting.

10 See Shoshana Felman's classic study on Don Juan and his scandalous performatives, *The Literary Speech Act: Don Juan with J.L. Austin, or Seduction in Two Languages*, translated by Catherine Porter. (Ithaca, NY: Cornell University Press, 1983).

11 See Freud's discussion on love and its opposites in "Instincts and Their Vicissitudes," *Standard Edition* XIV.

Works cited

Alonso, Carlos J. *The Spanish American Regional Novel: Modernity And Autochthony*. Cambridge: Cambridge University Press, 1990.

Bombal, Luisa Maria. *La amortajada* [1948]. 4th Ed. Barcelona: Editorial Seix Barral, 1992.

Brooks, Peter. *The Melodramatic Imagination*. New Haven, CT: Yale University Press, 1976.

Felman, Shoshana. *The Literary Speech Act: Don Juan With J.L. Austin, or Seduction in Two Languages*. Ithaca, NY: Cornell University Press, 1983.

Freud, Sigmund, and Philip Rieff. "Instincts and Their Vicissitudes." *General Psychological Theory: Papers On Metapsychology*. New York: Collier Books, 1963.

Proust, Marcel. *À la recherche du temps perdu*, I. Belgium: Bibliothèque de la Pléiade, 1966.

Puig, Manuel. *Boquitas pintadas* [1969]. Barcelona: Editorial Seix Barral, 1989.

Puig, Manuel. *El beso de la mujer araña*. 1st Ed. Barcelona: Seix Barral, 1976.

Puig, Manuel. *La traición de Rita Hayworth*. 1st Ed. Buenos Aires: Llibres de Mirall, 1968.

Sedgwick, Eve Kosofsky. *Between Men: English Literature and Male Homosocial Desire*. New York: Columbia University Press, 1985.

Sifuentes-Jáuregui, Ben. "Special Section: On Masculinities, Latin America and the Global Age: ¡ …es tu madre!: Pedro Infante and Melodramatic Masculinity." *Letr@S Hispanas*, vol. 11, 2015, pp. 133–146.

10

SEX WITH ALIENS

Dramatic irony in Daína Chaviano's "The Annunciation"

Matthew David Goodwin

Science fiction in Latin America has a long tradition going back at least to the eighteenth century, and while each Latin American nation has something of a science fiction tradition, it has been Mexico, Argentina, Brazil, and Cuba that have been the most prolific and so the most studied. Latin American science fiction has been well charted by scholars of Latin American literature and there are various studies of the history of the genre, in addition to anthologies and bibliographies. Rachel Haywood Ferreira has, for example, examined some of the most influential works of science fiction primarily from the nineteenth century in her study *The Emergence of Latin American Science Fiction*. J. Andrew Brown's thematic study *Cyborgs in Latin America* (2010) as well as a collection of essays *Latin American Science Fiction: Theory and Practice* (2012) edited by J. Andrew Brown and M. Elizabeth Ginway explore more recent works of fiction and film. The most commonly used bibliography is Darrell B. Lockhart's *Latin American Science Fiction Writers: An A-to-Z Guide* (2004) and the most representative anthology is *Cosmos Latinos: An Anthology of Science Fiction from Latin America and Spain* (2003) edited by Andrea L. Bell and Yolanda Molina-Gavilán. As it does in all of science fiction, sexuality appears as a common subject in Latin American science fiction, even while women writers have not been equally acknowledged in the field. Nevertheless, as Andrea Bell observes, "women are in the minority among Latin American sf writers, but they are an active minority and have been since the 1960s" (Bell and Molina-Gavilán 2003: 444). Two of the most prominent women writers who often write about sexuality have been Argentina's Angélica Gorodischer and Cuba's Daína Chaviano, both of whose works has increasingly been translated into English. This chapter examines the short story 'The Annunciation" (2003) by Daína Chaviano who frequently joins sexuality, religion, and mythology in her novels and short story collections.

Daína Chaviano's "The Annunciation" rewrites the annunciation story contained in the Christian bible and transforms it into science fiction.[1] In the original version of the annunciation in the gospel of Luke, the angel Gabriel comes to Mary to tell her that she will have a child and name him Jesus. The child will be conceived through divine intervention: "The Holy Spirit will come on you, and the power of the Most High will overshadow you" ("The Birth of Jesus Foretold"). Though Mary is frightened she accepts her fate. According to the Christian tradition, the conception of Jesus is a miracle in which the supernatural enters history and alters nature. Chaviano's "The Annunciation" retains key aspects of this original story. The central characters are all there (Mary and Gabriel, with Joseph on the margins), the story seems to be set in the same time and place, and the basic plot of an annunciation of the future pregnancy of Mary remains. The story, however, diverges sharply by changing the background scenario as well as the development of the plot. Most importantly, Gabriel is not an angel of God, but a space alien. He is a member of a group of aliens who have come to Earth and, it seems, have been interacting with humans for a while. And Gabriel comes not only to announce the conception of Jesus, but to enact it as well. Over the course of the story, Gabriel seduces Mary, they have sex, and Jesus is conceived. Rather than a divine father, Jesus has a super-powerful alien father.

Sex with an alien is as complex as sex with a human, and it involves all of the typical elements: the choice of partner, the control of reproduction, the impulses expressed, the biological systems involved, the intricacies of sexual pleasure, cultural norms and taboos, emotional resonances, and so on. But sex with an alien is different as well, and it is this difference that makes it so that the alien-human sexual encounter can be used to represent and explore alternate sexual interactions. Science fiction writer Samuel Delany who often explores sexuality in his work says in an interview: "That's what is liberating about alternative or alien sexualities —they are new and fantastic." He offers an anecdote as an example:

> When I went to my very first sf convention, which was Worldcon in 1966, I'd already published six or seven novels. A very young man came up to me and said, "You wrote a book called *Babel-17?*" I said "Yes, indeed I did." He said, "That stuff, where three people get together and they all do it at once . . . is that possible?" I said, "Yes." And he gave an immense sigh of relief and turned around and walked away. At which point I thought, "I am doing *something* right."
>
> *(Scott Westerfeld 2001)*

For Delany and others, science fiction provides an imaginative space, as well as the potential cover of allegory, to deal with at times difficult or taboo topics such as simultaneous multiple partners or same-sex encounters. Chaviano's "The Annunciation" certainly provides an alternate view of Mary's sexuality since she is converted into a fully human, fully sexual, person quite different from the Mary of the Christian tradition. The sexual encounter between Mary and Gabriel is in this respect an affirmation of female sexuality. At the same time, there is more to the story. Alcena Madeline Davis Rogan writes in regard to Delany: "… alien sex in Delany's account is not just a deconstructive treatment of the limits of desire—it is not, in other words, merely a catalog of strange and wonderful beings and their various interactions, a celebratory treatment of difference as such; although it certainly is also this" (2004: 450). Any complex depiction of sex will include the violence to women that has been a deeply entrenched part of the history of human sexuality. Such is the situation of "The Annunciation," in that Gabriel has come to Mary to announce that she will have a child and then he proceeds to enact this plan. He has not come to ask her if it's acceptable to have a child with him. In this light, the story, though it has comedic elements, is something of a science fiction horror story as well, an alien seducing a young woman for the benefit of the invading powers. Mary may be transformed through sexual liberation, but she is not in control of the reproductive act in which she is involved. That power is firmly in the alien hands of Gabriel.

This sexual power dynamic is constructed in a unique way in the story, specifically, through dramatic irony. Irony is a varied concept. In its most recognizable form, it is a rhetorical device in which what is overtly said is the opposite of what is meant. At other times, it refers to situations or events that are the opposite of what is expected. Irony can also be a more general perspective on life, a worldview, or even a philosophy (Colebrook 2004: 1). This chapter looks at a particular literary sort of irony called dramatic irony, understood to be a situation in which the reader knows or understands something that a character in the story does not (Baldick 2015). Dramatic irony opens up a kind of tension between the expectations of what will occur in the story, with a character believing one thing, and the reader another. Because of this tension, dramatic irony is common in tragedies, as well as in horror stories. By examining the role of dramatic irony in "The Annunciation" it can be seen how rich, subtle, and provocative the story is in regard to gender and sexuality and how it uses dramatic irony to develop a complex view of the alien-human sexual encounter.[2]

The primary dynamic of the dramatic irony in the story is formed between the character Mary and an ironic reader, or a reader who is performing the function of making an ironic reading the story.[3] The irony turns on the issue of the identity of Gabriel, with Mary and the ironic reader having different understandings of who Gabriel is. Mary believes that Gabriel is an angel of God while an ironic reader knows, according to the world of the story, that Gabriel is a space alien. In order to enact an ironic reading, the ironic reader must, more than anything, get the science fiction references. Some of the relevant references are that Gabriel says that he is from another planet, he seems to have special powers, the aliens have a spaceship, he uses modern scientific terminology, and so on. Mary hears these pieces of information, but she either does not understand them outside of a religious context or she completely does not understand what Gabriel is saying because the words or ideas are so foreign. The ironic reader, however, who understands the information revealed by Gabriel will come to the reasonable conclusion that Gabriel is a space alien.

Any individual with an ear to popular culture will be able to get the references and so this will include many readers. However, there will be a handful who are outside of popular culture streams. Even though the science fiction references are neither esoteric nor obscure, there certainly could be readers who will not get the science fiction references. The non-ironic reader, like Mary, will either misunderstand what Gabriel is saying or completely not understand what he is saying. There is also the possibility of a reader simply missing the references, an inattentive reader, for example. This is possible to a degree given that the story is a rewriting, and so the reader might just assume that the basic premise of the original story holds for this new version. All of these scenarios, and certainly many others, are possible. However, once the references are recognized by a reader as science fiction references, then the ironic reader will most reasonably choose to construct a science fiction account of what is happening in the story. In the words of Wayne Booth, this is an instance of "stable irony" in that there is little doubt as to the presence of irony and that "once a reconstruction of meaning has been made, the reader is not then invited to undermine it with further demolitions and reconstructions" (1974: 6). The dramatic irony set up between Mary and the ironic reader does not change in the story. Once the reader sees the dramatic irony, the ironic reader will believe that Gabriel is an alien throughout the story. By way of contrast, the dramatic irony of the story should be distinguished from the literary device of narrative ambiguity in which a story offers multiple explanations of some strange event but does not ultimately give clear support to one of the explanations, thereby keeping a significant degree of uncertainty.[4] In this case of dramatic irony, although there are two possibilities openly expressed as to the identity of Gabriel, it is clear in the world of the story that one of the identities is the true one.

Given how close, at least initially, the story is to the original, having the knowledge that this story is a rewriting of a bible story makes it a deeply rich experience. It is likely that many readers will have that experience. Juan Carlos Toledano Redondo writes that the "Annunciation is a myth/story that belongs with the Christian collective unconscious." He argues that in "Christian countries," and I think Cuba is included here, that most readers will know the original story even if they had never read the bible (2007: 37). Knowledge of the basics of the original story is definitely needed to understand some of the surprise and even comedy of the new story. However, it is not required to read the story ironically. All that is needed for that is that the reader recognizes the references to the supernatural, in particular, knowing that Mary believes something different from the ironic reader as well as having a basic idea as to what an angel is.

One of the first examples of dramatic irony that is dependent on a reader recognizing certain science fiction and supernatural references is the physical description of Gabriel:

> He was tall, and luminous white hair fell freely over his shoulders. His eyes sparkled red.
>
> His clothing was even odder than his physical appearance. He wore a tunic tightly fitted to his chest and fastened by a gold belt. Shoes that shone like polished bronze encased his feet. A transparent globe, similar to an aureole, surrounded his head. The stranger took the halo in his hand and gently placed it on a chair before speaking.
>
> *(Chaviano 2003: 262)*

This description of Gabriel is consistent with the traditional religious figure of an angel, though without the wings we typically associate with angels. The whiteness, the shining gold, the halo, all contribute to the reader recognizing Gabriel as an angel. Gabriel's name itself, as reference to the biblical Gabriel, makes the recognition secure. And later, and although he may be look "odd" from Mary's perspective, it is discovered that he is nevertheless attractive to her and she sees him as "handsome," in a way that is consistent with the conception of beautiful angels. At the same time, this description is also consistent with a science fiction humanoid alien in a classic "space-man" outfit. From the perspective of Mary, Gabriel is a religious figure, while for the ironic reader, this is a science fiction figure. One aspect of his appearance, the space helmet, makes the description of Gabriel particularly clear as science fiction. The oblique science fiction reference to a space helmet is apparent to the ironic reader as one cannot, after all, take a halo off.[5] And because this space helmet as well as the entire outfit is very much at odds with religious imagery, a comedic light-hearted tone is created for the ironic reader.

It is important here that this description of Gabriel is expressed not by Mary nor Gabriel, but by the narrator. It is the narrator who refers to the helmet as a "halo" rather than a "helmet." When Gabriel speaks to Mary and describes who he is and why he is there, he uses overtly science fiction terms such as "spaceship." The narrator, however, speaks using the language of Mary. In other words, the narrator's description is focused through the perspective of Mary who sees Gabriel as an angel of God. This general standpoint of the narrator, in fact, continues throughout the story, as the narrator calls Gabriel an "angel" rather than a being, alien, or some term more appropriate to science fiction. The narrator is significant in the construction of dramatic irony since it is the words of the narrator that are read ironically, that is, they point to another level of meaning. When the narrator says Gabriel is an "angel" the ironic reader does not take the narrator at its word and so the ironic reader reads it as "alien." The ironic reader, however, typically takes at face value the words of Mary and Gabriel. And, because Gabriel is the one who is himself an alien and is in the know about who the aliens are and what they are doing, the ironic reader believes what Gabriel says concerning them. The ironic reader is then correlated with Gabriel, at least in terms of what is believed concerning the aliens. The overarching constellation of characters, narrator, and reader is set up then between Mary/narrator and the ironic reader/Gabriel.

Mary believes that Gabriel is an angel and a messenger of God. He is visiting her to enact the divine plan of the conception of Jesus. The ironic reader, however, understands something different about why Gabriel is impregnating Mary. According to Gabriel, the aliens are intending to create a great and wise being who will become a leader of the aliens. He says that Jesus "is called to succeed

Sex with aliens

the great Iab-eh on the throne towards the march to Infinity," with Iab-eh being the current leader of the aliens (Chaviano 2003: 203). Furthermore, Jesus will serve the aliens in another way: "The fruit of this union will lead Iab-eh's spaceship to our own planet. The information must get there, and our wise men have decided upon the mixture of both races" (205). The aspect of Jesus leaving the planet is a sly reference to the ascension of Jesus into heaven. Furthermore, while the nature of the "information" is not completely clear, it is a reasonable guess that the aliens want genetic information of some kind. With these statements, it is known that Mary is simply a pawn in a larger cosmic purpose. The aliens want something from humanity and they are intent on getting it. At the same time, they believe themselves to be superior, and indeed, there is, like many alien narratives, a colonial element to the alien encounter. The aliens in "The Annunication" have come to Earth and are attempting to culturally influence the humans, all the while thinking that the natives do not understand. Gabriel says concerning humanity: "You haven't understood the half of our moral teachings. Instead of applying them, you've converted them into religion" (205). In this way, there is a sinister tone created by the overall plan of the space aliens that is very much not divine. It is true that there is a persistent tone of comedy in the story that is created through the dramatic irony. The comedy is in part based on the incongruity of science fiction and religious elements, that is, making use of the implicit taboo to reinterpreting a sacred text as popular literature. In addition, pleasure is generated for the ironic reader by understanding the references to science fiction that are somewhat hidden. However, the sinister tone resulting from ethical problems with the alien plan grow further.

Gabriel's general perspective on Mary is that she is inferior and his speech is often condescending towards her. In one instance when Mary is expressing how much she is attracted to him, Gabriel responds: "'Mary!' he exclaimed, moved, 'little thing'" (Chaviano 2003: 207) (*Pequeña criatura* in the original). The name he calls her is clearly one of condescension. The overall import of the line is that it indicates that her feelings or her experience are not actually important, that they are of a child, not of a superior being like himself. It is also significant to note that Mary's understanding of who Gabriel is and why he is visiting Mary is not simply based on her religious worldview. Gabriel believes that she is unable to completely understand what is happening, and though he does presumably tell her the truth in some respects, he also lies to her, manipulates her, and takes advantage of her misunderstanding of him as a messenger of God. This is seen in the seduction scene that follows their initial meeting:

He held her hands and kissed them.

"They are as soft as a dove's feathers," he said.

She blushed slightly.

"You're exaggerating. Surely, the wings of the celestial cherubs are much softer."
"Cherubs?" he let slip. "Oh, yes! But don't you believe such a thing. Of course, heaven
has much that is lovely, but I've never seen anything there as beautiful as your smile."

(205)

Gabriel, somewhat comically, forgets that Mary sees him as one of the angels and makes a mistake in questioning her about the angels. The façade comes quickly back as he continues manipulating her though her own beliefs. The dramatic irony in this case is not just formed through a belief system, but because Gabriel is lying, that is, Mary believes something different from the ironic reader because she is being misled. Gabriel also spins certain aspects of the aliens' plan as regards to Joseph:

"When must my husband know about this?" she asked him.

"As soon as he returns. At this moment he lies asleep along the road that leads to Nazareth."

Mary felt suddenly upset.

"Sleeping along the road to Nazareth? Heavens!"
"Do not be alarmed. The great Iab-eh is watching over his sleep."

The young woman was calmed.

(203–204)

Gabriel concludes the discussion of Joseph in a way that it seems Iab-eh is taking care of Joseph, whereas it seems more likely to assume that it is the aliens who are keeping Joseph asleep so that Gabriel can seduce Mary. Joseph is simply an obstacle to the overall plan of the aliens. Gabriel's lies and manipulation of the truth give further sign that something sinister is going on, and it begins to put the ironic reader in a difficult situation. It's not that the ironic reader begins to doubt Gabriel in terms of his identity. It is that the trust put in Gabriel does not extend to other aspects of his character. The text is constructed in some ways like the situation of a narrative with an unreliable narrator, except in this case, we have an unreliable character. In both of these cases, the reader must rely on a source of information that is untrustworthy or unethical in some way. That is, the ironic reader has a hard time trusting Gabriel will act justly, even though his is the voice of truth, or at the least the voice that the reader must follow.

Behind the alien's plans to impregnate Mary is a scientific principle that the aliens are following, made clear when Gabriel claims: "Eugenics has never failed, and you have been chosen" (Chaviano 2003: 203). As an early twentieth-century theory and social practice of attempting to "improve" humanity through breeding, Mary obviously does not know what eugenics is. The ironic reader, however, discovers that the aliens have been watching her, presumably studying the population, to determine the best candidate. Gabriel does not state why exactly Mary is chosen, but like many eugenics programs, it can be guessed that it have something to do with her race, as she is described as having white skin (202) or it may be because she is "beautiful" as Gabriel describes her[6] (203). It is also worthwhile speculating about who is really going to benefit from this pairing. It is possible that the humans might benefit from their union, assuming that Jesus has children, or it may be that the humans will benefit through the wisdom of Jesus which will help guide humanity. However, the magnanimity of the aliens seems thin, especially given Gabriel's lies, and so it seems that Jesus will probably most benefit the space aliens. The ultimate goal, after all, is that he leaves the planet to bring information to the home planet. What matters in eugenics is the product of sex, not so much the partners. Ultimately, it is significant that Gabriel and the aliens believe in eugenics, what has been generally discredited as a pseudo-science and as being responsible for some of history's worst atrocities.[7] That the space aliens believe in it is a testament to how far away they are from a contemporary ironic reader.

In addition to the reprehensibility of eugenics, there is also the seduction scene which provides more cause for the growing cognitive dissonance with Gabriel as the bearer of truth in the story. The overall feeling Mary has in the story is fear. Throughout the entire encounter, Mary is shown to be experiencing fear through a variety of descriptors: "troubled," "upset," "disturbed," "alarmed," "anguish," and "invaded by some vague and unknown fear." This fear never leaves and is only waylaid by her submission to him. Mary's reaction to the seduction fluctuates, and she responds both by submissively accepting the seduction on account of Gabriel's position of authority as an angel of God, and by resisting the advances of Gabriel:

Sex with aliens

"Your dress, doesn't it bother you?"

"Not at all! She protested weakly.

"But you are wearing so many things," he sighed.

"No, I assure you. Only what you see and…" lowering her voice modestly, "a very light tunic beneath."

"You should take it off. It's hot."

"The air is cool…"

His hands delicately undid the ties of her dress, and it fell to the floor.

Mary didn't dare protest for fear of offending him.

(Chaviano 2003: 206)

The implication here is that while she does in fact resist Gabriel, ultimately, Gabriel is able to take advantage of her submission to him. Furthermore, although resistant to his advances and although she does not completely understand what is happening, Mary is also sexually aroused. She experiences desire and responds sexually to Gabriel, feeling her body heat up and even going so far as to say "I feel so good that I don't know how I could have lived all these years so far from you" (207). She also seems to have a degree of playful sexual agency, as for example, when the narrator states: "She looked obediently at him. The angel of the Lord was certainly handsome" (204). This portrayal of Mary is quite different from the chaste Mary of the Christian tradition who would presumably not think such things. In the context of the portrayal of Mary throughout history, as Juan Carlos Toledano Redondo notes: "This fresh…new version of the Annunciation represents the possibility of women's enjoyment of sex by making the most pious of women enjoy it" (38). And Yolanda Molina-Gavilán places the alternate view of Mary in the context of the Latin American concept of *marianismo* which holds the chaste Mary as the ideal woman: "Chaviano's version of the annunciation attacks the concept of *marianismo* by challenging one of its most sacred bases, Mary's sexuality" ('Eugenic Orgasms?'). The depiction of Mary as a fully sexual person is an important liberation from past portrayals of women's sexuality.

From the perspective of the ironic reader who sees the lies, the manipulation, and the overall goal of the aliens, however, the sexual encounter seems more sexual coercion than "making love," the phrase that the *Encyclopedia of Science Fiction* uses as a description of the scene. While opinions will vary as to how to categorize the sexual encounter, it does seem to have elements of a rape. Given that Mary completely trusts Gabriel and is submitting to him because of religion, her ability to give consent here is almost non-existent. I think the best comparison, and one that is certainly evoked by the story, is the abuse of power by a religious leader. In these cases, a religious leader convinces a young person to have sex because it is God's will or something of the sort. The coercion in these cases does not happen through physical force but through social coercion, using religion as a weapon. Even still, there is certainly the possibility of force in the background. The seduction of Mary is not physically violent, however, Gabriel, as an alien, seems to have super-powers as well as a mandate to impregnate Mary. If Mary were to try to resist physically we can assume that she would have little chance of getting free.

In the act of sex itself, the very religious language of the event creates a distance between the ironic reader and not only Mary but Gabriel as well. While Mary conceives of the sex act through religious language, the ironic reader reads it as orchestrated sexual coercion. There are two elements of the scene which Gabriel explains to Mary using religious language. First, as Gabriel explains: "The sacred breath of Iab-eh will reach you through my person" (Chaviano 2003: 203). Iab-eh, as Chaviano explains, "is a personal version of the name Yahweh," indicating that Mary believes the act to be coming from God ("Planeta"). In addition, the sacred breath can certainly be read as a reference to the holy spirit in the original biblical story. The purpose of the breath of Iab-eh is mysterious. Perhaps it gives pleasure like a narcotic, which it seems to for Mary, or it may cause or aid in conception which would be consistent with the bible story. The second part is the "divine rain" which Gabriel says will come to Mary, bringing to mind the rape of Danae by Zeus who transforms into a golden rain (203). The ending of the scene has the two in bed without clothes, and Mary is "penetrated by an undreamed sensation of height and vertigo," and "…a hot shower had bathed the deepest part of her seed" (207). The ironic readers will recognize the sex and orgasm, Mary however also seems to be also having a religious experience. Ultimately Mary embraces the angel in the moment of orgasm: "'Gabriel,' she grabbed him tightly by the shoulders, 'You are…!'" (207). The implied conclusion to the exclamation is that he is a "God," giving a playful tone to the scene. Mary's capacity for sexuality runs quickly into a quasi-mystical sexual experience as the narrator notes: "The door of the kingdom opened before both of them" (207). But these expressions of sexuality, pleasure, playfulness, and mystical union do not negate the fact that Gabriel is posing as a religious authority and taking advantage of a young woman. In other words, if Gabriel were not using religious language and going along with Mary's belief that he is an angel, then she more than likely would have been more skeptical of Gabriel's intentions. By the same token, Gabriel's obvious enjoyment of the seduction and sex, as well as his declaration that he "loves" Mary (205), does not excuse him of sexual coercion.

Mary is in many ways representative of religion in the story. She believes and has faith, but this is not the problem with religion. The problem with religion in the story is the use of the religion by Gabriel. Likewise, Gabriel is in many ways representative of science, coming from an advanced and technological society. But the problem is not science per se, it is the use of eugenics, that is, the social policy surrounding science. In this way, the story is not a wholesale critique of either religion or science. The critique arises when these institutions are implemented in a way like the story so that they take control of the power of reproduction from women and put it into the hands of religious and scientific leaders.

The basic disjunction through religious language that is created between Mary and the ironic reader never does go away in the story. Rather, the story adds another layer of disjunction between the ironic reader and Gabriel. The ironic reader is initially paired with Gabriel as the voice of truth in the story. However, the correlation between the ironic reader and Gabriel seems untenable since he is depicted negatively, as the perpetrator of sexual coercion who uses religion as a weapon. Ultimately, the tensions of the story are never resolved, giving the story a powerful effect, and in addition to the provocative genre-blending of science fiction and religion, an ironic reading of the story reveals an element of horror.

Notes

1 The story originally appeared in 1983 as "La Anunciación" in the collection *Amoroso Planeta* (*Planet of Love*) (1983). The story was translated for inclusion in *Cosmos Latinos: An Anthology of Science Fiction From Latin America and Spain* (2003). Chaviano was born in Cuba in 1957 and moved to Miami, Florida in 1991. She explains that the move was in part motivated by the restrictive environment for writers: "There came a time when I felt I could not write what I wanted without posing a danger to myself. I had to take care of what I said. I hid to avoid signing those letters that the government forces artists to sign, saying they condemn this or that, even if one disagrees. It was very hard. I could not continue to live in a place where I was forced to say what I didn't want to say. I always refused to do it, but there came a time when I got tired of hiding and decided to leave" (Silvia Viñas 2010).

2 Linda Hutcheon in *Irony's Edge: The Theory and Politics of Irony* writes that "Ironic meaning comes into being as the consequence of a relationship, a dynamic, performative bringing together of different meaning-makers, but also of different meanings, first, in order to create something new and… to

Sex with aliens

endow it with the critical edge of judgment" (1994: 56). In other words, irony is not something you discover, but something you create in dialogue with the text. This perspective also has the consequence of bracketing the slippery questions of whether a text is truly ironic or what the author's intentions were. For this reason, I focus my analysis through the concept of an "ironic reader."

3   In my conception of this term, the "ironic reader" simply performs the function of reading ironically. Outside of this qualification there are no other implied characteristics such as whether they are religious or not, believe in angels or aliens in real life, and so on.

4   An example of narrative ambiguity is Isaac Bashevis Singer's short story "A Wedding in Brownsville" (1968) in which it is not clear whether the strange things happening to the protagonist are the result of him being dead, drunk, or the victim of food poisoning. All of these scenarios are possible, however, the story never makes it so that one is obviously true.

5   According to Wayne Booth, the first step in determining whether some part of a story is ironic is to reject the literal meaning, and the recognition of incongruity enables that to happen: "If he is reading properly, he is unable to escape recognizing either some incongruity among the words or between the words and something else he knows. In every case, even the most seemingly simple, the route to new meanings passes through an unspoken conviction that cannot be reconciled with the literal meaning" (1974: 10).

6   The mention of eugenics evokes the influence of eugenics programs in the Caribbean that not only supported the idea that the "white race" was superior but also supported an ideal of physical beauty. In Cuba, for example, "The government… made gestures of support, such as the beautiful baby contests, held by the Ministry of Hygiene and Welfare between 1915 and 1933" (Schell 2012: 2).

7   The sort of eugenics depicted here would be what is called "positive eugenics." According to Philippa Levine "Eugenic policies encompassed both "positive" and "negative" practices. Both focused on reproduction, but whereas negative eugenics stressed preventing it, positive eugenics sought to increase reproduction among the fit and socially valuable" (2017: 7).

Works cited

Baldick, Chris. "Irony." *The Oxford Dictionary of Literary Terms*. 4th Edition. Oxford, UK: Oxford University Press, 2015.

Bell, Andrea. "Science Fiction in Latin America: Reawakenings." *Science Fiction Studies*, 26:3, 1999, pp. 441–446.

Bell, Andrea L. and Yolanda Molina-Gavilán, eds. *Cosmos Latinos: An Anthology of Science Fiction from Latin America and Spain*. Middletown, CT: Wesleyan University Press, 2003.

"The Birth of Jesus Foretold." Luke (1:26–38). *The Holy Bible, New International Version*. Biblica Inc., 2011.

Booth, Wayne. *The Rhetoric of Irony*. Chicago, IL: University of Chicago Press, 1974.

Brown, J. Andrew. *Cyborgs in Latin America*. Basingstoke, UK: Palgrave, 2010.

Brown, J Andrew, and M. Elizabeth Ginway, eds. *Latin American Science Fiction: Theory and Practice*. New York: Palgrave, 2012.

Chaviano, Daína. *Amoroso Planeta*. Havana: Editorial Letras Cubanas, 1983.

Chaviano, Daína. "The Annunciation." In *Cosmos Latinos: An Anthology of Science Fiction from Latin America and Spain*. Edited by Andrea L. Bell and Yolanda Molina-Gavilán. Middletown, CT: Wesleyan University Press, 2003, pp. 202–207.

Chaviano, Daína. "Planeta." Received by Matthew David Goodwin, 3 June 2017.

Colebrook, Claire. *Irony*. London: Routledge, 2004.

"Daína Chaviano." *Encyclopedia of Science Fiction*. www.sf-encyclopedia.com/entry/chaviano_daina. Accessed 4 April 2017.

Davis Rogan, Alcena Madeline. "Alien Sex Acts in Feminist Science Fiction: Heuristic Models for Thinking a Feminist Future of Desire." *PMLA*, Special Topic: Science Fiction and Literary Studies: The Next Millennium, 119: 3, 2004, pp. 442–456.

Haywood Ferreira, Rachel. *The Emergence of Latin American Science Fiction*. Middletown, CT: Wesleyan University Press, 2011.

Hutcheon, Linda. *Irony's Edge: The Theory and Politics of Irony*. London and New York: Routledge, 1994.

Levine, Philippa. *Eugenics: A Very Short Introduction*. New York: Oxford University Press, 2017.

Lockhart, Darrell B. *Latin American Science Fiction Writers: An A-to-Z Guide*. Westport, CT: Greenwood Press, 2004.

Molina-Gavilán, Yolanda. "Eugenic Orgasms? A Fresh Look at Christian Mithology: Daína Chaviano's The Annunciation." www.dainachaviano.com/paper.php?lang=en&item=45#.WW1DkumQxPY

Schell, Patience A. "Eugenics Policy and Practice in Cuba, Puerto Rico, and Mexico." *The Oxford Handbook of the History of Eugenics.* Edited by Alison Bashford and Philippa Levine. Oxford, UK: Oxford University Press, 2012.

Singer, Isaac Bashevis. "A Wedding in Brownsville." *Short Friday and Other Stories.* New York: Farrar, Straus and Giroux, 1968, pp. 190–206.

Toledano Redondo, Juan Carlos. "The Many Names of God: Christianity in Hispanic Caribbean Science Fiction." *Chasqui*, 36:1, 2007, pp. 33–47.

Viñas, Silvia. "Hispanista: Interview with Daína Chaviano, Part I." Uptown Literati, 2010.

Westerfeld, Scott. "Space Cowboy: An Interview with Samuel R. Delany." *Nerve: Speculative Sex: The Science Fiction Issue*, 2001. www.nerve.com/dispatches/westerfeld/spacecowboy

11

VILLAIN OR VICTIM?

Undermining the memory of Japanese Peruvians in Augusto Higa Oshiro's *Gaijin (Extranjero)*

Shigeko Mato

"[M]y reading public is usually academic. Unfortunately, that's how it is," says Augusto Higa Oshiro, the author of *Gaijin (Extranjero)* (2014).[1] While he tried to publish the novel with Alfaguara, a leading Spanish-language publishing house, which can reach massive numbers of potential readers in the Spanish-speaking world, he is aware that he does not write for a mass audience. According to Higa, the problems that he intends to expose in his works and his "afflicted prose" ("la prosa castigada") do not attract the masses. At first glance, the author's awareness that his audience is limited to academics and that his "afflicted prose" is perhaps inaccessible for general public, seems to suggest that *Gaijin* should be read, not as a form of popular culture, but rather as a literary work of high culture mainly for critics in academia.

However, Higa does not invoke academic exclusivity in the novel. On the contrary, by employing an ordinary Japanese Peruvian woman's voice that orally recounts what she witnessed and experienced as a child, the author offers an ordinary oral practice of narrating anecdotes and experiences that challenges such exclusivity. His creation of an oral practice of telling stories about the past can be interpreted as a popular cultural form that dovetails with a new tentative definition of popular culture as "unauthorized culture" (Parker 2011: 165–67). In his article, "Toward a Definition of Popular Culture," Holt N. Parker refers to popular cultural productions as the works and practices of "those not recognized" as authors, experts, and professionals by institutions and authorities (165). Parker's new definition allows us to look into the following questions. Which institution(s) has (have) the authority to label which popular cultural forms as authorized culture (official culture) (166–67)? What happens to the resisting or rebellious function of popular culture against the official culture of dominant groups, once popular culture ceases to be unauthorized (166–67)?

Reading the oral practice of telling the past presented in Higa's *Gaijin* as a site of unauthorized popular culture can lead the reader to observe its resisting function that questions the unified collective memory of Japanese Peruvians constructed by the Japanese Peruvian Oral History Project (JPOHP). The JPOHP can be an example of showing how a popular cultural practice of oral history, once a site of unforgotten and unrecognized Japanese Peruvian voices against official dominant history, has been recognized and institutionalized as an official project by scholars and professionals. This recognition from the JPOHP may have brought an end to this oral history as popular culture, and thus as a problematizing force to the official dominant culture (Parker 2011: 167). If *Gaijin* is read side by side with the oral stories documented by the

JPOHP, the oral practice of telling the past in Higa's fiction serves to reveal what voices have been excluded in the JPOHP.

The JPOHP was established in 1991 by a group of Japanese Peruvians and their families who were interned in the U.S. relocation camps during World War II. Their intention was to record and preserve the memory of their unjust deportation and internment, as well as aiming to educate themselves and the public about the Japanese Peruvians' wartime experiences, while also demanding justice and redress ("What is the JPOHP?"). Thanks to the efforts of the JPOHP and the Campaign for Justice: Redress Now for Japanese Latin Americans! (CFJ) formed in 1996 ("Campaign"), the U.S. government officially offered an apology to the former Japanese Peruvian internees and their heirs (Small 2000: 250). The majority of the former Japanese Peruvian internees accepted a letter of apology and the redress of USD$5,000 per person from the U.S. government in 1998 (Small 2000: 253, "Campaign"), while some of them, seeing this as inappropriate and insulting, declined the redress (González "The Japanese-Peruvians"). The redress was only one fourth of the amount that the former Japanese American internees were granted in 1988.[2] Therefore, the surviving Japanese Peruvian internees of the Crystal City internment camp, the JPOHP and their attorney (Karen Parker), on behalf of Art Shibayama (Isamu Carlos Arturo Shibayama) and his brothers, filed a petition to the Organization of American States in 2003, demanding a more just and acceptable redress. To date, the Organization of American States has only considered the petition admissible, but has not yet given any answers to the plaintiff ("Report No 26-06," González "El drama"). While the Japanese Peruvians' pursuit and fight for justice still continues, the JPOHP and CFJ also continue to document their oral stories in order to raise public consciousness about this little-known part of WWII history and demand that the U.S. government grant the former internees a more just and proper redress.

There is no doubt that documenting the former Japanese Peruvian internees' testimonial oral stories and disseminating their stories to their community and others, has served to empower them in persevering in their efforts to obtain a sincere apology and proper redress from the U.S. government. However, in the process of collecting their oral stories with these focused goals in mind, the JPOHP tends to have created a predominant voice of victimhood, disclosing the sufferings and hardships caused by the U.S. government's violation of human rights, with the full cooperation of the Peruvian government. Without question, they are victims and survivors of institutionalized wrongdoing, yet by collecting and recording *their* side of this WWII history as victims and survivors, the JPOHP, whether intentionally or unintentionally, seems to have constructed a homogeneous and unified memory of victimhood that formulates a victim-victimizer binary relation that forgets other possible voices that do not fit in this binary model. If the JPOHP remains unconscious of this tendency for binary construction, it may fall into the peril of promoting an exclusionist vision of authenticity, projecting their stories as more "authentic" and "truer" than others. This tendency for exclusionist memorialization has been discussed by many theorists. In one work, Jeffrey K. Olick and Joyce Robbins have indicated how memory is used as a site of contestation for dominance in which "people and groups fight hard for their stories" (1998: 126), perceiving such a use of memory as a "vehicle[s] for establishing their power or, perversely, lack of power" (1998: 127). Olick and Robbins warn theorists and practitioners of memory studies and activists who use and present memories for the purpose of socio-political change to be able to recognize that recording memories as a unitary collection of "our own story" can lead to a reductionist demand for "an inversion of some past or a new monumental interpretation" (1998: 128).

Although the ultimate motivation and goal of the JPOHP have been to win fair redress, the JPOHP might also contemplate Olick and Robbins' concerns and consider the following questions, if it were concerned with avoiding becoming a reductionist project. Are there any alternative voices among Japanese Peruvians that do not see themselves and the former internees merely as victims? Are there any Japanese Peruvians who do not conform neatly to the profile of a Japanese Peruvian who underwent the confiscation of properties by the Peruvian government, the deprivation of human rights, deportation, and relocation to the U.S. internment camps? If so, how can these different voices be included in the project? How can these different voices not be forgotten, just as the unified voice of victimhood is recorded in order not to be forgotten? If the alternative voices are remembered along with the unified voice, how can and should the JPOHP pursue their goal of obtaining justice?

Many scholars who explore a relationship between oral history and collective memory have already responded to similar issues raised in these questions. For instance, Lynn Abrams draws attention to the responsibility of oral historians who attempt to compile people's recollections into coherent collective scripts, showing her concerns about the loss of individual memories which do not concur with the dominant cultural and socio-political agendas of their oral history projects (2010: 99–100). Anna Green also criticizes this trend among oral historians who "are increasingly focusing upon the ways in which individual recollections fit (often unconscious) cultural scripts or mental templates" and has underscored the importance of recognizing this tendency: "[O]ral history is converging with collective memory studies, within which individual memory is [...] subsumed under 'collective memory'" (2004: 35–36).[3] Similarly, in his study on the reconstruction and representation of diverse Cape Town residents' memories of apartheid in the post-apartheid present, Sean Field also asserts that although reconstructing a unified memory of the apartheid past brings a sense of solidarity to the fight against institutionalized oppression while developing public and political anti-apartheid consciousness, it also occludes other memories that do not share the same political agenda. Field warns oral historians to make sure "to record shared *and* unshared memories and interpret how these have shaped moments of unity *and* disunity" and "to think through how both shared *and* unshared memories influence the framing of dominant community stories" (2008: 117).

Higa's *Gaijin* displays "both shared *and* unshared memories" that exist in the Japanese Peruvian community, encouraging the reader to engage in observing how tensions between the two help constantly problematize the fixity of a dominant collective memory. Higa creates tensions between "shared *and* unshared" memories through a story about a Japanese immigrant, Sentei Nakandakari, who works in Lima in the 1930s and 1940s after arriving in Peru in 1923 from Okinawa. Throughout the novel, Nakandakari is depicted as an ambitious, greedy, shrewd, immoral, and heartless antihero who does anything to get what he wants and tries to separate himself from the Japanese immigrant community. However, he is, at the same time, described as a victim of the Peruvian and U.S. governments' anti-Japanese operations and persecution who shares the same sufferings with the other Japanese immigrants. Analyzing how *both* the avariciousness/immorality *and* victimhood of the protagonist are remembered in the novel, this study attempts to examine how the representation of the story about Nakandakari can offer an alternative memory which does not neatly align itself with the images of the Japanese and Japanese Peruvians' experiences projected through the JPOHP. By kindling this sort of negotiation with the dominant collective memory of the Japanese Peruvian community, this study also aims to argue that the story of Nakandakari, though it is a fiction, can serve to invite the reader to look into how and why a remembering of such a vicious and greedy Japanese immigrant should be included in the Japanese Peruvians' collective memory.

The novel opens with a scene in which Nakandakari gets off the bus in Lima, in rags and worn-out shoes, carrying no luggage, in order to start his new life, after having worked in haciendas north of Lima for eight years. He walks around the city and finds the marketplace where he visits his old friend, Ryochi Onaga, the narrator's father. Onaga provides Nakandakari with clothes, food, and a place to stay and helps him get financial credit from the Japanese loan association to get a street-vending cart.[4] It takes Nakandakari an agonizing six weeks to sell a shirt for the first time. At the moment of this first sale, he is overtaken by a frenzied exultation with the idea of selling, and he is now more determined than ever to make money. He does everything to attract customers, no matter how embarrassing his selling tactics can be. The narrator observes: "nada le hería, nada lo arredraba, sin pasado, sin tradición, sin memoria, Sentei Nakandakari no tenía ningún interés, excepto vender su mercancía, puesto que necesitaba salir cuanto antes de la pobreza, conseguir el rabioso dinero" (Higa 2014: 18). Nakandakari makes a fool out of himself, playing the *samisén*,[5] singing, and showing off his acrobatic flips in order to get attention. Although his customers repudiate or insult him because he is Japanese, and the other Japanese immigrants try to persuade him not to attract people's attention and to keep a low profile because of the increasing anti-Japanese sentiment, he continues to conduct his pretentious and flashy "performances" to make money.

Eventually, Nakandakari's vending cart business becomes steady, and he hires a young Japanese assistant Saburó Nakashima. Meanwhile, he finds a young Peruvian woman, Misha Arango, who works at a restaurant in Chinatown. He goes there for lunch every day at the same hour and sits at the same table to look at Misha. He is not physically or emotionally attracted to her, but he desires to marry her for his future business maneuverings. Misha's father is a primary school teacher and practicing Catholic who preaches Catholic doctrine on the street. In order to convince Misha's father that Nakandakari is also a believer and good man for his daughter, he pretends to be a devout Catholic and attends mass. He finally convinces her to marry him through his relentless stalker-like pursuits described as follows: "De manera que la conquistó, no con delicadezas, sino con sus férreos modales y el delirante acosamiento" (Higa 2014: 29). After successfully marrying Misha, his cart business flourishes with the help of his wife, who is friendly and enthusiastic about selling. He manages to pay off his debt and establish his own shop in Lima. But their marriage is nothing more than a convenient legal union for his economic success and is a forced pact for Misha. Nakandakari never has sex with his wife because he looks down upon her race: "en su irremediable orgullo, Sentei Nakandakari no se permitía tener intercambio carnal con mujeres que no fueran de su propia raza" (39). In their sexless marriage, however, Misha gets pregnant and gives birth to a son. It turns out that she and Nakandakari's Japanese assistant, Saburó Nakashima, have been having an affair, but their extramarital relationship does not bother Nakandakari. On the contrary, he continues to work with his wife and assistant without any jealous or angry feelings and focuses on his next move: to convince Misha's mother to run a brothel business with him, despite strong complaints and disapproval from the Japanese immigrant community.

Even with the increasing antagonism of the general public against the Japanese, and in spite of the moral disdain toward Nakandakari from his own community, Nakandakari's businesses keep growing. In fact, during the anti-Japanese riots rocking Lima, unlike the other shops owned by Japanese which are looted, Nakandakari's businesses are not attacked because his Peruvian wife and her mother are the legal owners. His manipulative calculations save him from losing his businesses, and they continue to grow even after the riot incident. However, his calculations cannot win over the outbreak of the Pacific War, followed by the attack on Pearl Harbor. He has to close his businesses and go into hiding for more than three and half years (1,320 days) until the end of the war. At the end, he dies alone, hating everyone and abandoned by everyone.

Nakandakari's story, from his arrival in Lima to his death, is told by an elderly woman, a daughter of Ryochi Onaga, his old friend from Okinawa, who crossed the Pacific Ocean together with him, to work in haciendas north of Lima as farm laborers. However, the narrator's identity is not revealed until the middle of the novel. At first, opening the novel and reading the first several sentences, the reader, without knowing who the narrator is, is led to believe that the story is and will be told from the perspective of an omniscient narrator in the third person. Higa employs a third-person omniscient narrative voice which predominates throughout the novel, but also inserts the narrator's direct commands in the second person in the opening section, as well as a narrative voice in the first person singular and plural in some areas.

By inserting direct commands, Higa sets out an atmosphere of storytelling in which the narrator tells the story of Nakandakari directly and orally to the receptor (reader/listener). The narrator interrupts the flow of the third-person narrative voice with her command, telling the reader to be sure to understand how Nakandakari appears in Lima: "Y de un modo u otro, *tenlo por seguro*, no era más que un ser insignificante, sin más equipaje que la ropa que llevaba puesta, un pantalón y una camisa desvencijada, sobre unos zapatones toscos, y un sombrero norteño" (Higa 2014: 9, my emphasis). The narrator repeatedly accentuates how destitute and ragged he is when he arrives in Lima, telling the reader to remember what he looks like: "*Recuérdalo de una vez,* así fue cómo llegó a estas calles atiborradas, al escabroso edificio del Mercado Central, y no estaba indefenso, ni sonreía, ni hablaba, solo miraba con sus ropas trajinadas, y el sombrero norteño, oliendo a bosta" (11, my emphasis). In her last command, she repeats the same: "Así fue como llegó, *recuérdalo bien*, sin un cobre en los bolsillos, oliendo a escoria, con las piernas descuadradas, el fuego de la avaricia en la mirada […]" (13, my emphasis). These imperative forms, though they appear only in the first section of the novel, set out to remind the reader that the story of Nakandakari is told at the present time and that it must be remembered now and for the future.

This narrative format may resonate with an oral storytelling in which a storyteller remembers and tells what she experienced in the past based on her memory in order to transmit the story from generation to generation. If the narrator insinuates, through the insertion of the imperative forms, that her story will be told based on her remembering what she witnessed and experienced in the past, she reveals, through the use of the second person plural "we" form, that she and her family were members of the Japanese immigrant community in Lima and that what she remembers about Nakandakari has been conserved and shared in the community.

One such memory of Nakandakari commonly conserved and shared in the Japanese community is his image as a greedy, selfish, and manipulative villain. The narrator, as a collective voice of the community, describes Nakandakari's arrival in the Japanese community in Lima as the advent of a cataclysm: "[…] amparado por Ryochi Onaga, consiguió un crédito de mercancías […]. Y ese fue el inicio de un cataclismo, sin que nadie lo pudiera evitar, de lamentables consecuencias *para nosotros*, pues el hombrecito no tenía paz, ni quietud, ni misericordia, ni consuelo […]" (Higa 2014: 13, my emphasis). "Nosotros" means the community of the Japanese immigrants and their descendants who position themselves in the binary relationship of us/Japanese and them/Peruvians. The Japanese community also identifies itself as an earnest, diligent, and moral group of people that encourages one another to keep a low profile in the Peruvian society where the escalation of anti-Japanese sentiment cannot be ignored. Nakandakari's flashy and exhibitionistic sales tactics do not fit well with this imagery of the Japanese constructed and accepted by the community. Thus, a group of people from the community tries to persuade Nakandakari to quit his showy performance:

> Sus propios paisanos, los Miyashiro, los Kaneku, los Nagashima, incluso Ryochi Onaga, lo venían a buscar quejumbrosos, y lo amonestaban por la locura de ejecutar maromas,

y que las reglas del comercio exigían mesura, pues estaban asustados con tanta fanfarria y tanto exhibicionismo, en la medida que *nos* agobiaba la campaña antijaponesa. [..].
[…] los *perujin* no *nos* querían, *éramos* desarraigados e insociables, […].

(Higa 2014: 20, my emphasis except "perujin")

The narrator shows that the Japanese approach Nakandakari as a group to try to convince the newcomer to behave as a good Japanese merchant like them, underscoring the oppositional relationship between us/Japanese/discriminated and them/Peruvians/discriminator.

However, Nakandakari declares that he does not conform to the value system of the Japanese community and has negative thoughts on the Japanese:

[…] pesnaba para sí: *oh los nihonjin, enjambre de bárbaros, emperrados y facinerosos.* Y no fueron una o dos noches, tal vez diez o quince, en esas reuniones con los paisanos, para recordarles que se llamaba Sentei Nakandakari, y que jamás se rendiría, pues su propia tragedia consistía en seguir existiendo, a rato como perro, a rato como árbol, sin gracia, sin consuelo, y sin pudor.

(21)

Nakandakari's nonconformist and unyielding attitude never disappears. On the contrary, he continues to cause more serious scandals and worries in the Japanese community. His plan to marry a Peruvian young woman, Misha Arango, is particularly scandalous, and as mentioned above, the entire community protests against this marriage. Again, the Japanese come in a group try to persuade him not to marry a Peruvian:

Había temor, miedo disimulado, sobre todo en los Miyashiro, los Taira, los Kaneku, los Ryochi Onaga, y el centenar de japoneses de los alrededores del Mercado Central. Todos comerciantes, mercachifles, abarroteros, vidrieros, hojalateros, pulperos, diestros curtidores, y confeccionistas de zapatos. Parecía una locura, era una provocación, no se podía enamorar a una criolla, los *perujin* nos van a matar, exclamaban, e invocaban a Sentei Nakandakari.

(25)

He impassively rejects this desperate petition from the entire Japanese community: "[…] él parecía irredimible, distante a las súplicas, sin mover los párpados, sin agitar los labios, ni siquiera oscilar el cuello, ausente, indefinido, no aceptaba ningún honor japonés, tampoco rumores, desacomodos […]" (25). Because of his obstinate and lustful ambition, selfishness, and lack of mindful attention to the warnings of the Japanese community, the distance between Nakandakari and the community is deepened.

Soon, this distance becomes even deeper, and there is finally a total separation between him and the community when he opens a brothel with his Peruvian mother-in-law. "[H]asta sus propios paisanos, los Kaneku, los Taira, los Ryochi Onaga, lo rechazaban y lo llenaban de injurias" (46) and for the Japanese community, he is "un canalla o un hombre despreciable" (51). No one approves what he does and how he behaves. The narrator inserts her first-person plural narrative voice to describe the disapproval of Nakandakari in the Japanese community:

[…] *éramos* gente decorosa, ocupados en el comercio de víveres, bazares, confecciones, maderas. […] *nuestro* trabajo era honorable, *resguardábamos* la moral, condescendientes con la propia familia, incapaces de transgredir las normas de la decencia. […] se hablaba

Villain or victim?

de Sentei Nakandakari, ese fantasma que tantos miedos arraigaba. […]. [Él era] tan despreciado por todos […].

(51, my emphasis)

The narrator accentuates the collective identity of the Japanese community as a group of decent, moral, and hardworking people and highlights the difference between us/the Japanese community and Nakandakari, who must be excluded from the community due to this difference. The use of the first-person plural narrative voice suggests that remembering Nakandakari as a phantasmagoric figure threatening the decency and morality of the Japanese community is shared among the Japanese as a collective memory.

However, it is not only the collective voice of "we," but also the narrator's individual voice presented by the "I" form that disseminates this message that Nakandakari as a menace to the Japanese community and thus deserves to be repudiated. As mentioned earlier, the narrator reveals her identity in the middle of the novel:

Y *hube* de verlo así muchas veces, por los recados que debía darle, tanto como que *era la hija de Ryochi Onaga* el *dokiusei* de Sentei Nakandakari, y quien lo ayudó a establecerse como ambulante en el Mercado Central. Sí, apenas *tenía ocho años, y me daba miedo* su rostro inexpresible, su cuerpo magro, sus manos y sus pies desapacibles, y esas bolsas inertes de sus ojos. Se decía tantas cosas de él, las atrocidades y trastornos que cometió.

(36–37, my emphasis except dokiusei)

The narrator confesses that as a child she personally knew Nakandakari through her father, remembering Nakandakari's frightening physical appearance and scandalous rumors about him. What she remembers as an individual person, needless to say, coincides with the collective memory shared in the Japanese community.

Further, this shared memory of the aversion toward Nakandakari becomes more aggrandized than before, when she narrates the incidents of rioting and looting which ruined many Japanese stores. She describes what happened to her family:

Mi propio padre Ryochi Onaga se defendió intrépido, pero sucumbió ante la barbarie, acabando mal herido, con su tienda asolada y *mi* madre llorosa e inconsolable. Ocurrió también con los Tsuha y su panadería, expresamente devastada por los ambulantes y vagabundos, […]. Nunca como aquel entonces *fuimos* tan denigrados, soportando amargas pérdidas, llantos dolorosos, humillaciones, impotencias.

(Higa 2014: 55, my emphasis)

She relates the devastation and agony that she and her family felt and immediately connects the reactions and feelings of her own family with those of many other Japanese people in Lima. While showing that her family and other Japanese families share the experience of this calamity, she emphasizes that Sentei Nakandakari is the only one who does not suffer from the same experience: "[…] turbas de saqueadores enloquecidos […] lograron arrasar los locales de los Kaneko, los Tsukazán, los Taira, pero no pudieron con el bazar de Sentei Nakandakari, pues enarbolaba bandera peruana, y la propietaria era Misha Arango […]" (55).

After the riot and looting, the already existing separation between the Japanese community and Nakandakari is further pronounced as a clear division between the victims who share the sufferings and the villain who takes advantage of anything even in the time of the calamity:

[F]uimos comprendiendo el arbitrario matrimonio de Sentei Nakandakari y Misha Arango. ¿No había sido un mero cálculo para protegerse a sí mismo? ¿Hasta qué punto Sentei Nakandakari no era más que un ser brutal? [...]. [A]l margen de la catástrofe y las familias japonesas en la orfandad, como si nada hubiese ocurrido, Sentei Nakandakari continuó vigilante en su intacto bazar de Mesa Redonda.

(Higa 2014: 55)

The narrator, shifting her individual narrative voice in the first-person singular ("Mi propio padre [...] acabando mal herido" and "mi madre llorosa e inconsolable") into the plural ("las familias japonesas en la orfandad") (55), demonstrates the solidification of her position as a member of all the Japanese families, beyond her own family. In other words, her individual recollection of her family's devastating loss and of Nakandakari's selfishness cannot be separated from the collective memory of the Japanese community.

It is not surprising or unusual to notice this close association between the individual memory and collective memory. Maurice Halbwachs' pioneering study of "collective memory" demonstrates that there is no individual memory that is not connected to a specific group memory. Halbwachs affirms that "[w]e can understand each memory as it occurs in individual thought only if we locate each within the thought of the corresponding group" (1992: 53). His often-quoted following words reinforce the interdependent relation between individual and collective memory: "While the collective memory endures and draws strength from its base in a coherent body of people, it is individuals as group members who remember" (Olick et al. 2011: 142). On the one hand, it is *only* when individual memory is located within a specific social framework and it is *only* through individual memory that collective memory can be articulated. However, on the other, it is important to note that since individual group members are different *individuals* who are most likely to belong to other social groups and have diverse experiences and thoughts, they may not share the exact same degree of remembrances. Because an individual member's viewpoint varies and changes, according to the social environments and spatio-temporal contexts in which they live, collective memory is formed, not as a result of a simple absorption of individual memories into one unified memory, but as a result of a complex combination of diverse collective experiences and thoughts which are constantly changing (142).

Halbwachs' understanding of the relationship between individual and collective memory can be useful for analyzing the relationship between the narrator's memory and the Japanese community's memory. When the narrator's memory is located within this specific group, her memory about the selfishness and viciousness of Nakandakari, needless to say, emerges as part of the group collective memory. Because of this social location, she can remember and trace back what she experienced and witnessed as a child when Nakandakari was around her family and the Japanese community. At the same time, it is through her individual memory that the collective memory, recreating the image of Nakandakari as a villain, is observed, and according to Halbwachs, this collective memory of Nakandakari "endures and draws strength [...] in a coherent body of people" (1992: 142).

At first glance, it seems that the narrator's memory of Nakandakari is located *completely* and *only* in the Japanese community's group memory and that the collective memory of Nakandakari in the Japanese community *steadily* and *coherently* "endures and draws strength" in the narrator's thoughts (1992: 142). However, as Halbwachs reminds the reader about an individual "viewpoint" on the collective memory, the narrator drops her own viewpoints while binding her recollections to the Japanese community's memory. Her memory of Nakandakari as a villain who has brought calamity to the Japanese community is still strongly recorded in her thoughts and awakened when she remembers how other Japanese, including her father, interacted with

Nakandakari. As seen above, she perceives him as the villain as opposed to the good of the community and shows, through her first-person singular (individual) and plural (collective) narrative voices, that this binary perception is commonly shared in the collective memory of the community. However, the narrator's third-person voice, which predominates the novel, allows her to step outside of her family and the community. From this position outside the community, she attempts to objectively project the *whole* aspects of both Nakandakari and the Japanese community, including different perspectives that do not correspond with the normalized images and opinions of the Japanese community. Her third-person narrative voice cannot be fully separated from the fact that it is the voice of a Japanese immigrant, Ryochi Onaga's daughter, whose memory is connected to the community's memory. However, her objective observations of Nakandakari and the Japanese community disrupt the binary imagery of Nakandakari as a villain and the Japanese community as a good group of people.

The collapse of the fixed image of Nakandakari as a villain occurs when the narrator insinuates certain similarities between him and the other members of the Japanese community. One similarity can be observed in the narrator's description of how her father started his small business. Her father, Onaga, and Nakandakari emigrated from the same village, Motobu, in Okinawa in order to work as contract workers in northern farmlands in Peru. Not only does Onaga carry the same background, he comes to Lima to look for a better life just as Nakandakari does:

> Ryochi Onaga se vino a Lima, trabajando incansable, constituyó una familia, y después de miles de peripecias, amarguras, sinsabores, ahorrando entre *tanamochi* o panderos con sus paisanos, se estableció en ese bazar del jirón Andahuaylas, incansable, ahorrador, y poco redundante.
>
> *(Higa 2014: 12)*

Although the narrator does not depict her father as a greedy, manipulating, and vicious person like Nakandakari, Onaga's determination to survive and then become financially successful echoes Nakandakari's desire to "salir cuanto antes de la pobreza" (18). Just as her father, Nakandakari tries to earn and save money. Nakandakari's perseverance for a better life has been perceived as emotionless aggression and selfishness among the Japanese community, but the narrator reveals the other side of his aggression and selfishness:

> [...] la cabeza se le llenaba de perversiones, ganas de arrojar, colgarse de la pared, perforarse el vientre con un cuchillo. [...]. [...] no había noche, no había descanso, no había lástima, ni pausa, ni quietud, él mismo era su vorágine, sin fondo, sin paz, y sin nostalgia.
>
> *(21)*

This revelation of Nakandakari's inner struggles hints that he is not a simple heartless villain, but that just as the narrator's father (and other immigrants) who underwent "miles de peripecias, amarguras, sinsabores" (12), he shares the similar feelings of torment and agony with them.

The narrator even goes on to analyze Nakandakari's mental struggles:

> Es posible, Sentei Nakandakari, tan despreciado por todos, luchaba consigo mismo, sin sosiego, sin pudor, como si ejerciera su propia destrucción. Tal vez era malsano, aquel ímpetu de ir contra la corriente, usufructuar el dinero envilecido, [...] y no tenía más remedio.
>
> *(52)*

Her analysis of Nakandakari's psychology does not change her perception of him as a villain, but insinuates that he may be mentally ill, unable to recover from his own agony, and this suffering may be a cause for his villainous behavior. Along with her speculation on his psychological state, the narrator also presents the fact that he suffers from recurrent nightmares. In his dreams, Nakandakari enters a labyrinthine space from which he cannot escape: "Aparecían perros bestiales, bramidos infamantes, devoraban y volvían a tragar sus piernas y su rostro, y otra vez Sentei Nakandakari se introducía en otro aposento, y era atrapado en una selva intrincada imposible de escapar" (Higa 2014: 60). The nightmares, according to the narrator, make him feel "inquieto, [...] perturbado en la dormitación, asfixiado en sus pesadillas" (60), and the depiction of his feelings of fear, restlessness, and suffocation exposes a vulnerability that he never shows in public. The narrator's interpretation of his inner struggles and exposition of his vulnerable side disturbs the firmness of the Japanese community's limited collective perception of him as a villain that does not see beyond the surface of his behavior.

As she raises a doubt about Nakandakari's fixed label as a villain, she also implies a skepticism about the engraved imagery of the Japanese community as the good—a group of honorable, ethical, and orderly people. The narrator recalls an incident that unveils the evilness of a Japanese immigrant, Agríe, who tries to persuade Nakandakari to close the brothel, insisting on the importance of preserving the dignity and honorability of the Japanese. Since Nakandakari does not pay attention to Agríe nor, indeed, to any advice from the other Japanese, Agríe attempts to handle Nakandakari's impassive unruliness with a final tactic—leaving Nakandakari a loaded gun and indirectly prompting him to commit suicide with the gun. Alone with the gun, Nakandakari puts the loaded weapon to his temple, but Agríe's operation fails. In the aftermath of that attempt at the ultimate coercion, there is no mention of a criticism against or punishment for Agríe's action. Instead, a group of Japanese people continues to reproach Nakandakari for his brothel business. This incident demonstrates that a member of this Japanese community that is proud of being honorable, ethical, and orderly, has attempted to lead a person to suicide. Is this not contrary to honorable and ethical behavior, a behavior to be criticized or punished? The revelation of this incident distorts the face of the good of the Japanese community.

Similarly, the imagery of the good becomes suspicious when attention is drawn to the Japanese community's discriminatory attitude toward Peruvians. As seen above, the anti-Japanese sentiment is diffused throughout the city and the country, and the Japanese community perceives themselves as victims of the anti-Japanese Peruvian society. The voices showing the Peruvians' hatred circulates in the community: "Los *perujin* no nos querían" (Higa 2014: 20); "nos agobiaba la campaña antijaponesa" (20); "nos desprecian los *perujin*" (37); and "los *perujin* nos aborrecían" (52). Although the Japanese people do not directly insult or attack Peruvians, the Japanese community is described as a closed and exclusionist society with an effective communal financial loan system, where only Japanese help one another and exclude Peruvians from working at their stores and playing together with their children. It is curious to note that only Nakandakari among all the Japanese people directly interacts with Peruvians and hires Peruvians for his brothel business. In other words, behind the face of the good, there exists a total exclusion of people of different race and culture from the Japanese community.

However, it cannot be denied that the Japanese community is the victim of the riots and looting, persecution, confiscation, and deportation—that is, they are the victims of the wartime. Yet, again the third-person narrator does not forget to objectively include the historical fact: "Japón se mantenía invicto y ocupaba los territorios de Corea y China" (Higa 2014: 23). This sentence makes the reader wonder why the narrator includes this statement and questions the meaning of "the victims of the wartime" constructed in the Japanese community. If the Japanese in Peru are the "victims of the wartime," then, how about the Korean and Chinese people whose lands

Villain or victim?

were occupied by the Japanese government? The narrator does not explicitly provoke the reader to contemplate this question, but her insertion of this sentence disturbs the memory of the Japanese community as a victim, raising a question of who the victim, villain, or perpetrator is.

Just as the imagery of the Japanese community as the good and the victim is dismantled, toward the end of the novel, the imagery of Nakandakari as a villain also becomes debatable. When the war breaks out and the "Japanese-hunting" starts, he goes into hiding, as do many other Japanese people. He has to close his businesses and hide in a small room back of his wife's parents' house: "[…] la cacería contra los japoneses se desataba. […]. Sentei Nakandakari permaneció escondido día y noche, sin atreverse a salir a la calle, sentado en una silla, observando inconmovible la verde pared, el techo viejo, y la cama destartalada" (Higa 2014: 66). Although Nakandakari's businesses are not confiscated by the Peruvian government because his properties are registered under Arango's name, the narrator does not describe him as a vicious and selfish person as she does when she remembers his calculating way for surviving at the time of rioting and looting. On the contrary, she portrays him simply as one more victim of the government's institutionalized "Japanese-hunting." The narrator objectively recounts what happens to the Japanese community:

> El gobierno confiscó las propiedades de los ciudadanos japoneses, encarcelaron dirigentes y personas con alguna fortuna. Cerraron los colegios nipones, cancelaron todas las licencias comerciales, no podían funcionar ninguna empresa, ninguna fonda, ningún bazar, ninguna vidriería. Hubo receso, muchos paisanos se escondieron por algún tiempo, sobreviviendo a duras penas, con sus hijos a cuestas, realizando negocios clandestinos […]. [E]n medio de esa confusión, cualquier extranjero japonés podía ser denunciado a las autoridades policiales.
>
> *(66–67)*

Nakandakari is depicted, no longer as a villain whose vicious and manipulative actions stand out, but as a "cualquier extranjero japonés," a faceless member of the Japanese community, who undergoes the injustice imposed by the government. Nakandakari's identity as a victim, for the first time, at the end of the novel, is explicitly revealed: "Nadandakari se encontraba en su reclusión, oculto y abrumado, consumando infamantes vueltas en su habitación, afrontando enardecido su propia derrota y humillación" (67). The narrator goes on to tell that he remains enclosed for 1,320 days until Japan's unconditional surrender, describing him as "un hombre consumado por el tiempo" (67), and that he loses his sanity, not talking to anyone, and dies in total desolation and abandonment.

The narrator's two contradictory memories of Nakandakari—one reconstructed within the collective memory of the Japanese community and the other reconstructed outside of the collective memory—are exhibited side by side, destabilizing the rigidity of the collective memory about his reputation as a villain. However, despite the narrator's depiction of Nakandakari as another victim of anti-Japanese oppression, her memory does not deny her perception of him as a villain. Again going back to Halbwachs' concept of "collective memory," he argues that even when a person leaves a group or marries, he or she does not lose completely the collective memory of the previous group or family. Rather, this person's traditions, customs, culture, and value system are mixed with those of the new family or new group's, and his or her previous memory is merged with the memories of the new group's, making a new collective memory (Halbwachs 1992: 74–83, 184–85). In the narrator's case, her memory of Nakandakari is located, not only within the Japanese community's collective memory that perceives him as a villain and the community as the good, but also within the value system that she has acquired so far.

Synthesizing and synchronizing the Japanese community's memory and other memories, the narrator negotiates with the Japanese community's collective memory, a collective memory whose binary perception of themselves as the good and the victim stand in opposition to Nakandakari as the villain and the Peruvian society as the perpetrator.

The narrator's contrasting perspectives, *both* as a member of the community *and* as a person who steps outside of the community, reveal tensions between the voice that supports the image of the Japanese community as a victim of the Peruvian racial anti-Japanese sentiment and Nakandakari's provocative and reckless behavior, on the one hand, and the contradictory voice that unsettles the fixity of the victimhood of the Japanese community, on the other. Such tensions between the enduring fixity of the collective memory and a fissure in the fixity recall Jeffrey Olick's statement. According to Olick, "[…] memory is never unitary, no matter how hard various powers strive to make it so. There are always subnarratives, transitional periods, and contests over dominance" (2003: 8). Although the narrator shares the collective memory preserved by the Japanese community which tends to insist on their unity, her other "subnarrative" voices fluster the sense of unity and make it variable.

Higa's *Gaijin* is worth being read on its own terms, but perhaps it is even more rewarding when read alongside with the JPOHP testimonial voices. One may say that it may be incompatible to compare and contrast a fiction and an oral history project. However, it is this fictional and imaginative space, residing outside of the specific academic or professional field of history and oral history, that allows the author to create and reveal an alternative view to the collective memory represented by the JPOHP. Then this alternative view depicted in the novel *does* provoke the reader to question the perpetuation of the unitary collective memory and begs for answers to the questions raised at the beginning of this study. Behind the neatly assembled collective memory of an oral project, are there any other voices that are excluded from the project? Should an alternative voice, like the narrator's voice describing Nakandakari both as a villain and victim, that does not fit in an oral project's agenda be included in the project? Being already recognized as "authorized culture" in the field of oral history, the JPOHP may fail to address these questions or to generate new ways of thinking about a non-conformist voice. In contrast, Higa's novel, as a popular cultural imaginative space, seems to affirmatively answer these questions by manifesting the narrator's "subnarrative" voices that ruminate over the forgotten and unshared memory and negotiate with the unified Japanese Peruvian collective memory.

Notes

1 Translation is mine.
2 In 1988, the redress of USD $20,000 per person was granted only to the Japanese Americans, not to the Japanese Latin Americans (Small 2000: 249; "Campaign for Justice;" González "The Japanese-Peruvians").
3 Similar statements by Green are also quoted in Abram's study (100).
4 The loan system established by a group of Japanese immigrants in the U.S. is called *tanamochi* or *tanomoshi*.
5 *Samisén* is a three-stringed Japanese traditional instrument.

Works cited

Abrams, Lynn. "Memory." *Oral History Theory.* London: Routledge, 2010. 78–105.
"Campaign for Justice: Redress Now for Japanese Latin American Internees!" *Campaign for Justice 2000–2015.* www.campaignforjusticejla.org/whoweare/index.html Accessed 11 July 2017.
Field, Sean. "Imagining Communities: Memory, Loss, and Resilience in Post-Apartheid Cape Town." *Oral History and Public Memories.* Philadelphia, PA: Temple University Press, 2008. 107–24.

Halbwachs, Maurice. *On Collective Memory: The Heritage of Sociology*. Translated by Lewis A. Coser. Chicago, IL: University of Chicago Press, 1992.

Higa, Augusto Oshiro. *Gaijin (Extranjero)*. Lima: Animal De Invierno, 2014.

Higa, Augusto Oshiro. "Augusto Higa: 'En literatura no hay consejos ni recetas.'" By José Miguel Silva. LIBROS A MÍ. *El Comercio.pe*. El Comercio, 28 December 2014. Accessed 24 July 2017.

González, Jaime. "El drama de los peruano-japoneses encarcelados en campos de detención en EE.UU." *BBC Mundo*. 9 January 2015. www.bbc.com/mundo/noticias/2015/01/141212_eeuu_peru_japoneses_campos_internamiento_guerra_mundial_jg. Accessed 11 July 2017.

González, Jaime. "The Japanese-Peruvians interned in the US during WW2." *BBC Mundo*. 22 February 2015. www.bbc.com/news/world-latin-america-31295270 Accessed 11 July 2017.

Green, Anna. "Individual Remembering and 'Collective Memory': Theoretical Presuppositions and Contemporary Debates." *Oral History*, 32:2, 2004. 35–44.

Olick, Jeffrey K. "Introduction." *States of Memory: Continuities, Conflicts, and Transformations in National Retrospection*. Durham, NC: Duke University Press, 2003. 1–16.

Olick, Jeffrey K. and Joyce Robbins. "Social Memory Studies: From 'Collective Memory' to the Historical Sociology of Mnemonic Practices." *Annual Review of Sociology*, 24, 1998. 105–40.

Olick, Jeffrey K. et al. eds. "Maurice Halbwachs (1877–1945)." *The Collective Memory Reader*. Oxford: Oxford University Press, 2011. 139–49.

Parker, Holt N. "Toward a Definition of Popular Culture." *History and Theory*, 50:2, 2011, 147–70. www.jstor.org. Accessed 25 July 2017.

"Report No 26-06 Petition 434-03 Admissibility Isamu Carlos Shibayama et al." *Organization of American States*. 16 March 2006. Inter-American Commission on Human Rights. 2012. Accessed 20 August 2015.

Small, Julie. "Epilogue." *Adios to Tears: The Memoirs of a Japanese-Peruvian Internee in U.S. Concentration Camps*. By Seiichi Higashide. Seattle, WA: University of Washington Press, 2000. 249–53.

"What is the JPOHP?" *The Morita family web page*. 15 September 2013. Accessed 18 August 2015.

12

ART, LITERATURE, AND MASS MEDIA IN PEDRO LEMEBEL

Juan Poblete

In an interview in Barranquilla given shortly before his death with John Better Armella, a gay Colombian crónica writer and poet, the Chilean crónica writer Pedro Lemebel (1955–2015), talked about the connection between his writing career and "Hablo por mi diferencia," a famous manifesto he read in 1986 in a gathering of the Chilean political left resisting the Pinochet dictatorship. "When I wrote Manifesto (*I Speak for My Difference*), someone paid me to publish it, and they asked for another text. So my chronicles were born out of the need to survive. It's worked out well, which is why I say with all the false modesty of a bald queen that, in Latin America, chronicles are what pays to get my hair done" (Better 2017: n.p.).

The story encapsulates a series of defining strands in Lemebel's writing: it combines a clear-eyed irreverence towards the importance of the literary and literary authorship, a dark humor that makes fun even of his own dying as a result of the larynx cancer that eventually killed him in 2015, the intensely autobiographical references to his humble origins in the past and their contrast with his high standing in the present of the Latin American literary field; and a full awareness of the economic basis of all life, literary and otherwise. When asked about being a cult author, Lemebel expanded: "I detest the machista mythomania that places literature at the center of everything and rescues accursed writers and hopeless alcoholics. Those kinds of comments make me unreachable, and I want to be out there in the street, on the sidewalk, pirated by clandestine commerce, within arm's reach where my public can grab me. I belong to the copular and popular class." In fact, since the Spanish original reads: "en la vereda, pirateado por el comercio clandestino, al alcance de la mano, donde mi pueblo me quiera coger" (Better 2017: n.p.). And "coger" is both grab and fuck, Lemebel was adding to those strands the close connection he saw between writing and sex, the copular and the popular, as the basis for a non-literary form of *ecriture* that could, simultaneously, be more than literary while literary, more than mediated, while mass-mediated, more than simply prestigious, transformational. The story also connects the manifesto's conceptual and performative power, as an intervention in a concrete socio-political situation, with Lemebel's own crónicas, and his understanding of them as propositional, interventionist, and provocative texts in a specific mediascape. It links the author's 1980s and 1990s art performances as part of the queer collective Yeguas del Apocalipsis (along with Francisco Casas) with Lemebel's 1990s famous written crónicas. It also, finally, defines the possibilities, challenges, and traps involved in developing a voice in a context that was generally hostile to such an endeavor.

Art, literature, and mass media in Pedro Lemebel

Lemebel was a writer who had thrown a triple challenge to the Chilean cultural and political establishment: he was gay in one of Latin America's—most traditional countries; he was defiantly working class and a communist sympathizer in a small cultural environment overwhelmingly dominated by the upper-class; and he was centrally a crónica writer and performing artist in a country known for its novelists and poets. That challenge had always meant fighting for the right, first, to have a voice and, then, be heard. Defined by the struggle to produce a new form of cultural practice—expressive of and truthful to the manyfold violences that for him defined Chile in the recent past, but also capable of reaching vast audiences through mass media in the present—Lemebel's best work took place in a challenging but exciting context for such a project. First the dictatorship and then the transition to democracy were decisively more interested in forgetting than in remembering, in moving on rather than in looking back. Insisting on a clean break with the dictatorial past while maintaining the basic tenets of its neoliberal social and economic model—a model specializing in the production of radically unequal development—the long governing center-left coalition generated from 1990 on, in its own sui generis mix of dis/continuity, a ground that was both difficult and fertile for Lemebel's *oeuvre*. (Poblete 2015)

In this context, I want to read here Lemebel's crónica work along three complementary lines, all connected to what I call processes of proletarianization. Those lines are: first, sexuality as revolutionary practice, culturally expanding the limits of the political; second, Lemebel's relation to mass media; and third, the crónica as mass-mediated text. Before I do so I need to explain what I understand by proletarianization.

There are two theoretical senses of proletarianization that are relevant to my reading of this self-declared proletarian loca's work: the first is positive and was originally proposed by Walter Benjamin in his classic essay "The Work of Art in the Age of Mechanical Reproduction." The second is negative and was first developed, partly in response to Benjamin, by Adorno and Horkheimer in their chapter on the culture industry, and more recently expanded by Bernard Stiegler. The first sees the potential of mechanical reproduction and the de-auratization of the work of art—the de-valuing by multiple copying through technological means of the original and exclusive culture of the bourgeoisie—as a radical proletarianization of art and its practices, a democratization of its creative and social possibilities. Here, new forces of production (technology) enable or make potentially viable new social relations (of production). The second position, the culture industry thesis, sees technology as an enabler of the deepening capacity of capitalism to penetrate the life of the proletarians, reaching not just their labor, but their free time and imaginations, and ultimately, their sensory and neural capabilities.

If every true economy presupposes among the participants a commerce of *savoir faire* (knowledge of how to do) and *savoir vivre* (knowledge of how to live), that is to say, an exchange of life and creative materialized ideas, French philosopher Bernard Stiegler's diagnostic on the destructive nature of contemporary capitalism is that it is not properly an economy but an anti-economy, reduced as it is to monetary exchanges. This anti-economy leads to: the destruction of *savoir faire* and *savoir vivre*, a mutation of the nature of work, and a functionalization of production, consumption, and social relations, now inseparable from the technological apparatus. This is part of a process of proletarianization that has, for Stiegler, at least three modern moments: it began in the nineteenth century with the destruction of the *savoir faire* of the workers (of their physical working gestures) by its transfer to the machines, which made possible the creation of a proletarian labor force. It continued in the twentieth century with the destruction of the *savoir vivre* of the workers qua consumers; and has gone on now with the crisis of such forms of production and consumption in a generalized process of cognitive and affective proletarianization. In such process what is alienated to the machines, what is externalized is, in addition to the *savoir faire* and *savoir vivre*, the *savoir theorizer*, i.e. the capacity that allows us to think our own experiences and produce knowledge. (Stiegler 2010, 30) The proletarians of the muscular system, so produced by the machine appropriation of their *savoir faire*, are now joined by the proletarians of the nervous system, who produce cognitive labor without controlling the knowledge thus produced. This process of externalization of memory in its various forms: bodily and muscular, nervous, cerebral, and biogenetic is what Stiegler calls grammaticalization. Once grammaticalized these different forms of memory can be manipulated by systems of biopolitical and sociopolitical control which regulate, in what the author calls a "general organology," the articulation of bodily organs (muscles, brain, eyes, genitals), artificial organs (tools and machines), and social organs (from the family to the nation as forms of organization of the social and its reproduction). (Poblete 2015)

There is, thus, a positive and a negative version of what proletarianization may mean, and, then, a third version of it, to which I will return later, that understand it as connected to the concrete forms of social memory and tools for thought and action available to a given community.

Discussing the connections between, on the one hand, digital technologies, such as social media and internet, and, on the other, transformational politics and social movements, Todd Wolfson proposes a dialectical approach capable of going beyond dichotomies that see technology as inherently revolutionary or as completely captured by neoliberal capitalism. Instead, Wolfson suggest we acknowledge the socio-economic embedding of (especially communications) technologies in capitalism while at the same time we recognize "that technological practice is a site of contested struggle, and technological tools can be utilized to create social change." (Wolfson 2014, 102) What matters then is not only which is the technological medium being used and what could be the logic of its internal functioning, but also the actual communicative practice of concrete actors involved in specific struggles in concrete circumstances.

Pedro Lemebel's crónica-based communicative and political practice is grounded then on two general forms of understanding proletarianization that I will study below in three parts. One is reactive to what it perceives as the partial theft of historical capabilities of the Chilean people by neoliberal capitalism (memory, capacity for struggle and change), and especially by mass-mediated communicational capitalism; the other is proactive as it proposes, first to re-appropriate, re-invigorate and re-collectivize the general aesthetic capabilities encoded and privatized by traditionally understood literature and mass media; and, second, to culturally expand the limits of what is politics and political. For Lemebel, as for Jacques Ranciere, art like politics, is, or should be, a practice suspending the rules governing normalized experience and their specific and historically determined distribution of the sensible (including forms of discourse, concepts of subjectivity, and objects of contemplation and thought). Art, like politics, strives, through "dissensus", to introduce heterogeneity into a normalized field of perception and action.

Sexuality as cultural expansion of the political

If for Ranciere politics is quintessentially the contentious dissensus that, in expanding the sensible, makes audible the voice of those who, under a particular form of political consensus, did not have a right to speak or could not be heard as political subjects, then Lemebel's artistic production is centrally political.

There are a few such subjects that are crucial to Lemebel's writing. They include, la loca (the gay voice and character that defines his crónicas), proletarian youth, many working class figures, and the disappeared, tortured, and violence victims during Pinochet's dictatorship.

As already stated, at the very beginning of Lemebel's work is the striking and forceful queer voice of the author of the manifesto "Hablo por mi diferencia" (I Speak for My Difference) which can now be read, retrospectively, as a full poetics for Lemebel's *oeuvre*. In the manifesto, this queer voice establishes two of its defining notes from then on, both of them developed here, paradoxically, in a tense dialogue not with the dictatorship, as it may have been expected, but instead, the political forces leading the resistance to and transition after Pinochet. This is because the so-called politics of consensus in Chilean political history was, Janus-like, two-faced: there were the limits imposed by the dictatorial power during the last part of the military regime and its aftermath from 1990 on; but, especially in post-dictatorship, there were also the self-imposed limits of a coalition of political forces ranging from the Socialist party to the Christian Democrats which understood politics as the art of the possible under the post-dicatorial circumstances. There is then in the manifesto, first, the defying tone, the dissensual challenge to a consensus that was as much cultural as it was political:

> I'm not a fag disguised as poet
> I don't need a disguise
> Here is my face
> I speak for my difference
> I defend what I am
> And I'm not so strange
> Injustice stinks
> And I suspect this democratic dance
> > *(Lemebel, "I Speak", n.p.)*

After a series of mass mobilizations that, in the wake of a major economic crisis, had broken the dictatorially imposed quiet of the first few years of the 1980s in Pinochet's Chile, by 1986, the so-called Opposition, a loose group of politicians and workers-lead movements, was in search of a peaceful strategy to, first, weaken and, then, terminate the dictatorship, in what would end up being a negotiated transition and transfer of power. Literally, dissensus was being shaped into what would eventually be called the politics of consensus, itself based on truth and reconciliation but not on justice. Then, secondly, there is in the manifesto the redefinition to what it means to be oppressed in Chile at the time:

> But don't speak to me of the proletariat
> Because to be poor and queer is worse
> One must be tough to withstand it
> It is to avoid the machitos on the streetcorner
> It is a father that hates you
> Because his son is a queen
> It is to have a mother whose hands are slashed by bleach
> Aged from cleaning
> Cradling you as if you were ill
> Because of bad habits
> Because of bad luck
> > *(Lemebel, "I Speak", n.p.)*

Beyond the repression of political activity during the dictatorship, beyond the very visible limits of and to what was political under Pinochet, there was a form of oppression nobody spoke of, a repressed subject against whom violence predated and would persist after the military government:

> Like the dictatorship
> Worse than the dictatorship
> Because the dictatorship ends
> And democracy comes
> And right behind it socialism
> And then what?
> What will you do to us, compañero? [...]
> Will the future be black and white?
> Day and night, without ambiguity?
> Won't there be a fag on some street-corner, destabilising the future of your new man?
> *(Lemebel, "I Speak", n.p.)*

The queer difference from which Lemebel's voice speaks, does so, explicitly, as a deconstructive device capable of disrupting the in-audibility of the popular gay subject in Chilean history. While sexual repression has had a long history in the country, the few signs of relatively open gay presence at the level of written discourse, what Juan Pablo Sutherland has called "el habla marica en la literatura chilena" (the gay speech or discourse in Chilean literature, Sutherland 2009, 23) had been almost exclusively upper class. In that context, Lemebel's voice was doubly disrupting: it cracked open the class-bases of "el habla marica" and it did so as a Communist sympathizer who forced the Chilean left to confront the limits of their own understanding of freedom, politics, and political agency:

> My manhood is to accept myself as different [...]
> I don't turn the other cheek
> Instead I present my ass, compañero
> And that is my vengeance [...]
> I will not change for Marxism
> That rejected me so many times
> I don't need to change
> I am more subversive than you
> *(Lemebel, "I Speak", n.p.)*

But Lemebel's re-writing of the limits of what is politics and political was also complemented by an equally critical position to what in the United States would be called identity politics. Like Manuel Puig before him, Lemebel was highly suspicious of the forms of gay identity they both came to know through popular culture and their visits to the United States. Lemebel decried the "cold pink spring" of the white, wealthy, and elegant gays of San Francisco "who only look at each other" (Lemebel 2012, 43) and disparaged "El prototipo gay de los 90 [...] misógino, fascistoide, aliado con el macho que sustenta el poder" (The gay prototype of the 1990s [...] misogynous, fascist-like, allied to the macho who holds power, in Schäffer, 59). Puig, on the other hand, had stated in a famous article called "El error gay" (The Gay Mistake) that "homosexuality does not exist. It is a projection of the reactionary mind" (Puig, 139). By that, the Argentine author meant that sex was a natural behavior with no particular moral meaning attached to it. Instead, what mattered morally and personally, was intense affective activity. Sex, Puig insisted, should not define the person who practices it with people of the same sex

Art, literature, and mass media in Pedro Lemebel

"because it has no meaning. […] What gives life, then, would be affect and not sex, and the latter would be simply the instrument of a purely affective impulse." (Puig, 139) Puig's conclusion, and the justification for his title, was the abolition of the categories of homo- and heterosexuality and the proclamation of free and uninhibited sexuality:

> "…I admire and respect the work of gay liberation groups, but I see in them the danger of adopting or vindicating homosexual identity as a natural fact, when, instead it is nothing but a historically and culturally constructed product, as repressive as the heterosexual condition."
>
> *(Puig, 141)*

As we have seen Lemebel had widely criticized traditional politics for their deafness to the forms of oppression experienced by homosexuals, for claiming the mantel of freedom while condoning or sharing conservative moralizations and condemnations of homosexual behavior. In *Háblame de amores* (2012), however, while celebrating the public affirmation of gay presence in Santiago since 1992 when, according to Lemebel, gay activists had first openly joined a political demonstration, he also criticizes the commodification of gay life and the self-absorbed gay lifestyles manifested in Bellas Artes, which he considered his neighborhood. So a new march in Bellas Artes, in support of the student movement demanding better and free education in Chile, becomes in this *crónica* the occasion for both a celebration of the fact that the gay community in the neighborhood joined the demonstration, and a mordant, while still sympathetic, critique of a certain form of gay politics that, for the author, is often incapable of looking beyond "sus pestañas mochas" (their fake and bad eyelashes) or the narrowly specific nature of their gay demands. Instead of the "homosexuality of design"—by which Lemebel refers both to professional gay designers that have taken over the neighborhood and the market shaped identity of upper class gay identities—Lemebel celebrates the presence of gays and lesbians "now in the streets demonstrating without fear for a collective cause" in support of the politics of others (Lemebel, *Háblame*, 230).

Lemebel's literature was thus born on two rhetorical and discursive gestures that would ground it for the next thirty years: the challenging and disrupting eruption of a voice that knows itself new and needed in Chilean history; and the claim to expand the definition and limits of politics and political subjects. This is what I call Lemebel's first proletarianizing move. This move, in full narrative display in Lemebel's only novel, *Tengo miedo torero* (*My Tender Matador*, 2001) participates in a discursive gesture of expanding the political by contrasting two main characters: the political fighter and his gay counterpart. The gesture itself has by now a significant tradition in Latin America. It includes Manuel Puig's *El Beso de la mujer araña* (*Kiss of the Spider Woman*, 1976), Senel Paz' *El lobo, el bosque y el hombre nuevo* (1990), and Tomás Gutierrez Alea's film (based on Paz' short story) *Fresa y chocolate* (*Strawberry and Chocolate*, 1993), and if one were to expand the definition to encompass homoeroticism, also Julio Cortázar's "Reunión" (1965) and Omar Cabezas' *La Montaña es algo más que una inmensa estepa verde* (1982).

Lemebel's relation to mass media

The second form of proletarianization in Lemebel's work is connected to his deep relation with mass media, mass-mediated culture, and popular culture in general. In order to grasp its importance for a reading of the author's work, we must first understand the specific media and social-scape of Chile in the roughly last half-century. During this period the country was the scene of three radical experiments at re-foundation, all connected by what sociologist José Joaquín Brunner has called the "overdetermining power of politics" (Brunner 1988, 48) and its ambitious claims to reshape the social and cultural realms. The three experiments were: the so called revolution within freedom of the Christian Democrats (1964–1970), the socialist revolution of Salvador Allende's Unidad Popular (1970–1973) and the military revolution (1973–1990) of Augusto Pinochet. What is characteristic of the latter, the most successful of the three examples, is the specific form its foundational ambition took. Instead of promoting a national-popular culture as the Christian Democrats and the Socialists had done, the dictatorship turned "as far as possible, the regulation of communicative processes over to the private circuits coordinated by the market" (Brunner 1988, 105) while simultaneously keeping for itself "the functions of ideological control and administration of said processes, thus actively intervening in the reorganization of the main cultural apparatuses." (105) From this moment on, the liberalization of cultural markets by the private sector would go hand in hand with the efforts of the military and intellectual elites to counter its potentially subversive effects in the social and values realms. Control and subjection were functions the military state entrusted, somewhat contradictorily, both to its repressive apparatuses and to the privatizing forces of the market and mass-mediated national and international culture, which was to replace the previous national-popular culture. But the contradictions were only apparent. The strict social control and the violent de-articulation of political forces (political parties, unions, local forms of association, etc.) were the necessary conditions and the opportunities to "liberalize" and privatize the economy, displacing the social coordination produced by the state by that generated by "the market community." (Brunner 1994, 251) Thus, authoritarianism and neoliberalism shook hands. This space—between a national-popular and an international globalizing culture, between tight political control and the alleged freedom of cultural consumption and communicational markets—is the discursive and performative arena for some of Lemebel's most important contributions to Chilean culture.

Since most of the democratic media during the seventeen-year dictatorship period was first shut off and then replaced by almost uniformly right-leaning outfits, a media landscape that lingered well into the transitional post-dictatorship, Lemebel's media participation always took place, in relatively smaller media. Among them: the independent biweekly *Página Abierta* in which some his first crónicas were published in the 1990s; the satirical weekly *The Clinic*, the communist party newspaper *El Siglo* and the weekly *Punto Final*, the independent feminist radio station Radio Tierra, in which for at least two years, twice a week, he had a ten-minute program of radio crónicas, read with music. The one exception was Lemebel's weekly one-page section—"Ojo de loca no se equivoca" (The Queer Eye Does Not Err)—in the government sponsored and nationally distributed newspaper *La Nación* during the first presidency of Michelle Bachelet (2006–2010).

In addition to the proletarian figures mentioned above—la loca, marginal youth, many working class figures, and the victims of political violence during Pinochet's dictatorship, some of which I will deal with in the next section—what Lemebel brought to each one of these media outlets was a deeply felt and deeply queer relationship with popular culture, especially with popular music. In fact, the Radio Tierra crónicas were compiled into a book, *De Perlas y cicatrices. Crónicas radiales* (1998). In it, Lemebel powerfully mixes two of his defining preoccupations: popular culture figures (especially from popular music) and the human consequences of political violence (especially the denunciation of crimes and the outing in post-dictatorship times of those who, in their media work, profited and collaborated with the dictatorship.) Right in the introduction, Lemebel acknowledges the limitation of his endeavor: the published crónicas cannot recuperate the affective contact music allowed him and his listeners to establish with historical and personal memories through the background sounds and the playing of songs from a series of highly melodramatic singers. In fact, the written texts should be seen as a "mute

Art, literature, and mass media in Pedro Lemebel

score" (Lemebel 1998, 5) that cannot encompass the communicative complexity of this form of intermedial performative contact. But if these crónicas are limited in their capacity to rescue the grain of the voice and the affective contact produced by the audible, they are fully capable of displaying one of Lemebel's writing's defining traits, the dialectics of memory against oblivion. In fact they can even explore some of the traps or blind spots of an exclusively affective relationship to popular culture and memory as in the text about Spanish boy singer star, Joselito, who is first fondly remembered for its singing and ultra-pious roles in a series of film during the 1950s and 1960s, and then debunked later in the text as a cultural creation of the Franco dictatorship in Spain, a fact about which Lemebel and Chilean listeners were completely ignorant. The memory/oblivion dynamic is always displayed in Lemebel's texts as a counter-response to the articulated forms of neoliberalism, seen as a social (anti) memory apparatus.[1] If neoliberalism could be said to be an active effort at forgetting in the constantly renovated presentness, the temporal and historical flatness of the always now, of and in the market, then Lemebel's writing is often a counter-discourse of memory, fighting for a piece of the attention market, a memory antidote using mass-mediated forms of communication to go against the grain of hegemonic media, deploying some of the master's tools to attempt a partial dismantling of the dominant social memory structure. As we will see, and Audre Lorde warned us about, those tools are suffused with and in power and they present risks and limitations of their own.

Neoliberalism as a social apparatus refers to the dual nature of neoliberal globalization: the imposition of both a new political economy (often times referred to as neoliberal trickle-down economics) and a new libidinal economy (based on the stimulation of individual consumption and debt), and above all, to their degree of imbrication and their contrast with previous forms of structuring the social, individual experience, and the historical relation of the present, past and future. In this context, citizens are turned into clients, social demands into technical problems of segmented markets, justice and equality into access to levels of consumption, and the social diluted into the permanent administration of the self, its credit rating and social, human, and economic forms of capital.

As a memory counter-discourse, the crónica in Lemebel is attempting to return to the popular Chilean subjects that which has been stolen from their consciousness in the permanent and banal show of media spectacles, what in the parlance of Chilean journalistic discourse could be called the 'farandulización de la vida' (the spectacularization of life). Against this *farandulización*, against the technical apparatus of anti-memory defining the neoliberal mediascape, but using similar mechanisms of affective capture and memory work, Lemebel deploys what could also be termed a counter-sentimental education, a consistent labor of reconnecting affective investment with true historical memory. In fact, for the author the latter's truest form can best be expressed only as a semi-articulated expression, a form of pure affective and discursive disruption:

> …en esos gritos, en esas consignas amortiguadas por el apaleo de la repre democrática, es en el único lugar donde la dignidad de la memoria anida inagotable. En esas explosiones de desacato, mujeres, estudiantes, jóvenes y obreros suman el sagrado derecho a la desobediencia…(In those shouts, in those chants softened by repression in democracy, is the only place in which the dignity of memory is nested inexhaustibly. In those expressions of dissensus, women, students, youth and workers gather the sacred right to disobedience.)
> *(Lemebel 2016, Kindle Locations 105–107)*

Lemebel's counter-memory work through strategic use of counter-spectacularization or *re-farandulización* can be clearly seen in action in one famous 2000 episode of Chilean TV history, recounted later by its protagonist in a crónica called "Una Molotov para la tele de ese tiempo" ("A Molotov for the TV of that epoch", in Lemebel, *Mi Amiga Gladys*). In it, Lemebel was invited as a guest to a variety show on TV called De Pe a Pa, hosted by Pedro Carcuro, a man originally known by Chileans as the quintessential narrator of the national soccer team's games, a man whose voice had become, during the dictatorship and after, synonymous with the truest depths of affection in Chilean popular culture. Because at the time this was one of the highest rated shows on TV, Lemebel knew from the beginning that it was a rare opportunity for a figure like himself to reach a truly massive national audience. He also knew, as he often put it, that in part he had been invited as a *rara avis*, a freak always worth seeing, a walking scandal. So, he delivered, but in his own terms, with a carefully staged plan:

> me enteré de que la hermana del comentarista, Carmen Carcuro, había sido militante del MIR y cruelmente torturada precisamente bajo la dictadura que saludaba con entusiasmo el televisivo animador. Y ese era un motivo, mejor digo, una molotov para la tele de ese tiempo, donde estas figuras de la entretención y el espectáculo se abanicaban con su apolitismo derechista. (I discovered that the sister of the broadcaster had been a member of the [leftist and heavily repressed political group] MIR and cruelly tortured under the same dictatorship the anchor always enthusiastically endorsed. And that was a reason, better, a molotov cocktail for the TV of that period, during which these entertainers fanned themselves in their apolitical right wingism.)
>
> *(Lemebel 2016, Kindle Locations 170–172)*

Thus Lemebel—already "metido en el show con mi bomba política oculta bajo la manga." ("lodged inside the show with my political bomb under my arm." Kindle Locations 177–178) and having been warned by an insider friend that "lo que tengas que decir dilo resumido porque te van a dejar para el final, te están acortando el tiempo" (Whatever you have to say, say it quickly because they left you for the end and they are shortening your time on camera" Kindle Locations 193–194)—used the final moments of the interview to say, to the astonishment of Carcuro:

> Quiero rendirle un homenaje a todas las mujeres que fueron torturadas y detenidas en la dictadura de Pinochet, en el nombre de tu hermana, Carmen Carcuro. (I want to pay an homage to all the women who were tortured during Pinochet's dictatorship, on behalf of your sister, Carmen Carcuro)
>
> *(Video. "El Día")*

As a sensational episode redefined, i.e. as a strategic use of the capture of the sensible, what popular TV by definition is, the moment perfectly encapsulates Lemebel's broader media mission. One he developed, in both his writing and his personal media appearances, to counter one aspect of the massmediatization of experience, the spectacle—i.e. its mediating as formatting, distancing, and shaping of experience—with a carefully choreographed interventionist situation. In so doing he used another aspect of the mass-mediated, i.e. its massive reach, to contradict its regularly amnesic effect, homeopathically refuting spectacularization with an equally powerful counter-spectacularization.

He succeeded. The next day, Chilean newspapers lead with the scandal one famous Pedro had supposedly created by uncovering the scandal the other famous Pedro had worked so hard to suppress. Lemebel had accomplished a "lemebelazo" whose effect he summarized as:

> Había intervenido en su propio escenario, la memoria impune de la televisión chilena. Y eso me hacía feliz [...]El tema farándula y dictadura estaba abierto." (I had

Art, literature, and mass media in Pedro Lemebel

intervened in their own scenario, the unpunished memory of Chilean TV. And that made me happy. [...] The issue of [the connections between] spectacle and dictatorship had been pried open.)

(Kindle Locations 245–249)

The true impact of this guerrilla-intervention in Chilean media can best be ascertained by considering two facts: first, that "the scandal" took place in 2000, i.e. already ten years into the so-called Chilean transition to democracy, and, secondly, by describing what Pedro Carcuro himself was to say about the episode fifteen years later. Interviewed in February 2015, a month and half after the death of Lemebel, Pedro Carcuro remembered:

Invitar a Pedro Lemebel era, en primer lugar, una incógnita. Era la primera vez que él iba a estar en un programa de audiencia masiva, además en vivo, cuando la TV abierta se manejaba con códigos muy distintos a los de ahora. Había mucha más timidez respecto a los temas que se trataban y a quiénes se invitaba. [...] Pero es evidente que entrevistar a Pedro Lemebel te provocaba un poco de cosquilleo en el estómago... Tú sabías que era un personaje fuerte que no tenía pelos en la lengua: decía lo que a él se le antojaba. (Inviting Pedro Lemebel was, first, a mystery. It was the first time he was going to be on a mass audience TV program, live, when open TV operated with very different codes from the ones it uses today. [...] But it is obvious that to interview Pedro Lemebel gave you some pause... You knew he was a strong personality who had no trouble saying whatever he wanted to say.)

("Pedro Carcuro", n.p.)

Carcuro's most telling comments about the situation, however, did not refer to Lemebel's performance but to the impact his words had had on the anchor himself:

Me descolocó, esa es la verdad, era algo que no esperaba para nada. Es como si estás en la playa bañándote y de pronto se te viene una ola gigantesca encima. [...] Y yo también, con el tiempo, he ido masticando los hechos con una perspectiva distinta. Él hizo un homenaje a las mujeres chilenas que estuvieron en la resistencia a través de mi hermana Carmen... Yo hoy me siento emocionado por lo que él hizo. Ésa sería la forma definirlo: me siento emocionado. (He threw me off, that is the truth, it was something I was not at all expecting. It is as if you are at the beach swimming and then a gigantic wave covers you. [...] And I too, over time, have been mulling over the facts with a different perspective. He paid an homage to the Chilean women who fought in the resistance through my sister Carmen... Today I feel touched by what he did. That would be the way to say it: I feel touched)

("Pedro Carcuro", n.p.)

Lemebel's use of the media as a counter-intervention space to contradict the effects of the media on social memory is a proletarianization insofar as he used the people's passions (soccer, TV, the spectacular, irreverence, the scandalous) to sensationally (i.e. aesthetically, sensorially) remind the people of that which their media consumption habits had occluded. Lemebel showed his public that their task was not simply watching popular TV but understanding its power and being critical about it, in the process creating a powerful moment of true and truly popular TV.

Juan Poblete

The crónica as mass-mediated literature

Mass media are for Lemebel always a place of existence and production of the social, outside the media nothing seems to count socially. But they are also a space that permanently and significantly affects and distorts that, which otherwise, exists outside them. For the author, literature is, on the other hand, both a space within which to produce and perform a freer self capable of confronting the limitations other social discourses, such as those of mass media, inflict on the subject, and a somewhat restrictive aesthetic straight jacket imposing rhetorical, thematic and discursive limits to that expression and, especially, to the author's capacity to reach an audience and intervene in his society. Lemebel's *oeuvre* is located precisely in the space between these two media specific forms of discursive possibilities and limitations.

In a 2012 piece I divided Lemebel's literary production into three stages: a first one defined by two great crónica books *La Esquina es mi corazón: Crónica urbana* (1995) and *El Loco Afán: Crónicas de Sidario* (1996); a transitional moment marked by *De Perlas y cicatrices: Crónicas radiales* (1998) and *El Zanjón de la Aguada* (2003); and a third and final phase, including *Adiós Mariquita linda* (2004), *Serenata cafiola* (2008), and *Háblame de amores* (2012). The principle organizing these three stages, I proposed, was the movement from a form of authorial voice based on the figure of "la loca" (or the queer flaneur) to another based on the figure of the literary author of great commercial success and national and international recognition. In all cases what defined the respective stage was also the mediation between the local, the national, and the global. (Poblete 2010)

Rather than repeating that full argument here and in order to conclude this chapter, I would like to develop, instead, a complementary and much shorter thesis on the nature of Lemebel's overall cultural project, and more specifically on the relationship between his literary and his journalistic efforts. Or, to put it more precisely, I propose that such project is defined by a constitutive contradiction or tension between what would be more appropriate to call two writerly impulses. One is democratic and expansive (the journalistic), the other individual, expressive, and, by definition, more restrictive (the literary). The figure of "la loca" presides and organizes the first and more literary epoch in Lemebel's writing, a period stylistically defined by the author's extraordinary exploration of the expressive possibilities of what I have called elsewhere his "barroco popular y urbano" (popular urban baroque) language.[2] That language serves as an expression for what Lemebel himself has called "la pasión ciudadanal" (a passion that is both a form of citizenship and the manifestation of a sexual desire that can also be political). That baroquely expressed passion combines then the effort to understand the actual life of the citizens (the people) with the erotic impetus of direct connection with their bodies. Such "pasión" thus mixes erotics and politics, desire and participation, knowledge and analysis, with ecstasies and libidinal energies. The result, in those two early books, is a form of participant ethnography, a new type of knowledge capable of illuminating the complexity of the urban milieu under neoliberal globalization. The instruments of this knowledge are both the eye and the pen and the anus and the phallus. They all see and write this city perceived from the "pasión ciudadanal." While la loca is clearly informed by Lemebel's own biography, what defines her discursive power—as both, the perspective organizing the world represented, and a participating character in that universe—is a certain form of analytical objectivity, a paradoxical de-personalization or de-subjectification. Asked in 1998 about his defense of the rights of minorities, Lemebel said:

> Pero yo no hablo por ellos. Las minorías tienen que hablar por sí mismas. Yo sólo ejec-
> uto en la escritura una suerte de ventriloquía amorosa, que niega el yo, produciendo

un vacío deslenguado de mil hablas. (But I don't speak for them. Minorities must speak for themselves. I only perform in writing a form of loving ventriloquy, which denies the self, resulting in a tongueless void of many speeches.)

(Lemebel, in Schäffer 1988: 59)

After a transitional period, what marks the second epoch in the author's *oeuvre* is, as already stated, a voice based on the figure of the commercially successful and renowned author. In this period, while Lemebel is not nearly as often writing about his passionate participant ethnographies, he finds a different way to turn his self into the vital matter animating the crónica. In this case, however, rather than the distancing of literary de-personalization that generates the characteristic mix of intense subjectivity and clinical objectivity of his first period—we read something else. What now produces the logic and organization of the texts is a different form of the biographical, one that both reaches out to a much broader public by privileging the content (a sustained commentary on popular culture, Chilean political life, and their connections) rather than the elaboration of the language, and the famously queer perspective of the well-known author, and places it at its very center, the very well known "Ojo de loca [que] no se equivoca." The eye has become more of a recognizable signature or a brand than a clinical instrument for dissecting and understanding the underside of the social.

But these two writerly impulses, what I have called here the journalistic and the literary, the expansive and the restrictive poles, are not exactly opposed but rather in tension throughout Lemebel's work. After all, all of Lemebel's books have been extraordinarily popular in Chile and elsewhere in Latin America, and for his most popular, working class readers, even Lemebel's most journalistic works have been a (perhaps rare) window into the literary.

Lemebel was of course fully cognizant of how difficult it was to find the right place and balance in a literary and social market defined by the rules of others, and characterized by its ability to commodify everything, including dissent. The sustained exploration of such a predicament is not one of Lemebel's minor accomplishments. His whole *oeuvre*—a significant redistribution of the sensible that, at a specific time in Chilean history, marks the gap between a poetics (a way of doing discourse) and an aisthesis (a horizon of affects) to include new boundaries between popular culture and elite culture, literature and mass media, the intellectual and the masses, the cognitive and the affective, the freer self and a freer and more just society—can now be considered a sharp comment on the challenges and paradoxes of successfully speaking from the margins, of building a career bringing to light what's repressed and marginal, of doing cultural work in Chile at the time of its neoliberal globalization. That was his third and, perhaps, most important proletarianizing move. Such proletarianization insist on combining his inclusive and restrictive writerly impulses with his *barroco popular* against neoliberalism, the literary and the journalistic in the development of a uniquely popular and literary voice in Latin America, as he eloquently put it in his prologue to *Serenata Cafiola*:

Podría escribir clarito, podría escribir sin tantos recovecos, sin tanto remolino inútil. Podría escribir casi telegráfico para la globa y para la homologación simétrica de las lenguas arrodilladas al inglés. [...] Podría escribir novelas y novelones de historias precisas de silencios simbólicos. [...] Podría escribir sin lengua como un conductor de CNN, sin acento y sin sal. Pero tengo la lengua salada y las vocales me cantan en vez de educar. [...] Podría escribir con las piernas juntas, con las nalgas apretadas. Podría guardarme la ira y la rabia emplumada de mis imágenes, la violencia devuelta a la violencia y dormir tranquilo con mi novelería cursi. Pero no me llamo así [...] Pero no vine a eso [...] No sé a lo que vine a este concierto, pero llegué.

(I could write very clearly, I could write without so many twists. I could write almost telegraphically for the world and the symmetrical homogenization of the languages kneeling before English. I could write novels and big novels of precise stories and symbolic silences. […] I could write without a tongue like a CNN anchor, without an accent and with no salt. But my tongue is salted and my vowels sing instead of educating. […] I could write with tight legs and a tight ass. I could hide my rage and the flowery rancour of my images, the violence returning the violence, and peacefully sleep with my pretentious novelties. But that is not my name […] But I did not come for that. […] I do not know why I came to this concert, but I am here.)

(Lemebel 2008: 11–12)

Notes

1 On neoliberalism as an anti-memory apparatus, see Moulián (1997).
2 For a relevant and comprehensive exploration of the baroque discursive tradition in Latin America and Spain, see Mateo del Pino (2013). For an excellent analysis of how the baroque image, the residual and kitsch in Lemebel are part of a communicational strategy to resignify mass media in the Chile of the Transition from dictatorship to democracy, see Sierra.

Works cited

Adorno, Theodor and Max Horkheimer. *Dialectic of Enlightenment*, London: Verso, 1997.
Better, John. "El Cuerpo castigado: Una entrevista a Pedro Lemebel", *Latin American Literature Today*, 2, April 2017.
Brunner, José Joaquín. *Un Espejo Trizado*, Santiago: Flacso, 1988.
Brunner, José Joaquín. *Bienvenidos a la modernidad*, Santiago: Planeta, 1994.
Cabezas, Omar. *La Montaña es algo más que una inmensa estepa verde*, La Habana: Casa de las Américas, 1982.
Cortázar, Julio. *Todos los fuegos el fuego*, Buenos Aires: Sudamericana, 1966.
Gutiérrez Alea, Tomás and Juan Carlos Tabío. *Fresa y chocolate*, ICAIC, 1993.
Lemebel, Pedro. *La Esquina es mi corazón*, Santiago: Cuarto Propio, 1995.
Lemebel, Pedro. *Loco Afán. Crónicas de sidario*, Santiago: Lom, 1996.
Lemebel, Pedro. *De Perlas y cicatrices. Crónicas radiales*, Santiago: Lom, 1998.
Lemebel, Pedro. *Tengo miedo torero*. Santiago: Seix-Barral. 2001.
Lemebel, Pedro. *Zanjón de la Aguada*. Santiago: Seix-Barral, 2003.
Lemebel, Pedro. *Adiós Mariquita linda*, Santiago: Sudamericana, 2004.
Lemebel, Pedro. *Serenata Cafiola*, Santiago: Seix Barral, 2008.
Lemebel, Pedro. *Háblame de amores*, Santiago: Seix Barral. 2012.
Lemebel, Pedro. "*Manifesto (I Speak for my Difference)*", translated by Sergio Holas-Veliz and Israel Holas Allimant, *Cordite Poetry Review*, 1 May 2015.
Lemebel, Pedro. *Mi amiga Gladys*, Argentina: Grupo Planeta, 2016.
Mateo del Pino, Angeles. "Barroco constante más allá de…" in Angeles Mateo del Pino et al. eds., *Angeles Maraqueros. Trazos neobraroc-s-ch-os en las poéticas latinoamericanas*, Buenos Aires: Katatay, 2013, 9–68.
Moulián, Tomás. *Chile actual. Anatomía de un mito*. Santiago: Arcis/Lom, 1997.
"Pedro Carcuro: Hoy me emociona lo que hizo Lemebel", *The Clinic*, 3 February 2015.
Paz, Senel. *El lobo, el bosque y el hombre nuevo*, La Habana: *Edición Homenaje del Ministerio de Cultura*, 1990.
Poblete, Juan. "Crónica y ciudadanía en tiempos de globalización neoliberal: la escritura callejera" in Graciela Falbo, ed., *Tras las Huellas de una escritura en tránsito. La Crónica contemporánea en América Latina*, Buenos Aires: Ediciones Al Margen/ Editorial de la Universidad de La Plata, 2007, 71–88.
Poblete, Juan. " De la loca a la superestrella: cultura local y mediación nacional en la época de la neoliberalización global" in Fernando Blanco and Juan Poblete, eds., *Pedro Lemebel. Discurso cultural, resistencia y comunicación en la época neoliberal*, Santiago: Cuarto Propio, 2010, 135–156.
Poblete, Juan. "The Memory of the National and the National as Memory", *Latin American Perspectives*, 202:43 (3), 2015, 92–106.
Poblete, Juan. "Pedro Lemebel: In Memoriam", *Journal of Latin American Cultural Studies*, 24:3, 2015, 287–289.

Puig, Manuel. *El Beso de la mujer araña*, Barcelona: Seix Barral, 1976.

Puig, Manuel. "El Error gay", *Debate Feminista*, 16, 139–141, 1997. Originally published in Spanish in *El Porteño*, IX, September 1990.

Ranciere, Jacques. *Dissensus. On Politics and Aesthetics*, New York: Continuum, 2010.

Schäffer, Maureen. "Pedro Lemebel. La Yegua Silenciada" (an interview), *Revista Hoy*, 9–15 February, 1988.

Sierra, Marta. "'Tu voz existe': percepción mediática, cultura nacional y transiciones democráticas en Pedro Lemebel" in Fernando Blanco and Juan Poblete, eds., *Pedro Lemebel. Discurso cultural, resistencia y comunicación en la época neoliberal*, Santiago: Cuarto Propio, 101–134.

Stiegler, Bernard. *For a New Critique of Political Economy*, Cambridge: Polity, 2010.

Sutherland, Juan Pablo. "Los efectos politico-culturales de la traducción del queer" in Sutherland, Juan Pablo ed,. *Nación Marica. Prácticas culturales y crítica activista*, Santiago: Ripio Ediciones, 2009.

"Video. El Día en que Lemebel descolocó a Carcuro recordando a su hermanan torturada", *The Clinic*, 24 January 2015.

Wolfson, Todd. *Digital Rebellion. The Birth of the Cyber Left*, Urbana, IL: University of Illinois Press, 2014.

PART III

Re-constructing silver screen imaginaries

13
NEOLIBERAL PIGMENTOCRACIES
Women and the elite body politic in neoliberal Mexican cinema

Ignacio M. Sánchez Prado

In his essay "The Nation and Its Women", Partha Chatterjee discusses the ties between nationalist discourse and a patriarchy that, in his words, "combined coercive authority with the subtle force of persuasion" (1993: 130). While his discussion focuses on the rise of Indian nationalism *vis-á-vis* the colonial State, Chatterjee's insights adequately illuminate the way in which Mexican post-Revolutionary culture used gender and the representation of women in order to construct a "cultural essence" that defined the nation in relation to both foreign culture and the life of subaltern subjects. Being mindful of the differences between India and Mexico, one can nonetheless draw the important departing points for my discussion from Chatterjee's conclusions. First, Chatterjee points towards the construction of "woman" as part of a recourse of essentialism that distances her and the nation from both the threat of cosmopolitanism and the understanding of the economic differences of the lower class (134). In other words, it is part of a set of cultural devices that have enabled the hegemonic rule of the elite by constructing identities and social behaviors that put social difference under erasure. Second, in Chatterjee's assessment, this culture exists and reproduces because of the willing participation of the middle classes in it, using even forms of apparently progressive cultural production to preserve hierarchies of race and gender within the social contract of the nation (134). If we focus for a moment on the way in which two great icons, Dolores del Río and María Félix, were shown in the cinema of Emilio Fernández, we can see some of the same patterns, including the presence of a national essence that is predicated on either traditional or community values embodied in woman. But an equally important point for my purposes is that these two icons match Chatterjee's insight about the middle classes more clearly: we see these two bodies, whiter than the average *mestizo* or indigenous citizen they were claiming to represent, as an elite constructed stand-in for the people that nonetheless exists at a distance from both cosmopolitan culture (as we see, for instance, in the erasure of Dolores del Río's Hollywood persona through Mexicanization) and from the lives and cultures of subaltern classes. In their foundational books on women in Golden Age Mexican cinema, Joanne Hershfield and Julia Tuñón have insightfully shown the disruptive nature of some of the images and figures of women in the context of the social modernization of the 1940s, which also, and paradoxically, were part of a normalization of cultural hegemony that appeared equally in the films of Fernández or Ismael Rodríguez, as it did in late muralism, literature and other cultural genres.[1]

In the following pages, I want to raise the question as to how this figure of woman as part of the repertoire of icons for nationalist hegemony becomes problematized into a set of images that seek to reconfigure her once the nationalist social contract breaks. In particular, my interest focuses on the ways in which the nationalist articulation of the female body withers and gives way to new forms of the elite body politic in the context of neoliberal cinema. I present these ideas as one of the scholars of Mexican cinema in the English-language academy who have recently published work that collectively engages the structural changes in the production and reception of Mexican cinema since 1988 and the effect of those changes in the aesthetics and ideologies of cinema.[2] Within this framework, I believe that the change of function of woman in Mexican cinema from the paradigm established by the Golden Age and by revolutionary nationalism to the predominant iconicities in the neoliberal processes has to do with a displacement of the representational claims of the elite from the national subject to the upper-class ideal represented by neoliberalism. There are of course significant intermediate figures that signaled the transition. The exploitation genres of the 1960s and 1970s, and actors like Isela Vega, Meche Carreño and Fanny Cano presented oversexualized figures that, accompanied by an increased visibility of queer subjects, presented a vision of sexuality that was, paradoxically, open and full of fears and anxieties.[3] At the same time, some iconic figures pulled in a different direction, in which women continued to embody forms of social disciplining in visual media, resisting the changes brought forward by the Mexican revolution. An example of this is Lucerito, a young woman who grew up in Televisa films and *telenovelas* and came to be seen as an embodiment of moral values and of ways to bring youth back to the moral fore.[4] And, finally, there is the case of La India María, a comedic character created by actor-director María Elena Velasco, perhaps the most commercially successful female filmmaker in the history of Mexican cinema, in which the stereotypical (some would say racist) ways in which indigenous women are represented are turned into a comedy that shed light on various important issues of race, gender and migration under the guise of light comedy.[5]

Starting in the late 1980s, as Mexican cinema gradually ceased to be a popular genre, and, as movie theaters privatized, the film industry turned itself towards the middle and upper classes.[6] What this meant is that the role of women in Mexican cinema lost the pedagogical dimension tied to national paradigms (and designed by the filmmaking class to engage working-class audiences) into a new economy of representation and desire in which women, both characters and the actors that portray them, come to represent constellations of race, gender and class particular to the subjectification of neoliberalism. My analysis here is focused in what I call woman as embodied neoliberalism, where the changes in the roles of women produced by late capitalism in Mexico reconvert themselves into imaginaries of a gendered middle and upper class that idealizes a self-referential identity of the elite that no longer needs to claim representation of the subaltern classes. To be sure, my point of course is not that we pass from a cinema that represents "the people" to one that does not, as I do not believe that such a cinema ever existed. Rather, I will claim that contemporary Mexican cinema operates in paradigms where the elite subjects it represents no longer feel the need to negotiate with any social subjectivity but their own. This is a major shift from the role of women prevalent in nationalist cultures like Golden Age cinema, and the correlation between woman and nation theorized by Chatterjee. Rather, we are seeing the figure of woman as the signifier of a body politic that is more narrowly defined as elites sustained on race dynamics such as "pigmentocracy", a term that has emerged to describe the role skin color plays in social and class hierarchy in Latin American societies that self-fashion as *mestizo* or racially mixed.[7] The elite body politic imagined by commercial films is tied to the assertion and privileging of a regime of neoliberal pigmentocracy, in which certain iconic white women actors perform, across a repertoire of characters with common traits, the embodiment of values tied to class in late capitalism – creativity, individualism, economic independence, technocratic professionalization and so on – in social types that elicit audiences desires and affects towards a naturalization of hierarchical social orders and even forms of feminism that are paradoxically tied to neoliberal subjectivities.[8]

The last iteration of nationalist bodies proper in Mexican cinema emerged, in my view, in three of the most important films of the 1990–1994 class of films, which developed within a context of unprecedented aesthetic and ideological diversity in the context of three phenomena: the dismantling of considerable parts of the State's structures of film production and exhibition, the emergence of a middle-class optimism resulting from the apparent success of the Salinas de Gortari reforms and the emergence of a new generation of filmmakers that no longer felt bound to the gritty art cinema paradigm established by *echeverrismo* or the populist bent of commercial cinema established by lopezportillismo.[9] Three films in particular – Alfonso Arau's *Como Agua para Chocolate* (*Like Water for Chocolate*, 1992), María Novaro's *Danzón* (*Danzón*, 1991) and Carlos Carrera's *La mujer de Benjamín* (*Benjamín's Woman*, 1991) – sought to reestablish a social contract in which cinema could reconnect with the audiences lost in the decades elapsed since the end of the Golden Age while accounting for the processes of cultural modernization brought forward by early neoliberal reform. These three films become interesting because they exhibit a certain degree of symbolic insufficiency of the iconic paradigms they seek to reactivate. Carlos Carrera's Natividad, (Arcelia Ramírez), for instance, is a young woman bored with the traditional life in her hometown, which, as an icon, she is supposed to embody. The main conflict of the movie emerges when title character Benjamín (Eduardo López Rojas) falls in love with her, and due to her reluctance, tries to kidnap her. The conflict deepens with the arrival of Leandro (Eduardo Palomo), a truck driver that represents, for Natividad, the possibility of breaking away from the small town. In this case, I believe that Natividad, whose sexuality and desire exceed the parameters of the national woman, represents the insufficiency of this figure to embody the values of a traditional society, which requires the enforcement of a violent and dark superego figure, Benjamin, to unsuccessfully keep her under tabs. Another problematic figure is Tita (Lumi Cavazos), from *Como agua para chocolate*. She is also a figure whose desire exceeds the parameters of the role of traditional woman, as manifested both sexually and in cooking. But a point that most critics forget is that she is in fact nothing but a precursor. We know that the conclusion of her story is that she ends up marrying an American and being part, through family connections, of the post-revolutionary elite. And, more importantly, we also know that her story is told by a nameless contemporary middle-class woman, also played by Arcelia Ramírez. Tita, thus, is not a repository of the national, but a woman whose struggle to liberate from those imperatives is a precursor for the individual modern identity of the narrator, Ramírez's character. Finally, a third case is María Novaro's Julia (María Rojo), from *Danzón*. This character is more interesting, because she is in fact a working-class woman whose economic world is about to be threatened by modernization (she is a unionized telephone worker on the eve of Telmex's privatization). However, Novaro's solution is very unsatisfying: at the collapse of the social benefits of the post-revolutionary welfare state, the traditional and conservative culture of *Danzón* becomes the symbolic refuge, in which a woman may reinscribe herself in the safety of the traditional order after confronting the pain and liberation of modernity.

In contrast to the exhaustion of the nationalist imaginary, Mexican filmmakers of the 1990s gradually developed a competing form of female iconicity, where woman no longer embodies the essence that shelters the nation from the threats of modernity or inequality, but someone whose body becomes the site of the purported emancipation neoliberalism promised, and the triumph of creative individuality heralded by neoliberalism. The founding character of this paradigm is Clarisa (played by Claudia Ramírez), in Alfonso Cuarón's *Sólo con tu pareja* (*Love in the*

Time of AIDS, 1991). Clarisa participates in the middle-class economy of the early neoliberal period in her work as a flight attendant, which, significantly, is one of the reasons why she is an object of desire for the protagonist, Tomás Tomás (Daniel Giménez Cacho), who falls in love with her while she rehearses her flight safety routine. What we see in this movie is a woman whose evident marks of class and whiteness relieve her from the duty of embodying any representational essence, becoming an individually discernible object of desire for the male gaze (because, ultimately, she is the one who stands out as a love interest of a womanizer who equalizes all other women as interchangeable). Another variation of this individual figure is Susana (Arcelia Ramírez) in Rafael Montero's *Cilantro y perejil* (*Cilantro and Parsley*, 1995), whose middle-class status becomes the condition of possibility of a process of individuation and self-discovery permitted by her divorce But perhaps the most iconic case of this in the 1990s is Gina (Diana Bracho), the protagonist of Sabina Berman's *Entre Pancho Villa y una mujer desnuda* (*Between Pancho Villa and a Naked Woman*, 1996). The movie focuses on a woman who seeks to emancipate herself from the structures of patriarchy and desire embodied by her lover Adrián (Arturo Ríos), a hyper-masculine left wing journalist, and by Pancho Villa (Jesús Ochoa), who shows up in spirit to advice Adrián on how to better subjugate Gina. The telling element, though, is that Gina is the co-owner of a *maquila*, a border sweatshop, and thus part of the emerging elite that directly benefits from of neoliberalism. In Gina, there is a fundamental shift, since the liberation of the body of woman from the constraints of the past is directly connected to the ideologies of individual success and entrepreneurship of neoliberalism. In all three cases, social and economic privilege begets an ideal of individuation that gradually emancipates a woman from her symbolic duties to the nation And, as is particularly evident in the case of Clarisa, the white *mestizo* image cultivated since the Golden Age is fading towards a new pigmentocracy, a new idea of white female beauty that becomes more marked than even the one prevalent in other audiovisual media, like *telenovelas*.

This form of class-determined white femininity operates in the creation of an idealized body politic of the elite that requires moving lower-class women to positions that do not assume a potential inscription into the sphere of the social. The economic dead-end deftly perceived by *Danzón* in the figure of Julia develops over the 1990s into a repertory of female characters who are marked more clearly as *mestizo* and who invariably fail in their engagement with the challenges of neoliberal contemporaneity. One may remember here Alma (Salma Hayek) in *El callejón de los Milagros* (*Midaq Alley*, Jorge Fons 1995). Just like the protagonists of classical films from the 1930s, Alma becomes a prostitute as a result of the failure of her "moral" male love interest to deliver a safe economic situation (he emigrates to the United States) and, of course, as a punishment for her reluctance to surrender to the laws of the traditional society of the *barrio* to which she belongs. Another example is Esperanza (Dolores Heredia) in *Santitos* (*Little Saints*, María Amparo Escandón 1998), a woman who faces the loss of her daughter and the challenge of modernization by sustaining a strong belief in a carnivalesque form of anti-modern religion, which shields them from the affective and economic challenges of the present. And, of course, the best know example is Susana (Vanessa Bauche) in *Amores perros* (Alejandro González Iñárritu 2000), a woman unable to decide between her role as a wife of a man who becomes a criminal in the face of his failure in dealing with neoliberalism, Ramiro, or as lover of her brother-in-law, who is able to game the neoliberal economy by participating in the underground economy of the dog-fight to finance a vague future. Susana, like Alma and like Julia, faces the failure to inscribe herself as an embodiment of the new social order, which results in the perennial failure of these female figures to inscribe themselves into the contemporary.

The ideal of the white neoliberal woman becomes hegemonic in commercial Mexican cinema after the year 2000, when films directed at middle and upper-class audiences who can afford a movie ticket in the newly privatized regime of film exhibition represent embodiments of the social ideal that Richard Florida has called the "creative class", the idea of a society predicated on the success of exceptional individuals driven by their creativity and personal freedom.[10] We can see, for instance, an evolution of women figures whose belonging to economic structures of the creative class allows them to embody a purportedly emancipated femininity in which their ability to conform to ideals of middle-class individuality results, paradoxically, in finding heterosexual love. (This is the case two of the most commercially successful romantic comedies of the past decade: *Ladies Night* (Gabriela Tagliavini 2003) and *Cansada de besar sapos* (*Tired of Kissing Frogs*.[11] In the first film, the two female protagonists, Alicia and Ana, work for an advertising company and are entangled in a love triangle with a co-worker. Then Alicia (Ana Claudia Talancón), a girl presented as innocent, falls in love with a male stripper, thus clearing the way for Ana (Ana de la Reguera) to date the co-worker. It is also interesting to note that Alicia is from the upper class, while Ana is from the professional middle class, and their friendship can be read as a gendered alliance between the two social groups in distributing the benefits, economic and symbolic, of neoliberal reform. *Cansada de besar sapos* is also about the love trials of a publicist, Martha (Ana Serradilla), who decides to try online dating to shop for a date better than her cheating boyfriend. And Clarisa has a descendant in the protagonist of *Te presento a Laura* (*Meet Laura*, Fez Noriega 2010), a Mexican version of the female type called "manic pixie dream girl", a girl whose quirkiness seems to exceed the parameters of middle-class values but ultimately becomes the instrument for the salvation of a middle-class boy.[12] The pinnacle of this type of femininity is seen in the movie *Niñas mal* (Fernando Sariñana 2007), a very popular movie whose success resulted even in the development of a Colombian TV series for MTV Latin America. All the main characters are girls from the middle and upper class who enroll in a finishing school to be able to learn their proper role in society. The movie focuses on Adela (Martha Higareda), the daughter of a conservative politician, who refuses to be the "good girl" that her father's political ambitions require. As expected, the movie resolves in a way that allows Adela to pursue her career as an actress and to be the "free spirit" who can move away from her class expectations. But the important thing to note here is not only that she can do that because she is wealthy (in this case, by being part of a ruling-class family), but also because all of the other girls in the finishing school occupy roles necessary for the maintenance of the neoliberal hegemony: Heidi (Alejandra Adame) attends the school to marry Kike Van der Linde (Víctor González), the young male son of an corporate tycoon; Pía (Camila Sodi) attends the school to adapt enough to society so she can go to her next step in life, a Ph.D. in economics in Harvard, which leads us to believe that she will be part of the technocratic class that manages the neoliberal consensus (her love interest is Adela's father policy coordinator); Maribel (María Aura) goes on to open her own finishing school, thus assuring the preservation of class privilege for women; Valentina (Ximena Sariñana), who we learn is a lesbian, becomes a singer and, as an artist, can stand-in as escape-valve for a sexual difference that can be processed in a way that does not threaten the economic consensus.

What should be obvious at this point is that this new form of idealized neoliberal womanhood is predicated in a freedom with two conditions of possibility: pre-existing economic privilege (none of these figures represent any kind of social mobility, making them far more assertive of elite status than telenovelas), and the willingness to accept individual freedom as a privilege that exists within the narrow race and class confines of the contemporary hegemonic elite. It is, in other words, a discourse meant to preserve the symbolic structures of class inequality without even making the gesture of any kind of pretended democratic inclusion.

To conclude, I want to turn my attention to two forms of feminine representation that, within the limits of a film industry still bound to an audience that can afford a ticket costing the same as a full day of Mexican minimum wage, seek to negotiate the expectations of this audience with a representation of the symbolic violence that underlies neoliberal privilege. One way in which this has happened has been through stories of middle- and upper-class teenagers who fail to participate in the system, or who for some reason refuse to do so, and are harshly punished for this. We can remember here the example of Renata, Higareda's breakthrough character from *Amar te duele* (*Love Hurts*, Fernando Sariñana 2003), a rich girl who falls in love with a lower-class boy and who ends up murdered by her rich former boyfriend, who echoes her family's strong resistance to her class-crossing love affair. Another telling example is that of Maru (María Deschamps) from Gerardo Naranjo's *Voy a explotar* (*I'm Gonna Explode* 2008). Marú becomes the love interest of the son of a congressman, who is rebelling against his father, and they decide to hide from the family and plot their life together. However, in the end, she also dies after being shot by accident. Finally, we have the example of Alejandra (Tessa Ía) in *Después de Lucía* (*After Lucía*, Michel Franco 2012), whose inability to adjust to the life of a middle-class school results in brutal bullying that also results in her death. As these characters emerged, some filmmakers in recent years have also developed female characters that contest neoliberal ideals from within: Carlos Reygadas' Ana (Anapola Muskádiz) in *Batalla en el cielo* (*Battle in Heaven* 2006), who becomes a prostitute as a hobby and who sleeps with the family driver, until she is, once again, killed. Blanca (Ana de la Reguera) from *Backyard/El traspatio* (Carlos Carrera 2009), who challenges the gender violence that underlies the femicides in Juárez, and Laura (Stephanie Sigman), from *Miss Bala* (2011), whose quest for neoliberal normalcy through the beauty pageant leads her to face the brutal violence of the drug war in Mexico. But, of course, these are all histories of defeat, as neoliberal Mexican cinema remains unable to produce a consistent imaginary of female agency that is not predicated in nostalgia for the past, preservation of elite values, or violent defeat.

Instead, in the past five of years we see a persistence in the celebration of elite values in films *Nosotros los nobles* (*The Noble Family*, Gaz Alazraki, 2013), which became for some time the highest grossing Mexican movie ever (and remains at number two). One of the protagonists, Barbie Noble (Karla Souza), is a shallow rich heir who is made to believe that her family lost all money. This forces her to work as a waitress in a cantina, where she rekindles her emotions for the family maid's son, Lucho, who gets her the job in the first place. When she finds out that her poverty was nothing but a ruse put together by her father, she nearly marries a gold digger, but ultimately ends up with Lucho. (Ianis Guerrero). While this movie no longer punishes class-crossing love, like *Amarte duele* did, her relationship with Lucho (just like a side plot with one of her brothers) suggests the possibility of inter-class relations as a way to place under erasure the social inequality that exists in Mexico and that, since 2014, is exploding across the country in insurgent movements and social mobilizations. It is not coincidental that *Nosotros los nobles* is the product of the Alazraki family, a billionaire clan with strong control of media and advertising industries in Mexico (they do advertising for Slim businesses, for example), and with strong political ties to the neoliberal incarnation of the Institutional Revolutionary Party (PRI). Barbie Noble is the new version of an elite that uses culture to negotiate with the inequality that benefits them. And Mexican cinema still cannot produce what it has never produced, a system of cultures and icons that more fairly and critically represents the gender, race and class violence and the insurmountable divisions that characterize modern Mexican society.

Notes

1 See Tuñón, *Mujeres de luz y sombra* (1998) and Hershfield, *Mexican Cinema/ Mexican Woman* (2012).
2 A description of this debate exceeds the extension of the present chapter, but four books on this subject are: MacLaird, *Aesthetics and Politics* (2013); Aldama, *Mex-Ciné* (2013); Smith, *Mexican Screen Fictions* (2014); Sánchez Prado, *Screening Neoliberalism* (2014).

3 On this matter, see Berg, *Cinema of Solitude* (1992: 125–30); Venkatesh, *New Maricón Cinema* (2016: 28–38); De la Mora, "Tus pinches leyes" (2009). A particular case is that of *Lola la trailera* (1983), which combines exploitation and female empowerment in a very unique way. See Benamou, "Con amor, tequila y gasolina" (2009).
4 For an excellent study of Lucerito, see Cosentino, "Televisa Born and Raised" (2016).
5 Finally, after many years of scholarly silence, a book on La India María is forthcoming. See Rohrer, *La India María* (2017).
6 For a study on trends in movie-going and the demographic changes that took place with privatization, see Rosas Mantecón, *Ir al cine* (2017: 231–92).
7 Although the term is frequently used in the press and scholarship, its proper theorization is a fairly recent phenomenon. For the most complete analysis of the term *vis-à-vis* concrete social practices in Latin America, see Telles and PERLA, *Pigmentocracies* (2014). For a recent (and controversial) assessment of the workings of racism in Mexico, see Navarrete, *Mexico racista* (2016).
8 In this assertion I follow Nancy Fraser's powerful study of the relationship between certain ideas of feminism and neoliberalism. See Fraser, *Fortunes of Feminism* (2013).
9 See, Sánchez Prado, *Screening Neoliberalism* (2014: 15–61).
10 See Florida, *The Creative Class* (2012).
11 For parallel examples on the relationship between romantic comedies and class, see Sánchez Prado, "Regimes of Affect" (2014). I have also written a more in-depth analysis of these two films in Sánchez Prado, "Humorous Affects" (2016).
12 The idea of "manic pixie dream-girl" was developed by critic Nathan Rabin as a parody of the stereo-typical woman in late 1990s romantic comedies. See Rabin, *My Year of Flops* (2010: 1–6).

Works cited

Aldama, Frederick. *Mex-Ciné. Mexican Filmmaking, Production and Consumption in the Twenty-First Century.* Ann Arbor, MI: University of Michigan Press, 2013.
Benamou, Catherine L. "*Con amor, tequila y gasolina.* Lola, the Truck Driver and Screen Resistance in *cine fronterizo.*" In Victoria Ruétalo and Dolores Tierney eds., *Latsploitation, Exploitation Cinemas, and Latin America.* London: Routledge, 2009. 171–84.
Berg, Charles Ramírez. *Cinema of Solitude. A Critical Study of Mexican Film, 1967–1983.* Austin, TX: University of Texas Press, 1992.
Chatterjee, Partha. *The Nation and Its Fragments. Colonial and Postcolonial Histories.* Princeton, NJ: Princeton University Press, 1993.
Cosentino, Olivia. "Televisa Born and Raised. Lucerito´s Stardom in 1980s Mexican Media." *The Velvet Light Trap*, 78, 2016. 38–52.
De la Mora, Sergio, "'Tus pinches leyes yo me las paso por los huevos:' Isela Vega and Mexican Dirty Movies." In Victoria Ruétalo and Dolores Tierney eds., *Latsploitation, Exploitation Cinemas, and Latin America.* London: Routledge, 2009. 245–57.
Florida, Richard. *The Rise of the Creative Class. And How It's Transforming Work, Leisure, Community and Everyday Life.* New York: Basic Books, 2012.
Fraser, Nancy. *Fortunes of Feminism. From State-Managed Capitalism to Neoliberal Crisis.* London: Verso, 2013.
Hershfield, Joanne. *Mexican Cinema/ Mexican Woman.* Tucson, AZ: University of Arizona Press, 2012.
MacLaird, Misha. *Aesthetics and Politics in the Mexican Film Industry.* New York: Palgrave Macmillan, 2013.
Navarrete, Federico. *México racista. Una denuncia.* Mexico City: Grijalbo, 2016.
Rabin, Nathan. *My Year of Flops. One Man's Journey into the Heart of Cinematic Failure.* New York: Scribner, 2010.
Rohrer, Seraina. *La India María. Mexploitation and the Films of María Elena Velasco.* Austin, TX: University of Texas Press, 2017.
Rosas Mantecón, Ana. *Ir al cine. Antropología de los públicos, la ciudad y las pantallas.* Mexico City: Gedisa/ Universidad Autónoma Metropolitana-Iztapalapa, 2017.
Sánchez Prado, Ignacio M. "Regimes of Affect. Love and Class in Mexican Neoliberal Cinema." *Journal of Popular Romance Studies*, 4.1, 2014.
Sánchez Prado, Ignacio M. *Screening Neoliberalism. Transforming Mexican Cinema 1988–2012.* Nashville, TN: Vanderbilt University Press, 2014.
Sánchez Prado, Ignacio M, "Humorous Affects. Romantic Comedies in Contemporary Mexico." In Juan Poblete and Juana Suárez, eds. *Humor in Latin American Cinema.* New York: Palgrave Macmillan, 2016. 203–22.

Smith, Paul Julian. *Mexican Screen Fictions.* Cambridge: Polity, 2014.

Telles, Edward Eric and the Project on Ethnicity and Race in Latin America (PERLA). *Pigmentocracies. Ethnicity, Race and Color in Latin America.* Chapel Hill, NC: University of North Carolina Press, 2014.

Tuñón, Julia. *Mujeres de luz y sombra en el cine mexicano. La construcción de una imagen, 1939–1952.* Mexico City: El Colegio de México/ Instituto Mexicano de Cinematografía, 1998.

Venkatesh, Vinodh. *New Maricón Cinema. Outing Latin American Film.* Austin, TX: University of Texas Press, 2016.

14

CLASS, GENDER, RACE IN RECENT FILMIC URBAN BRAZILIAN SPACES[1]

Samuel Cruz

The high concentration of cinemas has often exemplified a city's cultural offerings; and urban life has been a central concern of the films themselves. As pointed out by David Clarke, "Indeed, whilst the histories of film and the city are imbricated to such an extent that it is unthinkable that the cinema could have developed without the city, and whilst the city has been unmistakably shaped by the cinematic form, neither film nor urban studies has paid the warranted attention to *their* connection" (Clarke 1997: 1). Recently, Brazilian films have also been an important mechanism for helping audiences at home and abroad to perceive and better understand the city's role in perpetuating social injustice.

Scholars have understood cities as the pinnacle of human achievement. Robert Park notes that "Cities, and particularly the great metropolitan cities of modern times… are, with all their complexities and artificialities, man's most imposing creation, the most prodigious of human artifacts. We must conceive of our cities therefore… as workshops of civilization, and, at the same time, as the natural habitat of civilized man" (cited in Harvey 1973: 195). Cities, and more specifically the metropolis and megalopolis of our time, are definitely workshops of civilization. But the same workshop that serves as a creative space for the concretization of man's greatest dreams has been unable to meet the most fundamental aspirations of humanity, exacerbating instead socio-spatial inequalities. My purpose here is to discuss the nexus of contemporary Brazilian cinema and São Paulo, taking into consideration socio-economic and political issues related to class-specific, gendered, and racialized social spaces that have shaped São Paulo and Brazil at large. In the end, the city is incapable of creating attainable dreams and hope might be the last resort, for those who have hope.

São Paulo was founded on January 25, 1554. It is the largest city in South America and is one of the largest cities across the globe with an urban area of 590mi² and a diverse population of over twenty million people. In the aftermath of the military dictatorship (1964–1985), Brazil was profoundly impacted by neoliberal reforms which had numerous socio-economic consequences, including massive unemployment, escalating impoverishment, and detrimental distribution of wealth. As South America's most important city, São Paulo has experienced the material as well as social implications of such actions. At the material level, this city has witnessed the abandonment of public areas, the revitalization of some spaces as well as the promotion of urban fragmentation through the creation of wealthy enclaves.

The two films on which I ground my analysis, *Os Inquilinos* (2009) (The Tenants [Don't Like it, Leave!]), directed by the acclaimed director Sergio Bianchi, and *Linha de Passe*[2] (2008), directed by the world-renowned director Walter Salles and co-directed by Daniela Thomas, offer a critique of racial-, gender-, and class-related practices underlining these practices from different perspectives. Moreover, my goal in discussing how Bianchi, and Salles and Thomas portray cities, particularly the globalized metropolises of the South, is to offer a look into the great persistent inequalities observed in Brazilian society today.

Os Inquilinos

Sergio Bianchi's critically acclaimed *Os Inquilinos* (2009) offers avenues to explore larger socio-economic, cultural, and political issues related to São Paulo's urban space. I argue that the film charts and makes visible socio-economic, cultural, and political tensions in the city. The film reproduces the socio-spatial divisions that create symbolic and material urban elements such as the *favela*. *Os Inquilinos* does that by underlining class, gender, and race differentiation in São Paulo, showcasing socially and geographically isolated class. The tenor of the film's critique of socio-spatial stratification is Bianchi's known acid tone. Bianchi does not see a solution for the social problems he critiques in his films; in the end, the "lower" classes continue to be dominated.

Os Inquilinos is a cutting critique on the socio-spatial order. The film is set in a peripheral area of São Paulo, offering only a glance from a distance of the central and better equipped area of the city. Through composition, framing and camera movement as well as the mise-en-scène, the film builds a sense of social entrapment in order to critique larger class-, gender-, and race-related issues. Although *Os Inquilinos* centers its narrative on a working-class family and elite sectors are not directly represented, hegemonic discourses about the periphery play a fundamental role in the film's portrayal of race, class, and gender relations. This is done for instance through the representation of violence in other media such as television and literature in multiple scenes that showcase their effect on the main character Valter, his family, and other characters from peripheral neighborhoods.

Sergio Bianchi's so-called *Cinema Faca* (Knife Cinema) refers to his subtle, yet vicious indictment of dominant society as thoroughly corrupt and unable to solve endemic social problems that affect the working class disproportionately. *Os Inquilinos* builds a net of correlations that the film unfolds to discuss the social and material implications of living entrapped in and by the hardships of a huge metropolis. It is set entirely in the city's outskirts and privileges the perspectives of those who live there – particularly that of Valter, who works loading boxes at a fruits and vegetables warehouse, and his family.[3] The narrative foregrounds their experience of the precariousness of urban life, most notably the seemingly constant threat of violence, and lack of the right to the city. It also draws attention to the power of hegemonic discourses that associate the peripheral/marginal urban space with certain class, gender, and racial discourses. More specifically, by placing Valter's experiences at the center of the narrative, the film shows us the degree to which his perceptions of his surroundings are influenced by hegemonic discourses about the urban environment, especially those that associate violence with the (working) poor and Afro-Brazilians living in peripheral neighborhoods like his and the even poorer sections surrounding his neighborhood.

The film's suggestive title underscores the precariousness of life in Valter's neighborhood and, at the same time, points to the impossibility of any other choice. Is it possible to leave? Leave to where? The title refers to the neighbors who move in next door; and whose very presence seemingly endangers Valter's family, who see their home ownership as a sign of social mobility.

Class, gender, race in recent filmic urban Brazilian spaces

Highlighting the distances and differences that exist in a polarized society, *Os Inquilinos* positions the destitute as imprisoned by a system that privileges hegemonic elite.

Disenfranchisement and marginalization: Positioning gender and race

The opening scenes depict Valter's family dynamics. He lives with his wife Iara, and their two kids, Fernanda and Diogo, in a typical working-class neighborhood in São Paulo's periphery. We later learn that the neighborhood is called Vila Imperial (Imperial Village), a name that exemplifies Bianchi's characteristic use of irony. This is visualized in the film itself in shots of the neighborhood's modest, one to two story houses with limited amenities that in no way embody grandiose ambitions. Iara wants to move because this neighborhood is located near the dangerous *favela* depicted in the opening scene, but Valter insists on staying. As he points out, his father built the house in which they live "brick by brick" and for that reason he does not want to move. Through this interchange, the film reminds viewers of the ongoing challenges faced, generation after generation, by lower working-class families in terms of finding and maintaining their own homes.

Os Inquilinos interrogates daily practices of an interracial family, discussing long-standing practices of racial, gender, and class domination. The film underscores the still prevalent colonial practices of domestic service, as well as gender and racial dominance primarily through the characterization of Iara, a traditional housewife, who does all the domestic tasks. Most of the time she is in the kitchen, cooking, setting the table for the various meals we see the family eat together. Iara serves the family members. She gets the kids ready for school, cooks dinner and keeps a plate in the oven for her husband who often arrives back late after his night-school class. When he arrives home, he sits at the table and she serves him, a ritual that the film reinforces repeatedly. Iara also sews and does crochet. She says that she is thinking about teaching Fernanda how to crochet, and that at her age she already knew how to crochet. Moreover, the only time we see her leave the home is to attend a neighbor's party. Iara was raised to get married and take care of the family, following the patriarchal pattern. By portraying her in this way, *Os Inquilinos* offers a critique of the socially accepted stereotype of Afro-Brazilian women as domestic servants or social subordinates, a stereotype that can be traced back to the colonial period.

The film utilizes Valter's interracial family to comment on long-standing historical processes of racialization that often are overlooked even today. This family evokes characteristics of social patriarchy and *mestiço* essentialism, underscoring the Brazilian racial system, typically characterized as being based on appearance and phenotype. It is a fluid system where racial (self)identification may be circumstantial and anchored on bias, preference, convenience, and so on. The film's cast represents a palette of colors evoking miscegenation and the whitening process carried out by Brazilian elite in the aftermath of Lei Áurea.[4] Brazilian elite believed that European immigration, miscegenation, and low birth rates among Afro-Brazilians would be an essential part on the process of civilization and progress envisioned for the Brazilian nation (Caldwell 2007: 30).

The family depicted in *Os Inquilinos* functions as a miniature of the nation, racially and in terms of patriarchal gender norms traceable, in part, to the dominance of Catholicism. Nonetheless, the film subverts the social norm. Valter is white, Iara is a black woman who can also be characterized as a (sensual) *mulata*, and their kids can be identified as black or *morenos*. Iara is characterized as "feminine" (in the way she dresses, for instance), following an essentialist pattern. She is portrayed as a strong woman who urges her husband to take action and confront their neighbors' bad example and harmful practices, such as throwing loud parties with alcohol and women, that Iara can see from the kitchen window, located just a few feet away. As one of her female friends says, "My God, you can see everything from here." Extrapolating beyond the family, this scene underscores Brazilian phenotype classification and its apparent racial tolerance in presenting these women's convivial relationship.

The film underlines working-class efforts and struggles to overcome the difficulties of peripheral life and to achieve some level of socio-economic mobility. Besides working at the *entrepôt*, Valter attends school in the evening to achieve something else in life. School therefore becomes a tool in order for this family to carry out its dreams. He leaves early in the morning and arrives back home late at night, after school, a daily routine for millions of *paulistanos*[5]. The many shots depicting workers leaving to work, taking the bus and arriving home underline this common social condition. The film offers an insider's look at working-class life by depicting a working-class family that lives a simple life but has the basics that they need, that is, a house, and food on the table. The moments they can be together are mainly weekends. And their entertainment is reduced to watching TV, working around the house, and participating in the neighborhood's social events such as family parties and so on. In chronicling the family's routines, the plot encourages spectators to perceive and reflect on the exhausting rhythms of urban life.

Urban violence and the politics of representation

The opening sequence is pivotal to the film's critique of class inequalities. It starts with an extreme long shot of a "wall" of small houses built almost on the top of each other on a steep hill. They fill the entire screen for a few seconds and invoke sensations ranging from discomfort to dread as underscored by the first minor tone chords of Joseph-Maurice Ravel's gloomy *Un Grand Sommeil Noir*[6] in the background. First and foremost, the shot provokes a sense of entrapment. There seems to be no escape from that place because the usual urban spatial grid cannot be identified; there are no visible streets, and no open spaces. It is also disorienting because the image does not provide any clear sense of urban direction or recognizable landmarks.

The "flatness" of the shot (produced by a telephoto lens) emphasizes these feelings. The lack of deep space communicates a sense of being spatially entrapped that is highlighted by a dissolve into the second shot featuring a more distant frame of the same image. Rather than allowing us to see "more clearly," the second shot merely deepens our sense of the scale of this dehumanizing landscape. Both extreme long shots have in their center a tree surrounded by concrete and bricks. As the concrete's presence grows with the dissolve, the tree seems to shrink in the center of the image. In these early images, *Os Inquilinos* seems to echo the way in which the city's poorer neighborhoods have come to be visually imagined in the media – as if from a distance, by those who live elsewhere, as an endless sea of indistinguishable hovels.

With these opening shots, the film begins its reflexive commentary – foregrounding how the depiction of criminality and violence depends upon which perspective is chosen to tell the story. The next sequence, set in Valter's neighborhood adjacent to the *favela* just depicted, builds on the commentary of the film about the entrapping nature of marginal urban spaces; and how we perceive that urban environment. A high angle, crane shot slowly tilting down shows children playing on a narrow street at night; the shot evokes Brazilian urban cultural practices while also hinting at the probable safety of that place. The scarce material condition of the urban environment is reinforced. The narrow street, pure asphalt surrounded by concrete, resembles typical ones found in São Paulo's working-class neighborhoods.

The descending shot pans to the right, at the same time it dollies to explore the pro-filmic space, eventually focusing on a specific house with the neighboring one in the background. From the house comes the sound of a couple arguing. This opening track keeps us outside the house suggesting that the argument comes from the family, therefore positioning our perspective

Class, gender, race in recent filmic urban Brazilian spaces

to encourage us to make certain assumptions about the nature of poor neighborhoods. It suggests a pre-conceived idea that poor people are ignorant, violent, and uneducated. When we are allowed in the house in the following shot, the film encourages us to question those initial perceptions by offering us a different perspective: the sounds of the vicious argument are coming from the television set broadcasting the latest *telenovela*. The on-screen, argumentative white couple are represented as upper-class as evidenced by their clothes and the setting. In contrast to the contentious relationship presented on the small screen, we see an evening family gathering (Valter and his wife getting ready for dinner as Fernanda watches TV), pointing to harmony and happiness. Through this careful deployment of on- and off-screen sound and space, the scene destabilizes spectatorial assumptions about the correlation between poverty, race and fierce conflict.

In encouraging us to recognize our misperception about the origins or site of (urban) violence, this initial sequence anticipates one of the film's broader concerns. And in the process, the film establishes a parallel between the spectators and Valter's family. Whereas violent family relations might be expected in his neighborhood, Valter and his wife associate violence with the poorer communities located nearby. The idea of the *favela* is commonly charged with negative characteristics such as violence, misery, etc. Therefore, one avoids being associated with this kind of space as is the case of Iara who does not want her son to go near the adjacent *favela*.

Nonetheless, when someone from a better off socio-spatial reality looks at these two places, that is the main characters' neighborhood (Vila Imperial) and the *favela*, they both might be qualified as the latter, reinforcing the idea that periphery and poverty equals urban violence. The cinematography underlines this by blurring these distinctions as sometimes the shots do not make it clear where we are. Valter's home is visibly located on a high part of a street at the exact point where the street starts to descend a hill. External shots of his street frequently position his house in the foreground with the *favela* in the background. But because of the position of the shot, it is not possible to determine the distance between Valter's house and the neighboring *favela*. The daylight shots reinforce the image of the opening scene while the night shots completely blur any difference between the two places.

Even as *Os Inquilinos* encourages the audience to question their own assumptions about dominant representations of poverty, the film also demonstrates the effects of those same conventions on "the poor." As Valter and Iara sit on the sofa, an over-the-shoulder shot shows the TV in close-up from their perspective. They are watching the show "Brasil Urgente" (Urgent Brazil), an actual news show that frequently depicts tragedies that occur in São Paulo, usually involving violence.

Through the ubiquitous presence of the TV, the film suggests a common practice in Brazilian society, of being informed by dominant discourses through television. The TV show within the film emphasizes a connection between poor areas of the city and violence. The reception of this news by the family and its reaction underlines a distinction made by different areas of the city about their spatial perspective. The *favela* is seen by the working-class family as an Other, a different place. Dialogue reinforces Iara's positioning about her spatial location. According to her viewpoint she does not live in a *favela*. However, television and hegemonic discourse in general may not differentiate between these two locations, characterizing the whole area as a site of violence. In this regard, Bianchi seems to be echoing the perspective of Michel de Certeau who said:

> To write is to produce the text; to read is to receive it from someone else without putting one's own mark on it, without remaking it. In that regard, the reading of the catechism or of the Scriptures that the clergy used to recommend to girls and mothers, by forbidding these Vestals of an untouchable sacred text to write continues today

in the "reading" of the television programs offered to "consumers" who cannot trace their own writing on the screen where the production of the Other – of "culture" – appears. "The link existing between reading and the Church" is reproduced in the relation between reading and the church of media.

(1984: 169)

In other words, these repetitive, direct references to television suggest that the characters are passive "readers" lead by empty consumerism. Their understanding of themselves, of their neighborhood, and of the city at large is informed by television.

Linha de Passe

Salles's and Thomas's *Linha de Passe* shares *Os Inquilinos*'s concern for showcasing socio-economic inequalities in contemporary São Paulo and the concomitant socio-spatial distinctions between the city's center and periphery. *Linha de Passe* is interested in critiquing class, gender and power inequalities through a narrative focused primarily on the working class. Despite these similarities, Salles's and Thomas's film does not propose a direct critique of the power system ultimately responsible for the social gaps and material deprivations the film depicts. In depicting the hardships of peripheral life in São Paulo, the film addresses interiorized violence experienced by the characters in their daily fight for survival. The film shows that although violence seemingly presents itself as the last means of resistance for those trapped in an untenable situation, those on the periphery do not always opt for it. In doing so, the film humanizes the characters.

Rather than circumscribing the narrative within a working-class neighborhood, Salles's and Thomas's film allows us to travel between the outlying areas and the city center in order to interrogate the notion of social mobility. This plot structure allows me to identify a trope within the film that I will call "fluidity." According to the film, the city is alive. It is the site of constant movement depicted through numerous shots of over-passes and roads showing the on-going flow of traffic or endless traffic jams. At the same time, *Linha de Passe* makes clear that these physical flows do not allow for social mobility. The film conveys its critique through recurrent elements in the mise-en-scène, most notably, various means of transportation (bus, motorcycle, car) and references to water (the river, the shower, the drizzle[7] and repeated shots of a clogged sink at the main character's home). Salles and Thomas utilize these elements to demonstrate the asymmetry within the social fabric as well as in the city's built environment.

The film's narrative structure reveals these asymmetries by following the trajectories of the main characters between different spaces; patterning its development through the oscillation between scenes set in two different socio-economic spaces. Cleuza, the protagonist, is a white middle-aged pregnant single mother who works as a domestic servant for a middle-upper class family in an affluent neighborhood. She strives to survive as a low-income worker, commuting on the bus between her home on the periphery and her work in the center while hoping for a better future for her sons. She lives in a small house in a working-class neighborhood in the outskirts of São Paulo with her four sons Dênis, Dario, Dinho, and Reginaldo. She is an enthusiastic soccer fan who attends matches at the stadium as underlined by the film's opening scene. Her oldest son, Dênis is a *motoboy*[8] (a motorcycle courier). We follow him on his motorcycle through modernized areas of the city. Also, he has a child who lives with the mother who he sees occasionally. Dinho is a converted Evangelical Christian who works as a pump attendant at a gas station. Her third son, Dario, is about to turn 18 years old. He is an aspiring soccer player who dreams of becoming a professional as do millions of other young men who see soccer as the only escape from poverty. His age is becoming a problem, though, as professional teams tend

Class, gender, race in recent filmic urban Brazilian spaces

to invest in younger players. And Reginaldo, the youngest, a pre-adolescent kid with darker skin than his brothers, wants to meet his unknown father. In trying to do so he frequently rides the bus for hours in search of his father, who he knows is a black bus driver. Referring to his father he says, "He's a lot blacker than me, isn't he mother? If I'm this black, he must be like a charcoal!" (12'35"). Through the journeys of these various characters the film portrays an image of the working class that points to the dead-end journey through which these characters are traveling. Nonetheless, in the end the asymmetries the film showcases are reversed into hope, following Salles's humanizing tendency.

In comparison to *Os Inquilinos*, *Linha de Passe* offers a more vivid depiction about how racialized dynamics play out within families – even multiracial ones. Here the multiracial family does not follow the happy, balanced model portrayed in *Os Inquilinos* nor does it portray the patriarchal family pattern. *Linha* adds racial tension within the family, functioning as a synecdochical reference to the country's racial color categories and the frictions within it. Moreover, the references the film makes to blacks underscore the socially ingrained tendency to refer to blacks using pejorative language. At one point Cleuza calls Reginaldo, "Neguinho desaforado!" (insolent lil nigger!) (35'37"). Furthermore, Reginaldo says to his mother, "It's one more child we don't know who the father is," to which Cleuza replies, "I'm the father and mother of you all," underlining her role as a female household head.

Cleuza epitomizes the peripheral working-class women. She has to take the bus to work, leaving home at dawn returning to the periphery at the end of the day, an urban ritual followed by millions of workers. Talking about this daily ritual, Edward Dimendberg says, "For what belongs more to everyday life in centrifugal space than the daily commute, that ritualized movement between the urban center and its environs that organizes the schedules of so many who dwell within it?" (2004: 202). The film portrays Cleuza as part of this ritualized activity, stressing the dynamics of working class urban (im)mobility. She is a domestic servant who works for a middle-upper class family that lives in a comfortable apartment in a well-equipped area of São Paulo. The narrative places Cleuza in a pivotal position providing us with different class and gender points of view. Her incursions into the city offer a depiction of material differences and function as a vehicle to underline socio-economic differences caused by political-economic issues that result in social fragmentation.

By positioning Cleuza as a domestic servant, the film addresses noxious employment practices involving the working class that impede social mobility. Specifically, *Linha de Passe* emphasizes that her boss, Estela, has not provided her with a "carteira assinada," a governmental document that would guarantee certain economic benefits.[9] In so doing, the film makes visible the unfair working conditions of working-class sectors involved in the so-called "informal economy." This is underlined in a dialogue between Cleuza and Estela (63'27"). A pregnant worker who does not have the same productivity can be laid off and left with no safety net and no guarantee of any sort.[10] This issue of precariousness was foregrounded in a similar scene between Valter and his boss in *Os Inquilinos*. Cleuza's relationship with her boss underlines social imbalance resulted by lack of opportunities in terms of social mobility which would be facilitated for instance by education.

In addition to the film's critique of Cleuza's boss, *Linha de Passe* also utilizes her to demonstrate the correlation between education and social mobility. Estela is a well-educated professional woman who made her way into a comfortable lifestyle, as stressed by dialogue and cinematography.[11] Contrarily to Cleuza, she has a small family and a big apartment pointing to a connection between family planning and formal education. A woman's lack of qualification prevents her entry to the labor market through other professions and employment as domestic servant becomes the possibility of survival. Housekeeping is generally considered an unskilled function. In addition, the domestic worker is commonly considered a female profession and therefore is less valued. These dialogic and spatial interactions suggest that the better-educated one is, the more chances one has in terms of social mobility.

Even as the film holds up the importance of education, *Linha de Passe* questions how lack of education leaves working-class people with few opportunities for socio-economic advancement and with unsustainable fantasies. Class differences are highlighted by the relationship between the sons of the two families. Dario is invited by Cleuza's boss's son (who gives Dario one of his expensive soccer shoes) to come play soccer for his team in their building recreation area (39'). A commentary during the soccer game made by one of the well-off young men is that he invited the maid's son, who plays soccer well, with the only intention to beat the adversary, suggesting that he would not do so otherwise. The sequence interrogates class stratification. Dario's one-time incursion into the affluent youth's lifestyle and their home, partying with them and experimenting with drugs after the game, demonstrates the huge social gap faced by the country's youth and the poor's difficulty in terms of social mobility. It is evidenced by the contrast between Dario's life and the one to which he aspires. In Brazil, the possibilities for youth's socio-economic mobility, from poverty to a better economic and financial situation, are scarce. Like millions of young Brazilian men, Dario dreams to become a professional soccer player in order to move from poverty to wealth (replicating soccer idols' careers), most probably his only chance of social mobility. The film underlines this by showing a long line of youths applying for a tryout. His aspiration into wealth is stressed through his spatial experience at the affluent home. While he lives in a cramped small house with his mother and three other brothers (the youngest sleeps on the couch), the privileged kids enjoy much bigger houses filled with expensive appliances. The film underlines the material gap by the use of different lighting. The affluent space is shown in brighter light than the poor home, photographed in darker tones. Dinho's home's sink is clogged and in different moments it is emphasized as such. It is reason for anger because it does not function as it should. In one of these scenes Cleuza says, "Isn't there a man in this house to unclog this fucking sink?!" This symbolic feature points to a malfunctioning of their life in general. Also, the sink is portrayed in dark color and as being old. On the other side of the social spectrum, at the affluent home, their sink besides being bright and clean provides fluidity. At that end things work better and life seems to be easier when one has opportunities. Nonetheless, opportunity is scarce currency in an environment where inequalities abound.

As demonstrated above, *Os Inquilnos* and *Linha de Passe* offer a devastating critique of the numerous inequalities of contemporary urban life in São Paulo, but do so to different ends. As I have mentioned, Bianchi's cinema is known for its acid tone. In *Os Inquilinos*, the parallel established between the film's opening and ending reinforces the claustrophobic sensation caused by the film as well as the subjugation under which working class, women, and blacks live. The final bird's eye shot depicting workers walking in the street leaving for work as in a procession, or most probably the metaphor Bianchi would use would be that of oxen marching to death, matches similar early scenes offering a critique of an oppression system that incarcerates minorities in an indefinite loop. Walter Salles, on the other hand, is known for his somewhat milder, more humanist critique of social problems common to Brazilian society present in films such as *Central do Brasil* (1998) (Central Station). In the end, if Salles's *Linha de Passe* does not foresee the facile resolution of major problems, there is at least hope for the future, a feature not common in Bianchi's *oeuvre*.

Linha de Passe is not interested in exposing injustice against the oppressed with the same acid vigor as Biachi's film does. *Linha*'s interest is to present class, race, gender, and power differences, grounding its narrative on the working class without proposing a direct critique of the power system responsible for the social gaps and material deprivations the film portrays. The film is interested in talking about human beings interacting with a dehumanizing city. Violence against the destitute is shown less through externalized violent acts than as an internal process, manifested through their psyche. As opposed to *Os Inquilinos,* the characters in *Linha de Passe* are not presented as oxen hopelessly marching on an indefinite loop. In the end, there is hope; there is faith in humanity, as stated by the lyrics of the *samba* performed by Seu Jorge, *Juízo Final* (Final Judgement),[12] which is played during the film and accompanies the final credits as well. There is a path through which one can walk after a rebirth, or drive the bus for that matter flowing towards a better future, even when surrounding structures are falling apart.

Notes

1 I would like to thank Laura Podalsky, Bev Hogue, and Grace Johnson for their comments and suggestions on this article.
2 In soccer, pass line (linha de passe) is the exchange of ball between the players of the same team.
3 Valter works at Ceagesp – Companhia de Entrepostos e Armazéns Gerais de São Paulo, one of the world's largest warehouses of goods, state-run, located in Vila Leopoldina neighborhood in São Paulo.
4 Literally "Golden Law," this was the Imperial Law (officially law number 3.353), sanctioned on May 13, 1888 that abolished slavery in Brazil. It was signed by Princess Isabel (1846–1921).
5 Those who are born in the city of São Paulo, capital of São Paulo state.
6 *A Long Black Sleep,* "A long black sleep /Descends upon my life: /Sleep, all hope, /Sleep, all desire! I can no longer see anything, /I am losing my remembrance /Of the bad and the good . . . /Oh, the sad story!
I am a cradle /That is rocked by a hand /In the depth of a vault. /Silence, silence!"
7 São Paulo is known as "terra da garoa" [land of drizzle].
8 In Brazil all kinds of deliveries, from pizza to documents are usually done by motorcycle. Deliverers/drivers are called *motoboys.* They are part of the metropolises scenario. They are usually underpaid and have to work long hours in order to make a living. Some people, mostly young men, work part-time as *motoboys* in order to make some extra money. Fatal accidents are common among them. The newspaper Folha de São Paulo reports that in 2014 440 *motoboys* lost their lives in accidents (Pereira 2015).
9 The "carteira assinada" was created by President Getúlio Vargas in 1932 and in 1934 it became mandatory. It is an official document (in booklet format) issued by the Federal Government through the Labor Ministry that outlines the data about the worker's employment contracts and is used, among other things, to grant social benefits. For someone to be considered officially employed and therefore has social benefits rights, the job must be registered through this document, among other forms that have to be filled to the Ministry.
10 Mendonça and Jordão (2008): "According to IBGE data, there are more than 6.5 [million] domestic workers, of which 6.2 million are women. ILO data show that in 2006, only 27.8% of domestic workers had a formal contract. 75.6% of black women and 69.6% of non-black women domestic workers are not registered. According to data from the National Survey of Household Sample – PNAD (2006), in relation to the organization of the professional category, domestic employment is the one with the lowest union membership rate. In Brazil, only 1.9% of domestic workers are unionized."
11 In the scene when she is talking to Cleuza that she will have someone else to help with housekeeping, because of Cleuza's pregnancy, she says, "I have a patient in twenty minutes. I gotta go."
12 Composed by Nelson Cavaquinho and Elcio Soares. Lyrics: "The sun will shine once more/The light will reach the hearts/The seed of evil will be cremated /Love will be eternal again/It is the final judgment, the story of good versus evil/I want to have eyes to see evil disappear."

Works cited

Bianchi, Sergio, director. *Os Inquilinos (Os Incomodados que se Mudem)* [The Tenants (Don't Like it, Leave)]. Global Lens, 2009.
Caldwell, Kia L. *Negras in Brazil: Re-envisioning Black Women, Citizenship, and the Politics of Identity.* New Brunswick, NJ: Rutgers University Press, 2007.

Certeau, Michel de, and Steven Rendall. *The Practice of Everyday Life*. Berkeley, CA: University of California Press, 1984.

Clarke, David B. *The Cinematic City*. London: Routledge, 1997.

Cruz, Samuel. "São Paulo and Buenos Aires: Urban Cinematic Representation in Contemporary Latin America." Dissertation, Ohio State University, 2015.

Dimendberg, Edward. *Film Noir and the Spaces of Modernity*. Cambridge, MA: Harvard University Press, 2004.

Harvey, David. *Social Justice and the City*. Baltimore, MD: Johns Hopkins University Press, 1973.

Mendonça, Maria Luiza Martins de and Janaína Vieira de Paula Jordão. "Domésticas no cinema: identidade e representação." XXXI Congresso Brasileiro de Ciências da Comunicação, Sociedade Brasileira de Estudos Interdisciplinares da Comunicação, 2–6 September 2008, Universidade Federal de Goiás, Goiania. Conference Presentation.

Pereira, Elvis. "Número de Motoqueiros Mortos no Trânsito de São Paulo Volta a Subir." *Folha de São Paulo*, 5/10/2015, Section São Paulo. Accessed 6/7/2015.

Salles, Walter, director. *Central do Brasil*. VideoFilmes, 1998.

Salles, Walter and Daniela Thomas, directors. *Linha de Passe*. VideoFilmes, 2008.

15

EL ROC HA MUERTO, VIVA EL ROC

Countercultural heroines in Sergio García Michel's Super 8mm cinema

Iván Eusebio Aguirre Darancou

After a rapid industrial, economic, educational and symbolic modernization during the 1960s, Mexico City's countercultural spheres experienced a violent crackdown upon its musical spaces. Rock, which initially had made its appearance under state sponsorship as a way of gaining entry into (sanitized) global cultural flows, was quickly transformed into a tool against state-guided nationalism, an 'organic' phenomenon that rapidly led to social unrest due to bringing together youthful bodies into the same spaces.[1] The technological developments that led to the global explosion of counterculture also provided, besides the sounds of electronic music in rock, a powerful tool for the establishment of alternative forms of representation: Super 8mm film.[2] First introduced as a bourgeois commodity for family videos (and arguably always a contraption of privilege, as opposed to more horizontal technology in the form of musical instruments), Super 8mm film quickly became a tool for the counterculture, a weapon of ideological warfare whose intrinsic technical limitations made it the perfect medium to avoid capture by entertainment industries.[3] Super 8mm had the possibility of empowering movements of resistance, cultural representation and exploring non-industrial cinema, especially outside the context of Hollywood.

In the context of the 1970s and 1980s, the works of Sergio García Michel appear as the most daring, critical and exhaustive exploration of the possibilities of a countercultural cinema in Mexico. In the vibrant sphere of the early 1970s, when Super 8mm production and distribution was at its highest in Mexico, García Michel quickly became the vanguard of a movement that sought to respond to state authoritarianism by using film as a tool for political uses (in the style of Latin American 3rd cinema) or, more interestingly, as an instrument for raising consciousness but not directing, forming or programming a set of political actions. García Michel's films range from short three-minute clips to long-format rock operas. They are a collection of adventures that not only represent one of the culminating moments of *mexperimental* cinema (Lerner 1999) but also provide a concise and clear critique of the ways in which counterculture as a market-produced phenomenon could easily become a depoliticized and sanitized product.[4]

In this chapter I analyze how he represents and reassembles female sexuality, citizenship and political subjectivity by focusing on female protagonists who develop throughout his oeuvre into the founding figures of an alternative nation, enacting thus a gendered *mestizo* politics rooted in the countercultural milieus of the time. I underline how García Michel develops a critique of capitalist consumption and relations of production, as well as of the ease with which countercultural spheres can be commodified, especially for male citizens for whom the act of consumption does not entail an act of resistance as much as an act of (heteronormative) masculine power. And, I focus on this particular producer (as opposed to a grander approach to the variety of directors and producers who worked with Super 8mm) because in his lifework, he founds alternative nations outside the nationalist and capitalist hegemony contained in industrial spaces as much as symbolic regimes. After working briefly in advertising agencies, García Michel instituted several forums of Super 8mm projection and became a professor in various cinema schools, thus becoming, like writer and academic Margarita Dalton, an active builder of counterculture in a professional career as much as in cultural product.

With a price oscillating between \$1,800-\$7,000 pesos, a Super 8mm camera was not a cheap commodity, but compared with the expensive equipment required for big studio production, its presence in the cinematic spheres of the decades greatly horizontalized the means of production. As historian Álvaro Vázquez Mantecón has signaled in his most important recovery of the movement, Super 8mm quickly became an ubiquitous product for the up-to-date countercultural youth of the 1960s and 1970s.[5] In the years between 1970–74, there were over 200 films produced and over nine contests organized by various institutions, from cultural center/café Las Musas to the Secretaría de Cultura y Deportes of the Asociación Nacional de Actores (Vázquez Mantecón 2012: 19).[6] This hyperactive sphere was originally a response – genealogically preceded by the Concursos de Cine Experimental from the 1960s where Rubén Gámez released what can be considered México's most important contribution to global experimental cinema *La Fórmula Secreta* – to the "stop-and-go development of the cinematic industry" which oscillated between "complete liberalism on the one hand and state monopoly on the other" (Tompkins 2013: 21).

As Jesse Lerner documents, these spaces of exhibition became gathering spots for countercultural citizens of all ages, serving the same function as concerts and other socialization spaces (Lerner and González 2015: 85, 89). In the aftermath of the 1970s, García Michel (1945–2010) appears as a central figure in the countercultural vein of Super 8 production. In 1972, he publishes, with other *superocheros*, a manifesto titled "Towards the Fourth Cinema", seeking to problematize the effectiveness of "Third Cinema" in a repressive state that also subjectifies bodies in a capitalist society through democratic institutions allied with market forces, since,

> 8mm cinema can contribute greatly towards the collective escape from alienation and the formation of an active critical consciousness. 8mm cinema is called upon to be an antidote to the alienating media, giving back to the individual his/her function as subject, making him/her a direct participant in the work of cinema, since in traditional media and education the individual is a mere object.
>
> *(1999: 169)*

Thus, instead of trying to use cinema in a simple and direct engagement with an established language of political action – the same one that the state legitimized and recognized as valid political subjectivities to be dealt with – Garcia Michel and other countercultural *superocheros* seek to generate a "cinema that raises consciousness, but does not form it" (171). In this way, they sought to differentiate themselves from other (Super 8mm) directors who chose to document political movements in a more classical manner by generating alternative political subjectivities and positions rather than reproducing the same *mestizo* heteronormative and exclusionary structures.[7] In doing so, they exploit the inherent limitations of the film format (inability to record sound while filming and to mass produce copies from the reversible film with no negatives), to creatively assemble sound and music as forces of resistance and generate spaces of projection that serve as spaces of affective re-subjectification in communal relations.[8]

In 1970, the Art Centro Las Musas called for the First National Competition of Independent Cinema in 8mm, with the prize awarded by Luis Buñuel. A total of 20 films were submitted under the general theme of "Our Country," with a generally critical position towards the government after the events of 1968 and a decidedly countercultural aesthetic of rock music and youths (Vázquez Mantecón 2012: 47). Sergio García participated with the seven-minute short film *El fin/The End*.[9] In the aftermath of the violent and disruptive event that was Tlatelolco, García focuses on critically appraising the political and social actions available to youths in the context of post-Tlatelolco Mexico.

The film opens with a bearded man behind prison bars molded to outline the geography of Mexico, moving then to a hippie man who emerges from the forest and takes a woman to flee into the woods with "You Can't Always Get What You Want" by the Rolling Stones playing, thus already making a critique of escapist countercultural groups. Their sequence ends with them running into the forest, disappearing from society in an escapism that is heavily critiqued as depolitical and dangerous. The camera cuts to two youths around a campfire who are being chased by a charro, a priest, a businessman, and a bride, all representatives of the material and symbolic institutions that are capturing countercultural youth into nationalist *mestizo* subjectivities. One of the youths is caught and infantilized, while the other is murdered by the soldier among stone ruins, in a clear reference to Tlatelolco, the *Plaza de las tres culturas*. The surviving youth is later caught smoking marijuana by a businessman who substitutes it for Coca-Cola. *El fin* then passes to a sequence of images of the urban landscape seen through a kaleidoscopic effect, emphasizing the hallucinatory state of mind that consumerism and ideologization can enact upon a body, coupled with an accelerated soundbite of "(This Is) The End" by The Doors. The final scenes show the now-suited man driving a car, completely captured. García uses music to deterritorialize affects that are available to youth, released by the early years of rock and recaptured by the Mexican state: from The Doors, the music fades into Armando Manzanero, a melodramatic and romantic ballad singer. The soundtrack of the film becomes a "more potent force of deterritorialization than sight, because, as sound becomes more refined, it tends to dissolve and connects with other elements easily in a machinic way. The sound quality of a song exceeds the signification of its lyrics" (Powell 2007: 45). The Oedipal liberation that Morrison seems to imbue in the lyrics of the song are left aside to focus on the affective re-territorialization the song provides, machinically assembling rock music as a deterritorializing political force that can challenge subjectification, but not survive repression.

As Vázquez Mantecón signals, the short film becomes an "historia sobre el acoso sufrido por la juventud por parte del mundo de los adultos" (2012: 50); however, this basic manifesto of counterculture post-1968, ending with a sour note on the total capturing of the rebellious youth culture, contains two very prescient critiques. First, the film foregrounds the powerful affective forces contained in the act of consuming under capitalist relations: the businessman literally feeds the young man a Coca-Cola, and soon afterwards the camera shows a canted angle and explicitly altered gaze of rapid-fire images of the urban landscape. In doing so, García Michel demonstrates a conscious use of what Lerner terms the "syntax of consumerism" that he characterizes in Rubén Gámez's *La formula secreta* (1965), which also contains a scene of intravenous consumption of Coca-Cola. This coupling of a mass-consumer product with a hallucinatory state reveals an already critical position of the use of drugs within the countercultural communities of the moment, one that becomes more visible with the centralization of male bodies and the erasure of female bodies from the projection. Thus, in *El Fin*, more than celebrate the existence of *jipismo* in the Mexican context, which other directors such as Alfredo Gurrola did in his Super 8 recording of *Avándaro* (1971), García Michel begins to construct a gendered and critical history of the counterculture.

His second short film of 1974, the 20 minute long *¡Ah, verdá!/You thought so!* is a much more positive story of an urban guerrilla couple who bomb national monuments (the Monumento a la Revolución, the Palacio de Hierro and the newspaper *El Heraldo,* known mouthpiece of the authoritarian government), consume immanent nationalism in the form of *tortas,* and are persecuted by plainclothes policemen, representing the repressive forces of the state that kidnapped and murdered urban and rural guerrillas as well as rock bands. After the male youth is murdered by these, García's gaze focuses on the protagonist female character, who not only survives political repression but becomes the founder of alternative politics, showcasing the political actions available in social, sexual and bodily terms. In a countercultural swerve, the film shows the woman manually preparing lysergic acid, sowing *ololiuhqui* (hallucinogenic morning-glory seeds) and drugging a group of monks, turning this recaptured institution into an agent of social change. In turn, the liberated monks pour LSD into water supply tanks, while The Beatles sing "Good Morning", and effectively drug Mexico City society, with the camera skewing and chaotic electronic noise music playing to represent their *shared* and *communal* hallucinogenic state.

¡Ah Verda¡ quickly becomes a film of female protagonic heroism, marking a difference with other youth films such as José Agustín's mainstream *5 de chocolate y 1 de fresa* (dir. Carlos Velo 1968) in that female *jipitecas* are not seen only as sexual partners or even mischievous counterparts, but as citizens able to enact their own lines of flight and resist heteronormativity in any guise it presents. In a central scene of *El fin,* after the male youth is assassinated, the young woman mourns and buries him, and is then seduced and captured by a middle-upper class young man by the side of his pool. After he flirts with her and begins to make sexual advances on her, she represents her non-consent in various body language poses (due to the limitations of the format and sound recording) and plots a resistance, reaching over to grab the nutcracker they had been using to eat nuts and using it against the man, specifically his genitals. The camera suddenly zooms in on a pair of walnuts being broken apart and pans to his grimace of pain. Žižek defines freedom as "not a blissfully neutral state of harmony and balance, but the violent act which disturbs this balance" (2005: 186), and the violent act of castration becomes this moment of freedom from the heteronormative *mestizo* order that constructs counterculture as an object of cultural capital to be consumed. The pair is listening to rock music and enacting an apparent sexual 'liberation,' but the camera's gaze is careful to construct female pleasure as autonomous and unsubjugated from male power. What is more, in recognizing her sexual power but not placing it at center stage, the film constructs a non-reproductive countercultural nation where fertility in the female body is embraced as an integral part of femininity (she plants seeds) while rejected as being the only model for womanhood (in the style of the *mestiza* mother). In the same way, the acts of consuming LSD by the woman, the monks and the drugged-out city, become acts of violence in that they disrupt the affective forces of state and market epithumogenesis precisely through biochemically modifying the body itself.

García also dialogues with global countercultural film aesthetics. One scene where the couple hijacks a VW van to have sex on a plush carpeted interior is possibly a reference to *Barbarella* (dir. Roger Vadim, 1968) which also made a deep impression on countercultural sexual liberation due to the representation of female pleasure and its assemblage to political agency in the character of Jane Fonda. Another scene when the monks chase the woman and proceed to pour LSD in a silly and accelerated sequence instantly remits the viewer to the 1965 classic countercultural film *The Knack and How to Get It* (dir. Richard Lester). When speaking of *Altered States and Film,* Anna Powell foregrounds how "the automatism of cinema deterritorialises perception. Anomalous states of consciousness can be celebrated [for] their impact on the audience who partakes of their affective contagion" (2007: 22). The sounds-images in *¡Ah Verdá!* generate affective responses in the viewer, collectively gathered in the spaces he creates, rather than

El roc ha muerto, viva el roc

represent and celebrate hallucinated states as fetishized moments, grounding the consumption of drugs (but also global counterculture) as a political action with social consequences. With a rock soundtrack, moving images of urban landscapes, autonomous and empowered female sexual desire, global countercultural references and resignified nationalist aesthetics, *¡Ah Verdá!* re-presents the affective force of (countercultural) film, whose power is doubly exploded when one considers that this film, along with other Super 8 production, *had* to be viewed in collective spaces and not privately consumed.

After travelling to Cuba in the late 1970s, García Michel focused on the promotion of Super 8 film culture in Mexico City through the founding of the Foro Tlalpan for production, distribution and screening, as well as active participation in other forums and workshops. From 1985–1988, he films and produces *Un toke de roc/A toke of roc*, a pun on the drag of a marijuana cigarette known as a toke (in Spanish and English) as well as *tocada*, the word for an impromptu or underground rock concert. In the context of the overly sexualized film industry of the 1980s in the *fichera* and *sexycomedia* genres, as well as the abandonment of the Super 8 medium by many *superocheros* of the 1970s who move to larger formats, *Un toke de roc* reworks nationalism, the rock scene of the 1980s and countercultural politics through the affective forces of music and experimental film images, doubly resisting the commodifying aesthetic of the entertainment industry *and* the material formats and circuits which promoted mass-consumption.[10] Disillusioned with the transformation of drugs, especially marijuana, into commodities of the (illegal) market, García Michel focuses his story on female protagonists who engage the state and its heteronormative structuring of society through embodied, but not drugged, acts of resistance.[11] As Vázquez Mantecón (2012: 296) and Lerner (Lerner and González 2015: 85) have signaled, the film becomes a founding moment of an-other nation. I argue that its engagement with nationalism through quotidian acts of urban consumption and its reassemblage of the eponymous imagery of indigenous pasts (*mestizo* identity), urban statues (Mexican Revolution aesthetics), and collective *vecindario* living (Golden Age film heritage) becomes a blueprint of alternative interpersonal relations grounded in an ethical recognition of the marginalized other.

The film is a rock-opera with a prologue and three acts, musicalized with mainly live performances, as well as recordings, of Mexican rock bands from the period, which was experiencing a come-back with the appearance of Cecilia Toussaint, Rockdrigo González and the *guacarrock* aesthetic initiated by Botellita de Jérez. It tells the story of three young women who flee their capturing environments of family and institutions to form a commune with a young woman who dresses up as a nun while graffitying the city, only to be captured later by plainclothes policemen and tortured. The sole survivor escapes to a rock commune that is later raided, but she flees underground and disappears. Throughout the film, a super-heroine appears in key moments as the savior of both male and female rebels, transforming the global aesthetic image of the super-hero (tied to mass-consumption and countercultural spheres through the comic format) into a female citizen powerful enough to withstand and fight back against state violence, founding an alternative nation that can withstand time and violence.[12] The ending sequences serves as a critical documentary of the paradigm-shifting events of the 1980s: the earthquake of 1985, the 1986 World Cup and the ensuing protests which sparked the formation of the civil society networks that led up to the electoral challenges of 1988. García Michel also directs a very scathing critique of the sexualization carried out in marketing and how the visual imagery of capitalist consumerism subjectifies and generates a nationalistic epithumogenetic process that places women as only sexual objects.[13] Women in the film are not assembled in an essentialist manner, such as the one used by surrealism and similar aesthetics, but as a socio-political position that gathers its meaning from the relations between the female body and social, economic and political institutions. Thus, García uses female bodies to underline the presence and lineage of female rock singers and the importance of the participation of women in the countercultural struggle of the 1960s and 1970s, aside from being an object of free sexual love.

The prologue of *Un toke* sets up the parameters of affective engagement demanded by García Michel by showing a female sacrifice in an indigenous setting, with the heart being cut out to become the meat of a *taquería* and the protein in the preparation of an order of tacos a well-dressed woman consumes, all this musicalized by Silvestre Revueltas, one of the leading Mexican composers of the state-funded nationalism of the 1930s–40s. Thus, the film begins by foregrounding the processes of subjectification that are happening around female bodies, who literally *consume* the ideologies of femininity embodied in her dress and demeanor just as she consumed tacos. To counter this subjectification, García Michel seeks to generate a new visual and musical language, as Frederic Lordon calls for when critiquing neoliberal epithumogenesis, to remobilize affects grounded in individual bodies as social constructs; a new language that can not only rename things but break the orders of knowledge in doing so (2014: 64). This allegorical contextualization positions García Michel in relation to institutions and discourses of gender, aligning him closer with what Mexican philosopher Benjamin Arditi describes as the becoming minoritarian that characterizes 'marginal' urban societies, specifically in Mexico City, dissembling him from the commodification and fetishizing of countercultural bodies, acts and aesthetics.

The first act opens by denouncing the uncritical consumption of state nationalism mediated by capitalist economic structures, focusing on a male youthful rebel who steals from the woman and is pursued by a policeman, rescued then by a superheroine dressed in a red cape and eye-mask, speeding through the city on roller-skates, able to navigate the urban landscape in a smooth manner. García denounces as well the dirty war carried out by the state against urban and rural guerrillas in a shot that slowly pans down a newsstand, focusing on key code words in the newspapers documenting police violence while erasing its victims. The family and the school are both institutions of oppression and ideological subjectification through the isolation of the female body, where one girl experiences a typical middle class familial conflict while two others are caught in a music school with a music professor who acts more like a sexual predator than a purveyor of knowledge. Garcia condemns once more the explicit connections between sexualization carried out by advertising in an attempt to generate a consumer subject: the gaze of the camera focuses on billboards covering the urban landscape with hyper-sexual images of scantily clad women. But this process is broken through the foregrounding of a sexual female body who enacts her own processes of countercultural subjectivation/protection. The camera focuses on a woman who steals clothes from the high-end *Palacio de Hierro* department store by covering up her nude body with them, then draping a nun's outfit on top of all the clothes she is stealing, thus fighting sexualization while embracing her own body, and resisting the capitalist consumer model by literal property theft. The nun graffitis several political messages across the city, musicalized to a rock version of the Pink Panther theme: 'el roc ha muerto, viva el roc', 'cuidado con la neurosis en el poder', 'the dream is over'. After rescuing the fleeing girls from their dangerous encounters with male citizens who seek to abuse or rob them, the nun introduces them to the disruptive act of vandalism as a violent act of freedom literally engraved onto the urban landscape itself.

The second act shows the community the four women form in opposition to being absorbed and captured in the gender, sexual and social roles established for them.[14] They survive by stealing food and collaborating with street rock performers until agents of the state kidnap the rockers and destroy their homes. The act of constructing a second commune becomes then, in the face of the repression that seems to never end, an act of redemption that disrupts the exercises of sovereign totalitarian control; in refusing to submit to the plainclothes policemen, the female gang generates a community with strong alliances to other countercultural communes in the underground.[15] The love of thy neighbor and the strong social bonds that tie the women together are the visual representation of the immanence of redemption in an urban space, which only get stronger with the latter communes that appear, or the images of the people helping each other in the aftermath of the devastating 1985 earthquake, or the documentary of the political marches in 1986. All of these (sound)images come together in the affective experiencing of viewing the film to generate a thriving sense of community amongst the viewers, a construction of another nation which only they can access, through coming together to consume the film but also through imitating the micropolitics it showcases. The religious symbolism of the hippie woman *cum* nun points towards this neighborly love, in a lineage that García constructs since the short films of the 1970s. The second act ends with the capture of three of the women by plainclothes policemen, and the escape of the fourth woman.

The third act opens with images of tortured women, once again establishing a visual memory of the dirty war of the 1970s and 1980s. After the quake of 1985, the single woman left free graffitis "el sueño ha terminado/the dream is over," the Beatles lyrics referencing the quake but mostly the structural and symbolic violence that overpowers youth countercultural groups and literally ends dreams. This leads the woman to attempt suicide several times, her alternative and marginal subjectivity being under not only symbolic but mostly bodily attack, but the mysterious super-heroine rescues her as she falls from the building. Redemption then enters: the young woman is taken to a new rock commune where she is adopted by a ragtag group of musicians. Though police in the end also raid this commune, no rockers are captured this time and the super-heroine becomes the embodiment of the alternative countercultural nation that punishes the *per-judiciales* (*judicial* is the name of a federal police officer). When the policemen attack, they are defeated by this heroine shooting arrows from the rooftops, becoming in that moment the living statue of the *Diana cazadora* which crowns one of the most famous avenues in Mexico City, and which had become already a symbol of countercultural imagery in the film *Los caifanes* (dir. Juan Ibáñez, 1966). *Un toke de roc* ends with an allegorical walking away of the four women into facing traffic, seemingly disappearing from society by fusing into the flow of modern urban metropolis. By underscoring the agency of the four women walking hand in hand, García Michel resists the popular imagery of the metro or other phenomenon of urbanization as symbols of mass existence and chooses to focus on individual yet communal existence, as opposed to mass anonymity. I read Garcia Michel's only full-length fiction film as an example of the use of countercultural aesthetics and mediums to politicize rock as a social phenomenon, specifically directed against other more mainstream films such as *De veras me atrapaste/You Really Got Me* (dir. Gerardo Pardo, 1985) which make rock a simply escapist youth fantasy.

García Michel thus weaves the imagery of the nation in the bodies of the female citizens and statues who are subjected to stratified and static political subjectivities. By reactivating the revolutionary potential embedded in the symbolism conjured by post-revolutionary Mexican nationalism, *Un toke de roc* and his previous films empower countercultural youth with the same political validation of their founding moments. Furthermore, and what is most important, given the particular economic developments in the entertainment and film industries, in choosing a format that resists being commodified and mass-produced, García Michel constructs networks of communities who come together in specific spaces to consume these products and enact instances of redemption, recognition of the other, and national reassembly into legitimate political subjectivities. Sadly, Super 8mm made its last public appearance in 1989, when García Michel held the last exhibition of his films and shut down the Foro Tlalpan for Super 8 projection. The costs of developing the film and the advances in other formats gave way to other forms of cinematic resistance, embedded now in video formats and production circuits able to bypass the chokingly stagnant film industry of the 1980s and early 1990s.

Notes

1 "In emulating the hippies, Mexican jipitecas thus reappropriated a countercultural discourse grounded in their own indigenous roots yet dresses up as avant-garde. What is double ironic, moreover, is that the Mexican state facilitated this process by promoting an image of the nation abounding in indigenous cultures" (Zolov 2001: 257).

2 That is, "8mm can be shot by amateurs. 8mm is ubiquitous, and if often present when noteworthy events occur. 8mm can wait around where such events are likely to occur. 8mm equipment is non-threatening to people, and encourages spontaneous, unaffected, and intimate expression" (Gunter 1976: 20).

3 In the Brazilian context of countercultural *tropicalia* and other movement, Christopher Dunn signals how the youth "regarded Super 8 films as democratizing technology, in that almost anyone could use the camera to make what he called *cinema de invencao*. He sought to reclaim the ethos of mid-sixties Cinema Novo captured in Glauber Rocha's maxim that all needed to make a film was 'a camera in hand and an idea in the head'" (2016: 94).

4 Over his lifetime, he produced and directed over 30 films, almost all of them shot in Super 8mm format with a few forays into video production at the end of his career.

5 "El súper 8 se difundió rápidamente en la sociedad mexicana. Más allá del ámbito casero, muchos jóvenes aspirantes a cineastas participaron en cursos y talleres, con el objeto de filmar películas con un carácter más ambicioso. Para mediados de los años setenta las innovaciones tecnológicas y posibilidades del súper 8 crecieron de manera notable" (Vázquez Mantecón 2012: 15).

6 See Lerner and Gonzalez. *Mexperimental Cinema* (2015) and Vázquez Mantecón. *El cine super8* (2012) for a detailed account of this milieu.

7 "The distinction then between "Third" and "Fourth" cinema hinges then not on their identification with leftist politics of Third World liberation, something that the two share, but rather with a stance toward an imported youth culture [that] crossed paths with their Mexican contemporaries in chemically enhanced encounters" (Lerner 1999: 25).

8 As has been pointed out, "esta limitación técnica inicial determinó el surgimiento de una narrativa fílmica particular, situada a la mitad entre el arcaísmo de la expresión del cine mudo y la innovación contracultural" (Vázquez Mantecón 2012: 17).

9 This and the other films discussed can be accessed via YouTube.

10 The films *Bikinis y rock* (dir. Aldredo Salazar, 1972) and *De veras me atrapaste* (dir. Gerardo Pardo, 1985) are examples of this commodified and depoliticized representation of rock culture.

11 In this, he follows what Dunn has signalled for the Brazilian counterculture, where "the use of drugs for both recreational and 'mind-expanding' pursuits lost some of its hopeful innocence with the rise of violence associated with heavily armed narco-trafficking gangs and the state-sponsored militarization of efforts to control the production, sale and export of drugs" (2016: 202).

12 *Un toke de roc* "es una ironía sobre los emblemas oficiales de la mexicanas (la importancia del mundo prehispánico, el escudo nacional, el valor de los mariachis) … ya no hay una negación de la nación … sino la propuesta de una nación alternativa" (Vázquez Mantecón 2012: 296).

13 "One can use the word 'epithumogenesis' to name this second type of desire-producing work, a deliberate engineering of affects that is not always left to the great 'process without a subject' that constitutes the body's self-affections, but is as times steered toward very specific ends" (Lordon 2014: 51).

14 Arditi points out how "la comunidad no es una categoria unitaria y las diversas identidades colectivas no son entidades cerradas y autarquicas" (2011: 104).

15 Kenneth Reinhard speaks of redemption as "a kind of temporal bomb which the historical materialist can throw into the teleological historicism… redemption is not the final cause of history, but the interruption of the false totality of historical causality and contextualization by acts of critical creation and constellation" (2005: 20).

Works cited

Agustín, José, writer. *5 de chocolate y una de fresa*. Dir. Carlos Velo. AM Libre, 1968.

¡Ah, verdá! Dir. Sergio García Michel. Filmoteca de la UNAM, 2005 1974.

Arditi, Benjamín. *La política en los bordes del liberalismo. Diferencia, populismo, revolución, emancipación*. Barcelona: Gedisa, 2011.

Avándaro. Dir. Alfredo Gurrola. 1971. In *Three souls in my mind: una larga experiencia*. DVD. Video Group Empresarial, 2006.

El roc ha muerto, viva el roc

Barbarella. Dir. Roger Vadim. 1968. DVD. Paramount, 1999.

De veres me atrapaste. Dir. Gerardo Pardo. 1985.

Dunn, Christopher. *Contracultura. Alternative Arts and Social Transformation in Authoritarian Brazil*. Chapel Hill, NC: University of North Carolina Press, 2016.

El fin / The End. Dir. Sergio García Michel. 1968. In *Un toke de roc*. DVD. Filmoteca de la UNAM, 2005.

García Michel, Sergio. "Toward a Fourth Cinema". *Wide Angle*. 21.3. (1999): 70–175.

Gunter, Jonathan. *Super 8: The Modest Medium*. Switzerland: UNESCO, 1976.

La fórmula secreta. Dir. Rubén Gámez. 1965. DVD. 5 Minutes to Live, 2004.

Lerner Jesse. "Superocheros". *Wide Angle*. 21.3. (1999): 2–35.

Lerner Jesse and Rita González. *Mexperimental Cinema. 60 Years of Avant–Garde Media Arts from Mexico*. Michigan: Smart Art Press, 2015.

Lordon, Frederic. *Willing Slaves of Capital: Spinoza and Marx on Desire*. London: Verso, 2014.

Los caifanes. Dir. Juan Ibáñez. 1966. DVD. Distrimax, Videomax. 2003.

Powell, Anna. *Deleuze, Altered States and Film*. Edinburgh: Edinburgh University Press, 2007.

Reinhard, Kenneth. "Toward a Political Theology of the Neighbor" in *The Neighbor: Three Inquiries in Political Theology*, eds. Kenneth Reinhard, Eric L. Satner and Slavoj Žižek. Chicago, IL: University of Chicago Press, 2005. 11–77.

Tompkins, Cynthia. *Experimental Latin American Cinema*. Austin, TX: University of Texas Press, 2013.

Un toke de roc. Dir. Sergio García Michel. 1988. DVD. Filmoteca de la UNAM, 2005.

Vázquez Mantecón, Álvaro. *El cine super 8 en Mexico: 1970–1989*. México: UNAM/Filmoteca, 2012.

Zolov, Eric. "Discovering a Land 'Mysterious and Obvious': The Renarrativizing of Postrevolutionary Mexico" in *Fragments of a Golden Age: The Politics and Culture of Mexico Since 1940*, eds. Gilbert Joseph, Anne Rubenstein and Eric Zolov. Durham, NC: Duke University Press, 2001. 234–272.

Žižek, Slavoj. "Neighbors and Others Monsters: A Plea for Ethical Violence" in *The Neighbor: Three Inquiries in Political Theology*, eds. Kenneth Reinhard, Eric L. Satner and Slavoj Žižek. Chicago IL: University of Chicago Press, 2005. 134–190.

16

STARRING MEXICO

Female stardom, age and mass media trajectories in the 20th century

Olivia Cosentino

This chapter provides an alternative critical framework to the scholarly tendency to study Mexican female stars in terms of their crossover appeal – in particular, their ability to succeed in the U.S.[1] The Hollywood-centric approach obfuscates the majority of female performers who circulate within Mexico and Latin America. While the lack of critical attention within U.S. and U.K. academies about the composition and circulation of Mexican female stars within their own national and regional contexts is notable, it is also unsurprising due to Eurocentric and Hollywood-centric research focuses. Within the Mexican academy, star studies often take on biographic qualities, but lack criticism and/or critical theory.

This chapter engages classic star studies by extending Richard Dyer's concept of the "star image" – i.e. "constructed personages in media texts" – to the star's mass media trajectory and public perception as a whole (*Stars* 97). Mexican female stars have been studied in terms of the archetypes they represent (López 1993, Hershfield 1996, Tuñón 1998, Maciel and Hershfield 1999), but this disregards what Christine Geraghty characterizes as "the duality of image which is deemed to mark a star, a duality which emphasizes balance between the site of fictional performance and life outside" (184–5). Thus, stars are more than the characters they play. Dyer explains that the star image is "realized in media texts," including advertisements, interviews, press coverage, reviews and other public materials (*Stars* 1). Star image and overall reception of the star are included in this chapter because they influence both patterns of circulation and consumption. Approaching the star image through mass media trajectories provides two benefits: first, it allows us to consider female performers' agency in shaping their careers, instead of focusing on the men who "made" them.[2] Second, it offers a picture of the constant fluctuation of available mass media circuits within Mexico. I claim that stardom mirrors important transformations of dominant media in 20th-century Mexican mediascapes, and on the whole, the frequency of multi-platform stars (those who begin in one cultural industry and later move to others, capitalizing on pre-established fame) steadily increases as we move towards the 21st century. The star studies here are divided into three mass media starting points – film (Angélica María) in the 1950s, television (Verónica Castro) in the 1970s and music (Gloria Trevi) in the 1980s – precisely because those venues were the most salient way in each era to enter the Mexican media scene. This chronological analysis of stardom engages with the changing socio-cultural norms in Mexican mass media in order to juxtapose the relative sexualization of female stars in different eras. These star studies question the impact that the star's age and relative sexualization had upon the construction of their star image in media texts and, in turn, how that affected their mass medial movement and geographic circulation. I argue here that youth as it relates to sexuality paradoxically both impedes and enables the circulation and overall fame of Mexican female stars, depending largely on the media landscape and context from which they emerge.

This chapter first comments briefly upon the possibilities and limitations of the growing field of star studies. Then, it shows how stardom illuminates a larger panorama of changing mediascapes within Mexico. Reconstructing Angélica María, Verónica Castro and Gloria Trevi's star images through their mass media trajectories not only contextualizes the star within her own time, but offers a productive methodology for studying the circulation of Mexican female stars within national, regional (and sometimes worldwide) markets by interrogating the impact of intersections of gender, age and sexuality.

Mapping the field, carving a space

Star studies, like most sub-fields of film and media studies, frequently privileges Hollywood and/or European cinemas. Seminal works by Richard Dyer – *Stars* (1979) and *Heavenly Bodies* (1986) – set the field in motion and gave theoretical weight to the study of film stars through a semiotic and sociological approach. The early 1990s saw the publication of Christine Gledhill's edited volume *Stardom: Industry of Desire* (1991) and *Star Gazing* (1994) by Jackie Stacey, both of which delved into spectatorship and identification with stars from a psychoanalytic perspective. All aforementioned texts theorize solely from the abundant star system that Hollywood produced. Martin Shingler's recent textbook-like *Star Studies: A Critical Guide* (2012) compares star systems within Hollywood, Europe, Bollywood and China. The absence of Latin America is glaringly evident, and despite his acknowledgment of the exclusion of "Japanese, African and South American" industries, Shingler's goal is only to give "scholarly synthesis" of the "existing academic field," effectively proving that Latin America holds no place in the extant field of star studies (5).

There are two recent fluxes in the area of star studies; the first, a renovated focus on national and transnational stars predicated by this age of globalization, and the second, a deeper examination of the Latina/o body as portrayed, consumed and mediated by Hollywood. The phenomenon of the transnational – an important current focus across the discipline of film studies – has extended scholarly attention to some marginalized industries, but the studies rarely treat Latin American stars. Meeuf and Raphael's *Transnational Stardom* (2013) offers case studies on French, Japanese, Chinese, Thai, Bollywood and Iberian stars, yet the only "Latin American" who appears in the volume is Shakira. The vast majority of U.S. and European scholarly attention reinforces the hegemonic centrality of Hollywood by only acknowledging Latin American stars who have "made it" by successfully transitioning into the flows of U.S. culture. Stars like Dolores Del Río, Lupe Vélez, Rita Hayworth, Carmen Miranda, Salma Hayek and Jennifer López have been studied far more than their peers who never left Latin America.[3] The presence of Latinas in the public eye and their often-problematic representations have created an impetus for the growing field of Latina star studies, featuring paradigm-shifting work by Valdivia (2000), Mendible (2007), Beltrán (2009), Molina-Guzmán (2010), and Ovalle (2011). Although the Latina body and image within U.S. media has been carefully theorized, we must recognize that the same logics of gender, sexuality and especially, exoticization, cannot be generalized to female stars of Latin American origins that circulate mainly within that region. As products that circulate widely, Latina stars are constructed to be clear racial Others within the milieu of U.S. and global racial logics. Alternatively, Angélica María, Verónica Castro and Gloria Trevi – while sexualized in their own ways – were not exoticized racial Others because their star images were shaped to circulate within a more limited national and/or regional context where all three would be considered white.

Some scholarship in this star studies constellation has begun to question Hollywood hegemony, but those studies are not without limitations. O'Connor and Niebylski's volume *Latin American Icons* (2014) approaches "icons" from the field of cultural studies and do not engage with "media texts" as Dyer's methodology proposes. Interestingly, Kristy Rawson's chapter on Lupe Vélez focuses solely on her time "before Hollywood" in Mexico and the joint chapter from Janis Breckenridge and Bécquer Medak-Seguín frames Norma Aleandro specifically as the post-dictatorial, middle-class Argentine icon. Focusing on stars in their national contexts is laudable, yet it still does not consider regional implications of stars' circulation within Latin America where media moved fluidly in the 20th century. An article by Niamh Thornton offers a highly original approach, reading YouTube as the "new and dynamic source (and resource) for the constructed star image" of Mexican divas Del Río and Félix (65). While Thornton's study offers an innovative template for analyzing stars and 21st-century transnational fan communities in the internet age, my chapter addresses fan and media response *during* the height of the stars' fame. The pioneer of 20th-century Mexican star studies in the U.S. academy, Sergio de la Mora, has employed a queer lens to re-read male cinematic national icons like Pedro Infante or Arturo de Córdova through film and extradiegetic texts ("Lo queer"). De la Mora has also written on "Mexico's most notorious sex symbol," Isela Vega whose carefully constructed star persona exceeded her curious blend of sexploitation and art films ("Tus pinches" 245–6). As his work delves into questions of Mexican nationalism and *mexicanidad*, these studies do not consider the circulation of these stars within Latin America or worldwide. What is more, the studies cited here privilege cinema as the star-making medium, disregarding stars from other media like television or music. This chapter builds upon these contributions, but further considers the role that youth and sexuality play in the construction of female stardom.

Mapping trajectories

Portal 1: Film

The vast majority of women who entered the industry during the Golden Age of Mexican film (1936–1959) not only began in film, but their career trajectories stayed primarily within that medium. Mexican cinema was flourishing at that time and relied heavily on stars to maintain its status because "talented, charismatic, and attractive performers… could assure commercial success for even the worst of films" (Mora 75). Actresses like Silvia Pinal (b. 1931), Andrea Palma (b. 1903), Lilia Prado (b. 1929), and Marga López (b. 1924) cultivated significant careers principally within the film industry; Pinal boasts nearly 90 acting credits! It is important to note that the generation of Golden Age female stars entered the industry around age 20–30, meaning that while they were young, they were not youth stars. Rather, their age allowed for them to be sensualized into sexual objects of the male gaze without any moral ramifications.

A notable departure from this pattern – predicated, I argue, by age – is our case study: *la novia de México* (Mexico's sweetheart), Angélica María Hartman Ortiz (b. 1944). Initially constructed as a child star when her career began at age six in the Golden Age film *Pecado* (Luis César Amadori, 1951), Angélica María's transition to adolescence is marked in media texts. After a trip to the U.S. to visit her father for her 15th birthday, she returned to Mexico "transformed in a young lady (*señorita*)," ready to film *Las hijas del Amapolo* (Gilberto Martínez Solares, 1962) in which she sang *rancheras* (Peña 15).[4] Around this time, Angélica's career began to diversify: she starred in Televisa's telenovela *Cartas de amor* in 1960 and she recorded "Eddy Eddy," a pop

Starring Mexico

song, in 1962. Angélica María represents a significant change in the post-World War II market when youth became a marketable consumer category. She starred in a slew of moralistic youth-centric rock 'n' roll films – *Mi vida es una canción* (Miguel Delgado, 1963), *Vivir de sueños* (Rafael Baledón, 1964), *Perdóname mi vida* (Miguel Delgado, 1965), *Sólo para ti* (Ícaro Cisneros, 1966) – that nourished her singing career and solidified her status as youth superstar.

Angélica María's star image reflects a targeted appeal to younger generations that crossed national boundaries. By the 1960s, she was well-known through Latin America. A 1968 issue of the international film magazine *CINEavance* included letters to the editor from fans in Guayaquil, Ecuador and Honduras, which pointed to her transnational appeal likely due to her multi-media (film, music and television) career. In 1966, Angélica María traveled to Spain to film *Fray Torero* (José Luis Saenz de Heredia, 1966) precisely to compete with Spanish youth stars Rocío Dúrcal (also born in 1944) and Marisol (slightly younger, born in 1948), according to an interview conducted by Enrique Gómez Vadillo in *CINEavance* (20). Angélica María conjectures that she was well-received in Spain, "perhaps because it is intimately linked to all that is Mexican" (Gómez 20). Spain, unlike Hollywood, was a fairly small industry into which Mexican stars could easily transition without a language barrier, but this move also carried cultural capital. Gómez's article emphasizes how much the young star matured during her trip, shaping her even more into a role model for Mexican youth.

It is important to note that Angélica María's star image was never overtly sexual, always safely alluring as the idealized "novia de la juventud" that embodied Mexican values (Barajas and Moreno 105). Playing into this image, Angélica María was often portrayed as single in her late teens and 20s. In the magazine *Confidencias*, 21-year-old Angélica María was described as "a normal, healthy young girl (*chiquilla*) that many have idealized" as the "girlfriend one dreams about having all of one's life" ("Angélica María" 7). This accessibility was part of her great appeal to men, but also assured fans that she was not promiscuous. In 1967, the 23-year-old star graced the cover of *CINEavance* with the headline: "Angélica María wants a boyfriend." While inevitably sexualizing Angélica, the article focused on her desire to find and marry a man, reinforcing traditional conservative values. Angélica María's transnational appeal continued to expand into her late 20s as she appeared in telenovelas like *Muchacha italiana viene a casarse* (1971), which aired widely outside of Mexico and is said to be the first to break into the international market. Regardless of the increased signs of adulthood (marriage, a child, a divorce) in the press, her good girl, safely sexualized star image crafted in the 1960s remained iron-clad and emblazoned in the Mexican imaginary, even to this day. A May 2017 *Sopitas.com* article reported that Bono hit on Angélica María when U2 visited Mexico in 1992, but the ever-chaste diva apparently told him, "*Ahorita no joven* / Not right now, young man" ("WTF!?" n.p.). As the ultimate manifestation of her hold on the national imaginary, in 1991 fan Gustavo Maldonado Barajas founded the Museo Angélica María, located in Mexicali, Baja California, which houses an incredible collection of star texts (including 15,000 photographs) reflecting her star trajectory as the ideal "novia de México" (Gómez n.p.).[5]

Portal 2: Television (Telenovelas)

Most stars that entered the scene post-Golden Age (after 1959) did not begin their careers in the film industry, due to interwoven market forces including declining cinematic production in the 1960s and 1970s and the increasing popularity and availability of television. President Alemán's national address on September 1, 1950 marked Latin America's entrance into television broadcasting and inaugurated a new era in mass media consumption within Mexico (González de Bustamante 1). Companies like the multi-media conglomerate Televisa saw great opportunity in television, especially telenovelas and according to John Sinclair, Televisa's "Golden Age" occurred in the 1970s and 1980s (38–9). Television, Televisa and importantly, the telenovela, jumpstarted many careers, including that of Verónica Judith Sáinz Castro (b. 1952). Declared the "queen of Mexican television" by *Somos* magazine in 2003, Castro's trajectory illustrates two phenomena: first, the enmeshing of print culture and television to generate stardom and second, the internationalizing possibilities of working in telenovelas. Though young when she made her professional debut, Castro was never a "youth star" and exemplified fully adult sexualized stardom due to her emergence post-sexual liberation.

In Castro's case, print culture (newspapers and fotonovelas) worked together with television to skyrocket her to national fame with an overtly sexualized image. In 1966, Castro appeared in the fotonovela *La romántica Samantha*, where her photographs were used to illustrate a comic book-like story that ran in the magazine *Chicas*.[6] Other fotonovelas (1966–68) generated Verónica the necessary mediatic presence to begin working in television; first on *Operación Ja Ja* (1967), then commercials, and later a small role in the telenovela *No creo en los hombres* (1969). Famed Televisa host Raúl Velasco encouraged Castro to nominate herself for the annual amateur beauty contest, "El rostro de (the face of) *El Heraldo de México*," which ran from 1966–2003. When 18-year-old Castro won in 1970, Televisa broadcast *El Heraldo*'s awards show for the first time, marking a clear convergence of print media and television. Other post-1970 (in)famous winners of "El rostro" that later developed media careers include (rival) telenovela star Lucía Méndez in 1972, the singer Tatiana in 1984, the first lady of Mexico and former telenovela star Angélica Rivera in 1987, and actress/singer Aracely Arámbula in 1996. Importantly, Castro and other winners projected sexually explicit star images very different than that of Angélica María who, despite being active in the late 1960s, was likely not sexy enough to be awarded "El rostro." Castro exemplifies an unquestionably sexualized stardom. She was Mexican men's magazine *Caballero*'s April 1971 covergirl, which promised an "audacious article" on the star, implicitly alluding to her nudity inside. By the 1970s, this type of pornographic appearance was culturally normalized, whereas it likely would have ruined Angélica María's career and image. Most publicity from the 1970s and 1980s created an overtly sexual star image, like the cover of an Argentine *TV Guía* from September 1987 that features a scantily clad Castro inviting us to discover "Verónica's new love!" Leveraging her fame as the "face" of Mexico, Castro acted in various films in the 1970s and 1980s (notably, no *ficheras* or *sexycomedias*), but it was not film that boosted Castro's stardom to international heights.

Verónica's participation in Televisa's *Los ricos también lloran* (1979) – later called the "most famous Mexican soap of all time" (Matelski 65) – effectively branded her a national and international telenovela superstar, but importantly, led to distinctions in her sex appeal across borders. Besides garnering huge success within Mexico and Latin America, Castro's telenovela appears to have been broadcast to 127 countries, including "unsuspecting markets in Asia and Eastern Europe" (Rondero n.p.). Kate Baldwin notes that in post-Soviet Russia the telenovela "enjoyed the highest ratings of any TV show ever. It is estimated that 70 percent of the population, or 200 million viewers, tuned in regularly" (286). Baldwin claims that part of Verónica's "saliency as a cult figure" within Russia "can be found in her stereotypically visually marked 'ethnicity'" (296). She then mischaracterizes Castro as a "dark-haired, *dark-eyed*, tawny-skinned Mexican beauty" (296, emphasis added). Within Mexican star texts, Castro's penetrating blue eyes took center stage, as is the case for *El Heraldo*'s 1970 photograph of Castro as "the face" of Mexico, in addition to a 1970 ad for Nescafé where the ad's blue text highlights her wide, mascaraed light eyes. In 1990, film critic Jorge Ayala Blanco's interpretation of the Castro phenomenon pointedly describes her as "*ojiazul*/blue-eyed" (48). A recent article highlighting her career trajectory begins: "Vero's blue eyes appear from under thick bangs" (Reina 27). Clearly, Castro's (exotic) eyes have always been a signature feature of her star image and played into her sex appeal within Mexico. Baldwin's mistake gestures towards the need to understand stars within their national racial constructions because her "tawny skin" is indeed much lighter than many Mexicans and, though never outright mentioned, stars like Castro and Angélica María were celebrated within their country for their phenotypically European (i.e. not indigenous) appearances. As a testament to her sexualized, European look, post-*Los ricos*, Castro succeeded in Argentinean and Italian telenovelas, where she was known respectively as the "*Burbuja sexi*" and the "Mexican panther" (Saavedra n.p.). This sexualization varied within different markets and racial constructs, a complex phenomenon that I do not have space to fully unpack here; however, it is significant that across nations and even as she aged, Castro's star image is glued to sexuality. A 2017 *People en español* article declared: "Verónica Castro, a sexy grandma at age 64," gesturing to a different, fascinating interplay of *old* age and sexualization (Trejos n.p.).

On a final note, besides internationalizing stars, Ana López explains that "the telenovela star system has produced fascinating ancillary markets" where telenovela actors "have also become singers and entertainers and have spilled out on to other programs and media" (271–2). Castro is a compelling example of multi-platform stardom. She recorded the theme song, "Aprendí a llorar," for *Los ricos* and later, released a slew of albums in the 1980s, 1990s and 2000s. Castro also hosted a plethora of Televisa talk-shows after *Los ricos*, including *Mala noche… ¡no!* (1980) and the ambitious *Y Vero América ¡Va!* (1992), filmed across Latin America in celebration of the quincentennial. *Y Vero* reached "350 million spectators" in "25 countries," including Latin America, Spain and North Africa, thanks to developments in satellite technology and Castro's established popularity (Toussaint n.p.). Verónica has far from disappeared today; she is slated alongside Aislinn Derbez and Cecilia Suárez to star on a new platform – digital streaming – in Manolo Caro's Netflix series in 2018.

Portal 3: Music

Stars who entered the industry in the late 1970s or 1980s frequently began as singers and used their vocal talents to move to other forms of media, mainly television and sometimes film. A notable pathway was entering through children's media, specifically Televisa's television shows that featured young talent – like *Juguemos a cantar* (1982) or *Chiquilladas* (1982–1989). Stars like Lucerito (b. 1969), Thalía (b. 1971), Paulina Rubio (b. 1971) and Anahí (b. 1983) all initially positioned themselves with music and Televisa. Most then transitioned into Televisa telenovelas (youth-oriented and not), but did not launch film careers. Lucerito is an exception to this rule for her cinematic success in what I have previously called the Televisa youth star vehicle film; musically oriented, moralizing family melodramas that reached the top of box office charts and even beat out Hollywood youth films at the time (Cosentino 45). The reason most youth stars did not have film careers outside of this particular vein of Televisa film production is because the industry was dominated by *sexycomedias* (the 1980s follow-up to 1970s *ficheras*), certainly not the place for pre-teen aspiring actresses.

The Televisa trend continues in the case of Gloria de los Ángeles Treviño Ruiz (b. 1968), known by her stage name Gloria Trevi, who also began in music, but whose distinct, commercially sexualized star image indicates another pipeline to fame. Ironically, bad girl Trevi got her start by winning a 1983 contest sponsored by the Televisa show *XE-TU* that sought Lucerito's lookalike for the uber-popular telenovela, *Chispita*. A few years later, she joined *Boquitas pintadas* – a girl group managed by the infamous producer Sergio Andrade – and three years later, Trevi embarked on a solo career that would skyrocket her to fame.[7] In 1989, she debuted her untamed hair, racy, self-made outfits and scandalizing dance moves on Televisa's *Siempre en*

Domingo with "Dr. psiquiatra," a song she composed herself that proclaimed, "I'm not crazy, I'm just desperate/*desesperada*." This first appearance – which Televisa head Azcárraga is said to have disliked – embodies the constant tension that would follow between Trevi's agency in self-creating a rebellious star image and Televisa's institutionalization of Trevi's rebellion into profitable iconoclasm.

When considering Trevi's sexualized star image, it is important to keep Televisa in mind because Trevi's irreverence, to some degree, was captured and commercialized to create a money-making antithesis to good-girl youth star, Lucerito.[8] Well-managed scandals provoked by Trevi's rebellious style, candid discourse, and overt sexuality are a key feature to her star image. A wild-haired Trevi appeared on the cover of *TV y novelas* in 1991 with the quotation: "I scandalized Latin America, but they like it." In 1992, Trevi began to release *sexy-calendarios* as part of what Anne Rubenstein calls her "calculated outrageousness" that "distinguished [her] from other starlets" with the notion that "she controls her own products and image" (1). The calendar and its subsequent three editions were huge sellers despite attempts to censor it, though Rubenstein suggests that perhaps the threat of censorship might have made her calendar more popular (2). Symbolic of the subsumption of Trevi's irreverence to the money-making machine of Televisa, Rubenstein claims her calendar was even "printed by another Televisa offshoot" (167).[9] While Trevi appeared to be rebelling against all sorts of Mexican institutions, the young star's image was being monetized by the largest mediatic institution in all of Mexico, (and Latin America): Televisa.

In her mid-90s move from music to film star, Trevi projected a hybridized woman-girl, sexualized, yet family-friendly image. Trevi made three films in the 1990s with Televicine, Televisa's film production branch established in 1978 that also made Lucerito's youth films. *Pelo suelto* (Pedro Galindo III, 1991) featured songs from Trevi's recent album "Tu ángel de la guarda" and brought enormous financial success; *Dicine* reported that it was the top-earning Mexican film of 1991 with 11 million pesos in box-office returns ("Cuadro" 8). Trevi told *El Heraldo* she wanted youth and adults alike to enjoy *Pelo suelto*, which she thought would ultimately foster "family unity" (*El Heraldo* n.p.).[10] Trevi's films are certainly more risqué than Lucerito's; while Televisa actively de-sexualized Lucerito, Trevi's star image sought to merge overt sexuality and youthfulness. The press seems to have been extremely aware of these contradictions and tries to grapple with this as early as December 1989 when *El Nacional* described 19-year-old Trevi as: "Young in spirit and age… even so, she is a woman in every sense of the word (check out the photo if you don't believe it, dear reader), a young woman" ("Falta" 11). Later, Sergio Gonzalez Rodriguez reflects that Trevi's "half-naked image" on her polemical calendars "brings with it an ironic disdain for certain artistic conventions," especially the way in which the public images of 20-year-old singers are designed to have "the modesty of 15-year-olds with the bodies of 30-year-olds" (53). This awareness of the hypocrisy in Mexican society is exactly what Gloria sought to create with her well-planned, scandalous star image.

Despite Televisa's mediation, Trevi's star image often encouraged the public to question norms, instead of just promoting blind consumption, a factor that differentiates her from Angélica María and Castro. From the very beginning, young fans idolized and respected Trevi because she was "authentic" and unafraid to speak her mind, even about touchy topics like virginity, prostitution and politics (Aguilera and López Betancourt 1992: 43). During and after the Andrade scandal, Gloria's fans fiercely defended her innocence and she is known today as a key advocate and icon for the LGBTQ community. These connections allow her to reach beyond the commercialization of her rebellious star image to create real, positive change by encouraging fans to break barriers and embrace their true selves. Post-scandal, Trevi has proven that she is indeed "immortal" (the title of her latest album) by successfully reigniting her career and returning to her true passion: composing, singing and performing.

Starring Mexico

This chapter, more than anything else, considers a new methodology for studying Mexican female stars in a context outside of Hollywood. Studying stars points to macro trends, like the fluctuation of mass media availability and popularity, intertwining national and regional mediascapes, shifting standards of sexuality and the changes that globalization brings to stardom. Star studies also values the micro; stardom is personal, nuanced and often resistant to large generalizations. Star images are the product of a very specific construction for specific audiences in specific contexts. Contrasting stars that exist within the same national or regional imaginary can be helpful to differentiate the specificities of star images, especially for female stars because nearly all are viewed as sexualized (with the exception of national *abuelita* Sara García). Furthermore, my chapter shows the importance of tracing where stars work, what kinds of media they use and who owns that media in order to contextualize their star image and trajectory.

Circulation and mass-media trajectories as they relate to age, sexuality and star image as an analytical framework could easily be applied to the study of other female (and potentially male) stars within Latin America. Though my focus here is women, male stardom could also be considered through the lens of age, masculinity and sexuality, or contrasted with female stardom in terms of the career agency (i.e. decisions to move between media or how they got their big break) that female stars are often denied. What is more, as music, television and film moved fluidly throughout the region, a larger study on the circulation of Latin American stars in Latin America (or perhaps the Global South) would reshape our understanding of stars and mediascapes. Following the push of cultural studies, my chapter demonstrates the need to study all kinds of Latin American popular stars, in particular those who worked outside of film, or whose films were considered trash, because it was this popular media that Latin Americans vociferously consumed. Starring Mexico is a worthwhile step towards better conceptualizing cultural industries and the stars who often keep media alive.

Notes

1 I am grateful for the Felice M. Grad Endowed Scholarship and the Susan Pratt Munthe Award for Latin American Studies, which allowed me to conduct research in Mexico City. This chapter would not have been possible without assistance from Gustavo Fuentes González at Fundación Televisa, archivists at the Filmoteca Nacional and the Hemeroteca Nacional at the UNAM and Raúl Miranda at the Cineteca Nacional.
2 This is a pushback against defining women's success through men. In late 2016, a 100th anniversary edition of Mexican author Elena Garro's novel *Reencuentro de personajes* was released with a book band that read: "Octavio Paz's wife, Bioy Casares' lover, García Márquez's inspiration, admired by Borges." Though quickly retracted by the publisher after backlash, it is evident that sexist attitudes are still prevalent even (or especially) within intellectual communities.
3 For studies specifically on Del Río see Hall (2013) and Hershfield (2000).
4 All translations are my own. Occasionally I will leave words or phrases in Spanish when I think it will benefit the reader.
5 In summer 2015, I saw Angélica María perform in Mexico City at a 3 hour-plus concert called "Juntos otra vez," featuring rock bands and "youth idols" from the 1960s. Her voice was flawless and she whirled around the stage like no 71-year-old I've ever seen.
6 Space does not allow me to treat *fotonovelas* here, yet they are an important Latin American mass media phenomenon that requires more scholarly attention. For more, see Butler Flora (1980).
7 Andrade is important to Trevi's trajectory, but I refuse to deeply explore his role as it violates my intent to return agency to female performers. For more on Trevi and the Trevi-Andrade clan scandal in the late 1990s, see Sabina Berman's *Gloria* (2014).
8 More so than Lucerito, however, Trevi played both sides of the TV Azteca and Televisa rivalry, and even recorded with BMG Ariola Records – a company outside of the Televisa web. After many negotiations (and a snafu that involved selling TV Azteca rights to the behind-the-scenes footage of the photoshoot for her *calendarios*), Trevi eventually signed a six-year exclusivity contract with Televisa in 1996 for eight million pesos to make four telenovelas, six films and to host XETU Remix (García Hernández).

9 Though I do not doubt this, it has been impossible for me to confirm the printer/publisher of Trevi's *calendario*.
10 In the past, Trevi had been accused of breaking apart families when youth would follow her lead and leave their families to pursue their dreams.

Works cited

"Angélica María. La chica ideal." *Confidencias,* March 1965: 4–7.

Ayala Blanco, Jorge. "El Fenómeno Verónica Castro y sus Tres Caras." *El Financiero*, Mexico City, 29 August 1990: 48.

Baldwin, Kate. "Montezuma's Revenge: Reading *Los Ricos También Lloran* in Russia." *To Be Continued… Soap Operas Around the World*. Ed. Robert C. Allen. New York: Routledge, 1995. 285–300.

Barajas, Carmen and Silvia Moreno. *Angélica María: La novia de México*. Mexico, D.F.: Reader's Digest, 2005.

Beltrán, Mary. *Latina/o Stars in U.S. Eyes: The Making and Meanings of Film & TV Stardom*. Urbana-Champaign, IL: University of Illinois Press, 2009.

Berman, Sabina. *Gloria*. Mexico City: Planeta, 2014.

Butler Flora, Cornelia. "*Fotonovelas*: Message Creation and Reception." *The Journal of Popular Culture* 14.3 (Winter 1980): 524–34.

Cosentino, Olivia. "Televisa Born and Raised: Lucerito's Stardom in 1980s Mexican Media." *Velvet Light Trap* 78, Fall 2016: 38–52.

"Cuadro 1. Las películas mexicanas más taquilleras en el país." *Dicine* 45, May 1992: 8.

De la Mora, Sergio. "Lo *queer* en el cine clásico mexicano de Arturo de Córdova." *Miradas al Cine Mexicano* Vol. 2. Ed. Aurelio de los Reyes García-Rojas. Mexico City: IMCINE, 2016. 41–59.

De la Mora, Sergio. "'Tus pinches leyes yo me las paso por los huevos.' Isela Vega and Mexican Dirty Movies." *Latsploitation, Exploitation Cinemas, and Latin America*. Eds. Victoria Ruétalo and Dolores Tierney. New York: Routledge, 2009. 245–57.

Dyer, Richard. *Heavenly Bodies: Film Stars and Society*. New York: St. Martin's Press, 1986.

Dyer, Richard. *Stars*. London: BFI Publishing, 1998.

"Elemental, mi querido público: Gloria Trevi debuta en 'Pelo suelto'." *El Heraldo*, 11 July 1991: n.p.

"Falta creatividad a nuestros compositores: Gloria Trevi" *El Nacional*, 7 December 1989: 11.

García Hernández, Arturo. "Gloria Trevi: el recuento de los daños / II." *La Jornada*, 3 December 1999: n.p.

Geraghty, Christine. "Re-examining Stardom: Questions of Texts, Bodies and Performance." *Reinventing Film Studies*. Eds. Christine Gledhill and Linda Williams. New York: Oxford University Press, 2000. 183–201.

Gledhill, Christine. *Stardom: Industry of Desire*. New York: Routledge, 1991.

Gómez, Bernardo. "Angélica María: Museo de Angélica María en Mexicali." *YouTube*, commentary by Laura Tejada, 30 April 2008: youtube.com/watch?v=0WZKO99LUEM.

Gómez Vadillo, Enrique A. "La nueva Angélica María." *CINEavance* 92, 1966: 16–21.

González de Bustamante, Celeste. *"Muy buenas noches": Mexico, Television and the Cold War*. Lincoln: University of Nebraska Press, 2012.

Gonzalez Rodriguez, Sergio. "Gloria Trevi: semidesnudez persuasiva." *El Nacional,* 12 December 1991: 53.

Hall, Linda B. *Dolores del Río: Beauty in Light and Shade* Stanford, CA: Stanford University Press, 2013.

Hershfield, Joanne. *The Invention of Dolores del Río*. Minneapolis, MN: University of Minnesota Press, 2000.

Hershfield, Joanne. *Mexican Cinema, Mexican Woman: 1940–1950*. Tucson, AZ: University of Arizona, 1996.

López, Ana M. "Our Welcomed Guests: Telenovelas in Latin America." *To Be Continued… Soap Operas Around the World*. Ed. Robert C. Allen. New York: Routledge, 1995. 256–75.

López, Ana M. "Tears and Desire: Women and Melodrama in the 'Old' Mexican Cinema." 1993. *Feminism and Film*. Ed. E. Ann Kaplan. New York: Oxford University Press, 2000. 505–20.

Maciel, David R. and Joanne Hershfield. *Mexico's Cinema: A Century of Film and Filmmakers*. Wilmington, DE: Scholarly Resources, 1999. 249–65.

Matelski, Marilyn J. *Soap Operas Worldwide: Cultural and Serial Realities*. Jefferson, NC: McFarland & Co, 1999.

Meeuf, Russell and Raphael Raphael. *Transnational Stardom: International Celebrity in Film and Popular Culture*. New York: Palgrave Macmillan, 2013.

Mendible, Myra. *From Bananas to Buttocks: The Latina Body in Popular Film and Culture*. Austin, TX: University of Texas Press, 2007.

Molina-Guzmán, Isabel. *Dangerous Curves: Latina Bodies in the Media*. New York: New York University Press, 2010.

Mora, Carl. *Mexican Cinema: Reflections of a Society, 1896–2004*. Jefferson, NC: McFarland & Co, 2005.

O'Connor, Patrick and Dianna C. Niebylski. *Latin American Icons: Fame Across Borders*. Nashville, TN: Vanderbilt University Press, 2014.

Ovalle, Priscilla. *Dance and the Hollywood Latina: Race, Sex and Stardom*. New Brunswick, NJ: Rutgers University Press, 2011.

Peña, Mauricio. "Entrevista: La verdadera vocación de Angélica María." *Somos*, 1 January 1998: 10–25.

Reina, Elena. "'Tuve que hacerme un hueco entre los hombres'." *El País*, 23 July 2016: 27.

Rondero, Roberto. "A 30 años de 'Los ricos…'" *El Universal*, 8 April 2009: n.p. Web. 13 December 2016.

Rubenstein, Anne. *Bad Language, Naked Ladies, and Other Threats to the Nation: A Political History of Comic Books in Mexico*. Durham, NC: Duke University Press, 1998.

Saavedra, Lorena. "La actuación no ha sido su única disciplina artística." *Excelsior*, 16 July 1988: n.p.

Shingler, Martin. *Star Studies: A Critical Guide*. London: BFI/Palgrave Macmillan, 2012.

Sinclair, John. *Latin American Television: A Global View*. New York: Oxford University Press, 1999.

Stacey, Jackie. *Star-Gazing: Hollywood Cinema and Female Spectatorship*. New York: Routledge, 1994.

Thornton, Niamh. "YouTube: Transnational Fandom and Mexican Divas." *Transnational Cinemas* 1.1, 2010: 53–67.

Toussaint, Florence. "Y Vero America Va." *Proceso*, 25 July 2009: n.p. Web. 30 May 2017.

Trejos, Carolina. "Verónica Castro, una abuela sexy a los 64 años." *People en español*, 17 January 2017: n.p. Web. 1 June 2017.

Tuñón, Julia. *Mujeres de luz y sombra en el cine mexicano: la construcción de una imagen (1939–1952)*. Mexico, DF: Colegio de México y IMCINE, 1998.

Valdivia, Angharad N. *A Latina in the Land of Hollywood and Other Essays on Media Culture*. Tuscon, AZ: University of Arizona Press, 2000.

"WTF!? La historia de cuando Bono trató de ligarse a Angélica María." *Sopitas.com*, 12 May 2017: n.p.

Zulema Aguilera, Claudia and Gilberto López Betancourt. "Gloria Trevi: Apoyan jóvenes sus 'locuras'." *El Porvenir*, 23 October 1992: 43.

17
HEMISEXUALIZING THE LATIN LOVER
Film and live art interpretations and provocations

Paloma Martinez-Cruz and John Cruz

When the *Sense8* science fiction web drama (2015) connected eight strangers from different parts of the world and featured an Anglo transgender woman named Nomi (Jamie Clayton) and Lito Rodriguez (Spanish actor Miguel Ángel Silvestre), critics at large applauded the show's representation of LGBT characters. While the computer genius Nomi comes from a wealthy and conservative family in the US, Lito brings the element of imaginative sexuality, situational improvisation, and outsized empathy to harness the emotions of his psychically linked companions. We, too, are enthusiastic fans of the *Sense8* series. However, as Laura Fernández examines in this volume, we also share a complex and mixed response to Silvestre's Lito, who so robustly represents aspects of the Latin lover stereotype (why couldn't Lito be the computer genius?), even as he subverts heteronormative prejudice and provides a more thoughtfully styled Latinx imaginary than the vast majority of his Latin lover counterparts in popular culture. To wit, he is definitely *not* the "Guatemalan gardener Javier" who we are told seduces an underage Paula (Jane Lynch) in the film *The 40-Year-Old Virgin*. However, the faceless gardener alluded to in *The 40-Year-Old Virgin*, and the Lito character both have in common an overt, hyper-sensual nature that crosses into the realm of prohibited, but irrepressible, sexual drives.

As a Latin lover, Lito is certainly connected to this narrative of Latino sexuality, but, departing from the conventions surrounding the stereotype, the Lito story also liberates, as audience members empathize with his struggle to assess the totalizing destructiveness of homophobia in his life and career, and then follow him on his journey toward his eventual triumph as the out-and-proud face of LGBT resistance on a hemispheric level. As with the Lito character, our present findings reveal that the Latin lover has many valences in both film and live art performances and provocations that require us to consider his iterations as more than a mere Hollywood stereotype, but also as a symbol of hemispheric recovery from the pathologies of prescribed homophobia and oppressive masculinities.

In both Latin America and the United States, popular and scholarly arts and letters aided in the naturalization of a binary between Iberian and Protestant subjects that associated Latino males with voracious passion and sexuality, while ascribing to Anglo males the virtues of self-control and rationality. In contemporary discourse, we need look no further than President Trump's campaign trail and his infamous and inflammatory assertion that Mexicans are "rapists" to observe the reinvigoration of early 20th-century ideas about the dangers of Mexican and Latinx sexuality. The present chapter deals with the role of film and performance in the denigration of Latino male sexuality in ways that impact the political prospects of Latinx peoples in the scope of the United States national project and beyond, while also examining the transformative potential of the "hemisexual" prospects in the popular imagination.

Our study is hemi*spheric*, as we opted for a comparative interpretation of the bodies of knowledge and cultural production generated by U.S. Latin lovers as well as performances arising out of Latin American cinematic priorities, but it is also hemi*sexual*. The notion of hemisexuality, introduced here as an expansive gesture of solidarity for a range of sexual orientations and expressions, is rooted in the vocabularies of the Hemispheric Institute of Performance and Politics, founded in 1998 at New York University.

The Hemispheric Institute of Performance and Politics is a biennial Americas-wide network that convenes large-scale international gatherings, connecting artists, scholars, and activists. Originally inspired by tee shirts emblazoned with the word "hemisexual" that began to appear at the "Hemi" conferences in recent years, in our study, the word's generative potential attached itself to the political, geographic, and sex-positive capaciousness of non-heteronormative, Americas-based positionalities, allowing us to envision two distinct categories of Latin lovers: Hollywood's Latin lovers that rehabilitate the logic of White supremacy, and hemisexual Latin lovers that harness the potential of performance to advocate for new possibilities for Latino masculinities. The prefix hemi-, from the Greek word meaning "half," is joined with the Latin "sphera," constituting a round, solid body: a ball, a globe, or a celestial structure. The hemisphere, usually conceived as a division between north and south or east and west by an imaginary line passing through the poles, is articulated across Hemispheric Institute conversations as the region particular to the American continents and nations, emphasizing solidarity with its denizens experiencing the political, cultural, and material consequences of settler colonialism, neoliberal capitalism, and the administrations and technologies that institute and police capital's attending privileges and punishments. To the multivalent geographic designation expressed in the prefix hemi-, conference-goers have added the root "sexual" in order to express fidelity to the artistic and theoretical human rights movements of the Americas, and, at the same time, stand against all forms of sexual bigotry with this embodied gesture of resistance.

Our analysis finds particular resonance with the work of Daniel Enrique Pérez (2012), who focuses on the screen presence of the Latin lover to "highlight queer aspects of his identity while also underscoring the influence he has had on male aesthetics and on facilitating non-normative discourses on gender and sexuality" (Pérez 437). While foregrounding the non-heteronormative and ambiguous sexuality that is alternately celebrated or castigated in representations and plot lines involving Latin lovers, Pérez also interrogates the politics of sexual labeling. "I am not interested in labeling the Latin lover as gay, bisexual, heterosexual, or any other fixed category related to sexuality; none of these adequately permits the wide spectrum of ambiguities and contradictions that the Latin lover actually embodies to coexist" (438). His use of "queer" as a descriptor expands to include what Western categories would classify as non-heterosexual, but also incorporates "a multiplicity of subject positions with antithetical relationships to things that are considered 'straight' or normal" (438). Here, we sustain Pérez's observation that the Latin lover is not, nor was he ever, a symbol of heteronormative sexuality. However, our enthusiasm for this figure's radical ambiguities extends beyond his queering presence in film and performance to encompass the equally radical, and equally inflammatory, circumstance of the statelessness that is part and parcel of the Latin lover's sexuality.

First, we map the historical presence of Hollywood's Latin lovers and compare these to Latin America's onscreen traditions of masculine seduction. The Hollywood productions analyzed here include *The Four Horsemen of the Apocalypse* with Rudolph Valentino (Rex Ingram, 1921), *Latin Lovers* starring Ricardo Montalban (Mervyn LeRoy, 1953), *The Big Lebowski* featuring

John Turturro as "the Jesus" (Joel and Ethan Coen 1998), and *How to Be a Latin Lover* starring Eugenio Derbez (Ken Marino, 2017). We then consider the U.S. project of Latino representation in light of Latin American cinematic texts beginning with the French-Argentinian tango singer Carlos Gardel, and his crooning Mexican counterparts Jorge Negrete and Pedro Infante. Finally, we examine the live art persona developed by Colombian, Ohio-based performer and co-author John Cruz. By providing a comparative genealogy of the Latin lover's developments in film, and extending our analysis toward the live representation of the Latin lover, we submit that this figure continues to influence national attitudes toward Latino men, with hemisexualizing prospects that persist in spite of the Anglo dominance that is reasserted in the Hollywood version of this stereotype.

A genealogy of the Latin lover in the Americas

When Rudolph Valentino (1895–1926) starred in Rex Ingram's 1921 silent, epic war film *The Four Horsemen of the Apocalypse*, his interpretation of the lascivious playboy Julio Desnoyers inaugurated the cinematic Latin lover stereotype, offering an alternative representation of Latino masculinity to the Western film genre's proliferation of scowling, unwashed bandidos and classic male buffoons (Ramírez Berg 2002, 66–86). The darkly handsome Desnoyers character, who seduces married women and is more at home on the dance floor than in the traditionally masculine atmospheres of the business office or the battle field, establishes the criteria for Hollywood's Latin lover, which we describe here. First, Desnoyers and his successors are erotically dangerous, with a plot arch that very rarely culminates in the normalizing contract of matrimony. Promiscuous without fathering children, he produces distrust and aversion among members of polite society for acting on extra-conjugal and forbidden drives. Secondly, Latin lovers are passionate and emotive, rather than the sturdy, silent types so prized among U.S. cinematic masculinities (Ramirez Berg, Pérez, King). Refined and graceful, Latin lovers bear no trace of the boorishness associated with underclass ignorance: they dance with sophistication, croon sentimental melodies, converse with silver-tongued persuasiveness, and employ a piercing, yet irresistible gaze to entice and seduce.

Our analysis emphasizes not only the sexual ambiguity implied in the graceful mores of the Latin lover described above, but also his ambiguity with regard to ethnicity and nationality. To be a Latin lover, he must conform to an Ibero-Mediterranean appearance that is decidedly swarthy – never blond or blue-eyed – but also not mistakable for his mestizo, indigenous, or African-descended counterparts who share his regional and political cartographies in Latin America and the U.S. Moreover, the Latin lover is – must be – nationless. Often an Italian-American interpreting a Latin American, or a U.S. Latino of undefined provenance with a thick accent, the lover is characterized by cultural transience and shiftlessness, an instability that distances him from the possibility of being a serious prospect for either marriage or nation building.

According to Hurtado and Sinha in their recent volume *Beyond Machismo: Intersectional Latino Masculinities* (2016), manhood is perceived as "a developmental process that is reached when a person is responsible for raising a family" and is fundamentally relational, "as in belonging to a culture, a community, a family" (64). The U.S. Latino male respondents in their *Beyond Machismo* study coincided in the notion that the process of manhood culminated in marriage and procreation, with the concept of *belonging to a community or family* at the core of their understanding of masculinity. In this traditional understanding of Latino maleness, the effeminacy presented by the Latin lover erodes and threatens the values of power and domination that are so intrinsically tied to marriage and the formation of a nuclear family unit. But we also affirm here that the Latin lover's lack of belonging – his lack of a discernable socio-geographic root structure – is just as threatening as his non-normative sexuality.

Hemisexualizing the Latin lover

Cinema was not the first medium to establish the Latin lover's uncertain contract with nationality. In the dramatic and lyrical imagination of Europe, the first written version of the legend of Don Juan comes from the character Don Giovanni (Italian), the fictional libertine penned by the Spanish dramatist Tirso de Molina, whose play, *El burlador de Sevilla y convidado de piedra* (*The Trickster of Seville and the Stone Guest*) was first circulated in Spain around 1630. Lord Byron (1788–1824), Britain's most prominent figure of the Romantic movement, authored the mock-epic narrative poem "Don Juan" about a lustful Spaniard whose wanderlust and strings of seductions helped to seal an already well-developed notion about Roman masculinity at the advent of the Industrial Revolution.

After the fictional figure of Don Juan, Giacomo Girolamo Casanova (1725 to 1798) provided one of the Western imagination's earliest literary depictions of a historical Latin lover. Aided by his 12-volume autobiography that includes extensive details of his voracious sexual adventures, Valentino's early predecessor was born in Venice, and died in Castle Dux (Duchsov) in the remote Czech countryside. However, it was the Bibliothèque Nationale de France in Paris that eventually purchased the original version of his autobiography in 2010 for a record manuscript price of $9.6 million, consecrating Casanova's penned pages as a French sacred artifact on par with relics of saints and martyrs. Writing in Italian and French, and ending up in German-speaking Bohemia, Casanova neither married nor kept a permanent home (Perrottet 2012). This early playboy aristocrat of Roman extraction became a symbol for societal subversion, which is narrated as the sexual exploits of a man perilously adrift: the anti-hero, who, instead of concluding his epic journey on the road back to his place of origin to bring glory to his realm and kin, undertakes a journey away from home in express pursuit of sensual pleasures. The popularity of these early modern anti-heroes was such that the names "Don Juan" and "Casanova" continue to act as substitutes in the contemporary vernacular for society's insatiable womanizers, and films such as Jeremy Leven's *Don Juan DeMarco* (1994) starring Johnny Depp and *Don Jon*, directed by and starring Joseph Gordon-Levitt (2013) attest to the persistence of this protagonist in popular storytelling.

The power of this cultural motif in the Western imagination is evinced by the Latin lover's early iteration on the silver screen. The roaring twenties were a time of feverish change, when the U.S. economy experienced an emergent prosperity that was as unprecedented as it was unfamiliar. A new consumer society, with more of the population suddenly living in cities than on farms, was being redefined by the perplexities of new innovations such as radios, cars, and movie palaces that recalibrated the definitions of civic inclusion and the visual practices of spectators. The generation's corresponding symbols of sexuality gained purchase on the silver screen: if the adventurous, short-skirt wearing, rouge-kneed flapper represented the modern woman's escape from domestic confinement, then Hollywood's Latin lover became a stalwart in the U.S. cinematic and performatic imaginaries of sexuality and seduction. Cast in the starring roles of *The Four Horsemen* (1921) and *The Sheik* (1921), Valentino achieved stardom for his brooding-yet-irresistible sensuality in non-Western leading roles. Playing a matador embroiled in an extramarital, sadomasochistic affair in *Blood and Sand* (1922) further cemented Valentino's typecasting in silent films as the exotic seducer, whose deviant on-screen sensuality had off-screen implications that dominated newspaper headlines and society gossip about the supposed proclivities of the Roman-featured silent film star.

If the Latin lover had long served as a symbol for dangerous Latin sexuality in the West, it was during Valentino's era when his physical and psychological traits were systematically concretized. Paramount Pictures, in the hands of movie mogul Adolph Zukor, played a foundational role in the dissemination of Hollywood's Latin lover. Zukor believed that exclusive contracts with directors, writers, and stars, would make the company the sole proprietors of stand-out talent and enable Paramount to control every aspect of the business. Zukor's "stable of stars" concept lead him to hire leading celebrities such as Mary Pickford and later Valentino. After his successful work in *The Four Horsemen,* which had been produced by Metro Goldwin Mayor, his first movie for Paramount was *The Sheik* (1921). It was through this film Valentino became known as the "synonym of the romantic male," and catapulted Valentino to "the highest rank of stardom" (Eames, 23). Following this film, the quality of the films in which Valentino would star began to decrease. For example, the film *Monsieur Beucaire* (1924) was criticized for the use of flamboyant decoration in Valentino's costumes that made him look effeminate in the eyes of critics (Eames, 31). Despite these slights, his films continue to be successful due to the star power brought by Valentino, which centered on his designing gaze. His command of the star system allowed Zukor to put these elements together in order to catapult actors to stardom, despite the unevenness of a particular film's quality.

Valentino's power of seduction, along with continued speculations about his sexual preferences, continued long after his early death at the age of 31 caused by peritonitis. A rash of suicides among his female fans was reported by the press as the result of their grief at having lost their incandescent star, adding to the mythology surrounding the outsized force of his attraction. The Latin-ness of Valentino's magnetism was remarked in the Colombian magazine *El Gráfico.*

> Las Mujeres de todas partes del mundo, cansadas ya de rubios galanes de ojos azules, se volvieron locas ante el latino de pelo negro y ojos de mirada voluptuosa. Su sonrisa irónica y sus ojos de malayo tan pronto se adaptaban al carácter sensual del árabe o al fogoso español como al del correcto lord inglés o al del galante duque francés del siglo XVII / Women from everywhere had grown tired of the traditional handsome blond and blue eyed male actors. They went crazy for the Latin men with black hair and dark eyes and a voluptuous gaze. His ironic smile and his devious eyes adapted easily to characters like the sensual Arab, the passionate Spaniard, the well-mannered English lord, or the gallant XVII century French Duke.
>
> *(E. C., authors' translation, 2388)*

In terms of the film that first linked Hollywood's Latin lover to the problem of statelessness, in *The Four Horsemen,* Valentino's Julio Desnoyers is born to a family in which the patriarch, Julio's maternal grandfather, represents a poor Spanish immigrant turned landed gentry in Pre-First World War Argentina. Intertitles preface Valentino's famous tango scene with a warning: "Encouraged by an indulgent grandfather who was his ideal, what chance had Julio Desnoyers to be anything other than a youthful libertine?" (*Four Horsemen*). The tango dance takes place early in the character's progression, when Julio starts a fight to steal a dance partner from another suitor, then stuns and delights the unrefined bar crowd with his superior ability on the dance floor. When his French father relocates the family to Europe after his grandfather's death, Julio is depicted painting semi-clothed women in his personal studio where he creates portraits that the audience members of the generation would have interpreted as shockingly salacious. It is here in his studio that he seduces a married woman, stealing her virtue, and solidifying the observer's understanding that Julio's character is beyond moral redemption. He does find a kind of absolution at the film's conclusion, when he spills his blood and sacrifices his life in the fight for the allied forces. In this epic war film, we find the combined ingredients of Roman features, exceptional artistic ability, dangerous sexual liaisons, and the cultural ambiguities of Argentinean, Spanish, and French heritage that can only be reconciled through his ultimate sacrifice at the film's conclusion.

In the world of arts journalism and society columns, the characters Valentino interpreted caused his fans to swoon on a scale that had not yet been witnessed as such a widespread phenomenon, but the multiple displacements of normative sexuality and nationality were also the cause of acute ridicule and anxiety. As Gilbert King recalls:

But it was the *Chicago Tribune* that really set Valentino off. On July 18, 1926, the paper ran an unsigned editorial under the headline "Pink Powder Puffs" that blamed Valentino for the installation of a face-powder dispenser in a new public men's room on the city's North Side:

A powder vending machine! In a men's washroom! Homo Americanus! Why didn't someone quietly drown Rudolph Guglielmo, alias Valentino, years ago? ... Do women like the type of "man" who pats pink powder on his face in a public washroom and arranges his coiffure in a public elevator?

(King 2012: 4)

Valentino's career was plagued by fears of his "effeminacy," and the actor's own desires to repudiate these hostilities. As the *Tribune*'s above editorial makes clear, complete with shrug quotes around the descriptor "man," the Latin lover's explosive entry into cinematic relevance was, from its outset, under assault for its gender destabilizing potential.

A brief survey of early cinematic renderings of romantic male leads created for Latin American markets demonstrate a very different symbolic economy of masculine ideals in Latin American cinematic productions. Exemplified by Carlos Gardel, whose films were produced by Paramount for the Hispanic and French markets, and Pedro Infante and Jorge Negrete who epitomized the Mexican national project, these Latin American icons of the emergent masculinities that cinema had the power to produce convince us that only Gardel, in the hands of Paramount, can have been classified as a proper Latin lover. In Paramount's hemispheric framing aimed at different Latin American and European audiences, Gardel represents ambivalence of both sexuality and nationality. In contrast, the hyper-nation-ness of Infante and Negrete, in their elaborate charro outfits with flashy silver decorations on tight trousers, jackets and sombreros, connect masculinity to the patriarchal principles of, well, *patria*. This stands in stark opposition to the cosmopolitan outfits of Hollywood's Latin lovers, who are seldom associated with the symbols of regional folklore beyond a single feature film, and whose attachment to such regionalisms is understood as visual fiction, rather than authentic patriotism.

Following Valentino's sudden and tragic departure, Paramount saw in Gardel a new star for the film industry that was able to represent the ideal Latin lover. *Luces de Buenos Aires* (1931), Gardel's first film made by Paramount, depicts the protagonist Anselmo Torres, a romantic and bucolic gaucho owner of an *estancia* in the Argentinian pampas. Significantly, both Valentino and Gardel interpreted the Argentine gaucho in their first films: the latter distilled his seduction by his fiery tango movements while the former displayed his charm by singing dramatic and romantic tango songs. Doubtlessly, the tango functioned as the irrefutable representation of the Latin American male in early cinema: romantic, passionate, and predatory, like the allusions to violence in the choreographies fusing attraction and danger in dance. Through these depictions, the spectators were seduced by the vehement and sensual movements of the dancing and the nostalgic sound of the bandoneón combined with Gardel's baritone voice.

In terms of the gender ambiguity associated with his roles, Gardel departs from Valentino in significant ways. While he capitalized on his power of attraction as a virile male romantic lead, it must be noted that the cinematic representation of Gardel in his films presented him as the new Latin male "divo" that departs from the silent portrayals of Valentino as the Latin lover who seduces through the dance and the glance. Here, we employ divo as an extension of the "diva" category assigned to female singers and actresses recognized for their commanding presence both on stage and in life. As a male divo, Gardel's cinematic representation highlighted the glamour, flare, and screen dominance that is typically associated with female opera virtuosos.

For example, in Gardel's second movie *Melodía de Arrabal* (1932), Gardel portrays Ricardo Ramírez, a swindler poker player known for his card playing abilities and singing talent. In one of the scenes, Ramírez is in a private party where his romantic female interest Alina introduces him to a producer. After she finishes her song, she plays the piano and Ramírez sings "Cuando tú no estás." The film shows Ramírez singing from a balcony while he performs for an audience in a theater. In a medium shot, we see him behind a balcony which functions as a barrier between he and the spectator: as a divo, it is impossible for his public to approach him. Behind, the various assembled guests in attendance begin to move closer as they are hypnotized by his voice. The camera does not distinguish between the admiration garnered by women and men, who are both equally enthralled by his virtuosic performance. At the feet of the divo, both genders are mesmerized by his music that is as sentimental as it is gallant.

In Gardel's ensuing films, we see the same emphasis on medium shots that, on occasion, are combined with low angle shots and American (3/4) shots, producing a feeling of attending one of his performances live, and reinforcing Gardel's significance in both the cinematographic and discographic industries. Another example of Gardel as the seductive male divo can be seen in his film *Tango Bar* (1935). In the role of a young cabaret performer, he delivers a vocal performance that begins at the top of a flight of stairs on the deck of a ship looking down at a group of reveling Spaniards before he begins the dramatic descent that constitutes the signature choreography of the diva/o.

A more overt – even brazen – moment of same-sex attraction takes place in *Melodía de Arrabal* when the character Gutierrez, a fellow card shark, approaches Gardel's character Ramírez after observing him playing cards and singing. "Usted es un hombre joven y muy bien dotado," offers Gutierrez. In a serious tone, Ramírez ask, "¿Por la voz?," to which Gutiérrez responds, "Y por las manos." At the scene's conclusion, Gutierrez emphasizes the handsomeness of Ramirez's face. In his remarks about card playing abilities, Gutiérrez manages to reference sexual prowess. Although we never see any kind of sexual encounter between Ramirez and Gutierrez, the intimacy of the dialogue and tone of the scene erodes heteronormative orderings that would conventionally reinforce, rather than destabilize, Gardel's conquests of members of the opposite sex. Furthermore, the scene could be viewed as an extension of Gardel's off-screen life, in which he was suspected of keeping secrets about his sexual proclivities. Through the Gutiérrez-Ramírez chemistry, audiences are invited into the pleasures of same-sex attraction.

Our investigation of the Latin lover motif in Latin American markets found that Gardel, as a Latin lover-divo in the hands of Paramount, differed greatly from the hyper-masculinity and zealous patriotism of charro-macho films that enjoyed broad circulation among Spanish-speaking audiences. In the careers of Pedro Infante and Jorge Negrete, each personified the Mexican charro, who represented a passion for the rural landscape, and valued the importance of hacienda work upon which their power over the hearts of virtuous women was derived. The Infante and Negrete characters reinforce social gender conventions and the ideology of nationalism by virtue of a cinematic imaginary combining regional costumes, national song catalogues, an emphasis on the male-to-female serenade (with its concomitant allusions to marriage), and the centrality of the relationship between land and patriarch.

On the surface, the nation-ness of these charro suitors might be compared to the flamboyant costumes so central to Valentino and Gardel's screen images, but the costumes, in the world of Hollywood production values, recreated and helped to deepen U.S. notions of the exotic Other. In order to resemble the Arab leader known as the sheik, Valentino wore the primitive and extravagant "Arabic" outfits, while in *Blood and Sand*, he wore a flashy rococo bullfighter outfit. His costumes represented the archetypes that Hollywood employed to emphasize the difference between the foreign lover and the well-mannered White male. Moreover, the stereotypical

Hemisexualizing the Latin lover

costumes were part of the film's narrative structure in which spectators could easily identify different male "races," providing a visual shorthand for the ideology of Anglo superiority and non-White male deviance. The charro in Mexican cinema, in contrast, evokes an entirely different symbolic economy by which Mexican hyper-masculinity, read here as normative, results in the stabilizing principles of matrimony and regional rootedness. The charro, standing with his riding boots planted on bare earth, sending his devotion toward a demure young woman above, may well be envisioned as the antithesis of the filmic divo. Also, Infante and Negrete, as Mexican nationals who could not be interpreted as outsiders performing the roles of "exotics," were seen to inhabit the charro costume as both a birth rite and a national destiny.

Keeping Valentino and Gardel in mind as Paramount's foundational success with the Latin lover formula, the stereotype has never gone out of vogue. A fascinating take on the cinematic convention of the Latin lover is offered in the midcentury film *Latin Lovers* (1953). The film centers on the wealthy businessman Paul (John Lund) who has trouble proposing to his millionaire intended Nora (Lana Turner). Nora, in turn, is unconvinced that her suitors are not mere opportunists in pursuit of her fortune. When Paul's business dealings take him to Brazil, Nora follows him to see if the tropical holiday can help him escape the repressive caution that burdens their courtship, as a Brazilian dance instructor has told her that, "Things happen to a man in the air in Brazil. He knows what he wants and he takes what he wants. He takes a woman he wants."

Advised independently by their respective psychiatrists, the film asserts that the Latin American context can provide a scientific curative for the repression that keeps them from consummating their courtship and finding true happiness. When the potential groom-to-be ends up focusing on business in Brazil, Nora follows her analyst's urgings to be more impulsive, and she ends up giving her heart to the dashing Brazilian Roberto (Ricardo Montalban). Breaking off her near-engagement to Paul and agreeing to marry the stable owner Roberto, Nora is still afraid that her handsome new fiancé of modest means is just in it for profit. At the film's conclusion, she finally discovers what will make her most happy: she will give away all of her money to Roberto, so that the burden of wealth will be his to bear.

Latin Lovers departs from the script of the Hollywood stereotype in that it concludes in marriage, but it is a specific kind of marriage, in which the Anglo woman must relinquish both nation and fortune in order to belong to her lover's world. With Anglo and Latin American suitors pitted against each other, we see the clichés surrounding Latino sexuality depicted as a clear binary: while Paul is sensible and stoic, Roberto is glamorous and impulsive. While Paul respects her bodily boundaries, Roberto is always trying to insinuate himself in a dangerous seduction to which she mounts scant defense. Paul is uncoordinated and is laid up with an injury; Roberto is a talented horseman whose riding skills (ahem) cause her to swoon at first sight. He grabs and kisses her even before he speaks with her when she wanders through the stables in search of a second glimpse of him. And, on the dance floor, he chides her for being too stiff, and not having the play around the hips and shoulders that allow the women of his country to express themselves with abandon when the music starts to play.

In a twist on the Latino-sexuality-as-pathology trope, the film produces an extremely curious critique of Anglo sensuality as a condition that is intrinsically pathological. As an unsatisfied woman, whose Anglo suitor is unable to perceive or react to her obvious sentimentality and desires, the Brazilian male provides the curative for culturally induced frigidity and repression. Nora's analyst even provides a scientific rationale for her to behave more impulsively, and seize the opportunity to open to sensuality and impulse: a metaphorical doctor's note that saves her from the repression of Anglo courtship, and propels her to follow her innermost urgings. The presumably happy conclusion finds her giving away her fortune and her national residency – a total refutation of the logics of U.S. capitalist accumulation – to demonstrate her utter subordination to the husband-to-be. While the premise could not be a stronger bid for patriarchal social orderings and traditional gender roles, the film's sex-positive, hemisexual aspect allows for an alternative reading of Nora's total surrender of power. By prioritizing sensual pleasure, and even finding a scientific logic behind her need to obey her longing, her love for a Latino man and for Brazilian society reads as a life-affirming escape from Anglo sexual behavior that is framed as heavily oppressive, and signals the need for alternative routes towards personal completion.

While the Latin lover figure has qualifiable redeeming – or redeemable – virtues in *Horsemen* and *Latin Lovers*, in *The Big Lebowski* (1998), the defining characteristics of the Latin lover, such as dance, music, effeminate style, and dark seduction, are deployed in order to naturalize Latino male sexual depravity. A crime comedy film centered on the slacker Jeff Lebowski (Jeff Bridges) involves the mystery of how and why the young trophy bride Bunny Lebowski (Tara Reid) goes missing. As a White slacker whose only commitments are to smoking marijuana and to his bowling league, the film is not structured around the developments of a Latin lover figure. It does, however, feature a prominent scene that engages an extreme reproduction of this stereotype. Jesus Quintana, played by John Tuturro, is a star bowler on the competing team. Quintana wears a form-fitting lilac-colored body suit, a prominent hairnet covering oiled-back, dark hair, sports lengthy, painted finger nails, and he is shown to lasciviously lick his bowling ball. He cleans his bowling ball between his legs near the groin region with the kind of gusto associated with the pursuit of sexual self-gratification, and he refers to himself in the third person as "the Jesus" in a derisory, mock Cuban American accent.

Cinematically, the technique of triangulation, as set forth by Ramirez Berg (2002) by which two allies join together against a targeted third, is fundamental to the staging of the Latino male as an agent of sexual perversion. "The classical Hollywood film sets up a stereotyping triangle with the dominant ideal—the archetype protagonist—at its positive apex, the stereotype in the negative corner, and the viewer as the third—and ostensibly neutral—point of the triangle…" (62). In the Jesus scene, the triangle is formed by Walter Sobchak (John Goodman) the protagonist's best friend and fellow team member who narrates the backstory involving the Latino Other for the benefit of the Dude: "He did six months in Chino for exposing himself to an eight year old. He is a pedophile. Eight year olds, Dude." The two share this confidence while visually surveying Quintana's prowess on the lanes with evident envy. "Triangling helps ensure that the maximum number of viewers are fused … into the narrative in the "right" way—pro the Anglo dominant and contra the Other" (64).

The triangling that initially takes place between the film's hero and secondary character to establish the sexual corruption of the Latino Other is also deployed to convey Quintana's geographic transience. First, Tuturro's Jesus revisits the Hollywood tradition of Italian-Americans cast as Latino characters: Jennifer Esposito (*Crash*), Marisa Tomei (*The Perez Family*), Al Pacino (*Scarface*), and Madonna (*Evita*), to name a few. His heavy, mock Spanish Cuban accent might be a study of Al Pacino's Tony Montana, and, like his name, is clearly meant to be interpreted as a source of derision. While the name "Jesus" is common in Spanish- and Portuguese-speaking cultures, it is virtually non-existent as a first name in the Anglo context. Therefore, his "nobody fucks with the Jesus" is a tagline that produces laughter from the *fact* of his Latinidad as a source of bizarre eccentricity, which is then married to the sexual perversion that Quintana eagerly flaunts. Next, the conflation of international Latino identities is underscored by the use of Spanish flamenco to narrate the physical activity of someone whose speech pattern reveals him to be of Cuban origin. Finally, his geographic transience is emphasized when the cutaway shot that accompanies Sobchak's backstory exhibits Quintana going from door to door in his new neighborhood to inform the residents that he is a registered sex offender. The scene shows Quintana recoil in fear as a large, brutish looking Anglo man answers the door to his knock.

Hemisexualizing the Latin lover

We understand that the man who has come to the door will take pleasure in brutalizing Quintana, but we are not shown this inevitable sequence of events. Instead, the camera cuts back to the bowling alley, where Sobchak confirms to Lebowski that this is what has happened.

Although cinematically stacking the deck in favor of Anglo dominance, the Coen brothers' Latin lover is not represented without its requisite elegance. Quintana's athletic adroitness is Latinized, even lionized, by the scene's auditory information that equates bowling with dance. The Gypsy King's version of The Eagle's song "Hotel California" sounds thunderously when Quintana bowls a strike. Sung in Spanish, the flamenco singing style, characterized by extensive, raspy vibrato and the instability of timbre, conveys the Latino terrain of Otherness: we are to understand that the Jesus inhabits a realm of unfettered passions, as exotic as they are unintelligible to the monolingual English-speakers established as the "in" group by the Lebowski-Sobchak-Quintana triangle.

In terms of its legacy, *The Big Lebowski* is considered a national cult classic, and was selected for preservation in the National Film Registry by the Library of Congress, being deemed "culturally, historically or aesthetically significant enough for preservation" (Grow 2014). Currently, a spin-off based on John Turturro's Jesus Quintana, titled *Going Places*, is in post-production and was scheduled for a 2017 release date. Acting as writer and director, Turturro reprises his role of what might be Hollywood's most reprehensible cinematic Latin lover that relies on textbook stereotyping to sediment ideologies about the superiority of Anglo morality, and the predatory transience of Latino male bodies.

In Ken Marino's *How to Be a Latin Lover* (2017), the final film project analyzed in this section, the myth of the passionate Latino is both celebrated and subverted. In this light-hearted comedy, Eugenio Derbez interprets Maximo, a calculating gigolo who is caught with no back-up plan when his wealthy, 80-year-old wife leaves him for a younger car salesman played by Michael Cera. Forced to find another place to live, he moves in with his estranged sister Sara (Salma Hayek) and her bright, but socially awkward, son Hugo (Raphael Alejandro). While launching new schemes with his fellow career gigolo Rick (Rob Lowe), he manages to form sincere emotional connections to his sister and nephew. The film concludes with Maximo's final return to his life as a gigolo, but only after securing victories for his sister's career and his nephew's grade-school love interest that demonstrate that his redemption as a reliable member of the immediate family has been guaranteed.

Derbez as a Latin lover is clearly the film's first laugh. The official movie poster depicts him in a yellow Speedo-style swim suit, his body announcing the signs of encroaching middle age, and his facial features connecting Derbez to the aesthetic of Mexican *mestizaje*, rather than conserving the convention of a lighter, more European (or Europeanized) version of swarthy attraction. For his Spanish-speaking fan base, Derbez' attitude and carriage are more akin to a Cantinflas-as-Adonis visual than an Antonio Banderas type romantic lead. In fact, the impossibility of Maximo as a romantic lead is the obvious parody of the Hollywood stereotype, and this point is made on several grounds.

First, Maximo and his sister are clearly of Mexican descent, and the production centers on cultural pride as a source of spiritual and psychological alignment. In fact, the protagonist's work ethic, or his aversion to said ethic, stems from his father's early death produced by dangerous working conditions, suggesting the reality of economic exploitation as a defining aspect of bordered lives. While they are still young children, Sara asks Maximo what he wants to do as a career when he becomes an adult. Gazing longingly at a glossy page in a magazine depicting a wealthy older man with a dazzling trophy wife at his side, Maximo tells Sara that this is what he wants to be. Sara explains that to become a wealthy impresario, he will have to work extremely hard. After all, their father had always told them, "You get what you work for." Maximo clarifies that it is not the man's job in the image that he wishes to pursue, but *hers*. The film leaps ahead by some 25 years when Maximo awakens in a mansion made from his wife's money, and the spectator can recreate in their imagination the steps he took in order to fulfill his childhood dream to become a career Latin lover.

The film's objective is summed up by Derbez when he states in a *Los Angeles Times* interview, "The best way to break down a stereotype is to make fun of it." All of the Latin lover motifs are present and accounted for, but in ways that substitute audience sympathy for racial prejudice. The dance motif is repurposed as a way for Maximo and his sister to reconnect over a bottle of tequila in a "viva México" moment that repairs broken filial ties. Next, Maximo is penniless, and the seduction of wealthy, older women for him constitutes a job, rather than the pursuit of sexual pleasure. Audiences understand that, while living a life of exaggerated luxury, (preferring to ride a Segway indoors than to walk from room to room), he is also in charge of providing steady companionship to his legal wife in spite of his clear physical and emotional ambivalence about his spouse. In other words, although he is using her for her money, he, too, is being used, and inhabits a gilded cage devoid of emotional depth or meaning. When he finds realignment with the values of family and country, he goes back to doing the work – and it *is* work – of being the hired playmate of wealthy women.

This historical review of Hollywood's cinematic legacy of Latin lovers allows us to appreciate that this figure is most dangerous when he is shown to erode the national project as a carto-graphic Other. As with Priscilla Ovalle's assertion that the myth of Hollywood's dancing Latinas began with the Spanish Conquest and Manifest Destiny, and has endured through a succession of colonial relationships organized around the political categories of race, gender, and sexuality, "its visualization and perpetuation in the twentieth century…have relied on collapsed, codified, and reiterated depictions of dance and racialized sexuality that signify the Latina's amoral behavior and impermanence" (Ovalle, 2). Latin lovers, like Ovalle's dancing Latinas, rely on filmic depictions that include choreography, accented dialogue, costuming, and geographic imperma-nence to visualize and perpetuate the myth of Latino male depravity. Ranging from overt fear and revulsion toward Latino male sexuality, as with Valentino and Tuturro who are depicted as sexual predators in the flamboyant guise of the exotic Latino Other, to the problematic curative proposed by "South American" sensuality (Montalban), to the potentially empowering subver-sion of the stereotype (Derbez) who demonstrates the absurdity of this role while affirming the symbols of culture and family on his journey toward completion: when the Latin lover is shown as a threat to heteronormative masculinity and sexuality, this is invariably situated within the context of national ambiguity.

It must be emphasized that Hollywood's Latin lovers have an enormous role in the normali-zation of Latinophobia that overwhelms contemporary political discourses. The racist myth of Latino sexual pathology, situated within the context of political and geographic displacement, are combined with the national rejection of sexual ambiguities of any kind to produce and sus-tain fears of the Latino Other. After all, triangling worthy of the Coen brothers was vigorously deployed by Donald Trump on the campaign trail, who leaned conspiratorially toward his eager audiences to exploit their fears about Latino sexual degeneracy. And he was able to rely on these fears to send him all the way to the nation's highest office.

Hemisexual provocations: Meet Rrrricarrrdo

Our present section, based on two live art performance interventions conceived and performed by John Cruz at events coordinated and produced by Paloma Martínez-Cruz, represents a collaborative critical reflection that employs Cruz' first-person voice to maintain the intimacy and immediacy of the performance diary genre.

Hemisexualizing the Latin lover

My creation of the Latin lover performance persona, who I call Ricardo, initially arose from my gender identity as a homosexual man. An act of self-affirmation, this intervention allows me to embody different styles of seduction without discriminating among genders. At the same time, I speak from a subaltern positionality and seek to subvert heteronormative models with my performance. The Latin lover provides a vehicle for the embodiment of seduction that involves both men and women that would not be possible outside of this performance provocation for two reasons. First, a man who is "read" as gay is not convincing as a seducer of feminine subjects, and, in the second place, seduction of male subjects is repressed in public. As such, with Ricardo "the Latin lover," I embody seduction as a corporeal liberatory practice by creating targets of desire that subvert hetero- and homosexual categories.

Performed in 2014 at the Ohio State Union and 2016 at Wild Goose Creative (both in Columbus, Ohio), even though some audience members knew me and were aware of my sexual orientation, they still became involved with the performed possibility of seduction directed at both male and female participants. As Ricardo, the hemisexual positionality, both of the Latin lover as a known stereotype and my own identity as a gay male Colombian national based in the U.S., I blur the sexual and cultural categories until arriving at a non-binary space of pleasure that is not confined to specific audience members' bodily boundaries, but becomes a communally owned and fully participatory matrix of meaning.

My objectives during the performance are: first, from the perspective of the Latin lover as a Hollywood stereotype, to question the political and social discourses surrounding Latino men as an exotic body that threatens to destroy Anglo society; second, through the technology of seduction, to provoke sensorial stimulation without regard for the gender or race of the audience member who becomes the momentary target of Ricardo's desire.

My Latin lover performance is unscripted, but rather arises as an organic intervention that activates the possibility of seduction through visual and verbal cues. In terms of the gaze, I seek to maintain direct and sustained eye contact with an audience member accompanied by a confident and elegant stride. The unsolicited, sustained gaze engenders different reactions among the public. With this in mind, the interaction with the public determines the extent to which Ricardo can develop the seduction until he achieves his final objective: to take an assistant to an implied, off-stage room where no one can see or know what happens.

Various images and cinematic texts inform my representation of the Latin lover, along with personal experiences relating to the political categories that shape my social reality. The elasticity of my physical presence and gestures materialize the spectral and spectacular drama from the Latin lover of the silver screen. A cosmopolitan figure, he is the master of seduction and refinement. He is stylized, with slicked back hair, a classic dark suit, and an exaggerated presentation of masculinity that also incorporates somewhat effeminate mannerisms.

Ricardo's physical and emotional traits are culled from cinematic renderings. Most particularly, I draw on the mischievous gaze that Valentino directs at his would be paramour in which he raises a single eyebrow while *The Four Horsemen*'s intertitles read, "Why not come to my studio? There would be no harm. I promise to be good!" I have adapted this by saying, "Let's go to a dark room in back. It'll be our secret."

The name Ricardo serves as an auditory gesture in the performance. Among audience participants, the rhotic consonant "r" produces a trill vibration that emphasizes the Latinidad of the lover. Moreover, the rhotic pronunciation gives Ricardo a distinctive sonority that maximizes his sensual presence. This rolled rhotic is a stalwart among cinematic Latin lovers. As the early example of Carlos Gardel demonstrates, roles that featured trilled rhotic consonants in the first or last names are central to his film catalogue: Anselmo Torres in *Luces de Buenos Aires* (1932), Carlos Acuña in *Esperame, andanzas de un criollo en España* (1932), Juan Carlos Romero in

La casa es seria (1932), Roberto Ramírez in *Meloáia de Arrabal* (1932), Carlos Acosta in *Cuesta abajo* (1934), Alberto Bazan in *El Tango de Broadway* (1934), Julio Argüelles in *El día que me quieras* (1935), Ricardo Fuentes in *Tango Bar* (1935). The rhotic sound represents a direct signifier of the seduction of the Latin lover, serving as a synecdoche for the specific valences of "Latino" lust on the acoustic plane as listeners enter the space of Ricardo's exotic e-rhotic.

The first stage of Ricardo's seduction begins with the pursuit of a woman in the audience as a social and visual playfulness that erodes audience tension and subtly paves the way for the possibility of the seduction of men. It is productive to involve female spectators who are unaccompanied by male companions, as well as women who are clearly partnered by men in attendance that I approach with Ricardo's designs. On two occasions, married women with significant authority positions in the group have received Ricardo's attentions, leading to a heightened understanding of Ricardo's take-no-prisoners audacity, as well as the erosion of conventional hierarchies in place outside of the zone of the performance. At this point, there is laughter in the audience, but it is a distinctly nervous laughter. Both Ricardo's silent approach and his piercing gaze activate uncertainty and excitement among spectators, and Ricardo draws on this energy to fuel his provocation. They don't know what is going to happen, or how far I will go (Figure 17.1).

Generally, women who are there with a companion tell me right away that they are with someone, and they gesture to their date. This is where the Latin lover breaks from the institutional conventions of heterosexuality and monogamy, as he is not put off at all by her companion, but rather gamely proposes a different possibility. As Ricardo, I begin to expand my mark to include both the woman and her date when I ask, "Do you want to try something new?" However, when it comes to Ricardo's contact with unaccompanied men, the idea of seduction by another man implies a loss of the public face of their masculinity, and their emotive responses are brusque as they look for a way to avoid the gaze of the Latin lover who invites them into this moment of seduction. The stability of their masculinity within the social group becomes exposed and vulnerable: even if they spurn Ricardo's advances, they are still witness to his attentions and intentions

Figure 17.1 Morato, Fernando. Latin Lover Provocations: Performance by John Cruz. 2016.

in a way that implicates them in the web of his desires, and had just been visibly pleasured by Ricardo's attempts to seduce the women around the room that he approaches. Although they rebuff the Latin lover with hurried phrases and measured indifference, an unnamed possibility has been evoked and externalized that had been socially omitted before: a man just might become aroused by another man. By way of a conclusion to my Latin lover provocation, Ricardo's aim is to convince an audience member to go with him to a secret place, presumably to complete the cycle of seduction and engage in a bout of singularly passionate love making between two bodies that had never encountered each other before that moment.

Conversations with audience members following the Latin lover performances, both the ones who had been my unsuspecting marks, and those who had been witness to Ricardo's attempts to seduce others, continue to educate me about the hemisexual implications of the Latin lover. One audience-participant, a young man of Afro-Honduran descent, approached me to tell me that although he identified with his Latino culture, he understood that he was excluded from the range of the aesthetic conventions that define the Latin lover. His skin color and physical features did not correspond to Hollywood's representations of Latinos with exclusively Euro-Mediterranean features. This insight confirmed that the Latin lover could not be viewed as an inclusive metaphor for the image of Latino masculinity. Latinos, and here I specify male-gendered peoples of Latin American extraction contributing to the U.S. national project, imply a homogenous group inclusive of all races. Therefore, the light-skin privilege that construes a hemispheric category of vast entitlements in the political circumstances of the Americas are present in my indexing of this cinematic stereotype. Not all Latinos fall within the range of Hollywood's conventional Latin lovers. On the contrary, the logic of domination by a European-descended minority, narrowly associated with privileges of race and class in Latin American nations with majority indigenous, mestizo, and Afro-Latino populations, may inhibit the decolonial energies of the Latin lover as a performance provocation (Figure 17.2).

Figure 17.2 Morato, Fernando. Latin Lover Provocation: Performance by John Cruz. 2016.

In the spirit of Ricardo's provocation, "Do you want to try something new," my hemisexual project aspires to put the spectator on the border of their seat and ignite their minds with new possibilities that expand the relationships that define Latinx and hemispheric masculinities. How can Ricardo, through his joyful and playful performance, encourage the audience to expand the scope of what masculine identities can encompass? Also, how can Ricardo, through his words and gestures, help to transform the binary relationships and to contest the stereotype with its own absurdity? In the live art re-appropriation of a Hollywood stereotype, the hemisexualization of the Latin lover is achieved by activating a cartography of senses that defy the power grid that demarcates north to south or east to west, but instead envisions a plurality of sensual cardinal points through play. At the same time, the performance invites new dialogues about Latino male representations in the U.S. media industry, offering both a critique of Latinx depictions as irrational and hot blooded, while providing an open forum to acknowledge that not all Latinos will be hailed by Rrricarrdo as a vehicle for transformation: the Latin lover most certainly relies on race and class privilege to assert a cosmopolitanism that is rooted in Western (colonial) conventions of beauty and desire.

Do you want to try something new?

Peter Beinart's article "The Republican Party's White Strategy" appearing in *The Atlantic* (2016) explains that journalists who were shocked by Donald Trump's announcement that Mexican immigrants were "rapists" in his presidential campaign had not understood that Trump had a muse in the conservative political commentator and syndicated columnist Ann Coulter. Hitting bookstores two weeks before Trump entered the race, her book *Adios, America: The Left's Plan to Turn Our Country Into a Third World Hellhole* (2015), devotes six of the volume's 17 chapters to immigrants and rape. According to Coulter, a "Latin American rape culture" and "gusto for gang rape, incest and child rape," as opposed to the "unique sexual restraint of men of northern-European stock" accounts for the need to identify Latino males as sexual threats. Most succinct in her 2017 article titled, "To Say, 'Stop Raping Me!' in English, Press '1' Now," Coulter's conflation of the presence of undocumented Latino males and the increased threat of rape rises out of the same impetus to populate Hollywood films with the commodity of the immoral Latin lover. The sexually threatening Latino male has long provided an easy symbol for the assertion of northern and western European supremacy. Whether manifest as a fantasy heartthrob or as a flamboyant pedophile, Hollywood's Latin lovers signify a racially and geographically charged inability to control passions and sexual behaviors.

On the other hand, the hemisexual turn in Cruz' above live performance interventions begin with the premise that a loss of control can be a good thing. As with Montalban's Roberto, Ricardo invites audiences to participate in the Latino e-rhotic in order to liberate unspoken possibilities. The live evocation of the Latin lover disrupts prescribed gender roles by inviting audience members to participate in the playful, yet dangerous, prospect of an illicit Latinx lover and ionize sexual drives through the immediacy of the senses. The live play of the Latin lover performances enunciates a field of Americas-based awakening: neither homo- nor hetero-, the hemisexual gesture ignites an androgynous and erogenous electric spark by externalizing the channels of sexual desires and behaviors conventionally disciplined to obfuscate sexual impulse. Unlike Hollywood's Latin lover that rehashes colonial scripts of Anglo domination, the hemisexual Latin lover invites us to try something different: to transcend the boundaries prescribed by national borders and heteronormative institutions so that the Americas may be home to the emergence of masculinities defined not by patriarchal and colonial orderings, but by the creation of new spaces of radical inclusivity.

Works cited

Anderson, Tre'vell. "Eugenio Derbez Shares 'How to Be a Latin Lover' and Still Break Stereotypes." *The Los Angeles Times*, 27 April 2017.

Allen, Samantha. "What Makes 'Sense8' The Best LGBT TV Show". *The Daily Beast*. 5 May 2017. Accessed online 10 July 2017.

Beinart, Peter. "The Republican Party's White Strategy." *The Atlantic*, July/August 2016. Accessed online 23 July 2017.

Cruz, John. *Latin Lover Provocations." Swing State Latinx After the Trumpocalypse*. Wild Goose Creative, Columbus. 2 December 2016. Performance.

Cruz, John. "Performing the Latin Lover." *Hollywood's Latin Lover: Dominant stereotypes and media representations of US Latinos*. The Ohio State University, Columbus. 10 February 2014. Performance.

Dick, Bernard F. *Engulfed: The Death of Paramount Pictures and the Birth of Corporate Hollywood*. Lexington, KY: University Press of Kentucky, 2001.

Eames, John D. *The Paramount Story*. New York: Crown, 1985.

E. C. "Rodolfo Valentino." *El Gráfico*, no. 797, 1926, pp. 2388–89.

Grow, Kory. "'Big Lebowski,' 'Ferris Bueller's Day Off' Added to National Film Registry." *Rolling Stone*, 2014.

Hurtado, Aída, and Mrinal Sinha. *Beyond Machismo: Intersectional Latino Masculinities*. Austin, TX: University of Texas Press, 2016.

King, Gilbert. "The 'Latin Lover' and His Enemies" *Smithsonian Magazine*. 13 June 2012. Accessed online 28 June 2017.

Ovalle, Priscilla Peña. *Dance and the Hollywood Latina: Race, Sex, and Stardom*. New Brunswick, NJ: Rutgers University Press, 2011.

Pérez, Daniel Enrique. "(Re)Examining the Latin Lover: Screening Chicano/Latino Sexualities" in *Performing the US Latina and Latino Borderland*. Eds. Arturo Aldama et al. Bloomington, IN: Indiana University Press, 2012. (pp. 437–456).

Perrottet, Tony. "Who Was Casanova?" *Smithsonian Magazine*. April 2012. Accessed online 28 June 2017.

Ramírez Berg, Charles. *Latino Images in Film: Stereotypes, Subversion, and Resistance*. Austin, TX: University of Texas Press, 2002.

Sense8. Season 1, Netflix, 5 June 2015.

Filmography

Don Jon. Directed by Joseph Gordon-Levitt, Voltage Pictures, HitRecord Films, Ram Bergman Productions, 2013.

Don Juan DeMarco. Directed by Jeremy Levin, American Zoetrope, 1995.

How to Be a Latin Lover. Directed by Ken Marino, Pantelion and Lionsgate, 2017.

Latin Lovers. Directed by Mervyn LeRoy, Metro-Goldwyn-Mayer, 1953.

Luces de Buenos Aires. Directed by Adelqui Millar, Paramount Studios, 1931.

Melodía de Arrabal. Directed by Louis J. Gasnier, Paramount Studios, 1932.

Tango Bar. Directed by John Reinhardt, Paramount Studios, 1935.

The Big Lebowski. Directed by Joel Coen, Gramercy Pictures, 1998.

The 40-Year-Old Virgin. Directed by Judd Apatow, Universal Pictures, 2005.

The Four Horsemen of the Apocalypse. Directed by Rex Ingram, Metro Pictures, 1921.

18

TRANSNATIONAL QUEERINGS AND *SENSE8*

Laura Fernández

"If you don't mind, maybe you can explain one thing to me […] Who gives a fuck who I fuck?" ("Happy Fucking New Year" 2016). It is a good question and one asked by the *Sense8* character, Lito Rodríguez, while he battles paparazzi surrounding his Mexico City condo as he attempts to enter it, at the same time realizing someone has spray-painted the word "faggot" in huge bold letters on its façade. This scene comes to represent all Lito's worst fears come to light: having the world discover that he is gay and reject him for it. For a character as macho as Lito, having his homosexuality out in the open is cause for much distress. Having to come to terms with his sexuality in public against the hyper-masculine persona he plays in his films, becomes the foundation for his entire character in the show. This chapter examines how, even in a show with groundbreaking LGBTQ+ representations as *Sense8*, popular culture in the U.S. continues to rely on one-dimensional portraits of Mexico and its people, particularly in relation to sexuality.

The premise for *Sense8* revolves around eight individuals scattered across the globe who come to discover that they are all psychically linked to one another as "sensates." As they learn to harness their abilities after their "rebirth" in the first episode, they each begin to "visit" (appear and interact physically and emotionally with the other sensates) the others in their "cluster"—the term given to each group of sensates born together. Of the eight members in his cluster, Lito remains one of the secondary characters. The other sensates call on him only when they need someone to tell a convincing lie, because as an actor, Lito knows how to sell a lie, "You just look them right in the eye and you lie. It's what we do, it's called acting" ("Limbic Resonance" 2015). Much of his storyline deals with his coming to terms with being open to his sexuality and what that could mean for his career. By the end of the second season, Lito has publically embraced his homosexuality, was named São Paulo's Pride Parade's grand master, and has a Hollywood film project in the works in which he will play the lead in the film, *Iberian Dream*, centered on the love story between two men. And there is the crux of the issue—Lito is "free" to be whoever he wants, so long as it is not in a Mexican setting. For most of the first season, Lito is *terrified* that the press will find out that he is gay because for him that would be the end of his career, well, his Mexican career. He is perfectly happy to live with his boyfriend and have a life with him, so long as the Mexican people are left in the dark.

Don't get me wrong here, my point is not to disparage *Sense8*, I personally am a huge fan of the show and was just as devastated to learn that it was cancelled shortly after the premiere of its second season—and just as happy as the rest of the fandom to know that Netflix has greenlighted a two-hour episode to be released in 2018. According to a letter written by one of *Sense8*'s producers, Lana Wachowski, it was due in large part to the massive social media campaign the show's fans created petitioning Netflix to bring the show back, "The passionate letters, the petitions, the collective voice that rose up [...] to fight for this show was beyond what anyone was expecting. [...] Improbably, unforeseeably, your love has brought *Sense8* back to life" (@sense8). Part of the appeal of the show is its inclusion of LGBT+ representation—the show features a trans character played by trans actor, Jamie Clayton, and was created, written, directed, and produced by the trans Wachowski Sisters (most popularly known for their work in the *Matrix* series, though they were known as the Wachowski Brothers then). However, that spirit of inclusion only goes so far, seeing as Lito's character is played by the straight, Spanish actor, Miguel Ángel Silvestre, and Lito's boyfriend, Hernando, is played by the straight, Mexican actor, Alfonso Herrera. Here too we see a cultural clash in both the casting and the background of Lito's character. In the show, Lito is a half-Spanish, half-Mexican film star who portrays himself as a Mexican macho in his films.

Watching the series' Mexican plotline, I find myself asking: what counts as macho? Can one be queer and macho in a Mexican context? How does Lito's transnationality influence his characterization? Drawing on Judith Butler's theories on gender performativity and the previous literature on homosexuality in Mexico, the point of this investigation will be then, to highlight how *Sense8*, while groundbreaking in some regards, is unable to break the stereotyped mold of what counts as "Mexican" and the role of masculinity in a Latin American cultural context. While Lito's character is more of a complex representation of Mexican gender ideologies, the show's representation of Mexican culture in general leaves much to be desired; while gender and sexual identities are challenged in the show, culturally specific stereotypes fail to be questioned giving the show's American audience exactly what it expects in terms of what defines "Latinidad." I begin by outlining the complicated history of homosexuality in Mexico to better demonstrate how Lito both challenges and maintains those stereotypes.

It's not gay if you're a real macho: Passivity and Mexican queerness

In her work, *Gender Trouble,* Judith Butler illustrates why defining gender and sexuality is always such a complicated subject, and argues that such definitions must be contextualized given that gender is, "a shifting and contextual phenomenon, gender does not denote a substantive being, but a relative point of convergence among culturally and historically specific sets of relations" (1990: 10). In this way, gender is regarded as performative because it is not a norm, merely a set of culturally defined and regulated attributes, "the substantive effect of gender is performatively produced and compelled by the regulatory practices of gender coherence [...] gender proves to be performative—that is, constituting the identity it is purported to be. In this sense, gender is always a doing" (Butler 1990: 24–5). In the case of *Sense8*, what the Wachowski sisters are attempting to depict is their interpretation of homosexuality in a Mexican content. They label Lito a homosexual character despite his more feminine/queer behaviors, though as I will show, in the context of Mexican heteronormativity to be a "straight man," one cannot demonstrate any feminine qualities. While Butler argues that it is possible to "speak of a 'man' with a feminine attribute, whatever that is, but still to maintain the integrity of the gender," (24) in the conceptualization of Mexican masculinity and what defines a man as "homosexual" or not, performing a feminized version of male masculinity renders that performance void, and is built on a long history of stigmatization of homosexuality in Latin America.

As Martin Nesvig points out in his article, "The Complicated Terrain of Latin American Homosexuality," the stigma against homosexuality has a long-standing history in Latin America going back to the Spanish and Mexican Inquisitions where, "Mexico's Inquisition prosecuted a sodomite as early as 1542" (2001: 696) where the punishment for the "sin of sodomy" was death (697), though after the 18th century, "sodomy was generally no longer an executable offense" (710). From there, the next major moment in Mexican queer history occurred in 1901 where a private party was raided by the Mexican police and 41 men were arrested, half of whom were allegedly dressed as women. As Robert McKee Irwin writes, the incident became infamous, stating, "the party gained immense symbolic importance in Mexico as the number 41 itself came to signify male homosexuality. Perhaps more importantly, the event initiated the first significant discussion of same-sex sexual relations in Mexico since colonial times and raised questions about sexuality, masculinity, and Mexicanness itself that are still debated nearly a century later" (2000: 353).

The questions surrounding homosexuality in Mexico revolve around issues of masculinity, effeminacy, passivity, and dominance. What the scandal of the "Famous 41" demonstrates is how Mexican culture equates homosexuality with effeminacy, as coverage of the incident focused on perpetuating the stereotype of homosexuals as effeminate men: "Instead of unbiased descriptions of behaviors, desires, attitudes, or attributes that historians might hope to find, the only clear conception to emerge was a stereotype: 'From then until recent times in popular culture a gay has been a transvestite, and there has been only one kind of homosexual: the effeminate'" (Irwin 2000: 354). That effeminacy is marked by passivity, the "effeminate" male, the true homosexual, is the passive receiver of penetration, "homosexuality in Mexico is defined not by the biological sex of the participants but by the gendered roles that they perform in the sexual act. In this model only the *pasivo* [passive] participant is marked as homosexual" (Cantú 2002: 141). On the opposite side of the coin, the active man can evade the label of homosexual because the act of penetrating another is seen as a sign of masculinity and therefore not linked to the effeminacy of homosexuality, "In this macho world, where active men are macho men and only faggots and women are passive and penetrable and therefore weak, penetration takes on a cultural meaning beyond the sexual one [...] the act of penetrating another, regardless of the sex of that person, becomes and expression of masculine dominance and superiority, and it in no way impugns the macho status of a man" (Tate 2011: 104). While clearly such a definition does not apply to every homosexual in Mexico, that is the stereotype that has been perpetuated and that can apply across many Latin American borders: "Latin American sexuality is defined by a man's position as 'active' or 'passive' [...] There is agreement among these researchers that this view of sexuality is pervasive throughout Latin America [...] this definition of homosexuality by sexual position crosses all Latin borders" (104).

This notion of, "to be feminine is to be gay" (Tate 2011: 105), stems from Latin American conceptions of gender, specifically masculinity, as defined by a heterosexist, machista ideology, "the word [macho] connotes men who expect the superior place in a vigorously defended gender hierarchy and the societies informed by such a hierarchy" (Macías-González and Rubenstein 2012: 13). In his often-quoted work, "The Sons of La Malinche," Octavio Paz writes, "The *macho* represents the masculine pole of life. [...] The macho is the *gran chingón*. One word sums up the aggressiveness, insensitivity, invulnerability and other attributes of the *macho*: power. It is force without the discipline of any notion of order: arbitrary power, the will without reins and without a set course" (2002: 23). According to Paz. to "chingar" implies some act of violence, "an emergence from oneself to penetrate another by force" (21). Here again is the notion of masculinity inherently tied to action and penetration, "To the Mexican there are only two possibilities in life: either he inflicts the actions implied by *chingar* on others, or else he suffers them himself at the hands of others. This conception of social life as combat fatally divides society into the strong and the weak" (22).

In contrast to this idea of masculinity is Paz's concept of "La Chingada" as a representation of Mexican femininity and maternity, alongside the image of La Virgen de Guadalupe, both of whom represent passivity: "In contrast to Guadalupe, who is the Virgin Mother, the *Chingada* is the violated Mother. Both of them are passive figures. [...] The *Chingagda* is even more passive. Her passivity is abject [...] She loses her name, she *is* no one; she disappears into nothingness, she is Nothingness. And yet she is the cruel incarnation of feminine condition" (2002: 25). While Paz may not be explicitly equating masculinity and macho-ness with heterosexuality, the foundation is there—to be a man implies penetrating another, whereas whoever is the passively penetrated person, is feminine. This also implies that for the "active" homosexual, there is less stigma because they are not fully perceived as homosexuals: "masculine males who play the active insertor role in homosexual encounters do not appear to be generally conceptualized as *homosexuals* in Mexico. This lack of stigmatization provides prospective active participants with the important feeling that their masculine self-image is in no way threatened [...] a great deal of tolerance is extended to those masculine males" (Carrier 1976: 116). Though there is tolerance, and gay marriage is legal in Mexico City and in several states across the country (Masci 2017), a reoccurring theme in the literature on Mexican homosexuality is the need to restrict homosexuality to the private sphere: "They do not make bold statements or assert the power to be unapologetically and openly *gay* because they feel they have too much to lose. [...] If they were to break the culturally-accepted patterns of silence, they could severely jeopardize the relationships with their families [...] be fired from their jobs; and experience considerable discrimination" (Carrillo 1999: 235). This brings the conversation back to *Sense8*; in the following section I will analyze how Lito fits into the characterization of Mexican masculinity and how he is further exoticized due to his Spanish heritage, leaving him to play both the Mexican macho, and the Spanish Latin lover.

Lito Rodríguez: Professional liar by day, private queen by night

Lito's character straddles two tried and true stereotypes of Latin American men: he is at once the hyper-masculine macho (at least in his films) and he is also the hyper-sexualized Latin lover. His queerness adds a complicating dimension to that dichotomy, but even when he is outed in the beginning of the second season, it only serves to add the flamboyant and dramatic gay man stereotype to his character.

As all the sensates are being introduced, the first shot of Lito is him entering a church, drawing a gun, his face is cut up and bloodied, standing in front of the altar. The audience later finds him still in the church, this time telling the priest that he is there to "blow your fucking brains out" ("Limbic Resonance" 2015). It is then that the director yells cut and the audience is made aware that it was all an act and that Lito is not some murderous vigilante, but an actor. The scene later cuts to Lito in his trailer going over his lines, trying to get into his character of "Tino, el Caído," giving himself the reassuring pep talk that he is a man, all the while dealing with an impromptu erection (likely caused by the sexual activities of another member of his cluster). As he walks around his trailer going over his script and occasionally masturbating himself, his female costar walks in asking why he was so out of character during the shoot. She notices his problem and offers to help him find some relief when Lito shuts her down because, "There's nothing I'd like more, if only my heart did not belong to another" to which his costar replies, "She's a very lucky woman" before she leaves ("Limbic Resonance" 2015). At that point in time, the audience is not aware of the irony of that statement, given that Lito's hidden sexuality is not revealed until the middle of the second episode.

Is it in the second episode where Hernando, Lito's live-in boyfriend, is introduced after Lito attends a movie premiere with Daniela Velazquez on his arm. The viewer also learns that Lito is half-Spanish, as Daniela tells the reporter what an amazing dancer Lito is, to which the reporter responds, "Oh, it must be your Spanish blood right?" ("I Am Also a We" 2015)—it turns out that Lito's father was a flamenco instructor from Bilbao. After the premiere, Lito is once again propositioned, this time by Daniela, though again he responds in the negative and the next time the show focuses on his story, Lito is getting into bed waking up his sleeping boyfriend with a kiss. Daniela later ends up drunk at Lito's condo, pressuring him to let her in or else the paparazzi will find her there in the morning. Lito continues to make excuses to which a (sexually) frustrated Daniela exclaims, "It's just a little harmless sex, what is the problem Lito?" prompting a half-naked Hernando to respond, "The problem is honey, that you don't have a cock" ("I Am Also a We" 2015). It is then that Daniela realizes the truth (that she was being used by Lito as a cover) and agrees to be his live-in beard because, "this is going to be so good for you. I mean, you obviously need someone you can trust, right? Someone who can deflect the rumors? And if you know anything about me or my family, it's that I had to become an expert at doing such things" ("I Am Also a We" 2015). As the viewer learns later in the series, Daniela's family is involved in questionable importing/exporting enterprises, led by her abusive ex-boyfriend, Joaquín Flores, Lito's quasi-nemesis who outs Lito and Hernando's relationship in the second season.

While Lito may play the role of the macho action star in his films, he is depicted more as the Latin lover. He is constantly fending off advances of female costars and reporters, and in one scene a reporter asks him, "You've been involved in some of the steamiest scenes we've ever seen on television, what is the secret to be a great lover?" ("Demons" 2015). Lito's response leaves the reporter visibly flustered, proving that he can be quite the charmer. The Latin lover stereotype has been around since the early 20th century, and since its inception, the identity of the Latin lover has been constructed around, "the synthesis of eroticism, exoticism, and danger; he is attractive and irresistible [...] possesses three basic attributes: good looks, masculine features/behaviors, and ethnic markings (whatever may be construed as 'Latin'—dark hair, olive skin, a foreign accent)" (Pérez 2012: 439). In *Sense8*, Lito is doubly exoticized, first among American audiences as a Latin American heartthrob and sex figure (even though he is really from Spain), and secondly within the world of the show as a half-Spanish actor working in the Mexican film industry.

Lito fits the bill of the Latin lover well, given his response on how to appropriately display passion/desire onscreen, "you have to be selfless, the pleasure of your lover must become your own. But at the same time, you must also remain… selfish because wanting someone so much that it feels the same as the need to eat, or to breathe. This is where desire becomes love, I guess" ("Demons" 2015). As Lito is giving his answer, the scene cuts between Lito's interview and an intimate moment between Lito and Hernando where Lito engages in oral sex with Hernando in a public bathroom. From this sexually charged moment to the next time Lito appears in the episode, the eroticism follows him, because it is his flirtatious exercising and dancing with Hernando that helps prompt a cluster-wide orgy. As Lito and Hernando have sex, Daniela is seen watching and taking pictures of the pair, all the while masturbating because as she said earlier in the season, "It's so fucking hot, I can't even stand it" ("I Am Also a We" 2015) when picturing the two together. Miguel Ángel Silvestre, the actor who plays Lito, becomes *Sense8*'s perfect Latin lover since he ticks off almost all of the criteria: "good-looking, hypersexual, 'Latin,' masculine, dominant, self-centered, irresistible, dangerous, womanizing, and disrespectful of or violent with women" (Pérez 2012: 442). Though Lito is never violent with Daniela, he is willing to allow her to go back to the abusive Joaquín to protect his secret homosexuality, proving that though he is sympathetic to her abuse, he is still willing to put his career above her personal safety.

Though the Latin lover stereotype is steeped in queerness given that, "the display of the male body as erotic 'feminizes' the subject. [...] Men as sex objects are queer in the way they assume a passive role in exchange between viewer and subject [...] The Latin lover is by default non-heteronormative. His foreignness, promiscuity, and body are all sites for mapping queer identities," (Pérez 2012: 440–1) as I previously mentioned, homosexuality in the general Mexican context is equated with femininity. The penetrated man is the homosexual, with the active penetrator being able to avoid the label. In the show, Lito only announces publically that he is "a gay man" ("Isolated Above, Connected Below") once the truth has been revealed about his sexuality and he is acting as the Grand Marshall of the São Paulo Pride Parade—a position he only accepted after having rejected all the job offers his agent lined up because they involved him playing a sensitive or overtly effeminate secondary gay character who gets killed off. When the press initially questions Lito about the photos leaked of him and Hernando having sex, he is repeatedly asked if he is a homosexual/gay and to explain why he had been lying, he evades ever giving a direct response, stating that, "Labels are the opposite of understanding" ("Who Am I?" 2015). Given that he is never shown to be a *pasivo*, he could avoid the label altogether. According to the literature, because he is never shown to be penetrated by Hernando, he could maintain that he is not actually a homosexual.

Despite playing the active role in his relationship with Hernando, there are moments where Lito performs a much more feminine masculinity than what one would assume. Of all the sensates, Lito is depicted as the most "dramatic." After he is dropped by his agent because of the negative consequences of his outing, he is seen visiting in the background of the lives of other members of his cluster, often drunk, wearing a bathrobe, and eating ice cream, claiming to be mourning the death of his career. In the episode, "Art Is Like Religion," (2015) he is shown to be experiencing the menstrual symptoms of one other sensates, which he automatically associates with dying as he laments on the phone to Hernando, "I'm a fucking mess Hernando. I have a horrible pain in my stomach. I'm paralyzed. It feels like a tumor. You know cancer runs in my family Hernando, what if it's cancer? [...] Hernando please save me." A hilarious moment to be sure, but also not one to occur to any of the other male sensates in his cluster. Given his character's sexuality and the association between homosexuality and effeminacy, Lito can experience such feminine issues such as menstrual cramps and wild mood swings. Overall, his character becomes a source for comedic relief in the show, with his flair for dramatics at odds with the relative seriousness of the show.

While Lito may straddle the line between opposing stereotypes of the macho action star and the queer Latin lover, and thereby complicating the depiction of either one; the show does little else to challenge Mexican stereotypes. For instance, Daniela's jilted ex-boyfriend, Joaquín, only works to reify negative stereotypes held in the U.S. about Mexico and Mexican men. If any of the characters in the show can be described as machista, it is Joaquín. He epitomizes Octavio Paz's definition of the Mexican macho as the "gran chingón" (2002: 21) that uses his arbitrary power to violate and abuse others, in this case, Daniela. His defense for his abuse of Daniela is that, that is the way he was taught, "This is Mexico, I am a man. I was raised that way: you hit your woman to make her respect you" ("W. W. N. Double D?" 2015). Implicit to the characterization of Mexican culture is the idea of violence and despair. After Lito's photos are leaked online he is evicted from his condo and all his things are stolen. When Lito argues against the injustice, Daniela responds, "This is Mexico, sad truth is I've seen worse" ("Happy Fucking New Year" 2016).

The last major development in Lito's story involves him signing a Hollywood movie deal where he will star in a romance about two men, an offer that, as I mentioned before, he would never receive in Mexico. Kit Wrangler, the producer of the film (played by Andy Dick), is initially hesitant to work with Lito because, "I watch your films and I see the same male apery that has spread like a cancer through this industry, and I'm sure this meeting is a waste of my time"

("If All the World's a Stage" 2017). It was only Lito's speech at the Pride Parade that got him the meeting, and later after they sign the contract, Kit invites Lito to a party at his mansion, where all around are gay men in hot pants and little else. Lito sees Kit's Oscar prominently displayed and asks about it, to which Kit responds, "Hell yes I did. The minute I got home, dipped him head to toe in lube and took every golden inch up my ass" ("If All the World's a Stage" 2017). Lito is then changed out of his clothes in front of everyone to make him look more like character he is expected to play in the film, all the while Lito is looking around in almost stunned silence—quite a different reception than what he got back home. Even Lito's reception in Brazil was better than what he received in Mexico; in Mexico, he must deal with gay slurs being thrown at him, from Joaquín constantly referring to him as a "faggot" to having that word spray painted across his condo. In Brazil, he is welcomed by a group of fans, male and female, who see him as a champion of gay rights, even though before that he avoided fully identifying himself as gay. In the U.S., he is surrounded by gay men who flatter him and treat him to extravagant parties, playing to the notion of the U.S. as a "phallic dream" for repressed Mexican homosexuals, "in which queer Mexican men envision the United States as a sexual utopia, an erotic land of milk and honey" (Cantú 2002: 155–6).

What the show erases in Lito's cross-over moment, is the process of racialization that Latin Americans experience upon entering the U.S., which Suárez-Orozco and Páez propose as one of the key arguments for a panethnic Latino construct, "Latinos, we claim, are the offspring of these three broad sociohistorical processes: large-scale immigration, U.S.-Latin American relations, and racialization" (2002: 29). By crossing the border, Latin Americans become "othered," they do not fit into the U.S. black-white dichotomy, and the U.S. has a history of intolerance for those who transgress the racial norms. While for Lito the U.S. may represent a gay sanctuary, for many, "the United States represents anything but a space for tolerance, in large part because it is a space that racially marks him as other and without room for negotiation" (Cantú 2002: 156). Given the negative stereotypes held in the U.S. by political elites, the current desire to "build a wall" to keep out all the drug dealers and rapists comes to mind, "Latin Americans are depicted as racially and culturally inferior, ignorant, degraded, filthy, childlike, and essentially unable to govern themselves" (Suárez-Orozco and Páez 2002: 22). Lito and Hernando experience none of that, they are welcomed by Kit and his film crew and introduced to the sexually permissive utopia that is the United States, with Kit playing the role of the liberal elite who will guide Lito to the gay man's Promised Land. Mexico comes to stand as the land of sexual oppression, where Lito is hounded by paparazzi and faces discrimination in the workforce for his sexuality. While Lito's character may push the boundaries of who the stereotypical Mexican man is, Mexico itself is not given the same latitude.

Sense8 tells a complex, interwoven narrative about eight completely different people spread out across the globe. It has been lauded by fans and reviewers alike for its racial diversity and for its normalized representations of queer lives, especially those of trans individuals. I, for one, love the show and cannot wait for the follow-up series finale special, but even so, I argue that the Wachowski sisters could have pushed the boundaries more on its representations of Latinidad given that the show's major "Latin American" character is played not by a Latin American actor, but by a Spanish telenovela actor. He and his partner on the show also fail to push any casting boundaries, given that two white, heterosexual actors were chosen to play the lead gay characters. It is in the universe of the show that social boundaries become more nuanced. Lito, the closeted gay sensate in his cluster, straddles the line between Latin lover, Mexican macho, and drama queen. To his fans, Lito stands as a sex icon; in his films, he is the violent, sexual machista who can go from killing to having sex with a curvaceous woman in just a few seconds. In his cluster, he is the one called upon to create a scene or to tell a convincing lie or to generally pester (especially in the latter half of the second season) the other sensates with the drama caused by his sexuality.

Lito's sexuality on the show is depicted to be, more or less, in line with the general conception of homosexuality in Mexican culture. Lito is never shown to be the receiver of penetrative anal sex, and only publically admits to being gay after his career prospects in Mexico are ruined. Lito is able to maintain a macho identity in his films because he never openly discusses his sexuality, and since he is the "active" partner, his masculinity is not questioned. Despite that, given that the show is written and directed by Anglo-Americans, his characterization is masculine, but exoticized. To American audiences, he is the perfect sex icon: he is the tall, dark, and handsome Latin lover who represents, "The man every guy wants to be and every girl wants to fuck" ("W. W. N. Double D?" 2015), even if his actual Latinness is questionable (or simply nonexistent). While Lito's persona is a complex negotiation of various stereotypes, the Wachowski sisters do not hesitate to depict Mexico from an extremely negative viewpoint. *Sense8*'s Mexico is a homosexual's worst nightmare: a few gay Mexican extras approach Lito and thank him for what he has done, but they do so quietly and quickly retreat back into the background for fear of receiving similar treatment. Lito is obviously shocked at the open reception he receives in the U.S.—from the parties and the beautiful gay men that are everywhere, the U.S. is a gay paradise, something that is echoed by the trans character, Nomi Marks, who sympathizes with Lito's situation especially since she lives San Francisco and can take advantage of all its liberal glory.

What is erased in this gay utopia are the very real dangers that LGBTQ+ individuals face in the U.S. as well—the 2016 Pulse Nightclub shooting and the campaign against gender neutral bathrooms being only a few of the examples. It will be interesting to see how the series finale deals with Lito's story—will he return to Mexico to find a better situation or will he permanently remain in the U.S. where acceptance is so much easier to come by? My hope is for the former option to present a different Mexico, one that more aptly reflects the general tolerance found in the country for homosexuality, though given the limited timeframe allotted to tie up all loose ends, I predict Lito's storyline will end with him living happily ever after in the U.S. with Hernando and Daniela, ignoring the Mexican plotline altogether.

Works cited

"Art Is Like Religion." *Sense8*, Season 1, Episode 5. Released 6 June 2015, Netflix, www.netflix.com/watch/80025749?trackId=13752289&tctx=0%2C4%2C08b1fe57-6520-486b-a957-6b018c0a9e56-89291001.

Butler, Judith. *Gender Trouble: Feminism and the Subversion of Identity*. Routledge, 1990.

Cantú, Lionel. "De Ambiente: Queer Tourism and the Shifting Boundaries of Mexican Male Sexualities." *GLQ. A Journal of Lesbian and Gay Studies* 8.1–2 (2002): 139–166.

Carrier, Joseph M. "Cultural Factors Affecting Urban Mexican Male Homosexual Behavior." *Archives of Sexual Behavior* 5.2 (1976): 103–124.

Carrillo, Héctor. "Cultural Change, Hybridity and Male Homosexuality in Mexico." *Culture, Health & Sexuality* 1.3 (1999): 223–238.

"Demons." *Sense8*, Season 1, Episode 6. Released 6 June 2015, Netflix, www.netflix.com/watch/80025750?trackId=13752289&tctx=0%2C5%2C652947bc-a4a4-4154-ab22-288eb5f2fa7e-163243167.

"Happy Fucking New Year." *Sense8*, Season 2, Episode 1. Released 23 December 2016, Netflix, www.netflix.com/watch/80112878?trackId=14170068&tctx=0%2C0%2C4d387f6b-7bc1-4e0a-b704-e756d045ee28-533348903.

"I Am Also a We." *Sense8*, Season 1, Episode 2. Released 6 June 2015, Netflix, www.netflix.com/watch/80025746?trackId=13752289&tctx=0%2C1%2C652947bc-a4a4-4154-ab22-288eb5f2fa7e-163243167.

"If All the World's a Stage, Then Identity Is Nothing but a Costume." *Sense8*, Season 2, Episode 10. Released 5 May 2017, Netflix, www.netflix.com/watch/80057491?trackId=13752289&tctx=0%2C9%2C652947bc-a4a4-4154-ab22-288eb5f2fa7e-163243167.

Irwin, Robert McKee. "The Famous 41: The Scandalous Birth of Modern Mexican Homosexuality." *GLQ: A Journal of Lesbian and Gay Studies* 6.3 (2000) 353–376.

"Isolated Above, Connected Below." *Sense8*, Season 2, Episode 6. Released 5 May 2017, Netflix, www.netflix.com/watch/80057487?trackId=13752289&tctx=0%2C5%2C652947bc-a4a4-4154-ab22-288eb5f2fa7e-163243167.

"Limbic Resonance." *Sense8*, Season 1, Episode 1. Released 5 June 2015, Netflix, www.netflix.com/watch/80025745?trackId=13752289&tctx=0%2C0%2C652947bc-a4a4-4154-ab22-288eb5f2fa7e-163243167.

Macías-González, Víctor M. and Anne Rubenstein. "Introduction: Masculinity and History in Modern Mexico." *Masculinity and Sexuality in Modern Mexico.* Eds. Macías-González and Rubenstein. University of New Mexico Press, 2012. 12–25.

Masci, David. "Gay Marriage Around the World." Pew Research Center, Washington, D.C. 30 June 2017. www.pewforum.org/2017/06/30/gay-marriage-around-the-world-2013/#.

Nesvig, Martin. "The Complicated Terrain of Latin American Homosexuality." *Hispanic American Historical Review* 81.3–4 (2001): 689–729.

Paz, Octavio. "The Sons of La Malinche." *The Mexico Reader.* Eds. Gilbert Joseph and Timothy Henderson. Duke University Press, 2002. 20–27.

Pérez, Daniel Enrique. "(Re)Examining the Latin Lover: Screening Chicano/Latino Sexualities." *Performing the US Latina and Latino Borderlands.* Eds. Arturo J. Aldama, Chela Sandoval, and Peter Garcia. Indiana University Press, 2012. 437–456.

@sense8. "Death doesn't let you say goodbye. 2 hour finale episode in the works. Tell your cluster." *Twitter*, 29 June 2017, 11:39 a.m., https://twitter.com/sense8/status/880495946370568194.

Suárez-Orozco, Marcelo M. and Mariela M. Páez. "Introduction: The Research Agenda." *Latinos Remaking America.* Eds. Marcelo M. Suárez-Orozco and Mariela M. Páez. University of California Press, 2002. 1–37.

Tate, Julee. "From Girly Men to Manly Men: The Evolving Representation of Male Homosexuality in Twenty-First Century Telenovelas." *Studies in Latin American Popular Culture* 29 (2011): 102–114.

"Who Am I?" *Sense8*, Season 2, Episode 2. Released, 5 May 2017, Netflix, www.netflix.com/watch/80057483?trackId=13752289&tctx=0%2C1%2C652947bc-a4a4-4154-ab22-288eb5f2fa7e-163243167.

"W.W.N. Double D?" *Sense8*, Season 1, Episode 6. Released 5 June 2015, Netflix, www.netflix.com/watch/80025751?trackId=13752289&tctx=0%2C6%2C652947bc-a4a4-4154-ab22-288eb5f2fa7e-163243167.

19

GOOD GRINGOS, BAD HOMBRES

The postlapsarian films of Mel Gibson

Ryan Rashotte

It was springtime in Mexico City, and the boulevards were sweet on Jesus. Under the pink bloom of the jacaranda trees, amidst the Sunday throngs at Plaza Hidalgo; along the newsstands and across the racks of bootleg DVDs dividing the stalls of the *tianguis*, the image of Jesus—Jesus by way of James Caviezel—had flourished in the warming landscape. His shadows thriving under the imperious sun. His sorrows circling like the farewell notes of "Cielito Lindo" over the bust of a morose organ grinder.

I resented all this very deeply.

In the country I'd just departed, controversy over *The Passion of the Christ* had fallen to a weak cry; two borders south, stoked by fresh scandal,[1] it was once again a national uproar. And after a third day of Jesus Caviezel photo-bombing my selfies, and a third evening of chiaroscuro film posters flickering my subway ride into stations of the cross, the mimesis of sanctimony finally inspired me to lower my head and make a solemn and undifficult promise: from now on, I would avoid the cinema of Mel Gibson. *Amen.*

That promise remained undifficult for the next thirteen years, despite the Internet's habit of enabling my televisual nostalgia for the early 1990s, a period of happy times for me and for Gibson, when I was a suburbanite playing with toys a little late into preadolescence, and he was one of my favorite action figures. Murdoch, the good-looking rascal from the *Lethal Weapons*. Rick Jarmin, *Bird on a Wire*'s prince of bad behavior. Gene Ryack, Dale 'Mac' McKussic. Cocky, chummy, vulnerable men. Men whom saxophone licks trail from bedrooms to shootouts. Men who can cry on cue. Men who can kick very hard. Men who know their way around a pontoon boat. Molten layers of romance accrete beneath their modest chest hair. The collective noun for a group of women under their spell would be "a nudity."

It was through like etcetera that I and my more sensitive male classmates perceived Gibson in those years, whenever we were called on to challenge the Van Dammean and Schwarzeneggerian equivalents the duller boys plodded out at recess. I distinctly recall two occasions in grade seven in which friends asked me in confidence if their newly dropped voices sounded like Mel Gibson's ("'cause that's how it sounds in my head," one explained).

Of course, at that time, more mature fans had their own Gibsons. They had Gibson, the perpetual up-and-comer: a middlebrow actor always seemingly on the verge of real dramaturgical credibility. Longtime fan Pauline Kael described him as "passionate, shrewd, relentless."[2] In *The New York Times*, Caryn James called his *Hamlet* "strong, intelligent … visceral," and his film

Braveheart, which won five Oscars, including Best Picture and Best Director, "one of the most spectacular entertainments in years."[3]

Then there were other critics, just as discerning, who happened to have been acquainted with less discerning Gibsons. Audience members unamused by *Bird on a Wire*'s prancing homophobia, for instance, were probably keener to spot the red flags that surmounted each junket: Gibson's disparaging comments about homosexuals (pointing at his behind: "This is only for taking a shit"),[4] feminists ("[they] don't like me and I don't like them"), and evolution ("I think it's bullshit … how come apes aren't people yet?").[5] Not to mention the signs of anti-Semitism, which held the spotlight long after *The Passion*'s premiere. By the time of the Fall itself, lasting from 2006, year of the Sugar Tits Affair, to 2010, when a gossip website leaked audio recordings of Gibson verbally abusing his girlfriend,[6] most of us had accumulated enough moral and aesthetic evidence to sink Gibson from tragedy to farce. Hollywood imposed a five-year exile, during which the mirrored question resurfacing in those pristine blues eyes must have been, *how can I ever come back from this*? Through his scrappy charm, was redemption still possible, or had he finally gone too far?

A more appropriate question for the rest of us might be: who gives a bloody Caviezel? Certainly I didn't, at least until recently. By high school, I'd already moved onto cooler, more mysterious masculine icons: Johnny Depp, Jim Morrison, the Swayze-Reeves duo of *Point Break* (that yin yang of white halves). And last year, while Gibson was enjoying the first steps of Hollywood reinstatement (his 2016 film *Hacksaw Ridge* having received multiple Oscar nominations), Maverick Mel struck me as duller than ever. There's nothing more Hollywood trite than the bad boy's comeback, especially when it takes the form of a gloatingly big-budget analogy such as a planned sequel to *The Passion* (that's right, *Resurrection*).[7] (An earlier prequel was derailed—and this is way too good for an endnote—when the associates of the Sinaloa Cartel who purchased rights to its script fell afoul of the law[8].)

That Gibson's comeback is coterminous with Donald Trump's election, however, is something worth considering, and not simply because one early effect of Trump's victory seems to have been a massive reduction on the amount of public shame white men of the right are to endure for racist and sexist behavior. (At the time of press it remains to be seen what impact #MeToo will have on this particular demographic, whose offences often seem to encourage support along "anti-PC" lines.)

Though overly remarked, it's crucial to remind ourselves on a regular basis just how depravedly a contemporary presidential candidate brought racism—specifically anti-Latina/o rhetoric—into his platform of national revitalization. Trump may have established his political career questioning Obama's birth certificate, but the momentum of his vanity project of a presidential run can be traced to June 16, 2015, when his comment about Mexicans being drug-traffickers and rapists[9] achieved meme-status, activating the all-news-is-good-news, pattern-recognition strategy through which the rest of his campaign staggered to victory. Moreover, it established Trump's heroic image, in relief of a sweeping Mexican chaos, as the white strongman poised to keep the brown invasion at bay.

One major irony here is that, in his megalomania and misogyny, in his kitschy opulence and vulgarian sustain, Trump shares much in common with the drug traffickers he illogically equates with migrant workers. In studying these traffickers, a number of scholars, including yours truly, have attempted to catalogue the various narco personalities that proliferate in borderlands culture. Not archetypes, necessarily, but what Mark Cameron Edberg calls the "cultural personae … born in the nexus of class, power, national identify, and regional identity … who [represent] a whole aggregation of values and meanings" within the narcosphere.[10] The macho Robin Hood, whose crimes enrich his community,[11] for example, or the glamorous *patrona* with fangs of gold.

Through *corridos* and b-films, figures like these have held sway in the cross-border imagination for decades. But in the wake of Trump's rise, it's a different sort of narco persona that deserves scrutiny: the Gringo Savior, the white victim or hero who, in standing up to the brutality of narco Mexico and the "bad hombres" who rule it, secures his own masculine agency in the greater borderlands of North America.

This narco persona might be the most dangerous of all. Its dramatic resurgence in Trump signals that the eschatological narrative of the white man's demise is once again in jeopardy of being taken too seriously, the consequences of which for Latina/os and other minorities are now being felt with alarming force. And while no current celebrity has benefited more from its performance than Trump, he's not the only one to have successfully recuperated waning masculine energies by demonizing Latina/os, and specifically Latino men, in this manner.

This chapter will consider how Mel Gibson's recent "b-films"—*Get the Gringo, Blood Father* and *Machete Kills*—present Latino masculinity as a violent, socially destabilizing force to be contained by the Gringo Savior, who, in the process of containment, is able to redeem his own masculine agency (on- and off-screen), and safeguard the cultural authority of white masculinity at large in North America. I will also try to suggest how the films' redemptive narratives, and the ironic, kitschy, lowbrow pop-cultural aesthetics that convey them, creepily foreshadow Donald Trump's 2016 election.

The gringo rises

In the aftermath of his fall from grace, Mel Gibson's early cinematic attempts at reparation proved largely unsuccessful. 2010's *Edge of Darkness* failed to win fans with its *Taken* "homage," while *The Beaver* (2011), a depressing, somewhat schizophrenic drama about a depressive, severely schizophrenic father, faired even worse. Not until the 2012 release of *Get the Gringo: How I Spent My Summer Vacation* did Gibson's career show the first signs of successful rehabilitation, for despite having failed to receive a theatrical release in US, the film, co-written and -financed by Gibson himself, earned enough critical praise to hit 81% on Rotten Tomatoes, making it the highest-scored Gibson film since *Lethal Weapon II*.[12]

The film opens on a sunny day in the SoCal desert. A black Grand Marquis squealing down Route 151 toward the Mexican border, a convoy of police cruisers in its fast pursuit. When the driver, a much-aliased career criminal commonly known as "the Gringo" (Gibson), finally reaches the border fence, and spots a propitious mound of dirt in front of it, he hits the gas, attempting to propel his car over the border … [cue slow-motion] only to come crashing through its corrugated iron curtains to an inverted halt. Groggy, fuddled and now on the Mexican side of the law, the Gringo is apprehended by a pair of bumbling *federales*, who steal his suitcase of loot, and deposit him in prison under a made-up charge. This is where the adventure begins.

At first, El Pueblito seems a curious hell to our Gringo. Based on Tijuana's notorious namesake prison, it is less a jail than a carceral village of 6000, where small businesses (from video stores to drug dens) openly thrive, and where spouses and children live side by side with the male convicts. Corruption, squalor and violence finally forced the Mexican Army to shut down the real prison in 2002,[13] and it's around these characteristics that the film's "Locked Up Abroad" formula coalesces. Moments after being installed in a filthy holding cell, the Gringo is encircled by gangbangers, who stomp at him furiously while a brisk accordion-led *norteño* soundtrack completes the abuse: "torture by mariachi."

Once in the prison's general population, the Gringo is befriended by a ten-year-old boy ("The Kid," played by Kevin Hernandez) who abets his acculturation, and over time, as their bond strengthens, reveals the origins of his golden-child status within El Pueblito's criminal milieu. Owing to his rare blood type, the Kid is being kept as livestock by Javi (Daniel Giménez Cacho), the prison's narco *patron*, whose excessive drinking requires a reserve of fresh human livers. Though the Kid is determined to kill Javi and avenge his father (an earlier victim), when the time comes, it's the Gringo who'll be forced to step up, and out-scheme, out-punch and out-grenade the bad guys to save the Kid and "the Mother" (Dolores Heredia) from their tragic fate.

This rogue-makes-good character arc is vintage Gibson,[14] as is the prevailing moral confirmation of family as the fundamental social unit. What's new here are the winking nudges to Gibson's off-screen persona: gags about his proclivity for booze and cigarettes; the film's subtitle, "How I Spent My Summer Vacation," with its mischievous allusion to his Hollywood exile; and the stream of seedy, Peckinpah-grade[15] violence that steadily reminds us not only can the penitent Gibson take his licks ("A guy's gotta suffer," he told a preview audience, "There's gotta be obstacles to overcome, testicles to remove"),[16] he can do it with the maverick charm that won us over in better days. At times, this metadrama can seem a little too didactic. In one scene, an African-American woman curses out the Gringo for deceiving her, and then, a beat later, responds to his rectification by cackling, "That's good! You alright, man, you alright!" Is her sudden change of heart supposed to serve as a subliminal message for those of us who have yet to be won back? I'm probably overdetermining it, but it is worth remembering that Gibson himself co-wrote the screenplay.

Consequently, what's interesting about the film's exculpatory deprecation is that is seems to make a point of bypassing Hollywood mores in its appeal to a projected middlebrow "un-PC" audience. It does this most prevalently by insisting on the un-PC truism that men, regardless of race, are basically scumbags. Drinkers, cheaters, ballers and brawlers. The white US consulate official, a sweaty pervert looking for a bribe, the sleazy brown cops who blow their stolen loot on sports cars and prostitutes: this is a kingdom of assholes, violently selfish men driven to scale the pecking order, which here extends beyond prison into the ethically thin cirrus of American enterprise.

The polarizing difference, however, is that while white men in the film scheme and kill and use drugs on their way to the top, brown men in the film scheme and kill and use drugs and rape women and harvest children for their organs, while remaining trapped in the crowded lower tiers of this male hierarchy. Theirs is a scummier, more basic level of deprivation, endemic to the prison itself. It has irredeemably corrupted those it hasn't destroyed—and it has destroyed quite a few. The Kid's biological father, for example, a lowly narco-trafficker, was the first victim of his *patron*'s hepatic demand. He died long ago on the operating table, leaving his wife and son to fend for themselves in prison town. When he enters the film, it's through expository asides; his absence is non-spectral. Javi, the narco boss, and, by virtue of his authority, the film's other Latino father figure, is an effeminate lounge lizard lording over his garbage-dump fief in a bathrobe ("*El Jefner*," the Gringo dubs him). And somehow despite El Pueblito's surplus of male Latinos, it's not until the Gringo arrives that any man seems willing to take the Kid under his wing. Is it so surprising that the Mother, after delivering him a requisitely coy punch in the face, throws herself at the Gringo so Californianly?

This paternal unfitness, this deficit of good, productive Latino masculinity, is responsible for rousing the Gringo from his preternatural surliness to take up the compound "burden" of rearing the Kid (passing down fatherly bon mots: "A man who doesn't level with you [is] a man you can't trust"; replacing the Kid's cigarettes with nicotine gum and, in a final scene, lollipops); of sexually satisfying the Mother (which involves preventing her rape by a Latino inmate); and of becoming a suitable provider for his adopted family (hatching a scheme to kill Javi, and rescuing the Kid and Mother from El Pueblito once and for all).

In the final scene, we find the trio alone on a tropical beach, the Kid playing in the tide, Gringo and Mother cozying up in a hammock, clinking *cervezas*, "*por nosotros*." For the first time, and it seems almost to his own astonishment, the Gringo is happy. Happy because, in rescuing the Kid and Mother, he's transformed himself into the noblest articulation of man: Father. Or should I say *Padre*, Spanish having replaced English as the *lingua familiaris*. And not to belabor the obvious, but if you detect in the closing voiceover echoes of Gibson's own hero's journey—"for guys with my particular set of karmic could-bes, there was bound to be a bump or two down the road"—it makes his closing affirmation all the more resonant: "Ah what the hell, I'm going to enjoy what's left of the summer."

The gringo dies

The story of white heroism compelled by the overwhelming deficiencies of Latino men classifies *Get the Gringo* as a contemporary "white savior film," "the genre in which a white messianic character saves a lower- or working-class, usually urban or isolated, nonwhite character from a sad fate."[17] "[The trope's] imposing patronage," argues Matthew W. Hughey, "enables an interpretation of nonwhite characters and culture as essentially broken, marginalized, and pathological, while whites can emerge as messianic ... with their superior moral and mental abilities."[18] For generations, this Hollywood trope has helped secure the post-colonial hierarchies of race in North America,[19] and, in this regard, it's hard not to see Donald Trump as a beneficiary of its legacy. To better understand Trump's rise, let's look a little further in Gibson's filmography to a companion white savior film, 2016's *Blood Father*, directed by French action-auteur Jean-François Richet.

At first, *Blood Father* seems as different from *Get the Gringo* as veiny block of Bleu de Richet from the Kraft single slice. The straight-to-video *Gringo* delivers a cocky, but heart-warming take on its protagonist's messianism, whereas *Blood Father*, which premiered at Cannes, is ultimately much dourer in its veneration. What unites them, in addition to the campy, pulpy overtones, the rave reviews (*Blood Father* holds an 89% on Rotten Tomatoes, the highest score a Gibson film has received since *The Year of Living Dangerously*, with which it's tied),[20] and the metatheatrics (Gibson's real-life lapses are also mined to ironic effect), is the narrative trope of a chaotic narco Mexico enabling the gringo's self-awakening.

In *Blood Father*, the gringo is John Link, a grizzled biker who after thirty years of "drinking and drugging and fighting," and a sobering stint in jail, finds himself washed up in a trailer park in Indio, California. Rage still boils beneath his spry musculature (his grey beard and barbed facial creases makes him look at least a decade older than the Gringo); it heats his AA monologues to a threatening simmer. Only the hope that his runaway teenage daughter Lydia will return home can cool him down, though so far, the only manifestation of this hope has been the facsimiles of Picasso's Don Quixote he tattoos on the bodies of his fellow rednecks.

Lydia (Erin Moriarty), meanwhile, has been following prodigal footsteps: living in cocaine-fueled sin with Jonah (Diego Luna), the black sheep of the Juárez Cartel. When the psychopathic Jonah orders her to murder a (mostly) innocent white mother, Lydia demurs, and then accidentally shoots Jonah himself in the neck. Nowhere to turn, she flees to her father, and the two embark on an extended road trip, the police, the cartel and its army of heavily tattooed killers fast on their heels.

Hughey argues that "the 'stranger in a strange land' motif propels much of the rising action in white savior films."[21] *Blood Father*'s territory is more estranged than strange: a coastal mania of biker bars, stash houses, federal prisons and trailer parks. A pre-apocalyptic California peopled by rednecks, *cholos*, Aryans, *sicarios* with facial tattoos, off-the-gridders, conspiracy theorists, well-regulated militias of American crazypants. Everywhere the father and daughter escape reveals a new corner of an America pretty far from great: berserk and molting, nothing but fringe. Outrunning it resembles the only thing close to a sensible destination.

Organizing this fugitive journey are two confluent but repellant narratives of the white man's decline. The dominant strain, sincere and racist, is the story of John Link (*Mel Gibson, bro!*), a mean-ass son of a bitch doing everything he can to save his daughter from the savage narcos out to avenge their boss. This John Link refers to Mexico as a country of "turd factories" and "Zapotecan monsters." The subordinate narrative, expropriative and sarcastic—and much less persistent—is the story of John Link (*Henri, Mel Gibson!*), an angry nativist simpleton at home in a land of his own making. This is the narrative in which a sixteen-year-old Lydia can buy 600 rounds of 9mm bullets from the Walmart that refuses to sell her cigarettes. In the dominant narrative, Link says thing like, "[Mexicans] come up here, they're illegal and they take my job!" In the subordinate, he brain-farts in response to his daughter's retort, "So you pick oranges for a living?" The dominant narrative plays on what George Saunders calls the Trump supporter's "willingness to gloss over crudeness [as] ... an encoded sign of competence, strength, and reliability."[22] The subordinate, by mocking that crudeness, reveals the inherent incompetence, weakness, and arbitrariness of the film itself.

Consider the title: *Blood Father*. It sounds like the title of a bad poem, or a bad translation of one. Maybe it suggests "blood money," or "blood diamond," Gibson's character representing the film's tragically precious commodity: the tragedy of a white girl who'd desert her family for a psychotic Latin lover; the commodity of a white father who'd do something about it. What it does primarily, though, is foreground the film's puritanical fetishization of biological lineage. Partly why Lydia has run away from her mother's home (and into the arms of the corrupting Jonah) is a trio of stepdads who couldn't or refused to care for her properly. Only her "blood father" can protect her: first, by spectacularly killing off the criminals who mean her harm; second, by imparting the skills necessary to survive this lumpen America when he's no longer around. Those "skills" consist of sobriety, a grudging obedience to the rule of law, and most importantly, the self-awareness of your "Link" in the greater family, for just as in *Get the Gringo*, family here is the only real form of protection against the antagonist society. In the penultimate scene, after John Link kills the last of the *Juareneses*, he lays dying in his daughter's arms, and tells her: "You sure are a good girl." It's this confirmation, above all, that will secure Lydia's faith in her blood father, and see her through the darkness ahead.

The Trump campaign similarly infantilized its audience by offering up their inherent, all-purpose goodness as an entitlement to, and a remedy for, the devolving landscape of America. And like in *Blood Father*, Trump's notion of goodness was very much racially coded. Republicans had for generations pined to their base about a chimerical country of Mayberry communities, of sycamores pruned of their strange fruit. But Trump, the reality TV star, took this further by turning Latina/o scapegoating into a hallmark of his campaign. Little surprise that his rallies soon took on the historical drama of American elision, with his supporters pushing *others*, shouting, or beating them down, walling them off as a means of getting themselves closer to the righteous, angry father at center stage.

The gringo comes again

Freudian apocrypha has it that if a child had the power, he would destroy the world. Apocalypse by way of man-child is precisely what unfurls in Gibson's final white savior film, *Machete Kills* (2013), though the destroyer in question "is not really evil," according to director Robert Rodriguez. "He's got ... a very good plan ... but he's going about it the wrong way."[23]

Good gringos, bad hombres

A brief synopsis for readers unfamiliar with the *Machete* franchise: the titular character, a lithic Mexican *federal*-cum-migrant laborer-cum-mercenary-cum-Immigration Officer-cum-Secret Service of One (Danny Trejo) is caught up, between the blood-spattered hyphens, in the capers of cartels, corrupt senators, vigilante networks (pro- and anti-immigrant), killer priests, psycho prostitutes, shape-shifting bounty hunters, and the President of the United States, played by Charlie Sheen (rechristened Carlos Estévez).

Machete Kills, the sequel, adds to the melee one Luther Voz (Gibson), super villain extraordinaire, and prime mover of chaos. Voz is a millionaire with a penchant for sponsoring beauty pageants though the Trump allusions end here. A Silicon technocrat (Voz was partly based on Tesla CEO Elon Musk, who makes a cameo),[24] his primary business is arms manufacturing, and his real estate interests lie in outer space, where he plans to build a new civilization once he succeeds in "throwing the world into gargantuan, unrecoverable anarchy" (an outcome endorsed by many a celebrity Trumpist, from Steve Bannon[25] to Slavoj Žižek[26]). To ensure global annihilation, he's supplied North Korea, Russia, and the Mexican cartel with nuclear weapons, all of which are set to launch in 24 hours. "This world must end in order for a more perfect one to emerge," Voz explains. Gazing up at his space shuttle, he makes Gibson's final incarnation of the white savior explicit: "Noah had his ark? I got mine."

Like the Gringo and John Link, Voz is a strong PR vehicle for Gibson—and not despite, but precisely because he happens to be the first official villain Gibson's played in his 36-year career. It takes calculated humility for an accused racist to submit to the direction of the leading Chicano auteur, a filmmaker whose ironic sense of pop intertextuality is pitch-perfect, and whose original *Machete* sufficiently rankled Fox News and its jeremiahs of "reverse racism." (Conspiracy theorist and Trump *compa* Alex Jones denounced the film as "radicalized Latino culture ... playing to Hispanic supremacy").[27] For his part, Rodriguez, who wrote Voz with Gibson in mind,[28] set comparatively generous terms for the actor's penance. While the other Anglo villains in the *Machete* films tend to be bona fide bigots, cussers and swaggerers, all "beaner" this and "om-bray" that, Luther Voz, is as sophisticated as an OS update. The utopia he plans is practically Benettonian in its demography.

Nevertheless, while the other films are merely aware of it, *Machete Kills* is openly critical of its white messianism. Voz may not be a good ole boy, but his desire and repulsion for Mexican bodies reveals his complicity in the good ole hegemony. Voz so envies Machete's superlative Mexican genes, for instance, that he commissions them as the prototype for the galactic clone army that will safeguard his exodus from earth. He so admires Mexicans for their labor skills that he kidnaps them in droves to construct, and later serve on his space station. The message here is that exploitation without Skynyrd in the background can be even more virulent, and that what looks like a White Savior from this side of Mount Lee can appear as a Destroying Angel on the other. "He thinks he's God in heaven," Machete quips in steely deadpan, "so heaven must fall," forecasting a final sequel, *Machete Kills Again ... in Space*.

Though it's tempting to champion *Machete Kills*'s schlocky post-grindhouse irony as an antidote to the maudlin sincerity of a film like *Blood Father*, this, too, would be over-politicizing Rodriguez's work. As Frederick Luis Aldama argued of the original film, *Machete* shouldn't be reduced to propaganda: "There's a deliberate constructedness about it that foregrounds its playfulness and insistence that it be engaged with as an aesthetic, fictional artifact [of the grindhouse era]."[29] Moreover, to take the film as an antidote to political sincerity of the Trump campaign would elide the obvious fact that Trump used similar over-the-top theatrics on his "Make America Great Again" reality tour. We can't know how many of his supporters actually "took him literally, but not seriously,"[30] as the post-electoral meme suggested, but it's undeniable that those supporters found confirmation in all the braggadocio, hyperbole, and pure bullshit "not seriously" connotes. Saunders wrote of Trump's speeches how "oddly riveting [it is] watching someone take such pleasure in going so much farther out on thin ice than anyone else as famous would dare to go. His crowds are ever hopeful for the next thrilling rude swerve." This is also a fairly apt description of *Machete*'s narrative arc. The film's hyperbaric irony, which warps realism by increasing expectations for the outrageous, seems a piece with, less an interpellation of the Trump movement. It's no stretch to imagine Trump supporters whooping on Charlie Sheen's second-amendment-toting, border-defending "President of the United fucking States." With such fast-moving targets, the joke can be on everyone at once.[31]

All the same, I'm wary of lumping *Machete Kills* with *Get the Gringo* and *Blood Father* in one outsized Dumptean foreshadow. It's true that all three films present Gibson, and his characters, with racially coded opportunities for moral redemption. It's also true that, with varying success, each film relies on the ironic remove of its self-conscious "b-movieness" to temper the arrogance this redemption presupposes. But the very notion that Donald Trump and Mel Gibson should be considered companion "gringo saviors" in white American supremacy, if this was my thesis going in, in conclusion it strikes me as unfair. Mel Gibson's gringos are played by Mel Gibson, after all; Donald Trump is played by Donald Trump (among others). Good looks, a sweet voice, conceivable hair—such features were never part of Trump's genetic inheritance (which is why, without his father's head-start money, he probably would have failed as a conman). Gibson's charms might make it easier, or more difficult, for us to forgive him. But the important distinction, the sign pointed to over and over again by the biographical allusions in all three films, is that Gibson is genuinely contrite about his bad behavior, and he is willing to work for our forgiveness. Is Donald Trump capable of public humility? Has he ever apologized for anything?

When I was a grad student, with, let's say inflated expectations about my purpose in life, I believed it was the scholar's responsibility to push the discourse forward by identifying—and then laboriously decalcifying—any instance of racial, gender, sexual or class bias that inhibited the redemptive flow of otherwise progressive narratives. Now, in the wake of Trump's victory, I don't know if this deconstructive line is more prudent that ever, or if it's just all kinds of bananas. Maybe instead of reading the latest Toni Morrison novel for symptoms of unconscious hegemony, I should be on the lookout for sympathetic passages in the postlapsarian films of Mel Gibson: films which seem like obvious buttresses of the prevailing ideology; passages, which need not be subversive, but hopeful—hopeful in their attempts at inclusion.

The passage I have in mind is the final scene from *Get the Gringo*: Gibson and his Mexican lover on the beach, swaying in a hammock, his 'adopted' son playing in the sand. This is the idyll of homecoming, and the Gringo is truly at home here. His fluency in Spanish signals his assimilation into the Mexican family, while his tremendous smile shows the emotional growth that's allowed this to happen. That he and the Mother can form a relationship without any obvious sign of racial ambivalence might be significant,[32] though in the 2010s, it seems pretty standard, at least in Hollywood (*Blood Father*, with its reification of biological lineage, is the exception here). The impediment to their relationship was never explicitly race; it was the Gringo's inherent selfishness: his fear of self-preservation having blinded him to the needs, and the rewards of others. What he discovers in the end, 90 minutes after smashing through the US-Mexican border in that chaotic opening scene, is the overwhelming joy, the mutual awareness and the love of forming human bonds in these open borderlands. Of manifesting, in interlocked limbs, brown and white, the deep emotional links that undergird our shared mestizo world.

I don't mean to suggest this is a perfect ending. Critics who'd highlight its Cortesian paternalism wouldn't be wrong. But in Trump's America, where the prophets are only as good as their prophecies, there are absolutely worse endings in store, and more dangerous passions to suffer.

Good gringos, bad hombres

Notes

1 Having to do with its Adults Only rating. See Reed Johnson, "'Passion' engulfs Mexico." *Los Angeles Times* (March 20, 2004).
2 Quoted in Michelle Green, "The Dish from Down Under." *People* (February 4, 1985).
3 "Film Review: Braveheart: The Splashy Epic Finds New Life in the 13nth Century." *New York Times* (May 24, 1995).
4 Quoted in Elizabeth Day, "Mel Gibson: Saint and Sinner." *The Guardian* (5 June 2011).
5 Quoted in Todd Van Luling, "Mel Gibson's Sexist Interview Answers From 1995 Are Relevant Again." *The Huffington Post* (November. 4, 2016).
6 While I'm no believer in *in vino veritas* (a fallacy completely ignorant of chaos theory) and am very much a believer in the right to privacy (which the tape leaks violated), my main reason for glossing over these events is Foucauldian: the effects of Gibson's perceived racism, rather than its inherent validity, are what concern me in this chapter.
7 Ashley Lee, "Mel Gibson's 'Passion of the Christ' Sequel Titled 'Resurrection'." *Hollywood Reporter* (Nov. 2, 2016).
8 Luke Dittrich, "The Greatest Story Never Told." *Esquire* (July 25, 2014).
9 Michelle Ye Hee Lee, "Donald Trump's False Comments Connecting Mexican Immigrants and Crime." *Washington Post* (July 8, 2015).
10 *El Narcotraficante: Narcocorridos and the Construction of a Cultural Personae on the U.S.-Mexico Border* (University of Texas Press, 2004): 110–12; 120.
11 Edberg 111.
12 That is, if we dismiss the cartoon *Chicken Run* (2000), which received a 97%. Note that a lot of the praise was cagey (for *Gringo*, that is; *Chicken Run* is grandma-level beloved).
13 Greg Bloom, "The End of Baja's 'El Pueblito' Prison." *La Prensa San Diego* (September 6, 2002).
14 Incidentally, this isn't the first time a Gibson character has seen the inside of a Mexican jail. "Mac" McKussic from *Tequila Sunrise* spent two years of backstory learning to be a drug dealer in Mexican prison.
15 An influence noted by several critics. See, Peter Debruge, "Get the Gringo." *Variety* (April 20, 2012); Donald Liebenson, "Get the Gringo: Mad Mel Demolishes Mexico." *Roger Ebert* (May 2, 2012); Todd McCarthy, "Get the Gringo: Film Review." *The Hollywood Reporter* (April 20, 2012).
16 Quoted in Debruge (2012).
17 *The White Savior Film: Content, Critics and Consumption* (Temple University Press, 2014): 1.
18 Hughey (2014: 2).
19 Hughey (2014: 18).
20 Again, discounting the outlying magic of *Chicken Run*.
21 Hughey (2014: 29).
22 "Who Are All These Trump Supporters?" *The New Yorker* (July 11 and 18, 2016).
23 "Robert Rodriguez Talks Casting Mel Gibson in Machete Kills." *Access Hollywood* (October 3, 2013).
24 Jette Kernion, "Interview: Robert Rodriguez and Danny Trejo, 'Machete Kills' (Part One)." *Slackerwood* (October 16, 2013).
25 Philip Rucker and Robert Costa, "Bannon Vows a Daily Fight for 'Deconstruction of the Administrative State'." *The Washington Post* (February 23, 2017).
26 Žižek sees it is a necessary evil: "Yes, there is a great danger in Trump's victory, but the Left will be mobilized *only* through such a threat of catastrophe." "Slavoj Žižek on Clinton, Trump and the Left's Dilemma." *In These Times* (November 6, 2016).
27 Quoted in Alexander Zaitchik, "Does Robert Rodriguez's 'Machete' Advocate 'Race War'?" *The Huffington Post* (September 10, 2010).
28 "Exclusive! Mel Gibson Talks 'Machete Kills': 'Bad Guys are Always More Fun'." *YouTube* (July 19, 2012).
29 Aldama (2014): 125.
30 Coined by *The Atlantic's* Salena Zito. "Taking Trump Seriously, Not Literally." *The Atlantic* (September 23, 2016).
31 In his analysis of the original *Machete*, David Church makes a similar claim in arguing that the film's mix of irony and sincerity "[makes] difficult any blanket claims about the political valence of its reception.' *Grindhouse Nostalgia: Memory, Home Video and Exploitation Film Fandom* (Edinburgh University Press, 2015).
32 It was a main qualification for the "pure relationship" according to José E. Limón in 1998. See *American Encounters: Greater Mexico, the United States, and the Erotics of Culture* (Beacon Press, 1998): 193–206; 213).

Works cited

Aldama, Frederick Luis. *The Cinema of Robert Rodriguez*. University of Texas Press, 2014.

Blood Father. Directed by Jean-François Richet, Why Not Productions, 2016.

"Blood Father (2016)." *Rotten Tomatoes*, www.rottentomatoes.com/m/blood_father.

Bloom, Greg. "The End of Baja's 'El Pueblito' Prison." *La Prensa San Diego*, 6 September 2002, http://laprensa-sandiego.org/archieve/september06- 02/prison.htm.

"Chicken Run (2000)." *Rotten Tomatoes*, www.rottentomatoes.com/m/chicken_run.

Church, David. *Grindhouse Nostalgia: Memory, Home Video and Exploitation Film Fandom*. Edinburgh University Press, 2015.

Day, Elizabeth. "Mel Gibson: Saint and Sinner." *The Guardian*, 5 June 2011, www.theguardian.com/film/2011/jun/05/mel-gibson-beaver-saint- sinner-interview.

Debruge, Peter. "Get the Gringo." *Variety*, 20 April 2012, http://variety.com/2012/film/reviews/get-the-gringo-1117947416/.

Dittrich, Luke. "The Greatest Story Never Told." *Esquire* 25 July 2014, www.esquire.com/entertainment/movies/interviews/a23749/the- greatest-story-never-told-0814/.

Edberg, Mark Cameron. *El Narcotraficante: Narcocorridos and the Construction of a Cultural Personae on the U.S.-Mexico Border*. University of Texas Press, 2004.

"Exclusive! Mel Gibson Talks 'Machete Kills': 'Bad Guys are Always More Fun'." *YouTube*, uploaded by extratv, 19 July 2012, www.youtube.com/watch?v=YVNo2fZ_I4E.

Get the Gringo: How I Spent My Summer Vacation. Directed by Adrian Grunberg, 20th Century Fox Home Entertainment, 2012.

"Get the Gringo (2012)." *Rotten Tomatoes*, www.rottentomatoes.com/m/get_the_gringo/.

Green, Michelle. "The Dish from Down Under." *People*, 4 February 1985, http://people.com/archive/cover-story-the-dish-from-down-under-vol-23-no-5.

Hughey, Matthew W. *The White Savior Film: Content, Critics and Consumption*. Temple University Press, 2014.

James, Caryn. "Film Review: Braveheart; The Splashy Epic Finds New Life in the 13nth Century." *New York Times*, 24 May 1995, www.nytimes.com/movie/review?res=990CE2D71E3CF937A15756C0A963958260

From Mad Max to a Prince Possessed." *New York Times*, 19 December 1990, www.nytimes.com/movie/review?res=9C0CE7D81139F93AA25751C 1A966958260

Johnson, Reed. "'Passion' engulfs Mexico." *Los Angeles Times*, 20 March 2004, http://articles.latimes.com/2004/mar/20/entertainment/et-johnson20.

Kernion, Jette. "Interview: Robert Rodriguez and Danny Trejo, 'Machete Kills' (Part One)." *Slackerwood*, 16 October 2013, www.slackerwood.com/node/3884.

Lee, Ashley. "Mel Gibson's 'Passion of the Christ' Sequel Titled 'Resurrection'. *Hollywood Reporter*, 2 November 2016, www.hollywoodreporter.com/news/mel-gibsons-passion-christ-sequel-titled-resurrection-943363.

Liebenson, Donald. "Get the Gringo: Mad Mel demolishes Mexico." *Roger Ebert*, 2 May 2012, www.rogerebert.com/demanders/get-the-gringo-mad-mel-demolishes-mexico.

Limón, José E. *American Encounters: Greater Mexico, the United States, and the Erotics of Culture*. Beacon Press, 1998.

Machete. Directed by Robert Rodriguez, Troublemaker Studios, 2010.

Machete Kills. Directed by Robert Rodriguez, Troublemaker Studios, 2013.

McCarthy, Todd. "Get the Gringo: Film Review." *The Hollywood Reporter*, 20 April 2012, www.hollywoodreporter.com/review/mel-gibson-get-gringo-film-review-adrian-grunberg-314302.

"Robert Rodriguez Talks Casting Mel Gibson in Machete Kills." *Access Hollywood*, 3 October 2013, www.accesshollywood.com/videos/robert-rodriguez- talks-casting-mel-gibson-in-machete-kills-41844/.

Rucker, Philip and Robert Costa. "Bannon vows a daily fight for 'deconstruction of the administrative state'." *The Washington Post*, 23 February 2017, www.washingtonpost.com/politics/top-wh-strategist-vows-a-daily-fight-for-deconstruction-of-the-administrative-state/2017/02/23/03f6b8da-f9ea-11e6-bf01- d47f8cf9b643_story.html?utm_term=.2dcd5b57679.

Saunders, George. "Who Are All These Trump Supporters?" *The New Yorker*, 11 and 18 July 2016, www.newyorker.com/magazine/2016/07/11/george- saunders-goes-to-trump-rallies.

Tequila Sunrise. Directed by Robert Towne, Warner Brothers, 1998.

Van Luling, Todd. "Mel Gibson's Sexist Interview Answers From 1995 Are Relevant Again." *The Huffington Post*, 4 November 2016, www.huffingtonpost.com/entry/mel-gibson-playboyinterview_us_ 581a2ea7e4b0c43e6c1d92c0

Ye Hee Lee, Michelle. "Donald Trump's False Comments Connecting Mexican Immigrants and Crime." *Washington Post*, 8 July, 2015, www.washingtonpost.com/news/fact- checker/wp/2015/07/08/donald-trumps-false-comments-connecting- mexican-immigrants-and-crime/?utm_term=.0b6b6282e482.

Zaitchik, Alexander. "Does Robert Rodriguez's 'Machete' Advocate 'Race War'?" *The Huffington Post*, 10 September 2010, www.huffingtonpost.com/alexander-zaitchik/does-robert-rodriguezs-ma_b_712003.html.

Zito, Salena. "Taking Trump Seriously, Not Literally." *The Atlantic*, 23 September 2016), www.theatlantic.com/politics/archive/2016/09/trump- makes-his-case-in-pittsburgh/501335/.

Žižek Slavoj. "Slavoj Žižek on Clinton, Trump and the Left's Dilemma." *In These Times*, 6 November 2016, http://inthesetimes.com/features/zizek_clinton_trump_lesser_evil.html.

PART IV

Putting the feminist and queer pop in the pictorial arts

20

GRAFFITI IN LATIN AMERICA
Preliminary notes

Ilan Stavans

"Life Sucks without Graffiti"—the inscription, displayed in the 1990s in the Zehentgasse of Heilbronn, some 65 kilometers southeast from Heidelberg, Germany, summarizes the modern urban condition. But it also simplifies it. What life? And, more specifically, what graffiti?

I have spent the last half a decade traveling through Latin America. Among other endeavors, I focused on graffiti in metropolitan centers and, occasionally, also in rural landscapes, whenever possible interviewing *grafiteros*. I talked to them about money, racial, and gender issues. The last facet was insightful as I explored the unveiled world of sexual innuendos, which thrives in the culture. The experience was enthralling, to such degree that I am convinced this is a fertile field of academic scrutiny that deserves a patient, intelligent, coordinated transnational effort.

Most of the work I did on my own. My purpose was to decode the encryptions in a way that evidenced a universal graffiti syntax within the Latin American context.

On the surface, graffiti (from the Italian *graffito*, little scratch) is scribble—letters, drawings— on public surfaces. The common assumption is that such scribbles are essentially unruly, messy, and nonsensical, e.g., an affront to the mainstream aesthetics of a specific community. And that all graffiti is alike, regardless of context.

These are misconceptions. Graffiti might be anarchic but it is never chaotic. Indeed, it is an alternative form of order, a feature of the modern city that adapts itself to individual cultural climates. One might describe it as iconoclastic, nonconformist, even mutinous yet lucid, logical, and coherent. Graffiti delivers its message through transgression; it never gives up on the quest to signify. That signification is achieved through subversion. As a language, it features a general syntax. But each particular manifestation responds to identifiable forces, which need to be taken into account in order to crack the encryption.

The time I spent in Latin America enabled me to understand it as an ecosystem. Graffiti didn't show up in it at random. Its arrival in the 1960s fit into an environment that since pre-Columbian times has been geared toward the visual. Before 1492, indigenous cultures used languages that were non-alphabetical; languages that use hieroglyphs and other types of representation as semantic units. The arrival of the European colonizers (first the Vikings, and then the Spaniards and Portuguese) brought with them the imposition of a linguistic code that replaced glyphs with letters.

However, the visual remains in the substratum. Latin America is also a habitat where *Muralismo* has thrived across the board, from Mexico to Brazil, from Uruguay to Cuba. Important figures like *Los Tres Grandes*, Diego Rivera, José Clemente Orozco, and David Alfaro Siqueiros have incorporated historical, political, social, religious, and cultural elements into their frescos. Against this background, graffiti isn't just another artistic form. And while it has been perceived as "an urban pest," the illicit activity of youthful groups deemed vandals who perform it anonymously at night with stolen aerosol, the fact is that it is organically rooted in the region's past.

A dramatic change has taken place in Latin American graffiti since the turn of the millennium. This is especially obvious in the 2010s. Instead of resisting it, governments have been embracing it, blurring the line between fast-produced design and murals. In cities like Bogotá, libraries, schools, cafeterias, and other public sites have invited *grafiteros* inside to design large-size, colorful frescos using the same technique and ingredients employed on the street. The themes often play with surreal—e.g., "magical realist"—motifs. They are political. And they allow artists time to mature their aesthetic style.

In Colombia, I have seen friezes in Bogotá, a city at the forefront of this revolution, although others like Cali, Medellín, and Cartagena are also practitioners of this less confrontational, more harmonious face. Naturally, I noticed some discomfort, even resentment among the old guard. A few interviewees talked of treason, of younger artists selling out. They discussed with me the way Facebook, Twitter, Snapchat, and Instagram have redrawn the map, making graffiti less homegrown. Social media has created a transnational community of *grafiteros* that are in dialogue.

The topic of sexuality is front and center. With machismo at its core, Latin America is a polarized territory defined by strategies of conquest and submission—and by an unspoken grammar of sensuality. I can't begin to count the number of graffiti messages about gender relations, which are arguably the most prevalent. "¡*Lucía, eres mía para siempre!*," "*Gozo tu dulce jugo*," and "*Rafael y Marcela son pareja.*" Naked figures in the act of lovemaking, enormous penises, vaginas, and breasts, and all kinds of erotic imagery abound. At times I came across these signs scribbled on toilet walls and elsewhere in public bathrooms. Less frequently, they were visible in buses, trains, and taxis, as well as on sidewalks, cement surfaces, and tree bark.

Subjugation and gender fluidity are prime topics. A certain male was described as gay: "*Javier es marica.*" A woman was said to be a whore: "*Tu hermana me la mama.*" I saw numerous references to illicit liaisons and superhuman potency. More often than not, these messages were graphic rather than verbal. On occasion, they would also be confessional: "*Soy homo y te amo*" and "*Nadie lo sabe más que tú.*"

In the field notes I took during my Latin American travels there is a constant reminder of the tension between the local and the global. As a result of transnational forces and of the fast-speed communication that is achieved through the Internet and social media, the *grafiteros* I spoke to are attuned to graffiti elsewhere on the international scene. At the same time, all artists are by definition native, tied to a time and place. A reference to a politician, an event, a TV soap opera, and so on, serves as conduits to establish a connection with the audience. In other words, messages must be understood as part of a juncture (Figure 20.1).

Ideology and class are ubiquitous themes. Indictments are relentless to corrupt government figures, unpopular policies, and current scandals. In this regard, graffiti in Latin America voices popular sentiments not articulated in traditional forums. Presidents, ministers, mayors, and others are accused of inefficiency. Prison is invoked as punishment. At times, messages play with double-entendres. Other times, literary and philosophical references are made.

Expectedly, graffiti makes incessant reference to U.S. pop culture. In Venezuela, I saw references to President Nicolás Maduro as Dark Vader. Colonialism was invoked through the use of the McDonald's golden arches. And Donald Trump's image was defaced with obscenities, adorned with Nazi symbols, and likened to police brutality.

Figure 29.1 An example of *grafiterios*.

In terms of language, *grafiteros*, since for the most part they work in anonymity, use a daring lexicon. No phrase was too risqué. Blasphemies, expletives, and profanities abounded. "*Carbrón,*" "*Me cago en la virgen,*" "*Pinche mamón,*" "*Boludo,*" "*Chupa verga,*" and "*Te cojo en la cocina.*"

Another insight I had is that graffiti is more prevalent in times of social anxiety. The areas where I found it aren't known for offering community outlets where public expression might be crystalized. The result is a spontaneous manifestation of messages that struggle to convey people's deep unhappiness. In that sense, graffiti in Latin America looks for ways to bridge disparate groups. *Grafiteros* will post their art in middle- and upper-middle neighborhoods because they believe these are the places where their target audiences are to be found.

Likewise, I noticed that tourist areas are patrolled against graffiti. Seeking to protect the income from tourism, governments clean these areas on a regular basis in order to give foreigners a veneer of cleanliness. Yet tourists aren't easily fooled. They either travel outside their comfort zone, or else they are conscious that such tourist areas are artificial enclaves.

Ilan Stavans

Finally, while graffiti at times is made to symbolize a subconscious violence in the cityscape, Latin American metropolises have become acclimated to it, accepting it as an integral aesthetic component.

A few examples: When I visited San Juan, Puerto Rico was submerged in a financial crisis that had given place to a deep recession, $123 billion in debt and pension obligations, resulting in the government seeking bankruptcy relief in federal court. Evidence of that recession were everywhere to be seen: foreclosure signs, empty storefronts, public schools closed, and a growing homeless population. In reaction, a surplus of graffiti was available in the city.

Almost everywhere (the tourist areas were more emphatically policed), I came across multicolor scrawls, doodles, and other drawings, the vast majority reacting to political corruption, the colonial presence of the United States in the island, and in general to people's impoverished life. It was a well-known fact that in the last decade, approximately a fifth of the entire population—principally people from the middle-, upper-middle, and upper-classes—had left for the mainland. As a result, in their drawings *grafiteros* seemed to collectively react to the fracturing of Puerto Rican society (Figure 20.2).

Figure 20.2 An example of *grafiterios* in Puerto Rico.

At first the metropolitan authorities had tried to portray this artistic effervescence. But it had given up quickly, which was interpreted as an invitation to expand the possibilities of graffiti. I came across several neighborhoods that unofficially had been declared free graffiti territory, giving room to enormous murals obviously created without the fear of persecution. These astonishingly accomplished murals had more overt and clearly defined themes, such as the connection between sexuality and death and the celebration of Taino identity in a hybrid way that incorporated elements of 21st century pop culture (Figure 20.3).

In 2017, while admiring several San Juan friezes, I took note of the fact that in those more beneficial creative conditions, a few essential aspects of graffiti changed. Anonymity disappeared as artists whose activities were witnessed by the community became recognized figures. On occasion, they were also paid through a cooperative system. Aerosol was used most of the time but not always. Other pictorial ingredients were brought in, at times actively defying the concept of ephemerality, since a handful of frescos obviously were made to last. Plus, since these

Figure 20.3 An example of *grafiterios* in San Juan.

artistic pieces at times brought tourists to the neighborhoods, mechanisms were established to protect them.

Could any of the pieces have been taken out of San Juan and inserted in another Latin American milieu? Of course they could, but it would be like taking a cat out of its home. It would quickly lose a sense of place and die. In fact, one of the beauties of my trek was that I often visited areas in the company of friends who served as interpreters for me, explaining references I was unacquainted with. The references were only occasionally political. To a large degree, the graffiti I encountered there and elsewhere juxtaposed ideological with spiritual ingredients. This signaled to me a crucial ingredient in the study of this cultural manifestation: just as all art is local, so are all observations of it.

A similar experience occurred in Mexico City. In comparison to San Juan, the city is expansive, multilayered, and enormously complex. When I visited it in 2015, there were countless demonstrations of dissent against President Enrique Peña-Nieto and his wife, about the disappearance of 43 students in Ayotzinapa, about the assassination of journalists, and about Donald Trump's proposed building of a wall on the U.S.-Mexican border, among other subjects. There were more casual articulations in which a person professes eternal love for someone else or makes a promise whose contract is the writing on the wall.

Calaveras are a recurrent theme in Mexican graffiti. So are crosses, eagles, machine guns. In Ciudad Nezahualcóyotl, a municipality in the northern part of Mexico City, the graffiti I came across was less meticulously crafted than the pieces in Puerto Rico. They were done in defiance of authorities who refused to improve the sewer system or enhance security in the area. I was also struck by ungrammatical idioms, lack of accents, and typos (Figure 20.4).

In contrast, in Colonial Polanco, an affluent neighborhood where the Mexican elite frequently socializes, the graffiti I encountered was limited to a handful of street corners, which made it clear the neighborhood was heavily policed. At times images of Peña-Nieto with the words "*Asesino*" and "*Puto*" were painted over in white, only to resurface again. At one point, I saw a tribute to a famous Frida Kahlo painting in which the hearts of Peña-Nieto and Trump were connected through their arteries.

These graffiti pieces reminded me of the graffiti in Mexico City in the late 1960s, when a student movement against the ruling party PRI resulted in a massacre in Plaza de Tlatelolco. While artists had taken to the street to denounce a repressive government, they had done so incorporating elements of pop culture. There were references to *fútbol* stars and to the Olympic Games, as well as to Mickey Mouse. Likewise, during my recent visit I encountered expressions that used a saying by Bart Simpson or made a connection to *Transformers* and *The Planet of the Apes*.

In contrast, I find it extraordinary that during my various visits to Havana in 2013 and 2014, graffiti was almost nonexistent. Not in Havana Vieja, of course, for that is a tourist milieu, but in an assortment of popular neighborhoods. Its absence left me puzzled. This in part has to do with the system of governmental repressions in Cuba under Fidel and Raúl Castro. But similar systems existed in other nations I frequented that were either under a democratic or a dictatorial regime, yet they were invaded by all sorts of street scrabbling.

I wrote a variety of reflections about this absence in my notebook. The island has created channels of community participation that might silence graffiti. Plus, artists have become veritable entrepreneurs, granting them money-making outlet in the international scene that make graffiti a bad investment. Or social pressure is such that *grafiteros* are altogether sidelined. In any case, unlike other Latin American cities Havana was mostly clean.

This is troublesome, since life without graffiti does suck. It also sucks when graffiti isn't paid its due. Latin America is a large, heterogeneous territory. Looking at it *in toto* poses unique

Graffiti in Latin America

Figure 20.4 An example of Mexican graffiti.

challenges. Graffiti is a worthy area of exploration. No actual pest, it begs to be taken seriously—to be decrypted through in rational terms. My travels generated a substantial amount of material, including a large trove of photographs. I hope to systematically study this material in the near future.

An initial step will be to sort it out by theme. Sexuality might well be the place to start. This facet strikes me as invaluable. It is a tool to understand gender relations from an exceptional vantage point, since it makes understatements tangible.

21
GRAFFITI SCHOOL *COMUNIDAD*
A feminist arts pedagogy of empowerment

Guisela Latorre and Marjorie Peñailillo

Graffiti School *Comunidad*. These three words together evoke some inherent contradictions. What does graffiti have to do with schooling? What can we possibly teach through the use of graffiti, an often-criminalized urban art form? How can one build *comunidad* around a street practice that privileges the individuality of its practitioners? In this chapter, we will discuss how the convergence of these three words, far from representing contradictions, signify the building blocks for the radical practice of a feminist pedagogy. The Graffiti School *Comunidad* (GSC) is a community arts initiative based on collaborative workshops where participants not only learn creative skills inspired by street art practices, but also develop strategies of resilience and survival through a profound reconceptualization of the self and the collective. The GSC began in 2010 when a single graffiti workshop taking place in Valparaiso, Chile, led to a long-term project that brought together the non-hegemonic and alternative knowledges produced through street art and the emancipatory potential of feminist pedagogy. Though the GSC is adaptable to different social and geographical settings, it bears mentioning that the specificity of 21st-century Chilean culture and society provided a powerful impetus for the emergence of this initiative. The country's rich and complex tradition of street art—which includes graffiti but also muralism, public performance and other forms of expression—alongside the social movements that have defined its recent history, created a fertile ground upon which the GSC could grow and develop.

In what follows, we will be concerned with the various pedagogic tools deployed within the GSC, arguing that this initiative has generated productive and effective spaces where the power inequalities of traditional, top-down educational approaches can be challenged and deconstructed. Empowering students is at the center of the GSC's pedagogies and, as such, reflects the larger goals of a feminist education, as articulated by Jennifer Scanlon: "[Feminist pedagogy] encourages us to go beyond providing information to empower students so that they see themselves not only as victims of injustice but as people capable of creating change in society."[1] The insights contained in this chapter are also the result of the ongoing transnational conversations and collaborations that we, the authors of this text, have maintained with one another over the years since we first met in 2011. We are Marjorie "Gigi" Peñailillo, a Chilean graffiti artist and urban arts teacher active in the Valparaiso metropolitan area, and Guisela Latorre, a feminist scholar of Latinx muralism and street art who works at a large state university in the United States. It was Gigi who created the GSC and developed much of its curricula. The pedagogies that came to form this urban arts initiative emerged organically through her practice as a graffiti artist, her interactions with diverse communities on the streets and through her formal training in art and education in Chile. Guisela has worked with Gigi in refining the feminist language and intentionality of her pedagogies while also promoting the artist's work through her research and scholarship. Guisela also considers herself to be one of Gigi's students in the GSC, an identity she embraced when in 2016 she participated in a graffiti mural project lead by the artist. In sum, we are collaborators, colleagues and friends; our analyses in this text reflect the pedagogies of the GSC but also the collaborative relationship we have forged since 2011.

In conversations over the years, Gigi and Guisela have deeply influenced one another. Gigi made Guisela aware of the radical importance of graffiti as a pedagogical tool because it points to a legitimization of graffiti itself and to an implicit critique of an educational system that devalues street knowledges and practices. Moreover, the artist expanded Guisela's understanding of the possibilities for social justice in the practice of street art. The notion that a graffiti artist could become a teacher was transformative for her and so she began to think more deeply about the feminist possibilities inherent in collaboration. Ultimately, Guisela adopted many of Gigi's pedagogies in her own university classroom, in particularly those that pertain to methods and approaches that seek to legitimize and empower students. For Gigi this collaboration has meant gaining a deeper understanding of feminism beyond the limited and often negative connotations of the term that were prevalent in Chile during the first decade of the 21st century.[2] The conversations that Guisela established with Gigi focused on feminism's commitment to diversity, gender inclusion and egalitarian social relations which Gigi realized were also central to her praxis as an artist, educator and mentor. Guisela also impressed upon her the fact that feminism is concerned with social exclusion writ large, not just the one that is generated by gender oppression.

Most GSC sessions consist of arts workshops where participants work collaboratively to create a mural or graffiti piece in a public space. Gigi teaches them drawing and composition skills as well as how to master numerous spray paint techniques. Many of her students are school age children though she has also worked with adults, including senior populations. She has carried out many of these sessions within and outside of the public school system in Chile, often availing herself of state arts and education programs in the country. In recent years though, her work has attracted international attention, having received invitations to take the GSC to Brazil, Spain and the United States. Though Gigi works with communities of all gender expressions, women and girls are often enthusiastic contributors to her workshops, forming more than 50% of the GSC participants between 2015 and 2017. Two out of the eight projects she carried out during this time included all-women student bodies. The artist's commitment to gender inclusivity stems from her knowledge that graffiti, as well as other forms of street art, is dominated by men and that urban locales are still imagined as male discursive sites. Part of her praxis is thus about denaturalizing the connection between public space and maleness. Quite the contrary, for her, public spaces can also promote a certain openness and the opportunity for greater possibilities, ones not afforded within the confines of an institutionalized classroom. The movement of people within urban spaces can give us glimpses into the many possibilities of social action and learning in the public sphere.

In the course of her career as both a graffiti artist and educator, Gigi discovered the great pedagogic potential that existed in urban spaces and through the practice of street art. She realized that there was a strong relationship between art, public space and community building. In her work on graffiti pedagogy Janice Rahn insists that graffiti can provide educators with "an excellent example how individuals become self-motivated to learn through their involvement in community, collaboration and dialogue among peers."[3] But in order to promote that self-motivation it was critical to build up students' self-concept or *autoconcepto*, that is, the internalized perception and assessment of themselves. Driven by a social justice framework, in particular in the realm of education, Gigi understood that inequality could manifest itself through an individual's sense of self and that this *autoconcepto* was particularly damaged among the vulnerable populations with whom she worked. Vulnerable populations refer to communities that are neglected and at times even rendered invisible by the state. Susceptibility to systemic poverty, violence and forced displacement can be facts of their realities. Institutionalized forms of discrimination such as racism, sexism, homophobia and class bias further contribute to their experiences with structural inequality. Thus, working with a student's *autoconcepto* as an enclosed and solely individualized entity was insufficient when it came to these larger social problems. Gigi sought to impress upon her students the idea that a person's sense of self will always be dependent on that individual's relation to others. Was it then possible to promote a healthy *autoconcepto* among students within the urban space? Working in community settings and in a public space with the purposes of creating a graffiti mural allowed students to simultaneously build up their sense of self and their relationship with others who might be working on the same project. To that end, Gigi also works in developing an individual's social abilities which allow them to forge egalitarian relations with others.

Enhancing an individual's *autoconcepto* along with their ability to interact with others in egalitarian ways can be achieved by promoting dynamics of *otredad* or "othering" in any given pedagogic setting. We should make clear, however, that the GSC adopts a radical re-thinking of the concept of othering that subverts how the term has been understood in the U.S. and European academy. Within patriarchal, colonial and hierarchical contexts, *otredad* can function as a social mechanism that strips individuals of their humanity by always defining them according to their extreme alterity in relationship to a hegemonic "self." For example, psychoanalytic feminist scholarship has argued for decades against the objectification of women through the enactment and promotion of the male gaze in film and media, a process whereby women become the "other" and men adopt the hegemonic "self" or "I". Critical race and anti-colonial epistemologies also hold up *otredad* as an insidious social construct that has contributed to the marginalization and subordination of entire populations. Though the pedagogies of the GSC also understand the formation of the "self" through the existence of the "other," *otredad* within Gigi's pedagogic map focuses more on how to collectively build up a student's *autoconcepto* through a lovingly collective process. The goal is to have students realize that their *autonconcepto* takes on meaning in the ideas and thoughts of others whom they need to respect, validate and acknowledge. When participating in an arts activity within the GSC, a student's *autoconcepto* is redefined in a positive way through their relationship with others during the entire creative/productive process. This notion of *otredad* was largely inspired by the work of Mexican poet Octavio Paz who, through his writing, understood that his sense of self was incomplete or simply non-existent without the presence of others. In his 1957 poem "Piedra de sol" ("Sunstone") Paz proclaims the importance of our connection to others when building our *autoconcepto* but he also refuses to privilege a dominant or supreme "self" or "I" that must subordinate others. He insists that the "self" easily becomes the "other" in the minds of those who surround us by stating that "self" <u>must</u> also become the "other" in order to exist. In other words, *otredad* promotes the notion that the "other" is always contained in the "self." In her GSC pedagogies, Gigi activates the creativity in her students by coordinating and guiding their relationships with their peers and by encouraging in them a consciousness of *otredad*. These are the building blocks for creating an artistic community that does not need its participants to possess any particular technical abilities or art skills given that the pedagogic goal is to create a meaningful experience through collaborative work in a potentially disruptive urban space. This meaningful experience can only be forged if students and teacher alike actively embrace the notion that their subjectivity can only exist through the experiences of others.

Gigi created GSC in reaction to the rigid and static pedagogic approaches to education she witnessed in Chile, approaches that are not unique to the country. In other words, she reacted against what Paulo Freire called the banking style of education whereby the teacher "deposits" knowledge on students and they, in turn, "receive, memorize and repeat."[4] This banking approach prevents students from developing "a critical consciousness which would result from their intervention in the world as transformers of that world."[5] Moreover, the banking style of education also thrives when educators rely on static pedagogies that insist students should only act as passive receptacles of a teacher's banking practices. Gigi wanted to formulate a method of teaching capable of adapting to the changing needs of students, one that no longer held up the misconception that old educational paradigms of banking could still be effective on the millennial generations. One of those paradigms is the judgment and punishment system whereby teachers pass judgement on a student's work and then devise a series of punishments for unsatisfactory performance. Judgement and punishment is often put into practice when students fail to properly process a teacher's banking method. Errors, mistakes and missteps are reprimanded, as they are often a sign of failure. The only motivation for learning within this framework is the fear of receiving a negative evaluation or bad grade. In the GSC Gigi encourages students, in particular children, to value their so-called mistakes, to see them as an integral part of their artistic process. Because many of the GSC students come from the Chilean public school system, they had a tendency tear up their drawings in frustration when they saw that their work did not look "right"; in other words, they engaged in acts of self-punishment which mirrored the punitive practices they experienced in school. Low self-esteem is built through the negativity of such punitive practices so the work of the GSC is to break with many of the internalized notions of who the students are and what they can do. The moment they are able to break with those patterns of thought and create something they previously felt incapable of doing, teacher and student alike experience a moment of immense joy and satisfaction. When a student makes such a breakthrough, it becomes important for the teacher to highlight that accomplishment by sharing it with other participants in the workshop or class.

As an educator within the GSC the goal is not to teach "students" but to work with *people* in all the dimensions of their being. As such, the GSC's approach betrays affinities with Anita Revilla's concept of a muxerista pedagogy which seeks to understand a student's holistic needs and actively values their experiential knowledge.[6] These approaches, in turn, enable the teacher to legitimize a student's full personhood. When a student is afforded full personhood, a dynamic of respect and collectivity can occur. Personhood and respect can happen through simple gestures such as sharing a can of spray paint while working on a graffiti mural or having a conversation about what to create or plan out an arts project. Within the GSC Gigi seeks to construct a space that becomes a site of reciprocal trust, respect and collaboration, one that is inclusive of all levels of learning and abilities. This kind of space is necessary in order to establish a dynamic of creativity. Yet many educational systems, which include the great majority of those in Latin America and the United States, are not equipped to implement pedagogies that afford learners a sense of personhood because students themselves are not central axes in their policies. Quantifiable measures of "success," standardized testing and financial viability are often more important considerations when it comes to crafting policies in public education.

Moreover, Gigi tapped into the survival tactics often utilized by street artists who contend with the challenges of working in urban spaces but who also capitalize on the rewards afforded by those same spaces. Challenges can include harassment from passersby and law enforcement, as well as the unpredictable circumstances of working outside (such as bad weather, high foot and car traffic, etc.) Within the GSC, however, it was important for participants to appreciate the rewards and benefits of working on the street, the various different intimacies and relationships of trust that emerge organically from working together. Gigi has often commented to Guisela that her students, in the process of working collectively and in a public space, often let their guard down and share intimate aspects of their lives with other students and the teacher. The atmosphere of mutual support and legitimization that is often built within the GSC often leads to expression of intimacy and vulnerability among its participants. Moreover, doing collaborative work on the streets allows students to understand that creating art in a community setting—rather than an enclosed studio or classroom—also enhances their social skills and ability to relate to others in positive ways. Those relations may also extend to those communities that may live in the area where the work is being done. Regardless of whether the response of local people is encouraging or disapproving, the GSC expects students to treat these populations with respect, always legitimizing their right to assess the street art being created amidst their living spaces.

Within the GSC, deep reflections upon the role of the teacher are critical to the pedagogy of the project. The teacher must be in a constant state of transformation, always adapting oneself to the needs of students. Chicana feminist pedagogue C. Alejandra Elenes argues that transformative learning cannot happen if dualistic and monolithic teacher/student identities are maintained.[7] Teachers must understand the tremendous power they have over students and thus be careful not to wield that power in damaging ways. In her writings on feminist pedagogy, bell hooks observed the hurtful ways professors imposed themselves in her college classrooms, arguing that they "often used the classroom to enact rituals of control that were about domination and the unjust exercise of power."[8] This power is not just about affecting the students' future by granting them a good or bad grade, but it is also about having a decisive influence upon how they see themselves and their capacities. Upon learning their role in society teachers will inevitably transform themselves into social activists because they will gain a sense of tremendous responsibility. This transformation requires that educators routinely engage in the practice of self-reflection prompting them to constantly evaluate their praxis and question their ability to empower their students. Far from promoting self-doubt and insecurity in the educator, this practice allows for an honest assessment of the self with the purposes of avoiding complacency and gaining greater satisfaction in the practice of radical pedagogy.

Within the GSC, Gigi often takes on the role of a Creative Guide rather than a teacher. Creative Guides situate the process of learning/teaching within a horizontal and non-hierarchical context. They seek to systematically develop and explore the creative potential of their students and they do so by placing students at the center of an environment of equality, respect and collaboration. This environment, facilitated by the Creative Guide, yields multiple opportunities for creative development. Learning is guided and the modes of instruction are adapted to the individual needs of students. Gigi devised the pedagogical praxis of the Creative Guide from her experiences as a teacher but also as a graffiti artist working in urban spaces. These unique perspectives have allowed Gigi to become a Creative Guide who is able to conjugate various factors in her pedagogy: context, training, access, self-esteem and *autoconcepto*. Through this approach the Creative Guide can activate and accelerate a student's creative potential while also validating their experience and educational background. A graffiti pedagogy, Janice Rahn tells us, requires educators to do research "into the changes affecting the daily lives of their students."[9]

While the Creative Guide or teacher within the GSC labors to adapt to the needs of students, this instructor also encourages and expects certain adaptations and productive behaviors on their part. Thus, promoting the practice of *autorregulación* (self-regulation) becomes instrumental for the creation of a learning space in the GSC. The concept has been defined by Colombian critical pedagogues María Luisa Aguirre, Juan Carlos Mesa, Helen Morales and Eliana Saldarriaga as "the ability to control our own emotions and impulses in order to adapt them to a particular objective."[10] The idea is not to cut people off from their emotions but rather to direct them

Graffiti School Comunidad

in productive ways while also making them accountable for their actions. As a matter of fact, the Creative Guide needs to value and legitimize all emotions yet must also gently coax their students into evaluating their own internal processes. GSC workshops and sessions often consist of the co-creation of a mural, a graffiti piece or art project that requires participants to work collaboratively so *autoregulación* becomes a key component for that process. Challenges and difficulties will often emerge in a collaboration, so encouraging participants to reflect upon and productively manage their own emotional responses to the collaborative process will enhance the quality of a creative community. There is an important relationship between *autoregulación* and the methodology for collaborative projects that Gigi enacts in the GSC. This methodology seeks to consolidate a creative community that aspires to integrate all their participants, valuing the diversity of each group. Through the promotion of *autoregulación*, participants naturally develop social and emotional abilities such as respect and empathy. Even though these can be regarded as individual skills that students are encouraged to internalize through the process of *autoregulación*, these cannot be accomplished without forging loving relationships with others. Moreover, positive and constructive feedback from the Creative Guide and peers alike becomes the means by which *otredad* activates *autoregulación;* participants get the opportunity to see their creative development take shape in the eyes of others while at the same time understanding how their emotional self-awareness allows for creative exchanges to take place. Ultimately, *autoregulación* is about promoting the coalescence of an individual and group consciousness among GSC participants. When we gain an understanding of how we learn, what we like, how we communicate think and feel, we are able to consolidate the internal image that we have of ourselves, but we can't do so without regulating our subjectivity in relationship to those who surround us.

We will now turn to a specific practice enacted by the GSC in order to better highlight the feminist graffiti pedagogies described above. While we are aware that these approaches can be utilized in numerous educational contexts, not just within the GSC itself, we are also cognizant that the convergence of theory and practice can bring into sharper focus the real-world possibilities of a feminist urban pedagogy. Moreover, the pedagogic art actions outlined below will exemplify how these approaches to teaching art can be applicable and productive in transnational settings even though Gigi developed these techniques within the specificity of Chilean social contexts.

During the spring semester of 2016 Gigi accepted Guisela's invitation to The Ohio State University (OSU) with the purposes of creating a graffiti mural in the Department of Women's, Gender and Sexuality Studies (WGSS). The idea was for Gigi to instruct Guisela and the staff of the department on how to create a mural using graffiti techniques while also teaching us how to use the practices of *otredad* and *autoregulación* to work collaboratively with one another. It was during this collaboration that Guisela realized that her relationship with Gigi was not just that of a colleague and friend, but also that of a student and teacher. This invitation also coincided with Guisela's tenure as interim chair of the department, a position that allowed her to facilitate meaningful collaborations between Gigi and local communities. Guisela had entered into the chairship of a department that was quite unique in that the staff—Lynaya Elliot, Tess Pugsley and Jackie Stotlar (all graduates of our WGSS programs at the time)—actively participated in the feminist vision and mission of the department. The idea that Gigi could create a mural inside the departmental offices emerged organically from Guisela's conversations with the staff about the different ways they could enhance their own work space while also making it a welcoming environment for the feminist, queer, non-white and activist populations we served, be they students, faculty, other staff or community activists.

The process of creating the WGSS graffiti mural began with collective and transnational conversations between the staff, Gigi and Guisela over email and Skype prior to the artist's arrival in the United States. We hoped that the graffiti mural, situated at the entrance of our offices, would signal a shift in modes of thinking, indicating to those who visit our department that they are entering a space that promotes egalitarian and democratic social relations between students, faculty, staff and others at the university. We wanted to produce an image that was both specific but also broadly symbolic of a feminist and decolonial consciousness while also remaining attentive to the importance of a feminist education. The WGSS graffiti mural would focus on a single allegorical figure that could speak of the feminist intellectual mission of our department. This figure would then be surrounded by various attributes alluding to local indigenous environments in the state of Ohio. Gigi's experience with incorporating Andean indigenous motifs into graffiti aesthetics in Chile proved to be quite helpful in this respect. The staff shared various photographs and images of the local natural environment so that the artist could get a sense of our location while still in Chile. Gigi also proposed that the central allegorical figure reveal a maze of knowledge through its head, a motif that would allude to the power of feminist intellectual thought. As a result of these transnational brainstorming and dialogue sessions, Gigi created a digital sketch with the overall composition and design of the mural (Figure 21.1), an image that we approved as a group. During these online brainstorming sessions, Gigi actively built up our individual *autoconceptos,* as none of us had any experience with creating murals or graffiti and thus did not really feel confident in our ability to carry out this project. She actively legitimized our ideas and proposals by creating a truly exciting and innovative mural sketch. It was clear to us that the sketch came not from our isolated individualities but rather from our expressions of *otredad* whereby our unique contributions to the collaborative press were enhanced by the creative input of one another.

By the time Gigi arrived on the OSU campus, we had established a clear path toward the vision for this graffiti mural, though Lynaya, Tess, Jackie and Guisela were still unsure whether they were capable of turning that digital sketch into a wall image. Nevertheless, after numerous introductions, informal tours of the university campus and countless trips to local art stores for

Figure 21.1   Gigi (Marjorie Peñailillo), *Formación* (2016), digital sketch.

spray paint, latex, rollers, brushes and other arts materials, we all hit the ground running, so to speak. Gigi capitalized on the fact that Guisela and the staff had previously established a positive relationship of collaboration through which *otredad* and *autoregulación* were constant practices in the work space. But while we had worked collaboratively to run the department, cultivating a relationship of mutual respect and shared knowledge in the process, we were all new to the idea that we could be empowered as learning subjects through Gigi's community-based pedagogy.

Work began over a weekend when Gigi and Guisela prepared the wall for the mural by cleaning it and painting over it with a blue background using rollers and large paint brushes. Though this was a simple task, it was significant for Guisela who regarded that blue wall as an important foundation for the graffiti mural to come. After they finished this preliminary preparation, Tess joined the two to sketch out the mural's numerous figures using quick and sketchy lines with a paintbrush (Figure 21.2). Some feelings of uncertainty and self-doubt came over the group at that point, as we suddenly felt insecure about our ability to transfer the small digital sketch Gigi had made into the large-scale format of the wall. The artist understood that she had to build up our individual *autoconceptos*, in other words, she had to enhance our internal assessments of ourselves. She did so by putting her full trust in our abilities without having any prior knowledge of what we could actually do artistically. Jackie recalled being surprised by the level of participation that the artist expected from us: "I didn't necessarily connect that we were actually going to do it. I thought we would just assist, watch or do a backdrop, something really minimal. I didn't realize quite how much we were going to do."[11] Lynaya remembered

Figure 21.2 Tess Pugsley and Guisela Latorre working on outlines for *Formación* (2016). The Ohio State University, United States.

that when she began working on the wall she "was nervous and that made me feel apprehensive about it, but Gigi snuffed out my anxiety. She just didn't give [my hesitation] any airtime."[12] Indeed, Gigi expected deep involvement from us while also refusing to replicate or legitimize our own insecurities. She constantly praised our work in honest and thoughtful ways which further built up our *autoconcepto* as artists.

Gigi's approach to the WGSS graffiti mural consisted of building up the image in layers, with each "deposit" of paint adding greater complexity, volume and detail to the wall surface. Guisela came to realize that such an approach was also symptomatic of how she built up our *autoceptos,* one layer at a time. Our next step was then to paint the broad color areas of the graffiti mural. With Lynaya and Jackie now joining the crew, this stage required the use of spray paint for the first time in the process. But bringing out the aerosol cans brought back those feelings of uncertainty again, as Guisela, Jackie, Lynaya and Tess were particularly worried about being able to handle and control this medium. Unconcerned with our lack of experience, Gigi went to great lengths to instruct us on best practices in the use of aerosol, telling us that we should always direct the spray at an angle in relation to the wall while also advising us to keep the can in constant motion as to prevent unwanted drips.

What began as timid strokes on the wall on our part soon morphed into an all-out aerosol attack (Figure 21.3). The excitement of our group's new-found aerosol skills coupled with the realization that the general design of the mural was quickly taking shape filled us with a sense of exhilaration and euphoria. This excitement, however, did not mean that we abandoned the

Figure 21.3 Lynaya Elliott, Jackie Stotlar and Tess Pugsley working on *Formación* (2016). The Ohio State University, United States.

practice of *autoregulación*. We were all working within a rather crammed space, as the mural surface was a fairly small one (approximately 9 by 20 feet) so it was important that we respected each other's spaces and yielded opportunities to one another for self-expression. Such a dynamic would not have been possible without a conscious practice of *autoregulación*. When we finalized the details, volume and shading to the figures and objects in the iconography—as well as putting the finishing touches on the wall—the first WGSS mural at OSU had become a reality. The resulting composition and iconography of the WGSS mural centered around a central figure, a gender non-binary being, neither a man or a woman or perhaps both (Figure 21.4). This figure, rendered completely in shades of blue, appears to ascend from a body of water as they return the viewer's gaze. They wear a mask over their eyes, not unlike those worn in Andean indigenous ceremonies and rituals thus reflecting an important influence upon Gigi's work. From this mask, two large tree branches extend horizontally as they support local wildlife: a cardinal, a white trillium flower and a coccinellidae or ladybug. In the WGSS departmental website our group described the maze that is revealed through the central figure's head as a mind that is "visibly open to multiple and complex possibilities."[13] This iconography inspired us to title the mural, *Formación*, because, as we stated in our artists' statement, the concept represents "the constant state of becoming and formation that is at the core of non-oppressive and anti-colonial thinking. *Formación* thus celebrates ambivalent, in-between and continually evolving states of being."[14] The word "formación" also stood for our own learning process in the course of creating this graffiti mural. Working with Gigi helped us realize that learning and teaching too should always

Figure 21.4 Gigi (Marjorie Peñailillo), Lynaya Elliott, Guisela Latorre, Tess Pugsley and Jackie Stotlar, *Formación* (2016), graffiti mural, Department of Women's, Gender and Sexuality Studies, The Ohio State University, United States.

be in a constant state of formation, continually adapting itself to different circumstances and to the ever-changing and dynamic subjectivities of its diverse participants.

To conclude, in the GSC Gigi has developed radical pedagogies that aspire to empower students by working on their sense of self in relationship to others. This approach, however, has necessitated that Gigi challenge and resist the norms of institutionalized education in Chile and elsewhere. Such a posture has posed serious challenges for the artist who has faced rejection and lack of understanding from the Chilean educational establishment that is still invested in patriarchal and hierarchical models of education. It was both the innovative character of her work coupled with her inherent critique of hegemonic educational practices that Guisela sought to highlight in this chapter. It was also important for her to underscore how she gained a profound understanding of Gigi's pedagogies in the GSC by closely studying her theories but also by actively partaking in an arts project guided by the artist. We thus endorse the nexus of collaboration, sustained dialogue and embodied practice that allowed us to write this chapter, for the convergence of these three epistemologies generated a dynamic space for us to theorize about feminist arts pedagogies.

Notes

1   Jennifer Scanlon, "Keeping Our Activist Selves Alive in the Classroom: Feminist Pedagogy and Political Activism," *Feminist Teacher* 7:2 (Spring 1993), 8.
2   For more information on the contemporary Chilean views and discourses on feminism and gender inequality see Claudia Mora, ed., *Desigualdad en Chile: La Continua Relenacia del Género* (Santiago: Ediciones Universidad Alberto Hurtado, 2013).
3   Janice Rahn, *Painting Without Permission: Hip-Hop Graffiti Subculture* (Westport, CT: Bergin & Garvey, 2002), 187.
4   Paulo Freire, *Pedagogy of the Oppressed,* 30th Anniversary Edition, translated by Myra Bergman Ramos (New York: Continuum, 2005), 72.
5   Ibid., 73.
6   Anita Tejerina Revilla, "Muxerista Pedagogy: Raza Womyn Teaching Social Justice," *The High School Journal* 87:4 (April–May 2004), 83.
7   C. Alejandra Elenes, "Transformando Fronteras: Chicana Feminist Transformative Pedagogies," in *Education Feminism: Classic and Contemporary Readings,* eds. Barbara J. Thayer-Bacon et al. (Albany, NY: State University of New York Press, 2013), 344.
8   bell hooks, *Teaching to Transgress: Education as the Practice of Freedom,* Kindle Edition (New York: Routledge, 1994), location 135 of 3427.
9   Rahn 183.
10 María Luisa Aguirre Osorio et al. "La comunicación asertiva: Herramienta de la práctica pedagógica que permite mediar las dificultades en el aprendizaje," Proyecto y Práctica Pedagógica, Licenciatura en Educación Especial, Universidad de Antioquia, Medellín, Colombia, 2008. Online text: http://ayura. udea.edu.co:8080/jspui/bitstream/123456789/814/1/D0207.pdf (accessed on September 10, 2017).
11 Interview with Lynaya Elliott, Tess Pugsley and Jackie Stotlar, Columbus, Ohio, May 9, 2017.
12 Ibid.
13 "New Mural in WGSS Office," March 31, 2016, Department of Women's, Gender and Sexuality Studies, The Ohio State University: https://wgss.osu.edu/news/new-mural-wgss-office (accessed on September 11, 2017).
14 Ibid.

22

CONTEMPORARY AMERINDIAN IMAGINARIES AND THE CHALLENGE OF INTERSECTIONAL ANALYSIS

Arij Ouweneel

Over 20 years ago, I visited the art gallery of Maya painter Salvador Reanda Quiejú in Santiago Atitlán, Guatemala. Santiago is a Maya city, not a town or a village. Its inhabitants consider themselves city dwellers, not peasants. "We have always been urbanites," one of the Tz'utujil Maya neighbors of Reanda Quiejú told me. "Chuitinamit [the pre-Hispanic name of the city] was not as big as Tenochtitlán [the Aztec capital] but life was the same." True or not, most of Santiago's 45,000 Tz'utujil Maya see themselves as modern, globalized citizens. Some 1,500 miles to the Southeast on the continent, Aymara painter Rosmery Mamani Ventura shares a similar lifestyle. El Alto, bordering Bolivia's capital La Paz, truly is a huge, globalized city and its 675,000 Aymara speaking inhabitants do indeed lead the life of our contemporary urban times. However, when they express themselves in art, old themes loom up. For example, the major role of the elderly and the ancestors return time and again in their work, as do community activities and cyclical time. Sara Shahriari from the *Indian Country Today* website asked Rosmery Mamani "What attracts you to portraits?" The painter responded: "With a portrait it is as if that person is gazing at you and saying 'Look at me. I am telling you this, I feel this,' and that attracts me to portraiture, because it makes direct contact with the viewer. I love to draw elderly people, children, and women—I've also drawn men but not often, mostly older women. [...] The women who come to ask for money in the streets are people from my communities, they are my own blood, my own people, and that's why I want to draw them—because I am myself, and I see myself in them." (Shahriari, 2013)

Respecting and even venerating the elderly and the ancestors as the caretakers of communities is typically Amerindian and that is what unifies the paintings by Salvador Reanda Quiejú and Rosmery Mamani Ventura. All over Latin America, Amerindian groups, associations, communities and individuals use the creative media of textiles, of canvas and city walls, of theater stages and public places, of fiction and documentary film screens, of video clips and festival stages, and the power of the printed word to protest against the effects of nineteenth and twentieth-century internal colonialism, against contemporary neo-colonial tendencies of mining and timber logging, against social and economic exclusion, and cultural and social inequalities, usually pointing at the intersectionality of power arrangements behind most of these wrongs—today sometimes specified as *colonialidad* (Quijano, 1992 and 2000). In many instances, their works of art plead for socio-cultural decolonization. This falls within the parameters of intersectionality research

(Simien and Hancock, 2011; Choo and Ferree, 2010; Cho et al., 2013), but most of it would fall under the denominator of identity, not gender or sex in particular. In fact, in a volume on intersectionally stigmatized groups and populations, addressing in particular the intersection of sex and gender, the Amerindian world seems to contribute with silence.

To do or not to do

What is Amerindian? The Cacaxtla "Battle Mural" to the South of the city of Tlaxcala, Mexico, made around the year 700, shows a bloody scene with Jaguar Knights slaughtering Eagle Knights (Lombardo, 1986). It is a sacrifice or ritual combat, organized to end certain cycles and start new ones. Because the goal of the battle had been blood sacrifice, not victory, the captured Eagle Knights were probably not defeated but sacrificed to feed the divine powers. For the rulers and "victors" it meant "to feed and be fed," as historian Susan Ramírez once explained the crux of pre-Hispanic—and post-Conquest—Andean culture (Ramírez, 2005). It seems that in general terms in the Amerindian world, the victor would be caretaker and the defeated the one that is taken care of. Such sacrifices were often to end a cycle and start a new one. The sheer consequence of this type of cyclical thinking is an attitude of *non-defeat* in which the ones with the Upper Hand (the sacrificers, the "victors of the battle," the "conquerors") *take care of* the ones who ended up with the Lower Hand (the ones being sacrificed, the "conquered") (on non-defeat see also: Gose, 2008, who argues that in the Andes, conquerors were usually symbolically received as ancestors or as a group of people with a common ancestor).

The story told on the Cacaxtla murals is pre-Hispanic, therefore: indigenous. Can we see the paintings by Salvador Reanda Quiejú and Rosmery Mamani Ventura as such? No doubt, in our popular, political, journalistic, and scholarly work we would *ethnotype* them as "indigenous"—or as *indígenas* in Spanish. Rooted in commonplace and hearsay, ethnotypes are based on stereotyping of "ethnically" labelled categories of self and other in communication and interaction (Leerssen, 2016; Beller and Leerssen, 2007, xiii). This means that it may not be relevant to look for the "real" person behind the ethnotype, but focus instead on the use of ethnotypes by the artists or the public, thereby working with "*imaginated*" (Beller and Leerssen 2007, xiv; italics in original) characterizations and attributes that are difficult to articulate with social science research or statements of fact. After several decades reading into the cultural and social science scholarship of "ethnicities" in Latin America, I believe this is how such "ethnicities" work. I seriously doubt if we can be sure who is *indígena*, *mestizo* or *cholo* (see also Canessa, 2007 and 2012). The "indigenous" today has become a wide array of viewpoints and articulated to large variety of cultural products that go beyond set identities. This would make it very difficult indeed to establish beyond doubt and debate what is for example "indigenous" art and what is not.

My hesitation is underscored by studies like Roger Magazine's *The Village is Like a Wheel* (2012). The village in question is Tepetlaoxtoc in the Texcoco area east of Mexico City. In the Spanish era it was a *pueblo de indios* and fell under the jurisdiction of the *república de indios* and its *juzgado de indios* (Borah, 1983; Ouweneel, 1996). Magazine suggests that if we would map local culture, we could end up filling in a cultural continuum. Despite the rural occupation of fattening cattle, the villagers are occupied with other typically urban capitalist activities such as wage labourer in construction work, salaried employee in the city, or worker in a *maquila* assembling clothes, all of which posit them on the continuum near or among the city people of adjacent Mexico City. Their patterns of consumption are almost "city-like" in that they buy machines and urban household goods including televisions and computer gear. The dichotomous approach of "indigenous"/"non-indigenous" is hard to verify, also because the designations *nahua* and *indígena* are gradually disappearing from the Texcoco area. The old language is

Contemporary Amerindian imaginaries and the challenge of intersectional analysis

still spoken in parts of the towns in the area, but in general Spanish has become more prevalent over time. In Mexico City, I remember, people spoke of them as *mestizos*; others did see them as *indígenas*. *Mestizos* are categorized in a biological way as "mixed bloods." But very little of this "mixing" can be recognized in Tepetlaoxtoc—or, indeed, elsewhere.

Nevertheless, in Tepetlaoxtoc the population enthusiastically cherishes a communal way of living that Magazine describes as "motivating others to act." These "communal ways of living" would certainly qualify elsewhere in Latin America as *indígena*, as for example for the Mapuche in Chile. The "collective" action finds its quintessential purpose in making other community members be active in *doing* things together for a common purpose. The family functions not simply for biological reproduction but also for a kind of reproducing this *doing*. Helping and assisting family members is not an end in itself; it is the means to creating active subjectivity in each family member. The same can be said of the local fiesta system: the fiestas are not an end in themselves, but a means to *activate* the community members by coaxing them to work together, or, better perhaps, to perform being the community. The "community" does not collectively produce artefacts like fiestas and family networks, but through these artefacts produce *itself* as active subjectivities in its constituting members. Community members, who do not participate this way, fall outside the community; outsiders that actively participate are welcomed in.

These activities in Tepetlaoxtoc have ancient roots but they are not recognized by the people themselves as something *indígena*. This is because the usual mode identifies the "indigenous" by its produced artefacts as identity markers—such as traditions, social structures, rituals, myths, and so forth. Magazine argues that the "indigenous" "had never defined themselves in terms of things [...] that they had produced and possessed, and so such a definition had to be invented for the sake of government agencies or other actors that do recognize another through its culture" (Magazine, 2012, p. 105). Magazine maintains that identity markers in the Texcoco towns have little meaning for people "who do not share our [global northern] notions of culture, self, and otherness" (105). For these townspeople, their cultural products are conduits or by-products of "actions directed toward the production of active subjects"; of a *doing* that would involve individuals together. Note that this moves away from the traditional way of looking at *indígenas*, *cholos*, or *mestizos* from a personality theory framing—as integrated "people"—towards a theory of action. Venerating ancestors, filial piety, the attitude of taking-care, feeling non-defeated (*Oppressed But Not Defeated* says Rivera Cusicanqui, 1987), and bringing the community into motion are *doings*.

In line with Anna Carasthathis's (2013) ideas of identity categories as potential coalitions, I prefer to use the word *Amerindian* as a genealogical container concept for *indígenas*, *mestizos* and *cholos* alike. This can be underpinned using the insights of cognitive science. A cognitive scholar tends to look at what people *do* and much less so at what people *are* (if this is at all possible), or *say* what they are. In this case, the concepts point at *doings* that have a shared genealogical history of pre-Hispanic past and/or 300 years under Spanish rule and its prolongation under the national rule in the nineteenth and twentieth centuries. For centuries they were part of the doings of the members inscribed in the *república de indios* as *indios*, and also later, at least until the 1990s (as I can tell from ethnology), many were still seen as *indios*; later as *campesinos*. Action and behavior embedded in this shared history of how to do things are encoded in the brain in the form of cognitive schemas. Although in different scholarly fields these cognitive mental representations are also known as mental models, cultural scripts or frames, I prefer the word schema. Cognitive schemas are the building blocks of memory, using real or imagined knowledge of a class of people, objects, events, situations, and behavioral codes, in order to act and behave (Nishida, 1999, 775).

This does not mean that we may identify *Amerindian doings* (acts, actions, behavior) in for example works of art regardless of the person who made it. Therefore, I believe we have at least two parameters more. The second parameter says that an "Amerindian doing" must be made by people who share more than one Amerindian schema. This means that if I make a painting of an old Maya it is not Maya art. Furthermore, the definition of Amerindian also requires that at least a third parameter is involved: an Amerindian family genealogy. Specific schemas do not come by themselves. Cognitive schemas contain encoded information relevant in particular situations, places or between groups of people—believed likely to occur and used to guide our behavior in familiar situations. That is the reason to recognize complexes of local schemas as the culture people inherit. Cognitive schemas "live" at a certain spot in time. They are handed over generation by generation through *doing*—including storytelling. People who share these parameters share a number of cognitive schemas encoded in their memory and may therefore be seen as an Amerindian mnemonic community. I believe that *indígenas*, *mestizos* and *cholos* do form an Amerindian mnemonic community. So, instead of discussing *Amerindian* imaginaries I like to focus on Amerindian *imaginaries*.

Maya voices

The art of Maya painters like Salvador Reanda Quiejú falls within the Amerindian schemas discussed above. In the 1990s, the artists from the Tzútuhil towns at the border of Lake Atitlán in Central Guatemala—Santiago Atitlán, San Pedro la Laguna and San Juan la Laguna—and the Kaqchikel town of San Juan Comalapa painted Mayan "communities in action"; in the Arte Naif style (Cofiño et al, 2001). The number of painters is significant. A decade ago, San Pedro la Laguna, for example, counted a population of about 10,000 but had 40 oil painters. These Mayas are self-taught and all paint with oil on canvas although some do also make watercolors; in San Pedro and San Juan entirely with brushes. The first painter in San Pedro, Rafael González y González, made his first painting in 1929 with mixed aniline dyes and the sap of a local tree; and with brushes made from his own thick hair. He later trained some of his children and grand-children in painting. In Santiago Atitlán, the first painter was Juan Sisay and he began painting around 1950. He had exhibitions and won prizes for his paintings in the US and Europe. Over the years, a local style emerged in Santiago and the Tz'utuhil towns.

The Maya paintings seem to be intended as a device to protect Maya culture by educating the Maya audience—and the tourists as well—on how things are being done in their world. The paintings are a motivating force. In the globalizing culture full of exchange by tourism and after a few decades of devastating civil war followed by the rapid expansion of Radical Evangelical Protestantism, the old ways in the Maya towns are under threat or have disappeared. But by looking at the future by looking at the past, we see how the work on the land should be done—especially collective work in the coffee fields—and how women should work at the looms at home. Another theme is the adoration of the saints in general; at home, in church, on the street (processions). These are activities especially under pressure these days; but nevertheless, painted with love and consent, so it seems, by evangelical Maya painters. In short, their paintings are rather conservative. A good example is Miguel Chávez from Santiago Atitlán. We see village leaders—men, as always—asking the saint for support. What appears to be one of their wives sits on the ground, assisting them. To the left stands the powerful, wealthy and popular saint Maximón, who fulfills spiritual, political and material wishes—as long as he receives "appropriate" gifts, because he feeds after being fed (Carlsen, 1997, pp. 152–153).

A change of medium does not help. For example, if we look at the emerging Maya hip-hop culture in Guatemala's rural areas, we notice again the absence of the more common themes in intersectionality research. Maya rappers of the Balam Ajpu band—Tz'utu Baktun Kan (René Dionisio), M.C.H.E. (Yefry Pacheco), Dr. Nativo (Juan Martínez) and Danilo

Rodríguez—use their trade to educate local youngsters about traditional Maya values in the cities of Quetzaltenango and San Marcos, and the smaller town of San Pedro la Laguna (Agencia AP, 2015). Also the four boys of the Tihorappers Crew from Tihosuco in Quintana Roo (Yucatan, Mexico) rap about their life—a "happy life," they say: proud to be Maya, proud to be Mexican, happy to live in peaceful surroundings—to express a socially traditional worldview. Nevertheless, after they posted their song in Maya and Spanish "Estoy Contento" ("I Am Happy") on YouTube, it went viral in no time; eventually reaching over 2.5 million views within a few weeks (Hablutzel, 2016). Band member Christian Augusto (Hablutzel, 2016): "Besides singing in our native tongue and experimenting in a genre that its very interesting, we share our experiences and try to do so in a positive manner. That is why we had such a great response from cyber users all over the world."

However, scholars who like to map themselves "in service to social justice," as Patricia Hill Collins, one of the main theorists of intersectionality, once discussed a few years ago (Collins, 2012), would welcome the contribution to popular culture of *mestiza* Rebeca Lane; she auto-ethnotypes as *mestiza de ascendencia indígena*, mestiza from indigenous origins; and as a bisexual/lesbian. Lane was born into a middle-class family in Guatemala City. Although as a graduated sociologist she published about urban tribes and youth culture—next to a series of poems—she uses rap and hip-hop to reach a larger audience. Also, rap serves her well to fight a culture that made it possible that someone could rape her at 15. She had an abortion. Afterwards, Lane participated in the movement "Ni Una Menos" to protest against violence against women. Since 2000, some 10,000 women have been killed in Guatemala City alone. She lost an aunt—kidnapped and disappeared—during the state terror of the 1980s. She took part in theater plays that speak out for women's rights such as "Las Profanas" (2009), "El Juego" (2009) and "Histéricas y no tanto" (2013), and a comical hip-hop musical (Lane, 2016; Bosch, 2016). In her art she follows Chilean rapper Ana Tijoux, another mestiza fighting discrimination, racism and sexism.

The tyranny of time

The intersection of sex and politics brings us to "cinemasturbation" (Melebeck, 2008). The cinematic masturbation trope uses masturbation on screen to indicate the character's impotence or frustration. Typically, the character is involved in political issues. Several fiction films use the trope: Pablo Larraín's *Tony Manero* (2008, Chile), Carlos Reygadas' *Batalla en el Cielo* (2005, Mexico; *Battle in Heaven*); Josué Méndez's *Dioses* (*Gods*, Peru; 2008); Diego Lerman's *La mirada invisible* (2010, Argentina; *The Invisible Eye*), Murilo Salles' *Nome Próprio* (2007, Brazil; *Camila Jam*), and Marialy's short *Blokes* (2010, Chile). The cinemasturbating characters feel desperate to resolve the situation they are in and realize that they do not know a way out. Another example is the Mexican feature film *Año Bisiesto* or *Leap Year* (2011), directed by Australian playwright and filmmaker Michael Rowe. The film is co-written with Lucía Carrera, who introduced the Mexican elements; no doubt in close cooperation with actress Mónica del Carmen, who is from the former *pueblo* Miahuatlán, Oaxaca. In a television interview Rowe admitted that there were improvisations, causing details to enter the diegesis intuitively and unconsciously. No doubt, also working with the actress for two months before shooting the film must have influenced these details ("Entrevista," 2010). Therefore, the particular narrative of *Leap Year* grows out of the details, bottom-up, into the core of the story of journalist Laura.

Laura (Mónica del Carmen) is a 25-year-old immigrant from a former *pueblo de indios* in Oaxaca who now lives in a small rented apartment in Mexico City. Chronicling what ought to have been the last month of Laura's lonely life, the film is mainly set in one room only, with just a few speaking parts. Having lost her father on the previous February 29, four years earlier, she is certain that she will die the coming 29th. Laura lays about, picks her nose while typing, eats cheap food straight from the tin, has a series of one-night stands she barely enjoys, and she masturbates regularly, mainly while observing the couple across the courtyard—a typical cinemasturbation that represents her impotence to integrate in the city as a migrant and have a "normal" relationship. The only loving relationship in her present days is with her younger brother Raúl (Marco Zapata) who turns up when he is expected as well as when he is not. He still lives in Oaxaca. Signs of a doomed future abound: her relationship with her mother—through a cellphone—deteriorates rapidly, her employer lets her go, and her one-night stands result in a relationship only with Arturo (Gustavo Sánchez Parra), who loves his sex kinky and violent, and we see him slapping and whipping her. However, Arturo, a man in his 40s, is also the first to show some affection and interest in her. Because the sex grows more violent during the month—Laura being asphyxiated and urinated on, and, finally, being burned with cigarettes—and while conscientiously crossing out the calendar of February and realizing that time is running out, Laura invites Arturo to kill her on that doomed 29th—looking at her kitchen knife, Laura recognizes the opportunity (see Figure 22.1). That fatal day, however, expecting Arturo, Raúl shows up. After a small nervous breakdown, Laura takes up life anew, for although nothing gory happened that 29th, after the intervention of her brother Laura could start a new cycle with her brother as urbanites in Mexico City.

Here we realize that Laura's impotence as a migrant is not the only way to look at the film. The idea that time poses a threat, that it can be experienced as tyranny, has developed into a specific Amerindian chronotope (Gossen, 1999; see also the essays in Bender and Wellbery, 1991). Through Amerindian lenses (Bem, 1993), *Leap Year* can indeed be seen as another example of the tyranny of time: another cognitive schema to feed Amerindian imaginaries. As many anthropologists would underscore, members of the Amerindian mnemonic community experience

Figure 22.1 Laura (Mónica del Carmen), *Año bisiesto* (*Leap Year*, 2011), with the knife.

themselves as being in a landscape with the past in front of them and the future behind them. Members of the Amerindian mnemonic community may experience historical patterns more or less like a cycle of maize: seeds grow the same way, agricultural labor is usually always the same, but both are not literary identical. You cannot sow the same seed twice and labor is dependent upon weather conditions as well. It is believed that, humans may influence the cycles by offerings and sacred rituals (Gillespie, 1989; Randall, 1982). This idea was regenerated in the Amerindian world by almost any generation (place, time) for centuries in a row and well into contemporary Latin America. However, there is more, because sometimes between cycles, at moments of disarray and chaos, an Intervening Agent is needed; usually during chaotic times. In *Leap Year*, Laura's brother Raúl plays the part of the Intervening Agent.

In *Leap Year*, Laura continually saw the past of the previous February 29 in front of her. She therefore knew what would happen, read all the signs according to this Amerindian story schema, and acted accordingly by inviting Arturo to end her life. Calendar, loneliness and increasing failure brought Laura to trigger her Mexican time schema. Rowe told his interviewer for the *Producers' Cannes Press Kit* that the script had indeed started as a story about a conservative woman who accepted a sadomasochistic relationship in order to keep her lover from leaving (*Producers*, 2011). True, in general terms this would make *Leap Year* a film about a relationship of power between a *blanco* or *mestizo* and an *indígena*. Although many Mexicanists would agree that this is the storyworld of the Mexicans, it does not explain the conscientiously crossing out of the days on the calendar, the fatal date of February 29, or the ritualistic manner in which Laura prepares her sacrifice. Neither is the remark that Laura suffers from a guilt-ridden relationship with her deceased father. What drives Laura from scene to scene is the inevitability of the drama at the 29th. Whatever the origins of the drama—guilt-ridden or not—she clearly knows there is no escape from the tyranny of time. The disasters in her personal life followed by a cumulative, destructive sadomasochistic sex are its signs. Therefore, Laura decides to pursue this predestined history. That she takes this initiative is Mexican, Rowe said to his interviewer (Jordán, 2010). Therefore, at the end of the film Laura starts influencing and guiding the direction of time towards the fatal date of her sacrifice.

Concluding remarks: Fighting racism and sexism

At the end of this chapter, it is clear that for Amerindian mnemonic community art, the intersection of gender and sex cannot end without intersecting also with race. Perhaps Peruvian painter Claudia Coca is the champion of this, portraying the Amerindian heritage as one—unifying *indígena*, *mestizo* and *cholo*—in order to fight injustice, exclusion and racism from the side of the powerholders in her country: as a female painter, she indeed discusses identity categories as potential coalitions to endorse decolonization. European descendants, who are ethnotyped as *blancos*, *criollos*, or *ladinos* and who have the Upper Hand, would have to hand over that Upper Hand to the *indígenas*, *mestizos*, *cholos*, and *afro-latinos* who have had until that moment the Lower Hand. In Peru, the former position is called *hanan*, the latter *hurin*. As said, the Non-Defeat Schema holds that the hurin side has the right to remove the hanan side from power—which would be a *pachacuti* or turnover—if the latter would not fulfil its promise of "taking care," also called *buen gobierno*. Coca has several paintings instigating the need to pachacuti. *Plebeya 3* (2007) is one of them. The text reads: "Our blood is not different, Lord. Neither is our heart, Lord. So why are we humans not all of equal value?" This short stanza comes from the waltz "El plebeyo" (1930) sung by Alcides Carreño and written by Felipe Pinglo Alva (Caffelli, 2010). *Plebeya 3* is the third in a row of a series on racial discrimination in Lima. Both Pinglo's waltz and Coca's painting express sadness on the incomprehensible and iniquitous consequences of the supposed supremacy of the "white race." As a self-declared *mestiza* (*chola*), Coca declares her solidarity with the population of Andean descent (see the documentary *Pintura Contemporánea Latinoamericana*, 2011; also Shaw, 2011).

Coca believes with many Peruvians that ethnotyping in her country is part of a deeply racist culture: "It's the fear and rejection of the other," she said in an interview (Almenara, 2014). "Many times we are racists out of innocence, out of ignorance, because of our education; of what we learn from textbooks of Peruvian history; of what we saw the way our grandparents have been treated. All of Peru has been built with this sense of shame, above all with this blot of having Andean ancestors" (Almenara, 2014). What plays a part here is that in popular parlance—and also in general academic language—the word *mestizo* refers to a *loss*, to a negation. People ethnotyped as *mestizos* are not *indígena* anymore; only *true indígenas* have the right to be called indigenous. Coca refuses to look at the ethnotyped categories of *mestizo* and *cholo* as loss: "My work serves to demonstrate that mestizaje is enrichment" (Almenara, 2014). Perhaps the appropriation of a negative hetero-image as proud auto-image will help: an idealization of what is seen as the *mestizo* body. In truth, she said, this is urgently required because the ethnotyped *mestizos* have a problem in distinguishing their own "race" ("reconocerse en su propia raza") ("Claudia Coca," 2014). Personally, Coca only felt discrimination in the personal sphere, she said. The mother of one of her boyfriends, for example, had said to her son that she did not like her much "because of the way she was," *chola*. She also remembers that as a child she looked into the mirror, thinking: "If I'm so pretty, why don't they gaze after me?" It is this prejudice that should bring female artists from the Amerindian mnemonic community to contest without hesitation, racism and sexism.

Works cited

Agencia AP. "Raperos guatemaltecos promueven el maya a través del hip hop." *Prensa Libre*, 21 February 2015, www.prensalibre.com/noticias/comunitario/Raperos-guatemaltecos-idioma-Maya-hip_hop-musica_0_1307869225.html. Accessed 20 July 2016.

Almenara, Alonso. "Mi trabajo es mostrar que el mestizaje es un enriquecimiento." *LaMula.pe*, 20 July 2014, https://redaccion.lamula.pe/2014/07/30/mi-trabajo-es-mostrar-que-el-mestizaje-es-un-enriquecimiento/alonsoalmenara/. Accessed 12 October 2014.

Beller, Manfred, and Joep Leerssen, eds. *Imagology: The Cultural Construction and Literary Representation of National Characters. A Critical Survey*. Amsterdam: Rodopi, 2007, pp. xiii–xvi.

Bem, Sandra Lipsitz. *The Lenses of Gender: Transforming the Debate on Sexual Inequality*. New Haven, CT: Yale University Press, 1993.

Bender, John, and David E. Wellbery, eds. *Chronotypes: The Construction of Time*. Stanford, CA: Stanford University Press, 1991.

Borah, Woodrow W. *Justice by Insurance: The General Indian Court of Colonial Mexico and the Legal Aides of the Half Real*, Berkeley, CA: University of California Press, 1983.

Bosch, Andrea. "Rebeca Lane: 'Soy hija de la guerra'." *Pikara Online Magazine*, 11 November 2016, www.pikaramagazine.com/2016/11/rebeca-lane-soy-hija-de-la-guerra/. Accessed 12 December 2016.

Caffelli, Paolo. "Los 10 mejores valses peruanos." *Rincón Peruano*, 1 September 2010, http://rinconperuano.com/musica-criolla/10-mejores-vals-peruanos. Accessed 10 October 2013.

Canessa, Andrew. *Intimate Indigeneities: Race, Sex, and History in the Small Spaces of Andean Life*. Durham, NC: Duke University Press, 2012.

Canessa, Andrew. "Who is Indigenous? Self-Identification, Indigeneity, and Claims to Justice in Contemporary Bolivia." *Urban Anthropology*, Vol. 36, No. 3, 2007, pp. 195–237.

Carasthathis, Anna. "Identity Categories as Potential Coalitions." *Signs*, Vol. 38, No. 4, 2013, pp. 941–965.

Carlsen, Robert S. *The War for the Heart and Soul of a Highland Maya Town*. Austin, TX: University of Texas Press, 1997.

Cho, Sumi, Kimberlé Williams Crenshaw and Leslie McCall. "Toward a Field of Intersectionality Studies: Theory, Applications, and Praxis." *Signs*, Vol. 38, No. 4, 2013, pp. 785–810.

Choo, Hae Yeon, and Myra Marx Ferree. "Practicing Intersectionality in Sociological Research: A Critical Analysis of Inclusions, Interactions, and Institutions in the Study of Inequalities." *Sociological Theory*, Vol. 28, No. 2, 2010, pp. 129–149.

"Claudia Coca y el laberinto de la choledad." *Peru.21*, 20 July 2014, http://peru21.pe/espectaculos/claudia-coca-choledad-racismo-muestra-discriminacion-2192697. Accessed 12 December 2014.

Cofiño, Lucrecia, Lucrecia Méndez de Penedo; Unesco; Fundación Paiz; et al. *Arte naïf: pintura Maya guatemalteca contemporánea*. Paris: UNESCO; and Guatemala: Fundación Paiz para la Educación y la Cultura, 2001.

Collins, Patricia Hill. "Looking Back, Moving Ahead: Scholarship in Service to Social Justice." *Gender and Society*, Vol. 26, No. 1, 2012, pp. 14–22.

"Entrevista Año Bisiesto con Monica del Carmen, Michael Rowe y Gustavo Sanchez Parra, 1ra parte." *YouTube*, uploaded by Homocinefilus, 6 October 2010, www.youtube.com/watch?v=Ytfq82e0rCI. Accessed 14 April 2017.

"Entrevista Año Bisiesto con Monica del Carmen, Michael Rowe y Gustavo Sanchez Parra, 2da parte." *YouTube*, uploaded by Homocinefilus, 6 October 2010, www.youtube.com/watch?v=Cuo2Rbxv__k. Accessed 14 April 2017.

Fischer, Edward F. and Peter Benson. *Broccoli and Desire: Global Connections and Maya Struggles in Postwar Guatemala*. Stanford, CA: Stanford University Press, 2006.

Gillespie, Susan. *The Aztec Kings: The Construction of Rulership in Mexican History*. Tucson, AZ: The University of Arizona Press, 1989.

Gose, Peter. *Invaders as Ancestors: On the Intercultural Making and Unmaking of Spanish Colonialism in the Andes*. Toronto: University of Toronto Press, 2008.

Gossen, Gary H. *Telling Maya Tales: Tzotzil Identities in Modern Mexico*. New York: Routledge, 1999.

Habluzel Pelayo, Andrea. "Preserving Mayan Language with Rap: A Group of Young Men Rap to Preserve and Promote Their Native Tongue." *Mexico News Network*, 2 July 2016, www.mexiconewsnetwork. com/art-culture/preserving-mayan-language-rap/. Accessed 20 July 2016.

Jordán, Carlos. "En México se vive un matriarcado irreductible." *Imcine*, 9 October 2010, www.imcine.gob. mx/en-mxico-se-vive-un-matriarcado-irreductible.html. Accessed 15 November 2011.

Lane, Rebeca. "About." Personal website, www.rebecalane.com/about. Accessed 24 April 2016.

Leerssen, Joep. "Imagology: On Using Ethnicity to Make Sense of the World." *Revue Iberic@l*, No. 10, 2016, pp. 13–31.

Lombardo, Sonia. "Las pinturas de Cacaxtla." *Historias*, Vol. 12, 1986, pp. 3–21.

Magazine, Roger. *The Village Is Like a Wheel: Rethinking Cargos, Family and Ethnicity in Highland Mexico*. Tucson, AZ: University of Arizona Press, 2012.

Melebeck, Julien. "Work in Progress: CinémasturbationS." *Nisimazine*, 18 May 2008, p. 7.

Nishida, Hiroko. "A Cognitive Approach to Intercultural Communication Based on Schema Theory." *International Journal of Intercultural Relations*, Vol. 23, No. 5, 1999, pp. 753–777.

Ouweneel, Arij. *Shadows Over Anáhuac. An Ecological Interpretation of Crisis and Development in Central Mexico, 1730–1800*. Albuquerque, NM: University of New Mexico Press, 1996.

Pintura Contemporánea Latinoamericana, Santiago de Chile: Celfin Capital, Cazuela Films, 2011.

Producers' Cannes Press Kit found at: www.berlinbabylon14.net/ger/presse2010/presskits/press_mexiko.pdf. Accessed 15 November 2011.

Quijano, Aníbal. "Colonialidad y modernidad/racionalidad." *Perú Indígena*, Vol. 13, No. 29, 1992, pp. 11–20.

Quijano, Aníbal. "Coloniality of Power, Eurocentrism, and Latin America." *Nepantla: Views From the South*, Vol. 1, No. 3, 2000, pp. 533–580.

Ramírez, Susan E. *To Feed and Be Fed: The Cosmological Bases of Authority and Identity in the Andes*. Stanford, CA: Stanford University Press, 2005.

Randall, Robert. "Qoyllur Rit'i, an Inca Fiesta of the Pleiades: Reflections on Time and Space in the Andean World." *Bulletin de l'Institut Français d'Études Andines*, Vol. 11, Nos. 1–2, 1982, pp. 37–81.

Rivera Cusicanqui, Silvia. *Oppressed But Not Defeated. Peasant Struggles Among the Aymara and Qhechwa in Bolivia, 1900–1980*. Geneva: United Nations Research Institute for Social Development, 1987; translation of *Oprimidos pero no vencidos: luchas del campesinado aymara y qhechwa, 1900–1980*. La Paz: HISBOL & CSUTCB, 1984.

Shahriari, Sara. "Drawing the Dispossessed: Bolivian Artist Rosmery Mamani Ventura." *Indian Country Today* 25 May 2013, https://indiancountrymedianetwork.com/news/indigenous-peoples/drawing-the-dispossessed-bolivian-artist-rosmery-mamani-ventura/. Accessed 12 April 2017.

Shaw, Edward. *Pintura contemporánea latinoamericana*. Santiago de Chile: Quad Graphics and Celfin Capital, 2011.

Simien, Evelyn M., and Ange-Marie Hancock. "Mini-Symposium: Intersectionality Research." *Political Research Quarterly*, Vol. 64, No. 1, 2011, pp. 185–186.

Vich, Víctor. "Desobediencia simbólica. *Performance*, participación y política al final de la dictadura fujimorista." In *La cultura en las crisis latinoamericanas*, edited by Alejandro Grimson. Buenos Aires: Clacso, 2004, 63–80.

Wiener, Gabiela. "Si soy bonita, ¿por qué no me miran?" *La República*, 17 August 2014, www.larepublica.pe/17-08-2014/si-soy-bonita-por-que-no-me-miran. Accessed 20 August 2014.

23

THE PHOTOGRAPHY OF THOMAZ FARKAS AND THE ESTÁDO DE PACAEMBU

A theatre of Brazilian male homosociality

David William Foster

Inaugurated in 1940, and extensively renovated for the 2014 Olympics, the Estádio de Pacaembu (officially known as the Estádio Municipal Paulo Machado de Carvalho), located in the middle-class neighborhood of Consolação,[1] in central São Paulo, was originally meant to promote the social-nationalistic programs of the Getúlio Vargas government.[2] Vargas came to power via a military coup in 1930 and declared in 1937 a new vision for Brazil called the Estado Novo (which lasted until 1945). How much the Estado Novo was fascistic in nature has been extensively debated, but there is no question that Vargas intended to follow the rule of his European social nationalism mentors in making sports an integral part of the mass mobilization of the populace in the form of unquestioned and unquestionable so-called Brazilian populist values. I have written elsewhere about how the German-Swiss immigrant photographer Hildegard Rosenthal (1913–90), who undertook the first systematic photographic project of the city of São Paulo, provided memorable historic photographs of the fascistic display of the inauguration of the Pacaembu in 1940 (Foster 2011: 55–68). Rosenthal, for personal reasons, discontinued her photographic work on São Paulo. It was left to others to focus on the actual uses of Pacaembu for actual sports events, paradigmatically soccer, which went on to become the largest-grossing sport in Brazil and, increasingly and far beyond Vargas's interest in the ideological uses of populist events, one of that country's most complex sports phenomena. Indeed, soccer journalism, in multiple media venues, is a major cultural undertaking that has yet to be systematically examined for its contributions toward solidifying the sociohistorical meanings of soccer in Brazil, far, far beyond whatever meanings Vargas originally had in mind.

One of the major photographers who has focused his energies on soccer at the Pacaembu stadium, thereby contributing to its perception as a significant institution of São Paulo's urban history, is Thomaz Farkas (1924–2011),[3] also himself a foreign-born immigrant (Hungary). Throughout his long career Farkas, who may be considered one of Brazil's premier professional photographers, did extensive work all over the country. But he was particularly involved in capturing São Paulo's growth, which has been meteoric in the twentieth century, as well as the project for the creation of the modernist capital of Brasília.

Farkas's photography, exclusively in black and white, is marked by the sociocultural phenomenon of homosociality.[4] To put it bluntly, the universe of his art is that of man. While women do appear in a few of his images, it only serves to remind us of how dramatically the many public spaces that Farkas photographed were essentially spaces occupied by a hegemonic masculine presence. This quality is unquestionably present in Rosenthal's work as well: indeed, she is reputed to have used her female personal assistant in some of her compositions to provide some balanced gender representation, as the lack of respectable women in public in Brazil must have been a shock to someone arriving from Weimar Germany. In both instances, however, it is clear that the respective photographic projects are characterizing the gender exclusivity of public spaces, at least as far as an allegedly decent, bourgeois society is concerned.[5] Although one does not want to overgeneralize here, but the predominantly male population of photographic universes such as Farkas's and Rosenthal's is due to the fact that it was simply unacceptable for women of a certain social standing to be alone and unaccompanied in public spaces. Women did go out in public with other women, if not with a proper chaperon (a male family member or an older woman), than with another woman or as a group.[6] Thus, the generalized homosociality of Rosenthal's urban photography of the late 1930s is matched by the similar social phenomenon of Farkas's soccer photography for at least two decades after the inauguration of Pacaembu in 1940. Women did attend soccer matches: this was in part an extension of the class restrictions on paying customers (as opposed to those who saw the matches from external vantage points, as will be commented on below). But even the most superficial perusal of the work represented in Farkas's dossier *Pacaembu* reveals the prevalently masculine audience and therefore the primacy of homosocial interactions.

"Homosociality" has become rather a trendy term, and I must emphasize that I use it here neither as a euphemism or a code word for homosexuality, even though homosexuality may be viewed as a form of a homosociality or as one of its enactments. Whether understood as exclusively male in reference (focusing on the hegemonic power relations between men) or when used with reference to women (either to refer to the reduplication by some women, feminist or otherwise, of the power relations between men or as a sororial bonding between women to resist the impositions of hegemonic male power relations), the concept of homosociality examines the interrelations of same-sex subjects. Homosociality may be understood as the way in which men consolidate, if not render invulnerable, their structures of bonding for the purpose of social dominance. In the process, it may refer especially to those activities that promote that bonding, such as same-sex societies and same-sex privileged activities like the play together or the observing together of sports. On the other hand, homosociality may be viewed as a gateway opportunity to extended same-sex bondings, such as homoaffectivity (the affective pulsion between men and, perhaps, forms of displaying that pulsion) and homoeroticism (anyone of the feelings and representations of those feelings whereby homoaffectivity segues into what is generally understood as homosexual behavior, albeit perhaps more situational than as the consequence of a psychoanalytical conception of deep personal identity).[7] I think that it is important to make a distinction between an attributable, if not explicit, goal of studying homosociality as it occurs in a social institution like sports and, more particularly, soccer and the inevitability of the representation of homosociality because of the unquestioned nature of the social phenomenon being examined. Thus, for example, by saying that life aboard a military ship is predominantly masculine may either lead to an interest in analyzing the dynamics of that circumstance, or it may merely be stating the obvious and undertake to represent that social reality without directly devoting any particular attention to that fact. What emerges circumstantially, however, may be quite another matter. This, I would argue, is what constitutes the most legitimate approach to Farkas's extensive photography of Pacaembu.

The fact that Farkas was so intrigued by the many dimensions of soccer is most assuredly the consequence of its growing importance in Brazilian society, on the cusp of its transition from the diversion of a privileged social class to contemporary mega-commercialization, passing through the determining effect of its manipulation by Vargas's version of the social nationalist state as given status as an institutional paradigm through the construction and eventual utilization of

The Photography of Thomaz Farkas and the Estádo de Pacaembu

the Pacaembu stadium. If Pacaembu is an icon of Brazilian soccer, it is also a major focal point in the construction of soccer audiences, whereby the casual spectacle of soccer as a gentleman's sport crystallizes around projects of a specific nationalistic ideology. The audience for soccer that Pacaembu constructs, and that Farkas so diligently immortalizes in photographs that are only now beginning to be understood as of intense sociohistoric and documentary value just happens, so to speak, to be a homosocial one.

Yet the dynamics of soccer audiences certainly and undeniably echo the masculinist world of the Estado Novo as part of a long line of political projects to affirm male dominance in Brazilian society. This urgency of domination was capped most recently by the long chain of authoritarian dictatorships 1964–85, whose demise has still not fully consolidated a pluralistic society for Brazil, even if soccer may no longer be considered iconic of prevailing social ideologies. Soccer is now more iconic of prevailing late-capitalistic and globalized economic processes of which the Brazilian Everyman (the sexist denomination still has currency) is now not always a fully enabled consumer. In all of these cases, Farkas cannot be demonstrated to have been specifically interested in the homosocial configurations of the soccer audiences, whether ideologically or commercially constructed. But the simple fact that the audiences were, and have remained, if not quite so unanimously, homosocial, makes it possible to approach his photography in these terms. The questions to be answered, therefore, are: What does it mean that soccer audiences are so much a man's world? What does it mean as regards the interactions between spectators and between spectators and, of course, unvaryingly masculine players? And what does this compact universe of pitch and stands signify in terms of the urban space that envelops Pacaembu and yet of which it is such a symbolic institution?[8]

We begin, then, with one of Thomaz's many views of the spectators assembled for a match at the Pacaembu stadium. As is customarily, the stands are packed, shoulder-to-shoulder on presumably hard concrete bleachers, which are unquestionably a test in the endurance of discomfort during the extended time period of the match (wooden benches would not be likely because they would not stand up very long to the heavy rains São Paulo experiences). What is singular about this and other photographs that focus on spectators is, precisely, that spectators are the subject of the photograph and not the game itself.[9] Indeed, Farkas's photographs rarely focus on the pitch. There are some team photographs on the field and a few action shots. But in general the pitch is either absent or only partially to be seen (as in this photograph), and then devoid of any presence of the players. Indeed, the fact that only a sliver of the pitch is seen and that it bleeds off the left margin of the photograph is especially eloquent in denying the importance of the game in and of itself: it is as though the camera were deliberately ignoring the game, and the insignificant sliver of the pitch that is included in a sense affirms its lack of importance. Since nothing is going on in the small segment the camera incorporates, it might as well have shifted to the right and eliminated any view of it at all. The result is in a sense contradictory. The whole purpose of the event for which the spectators have assembled is the game going on down below their assembled human mass, and yet we can see nothing of that game going on, nothing of what was the core motive for this human assembly in the first place: the absent players and their sports competition is the purpose of this human assembly, but that purpose is not only not given any direct representation, but the partial representation of an empty slice of the playing field undercuts the importance of that space as a motivation for the human act of social congregation. If one did not understand the intense allure of soccer and the confluence of people it is capable of generating, one could well assume that the importance of assembly is assembly in and for itself, with no external motivating impulse.

To be sure, that is the point of Farkas's photograph: the importance of assembly in and of itself. Indeed, for the time in which the photograph was executed (best documentary evidence indicates the span 1942–1946), soccer would have been the principal motive to bring people together in a mass display of human subjects. This is a time prior to the practice of sociopolitical demonstration in São Paulo, which is still a relatively tranquil and even provincial city. It is certainly well before the Avenida Paulista, the principal metropolitan thoroughfare of the city and today the financial nerve center of the country and the Latin American continent, became the site for the largest gay rights parade in the world, long before the Paulista could be closed down on Sundays and converted into a several kilometers-long pedestrian mall and the popular venue for a massive city fair, long before it made the transition from a boulevard lined by mansions to a broad avenue lined by institutions of international banking. The São Paulo of the early days of the Pacaembu's draw as the principal soccer stadium in the country,[10] although already a dynamic city, was nevertheless quite bourgeois in its daily life, with a strong enforcement of the "ordem y progresso" motto that appears on the national flag. Never the capital city of Brazil (which has had four established capitals during its unified administrative history) and still not yet the cultural center of the country (Rio would remain that until well into the latter quarter of the twentieth century), São Paulo could only be characterized as irremediably staid.[11] If today São Paulo is now the quintessential postmodern city of Brazil, with all the teaming masses of humanity in full public view that that elastic term implies, at the time of Farkas's photography, the soccer stadium would have very much been the premier place for the mass assembly of humanity.

And exactly what does this humanity look like under the scrutiny of Farkas's camera? What it is that Farkas is seeing that he would transmit as the testimonial of his photographic texts? Since cultural production inevitably involves implicit messages (even the explicit rationales artists may give for their texts is suspicious in nature, as we have no way to objectively gauge if that is, in fact, what they have done, or to gauge if what they have done was in fact the impetus to textual production that they aver), we can only examine the text and report that what we are able to discern must necessarily (the accidents of reporting not withstanding[12]) correspond with what was of motivating interest to the photographer as he effected his image.

As one looks fixedly at Farkas's image, one stands out, very much as a Barthrian punctum (i.e. the "surprise" element in a photograph that seems to disrupt its placed representation surface)[13] is the dominance of the male fedora, the essential head covering of respectable men of the era. Certainly, the fedora is accompanied by the *de rigueur* masculine streetwear: a suit with a white shirt and tie; occasionally a vest that was an integral part of the three-piece suit. Proper socks and shoes would also be required, and everything would be touched off by a matching hat. In the image, we see some men covering their heads with a newspaper, and one wonders if it is because of the sun (never that intense in the temperate climes of São Paulo) or because of the social irregularity of lacking a proper *chápeu*; some men are also wearing caps, either those that are part of a uniform or the informal cap of men of lesser social standing. Even the vendors are wearing hats, and there is only a handful of men with no head covering. It is important to note that Pacaembu marks the transition of soccer from a gentleman's sport to an officially competitive one, as has been remarked above, either for sociopolitical reasons or for commercial ones. Yet the Farkas's audience is still notably classist in nature, the consequence of abiding restrictions on access to social space (as in the United States, attendance at film showings in Brazil at the time required men to dress in business clothing), not to mention the inevitable segregation, as is the case today, imposed by the high cost of tickets.

But what is noteworthy about the fedora (as opposed to the casual cap) is the way in which it sets off the human face by being larger than the head it covers; this is, incidentally usually also the case with uniform caps, especially the high-peaked military variety the German Nazi army exported to certain Latin American countries). In this sense, the fedora neither complements nor sets off the male head, but dominates it as a symbol of masculinity, much as the

The Photography of Thomaz Farkas and the Estádo de Pacaembu

extravagant and elaborate headpieces for women a generation or so earlier were a triumphant sign of privileged femininity. Indeed, such a symbol not only refers to masculinity in general, but to a particularly well-placed version of it, since the men so dressed constitute the controlling nucleus of a male-dominated society.

Seen in this way, the male hat in this photograph attests to the link between the circumstances of this assembly and hegemony of assembled masculine social dominance: that is, there can be no question (as there might be if the men were all dressed in the uniforms of day-wage factory workers) that what we are viewing is a synecdoche of Brazilian male homosocial society. Moreover, these men are drawn together by a sports event, not any event, but one that has already affirmed itself as a paradigmatic focal point of masculine identity.[14] Soccer will grow in importance as integral to the Brazilian sociocultural imaginary, coming to assume all sorts of important dimensions, as can be attested to by the proliferation, especially in recent years, of cultural productions that index the soccer event and invest it will all sorts of ideological and identitarian elements.[15] The effect of Farkas's photograph, focused as it is from a corner of the stadium that allows for the full sweep of the cascading seating that extends from the fairly clear detail of the lower right to the blurred masses that stretch outward toward the three other quadrants of the frame, is that of a uniform swarm.

Individuating distinctions are impossible to perceive in most of the photograph, and even where they are most distinguished, in the lower right-hand corner, it is difficult to perceive much more than general characteristics. One could indulge here in the metaphor of the beehive, with the concrete confines of Pacaembu circumscribing the legitimate space of the constituents, holding them in and ensuring they are focused on the task at hand, which is here to be spectators of the defining social event that is the soccer match. Certainly, these men are not all the same in any number of differing ways, from facial features and bodily comportment to their inner lives. But they are unified in social comportment in their commitment to the soccer event and to the affirmation of the universe of soccer as that of a determining social universe: that of white men of a certain socioeconomic standing and committed to the so-called normal values of Brazilian male citizenship. By "normal" I mean here the sort of unquestioned ground-zero of unmarked social intercourse that in no way signals deviance from the unspoken consensual standards of the day, which in this case would be the easy camaraderie of the shared interest in the sporting event, but would extend to an open-ended inventory of ancillary qualities engaged in a mutual interaction that overdetermines social class, no matter how broadly defined. This might include sociolinguistic characteristics, such as, a shared Brazilian colloquial norm that is not as far removed from an academic standard as might be, say, the aforementioned day-wage factory workers. It would definitely include the social norms of appropriate dress for public venues, at a time in which there were no alternative, logo-based and team-affiliated casual wear that today one might typically wear to a soccer match. And it would include the norms for "real man" behavior in public, not just the street in general, but the distinctive space of the soccer stadium.

Such norms would include not only putatively correct ways to behave in concert with the rest of the crowd, including the cramped quarters of shared spectator seating (e.g., what the rules are for bodily contact include shared enthusiasm relative to triumphant scoring) and even the shared space of stadium bathrooms. Needless to say, any sign of homoaffectivity would be likely censored even if it did not provoke a violent reaction, and yet there is a shared intimacy in the confines of the soccer venue that is unique (and rather quite different from the possibility of being jammed together with other bodies in the briefer trajectory of an urban bus route). The shared values of the sports event can only prevail if there is the preexisting condition for their shared importance, which is the universe of shared homosocial membership. Even today, where that shared homosociality may segue into manifestations of shared homoaffectivity (e.g., a buddy-like relationship that is reinforced by shared sports identities), the sustained fiction of the stadium, while no longer a privileged masculine space, but yet nevertheless one that remains primarily dominated by privileged masculine commitments, is that all of the spectators are acting in concert in the defense of a hegemonic ideology of identity and purpose. It is for this reason that the observer of Farkas's photograph is hardly surprised by the social consistency, so to speak, of the spectators it portrays.

Unified masculine social agency of a different sort is envisioned in one of the several images in which the camera is turned on the faces of the crowd. Since the soccer match and the immediate action transpiring on the pitch, is presumably the most important feature of a stadium-based event, the directing of the camera, in a reverse shot from what is expected, not only accords primary importance to the assembled spectators, but it denies, so to speak, the primary significance of what is transpiring on the pitch. The customary dynamics of the role of the camera in recording a soccer match would be in reiterating the view of the spectators, in a process whereby the view of one of the spectators (the cameraman) functions synecdochally for the collective view of the spectators among whom the cameraman stands. Thus, when we have an occasion in which a match is being recorded by a camera, whether still or motion-picture, we accept the legitimacy of the collective point of view the cameraman effects, and are grateful when that point of view is enhanced by other parallel ones coming from different cameras or from the moving around of one, or a combination of the two. Properly photographed, the resulting images give us the sense of being in the stadium and of even being in a privileged place there, as the camera achieves perspectives that one might not obtain from any fixed vantage point in the bleachers. Presumably in this process, the players are not watching the spectators, but are rather concentratedly involved in, as the saying goes, keeping their eye on the ball—which does not exclude the occasional, and usually noteworthy, interaction between player and spectator, especially when insults or aggression are involved from either or both parts. Yet, routinely, it is as though there were a one-way mirror between the pitch and the audience, such that there are eyes/cameras watching the game, but not eyes/cameras watching the audience, save for the occasional pan or other shot of the latter under specific situations (i.e. to remark on the particular fervor of the fans). But it is not the sort of sustained gaze that the audience is directing toward the players, or that one would assume the camera is so directing in the name of the audience.

Thus, when Farkas archives a view of the audience, as he does here and in other photographs included in *Pacaembu*, it is because he is finding other ways of focusing on the anonymous assembled fans as more important for his understanding of the sports event than named and numbered stars of the pitch are. The notion that Pacaembu is defined by a particular type of spectatorship and that Pacaembu functions to assign a particular identity to spectators are two sides of the same coin: the role of Pacaembu in institutionalizing Brazilian soccer. Thus, we would expect the audience of this image to be in no way substantially different from that of the previously examined photograph. Aside from focusing more intimately on the members of the audience than was possible with the longer-range take of the previous image, the close-up of this photograph is able to more concretely contextualize the spectators as part of a systematized theatrical event and not as just an under-individuated mass.

For example, we can see in detail how the space of the spectator has its own architectural distinction: it is not merely an undefined vantage point from which to watch the prioritized stage of the pitch as the principal point of interest for the stadium as physical space and as institutionalized setting. Farkas's reverse shot makes the area of the spectators into a stage as well, of which we, as the viewers of the photograph, become spectators of another order, whether contemporaneous or posteriorly as a defined subsequent historical moment (i.e. the specific moment now in which we are considering what ideology of soccer is being portrayed by this

The Photography of Thomaz Farkas and the Estádo de Pacaembu

image taken seventy-five years ago). Toward the end of understanding the configuration of the setting, then, we observe the importance of the restraining rail, which both holds back the crowd, supposedly in moments of great frenzy, and demarcates the frontier between the two sides of the one-way mirror in which it is legitimate for the spectators to view the players, but not, in the due course of the game, for the players to view (at least no more than in passing) the spectators. The camera violates the presumed directional impediment on the act of viewing, to give us, as I have already insisted, the sense of how the spectators may be here more important than the players. The constructed space of the so-called viewed stage of the spectators is further underscored by the geometrically positioned columns in the background, integral to sustaining the structure where their "theatrical event" is taking place.

We have already established what the importance of the archived spectators is, as the greater detail shows us that we once again have at issue a virtually unanimously all-male assembly,[16] one that is dominated by the prescribed public male dress of the day and includes improvised headgear made from newspapers by those lacking the proper fedora. Here we can see the multiplicity of responses to the game unfolding before them, from passivity to emotional responses, both favorable (the man standing in the white coat on the right) and regretful (the man standing in the black coat on the left). This disjunctive and symmetrical display is almost as if it were staged for the camera. There is a variety of response from other members of the audience, from what looks like a prayer for the soul of a player (lower right), to studious contemplation (the two men in the center, one clasping both hands, as though lamenting a particular play); the other shielding his eyes with his left hand, lost in thought. These are perhaps not particularly notable poses but they do individuate the spectators within their compact and unvaried display of the homosociality of the institution, reduplicating as audience the unvaried masculinity of the game. Farkas certainly has no discernible critical commentary to make on such a social configuration, nor is there any hint of irony, no gesture of the deconstruction of such a state of affairs. Certainly, one is confident in assuming that he would have found nothing strange or unusual in either the fact that the universe of the players is strictly masculine, that the universe of the spectators (although with possibly a few exceptions noted here) is strictly masculine, or that the conjunction of the two universes reduplicates the strictly masculine universe of Brazilian public life at that time in São Paulo. Hildegard Rosenthal, as a woman (and also as a foreigner like Farkas), found it possible to deploy an ironic tinge to her portrayal of the totally masculine public space she encountered in her rounds of the city, about a decade before these images were executed. Regrettably, although understandably—what, indeed, might have been her point of entry into this unalleviated masculine universe, the opportunity for her gaze upon it?—one can only imagine bemusedly what might have been the reaction of the assembled spectators at the Pacaembu to the intrusive presence of this diminutive woman and her photographic equipment. Quite literally, there is structurally no room for its insertion.

The third set of photographs in *Pacaembu* that I would like to comment on represent the excluded third, the banned other that might disrupt the binary conjugation of the players and privileged spectators. It is the audience that is literally prevented entrance into the stadium. But that excluded audience finds, as the subaltern is often wont to do, its own unassigned vantage point and the interpretation of the social proceedings it constructs from that vantage point. Concomitantly, as archived photography, Farkas's images are also speaking to the way in which we are constructed as observers of the impermissible spectatorship of the excluded other. In reality, I am referring here to two images, where the second is a virtual extract of the first one.

The first of the two shows two groups of spectators who are presumably watching a match from outside the stadium, taking advantage of the hilly contours of São Paulo to look down into the stadium from a knoll above. One group appears essentially to be a duplication, in their features, of the spectators within the stadium. Thus, we see the mass of the seated audience as a horizontal band that traverses the photo, anchoring its visual reference, as do so many of the photographs in *Pacaembu*, to the phenomenon of sports spectatorship. Although one young man can be identified, wearing a shirt but no tie, jacket, or hat, the several dozen external spectators are all "properly" dressed middle-class white men, the quintessence of the spectators of the day as Farkas visualizes them. Presumably they could all pay to have seats in the stadium, and various inconsequential casual reasons may be adduced for why they aren't: no remaining seats, lack of cash for the moment to pay for an entrance ticket, lack of time to stay for the whole match—that is, nothing that would challenge the integrity of the institution. The lone young man, curiously, is more interested in directing his gaze toward the camera than toward the goings on within the stadium, which do seem fully to engage the casual spectators.

Far more interesting is the casual group that disrupts the fairly trivial nature of a photograph of a handful of nonpaying onlookers, and that is the cluster of a half dozen boys who have shimmied up a denuded tree to ensure an even better nonpaying view than the formally attired spectators below them.[17] These are not ragtag children, as they are decently dressed as one might expect of children in that solidly middle-class neighborhood to be. Like their adult counterparts, they are staring toward the pitch, and it is clear they find the winter-time tree a viable substitute for stadium seating. Paralleling the young man on the ground, one of the kids in the tree is looking toward the camera, which only serves to emphasize how the others are fully engaged with action on the pitch. They have comfortably installed themselves in the branches of the tree, and this vantage point provided by the landscape from before the construction of Pacaembu correlates with the casualness of spectatorship for an excluded masculine subset (because they are children, because they are not properly dressed, and/or because they cannot afford the cost of attendance) as opposed to the constructed audience (in the terms described above) that is of a whole with the constructed institution of the sports stadium.

In the case of the second photograph, which I propose is something like an extract of the first, although it is not fully evident that it is the same tree or the same group of children, we have an image of the spectators viewed from the perspective I have described above for the shot of the soccer audience from inside the stadium. That is, the camera sees the children looking at the game; none of them here looks toward the camera. The tree on which they are perched, like birds avid for a glimpse of the pitch, is now seen not quite as denuded, and the way in which one boy has perched his shoes (which he has presumably removed to shimmy up the tree) on the ends of stumps of tree branches, may be viewed as naturalizing the shoes, and therefore the boys, of which they are a synecdochal icon, as much a part of the tree as the remaining wisps of leaves we can see. Taking advantage, I repeat, of the natural setting—the raised knoll, the convenient tree "left over" from the clearing of the area for construction—this group of boys is a marginal discordant note to the carefully built environment of the huge stadium inserted into a placid suburban neighborhood (or it was when the stadium was inaugurated in 1940), bringing with it a complex institution of a well-defined political ideology: soccer as a master metonymy for an emergent national myth of Brazilian social and cultural solidarity as defined by a privileged masculine class for which it is enacted with the assumption and expectation that that class will enthusiastically endorse it. Soccer, of course, did not remain a static mythifying force in Brazilian society, and it went on to become highly commercialized and intensely driven by multiple class interests, albeit with the popular class coming to constitute its most stridently evident face. It will become the task of other photographers (paradigmatically, the vast enterprise of sports photojournalism and television coverage) to provide macro-images of that evolution. Farkas's work, however, remains historically archived as a masterful representation of the emergence of professional soccer, highly circumscribed by prevailing ideologies, into the Brazilian national consciousness.[18]

The Photography of Thomaz Farkas and the Estádo de Pacaembu

Notes

1 Close to the stadium is Higienópolis, what the Brazilians call a *bairro nobre* (noble neighborhood)—that is, an upper-middle-class area; one of the features of Higienópolis is that it is home to the city's most prosperous Jewish community. There are many factors that played a role in the location there of São Paulo's first major sports stadium (for notes on Pacaembu's importance, see Kfouri 2014, and see Atique et al. 2015 regarding the importance of Pacaembu and the development of São Paulo). However, the undeniable implication, borne out by the early history of soccer, is that of an upper-middle-class undertaking, which around the mid-fifties was still being idolized by being called the *jogo benito* (beautiful game; see Bocketti (2016) for pertinent history here). This denomination is a far cry from the subsequent and current sociological reality of soccer as a ground-zero populist sport that has, nevertheless, followed the late capitalist model of the profound commercialization of all of its aspects, including the full apparatus of the star system for the players. In this sense, public access to the soccer stadium has come full circle: if in its late nineteenth-century origins, it was socially accessible only to upper social strata, today it is accessible, because of its commercialization and steep ticket prices, only to upper financial strata; the masses now watch soccer matches on TV or listen to them on the radio. Nevertheless, there is wide agreement over the belief that soccer distills the essence of Brazilian national identity. I would like to thank my colleague Patrick T. Ridge for providing me insights into the ideologies and practice of Brazilian football; his dissertation (Ridge 2017) is cited. See Toledo (2015) on the vertiginous development during this period.
2 The importance of soccer stadiums for modern Brazil, especially since the Estado Novo period of Getúlio Vargas, is studied by Kittelson (2014); Gaffney examines the importance of soccer stadiums in the history of Argentine and Brazilian popular culture. Unfortunately, he does not discuss Pacaembu; for an account of the construction of the Pacaembu, see Ferreira (2008). The universe of the stadium and soccer in the formation of Estado Novo masculinities is examined briefly by Franzini (1998). See also Archetti (1999) on the role of sports, most notably soccer, in the formation of Argentine masculine identities. Machado and Banchetti (2009) discuss in detail the role of Pacaembu in Vargas's governing ideology, Mehrtens (2010) discusses the political give-and-take in the planning of the Pacaembu project, and Negreiros (2003) focuses on the overall role of soccer as a tool for the fascist-like construction of Brazilian national identity.
3 Information, much less critical commentary, on Farkas is scarce, as it is for most Latin American photographers. Not only is there no Wikipedia entry for him, but a search of the database of the Instituto Moreira Salles, the principal institution in Brazil that curates that country's photographic production, yields no results, despite the fact that IMS has become the repository of the archives of his photographic production and his extensive personal library. On Farkas's importance in the emergence of Brazilian art photography, see Leite and Silva (2012).
4 Sedgwick (1985) is the obligatory starting point for the concept, although it has been considerably elaborated in subsequent use. A recent study such as Ward (2015), although it does not cover sports, is important for the way in which homosociality bleeds off into ritualized homoerotic behavior. Foster (2012) examines the representation of homosocialism in the men's locker room in the photography of Marcos López.
5 Margerith Rago (1991) examines the phenomenon of entrance of "good" Brazilian women into prostitution as a means of escaping the cloistering of so-called decent women in Brazil, a practice that lasted until well into the 1960s. The women described by Ragu were "exiles" from that cloistering, as was also the case of social rebels like the inimitable Patrícia Galvão (known as Pagu; 1910–62). There is a scene in Normal Bengell's biographic film, *Eternamente Pagu* (1987) in which Pagu and some of her young classmates are verbally attacked in the street as vulgar "public" women by a group of male law students for the temerity of their antics, including smoking, in full view.
6 This was particularly true when there emerged the practice of women-only matinees in movie houses; see Conde (2012: 136–39).
7 Much has been written about the so-called messing around between men in structured homosocial settings, such as initiation rituals (see Ward 2015 on fraternities and the military, where the men involved will nevertheless claim emphatically to be heterosexual; see Sebreli 1998 with specific reference to soccer).
8 Gallo, with reference to Mexico City, views the soccer stadium as one of the five major technological innovations of the early twentieth century that have a significant impact on cultural production (2005). The other four are cameras, typewriters, radio, and cement. Farkas's stadium photography, therefore, exemplifies the conjunction of two of these innovations in the service of cultural formations. Mexico's

first stadiums, the Nacional in Mexico City and the Xalapa in Veracruz, date from the mid-1920s and were also the result of ideological considerations of the importance of sports for nationalistic identity consolidation, which became the dominant political project in Mexico following the 1910 Revolución Mexicana in the second decade of the new century. Atique et al. (2015) also discuss the cement-based physical reality of Pacaembu and its importance for the São Paulo urban landscape.

9 One can turn to a textbook source on sports photojournalism to understand the importance of keeping the camera focused on the action on the field. See *Digital Sports Photography*: "Story editors usually want photos to display something pertaining to the piece, and the best way for sports photographers to do this is by getting images of the key play and players. I can't stress that enough" (2008: n.p.). This is a pretty elementary observation, but it is significant that the author believes it needs to be made.

10 At least until the construction of the mammoth Maracaná stadium in Rio de Janeiro for the 1950 Olympics.

11 An excellent way to understand what São Paulo was like in the 1940s and 1950s is to visit Curitiba, the capital of Paraná, 45 minutes by air south of São Paulo. While a dynamic city with excellent cultural creativity, Curitiba nevertheless continues to manifest the staid bourgeois decency that was still the hallmark of São Paulo seventy-five years ago.

12 Events that are, to be sure, legendary, especially in photography, which is likely to encompass more than the photographer intended or to include happenstance intrusions. A notable meditation on this circumstance is to be found in Julio Cortázar's short story "La babas del diablo" (1959) (the basis for Michelangelo Antonioni's 1966 film *Blow-Up*), which focuses on the unintended capture by a photographer of a scene of a child's sexual molestation. Cortázar's story emphasizes the impotence of artists to affect the human drama being recorded, but the story has often been read in terms of the so-called accidents of artistic production, particularly something as difficult to control as the field of the photographic lens.

13 The reference is to Roland Barthes's fundamental formulation in his *Camera Lucida* (1981); see the essays analyzing the nature of Barthes's formulation in Batchen (2009).

14 Archetti (1999) has studied the role of soccer in the formation of prevailing and privileged masculine identity with specific reference to Argentina, although the same may now be said with respect to forging hegemonic masculinity throughout Latin America.

15 The recent work of Patrick T. Ridge (2012), as represented in his essay in this volume, exemplifies very well the interest in analyzing these elements in Brazilian soccer. See also the work by Shawn Stein. Much similar bibliography now exists for Argentine soccer, going back at least to Juan José Sebreli's (1998) work cited previously.

16 Farkas does include in *Pacaembu* one telling image of a group of ten women dressed in uniform, accompanied by two other women nicely dressed for a social outing (chaperons?). The uniforms, a pants and jacket combination, of the first group of women bear the inscription ITAPIRA, which is the name of a municipality in the state of São Paulo. One sees these women as an early version of cheerleaders, although it is not exactly clear how they function. Women did attend soccer matches, but only under highly restrictive conditions, and probably most definitely not as "walk-in" patrons.

17 Farkas comments on this and similar images: "Nos anos de 1940, a cidade começava a anunciar a confusão e o tamanho a que chegaria hoje. Para o futebol no Pacaembu, ia-se d eterno e chapéu(as vezes de gravata...). A garotada porén tinha a melhor visão, naturalmente degraça, através das grades e por cima das árvores" (Farkas, *Thomaz Farkas* 2002: 11)

18 Despite the clear importance of soccer and the Pacaembu in Vargas's nationalist agenda, it is curious that Williams (2001) does not discuss either of the two or mass-spectator sports in his important study on the cultural wars Vargas unleashed.

Works cited

Archetti, Eduardo. *Masculinities: Football, Polo and the Tango in Argentina*. Oxford: Berg, 1999.

Atique, Fernando, Diógenes Sousa, and Hennan Gess.. "Uma relação concreta: A prática do futebol em São Paulo e os Estádios do Parque Antarctica e do Pacaembu." *Anais do Museu Paulista* n.s., 23.1 (2015): 91–109.

Barthes, Roland. *Camera Lucida: Reflections on Photography*. Translated by Richard Howard. New York: Hill and Wang, a division of Farrar, Strauss and Giroux, 1981.

Batchen, Geoffrey. *Photography Degree Zero: Reflections on Roland Barthes's* Camera Lucida. Cambridge, MA: Massachussets Institute of Technology, 2009.

The Photography of Thomaz Farkas and the Estádo de Pacaembu

Bocketti, Gregg. *The Invention of the Beautiful Game and the Making of Modern Brazil.* Gainesville: University of Florida Press, 2016.

Conde, Maite. *Consuming Visions: Cinema, Writing, and Modernity in Rio de Janeiro.* Charlottesville, Virginia: University of Virginia Press, 2012.

Cortazar, Julio. "Las babas del diablo" (1959). In *Relatos.* Buenos Aires: Editorial Sudamericana, 1970. 520–538.

Digital Sports Photography. Eds. G. Newman Lowrence *et al.* 2nd edition, Boston: Course Technology, 2008.

Eternamente Pagu. Dir. Norma Bengell. Brazil. Sistema Globo de Comunicação, 1987. Farkas, Thomaz. *Thomaz Farkas.* São Paulo: Editora da Universidade de São Paulo, 2002. *Farkas, Thomaz. Thomaz Farkas, Pacaembu.* São Paulo: Dórea Books and Art, 2008.

Ferreira, João Fernando. *A construção do Pacaembu.* São Paulo: Paz e Terra, 2008.

Foster, David William. "Homosocialism: Homoeroticism in the Photography of Marcos López." *Dissidences* 1.1 (2012): 1–21.

Foster, David William. *São Paulo: Perspectives on the City and Cultural Production.* Gainesville, FL: University of Florida Press, 2011.

Franzini, Fábio. "Fútbol, identidad y ciudadanía en Brasil en los años 30." *Lecturas: educación física y deportes* 3.10 (1998): 1–9.

Gaffney, Christopher Thomas. *Temples of the Earthbound Gods: Stadiums in the Cultural Landscapes of Rio de Janeiro and Buenos Aires.* Austin TX: University of Texas Press, 2008.

Gallo, Rubén. *Mexican Modernity: The Avant-Garde and the Technological Revolution.* Cambridge, MA: Massachusetts Institute of Technology, 2005.

Kfouri, Juca. "Pacaembu." In *Thomaz Farkas, Pacaembu,* São Paulo: Dórea Books and Art, 2008.

Kittleson, Roger. *The Country of Football: Soccer and the Making of Modern Brazil.* Berkeley, CA: University of California Press, 2014.

Leite, Marcelo Eduardo Leite, and Carla Adelina Craveiro Silva. "Diálogo em preto e branco: a experiência moderna na fotografia brasileira." *Mediação* 14.15 (2012): 14–34.

Machado, Felipe Morelli, and Luciano Deppa Banchetti. "Nas arquibancadas e nas tribunas! O binômio futebol/política na vivência dos estádios durante o governo Vargas: Pacaembu e São Januário." *Mnemosine* 5.2 (2009): 80–93.

Mehrtens, Cristina Peixoto. "The Pacaembu Scheme, March 1933." *Urban Space and National Identity in Early Twentieth Century São Paulo.* New York: Palgave Macmillan, 2010. 140–46.

Negreiros, Plínio José Labriola de Campos. "Futebol nos anos 1930 e 1940: construindo a identidade nacional: Soccer in the 1930's and 1940's: Building the National Identity." *História: questões & debates* 39 (2003): 121–51.

Rago, Margareth. *Os prazeres da noite: prostituição e códigos da sexualidade feminine em São Paulo (1890–1930).* Rio de Janeiro: Paz e Terra, 1991.

Ridge, Patrick Thomas. *From Sport to Spectacle: An Archaeology of Latin American Soccer.* Unpublished doctoral dissertation, Arizona State University, 2017.

Sebreli, Juan José. *La era del fútbol.* Buenos Aires: Editorial Sudamericana, 1998. Originally published as *Fútbol y masas.* Buenos Aires: Editorial Galerna, 1981.

Sedgwick, Eve Kosofsky. *Between Men: English Literature and Male Homosocial Desire.* New York: Columbia University Press, 1985.

Toledo, Roberto Pompeu de. *A capital da vertigem: uma história de São Paulo de 1900–1954.* Rio de Janeiro: Objetiva, 2015.

Ward, Jane. *Not Gay: Sex Between Straight White Men.* New York: New York University Press, 2015.

Williams, Daryle. *Culture Wars in Brazil: The First Vargas Regime, 1930–1945.* Durham, NC: Duke University Press, 2001.

PART V

Bend it like *Pelé*

24

A "FRIENDLY" GAME

Homoaffectivity in *Club de Cuervos*

Patrick Thomas Ridge

Down one to Venezuela during the 2016 Copa América Centenario, Mexico's Jesús Corona would score one of the most jaw-dropping goals of the tournament, dribbling through five defenders and burying a shot into the back of the net. After beating his chest to his cheering compatriots in the stands, "Tecatito"—as he is popularly known—enjoyed the celebratory embrace of his fellow teammates, a group bear hug that honored his heroics. Although men's soccer in Mexico represents one of the most influential discursive sites for constructing masculinity, homoaffective acts shared by the country's "toughest" *machos*—most commonly, hugs, kisses, and butt-slaps following goals—prove the game's capabilities for challenging heteronormativity.

While a critical interpretation of these athletes' behavior helps to deconstruct Mexico's dominant masculinist narratives, a queer analysis of cultural production on soccer also provides an alternative view of the so-called "man's game." Most notably, the sporting protagonists of Gary "Gaz" Alazraki and Michael Lam's *Club de Cuervos* (2015–)—Netflix's first Spanish-language comedy series—exhibit the same type of on-field behavior as the above-mentioned Mexican National Team. Furthermore, scenes filmed in the team's locker room not only present the nude bodies of these men during shared shower time, but also the man-on-man antics that perturb the gender norms established through homosociality. Contrary to previous studies that focus predominantly on themes of masculinity and nationalism, the following pages analyze how men's soccer in Mexico—revised by Netflix's popular streaming series—provides participants with one of the only cultural "arenas" for overt expressions of friendship and affection. Nonetheless, this study also considers how dominant discourse often disguises these acts with narratives of teamwork and brotherhood.

Performing masculinity on the pitch

Before understanding the discursive ties between men's soccer and masculinity, one must consider how gender has been constructed within Mexican society. As R.W. Connell importantly notes, distinct masculine traits are attributed to men within different cultural settings. The concept of hegemonic masculinity demonstrates how these cultures idealize traditional masculine traits like toughness and competitiveness in order to establish male dominance, while also subordinating women and marginalizing gay men (1990: 94). In Mexico, Robert McKee Irwin proposes that masculinity is not only defined by the traditional male-female binary, but also by gender performance. Using Judith Butler's notion of the concept developed in *Gender Trouble* (1990), he notes the presence of a certain continuum that ranges between different degrees of an individual's supposed manliness or effeminacy whereby men perform their masculinity through successful competition or the completion of ritualized acts (Irwin 2003: xx–xxi). Here, it is important to note the discursive influence of Octavio Paz and his *Laberinto de soledad* (1950, reprinted in 2007). Paz suggests that men prove their manhood through the active penetration of the passive, and therefore "weak" individual (2007: 165). Although this penetrated man is deemed homosexual or effeminate in Mexican culture, the penetrator preserves his masculine heterosexual identity (Carillo 2003: 357; Irwin 2003: xxiii–xxiv). But as Irwin points out, this active/passive dynamic is symbolic, and men often enhance their masculinity by successfully dominating or "penetrating" their weaker adversaries in trials of wit, authority, and force, social interactions that produce "manly" winners and "feminized" losers (2003: xxiii).

Taking these notions into consideration, one sees how sports such as men's soccer—intense competition between two teams where the so-called winner penetrates an opponent's goal—reaffirm dominant constructions of masculinity. On a stage for gender performance, players become central parts in the construction of modern Mexican masculinity and nationhood (Venkatesh 2011: 31). Men reproduce dominant *machista* (male chauvinist) social tendencies as powerful, passionate, and hard-working actors on the field of play. Furthermore, when presented as winners, these men are framed as the dominant sex within Mexican society, especially when women appear in supporting roles as player wives or fans (Gutiérrez 2009: 1–3). Finally, the display of the male body in these athletic performances, as well as its adherence to the game's rules—men continue to occupy a vast majority of positions within soccer's governing bodies—further establishes men's supposed superiority both on and off the field (Connell 2005: 54).

Soccer and homosociality

Along with these athletic performances, discourse and behavior within these sporting spaces tends to uphold established gender norms. In her seminal text *Between Men* (1985), Eve K. Sedgwick proposes that homosocialism—hierarchical social interactions between men in exclusively masculine spaces—serve to preserve and perpetuate patriarchy, often through ideological homophobia and/or homosexuality (1985: 25). Representing these types of male-dominated venues, David W. Foster adds that soccer stadiums and sports bars in Latin America have historically allowed male fans to uphold this patriarchal social order, principally through the use of homophobic language and comportment, along with the exclusion of women (1999: 17; 2003: xiv–xvi). Eric Anderson suggests that these aggressive actions—coined *homosocial patrolling* in his study—allow men to establish their dominance and marginalize their supposedly weaker counterparts (2014: 218). Furthermore, male athletes often reaffirm their masculinity by acting "gay" with their peers. This behavior—deemed *ironic heterosexual recuperation* by Anderson—includes mocking homosexual desire and performing stereotypes of gay men (2014: 91–92). Along with these heightened levels of homophobia and sexism, figures of authority, such as coaches, typically urge players to adopt warrior-like attitudes, and those that fail to do so are often deemed "weak," thus lacking the necessary talent for on-field success (Anderson 2014: 83).

Off the field, the yelling of *puto* in Mexican stands represents one of the most popular of these homophobic discursive practices. Fans typically hurl the insult at the opposing goalkeeper after goal kicks. Like Paz's symbolic model mentioned above, the chant stigmatizes the inferior participant on the field of play. Even though the term is resignified in certain social settings—often used jokingly between close friends in Mexico—it still retains its original semantic meaning, one that is synonymous with words like *marica*, *mariposa*, *mujercito*, and *afeminado*, all loosely meaning "fag," "girly," or "sissy" (Azamar Cruz 2015: 479). Despite numerous fines in recent years from soccer's governing bodies, the Federación Mexicana de Fútbol Association (FMF) continues to defend the chant as part of the normal conduct of Mexican daily life, although some argue that this defense also protects the interests of Televisa and TV Azteca, some of the Mexican national team's largest financial backers (Pons 2014: 79–80; for a more detailed analysis of this topic and the critical response of the Mexican chronicle, see Ridge 2017). Thus, players, coaches, fans, and even Mexico's soccer institutions tend to normalize this type of homophobic behavior.

Regarding the presence of women in these spaces, nationalist discourse has typically helped to sideline these participants. For instance, masculinity has historically served as the defining lines for national identity (Mosse 1996: 7–9). Thus, sports like men's soccer provide a way to reaffirm notions of masculinist nationalism (Nadel 2014: 219). As a result, those that perturb the heteronormative pact within homosocial space—the transgressive woman or effeminate man— serve as a threat to the patriarchal domain. Mexican women are continuously discouraged to play soccer due to the game's supposed "masculinizing" effects, as proved by the criticism experienced by talented players like Maribel Domínguez in recent years (Nadel 2014: 232–34). Up until 1971, it was still widely believed in Mexico that women playing soccer would potentially damage reproductive organs (Martínez 2006: 14; Nadel 2014: 229). Others propose that cultural myths such as the Virgin/Eve and/or Virgin of Guadalupe/Malinche dynamic have often deterred women from the public sphere, and this includes the participation in *porras*, a regional term used for fan groups (Magazine 2007: 101–04). So, both the homophobic discourse and exclusionary practices of soccer's traditional homosocial spaces have helped to reaffirm patriarchal social order.

Soccer's homoaffectivity: Perturbing masculine myths

While these power dynamics reaffirm conventional notions of Mexican masculinity, scholars like Irwin propose that male homosocial bonding also contributes to the discursive constructions of the nation, albeit in a conflictive manner (2003: xxvii–xxviii). At the end of the 19th century, he explains that discourse regarding homosexuality threatened to delegitimize these bonds, but equating homosexual men with effeminacy served to uphold traditional homosocial relations between *machos* (Irwin 2003: 227). Although Irwin explores these male-to-male bonds in Mexican literature, men's soccer offers a unique point of departure from traditional discourses surrounding masculinist nationalism, especially considering the game's homoaffective acts. As Jane Ward suggests, space becomes a central factor in deeming this behavior queer or straight. Depending on the setting and corresponding cultural narrative—one thinks of the bodily contact involved in military or fraternity hazing—sexual touching between male bodies can be coded as "normal" (2015: 192–93, 208–09). Homoaffective acts—forehead kisses or butt-slaps—are particularly prevalent among Mexican men that publically identify with heterosexism, a social process that Carillo calls *mayor acercamiento corporal* (2003: 359). Since soccer has been historically coded in masculinist terms, few question the affective comportment exhibited by soccer's *machos*. Thus, the soccer pitch in Mexican culture offers one of the few public venues that permits the free expression of homosocial desire whereby celebratory touching can occur without fear of penetration (Venkatesh 2011: 33).

Despite these open displays of affection, institutional and team entities have often tried to suppress this contact. Enrique Serna points out these suppression tactics in "Orgías futboleras," claiming that FIFA's attempts to ban post-goal celebrations represent a strategy to limit player affection (2008: 62). Both Serna and Juan José Sebreli (2005) also show how this policing extends to a team's coaching staff. They use the example of Daniel Passarella, the former head coach of the Argentine national team that banned homosexual players and required military-like order (Serna 2008: 63; Sebreli 2005: 264). Even though today's players exhibit non-heteronormative behavior, these institutional measures demonstrate how the soccer field continues to employ a normalizing gaze on men's bodies. But as Vinodh Venkatesh suggests when commenting on Serna's text, critical attention to Mexican footballers allows readers and spectators to question and reformulate the representation of masculinity in contemporary Mexican society (2011: 35).

Technologies of gender: Constructing on-screen soccer heroes

Television and film have fulfilled a key role in disseminating these heteronormative ideologies to the masses. For instance, Teresa de Lauretis notes that cinema serves as an important technology for constructing gender (1987: 18). Applying this model to Mexico, Sergio de la Mora demonstrates that national cinema has proved instrumental in inventing the idea of the Mexican *macho*, most notably his study references the *charro* protagonists portrayed by Pedro Infante during the country's golden age (2006: 6–7; 83–84). Likewise, typical portrayals of effeminate gay men—popular, for instance, in the *fichera*[1] films of the 1970s and 1980s—reaffirmed the traditional gender binary and "normalcy" of heterosexual masculinity (Mora 2006: 113–15), serving as what Vito Russo deems "yardsticks for measuring the virility of the real men around them" (1987: 16).

The screening of sport further facilitates these constructions. Televised sports continue to privilege dominant representations of masculinity that are marked by athleticism, muscularity, strength, and power (Swain 2000: 101). For example, in Mexico, mainstream coverage tends to exalt the men's national team, highlighting the heroics of players like Guillermo Ochoa, Rafael Márquez, or Javier "Chicharito" Hernández. Additionally, the male protagonists of sports films tend to exhibit masculine characteristics such as hard work, self-reliance, and a responsibility to others (Baker 2003: 75). Most women in these texts also help to reaffirm patriarchal authority by posing as dependent supporters and/or fans of their male counterparts (Baker 2003: 50). Popular Mexican sports films such as Carlos Cuarón's *Rudo y Cursi* (2008) adopt this narrative structure. While the comedy presents the professional trajectory of two small-town brothers (Gael García Bernal and Diego Luna) and their struggles to reach Mexico's top-tier soccer leagues, women remain on the sidelines as their supporting wives or girlfriends, as demonstrated by Adriana Paz's and Jessica Mas's characters. These narrative formulas also appear to reflect the dominant media portrayals of women in sporting settings, images that not only frame these individuals as WAGs (wives and girlfriends) and mothers, but as seductive and sexy for the male viewer (Binello and Domino 1998: 217–18). While cameras often zoom in on these supporters during league games, broadcasts also feature women that participate as sideline reporters and *porristas* (cheerleaders) that interview or cheer on their male counterparts, a juxtaposition that symbolically reinforces the traditional gender binary.

Likewise, scenes filmed in homosocial settings such as the stadium, locker room, and sports bar exhibit the "normalized" homophobic and sexist dynamics associated with sports. Venkatesh notes that male subjects in these settings—just like their off-screen counterparts—must follow a certain spatial contract that falls in line with heterosexism. By performing their "appropriate" gender role—for instance, the viewing of sports—men in these spaces uphold the dominant structures of patriarchy, like those present in the neighborhood bar (2016: 70).

However, viewed from a different optic, the filming of homosociality can serve to deconstruct or question conventional *macho* behavior. Thus, queer readings of straight culture, as Alexander Doty proposes, can challenge established sexual and gender categories (2012: xv–xvi).

Taking this into account, one not only recognizes the queer elements of soccer, such as the mentioned homoaffective behavior between the game's supposed *machos*, but also the male-to-male contact between half-naked bodies in popular spectator sports such as lucha libre, Mexico's form of professional wrestling characterized by participants' colorful masks and ensembles. Typically framed as masculine heroes within these spaces, few have questioned the sexuality of these competitors, despite the obviously queer elements of these spectacles.

Similarly, these cinematic and sporting settings often permit the male gaze on men's bodies. In her work, Laura Mulvey suggests that the camera typically projects the active male gaze upon the passive female subject in cinematic narratives, thus allowing for the spectator to identify with the men on the screen (1989: 19–21). However, in hero and action genres—along with other narratives that include fights, battles, and for the sake of this study, athletic competitions—men become objects of this voyeuristic gaze from both the spectator and other male characters (Neale 1993: 16), although sexualized images of the male body in sports films often occur within the context of female desire (Baker 2003: 92). Sporting spaces such as the gym and locker room also allow men to experience the autoerotic or homoerotic gaze facilitated by the prevalence of mirrors and shared shower time, even if the latter is discouraged (Venkatesh 2016: 158). The nude images of men in these shower scenes often capture fetishized images of the body, thus challenging the viewer to contemplate same-sex desire. Furthermore, the framing of the nude male body from behind can prove suggestive of its penetrability or potential loss of masculinity (Lewis 2009: 179–83).

Although men's soccer in Mexico—and its media and screen portrayals—has historically served to reaffirm conventional norms of masculinity, an analysis of Netflix's *Club de Cuervos* will demonstrate that these sporting *machos* exhibit non-heteronormative behavior both on and off the field, specifically through celebratory affection, locker room antics, and same-sex glances. As Rebecca Feasey concludes in her study on masculinity and popular television, alternative masculine personas—such as the "sensitive" and family-oriented David Beckham—have emerged to challenge stereotypes of the misogynist and homophobic footballer (2008: 102–03). A similar process has occurred in Mexican soccer since players like Guillermo Ochoa—the goalkeeper regularly sports long, curly hair and headbands on the pitch—break with the established *macho* norm (Gutiérrez 2009: 2). Like these alternative representations of the male athlete, a critical analysis of Netflix's popular series allows audiences and fans to contemplate and redefine the notion of masculinity within Mexican soccer and culture.

Club de Cuervos: Deconstructing the Mexican *macho*

Netflix has quickly become one of the most popular modes for cultural consumption. Due to its easily accessible platform—viewers can stream shows or movies on their smart devices, computers, or televisions—series like *Club de Cuervos* (2015–) facilitate the dissemination of Mexican cultural production. Furthermore, and unlike cable television, the net-streaming service releases all episodes of its series at the same time, often resulting in the current phenomenon of binge-watching. Thus, as a technology of gender, soccer-themed shows like *Club de Cuervos* are easily capable of embedding and distributing the game's heteronormative ideologies to the masses, particularly through its masculine personas, *machista* discourses, and male-dominated storylines.

Created by Gary "Gaz" Alazraki and Michael Lam and first released in 2015, the comedic drama represents the first of a wave of Spanish-language series—other notable examples include *Narcos* (2015–) and *Cuatro estaciones en La Habana* (2016–)—released by Netflix. The U.S. company originally approached Alazraki—the Mexico City-based director achieved mass success with the comedy *Nosotros los nobles* (2013)—with hopes of creating a series that would reach the Latin American market. Besides its transnational production, the show's Mexican creators also worked with American and *Californication* (2007–14) screenwriter Jay Dyer to develop the series (Zax 2015). Additionally, the show boasts a variety of different directors and writers for each episode, not to mention actors from the United States and multiple Spanish-speaking nations. While Alazraki directs the bulk of the series, other notable Mexican directors—such as Carlos Armella and Mariana Chenillo, known for their work on *En la estancia* (2014) and *Cinco días sin Nora* (2008), respectively—have collaborated. As a result of this transnational production formula, the show has not only reached audiences in Latin America, but also Spanish-speaking viewers in the United States, and considering the recent surge in soccer's popularity north of the border, one could argue that Anglos have begun to stream with English subtitles.

Like other texts belonging to the television genre, the show's drawn-out episodic format parallels with the novel, thus allowing for more character development in comparison with the typical two-hour formula employed by classical cinema. The series focuses primarily on the upper-class Iglesias family and the feud between Chava (Luis Gerardo Méndez) and Isabel (Mariana Treviño), siblings that debate over the ownership of their family's most prized possession: Los Cuervos, a soccer club located in the fictional Mexican city of Nuevo Toledo. After their father—the team's owner—dies suddenly of a heart attack, the two heirs feud over who will take over the club. Despite Isabel's advanced administrative experience and her brother's managerial incompetency and frivolousness, Chava receives support from his male colleagues and is accepted as president. While season one presents the brother's absurd goals of turning the modest club into the Real Madrid of Latin America, Alazraki's recently released follow-up satirizes the gender politics involved with soccer, specifically Isabel's struggles as the new team owner and her attempts to gain the respect of the men around her. The series explores several themes currently associated with Mexico's most popular sport, among them corruption, club management, the role of the media, and the effects of soccer on social identity. Although an extensive commentary on the sibling feud and Isabel's stint as team owner would expose the sport's historic exclusion of women—both on and off the field—this study examines how the series offers evidence of the game's homoaffective acts in an effort to deconstruct typical representations of Mexican masculinity.

Surprisingly, as a show dedicated to the sport, few scenes occur on the pitch, a narrative trend of other soccer-based series such as HBO Brasil's *'(fdp)* (2012) and the Colombian telenovela *La selección* (2013–). While on-field sequences often advance the plot in these narratives, they simply lack the genuine excitement and "beautiful" plays associated with live television broadcasts,[2] perhaps a result of their low-entertainment value and overall omission. *Club de Cuervos* does present the drama related to the team's triumphs and descent from the first division, but most of the narrative action and conflict between players, coaches, fans, and team administrators occurs off-field in the stands, locker rooms, club offices, and the city of Nuevo Toledo. Nonetheless, scenes that capture the on-field action reproduce the elevated masculine performances associated with soccer. These sequences not only oscillate between shots of the Cuervos players and their cheering supporters in the stands, but also the referenced post-goal celebrations. For example, under the direction of newly hired coach Pausini (José Carlos Rodríguez) in "Afortunado en jugar," the starting eleven dance and embrace each other as they celebrate a victory that saves their hopes of playing in the post-season Liguilla, hinting at the space's capability of enabling homoaffectivity.

Despite these on-field displays of affection, most of the show's male-on-male antics occur in the locker room, a setting that highlights the sport's homosocial dynamics. Previously mentioned, the first season of the series revolves around Chava's administration, and both the

A "friendly" game

stadium and its components function as a hierarchical masculine space where the owner offers recommendations to the coach, he then gives orders to the team captain, and the players obey their superior. Aside from its hierarchical structure—central in Michel Foucault's theories on power (1995: 170)—the setting allows for the show's male characters to establish their supposed dominance and heterosexuality through homophobic and sexist discourse, at times addressing each other with "puto" o "niñas." However, like Carillo (2003) proposes, the assumed heterosexuality of the men involved with the club permit a heightened frequency of bodily contact without perturbing the pacts of homosocialism. For example, the multiple scenes of pep talks shot in this environment exhibit the affective touching and embraces associated with team huddles. Some of these shots even suggest how homoaffectivity quickly segues into homoeroticism, especially due to the hypermasculine environment. In season one's finale, Rafael's (Antonio de la Vega) pep talk is so effective that it arouses Potro (Joaquín Ferreira), as demonstrated by a close-up on the erected contours of the man's white shorts. Presented with a comedic effect, Alazraki appears to satirize the non-heteronormative behavior prevalent in these settings.

Nonetheless, the most intimate of these acts occur in the showers. Different from the censorship standards of nudity on cable television, the streaming series offers multiple images that expose the male body. For instance, in "Respuesta uniforme," a full shot captures the nude backsides of three Cuervos players as they take their post-practice showers. Although some of these men avert their eyes from their fellow teammates, thus preserving homosocial order, others like Potro pat Tony (Juan Pablo de Santiago) on the back, and in one instance, the former even casts a downward gaze towards his younger counterpart. While the images of the men's exposed backsides present alternative representations of the soccer *macho*, particularly the male body's penetrable vulnerability, Potro's glancing allows the viewer to contemplate same-sex desire. Not only this, the masculine-coded space permits teammates to joke with each other in the nude. Later, in "Barreras para salir," one of Cuervos' Brazilian players,[3] conveniently nicknamed Río (Gutemberg Brito), repeatedly squirts shampoo on top of Cuau's head (Said Sandoval) as the man furiously attempts to rid his hair of the suds (see Figure 24.1).

Figure 24.1 Film still from from *Club de Cuervos* showing players in the shower.

Like the customary towel slapping found in the locker room, the liquid establishes a symbolic bodily connection between players. Furthermore, one can point out certain homoerotic elements of this act, particularly considering the parallels between the streams of shampoo and other bodily fluids.

One of the most convincing examples of homoaffectivity occurs when the players sing to Moisés (Ianis Guerrero) after his wife publically forgives him for his extramarital escapades. As the men bellow the chorus of José José's "Lo pasado, pasado" when they surround their captain, a giddy Potro touches and caresses Moisés's nipples. The use of *mise-en-scène*—the camera frames the Argentine player from the waist up with a white towel wrapped around his head—gives Potro an effeminate look, but his tattoos, as well as his defined pectorals and abdominals, help to blur lines between normative and non-normative masculine behavior and identity (see Figure 24.2). Echoing Anderson's (2014) theory on *ironic heterosexual recuperation*, the joking mood of these men's same-sex touching appears to reaffirm their masculine identities. Additionally, Moisés's confirmed heterosexuality and conventional *macho* behavior—his marriage to Ximena (Eileen Yañez) and his extramarital affairs, respectively—enable an increased amount of intimate contact between the men without jeopardizing their masculinity.

Potro represents one of the most central masculine characters in most of these locker room scenes, especially since the directors almost always present the Argentine with little or no clothing. Some sequences even offer full-frontal images of the man. The most revealing of these occurs in "Aitor," an experimental episode shot in the style of *Nación fútbol*, the series' fictional sports highlight show. A full-body profile shot exhibits a naked Potro extending his hand to greet the club's newly signed superstar, Aitor Cardoné (Alosian Vivancos) (see Figure 24.3). Although the shot displays the former in the nude, a large rectangular box reading "censurado" hovers above the player's penis. Aside from the virility suggested by the man's nickname—colt or stud in Spanish—the exaggerated use of censoring emphasizes Potro's well-endowed member. As Peter Lehman proposes, the framing of the large or erect penis in film serves as a symbol of masculine identity (2007: 10). Combined with the hypermasculine stadium setting, the player's

Figure 24.2 Film still from *Club de Cuervos* showing players in the locker room.

A "friendly" game

Figure 24.3 Film still from *Club de Cuervos* with full-body profile shot of Potro.

overtly virile representation allows for his intimate actions to be codified as straight behavior. Likewise, due to the character's inflated masculinity, both the spectator and his fellow teammates are led to assume his heterosexuality.

Although heightened levels of intimate physical contact occur within this space, these men also engage in non-heteronormative verbal and visual exchanges. For example, "size" serves as a common topic of conversation in the locker room, particularly after Aitor's transfer to the club from FC Barcelona. Fashionably clad and sporting his own line of cologne, the recently signed Catalonian represents a stereotype of the European footballer, reminiscent of players like Real Madrid's Cristiano Ronaldo. For example, the Portuguese national and five-time Ballon d'Or winner has an underwear deal with Calvin Klein. After showering, the camera focuses in on the club's new superstar as he redresses. The ensuing editing techniques—an eyeline match that links Cuau and Potro's eyes with Aitor's naked backside as he carefully situates his sizable member into his briefs—enables the viewer to occupy the homoerotic gaze. Stunned by the superior size of his new teammate's "equipment," Potro utters "es impresionante." Despite their supposed masculine identities within the sporting space, the men's verbal praise and fetishizing gaze suggest same-sex desire.

This male-on-male looking is replicated by Goyo (Emilio Guerrero) and Félix (Daniel Giménez Cacho) in "Descenso." The former coach and vice president of los Cuervos now take the reins of Los Carneros, a league rival, and while the two attend the league's annual draft, they scope out potential prospects on a local beach. The camera tracks the middle-aged men—pictured shirtless with unflattering builds—as they stroll the sands and first glimpse two young women in bikinis. However, Félix urges his colleague forward to view their main specimens, a group of young soccer prospects that perform drills for their onlookers. Again, the camerawork and editing establish links between the men's gaze and the youthful bodies of the soccer players (see Figure 24.4). Although the sequence might not overtly exhibit the homoerotic gaze present in the mentioned locker room scenes, the images do suggest how soccer enables men to freely gaze at the male body, an act often suppressed in other settings.

Figure 24.4 Film still from *Club de Cuervos* showing former coach and vice-president of los Cuervos scoping out potential prospects on a local beach.

However, these intimate gazes and bodily contact tend to change if one breaks with the masculine code of homosocialism, exemplified by the discovery of Aitor's sexual preferences at the end of season one. When Chava and the club's superstar throw a party, the inebriated Aitor attempts to touch his owner's penis during a shared trip to the bathroom. Even though the player has just finished having sex with various women in the previous scene, thus inflating his masculinity in the eyes of Chava, the advance violates homosocial norms and the owner quickly retreats.

The Mexican public reacts in a similar way when news emerges that Aitor and his manager have been carrying out a relationship behind closed doors. Keeping in mind the historic beliefs regarding Mexican men's soccer and masculinity or even the FMF's recent defense of *puto* chants, Alazraki again satirizes these conservative attitudes by juxtaposing Nuevo Toledo's homophobic reaction with those outside of Mexico. For example, while a news report shows demonstrators using the Cardoné jersey as a symbol for gay rights in Amsterdam, the subsequent images present protestors in Nuevo Toledo shouting "culero" and holding signs that say "PutX Aitor" [sic]. The news sequences also include an interview with the local Catholic priest, and his response echoes the crowd's homophobic attitudes: "Somos un equipo de tradición familiar. No aceptamos estos tipos de conductas." The scenes demonstrate how sports like soccer—and its supporting institutions such as the FMF or the Catholic Church—help to reaffirm dominant gender ideologies. Despite his superior athletic talent, Aitor's non-normative behavior strips him of his masculinity, resulting in his classification as the "penetrated" or "inferior" man by many Mexican followers.

Likewise, these attitudes extend to the locker room. Even though Chava publicly backs the personal preferences of Aitor during a team meeting, his teammates greet him with the typical discourse associated with *homosocial patrolling*. While some yell "pinche puto," others have taped a piece of paper in his locker that reads "soplanucas" and "muerdealmuadas" [sic]. Besides this, the intimate contact shared between the men and Aitor decreases dramatically.

A "friendly" game

Different from the homoerotic gaze employed in previous scenes, the players now exaggerate their disgust as the Catalonian drops his drawers. As Carillo explains, heterosexual men typically engage in less intimate contact when they discover another's homosexual identity (2003: 359). Thus, in an act to preserve their masculinity and protect patriarchal order within the sporting setting, the players carry out overt performances of heterosexuality, sexism, and homophobia. Furthermore, and similar to the portrayals of gay men in the mentioned *fichera* films, Aitor's juxtaposition to his other teammates helps to inflate the masculinity of these surrounding characters.

Men's soccer continues to represent one of the most influential cultural entities that facilitates the construction of the Mexican *macho*. The carefully crafted images of these men in television and media provide the dominant molds for the country's modern masculine heroes. However, a queer reading of the sport and cultural texts like *Club de Cuervos* allow viewers to question these conventional representations, as well as the associated heteronormative behavior. The streaming series' easily accessible episodes expose soccer's overt displays of homoaffectivity, images that deconstruct the idea of the tough, stoic, and supposedly straight *macho*. Although these sequences often exhibit these players' masculine performances—whether it be their on-field dominance or off-field discourse—they also demonstrate that the stadium creates a space where men can publicly enjoy each other's friendly embrace, behavior that is suppressed in other social settings. Nonetheless, as revised by Los Cuervos's reaction to Aitor, these playful displays of affection are reserved for the game's heterosexual participants, a process that reinforces heteronormative patriarchy.

Notes

1 These low-budget Mexican sex comedies—often taking place in homosocial spaces such as the brothel or cabaret—achieved commercial success during the 1970s and 1980s. According to González Rodríguez and Mora, the themes of these films coincide with the sex-related transformations within modern Mexican society, among these, the boom of the sex industry, the greater objectification of the female body, and the public recognition of homosexuals (González Rodríguez 1990: 76–77; Mora 2006: 111).
2 Hans Gumbrecht proposes that the unexpected, beautiful play represents one of the most fascinating phenomenon for fans of sports like soccer (2006: 184–95). Likewise, Juan Villoro, Mexico's most published intellectual and chronicler working with the sport, suggests that the lack of literary texts on soccer can be attributed to the game already generating its own epic, tragic, and comedic elements (2010: 21).
3 The inclusion of Brazilian (Río) and Argentine (Potro) characters on a team from Mexico's first division demonstrates the game's current globalized state. For more on this topic, see Fiengo's "Gol-balización" (2003).

Works cited

Alazraki, Gary, dir. *Nosotros los nobles.* Alazraki Films, 2013.
Anderson, Eric. *21st Century Jocks: Sporting Men and Contemporary Heterosexuality.* New York: Palgrave, 2014.
Azamar Cruz, César Ricardo. (2015). "Del 'puto' (amistoso) a la 'bitch' (de cariño): el insulto como manifestación de violencia de género." *Memoria del coloquio de investigación en género desde el IPN* 1.1 (2015): 471–485.
Baker, Aaron. *Contesting Identities: Sports in American Film.* Urbana IL: University of Illinois Press, 2003.
Binello, Gabriela, and Mariano Domino. "Mujeres en el área chica." *Deporte y sociedad.* Ed. Pablo Alabarces, Roberto Di Giano, and Julio Frydenberg. Buenos Aires: University of Buenos Aires, 1998. 211–26.
Butler, Judith. *Gender Trouble.* New York: Routledge, 1990.
Carillo, Héctor. "Neither *Machos* nor *Maricones*: Masculinity and Emerging Male Homosexual Identities in Mexico." *Changing Men and Masculinities in Latin America.* Ed. Matthew C. Guttmann. Durham, NC: Duke University Press, 2003. 351–69.

Club de Cuervos. Alazraki Films, 2015.

Connell, R.W. "An Iron Man: The Body and Some Contradictions of Hegemonic Masculinity." *Sport, Men, and the Gender Order: Critical Feminist Perspectives.* Ed. Michael Messner and Donald F. Sabo. Champaign: Human Kinetics, 1990. 83–95.

Connell, R.W. *Masculinities.* 2nd ed. Berkeley, CA: University of California Press, 2005.

Cuarón, Carlos, dir. *Rudo y Cursi.* Focus Features, 2008.

Doty, Alexander. *Making Things Perfectly Queer.* Minneapolis, MN: University of Minnesota Press, 1993. *(fdp).* Prodigo Films, 2012.

Feasey, Rebecca. *Masculinity and Popular Television.* Edinburgh: Edinburgh University Press, 2008.

Fiengo, Sergio Villena. "Gol-balización, identidades nacionales y fútbol." *Futbologías: fútbol identidad y violencia en América Latina.* Ed. Pablo Alabarces. Buenos Aires: Clasco, 2003. 257–71.

Foster, David William. *Gender & Society in Contemporary Brazilian Cinema.* Austin, TX: University of Texas Press, 1999.

Foster, David William. *Queer Issues in Contemporary Latin American Cinema.* Austin, TX: University of Texas Press, 2003.

Foucault, Michel. *Discipline and Punish: The Birth of the Prison.* 2nd ed. Translated by Alan Sheridan. New York: Vintage, 1995.

González, Rodriguez, Sergio. *Los bajos fondos: el antro, la bohemia, el café.* Mexico City: Cal y Arena, 1990.

Gumbrecht, Hans Ulrich. *In Praise of Athletic Beauty.* Cambridge, MA: Harvard University Press, 2006.

Gutiérrez, Luis Adrián Calderón. "Masculinidad y fútbol en México." *El tlacuache* 393 (2009): 1–3.

Irwin, Robert McKee. *Mexican Masculinities.* Minneapolis, MN: University of Minnesota Press, 2003

de Lauretis, Teresa. *Technologies of Gender: Essays on Theory, Film, Semiotics, Cinema.* Bloomington, IN: Indiana University Press, 1987.

Lehman, Peter. *Running Scared: Masculinity and the Representation of the Male Body.* Detroit, MI: Wayne State University Press, 2007.

Lewis, Vek. "When 'Macho' Bodies Fail: Spectacles of Corporeality and the Limits of the Homosocial/sexual in Mexican Cinema." *Mysterious Skin: Male Bodies in Contemporary Cinema.* Ed. Santiago Fouz-Hernández. New York: I.B. Tauris, 2009. 177–92.

Magazine, Roger. *Golden and Blue Like My Heart: Masculinity, Youth, and Power among Soccer Fans in Mexico City.* Tucson, AZ: University of Arizona Press, 2007.

Martínez, Maritiza Carreño. "Fútbol femenil en México 1969–1971." M.A. Thesis, Mexico City: UNAM, 2006.

Mora, Sergio de la. *Cinemachismo: Masculinities and Sexuality in Mexican Film.* Austin, TX: University of Texas Press, 2006.

Mosse, George L. *The Image of Man: The Creation of Modern Masculinity.* New York: Oxford University Press, 1996.

Mulvey, Laura. *Visual and Other Pleasures.* New York: Palgrave, 1989.

Nadel, Joshua H. *Fútbol!: Why Soccer Matters in Latin America.* Gainesville FL: Florida University Press, 2014.

Neale, Steve. "Masculinity as Spectacle: Reflections on Men and Mainstream Cinema." *Screening the Male: Exploring Masculinities in Hollywood Cinema.* Ed. Steve Cohan and Ina Rae Hark. New York: Routledge, 1993. 9–20.

Paz, Octavio. *El laberinto de soledad.* 13th ed. Madrid: Cátedra, 2007.

Pons, Juan Carlos Cabrera. "Puto: normalización institucional de la discriminación en el fútbol." *Desbordes* 5 (2014): 77–84.

Ridge, Patrick Thomas. "Mexico 'on Top:' Queering Masculinity in Contemporary Mexican Soccer Chronicles." *Perspectives on the U.S.-Mexico Soccer Rivalry: Passion and Politics in Red, White, Blue, and Green.* Ed. Jeffrey Kassing and Lindsey Meân. New York: Palgrave, 2017. 123–144.

Russo, Vito. *The Celluloid Closet.* Rev. ed. New York: Harper & Row, 1987.

Sebreli, Juan José. *La era del fútbol.* 4th ed. Buenos Aires: Debolsillo, 2005.

Sedgwick, Eve K. *Between Men: English Literature and Male Homosocial Desire.* New York: Columbia University Press, 1985. *La selección.* Caracol Televisión, 2013–.

Serna, Enrique. "Orgías futboleras." *Giros negros.* Mexico: Cal y Arena, 2008. 61–63.

Swain, Jon. "The Money's Good, The Fame's Good, The Girls are Good." *British Journal of Sociology of Education* 21.1 (2000): 95–109.

Venkatesh, Vinodh. "Androgyny, Football, and Pedophilia: Rearticulating Mexican Masculinities in the Works of Enrique Serna." *Revista de literatura mexicana contemporánea* 49 (2011): 25–36.

Venkatesh, Vinodh. *New Maricón Cinema: Outing Latin American Film.* Austin TX: University of Texas Press, 2016.

Villoro, Juan. *Dios es redondo.* 2nd ed. Mexico: Planeta, 2010.

Ward, Jane. *Not Gay: Sex Between Straight White Men.* New York: New York University Press, 2015.

Zax, David. "The Creative Team behind 'Club de Cuervos,' Netflix's First Spanish-Language Series." *Fast Company.* Fast Company & Inc, 19 August 2015.

25

READING RACE AND GENDER IN *THE BLACK MAN IN BRAZILIAN SOCCER* AND BEYOND

Jack A. Draper III

Since the early twentieth century, women and men of various races have played soccer recreationally. Up until the 1920s, the involvement of working class and non-white men in the top Brazilian leagues was heavily contested, while women were entirely excluded, placing Afro-Brazilians and women in parallel marginal positions with respect to the top flight of soccer in Rio de Janeiro and São Paulo.

Mário Filho's *O negro no futebol brasileiro* tells the story of how black soccer players struggled to break through the unofficial color line in the sport in Brazil, consolidating their position by the time the sport was professionalized in the 1930s. Women in this history, however, are not represented as players and are primarily represented as fans in the stands, or playing supporting roles to their husbands, from team presidents to coaches. Even in this role, in Filho's narrative, they had largely disappeared by the 1930s. This inclusion of working-class, black and mixed-race males in the sport even as women were increasingly marginalized should be understood as inherent to the formation of a sense of Brazilian nationhood tied to the national soccer team, emphasizing its collective strength, skill and increasing dominance internationally as key rallying symbols of national progress and development. Of course, this racial integration of the sport was linked to the popularization of the social/racial democracy ideology with the help of sociologist Gilberto Freyre in the 1930s. Even so, Filho does not depict integration as a smooth, accommodating process of hybridization for non-white players. What he reveals instead is the reality of the so-called racial democracy—rather than a tamed hybrid of racial mixture producing a hegemonic *mestiço* (mixed-race) subject, Filho demonstrates a hyper-consciousness of racialized features in the context of soccer celebrity and thus a *savage hybridity* (Moreiras 2001) that destabilizes the very notion of the hybrid nation. The figure of Pelé enters into the narrative towards the end as another destabilizing force, linking blackness, pride, and power to an unprecedented degree. On the other hand, women are increasingly excluded from the national soccer narrative as a subaltern population that helps define the gendered identity of soccer in its absence.

Woman as subaltern in the world of soccer and soccer narratives

Filho entirely ignores the possibility of women playing soccer. Women help to gender the soccer audience in his narrative, however, and Filho draws a parallel between the elite female crowd of rowing and regattas and the female audience members in the *arquibancadas* or grandstands

Reading race and gender in The Black Man in Brazilian Soccer *and beyond*

of the early soccer matches in the first three decades of the century. This specific gendering of the crowd, along with the occasional involvement of owners', coaches' and club members' (white, wealthy) wives and other female relatives in hosting or cooking meals for the players, or attending club soirees and cocktail parties, is explained as part of the general atmosphere which the soccer traditionalists of that era wished to maintain, an era in which "the grandstand of Fluminense [soccer club] resembled a bouquet of flowers [...] [and] in which soccer was a chique thing (a arquibancada parecia um *bouquet* de flores [...] [e] em que o futebol era coisa chique)" (Filho [1964] 2003: 70). The *saudosistas* (nostalgics), as Filho calls them, wished for the sport to remain elite and exclusionary, and the audience which best represented such a state of affairs were the women of elite families, dressed in their Sunday best to attend a soccer match, and presumably eyeing the sons of elite families on the field as potential paramours and future husbands (or alternatively as family or family friends). A sports magazine in Natal even argued for a social "cleansing [limpeza]" of the clubs in 1921, removing lower class and "uncultured [mal educados]" players from the teams and replacing them with "decent lads [rapazes decentes]" who have 'representation in society [representação no meio social]" (Santos 2009: 191). According to this same author, such a social cleansing would give "much satisfaction [muita satisfação]" to female fans (Ibid.). The homogeneity of spectators and players in terms of class (and necessarily race as well, due to the existent racial-class hierarchy in the country) allowed for an atmosphere that was deemed appropriate, safe and pleasing to upper-class women (or "genteel sportwomen [gentis sportwomen]" as one Minas Gerais paper called them), allowing them to be public aficionados of the young sport and frequent attendees at matches (Santos 2009: 184).

Once soccer had been consolidated as a national sport in Brazil that could incorporate the working-class and lower classes as well as non-whites (by the 1930s), Filho's narrative no longer references female fans. It seems the crowd can no longer be gendered female in this interclass, interracial atmosphere. What Archetti (1996) writes of Argentina was becoming equally true in Brazil, though with important racial variations: "football [soccer] is not only an eminently masculine social arena but it is also associated historically with the construction of national identity through the international successes of the national team and the 'export' of great players to Europe" (34). As was also the case for South American rivals/neighbors Argentina and Uruguay, soccer in Brazil was now a national sport, associated with masculinity, virility and national strength and skill, rather than the more ambiguous gender associations of the sport during the amateur era, during which it was more associated with gentlemanly behavior and considered less manly than rowing, according to Filho. Indeed, in an infamous 1923 incident of soccer violence perpetrated by white, elite fans of Flamengo against the fans of the very successful, racially integrated Vasco da Gama team, it was the rowing team that served as "hooligans" in the crowd. Members of the Flamengo rowing club felt so threatened by the idea of their club's elite, white soccer players losing to an excellent, multi-class and interracial Vasco da Gama side that they brought their oars to the stands and proceeded to beat the opposing team's fans with them to keep them from cheering for Vasco (Filho [2003] 1964: 124–126). Vasco lost this battle but won the war, becoming that same year the first "team of whites, mulattoes and blacks, all mixed together [time de brancos, mulatos e pretos, tudo misturado]" to win the Rio championship (Filho [2003] 1964: 124).

At the same time that soccer became more associated with virility, masculinity, racial mixture and nationhood in the 1930s, public calls for the official exclusion of women from soccer leagues became much louder, culminating in a law which prohibited women from playing organized soccer in 1941, a ban which would last until the 1970s (Nadel 2014: 218–219). Thus we can see both in Filho's narrative focused on black and mixed-race soccer players, and in the wider society, increasing restrictions on women's participation in the sport, and even on their symbolic association with it. Even as the genteel, feminized space of the arquibancadas disappears from the soccer matches of the 1930s in Filho's history, the Vargas regime was encouraged, by those who claimed soccer "endangered girls' and women's reproductive capabilities," to legally restrict the participation of women as players, ultimately taking this prohibitive action in the early 1940s (Nadel 2014: 218). Both soccer journalists/historians and the Brazilian politico-juridical regime began to feel a greater need to "police" the gender boundary between sports like tennis and volleyball deemed more appropriate for women, and the putatively male world of soccer, represented most famously by the skills, style and virility of the increasingly multiracial male national team and their struggles for dominance in the international arena.

Filho's savage hybridity: Racial integration of soccer and the persistence of the color line

Unlike the experience of women, whose exclusion from soccer worsened over the course of the 1920s and 1930s, Afro-Brazilians and other players of color managed to make major headway and become part of the starting 11 of both the national team and many professional clubs in Brazil by the 1930s. They were able to overcome the conjoined obstacles of racism and classism in order to break into the sport, and thus also were included in the constructions of nationhood and masculinity under the regime of Brazil's first populist president, Getúlio Vargas (1930–1945). But this process was by no means a smooth one, and the development of the hybrid or *mestiço* nation was uneven and heavily contested by an ideology of whitening well into the 1950s at least, as demonstrated by Filho's detailed look at race relations and racial perceptions in Brazilian soccer over that period. On a local textual level, Filho does a large amount of "racial reading" of individual players in order to situate them in the Brazilian race/color continuum. Filho's typical strategy is to describe skin color, hair type, and sometimes facial features in order to classify players as black or mulatto (both of whom he includes in *negro* identity). He then discusses the player's own self-identification, often with a lighter skin color or in a category less associated with blackness such as *caboclo*. In what follows, I explore this process of racial reading and the complex interplay between empowering black identity and the racial readings of players, coaches, fans and the media in an era when whiteness was still a status marker sought after by players of diverse racial backgrounds, and blackness was often described as a "curse" to be overcome.

Although the players, major club members/presidents, and fans in large part still viewed soccer as the domain of the elite "sportmen" in the early 1920s, at that point there were already some who thought that playing ability should be the primary concern. One columnist in 1921 wrote that, in the face of demands like the one noted above for the "social cleansing" of lower- or working-class players from soccer clubs, the clubs should instead reward players for their performance, no matter their social class, leaving good players on the team even if not members of elite society (Santos 2009: 192). Not coincidentally, this is the time period when multiple non-white players begin to find a way into the starting 11 of some of Rio's major clubs in Filho's narrative. The example of the great success of black players such as Isabelino Gradín on the Uruguayan national team also served as a competitive motivation to allow a softening of the color line in Brazil. One illustrative case is that of Manteiga, who was discovered at the small club of Mauá by the director of América soccer club, Jaime Barcelos. Like other managers of top teams looking for talent, Barcelos had begun scouting clubs by the port and in working-class neighborhoods, and happened to come across Manteiga in this team composed of sailors in the navy (Filho [2003] 1964: 112–113). Upon first mentioning Manteiga in his narrative, Filho labels him a mulatto, but then performs a further racial reading of his facial features and even his personality: "A mulatto with black features, the nose flat, the mouth with fat lips. But with

Reading race and gender in The Black Man in Brazilian Soccer *and beyond*

the delicacy, the softness of a mulatto [Um mulato de feições de preto, o nariz chato, a boca de beiços grossos. Mas com a delicadeza, a macieza de um mulato]" (Ibid.: 113). Filho proceeds to describe the great difficulties Manteiga had because of his physical appearance, even as he was breaking down racial barriers to become one of the first black players on América's team. In contrast to that of Manteiga, we can consider the description of Arthur Friedenreich, a player of mixed African and German descent who had already played on the Brazilian national team in 1919. Filho describes Friedenreich as "a mulatto that wanted to pass as white […] with green eyes, a brown face with light-olive complexion [but with hair that was] hard, rebellious (um mulato que quisesse passar por branco […] de olhos verdes, um leve tom de azeitona no rosto moreno […] [o] cabelo […] duro, rebelde) (Filho [2003] 1964: 61). In Filho's narrative, Friedenreich's desire to pass as white, along with his relatively light skin color and green eyes, allowed him, along with his amazing soccer skills, to be an exception on an all-white Brazilian national team and the various all-white clubs he had played on since 1909.

In the general context of Filho's writings, we should not understand physical appearance to be any concern of his personally with regard to the fitness of a player and whether they should be chosen for a team. Filho makes it clear that his primary concern is meritocratic—great players, whatever their race, should be recruited by Brazilian clubs and the national team. This was a position he had held since his beginnings as a sports journalist in the early 1930s (Pereira 2000). Filho's attention to racialized physical features should be understood as an attempt to frame the way the players are treated at that point in history by the general soccer community, including other players, coaches, club management and fans (of their own club and rival ones). Returning to the example of Manteiga, Filho emphasizes that despite the "fineness" and "softness" of his demeanor, and his great skill with the ball which earned him a position on a major Rio de Janeiro team, he continued to face significant discrimination from fellow players as well as fans and club members due to being a man of mixed race who nevertheless was unable to hide his Afro-Brazilian racial features (Filho [2003] 1964: 113–117). Upon Manteiga's arrival at the club for the start of the 1921 season, nine members of the team, generally described as members of white and wealthy families, quit in protest. One black player (also identified as mulatto) named Miranda was already on the team, and the protesting white players (many from the wealthy Borges family) claimed that two mulattoes on the team was too many. Emphasizing again the involvement of the "sportwomen" of elite families at this time in soccer clubs, Filho notes that two players who were romantically involved with female members of the Borges family distanced themselves from the club and stopped playing, while not officially terminating their memberships. This distancing is described by Filho as a result of "[t]he Borges women supporting their brothers, demanding from their boyfriends, fiancés, husbands, an attitude against Manteiga ([a]s Borges apoiando os irmãos, exigindo dos namorados, dos noivos, dos maridos, uma atitude contra Manteiga)" (Filho [2003] 1964: 114). Twenty-four other players agreed to stay on the team and play with Manteiga, indicating, along with the decision of club management to stand behind Manteiga, a growing acceptance of non-white players, especially those who were uniquely talented athletes. Nevertheless, despite Manteiga's relatively successful performance on the field afterwards playing for América, his struggles with integration into a mostly white team did not stop at mere resistance to his membership.

Filho goes on to describe what the process of integration actually looked like in this early era, emphasizing the psychological impact on an Afro-Brazilian player. Manteiga is generally described as very timid, uncomfortable, and walking on eggshells in any of his interactions with fellow players or club members off the field. In the locker room, while other (white) players would enter into more intimate contact with him such as "slapping his stomach [dar palmadinhas na barriga]," Manteiga himself was "[c]alling everyone mister, taking his hat off

Jack A. Draper III

when anyone approached to speak with him ([t]ratando todo mundo de senhor, tirando logo o chapéu quando alguém se aproximava para falar com ele)" (Filho [2003] 1964: 115). Generally Manteiga would not hang around the locker room or clubhouse to socialize, finding a way to slip out quietly after training sessions and matches. We can understand his behavior as certainly influenced by the controversy and conflict that had arisen upon his joining the club, but also that of a man who was completely unfamiliar with the elite, white social sphere of the majority of the players on the club. He was a migrant from Bahia whose primary social contacts outside his native state had been other sailors in the navy prior to joining this club full of genteel sportsmen and women (as a player, he was also another member of the club). Thus it is not surprising that his experiences with the club away from practice and matches is described as all the more alienating, despite not involving any direct discrimination. Filho describes Manteiga as being afraid to enter América's social hall, a space in which players would typically mingle with members of the club, men and women alike. "He didn't even have the courage to look [nem tinha coragem de olhar]" when he passed by the social hall, afraid that someone he knew would see him and oblige him to enter, and in his entire season as a player with América he "never entered [nunca entrou]" the building (Filho [2003] 1964: 115).

Clearly a social and psychological barrier existed for Manteiga which he was unable to fully cross. This barrier becomes all the more obvious in the exceptional case when Manteiga was given a direct invitation and socially obliged to attend a cocktail party in the restricted social sphere of club-member João Santos's house. Filho first explains how this occasion was envisioned in advance by the elitist families whose members had left the club in protest against Manteiga's inclusion on the squad:

> Something that the Borges and Curti families had always imagined as the height of absurdity: Manteiga at a cocktail party at João Santos's house. An elegant gathering, with young ladies [Uma coisa que os Borges e os Curtis sempre tinham imaginado como o maior dos absurdos: Manteiga num cocktail da casa de João Santos. Uma reunião elegante, com moças].
>
> *(Filho [2003] 1964: 115)*

Filho emphasizes the elegance of the party and the presence of daughters of elite families as key factors which, for the most prejudiced members of the club, made the attendance of a black man of humble origins a most absurd idea. As with the traditional sections of box seats at the major club matches, an elite space that is gendered as female ("It even seemed there would be a dance, the windows open, decorated with young ladies [Até parecia que ia haver baile, as janelas abertas, enfeitadas de moças]") generates a paranoia or repulsion towards blackness, perhaps accentuated all the more by the private ambience of the home (Ibid.). Going further, Filho emphasizes that the situation was probably the most uncomfortable for Manteiga himself, despite being an invited guest at the party. While all the other players there seemed right at home, Manteiga stood awkwardly, "without raising his timid eyes of a lamb from the design on the carpet [...] hiding himself (sem levantar os olhos mansos, de cordeiro, do desenho do tapete [...] escondendo-se)" (Ibid.).

Back on the field, Manteiga was doing well and scoring goals, putting América in reach of the Rio championship in its final tie-breaking match against Flamengo. When América lost this match, Filho emphasizes that "[n]o one felt [the defeat] more than Manteiga ([n]inguém sentia mais [a derrota] do que o Manteiga)" (Filho [2003] 1964: 117). It is evident that Manteiga, and other black players of the era, felt a unique pressure to perform at their peak and win championships in order to prove their worth—above all they felt they had to outperform the white players who would likely be favored over them, all things being equal, in terms of results. In this vein, Filho writes of the 1923 Vasco da Gama club, "Between a white and a black, the two playing the same, Vasco would stick with the white [Entre um branco e um preto, os dois jogando a mesma coisa, o Vasco ficava com o branco]" (Filho [2003] 1964: 120).

Considering Filho's telling of Manteiga's story in general, the most striking aspect is his decision not to portray the entry of an Afro-Brazilian as a star forward into a major club in 1921 as a triumph of racial democracy. Instead, Filho focuses on the inertia against such change that continued to exist and be felt very clearly by Manteiga in every aspect of his involvement with the América club. Having identified him clearly as a mulatto of obvious African descent in appearance, Filho's description of the racial-class discrimination (explicit and structural/implicit) against Manteiga from within his own club also problematizes any notion of the mulatto as a symbol of smooth racial mixture and harmony, a symbolism which had become prevalent in the national imaginary by the time Filho's book was published in its first edition in 1948. Thus Filho portrays in the story of Manteiga, and those of many other black players as well as some coaches, a savage hybridity involving social tension and struggle, rather than the more tamed, assimilative, conciliatory hybrid process associated with Freyre's theory of social/racial democracy.

The color line as challenged and experienced by a pioneering black coach: Gentil Cardoso

By 1933, black players had established themselves as a force to be reckoned with and they would become major participants in the dawning era of professional soccer. In that same year, the director of the elite soccer club of Fluminense made it clear that, as a professional team, his club would be looking for talent from all races (nevertheless, Filho emphasizes that white players were still preferred, all things being equal) (Filho [2003] 1964: 193). Professionalization favored both non-elite and non-white players, since having a significant amount of leisure time for training (as did the "sportmen" of old in their cult of gentlemanly amateurism) would no longer be an advantage. However, the question of black coaches was another matter. Fluminense would not have its first black coach until the following decade, in 1945. This coach, Gentil Cardoso, is the primary example of an Afro-Brazilian in this position of team leadership in the entirety of Filho's narrative (covering the period 1904–1961). This is hardly surprising, as Afro-Brazilians have very rarely been given opportunities to coach—even as recently as 2015, there was only one black coach out of 20 in Brazil's top national league (Borges 2015). (Internationally, the situation is not much better, with only four black coaches out of 92 in the clubs of the Premier and Football Leagues of England, despite 25 percent of the players in those leagues being black in 2014 (Lewis 2014).) In any case, Cardoso seems to have been the first Afro-Brazilian coach of any major club in Brazil, and likely one of the earliest in the world in a multiracial league (in fact, he was already coaching Bonsucesso, one of Rio's major clubs, in 1931).

Nevertheless, as with his narrative about the player Manteiga, Filho does not spend much time celebrating the historic and groundbreaking nature of Cardoso's appointment at Fluminense, nor his earlier coaching positions at Vasco da Gama and Bonsucesso. Instead, he continues in a narrative framework of savage hybridity, emphasizing the embattled psychological perspective of an isolated black coach in the 1940s and 1950s, and the inertia that coach feels working against his efforts to keep his job, even with great success on the field. Before describing the experience of Cardoso's first season as Fluminense's coach, Filho makes it clear that this coach is far more publicly vocal about his experience of racism than Manteiga had been two decades before, nor does he seek to hide his black identity like some players. At the same time, one notes in this description of Cardoso's views a very negative notion of black pride on the part of Filho, one which he would revise in the later edition of his book published in 1964, especially in his representation of Pelé:

> Gentil Cardoso never denied the condition of being black. On the contrary: it was like he proclaimed it. Not out of racial pride, in a reverse racism: out of suffering. Less due to his color, which God had given him, than due to the obstacles he perceived, in every sphere, put up against the man of color in Brazil.
>
> If he were not black, he would be directing great clubs, they would not deny him the honor of coaching the Brazilian national team. Who had been the first Brazilian coach, a real coach? The black Gentil Cardoso, using a blackboard and everything, with tactics drawn on it in chalk, the introducer of Chapman's system in Brazil.
>
> [Gentil Cardoso nunca negou a condição de preto. Pelo contrário: como que a proclamava. Não por orgulho de raça, num racismo às avessas: por mágoa. Menos da cor, que Deus lhe dera, do que da prevenção que vislumbrava, em toda parte, contra o homem de cor no Brasil.
>
> Se não fosse preto, estaria dirigindo times de grandes clubes, não lhe negariam a honra de treinar o escrete brasileiro. Quem fora o primeiro técnico brasileiro, técnico mesmo? O preto Gentil Cardoso, usando quadro negro e tudo, com táticas desenhadas a giz, o introdutor do sistema de Chapman no Brasil.]
>
> (Filho [2003] 1964: 248)

Taking Cardoso's perspective in a version of free indirect narrative, Filho highlights the injustice that a successful coach, who had brought significant tactical innovations to the Brazilian game, was viewed as inferior to white coaches solely due to the color of his skin, and thus was still hitting a glass ceiling in terms of the opportunities he was given. Indeed, in terms of the national team, Cardoso was only ever allowed to coach five matches—this was in 1959 and not even against international opponents, but rather against club sides in a regional tournament within Brazil (Borges 2015). (In the history of soccer in the country, Brazil's national team has only ever had one other black coach, and that was only for one match in 1991.) In any case, Cardoso still managed to have an illustrious career, coaching virtually every major Rio de Janeiro club and some in São Paulo, Recife and Portugal as well while winning multiple championships.

Gentil Cardoso's career success is certainly appreciated by Filho, but the stories he tells of Cardoso's experiences coaching Fluminense and Vasco da Gama to championships in the 1940s and 1950s are focused on Cardoso's struggles to keep his position notwithstanding his obvious coaching ability. Cardoso very clearly pins blame on racial discrimination for his being replaced by white coaches despite excellent performance, and Filho's narrative tends to confirm this perspective. In his 1952 season with Vasco da Gama, Cardoso is depicted as sensing a threat of replacement by the white coach Flávio Costa from the beginning of the season. Cardoso's nickname was "Moço Preto [Young Black Man]", and so he considered the competition to be between Flávio Costa, the "'Moço Branco' [Young White Man]," and himself, the Moço Preto (Filho [2003] 1964: 306). Cardoso's team won the Rio championship that year, but even as he celebrated in the locker room after the championship match, proclaiming that "The masses are with me! [As massas estão comigo!]", an influential club member confronted him with disrespect: "Shut up! You, sir, are nothing more than an employee of the club! [Cale-se! O senhor é um simples empregado do clube!]" (Filho [2003] 1964: 307). Cardoso responded angrily to this disrespect, and was promptly fired for himself disrespecting an important (white) club member. Filho explains that Cardoso saw this as "another proof of racism [mais uma prova de racismo]" and that "a curse was pursuing him: that of being black [uma maldição o perseguia: a de ser preto]" (Ibid.). Notable here is that Cardoso was standing up for himself against a white power structure in the club, which did not accept his challenge. He was however able to find employment at another major team shortly thereafter, namely Botafogo, where he would discover one of the greatest black players in Brazilian soccer history—Garrincha.

Filho then contrasts Cardoso's vision of his blackness as an inescapable curse with the racial identity of the Fluminense player Robson, in order to suggest that players at that time were more able to feel they had transcended their blackness. Filho tells a story which ends with Robson commenting to another player "I once was black and I know what that's like [Eu já fui preto e sei o que é isso]" (Filho [2003] 1964: 308). In addition to being a reflection of the survival from the period of slavery of an ideology of whitening which equates social mobility with becoming "whiter", Robson's statement is highlighted to demonstrate that players apparently did not understand their blackness to be as much of a limiting factor as it was for a coach, that is, "[h]owever black [a player] was he mixed with whites, as if he were white ([p]or mais preto que fosse [o jogador,] se misturava com os brancos, como se branco fosse]" (Filho [2003] 1964: 307). A black coach's job, on the other hand, placed him in a more intellectual sphere, the sphere of management where he was clearly more likely to be questioned and challenged by whites in the club hierarchy. Unfortunately, the situation of Gentil Cardoso described by Filho in the 1940s and 1950s continues to be the experience of black coaches to this day in Brazil. Up to the present decade, coaches such as Lula Pereira complain of racism preventing them from being hired (R7 Esportes 2014), and physical education scholar Osmar de Souza Jr. asserts that black coaches are still held to a higher standard than whites by both fans and club, and are quickly replaced by white coaches when they fail to meet this higher standard (Borges 2015).

From color line to gender line in Brazilian and international soccer

In scholarship related to Mário Filho's narratives on Brazilian soccer, it is typical to conflate his perspective on race relations with that of Gilberto Freyre (e.g. Pereira 2000: 343–344; Wisnik 2008 239–240[1]). No doubt this conflation was encouraged by Freyre, and even Filho himself to a certain extent, through the inclusion of Gilberto Freyre's preface in the first edition of *The Black Man in Brazilian Soccer*, which frames Filho's text as a kind of further proof of Freyre's theory of Brazilian social/racial democracy in the realm of sports. It should be evident at this point that my reading finds greater divergence between the two authors in this area—Freyre's theory of transculturation between indigenous, Euro- and Afro-Brazilian peoples yielding a harmonious, tamed national hybrid is implicitly called into question by the savage hybridity of Filho's history of black Brazilians' struggles to cross the color line in soccer. Filho's story does end with a triumphant vision of Pelé embracing his black identity even as he becomes the "king" of Brazilian soccer, a stark contrast with the story of Manteiga 40 years earlier. Rather than reflecting Freyre here though, the celebration of blackness is more in tune with the perspective of the contemporary *negritude* movement in Francophone literature, and in Brazilian culture, Vinícius de Moraes's play *Orfeu da conceição* (and its film adaptation *Orfeu negro/ Black Orpheus*) and the work of Abdias do Nascimento's Experimental Black Theater in the 1940s and 1950s. The triumph of Pelé as a black player also anticipates the emphasis on black pride of the Unified Black Movement (*Movimento Negro Unificado*) beginning in the 1970s. This is not a discourse that Pelé himself was explicitly foregrounding in the early 1960s—Mário Filho's interpretation that Pelé was not only the king of soccer but very much a national hero embracing black identity should be understood as an anti-racist politicization of the soccer star, a culmination of Filho's many earlier racial readings of players who had not assumed their blackness with pride as Pelé was now able to do.

Yet it would only be in the decades subsequent to the publication of *The Black Man in Brazilian Soccer*'s second edition that such a project of inclusion and uplift could be imagined on behalf of women. This project would involve the gradual weakening of the ban against women's soccer in Brazil and other countries, with an increasing amount of amateur play and competition at the grassroots level and subsequently more organized leagues and international competition in the 1970s and 1980s. Parallel to the color line battled for much of the last century in soccer, the gender line has been a major area of struggle in recent decades and is still a significant factor limiting the acceptance and success of women's soccer leagues around the globe. After the bans on women's soccer started to be lifted in the 1970s, the cultural/social inertia and psychological battles women have had to fight in Brazil, Latin America, the US and elsewhere, echo the experiences of players like Manteiga in the 1920s, and Coach Cardoso in the 1940s and 1950s.

One might assume that solidarity has been an easier path for women as a group, since there was no need for a project like Filho's racial readings of all black players to encourage the identification of women as one group. Yet as women entered a world of soccer that had been coded as masculine for many decades, their own femininity was stereotyped or questioned by critics and even their own families. From Mexico to Brazil in the 1970s and 1980s, women were either hyper-sexualized and thus not taken seriously as players, or accused of going against their feminine nature (i.e. challenging traditional gender norms) and thus being perverted by the sport into tomboys and/or lesbians. Prominent players from Brazil and other Latin American nations, who would as adults participate in the top echelons of national and international soccer, have reported that they experienced punishment and violent intimidation from their parents and siblings when they attempted to play soccer in their childhood years (Nadel 2014: 229; 232–235). Cultural and social change along the lines of the shift in attitudes about black identity in Brazil would be necessary in order to accommodate a rising generation of diverse, talented and highly motivated female athletes.

This became the democratizing struggle for female soccer players equivalent to that of black players in the previous era—to convince soccer aficionados, through a combination of their performance on the field and a valorization of their own identities as women, that their gender was legitimate in this context and was not erased or perverted but instead should be understood as part of a broader, multi-gendered (not to mention non-homophobic) understanding of the sport. The hybridization process here applies not to race but to the gendered understanding of the identity of a soccer player—which through the efforts of female athletes on the field and off has become far more associated with a spectrum of genders, instead of the stereotypically masculine connotations of yesteryear. Much like the integration process for Afro-Brazilians in the sport, women's integration should be understood as a savage hybridity, one which has had to overcome much stigma and social inertia and still has a long way to go to achieve parity with men's soccer in terms of support from public and private sectors (women, of course, have the added difficulty of being segregated into their own leagues by gender and thus having to popularize those leagues in competition with men's leagues). Taking into consideration the resonance between challenges to color and gender lines in soccer, we can see how truly fitting it is that Pelé was there to congratulate the outstanding female players of the first Women's World Cup in 1991, in which Brazil's women participated along with an international group including Japan, Germany, Sweden and the eventual winners, the United States (Lisi 2013: 17). Thirty years after Filho had celebrated his rise to prominence as the culmination of black players' contributions to the game, along with the start of a new era in which those contributions could be assumed with pride by Afro-Brazilians, Pelé was there to support the beginnings of a similar era for women.

Reading race and gender in The Black Man in Brazilian Soccer *and beyond*

Note

1 José Miguel Wisnik, in this passage likening Filho's narratives on soccer to Freyre's focus on miscegenation in Brazil and the development of a so-called "racial democracy," himself acknowledges that Filho does not hide "evidence to the contrary [sinais contraditórios]" (239). My contention here rests on exactly this aspect of Filho's historical narrative—especially in *The Black Man in Brazilian Soccer*—whose savage hybridity emphasizes the resistance to racial integration and equality which black players, coaches and fans came up against all too often. On the other hand, Fatima Martin Rodrigues Ferreira Antunes (2004), in her extensive analysis of Filho's sports journalism, does not emphasize an affinity with Gilberto Freyre's work among the major themes Filho covered related to soccer and national identity.

Works cited

Antunes, Fátima Martin Rodrigues Ferreira. *"Com brasileiro não há quem possa!": Futebol e identidade nacional em José Lins do Rego, Mário Filho e Nelson Rodrigues / "With Brazilians, No One Can Keep Up!": Soccer and National Identity in José Lins do Rego, Mário Filho and Nelson Rodrigues*. São Paulo: UNESP, 2004.

Archetti, Eduardo P. "Playing Styles and Masculine Virtues in Argentine Football." In *Machos, Mistresses, Madonnas: Contesting the Power of Latin American Gender Imagery*. Eds. Marit Melhuus and Kristi Anne Stølen. London: Verso, 1996: pp. 34–55.

Borges, Pedro. "Quem pensa, quem faz"/"He Who Thinks, He Who Does." *Alma Preta/ Black Soul*. 19 October, 2015. Web. www.almapreta.com/editorias/realidade/quem-pensa-quem-faz. Accessed 10 March 2017.

Filho, Mário. *O negro no futebol brasileiro/ The Black Man in Brazilian Soccer*. Rio de Janeiro: Editora Mauad, [2003] 1964.

Lewis, Tim. "Why Are There So Few Black Football Managers?" *The Guardian*. 14 December 2014. Web. www.theguardian.com/football/2014/dec/14/why-so-few-black-football-managers. Accessed 10 March 2017.

Lisi, Clemente A. *The U.S. Women's Soccer Team: An American Success Story*. 2nd ed. New York: Taylor Trade Publishing, 2013.

Moreiras, Alberto. *The Exhaustion of Difference: The Politics of Latin American Cultural Studies*. Durham, NC: Duke University Press, 2001.

Nadel, Joshua H. *Fútbol!: Why Soccer Matters in Latin America*. Gainesville, FL: University of Florida Press, 2014.

Pereira, Leonardo Affonso de Miranda. *Footballmania: Uma história social do futebol no Rio de Janeiro, 1902–1938/ Soccermania: A Social History of Soccer in Rio de Janeiro, 1902-1938*. Rio de Janeiro: Nova Fronteira, 2000.

R7 Esportes. "Conheça os únicos técnicos negros do futebol brasileiro"/"Get to Know the Only Black Coaches in Brazilian Soccer." *R7 Esportes/ R7 Sports*. 23 November, 2014. Web. http://esportes.r7.com/futebol/fotos/conheca-os-unicos-tecnicos-negros-do-futebol-brasileiro-23112014#!/foto/4. Accessed 10 March 2017.

Santos, Ricardo Pinto dos. "Tensões na consolidação do futebol nacional"/"Tensions in the Consolidation of National Soccer." In *História do esporte no Brasil: Do império aos dias atuais/ History of Sports in Brazil: From the Empire to the Present Day*. Eds. Mary Del Priore and Victor Andrade de Melo. São Paulo: UNESP, 2009.

Wisnik, José Miguel. *Veneno remédio: O futebol e o Brasil/ Poison Cure: Soccer and Brazil*. São Paulo: Companhia das Letras, 2008.

26

HARD PUNCHES, VULNERABLE BODIES

Latin American boxing films and the intersections of gender, class, and nation

Mauricio Espinoza and Luis Miguel Estrada Orozco

In addition to his prolific and influential career as a poet and political activist, Mexican American Rodolfo "Corky" Gonzáles was also an accomplished boxer.[1] Like most Latin Americans and U.S. Latinos who have made a name for themselves and their countries/communities in the ruthless sport of boxing, Gonzáles grew up in a tough barrio amid poverty. Why does boxing continue to draw attention despite its inherent violence? Some sociologists claim that it provides a means to survive in economically hard-hit urban areas. In fact, "the greatest numbers of fighters have come from the ranks of the most impoverished segments of society" (Heisnaken 2012: 2). Mexican boxers and boxers of Mexican origin have been a constant presence in the sport in the United States since the 1920s, like California native Bert Colima or Mexicans Rodolfo Casanova, Alberto Arizmendi, Manuel Villa, and Luis Villanueva (Maldonado and Zamora 1999: 32–33). For the past few decades, boxing in the United States has been dominated by people of color, "with Latinos generally controlling the lighter weight categories and African American boxers heading the divisions from middleweight upward" (Heisnaken 2012: 2). In Latin America, boxing has become one of the most popular sports alongside soccer and baseball—and in countries such as Cuba, Nicaragua, and Puerto Rico, boxing is only rivaled by baseball. The region has produced legendary pugilists that have left a permanent mark on the world stage and in their countries' national imaginaries: Argentine Carlos Monzón, Puerto Rican Félix "Tito" Trinidad, Mexican Julio César Chavez, Nicaraguan Alexis Argüello, and Panamanian Roberto Durán, just to name a few.

For almost a century now, boxing has had a close and almost natural relationship with film. The fighter became a popular figure in Hollywood cinema with the advent of sound and appeared in over one hundred feature films released between 1930 and 1960 (Grindon 2011: 3). Later, the screen boxer experienced a comeback in numerous films, including the famous *Rocky* series (1976–2006). More recent movies such as *Million Dollar Baby* (2004), *Cinderella Man* (2005), *The Fighter* (2010), and *Southpaw* (2015) have kept this genre relevant among new audiences. U.S. Latino and Latin American boxers (historical as well as fictional) have also been the subject of films produced both in the United States and south of the Rio Grande. *The Right Cross* (1950), *The Ring* (1952), and *Requiem for a Heavyweight* (1962) all feature Latino boxers. The Mexican golden age of cinema also delved into the boxing genre, starting with Alejandro Galindo's masterpiece *Campeón sin corona* (1945) and iconic movies such as *Pepe El Toro* (1953), starring Pedro Infante. In the twenty-first century, a number of films and television series have brought attention to Latinos as a dominant boxing force—including *Price of Glory* (2000), *Girlfight* (2000) *Resurrection Blvd.* (2000–2002), *The Kid: Chamaco* (2009), and *From Mexico with Love* (2009). In this article, we explore how two recent boxing films—*La Yuma* (Florence Jaugey, Nicaragua, 2009) and *Hands of Stone* (Jonathan Jakubowicz, Panama/United States, 2016) portray and interrogate the figure of the boxer in Latin America, while exploring the relationship between this cultural phenomenon and issues of gender, class, and nation that go well beyond the ring.

Boxing and film: A match made in ringside heaven

For the occasional observer, boxing is coded not by its history but by its mass media portrayals. In the twentieth century, first cinema and then television drew from several stereotypes and narrative paradigms that preexisted in the boxing lore and helped make them part of popular culture (Wacquant 1992: 221). Furthermore, film and TV have had a significant influence on boxing aesthetics. According to David Scott, the Hollywood cinema of the 1920s "glamorized" the appeal of rough, strong men and turned them into mainstream entertainment (2008: 21–22). In the following decade, public exposure via newspapers and film expanded the perception of pugilists as fighters admired by men to also become sex symbols desired by women (Boddy 2008: 218–224). Later on, postwar-era TV in the United States "transformed prizefighting from a closed attraction to a mass spectator sport" (Sammons 1988: 135); but more importantly, a multimillion-dollar spectacle to be watched in the living rooms of the men who returned home from war (Rondinone 2013: 22–26). Aesthetics is not the only aspect of boxing that mass media have both drawn from and actively influenced. Boxing has proven to be appealing to the eye for reasons beyond the thrill of watching two people fighting. The fight appears to be a metaphor or a "focus of profound identification" (Scott 2008: xxviii), and the fighter "a potential hero, a symbol of personal, communal, or racial investment" (xxviii). The power behind that symbol has been one of the components of the well-known formula of telling the story of a boxer as a race, class, or national hero, or a boxer as the ultimate expression of what being a *real man* is all about.

While boxing has become ingrained in popular culture and national imaginaries through literature, journalistic chronicles, TV broadcasts, and other media, "no art has shaped our perception of the boxer as much as motion pictures" (Grindon 2011: 3). This connection between boxing and cinema is expressed through certain narrative and visual conventions that have developed over time and which mold our understanding and expectations of pugilist-themed movies. First the paradigmatic narrative in boxing storytelling is stable and predictable. Even if the film is biographical and the real-life events of the boxer do not necessarily adjust to the formula, the path of the fighter in cinema is known beforehand and mirrors the heroic path described by Joseph Campbell in his 1949 seminal work *The Hero with A Thousand Faces* (Kring-Schreifels 2016). Although variations occur in individual films, the basic plot of the boxing movie (biographical or not) is usually organized around the rise and fall of the fighter's career (Cook 1982: 42). According to Loïc Wacquant, one common myth that is reproduced in boxing movies (and which is particularly helpful to our analysis) is that of the "hungry fighter" (1992: 221). Even though boxers generally come from underprivileged strata of society, a fighter who comes from the very bottom is very unlikely to fulfill the life of discipline required by boxing, but mass media has favored these stories because of the evident attraction they generate (Wacquant 2006: 53). The narrative trope of the hungry fighter—hungry in the literal, bodily sense but also hungry for social recognition, economic well-being, justice, freedom from oppression, etc.—also helps bring together the discourses of class and ethnicity/race. As Leger Grindon explains, the lower-class origin of the screen pugilist was already an established convention in cinema's early sound period. However, by the late 1930s the boxer had become clearly marked as an ethnic outsider (and later a racial outsider), too: "Prizefighting became an avenue to acceptance by the dominant culture and a means of resisting oppression" (2011: 156).

The narrative of the hungry fighter presents another appealing feature besides its obvious dramatic arch. Boxing has long been seen, along with other sports, as an option for social mobility. In a capitalist system that excludes and marginalizes certain members of society, sports are regarded as an open door for whomever has the right set of skills and mental toughness to reach the top. This is not entirely true in real life, but according to Jeffrey Sammons it is an important reason for justifying the existence of a violent sport in an era that appears to openly reject most forms of violence. For Sammons, "boxers become an integral element in a belief system that thrives on the willingness of an overwhelming majority of its faithful to dream the impossible—that success is there for the striving" (1988: 236). Boxing is thus presented as a sport with "redeeming social values" and is "directly associated with American strength and spirit" (Sammons 1988: 236). As we will see in this chapter, boxing can also be related to similar values in other societies. However, as Wacquant argues, the actual probability of successful social mobility through boxing is slim at best (with *La Yuma* being a perfect example of this reality). Despite this disconnect between film narrative and real life, boxers from marginalized sectors of society do embody many positive values within their neighborhoods or social groups. They can earn a degree of respect seldom granted and establish bonds far more functional and sociably accepted than those generated by the gangs that prowl the same areas where these boxers come from (Wacquant 1995: 516–519).

In addition to employing the hungry fighter and other myths, the boxing film genre has acquired unity and flexibility over time by exploring a series of dramatic conflicts that represent important social problems. Grindon has identified six key conflicts present in boxing movies, though not all of them necessarily appear in every film:

> the conflict between body and soul or material versus spiritual values; the conflict between individual competition fostered by market forces versus human cooperation and self-sacrifice; the conflict between integration into mainstream society versus loyalty to the marginalized community from which the boxer hails; the conflict between the manly ethos of the ring and a woman's influence, which leads to a masculinity crisis; the conflict that arises when anger at injustice clashes with powerlessness to eliminate oppression; and the conflict between stoic discipline in the face of life's cruelty and displaying sensitivity toward others
>
> *(2011: 6–7)*

Finally, boxing films can be analyzed through the way they follow or depart from established visual or mise-en-scène conventions of the genre. According to Grindon, the boxing movie thrives on a principle of "intensified realism," which reaches its apex in the narrative and visual power of the fight scenes: "[T]hese films integrate the development of the fight with the dramatic conflicts propelling the plot. The boxing sequences serve as the genre's distinctive spectacle, physical action that punctuates the plot at key intervals like song and dance numbers in a musical. The typical Hollywood film moves steadily toward an extended bout that brings the movie to its climax" (2011: 23). As Grindon explains, the boxing genre's preoccupation with visual realism has led to a desire "to replicate the experience of the fan at ringside" (2011: 23). This typically includes the camera recording the action just above the ropes, through them, or at a low-angle under the ropes, as if the film's viewers were at a ringside seat. Meanwhile, the composition shows both boxers from head to toe, "capturing their full movement like the choreography of two dancers" and establishing "the foundation for the visual action" (Grindon 2011: 23). There are, of course, some variations that have been incorporated over time and with changing filming technologies: shots within the arena, aerial shots, overlapping images of boxers and the crowd, closer shots of the boxer inside the ring, headshots of fighters taking a punch, detail shots of the boxer's fist hitting the opponent, slow-motion effects to enhance the dramatism of taking a punch or falling down, etc. However, even in recent film, "these variations are exceptions to the standard ringside position [...] from "the fan's ideal perspective" (Grindon 2011: 24).

Portraying 'real men': Masculinity and its problems

Boxing and masculinity share a "distinct historical link" (Gems 2014: 210). One can easily suspect why masculinity has been in boxing's foreground quite often and in a more powerful and direct way than in most sports. Norbert Elias recognizes that sport spectacles seek to elicit in audiences some of the emotions and sentiments of war, but in a controlled and non-deadly manner and with less visible violence (1986: 48–51). Though regulated and further reduced over time, combat and violence are still present in boxing. For Joyce Carol Oates, pugilism's appeal in our "civilized" world may derive from it being a "remnant of another, earlier era when the physical being was primary and the warrior's masculinity its highest expression" (2005: 77). Oates takes the link between boxing and masculinity to the limit: "Boxing is for men, and is about men, and *is* men" (2005: 72). Boxing seems to be a sport "designed to *test, perform* and *sustain* masculinity, with the vision of the masculine it engenders a particularly violent and predatory one" (Delgado 2005: 197). In Fernando Delgado's analysis, this predatory view of masculinity goes beyond the performance in the ring and it is "linked to other constructions and media articulations of boxers over the course of several generations" (2005: 198). Boxers like Mike Tyson, Jake LaMotta, and Durán have been portrayed as the ultimate combination of what Delgado calls violence and malevolence.

This historical link between boxing and masculinity is as tight as the one between masculinity and power, and the one between machismo and Latin American culture as perceived in the United States (Basham 1976: 126). It is important to point out that masculinity is not an all-encompassing term directly related to the physical genitalia, but is a notion derived from a social system. It is, in Connell's words, "simultaneously a place in gender relations, the practices through which men and women engage that place in gender, and the effects of these practices in bodily experience, personality and culture" (2005: 71). Limited as this definition can be, it gives us a starting point for two of Connell's illuminating suggestions: different societies define the concept of "masculinity" in their own terms and there can be many masculinities within a society.

"Hegemonic masculinity," for Connell, is the masculinity that legitimizes patriarchy, but it also corresponds with cultural ideals and institutional powers (2005: 77). It is no surprise that in the Western societies that Connell describes, hegemonic masculinity is also white, capitalist, and heterosexual. On the other hand, "marginalized masculinities" result from the "interplay of gender with other structures such as class and race" (2005: 80). Their relationship with the hegemonic masculinity is conflictive, since in a way they can help sustain the cultural ideals of a certain type of man for the patriarchy, but they can also challenge the authority of the dominant group. Connell himself thinks of black athletes as prime examples of hegemonic masculinity whose fame and wealth "does not yield social authority" (2005: 81). Not surprisingly, the media tends to emphasize malevolence and violence when writing about or portraying boxers of color such as Tyson and Durán, while downplaying their athletic success. The close link between boxing and masculinity is also reproduced in cinema. As Séan Crosson indicates, "film has had an important role to play in affirming the prominence of men in sport, with male physicality a prominent feature in many films" (2013: 104).

The irruption of the feminine in boxing

Women's presence in boxing is not an anomaly, but rather an irruption onto a realm traditionally construed as masculine. Hortensia Moreno's research on the development of women's boxing in Mexico is one example of the challenges women face in a country where machismo is predominant. The practice of a "manly" sport by a woman implies challenging roles and structures. First of all, women's boxing contests normative notions of the body. Since the female body has been traditionally thought to be fragile and weak in comparison to the male body, the first challenge occurs long before a fight is publically staged: at the gyms. Mexico City's 1947 ban on women's professional boxing was finally lifted in 1999, after a legal fight led by boxer and law student Laura Serrano. By the time Moreno started her research in 2005, despite the growing popularity of the sport thanks to fighters such as María "Guerrera" Torres, the lifting of the ban was still fresh in boxing people's mind (Moreno 2015: 197–199). Both trainers and pupils were simply unaccustomed to the presence of women in their gyms. This is not unlike what Rene Denfeld (1997) recounts about her own experience when she started boxing in New York City, where women's amateur boxing was allowed only since 1993. One of the main objectives of Denfeld's book is to debunk the theory that women are just not as aggressive and violent as men. Stamina, but specially aggressiveness and proclivity to violence, are at the core of the rejection women face at gyms in both Denfeld's narration and Moreno's research. The argument is that those things are not "natural" to them. What we see, as the quantitative data compiled by Denfeld suggests, is not that women are not fit for fighting, but that they are systematically rejected as fighters. Moreno parallels these attitudes with Simon de Beauvoir's passage in *The Second Sex* (1971), where the French philosopher expresses that in a society that values putting your own life in danger more than giving birth to it, the curse of women is to be excluded from the warrior's path (Moreno 2015: 64).

This concept of a fragile body leads to the stereotype of a non-aggressive gender (Denfeld 1997: 40–45), and because of that, to a social role with particular attributes. They are all characteristics that "differentiate men from women *and* define and legitimate their superiority and social dominance over women, then these characteristics must remain unavailable to women (Schippers 2007: 95). Since aggressiveness has been identified so closely with manliness, Denfeld has suggested that the real risk in regulating amateur or professional fights between men and women is not, as it has been suggested, that women may get hurt, but "it's the fear that, given an opportunity, a woman matched against a man just might, as horrible as it sounds beat the dickens out of him" (1997: 35). In other words, women's boxing as well as pop culture portrayals such as the 2000 movie *Girlfight* (where the protagonist, Diana Guzmán, spars against her male love interest Adrian Sturges), challenge "the *idealized relationship* between masculinity and femininity" (Schippers 2007: 94). In Moreno's interviews, the other recurrent challenge in the immediate experience of women boxers is their acceptance by family and society (2015: 271–281). Since these women do not fulfill their expected roles in society, rejection and lack of support are common, something that is made evident in *La Yuma*.

Finally, the media's perception of female boxing is the last stage on a long continuum of challenges. The bibliography on how female athletes are perceived is extensive, since it brings the individual experience into the social discourse through the portrayal of salient figures. Sometimes, the portrayals are more revealing of society's prejudices than of athletic performance or personal character itself. As Oates has indicated, the male-dominated realm of boxing has labored to exclude women to the point of making female boxers a parody, a cartoon, and a monstrosity (2005: 73). This has translated into popular culture representations. According to Moreno, "the image of female athletes in the media move from invisibility to objectification, without ever really consolidating themselves in the public consciousness as representative figures of national reverence" (2015: 197). Traditional roles for women in boxing films have included female boxers for comic and absurd purposes, such as in *Comedy Set-To* (1898) and *The Gordon Sisters Boxing* (1901). Women also play the role of the wife or partner who eventually supports or inspires the boxer (Adrian in *Rocky*), or an unfaithful and untrustworthy character who fouls up relationships, coming in between a boxer and his manager (Crosson 2013: 106–110). Since the middle of the twentieth century, "women began to feature more frequently in sports films. Indeed, these women now appeared in roles and possessed qualities perceived historically as masculine, such as authority, strength, aggression, force and intellect" (Crosson 2013: 111). According to Crosson, these strong women may pose a threat to patriarchy, which tries to contain them through three principle means in sports films: through the negative or comic portrayal of women in positions of authority; by positioning leading sporting females under the guidance and authority of men; or through the sexual objectification of women for male gratification. Such depictions of women "may ultimately reflect anxieties regarding masculinity itself and represent an attempt to reassert masculine authority and patriarchy" (Crosson 2013: 112).

The fists of a nation: Durán, masculinity, and U.S.–Panama relations

The 2005 documentary *Los puños de una nación*, by Panamanian director Pituka Ortega-Heilbron, portrays the Central American nation's struggle to find a sense of identity in the second half of the twentieth century. The country's leader, General Omar Torrijos, sought to broker a deal with the United States in the 1970s that would hand the Panama Canal (and a sense of national autonomy) to Panamanian control. Against this political background, boxer Roberto Durán (1951)—better known as "Manos de Piedra," or Hands of Stone, because of his devastating punching power—was quickly rising among boxing's international elite and became the perfect hero in his country's quest to reclaim national pride. It is this combination of nationalism and hypermasculine heroic achievement that is explored in the biopic *Hands of Stone*, which chronicles Durán's life from his impoverished childhood through his light middleweight title fight against American Davey Moore in 1983. Durán is considered one of the best lightweight pugilist of all time (Gems 2014: 183), having won world titles in four different weight divisions during a long career that spanned from 1967 through 2002. Shortly after his retirement, *Ring* magazine named him the fifth greatest fighter of the last 80 years (Iber et al. 2011: 264).

That boxing, nationalism, and masculinity would coexist in a film such as *Hands of Stone* is anything but unusual. Michael Billig has argued that modern sport has a social and political significance that "extend[s] through the media beyond the player and the spectator by providing luminous moments of national engagement and national heroes with whom citizens can emulate and adore" (1995: 120). Additionally, sport and the nation are both "historically male-centered as practice and spectacle" (Fernández L'Hoeste et al. 2015: 14). The particular nationalism that is explored in the Durán story (not just Panamanian or Latin American pride but also anti-United States sentiment), also transcends the film's historical timeframe and spills over into today's tense U.S.–Latin American relationships. When asked about the reason for filming this movie, Venezuelan director and screenwriter Jonathan Jakubowicz has repeatedly stated that the world is in dire need of a Latin American hero: "When Donald Trump describes Mexicans as rapists, drug dealers, illegal immigrants and criminals, he's describing 90% of the roles Latino actors have played in Hollywood movies and TV shows for the last hundred years" (Betancourt 2016). *Hands of Stone* is, then, Jakubowicz's effort to change this paradigm through a story told by a Latin American from a Latin American perspective.

According to Michael Donoghue, both Durán and Torrijos embodied the powerful machos who changed the paradigm in U.S.–Panama relations (2015: 18). Panama, a nation feminized by the U.S. occupation of the Canal Zone through military and economic dominance, found in Torrijos' intransigence and in Durán's vicious knockouts against "gringos" the means to reinstate the powerful male at the center of its national identity, which Donoghue calls "Isthmian machismo" (2015: 21). It is no surprise, then, that the film starts with the extradiegetic sound of a Panamanian broadcaster saying that Torrijos has guaranteed Durán's victory against American Sugar Ray Leonard. Though brief, this snippet of sound helps frame the entire movie as a long nationalist bout. A boisterous, threatening, violent, all-out macho boxer who would not be dominated by anyone, Durán was an instant success in times of U.S. political and military intervention in Latin America. The film depicts this masculine/nationalist discourse through several key scenes. Early on, during a 1964 protest against the U.S. occupation of the Canal Zone, a young Durán steals mangos to feed his starving family and friends and manages to escape American soldiers. Later, as he begins his training under Jewish American manager Ray Arcel, Durán stares down an armed U.S. guard from the other side of the fence that divides Panama City from the Canal Zone.

As Durán's success and fame increase, Jakubowicz moves away from shots that simultaneously show U.S.–Panama confrontation to scenes that work through either supplementation or juxtaposition—highlighting the increasing complexity and historical significance of the events depicted. For example, the scene depicting the signing of the agreement between Torrijos and President Carter to hand over the canal to Panama (which generates excitement for Durán and his fellow Panamanians), is punctuated by several subsequent scenes that culminate with Durán's historic 1980 victory over Leonard—all of which show Durán in his prime macho public persona, questioning Leonard's (and by extension, the United States') masculinity and legitimacy. The extent by which the two fighters are depicted as symbols that represent their respective countries is summarized in the way Felicidad (Durán's wife) speaks to her husband: "If you want your people to be proud of being Panamanian, this is the one you need to beat [pointing to a picture of Leonard in *Ring* magazine]. That clown[2] is the symbol of American sports. If you want the treaty to mean something for Panama before 1999, destroy their idol and make them respect us" (*Hands of Stone*).[3] By contrast, Durán's humiliating defeat in the rematch against Leonard (the infamous "no más" fight) is followed by shots that show Durán drunk, lying on a couch; news footage of a defiant President Reagan saying the U.S. will keep the canal; and the announcement that Torrijos has died. In other words, national redemption and defeat are conditioned by the boxer-hero's ring performance and the state of his masculinity.

While Durán's machismo was one of the main reasons Panamanians and Latin American fans loved him, it is also a problematic and controversial feature to present to audiences (especially American audiences) as a positive attribute. How can someone make a hero out of the macho? The answer is at the center of the aesthetics of *Hands of Stone*. The masculinity at odds here is the masculinity of the Other, in this case, the Latin man, as perceived stereotypically from an American point of view. Jakubowicz's challenge is to move Durán from an undesirable masculinity to something closer to the "right type" of masculinity—that is, one that is heroic, symbolic, and redeeming because of its social roots and national identification during a time of need for his country. The director accomplishes this by portraying Durán as aware of his status as a national symbol who defeats selfish appetites to find redemption. This process, however, takes time and compromise—and will require emphasizing the boxer's inevitable downfall, a component of boxing films' traditional master plot that Grindon refers to as "debauchery" (2011: 13). In addition to losing to Leonard and having his masculinity challenged, Durán turns to drinking, overeating, cheating on his wife, abandoning his family responsibilities, and turning on his friends and community. The film manages to humanize Durán and take the edge off the negative aspects of his machismo by showing a renewed man who fights for conviction and not for glory—he tells Felicidad that "I don't need to be the champion, but I need to fight" (*Hands of Stone*). Durán also restores relationships with his wife, his children, and Arcel; apologizes to Leonard for the sexually charged insults he had hurled at his wife; and goes back to training in the gritty barrio where he first developed his toughness. When he is shown back in the ring in the final fight scene against Moore, the narrative and visual emphasis is no longer fixated on the Panama versus U.S. confrontation but on the need for redemption. The film's last shot is a panoramic view that places Durán standing on the ropes with his arm raised in victory, surrounded by family, friends, trainers, and supporters—an emphasis on community over individual achievement.

There are several narrative and visual conventions of boxing cinema that are employed in *Hands of Stone*, and which help underscore some of the key themes explored in the film. First, this movie is clearly structured around the myth of the hungry fighter. Durán grew up in El Chorrillo, a notorious slum of Panama City, fatherless and in extreme poverty. As mentioned before, the first time we see Durán in the film, he is risking his life to bring food to his family and friends. Life in the poor barrio is tough, and young Durán quickly learns to use his fists and nurture his intimidating macho personality to make money and survive. Consequently, class is inextricably tied with gender and nationalism in the movie, as Durán's disadvantaged socioeconomic origin conditions charge his hypermasculinity and his relentless desire to avenge his "feminized" country. Durán's hunger (both literal and figurative) is employed throughout the entire narrative. As an adult, he is shown eating one of every flavor of ice cream he can find, because such simple pleasures were denied him as a child. He is hungry for happiness, pursuing the beautiful and aptly named Felicidad even though she comes from a privileged background. When Arcel announces Durán to the U.S. boxing world, he describes him as "a true hungry fighter, like in the old days" (*Hands of Stone*). Finally, after his victory over Leonard, he begs Arcel to leave him alone: "I don't want to fight [...] I'm hungry. I just want to eat. I want to enjoy what I have" (*Hands of Stone*).

Jakubowicz also incorporates and explores several conflicts in the plot to represent Durán as a foul-mouthed macho with highly redeemable qualities. After Durán becomes a star, the film shows him returning to his barrio and sharing his money with the people there. During his downfall, he lashes out at his family and neighborhood friends, some of whom ostracize him. To begin his road to redemption, he is shown participating in a religious pilgrimage in Panama and being humbled by fighters at a local prison. These actions and events coincide with the material versus spiritual values conflict, and the integration into mainstream society versus loyalty to the marginalized group conflict. Durán is also conflicted by the oppressive treatment of Panamanians at the hand of Americans, which propels him during the entire movie to seek justice through his actions in the ring. Finally, the film relies on conventional ringside camera shots to convey the historical nature of the bouts depicted. This visual representation is best suited for a biopic, as it allows the movie to create the illusion of recreating boxing history the way most people would remember it: through the ringside shots typical of TV broadcasts.

The limits of myth: La Yuma and gender precarity

In her research about female boxing in Mexico, Moreno asks, "Can a female athlete embody the spirit of a nation?" She seems to answer her own question: "The study of sports teaches us that the essence of the practice traditionally lies in the construction and consolidation of masculinity" (2015: 182). In the case of *Hands of Stone*, we know well before watching the film that yes, a male boxer such as Durán can and did capture the spirit not just of the Panamanian nation but of all of Latin America because of the anti-imperialist symbolism he came to embody. *La Yuma* is a different type of film, with a different type of hero, and with a significantly different narrative outcome. As a fictional movie, it is free from the constraints of historical representation inherent to a biopic like *Hands of Stone*, even with all the liberties that such "based on real-life events" films still take. We can see these differences in the way the bouts are photographed in *La Yuma*, with less emphasis on ringside shots and more attention paid to showing individual female boxers engaged in fighting through closer shots. This freedom allows director Florence Jaugey to craft an original story that explores some of the most pressing social and economic issues facing contemporary Nicaragua, the Western hemisphere's second poorest country ("Nicaragua"). Yuma (played by Alma Blanco) is a young woman who lives in a slum of Managua with her mother, three siblings, and her mother's live-in boyfriend. Her brother and most of her friends are members of a gang of low-level thieves and drug users. Yuma works in the neighborhood's second-hand "American" clothing store and trains at local gyms with the goal of becoming a professional boxer. The deplorable conditions in which Yuma lives are visually represented in the film by a documentary style of shooting that allows viewers to witness makeshift houses, stray dogs wandering dirt streets, unemployed youth, and criminal activity. The visuals are complemented by the soundtrack, which both diegetically and extradiegetically tell stories of gun violence, drugs, and migration to neighboring Costa Rica (where many poor Nicaraguans go in search of better opportunities).

The two basic narrative elements expected from a film featuring a female boxer protagonist are present in *La Yuma*: the insertion of a female character into an activity perceived as manly and the struggle for a better opportunity in life. It's important to point out that Yuma's boxing career is presented to the audience right before she makes her professional debut. The notion of Yuma already being a trained amateur boxer helps the spectator understand that her personal curiosity has been satisfied and that preliminary social resistance has been vanquished. This does not mean that Yuma's interest in boxing is fully accepted by her surrounding world. Her friends from the slum, her family, and even her love interest, Ernesto (who would be expected to be more open-minded) challenge her constantly. The poor people from the slum find the exercise of fist-fighting unfit for women, expressing their opinions through sexist and even sexualized terms. For example, her mom's boyfriend questions whether Yuma is a "real" woman because of her muscular arms, tomboy appearance, and rough mannerisms, which the camera displays constantly throughout the film. Upon seeing Yuma walk past him in a towel, he says: "How sexy! I hadn't realized until now your daughter is a woman" (*La Yuma*).[4] Right before that, the boyfriend had said that Yuma was a "wild animal" that needed taming, and that he knew how to do it (meaning, raping her). Scarlet, the clothing store's owner, tells Yuma that she's a pretty girl so she should "dress sexy" and is aghast at the fact that "women are even boxing now" (*La Yuma*). Meanwhile, Ernesto (a middle-class journalism student who is removed from the harsh realities of the slums), finds the very exercise of any kind of violence incomprehensible. However, in the boxing gyms, there is no resistance toward female boxing. Yuma does not encounter the lack of interest from trainers that we can read in accounts like the one by Denfeld, or referred to by Moreno.

One major achievement of this film is the way it approaches gender issues, not overstressing them by grandiloquent discourse but showing them via concrete portrayals and conflicts.

Hard punches, vulnerable bodies

In this sense, the director succeeds in conveying that Yuma does not find her inner strength and assertiveness through boxing. She boxes because she already confides in her own agency. When Ernesto asks her why she boxes, she simply replies: "Because I like it" (*La Yuma*). Boxing helps Yuma not to shy away from violence against men when they present a threat, as when her mom's boyfriend tries to abuse her younger sister Marjorie. The way her character is portrayed leads the audience to believe that Yuma would have behaved the same with or without her pugilist training. Yuma already lives in a world where gang violence is common, and she sometimes participates in gang fights and socializes with gang members. Regardless of the situation, she stands her ground. One can easily believe that the practice of boxing has helped Yuma build her confidence, but it was never entirely dependent on it. Unlike Durán, who is constantly asserting his masculinity through verbal attacks laced with machismo and sexual references, Yuma expresses her confidence mainly through non-verbal communication: mean stares with arms crossed. When she speaks, she goes to the point: "Everybody tries to boss me around. But I don't have an owner" (*La Yuma*).

Another accomplishment of the film is the way it subverts gender expectations and questions patriarchal norms, especially when compared to *Hands of Stone*. The most evident of these depictions is the fragility of Yuma's love interest, Ernesto. He is not prone to physical violence, he does not seem physically fit nor menacing, and he certainly cannot stand his ground in dangerous situations (he's beaten up by Yuma's brother and another gang member). He is not the stereotypical macho, although his masculinity is never challenged. The masculinity that is actually challenged is the one of Yader, Yuma's first trainer who moonlights as a stripper. He has a small boxing gym, but he takes his clothes off for women. His physicality is made for war but is used for pleasure instead. Toward the end of the movie, he starts a relationship with Scarlet, the much-older businesswoman who can be his provider. While Yader is presumed to have been a gang member in the past, he has chosen to leave the life of "debauchery" and seek other opportunities because "one has to seek his own path" (*La Yuma*). Yader departs from gender expectations by forsaking violent behavior, but his body is sexually objectified, which is also problematic. Surprisingly, Yuma's transgender neighbor, La Cubana, is seldom challenged or questioned because of her appearance or sexual preference. In fact, Yuma is more questioned for transgressing gender roles through her appearance and her interest in boxing than La Cubana is for her sexual inclination and her open activities as a prostitute. However, when confronted about the sexual abuse of Marjorie, the mom's boyfriend calls both Yuma and La Cubana "mariquitas" (little faggots)—a clear sign that such men cannot stand having their masculinity challenged by women with non-conforming gender identities. But overall, the film depicts a world where gender roles are changing despite the fact the members who perform their gender roles in more traditional ways do not realize or accept it. Case in point: when Yuma gets a black eye in a sparring session, it is difficult for her to convince people she was not the subject of gender violence.

Issues of class and violence go hand in hand in the film. When Ernesto and his ex-girlfriend are beaten up, Ernesto blames Yuma and claims that violence is the only world she understands—automatically associating her socioeconomic class with violent behavior. Ernesto fails to realize that contained violence is different from criminal violence and that, in a certain way, they oppose each other. He likes Yuma for being "rara" (peculiar), but when one aspect of her world's reality irrupts into his much safer middle-class realm, he feels threatened and is unable to see past class differences anymore. Slum boxers like Yader and Yuma do not engage in illegal activities, but for Ernesto and his class mindset, they and the gang members are all the same. Connections between boxing, class, and nation are also challenged in *La Yuma*. Just like Durán, Yuma is a hungry fighter straight out of a Central American slum. However, the hungry fighter myth does not shape *La Yuma*'s narrative. In *Hands of Stone*, Durán's boxing career is set against the backdrop of a nationalist confrontation, with a clearly defined enemy. Even after achieving success and riches, Durán returns to his barrio and engages with the world he knows. In *La Yuma*, the limitations of this myth are made evident. Boxing is never going to make Yuma rich because there simply isn't money in female boxing. After winning in her professional debut, a neighbor tells her: "You're famous now." She responds: "But I'm still broke" (*La Yuma*). Yuma simply wants to get out of the slum, escape her oppressing reality. When she finds out Ernesto's father lives in Miami and pays for his education, she says: "What I would give to have that visa and get the fuck out of here" (*La Yuma*). Unlike Yuma, Ernesto expresses his love for his country and desire to stay. If there's a national enemy in La Yuma, it's not the United States: it's the very country that has failed its most vulnerable citizens.

When Yuma manages to leave the slum, it's not in the way she and the audience would have desired or imagined. Having rescued her younger siblings from the abusive boyfriend and the indifferent mother, Yuma agrees to fight other women at a circus that just stopped by the barrio in order to make money. The match inside the circus tent is visually presented as a carnivalesque affair, with clowns in the ring and foreground shots of lions yawning—confirming what Oates and Crosson have stated about female boxing being typically portrayed as comical and cartoon-ish. Yuma's exit is in a circus wagon, a final scene that parodies the cowboy movie's convention of showing the hero ride into the sunset. It is painful to see that she must turn from boxer to clown in order to support her siblings. Yuma herself states that the most important thing is to find a way to gain economic independence, no matter what people think about her. Her triumph is far more practical than the fairy tale of the boxing champ. Despite the fact that female boxing has earned a place inside the gym, the world is less merciful than the cruelest sport. Yuma does not get a professional fight as soon as expected, so she opts for a way out instead of a way up. Movement and independence are more urgent than fulfilling a sports narrative.

A comparative analysis of *Hands of Stone* and *La Yuma* allows us to explore the ways in which contemporary Latin American cinema has engaged with issues of gender, class, and the nation through the figure of the boxer. Jakubowicz has constructed a narrative in which hypermascu-linity and anti-imperialism are embodied in the figure of boxer Roberto Durán, whose fighting prowess and proud machismo are portrayed as emblematic of Panama's struggle to free itself from U.S. "feminizing" domination. The film is successful in dramatizing this confrontation through the use of boxing cinema conventions, particularly the myth of the hungry fighter. However, the movie's brave criticism of U.S. interventionist policies in Latin America is unfortunately undermined by the emphasis given to the relationship between Durán and American manager Arcel, who is portrayed as a surrogate father figure to the boxer. Arcel's job is to "discipline" the talented but unpredictable Durán so he can have a chance to become a world champion. While softened (Arcel tells Durán he doesn't need his training skills to succeed), the symbolism of this paternalistic relationship has clear colonial undertones: like Panama, Durán has raw talent but needs the help (intervention) of an American to polish him and make him successful. This is similar to the argument that the canal should not be handed over to Panamanian control because this developing nation wouldn't know how to run it. Meanwhile, *La Yuma* does a remarkable job of challenging normative gender roles and expectations through its female boxer protagonist and other characters, as well as pulling no punches in portraying the failures of the nation to its most vulnerable citizens. Through the appropriation of certain values and characteristics Latin American societies consider "masculine," Yuma disrupts the relationship between genders and, because of that, the power balance. Ultimately, the cinematic portrayal of the female boxer is the portrayal of a failed system of acquisition of power: certain individuals cannot have access to it, even if they have the right tools and play by the rules of the game.

Notes

1 In his 1967 poem "I am Joaquín," Gonzáles uses boxing as a metaphor for civil rights struggle.
2 Durán repeatedly called Leonard a "clown" and a "ballerina," mocking the boxer's signature dancing style in the ring. He also resented Leonard's "privileged" upbringing and the attention media paid to his made-for-TV appearance: "I didn't like Leonard because he was the pretty boy for the Americans and I didn't care less about him. I used to tell myself that I was going to beat the shit out of that American so he will respect us Latin Americans" (qtd. in Giudice 2006: 181).
3 Translated from the Spanish by the authors. In the film, some characters speak in Spanish and some in English. Durán (played by Édgar Ramírez) uses both languages, depending on who he's talking to.
4 All quotes from *La Yuma* have been translated from the Spanish by the authors.

Works cited

Basham, Richard. "Machismo." *Frontiers: A Journal of Women Studies*, vol. 1, no. 2, 1976, pp. 126–143.
Beauvoir, Simone de. *The Second Sex*. Translated and edited by H. M. Parshley. New York: Knopf, 1971.
Betancourt, Manuel. "'Hands of Stone' Director on Why Making a Hollywood Film About Successful Latinos Is Impossible." *Remezcla*, 15 June 2016.
Billig, Michael. *Banal Nationalism*. London: Sage Publications, 1995.
Boddy, Kasia. *Boxing: A Cultural History*. London: Reaktion, 2008.
Connell, R. W. *Masculinities*. Berkeley, CA: University of California Press, 2005.
Cook, Pam. "Masculinity in Crisis?" *Screen*, vol. 23, no 3–4, 1982, pp. 39–46.
Crosson, Séan. *Sport and Film*. New York: Routledge, 2013.
Delgado, Fernando. "Golden but not Brown: Oscar De la Hoya and the Complications of Culture, Manhood, and Boxing." *The International Journal of History of Sport*, vol. 22, no. 2, 2005, pp. 196–211.
Denfeld, Rene. *Kill the Body, the Head Will Fall: A Closer Look at Women, Violence, and Aggression*. New York: Warner Books, 1997.
Donoghue, Michael. "Roberto Durán, Omar Torrijos, and the Rise of Isthmian Machismo." *Sports Culture in Latin American History*, edited by David M. K. Sheinin. Pittsburgh, PA: University of Pittsburgh Press, 2015.
Elias, Norbert. "Introduction." *Quest for Excitement: Sport and Leisure in the Civilizing Process*, edited by Eric Dunning. Oxford: Basil Blackwell Ltd, 1986.
Fernández L'Hoeste, Héctor et al. "Introduction." *Sport and Nationalism in Latin/o America*, New York: Palgrave MacMillan, 2015, pp. 1–26.
Gems, Gerald R. *Boxing: A Concise History of the Sweet Science*. Lanham, MD: Rowman & Littlefield, 2014.
Giudice, Christian. *Hands of Stone: The Life and Legend of Roberto Durán*. Lancashire, UK: Milo Books, 2006.
Grindon, Leger. *Knockout: The Boxer and Boxing in American Cinema*. Jackson, MS: University of Mississippi Press, 2011.
Hands of Stone. Directed by Jonathan Jakubowicz, The Weinstein Company, 2016.
Heiskanen, Benita. *The Urban Geography of Boxing: Race, Class, and Gender in the Ring*. New York: Routledge, 2012.
Iber, Jorge et al. *Latinos in U.S. Sport: A History of Isolation, Cultural Identity, and Acceptance*. Champaign, IL: Human Kinetics, 2011.
Kring–Shreifels, Jake. "Why Hollywood Is Still So Obsessed with Boxing Movies." *Esquire Magazine*, 18 November 2016.
La Yuma. Directed by Florence Jaugey, Camila Films, 2009.
Maldonado, Marco A. and Zamora, Rubén. *Cosecha de campeones. Historia del box mexicano I. (1895–1960)*. Mexico: Editorial Clío, 1999.
Moreno, Hortensia: "Women Boxers and Nationalism in Mexico." *Sports and Nationalism in Latin/o America*, edited by Héctor Fernández L'Hoeste et al. New York: Palgrave MacMillan, 2015.
"Nicaragua." Forbes, www.forbes.com/places/nicaragua/. Accessed 10 July 2017.
Oates, Joyce Carol. "On Boxing." *On Boxing*. Updated and expanded edition. New York: Harper, 2005.
Rondinone, Troy. *Friday Night Fighter: Gaspar 'Indio' Ortega and the Golden Age of Television Boxing*. Chicago, IL: University of Illinois Press, 2013.
Sammons, Jeffrey T. *Beyond the Ring: The Role of Boxing in American Society*. Chicago, IL: University of Illinois Press, 1988.
Schippers, Mimi. "Recovering the Feminine Other: Masculinity, Femininity, and Gender Hegemony." *Theory and Society*, vol. 36, no. 1, 2007, pp. 85–102.

Scott, David. *The Art and Aesthetics of Boxing.* Lincoln, NE: University of Nebraska Press, 2008.

Wacquant, Loïc J.D. *Entre las cuerdas. Cuadernos de un aprendiz de boxeador.* Translated by María Hernández. Buenos Aires: Siglo XXI Editores Argentina, 2006.

Wacquant, Loïc J.D. "The Pugilistic Point of View: How Boxers Think and Feel about Their Trade." *Theory and Society*, vol. 24, no. 4, 1995, pp. 489–535.

Wacquant, Loïc J.D. "The Social Logic of Boxing in Black Chicago: Toward a Sociology of Pugilism." *Sociology of Sport Journal*, vol. 9, no. 3, 1992, pp. 221–254.

27

"THE BLIZZARD OF OZ"

Ozzie Guillén and Latino masculinities as spectacle[1]

Jennifer Domino Rudolph

On June 16, 2006 a conflict arose between then Chicago White Sox Manager Ozzie Guillén and *Chicago Sun Times* sports columnist Jay Mariotti regarding Mariotti's article, "Judgment Call: Time to Worry About Ozzie?" in which he criticizes Guillén over a hit-by-pitch incident. In that article, Mariotti refers to Guillén as "the Blizzard of Oz" and questions his ability to lead the team. The incident follows established, though problematic, Major League Baseball practice where Guillén ordered rookie relief pitcher, Sean Tracey to hit Texas Ranger Hank Blalock after Ranger's pitcher Vicente Padilla had hit White Sox catcher A.J. Pierzynski with pitches in his first two at bats. When Tracey failed in his retaliatory hit attempt, Guillén showed his frustration, resulting in Mariotti characterizing him as "crazy" and via mob epithets such as "thug" which prompted Guillén to call Mariotti a "fucking fag." The resolution of this incident involved Guillén attending sensitivity training amid criticisms that he was culturally deficient, uneducated and thus "didn't know any better."

This conflict typifies representations of Guillén among media and fans as a passionate and erratic Latino. These representations dovetail with well documented stereotypes of Latinos in media, popular culture, and baseball. The Guillén case also helps us to understand the ways that Latino masculinities intersect with race and spectacle.[2] Indeed, as a wealthy, Venezuelan-born elite player and manager in MLB (Major League Baseball), Guillén, along with Latin/o[3] American MLB players/managers stands in for a much larger group of Latino men as non-Latinos, particularly White Americans, use him to construct their ideas about who Latinos are and what their place is in US society. The fact that many such players and managers, are viewed through a lens of irrational masculinity and scandal signals larger issues around race and equality in the United States as these representations may be used to justify both White supremacist public policy and individuals' perceptions and treatment of Latinos. As such, I will examine a key moment near the end of Ozzie Guillén's managerial career with the Miami Marlins when he stated that he "respected Fidel Castro." I use a theoretical perspective combining Latino masculinities and spectacle to elucidate the ways that Latino masculinities as spectacle contribute to racial formation.

Setting the stage of Latino spectacle: Race, masculinities and media

Understandings of famous bodies such as that of Ozzie Guillén emerge within a context informed by the larger history and construction of race and masculinities in the United States.

Michael Omi and Howard Winant (*Racial Formation in the United States*, 1994), Eduardo Bonilla-Silva (*Racism without Racists*, 2014), and Joe Feagin (*The White Racial Frame*, 2013) have all demonstrated how race in the United States operates on a White/non-White binary. Whiteness emerged historically as a shifting category linked to power and privilege where those who have access to Whiteness stubbornly protect their position of power and continue to limit its access for those not considered to be White. These scholars further argue that "racial formation" (Omi and Winant 1994: 55) is a project constantly under construction, termed a "racial project," which continues to operate and adjust according to societal and political circumstances.

Gender intersects with race in our understandings of Latino masculinities. Masculinity, like race is a construct informed by history and power relations. Latino masculinities stem from imperialist and colonial relations between Europe and the Americas, as well as within the Americas, specifically the relationship between the United States and Latin America. As Aída Hurtado and Mrinal Sinha argue in *Beyond Machismo: Intersectional Latino Masculinities*, this history has resulted in popular understandings of Latino masculinities in the US almost exclusively through the limited lens of machismo which has "cast an entire hemisphere as the epitome of male patriarchal privilege and small-mindedness" (2016: 11). Instead, Hurtado and Sinha attend to intersecting statuses like race, class, gender/sexuality and ability in their understanding of Latino masculinities within this history.

For a long period after the Cuban Revolution of 1959, revolutionary leader Fidel Castro would attract a firestorm of resentment and political policy in the US among Cuban exiles as well as the US government. In its unwillingness to conduct diplomatic relations with what it identified as a communist regime, the US state sustained an embargo which only during the presidency of Barak Obama showed signs of lifting. Related to this rejection of the communist Cuban state, the US government initially welcomed Cubans who were considered refugees, primarily a White professional class in the 1960s, though these dynamics would change with the Mariel Boatlift in 1980 which brought a more racially and economically mixed group of Cubans. This political reality set Cubans apart from other Latin Americans who could not immigrate to the US as easily and thus caused resentment between Cubans and other Latin Americans. This reality also demonstrated to Latin Americans the extent and ways that the US would wield its economic and political capital in the region, cementing a collective narrative of struggle in the face of US imperialism. Sustained immigration of Cubans of various races and social classes resulted in adjustments to the refugee status afforded to Cubans, such that undocumented Cuban immigrants have been increasingly "repatriated" off the coast of Florida before they reach US soil, termed "wet foot, dry foot." As Cuban arrivals included more people of color and poor people, the interception and deportation of Cuban immigrants illustrates how race and class intersect not only with media representation and reception, but also politics and the law. This history constitutes a watershed moment in the history of Cuban-Americans such that an off the cuff comment by a Venezuelan athlete ignites a backlash resulting in a media scandal.

Within the US context, this history intersects with the racial formation mentioned above which continues to deny most Latino men access to the power and privilege associated with Whiteness. These historical narratives of colonization, race, and masculinities manifest in the present via globalized economies and hemispheric power differentials which subordinate Latin America to the United States (see Brotherton and Kretsedemas *Keeping out the Other: A Critical Introduction to Immigration Enforcement Today*, 2008; Chavez *The Latino Threat: Constructing Immigrants, Citizens and the Nation*, 2008; Mirandé *Hombres y Machos: Masculinity and Latino Culture*, 1997). This has resulted in sustained migration from Latin America to the United States, placing many Latino men in lower-wage sectors of the economy and channeling them into informal, and sometimes illegal sectors of the US economy. MLB reproduces this colonial dynamic in its recruitment and training procedures in the Caribbean basin as a source of cheap talent, such that its ranks at both the major and minor league levels include at least 25% Latinos, the majority born outside the United States. Players and managers at the major league level like Guillén simultaneously challenge and uphold these hemispheric power differentials via media spectacles in which they are enmeshed to perpetuate the hemispheric colonial and racial hierarchy disfavoring Latino men.

Media production continues to play a significant role in formations of social positions and hierarchies with regard to Latinos. Based on the research of George Gerbner, in *Television and its Viewers: Cultivation Theory and Research* James Shanahan and Michael Morgan (1999) document how media production and consumption fuel many people's understandings of the world, especially of people different from themselves, with whom they have limited face to face interaction in their daily lives. Outcomes of this include the potential legitimization of stereotypes and famous members of a community as stand-ins for the community at large, or a significant burden of representation where relatively few individuals come to represent a much more nuanced and complex reality. For Latino men in particular, the implication is that their social positions and access to resources may be linked to a limited set of representations related to violence, invasion, dishonesty, and lack of stability which negatively affect outcomes.

Charles Ramírez-Berg (*Latino Images in Film: Stereotypes, Subversion, Resistance*, 2002), Clara Rodriguez (*Heroes, Lovers, and Others: A History of Latinos in Hollywood*, 2004) and Angharad Valdivia (*Latina/os and the Media*, 2010) have mapped the range of representations of Latino men over the history of media production in the US, including the Latin lover, outlaw-cum-gang member, and perpetual immigrant invader. Steven Bender (*Greasers and Gringos: Latinos, Justice and the American Imagination*, 2003), has linked these media portrayals and conventional wisdom about Latino men to adverse lived outcomes with the US legal system. In *Invisible No More: Understanding the Disenfranchisement of Latino Men and Boys*, Pedro Noguera, Aída Hurtado, and Edward Fergus (2012) extend this argument to outcomes in education, employment and incarceration. In "Latino Masculinities in the Post-9/11 Era," Hernan Ramirez and Edward Flores (2013) similarly argue that the dominant representations of Latinos men as immigrant laborers and gang members render them simultaneously invisible, engaging in low-wage, behind the scenes work such as gardening, while at the same time hyper-visible as threats to the nation as violent gang members. This representational context shapes media content depicting Latin/o American MLB Players. As Adrián Burgos Jr. (2007) argues in *Playing America's Game: Baseball, Latinos and the Color Line*, media workers often purposely include non-standard English grammar in addition to the above tropes in the content they produce on Latin/o American players.

Ozzie Guillén and Latino racial spectacle

Along with media representations and work on Latino masculinities, the idea of spectacle, specifically what Jonathon Markovitz (2011) has termed "racial spectacles" informs our understanding of Ozzie Guillén and social positions of Latino men in the US more broadly. The work of Guy Debord shapes much current theorization of spectacle. Debord understands spectacles as images connected to social relations and to the power structure of capitalism where the images serve the greater goals of those at the top (1967: section 5). Douglas Kellner departs from Debord in that while he agrees that spectacles form the base of social relations, he takes issue with the passivity and top down nature of Debord's definition, arguing instead that spectacles create opportunities for tension and resistance, not mere passive acceptance on the part of oppressed groups (2003: 11). Combining and amplifying Debord and Kellner's definitions, Markovitz defines racial spectacles as media events which engage various media platforms and technologies and function as "instruments of socialization" (2011: 2). Following the critical race work of Eduardo Bonilla-Silva and Michael Omi and Howard Winant, he goes on to emphasize that these events create national dialogues on race and thus contribute to national "racial formation in which categories of race are continually contested and reconstructed" (2011: 3). Markovitz also views racial spectacles from an intersectional perspective, stating that issues of class and gender/sexuality must also be taken into account in understandings of racial formations fueled by these spectacles. Kellner and Marovitz emphasize that racial spectacles are constantly under construction and negotiation by individuals and that they are never complete nor definitive.

Indeed, media spectacles such as that of Ozzie Guillén, as well as the idea of "spectacular bodies" developed by Susan Jeffords (*Hard Bodies: Hollywood Masculinity in the Reagan Era*, 1993), Yvonne Tasker (*Spectacular Bodies: Gender, Genre and the Action Cinema*, 1993), and Daphne Brooks (*Bodies in Dissent: Spectacular Performances of Race and Freedom, 1850–1910*, 2006) engage the dynamics of racial formation above as they relate to collective memory. Jeffords, Tasker and Brooks posit that spectacular or famous bodies such as that of Guillén stand in for the ordinary bodies and national ideologies enmeshed in the gendered and raced social structure of the United States, both perpetuating and resisting historical narratives of race and power. Spectacle and spectacular bodies, in turn, fold into the collective memory, a memory which also informs media audience reception as it happens. Maurice Halbwachs characterizes the relationship between past and present in collective memory as follows, "the past is preserved but it is reconstructed on the basis of the present" (1992: 20). Darnell Hunt expands this definition with regard to race and positionality via "intertextual memory" in stating that understandings of the past act as a "prism [that] refracts the content of media texts in ways that resonate with the 'real' and mediated experiences of individuals" (1999: 43). Markovitz, Halbwachs and Hunt's definitions of racial spectacles shape the present analysis of Ozzie Guillén and Latino masculinities in that the constructions and reconstructions of the past interlock with politics and social structure as audiences consume media spectacles as they unfold, in this case US/Cuban relations. The ways that individuals (re)construct unfolding racial spectacles through their understandings of the past and present manifest themselves in policy and social structure as well as lived racialized experiences, as we shall see in the analysis of Guillén's comments about former Cuban leader, Fidel Castro.

"The Blizzard of Oz" moves to Miami

By the time Guillén parted ways with the White Sox organization in 2012, he had gained a reputation among media workers, baseball organizations and fans alike as a volatile Venezuelan who could fire up players but also divide organizations due to his irrationality and outspoken nature. When Guillén accepted a position managing the Miami Marlins, *Sports Illustrated* coverage of the move focused on the team's big spending on talent and a new ballpark through metaphors of mental illness. A March 5, 2012 cover story featuring Guillén and shortstop José Reyes titled "Marlinsanity?: Betting that Binge Spending, a Psychedelic Park and Mad New Talent Will Create Baseball Mania in Miami" indexes images of mental instability through "insanity" and "madness" to explain changes made by the Marlins organization particularly to cater to Miami's large Latino/a population, many of whom are from the Caribbean where baseball enjoys a high level of popularity. Guillén would only briefly stay with the Marlins organization. He was fired amid a series of controversies on October 23, 2012, after one season with the team.

All of these measures to improve infrastructure and talent were meant to awaken baseball interest in arguably the most Latino/a city in the US, where such interest had not materialized since the formation of the Marlins organization as the Florida Marlins in 1993. The *Sports Illustrated* article evinces latinidad—a sense of shared struggle amid the colonial history of Latin America among ethnic groups captured under the label "Latino"—and aggressive masculinity in its description of the locations of the ticketing office and ballpark as well as the hiring of Guillén:

> To make good on one of the biggest gambles in baseball history, the Miami (né Florida) Marlins have established their ticket sales headquarters above a small medical center on a corner lot in Little Havana, abutting a fenced-in yard of squawking chickens. Catty-corner to the two-story building, as if it had recently come to rest after an interstellar mission, is soon-to-open Marlins Park, a sleek Kubrickian vision of white stucco, metal and glass that cost $515 million, seats 37, 442, and has a retractable roof that closes in 13 minutes.
>
> *(Reiter 2012: 36)*

The article describes Guillén's entrance to the Marlins organization and to their physical facility as follows:

> Then an accented voice boomed from the doorway of the room: 'Hey, for f——$10 million, I'd f——fly from the moon!' It was Ozzie Guillén, who after eight brash, generally winning and invariably profane seasons as the White Sox manager, replaced the re-retiring McKeon last September. Guillén, who received a four-year, $10 million contract, wasn't brought in merely to be a manager. He is expected, with his honest energy and loose-cannon quotability, to give the franchise a dose of personality and help invigorate the Marlins' fan base.
>
> *(Reiter 2012: 37)*

These two quotes illustrate the ways that aggressive Latino masculinities fuse with the particular latinidad of Miami and the marketing of baseball to a fan base of Latino/as. Presumably, fans would identify with Guillén's Marlins playing in a ballpark described in garish terms in Little Havana, among the ubiquitous chickens associated with Caribbean diet, sport, and cockfights. Marlin's leadership also courted non-Latino/as whose interest presumably would awaken amid Guillén's performance of masculatinidad, feeding into long held perceptions of Latino men in entertainment. I use the term "masculatinidad" here in accordance my previous research (*Embodying Latino Masculinities, Producing Masculatinidad),* in which I develop the construct as a way of unpacking the tensions of performances of masculinities and latinidad. Masculatinidad questions the extent to which performances of Latino masculinities that index aggression, passion and capital acquisition both advance and limit Latino/a identities in the public sphere.

Such masculine performances would get Guillén in trouble early in his Marlins career. In an interview with *TIME* magazine's Sean Gregory on April 9, 2012, Guillén stated, "I respect Fidel Castro. You know why? A lot of people have wanted to kill Fidel Castro for the last 60 years but that [expletive] is still here."[4] These remarks sparked a firestorm among Miami's staunch anti-Castro Cuban population that would contribute to Guillén's separation from the Marlins. This demonstrates the link between sports, politics and the sustained Cuban power base in Miami. The Marlins suspended him for five games as a result of his remarks. As soon as the story broke, the anti-Castro Cuban and Latino/a communities of Miami as well as the Marlins' front office reacted. Local politicians including Miami-Dade Mayor Carlos Gimenez and Joe Martinez, Head of Miami-Dade Board of County Commissioners implored the Marlins to address Guillén's remarks, asking for his resignation. Cuban exile group Vigila Mambisa planned a boycott (Ortiz 2012).[5] Indeed, those boycotting the Marlins protested outside Marlins' Park carrying signs bearing Guillen's name in a circle with a line through it, with the caption "NO APOLOGIES, FIRE HIM NOW."

In response, the Marlins issued the following press release, "There is nothing to respect about Fidel Castro. He is a brutal dictator who has caused unthinkable pain for more than 50 years. We live in a community filled with victims of this dictatorship, and the people in Cuba continue to suffer today" (Ortiz 2012).[6] Guillén similarly retracted his comments evoking latinidad in his apology to the Cuban community, "I feel sad because I know I hurt a lot of people. I'm Latino. I live in Miami. I have a lot of (Cuban) friends and players. They know who I am. They know how I feel" (Ortiz 2012).[7] Guillén subsequently gave a press conference at Marlins' Park to repair his standing in Miami's Latino/a community.

At the 2012 press conference posted to YouTube by DailyWorldwideNews, Guillén spoke in Spanish and English to address the community he had unintentionally hurt with his remarks, beginning the conference in Spanish and switching to English during the question and answer period when requested to do so by a reporter. Guillén's apology and remarks focused on his regret at having hurt the Latino/a community and how a miscommunication and misunderstanding with the *TIME* reporter resulted in his remarks. Guillén frequently cited miscommunication and his limitations in English when reporters asked him to clarify his comments, insisting that his intention was to say that he wonders how it is possible that someone who has done so much damage could still be in power. He stated this clarification in Spanish as follows, "¿Cómo era posible que una persona que ha hecho tanto daño en el mundo esté en el poder [How was it possible that a person who has done so much damage in the world still be in power?]?[8,9]

In addition to his explanation based on language, Guillén expressed his regret and sorrow as a Latin/o American and as a representative of the Latino/a community; "I don't represent just myself. I represent Latin America. I represent the ball club, and I represent the organization."[10] Acknowledging his error in judgment, Guillén stated "He herido a una comunidad, a toda Latinoamérica [I have hurt a community, all of Latin America]."[11] He most strongly connected himself and his apology to a group identity, "A toda la familia cubana, nuevamente, mi perdón, mi cariño, y espero que cuando salga de aquí, entienda mejor y sepa un poco quién es esta persona y de verdad qué es lo que siento por ellos y por el régimen castrista y por el régimen de Venezuela, y el de Nicaragua, y el de Ecuador, y el del Perú, y lo que Ud. quiera [Again, to the entire Cuban family I beg your pardon and give you my affection, and I hope that when you leave here you understand a bit better and know a bit more who I am and what I truly feel for you and for the Castro regime and the regimes of Venezuela, Nicaragua, Ecuador, and Peru and wherever else]."[12] Through the description of the "Cuban family," as well as the mention of several Latin American countries, Guillén deploys a heteropatriarchal latinidad that cuts across Latino/a communities and the collective memory of political struggle in Latin America in an attempt to defuse the charged political nature of the mention of Castro. He implores the audience to accept the sincerity of his apology because this was only the second time in his managerial career that he is apologizing; the first was when he questioned Alex Rodríguez's Dominican nationality when Rodríguez played for the Dominican World Baseball Classic team.

During the question and answer period, Guillén continued to negotiate his two languages, as well as a reporter asking him if this was another example of his craziness and erratic behavior, to which Guillén responded, "No soy loco [I'm not crazy]," instead explaining his remarks as a lapse of respect and communication. This is consistent with the tone of "the Blizzard of Oz" that has become ubiquitous in media representations of Ozzie Guillén. He insisted that he will work to mend his relationship with the aggrieved Latin/o American community via a Spanish saying, "las palabras, se las lleva el viento, las acciones se quedan" roughly equivalent to the English "actions speak louder than words."[13]

The YouTube posting of Guillen's press conference generated a 57-comment stream as of March 10, 2015 debating the following topics: Cuban nationalism, "American" nationalism, freedom of speech, masculinity, and the role of the media. Quotes from two commentators particularly capture the tensions around media and Latin/o American masculinities at the heart of this study. These comments illustrate the tensions around narrative construction of racial spectacles as the first contests capitalism and privatization as anathema to freedom while the second highlights White masculinity via the machismo metaphor usually attributed to Latino men. Raul Gomez stated:

I guess there are a lot of Cubans in the US, especially in Florida, who don't like the idea of freedom of speech, like the MLB and the privatized, biased media. The media wants to make a big deal about [that] so the people don't even dare to speak their minds. That is why they made Ozzie apologize (poor fool). It is anti-American to not let someone speak their mind. Freedom? In the US? LOL... don't make me laugh. Who should really be apologizing?[14]

Gomez's comments reflect a knowledge that media outlets construct the news content that we all consume and are complicit in market-driven production of stories to awaken interest and generate nationalism via spectacle. He further implicates MLB as part of the problem as their response to the incident shows more of a concern for image and profit than for human dignity and freedom. In this way, Raul Gomez uses the racial spectacle of Guillén's remarks to resist what he deems neoliberal privatization located in the media and MLB itself.

Conversely, with respect to masculinity and machismo, a masculine behavior and performance specifically attributed to Latino men, a second YouTube user, Kemiztri commented, "AT THIS POINT AMERICANS ARE VERY DOCILE; LOOK AT AMERICAN MEN THEIR BECOMING MORE FENEMIZED??? LOOK THEY SAY HOW MACHISMO IS BAD AND YET THEY DONT REALIZE MACHISMO IS WHAT MADE THE USA… ITS AMAZING HOW MEN ARE DUMB DOWN…"[15] This second commentator shows a clear anxiety around a perceived threat to White masculine power in his appropriation of machismo to defend European colonization of the United States. The use of all caps visually captures the intense anxiety of the commenter. This comment represents a disturbing justification of historical violence against people of color by way of a gendered construct associated with a racialized group, Latino men. This commenter advocates for White masculine violence as a point of nation building as well as maintenance of the nation in the present moment in the face of threat to an undefined "American" machismo which presumably grants unchecked power to White men over all others. In its evocation of the European colonization of what is now United States territory, this comment, and by extension the Guillén/Castro spectacle, deploys a Eurocentric narrative, embedded in the hegemonic collective memory of White Americans, to erase a racist historical legacy that continues to contour power relations in the Americas in the present moment.

Contextualizing Guillén's Latino racial spectacle

As such, both Guillén's apology and the comments cited here must be contextualized within a wider context of Latin American and particularly Cuban/US relations. As evidenced by the varied reactions from MLB, Guillén and YouTube commenters, this incident constitutes a racial spectacle in that individuals and institutions read and understand this media event via varied social positions and collective memory of relations between the US and Latin America.

The Guillén/Castro controversy, especially Guillén's assertion that he respects Castro's ability to remain in power despite having hurt so many, further highlights the ways that gendered masculinist discourses circulate via racial spectacles.

In this way, the media spectacle surrounding Ozzie Guillén's remarks about Fidel Castro illustrates the socio-political tensions around Latino/as in the US, especially Latin/o American masculinities which are understood by fans and media through optics of aggression, passion, irrationality and criminalization. Guillén does indeed provoke debate via his performance of self as he engages questions of politics, masculinity and power within MLB and media as both provide a forum for and embellish incidents of "the Blizzard of Oz." As such, Guillén, media workers and fans all collude in the perpetuation of the masculine Latino threat dating back to the early days of Hollywood and the *bandido* figure, which has evolved into the dictator/urban criminal, and I would argue the outspoken, wealthy, retired athlete that is Ozzie Guillén. The fact that Guillén understands the dominant perceptions of his actions and the market value of them as fodder for media workers to make money and on-line commentators to process Latin/o American social, political, racial and gender issues pushes us to critically engage class and Latin/o American masculinities in baseball because, to some extent, Ozzie Guillén's economic capital allows him a level of power in the public sphere afforded to few men of any ethnic or racial group. While there are consequences such as with the Cuban/Latino/a community in Miami, constructions and receptions of Guillén buttress a socio-racial hierarchy that benefits him as an individual while the larger Latin/o American community continues to suffer the material consequences of the stereotypes ascribed to him. Returning to Markovitz's construct, this, and other racial spectacles serve to distract individuals from the social, racial, political and gendered structures that contour their daily lives even as they provoke larger conversations around resistance and gendered racial formation in the United States.

Notes

1 I am grateful to María Elena Cepeda and Frederick Luis Aldama whose insights greatly strengthened this piece.
2 I use masculinities in the plural throughout to underscore the fact that there are multiple meanings and performances of Latino masculinities, and to discourage readers from reading Latino men exclusively through the popular conceptions of machismo associated with violence and womanizing.
3 I use Latin/o American throughout to capture the transnational identities of Latinos and Latin Americans born and living throughout the Americas.
4 http://content.time.com/time/magazine/article/0,9171,2110450,00.html. Accessed 10/16/2014.
5 http://usatoday30.usatoday.com/sports/baseball/nl/marlins/story/2012-04-09/ozzie-guillen-castro-controversy/54136806/1. Accessed 10/19/2014.
6 http://usatoday30.usatoday.com/sports/baseball/nl/marlins/story/2012-04-09/ozzie-guillen-castro-controversy/54136806/1. Accessed 10/19/2014.
7 http://usatoday30.usatoday.com/sports/baseball/nl/marlins/story/2012-04-09/ozzie-guillen-castro-controversy/54136806/1. Accessed 10/19/2014.
8 www.youtube.com/all_comments?v=RXSN7vodSJU. Accessed 10/20/2014. Note that all YouTube comments are reproduced as they appear on the site. Corrections or clarifications will be made when the meaning or context is unclear.
9 All translations are mine.
10 www.youtube.com/all_comments?v=RXSN7vodSJU. Accessed 10/20/2014.
11 www.youtube.com/all_comments?v=RXSN7vodSJU. Accessed 10/20/2014.
12 www.youtube.com/all_comments?v=RXSN7vodSJU. Accessed 10/20/2014.
13 www.youtube.com/all_comments?v=RXSN7vodSJU. Accessed 10/20/2014.
14 www.youtube.com/all_comments?v=RXSN7vodSJU. Accessed 10/20/2014.
15 https://www.youtube.com/all_comments?v=RXSN7vodSJU. Accessed 10/20/2014.

Works cited

Bender, Steven. *Greasers and Gringos: Latinos, Justice and the American Imagination.* New York: New York University Press, 2003.

Bonilla-Silva, Eduardo. *Racism without Racists: Color-Blind Racism and the Performance of Racial Inequality in America.* Lanham, MD: Rowman and Littlefield, 2014.

Brooks, Daphne. *Bodies in Dissent: Spectacular Performances of Race and Freedom, 1850–1910.* Durham, NC: Duke University Press, 2006.

Brotherton, David and Philip Kretsedemas, Eds. *Keeping Out the Other: A Critical Introduction to Immigration Enforcement Today.* New York: Columbia University Press, 2008.

Burgos, Adrián. *Playing America's Game: Baseball, Latinos and the Color Line.* Berkeley, CA: University of California Press, 2007.

Chavez, Leo. *The Latino Threat: Constructing Immigrants, Citizens, and the Nation.* Stanford, CA: Stanford University Press, 2008.

Debord, Guy. *Society of the Spectacle.* Detroit, MI: Black and Red, 1967.

Feagin, Joe. *The White Racial Frame: Centuries of Racial Framing and Counter-Framing.* New York: Routledge, 2013.

Halbwachs, Maurice. *On Collective Memory.* Translated and edited by Lewis Coser. Chicago, IL: University of Chicago Press, 1992.

Hunt, Darnell. *O.J. Simpson Facts & Fictions: New Rituals in the Construction of Reality.* Cambridge, UK: Cambridge University Press, 1999.

Hurtado, Aída and Mrinal Sinha. *Beyond Machismo: Intersectional Latino Masculinities.* Austin, TX: University of Texas Press, 2016.

Jeffords, Susan. *Hard Bodies: Hollywood Masculinity in the Reagan Era.* New Brunswick, NJ: Rutgers University Press, 1993.

Kellner, Douglas. *Media Spectacle.* New York: Routledge, 2003.

Mariotti, J. Judgment Call: Time to Worry about Ozzie. *Chicago Sun Times.* June 16, 2006.

Markovitz, Jonathon. *Racial Spectacles: Explorations in Media, Race, and Justice.* New York: Routledge, 2011.

Mirandé, Alfredo. *Hombres y Machos: Masculinity and Latino Culture.* Boulder, CO: Westview Press, 1997.

Noguera, Pedro, Aída Hurtado, and Edward Fergus, Eds. *Invisible No More: Understanding the Disenfranchisement of Latino Men and Boys.* New York: Routledge, 2012.

Omi, Michael and Howard Winant. *Racial Formation in the United States: From the 1960s to the 1990s.* New York: Routledge, 1994.

Ortiz, Jorge. "Ozzie Guillén on the hot seat over Fidel Castro remarks" http://usatoday30.usatoday.com/sports/baseball/nl/marlins/story/2012-04-09/ozzie-guillen-castro-controversy/54136806/1 April 10, 2012. Accessed 10/19/2014.

Ramirez, Hernan and Edward Flores. "Latino Masculinities in the Post-9/11 Era." In Eds. Michael Kimmel and Michael Messner. *Men's Lives.* Boston, MA: Pearson, 2013.

Ramírez-Berg, Charles. *Latino Images in Film: Stereotypes, Subversion, Resistance.* Austin, TX: University of Texas Press, 2002.

Reiter, Ben. "Marlinsanity?: Betting Big that Binge Spending, a Psychedelic Park and Mad New Talent Will Create Baseball Mania in Miami." *Sports Illustrated,* March 5, 2012.

Rodriguez, Clara. *Heroes, Lovers, and Others: A History of Latinos in Hollywood.* Washington DC: Smithsonian Books, 2004.

Shanahan, J and Michael Morgan, Eds. *Television and its Viewers: Cultivation Theory and Research.* Cambridge, UK: Cambridge University Press, 1999.

Tasker, Yvonne. *Spectacular Bodies: Gender, Genre and the Action Cinema.* New York: Routledge, 1993.

Valdivia, Angharad. *Latina/os and the Media.* London: Polity, 2010.

PART VI

Alt-hemispheric sound and body performatics

28

SOMOS MUJERES SOMOS HIP HOP

Feminism and hip hop in Latin America

Melissa Castillo-Garsow

There's a new wave of feminism in Latin America. It is a thriving movement adopted by and spearheaded by a diverse generation of young women who are not just outspoken but unapologetically hip hop. In "Latinoamérica Unida," the title track of the 2015 album from the female collective Somos Mujeres Somos Hip Hop—a group composed of twelve women representing ten countries—the performers take turns demonstrating the significance of hip hop feminisms as a way to combat gender inequality in Latin America. According to MC Rebeca Lane, "Feminism for me and for us and many women in Latin America it's not about a book, it's not about theory, it's not about academics. It's about how you feel and how you want to live your life without machismo." Although their exact interpretation of feminism may differ, as demonstrated by the individual songs which make up the rest of the compilation, their central argument is clear and unified. MC Roja of Ecuador describes the inspiration:

> There are women across Latin America that see feminism, not as a way of women dominating, but about equal opportunities for everyone. So we decided to start Somos Mujeres Somos Hip Hop as a Latin American wide project. We ended up with a group of twelve women representing ten countries all using music to address different social issues.
>
> *(Rima Roja en Venus 2015)*

The entire album is a powerful testament to the diversity of strong female feminist voices not just in Latin America in general but Latin American hip hop specifically. Composed of Nakury Del Patio (Costa Rica), Vaio Flow (Argentina), Rima Roja En Venus (Ecuador), Dania Neko (Chile), Audry Funk (Mexico), MC Jana (Colombia), Nina Uma (Bolivia), Anarkia Ruiz (Venezuela), Lenys Merkdo (Colombia), Rebeca Lane (Guatemala), Sipas Crew (Peru), each of the MCs on the album performs a solo song touching on issues relating to women in their personal and regional context as well contributing an eight-bar segment to the final track. What unites these diverse women is their conviction that Latin America needs feminism, and that feminism means women working together.

The album's twelve tracks pulse with attitude and skill, ranging in style from the melodic sound of Chile's Dania Neko to the coarse, guttural flow of the Colombian MC Jana. "Kutipakuy" (meaning "to ruminate"), a song by Peru's Sipas Crew, a trio of MCs from Portada de Manchay I, Lima, peppers Quechua words over a heavy charango beat while Lenys Merkdo from the northern coast of Colombia demonstrates her reggae and R&B backround. With confidence and swagger, they assert their hip hop dexterity, their relevance as women in a hip hop arena while also narrating the history of gender marginalizations as well as the way women have fought back, both past and present. Here, MC Anarkía's track shines, splicing images of slave and labor abuse against images of female activists and revolutionaries throughout the Americas. Powerfully, these women are black, indigenous, and everything in between. This diversity of hip hop feminism is most visually and auditorily powerful in the music video to "Latinoamérica Unida" which was composed of clips filmed individually. For eight bars we are transported to a skatepark in Quito where pink-haired MC Venus turns her head to show a jaguar tattooed over one ear. Then we move to a rooftop in Puebla, Mexico, as dreadlocked Audry Funk picks up the beat; to downtown Caracas, where Anarkia Ruiz climbs a statue of Simón Bolívar. Building on Bolívar's vision of Latin American unity and independence, Somos Mujeres Somos Hip Hop present a call for Latin American women to unite in the common cause of female independence. Thus, in the chorus they come together as united voice for gender equality, that is nevertheless composed of many different voices and ways of being a woman:

Hoy hacemos el stop	Today we stop
nadie tiene el control	No one is in control
levantamos la voz	We raise the voice
Latinoamérica	of Latin America
Hip Hop unida esta	united in Hip Hop
hombres mujeres van	men women with
sentido del igualdad	a sense of equality
eso queremos	that is what we want.

(Chorus from "Latinoamérica Unida"
by Somos Mujeres Somos Hip Hop [2015])[1]

In this chapter, I provide a brief overview of feminist hip hop scholarship as well as hip hop feminism in Latin America before exploring three of the Somos Mujeres Somos Hip Hop rappers' personal interpretations. While Rebeca Lane of Guatemala focuses on violence against women, Audry Funk's message empowers women via self-acceptance. Alongside MC duo Rima Roja en Venus of Ecuador, they argue for the power of female-founded and led hip hop collectives that are not exclusionary of men but in which men must enter female spaces, not vice versa. Together they put forth a community form of feminism that is built on self-sustainable networks (Mackey 2016) and a form of "intersectionality" based in the diversity of Latin American cultures. A term coined by American civil rights advocate Kimberlé Crenshaw to describe overlapping or intersecting social identities and related systems of oppression, domination, or discrimination, intersectionality here highlights the way the MCs bring to light the way racism and prejudice particularly against indigenous peoples heightens forms of violence against women (Crenshaw 1991; McCall). Thus Lane, Funk, and Rima Roja en Venus are part of a new generation of Latin American female MCs whose lyrics don't just touch on issues facing the region's women, they also celebrate the resistance and courage it takes to claim space as a woman at all.

"We all come from a very machista culture": Hip hop in Latin America

As my edited volume, *La Verdad: An International Dialogue on Hip Hop Latinidades* (Castillo-Garsow and Jason Nichols 2016) outlined, over the past forty years, hip hop has grown from its

South Bronx origins into a multilingual, multiethnic, intergenerational, global yet localized and regional collection of cultural expressions. From the beginning, descendants of Latin American immigrants in the United States were instrumental in the foundations of hip hop's four elements, but since the 1980s that cultural exchange has expanded by traveling to Latin America. As a result, hip hop in Latin America has grown to the point where Latin American artists are important influences for some US Latino and non-Latino artists, traveling around the world and performing in large non-English-language showcases.[2] I co-edited *La Verdad* with Jason Nichols because even with that volume, very little work exists in English on Latin American hip hop; furthermore, even in the context of global hip hop, Latin America is often overlooked, and discussions of women in hip hop are even more scarce.[3] There is an important body of scholarship (in addition to journalism) about hip hop written in Spanish, Portuguese, and French; however, this work is very little referenced within a US scholarly canon.[4]

Nevertheless, as Sandra Álvarez outlines, hip hop did not just arrive to Latin America, but did so in a time and context that makes female participation even more significant. As she describes:

> Al igual que en EEUU, el rap latino funcionaba como un amplificador de realidades sociales concretas, por lo que no es extraño que fuese permeable a las heridas históricas (regímenes militares, feminicidio, profundas brechas económicas) que el mapa latinoamericano arrastraba durante un largo tiempo. De esta forma, junto a las expresiones más lúdicas del género, se desarrolló un foco de resistencia desde el que se devolvía al rap su condición de herramienta de combate. Es en estos márgenes donde se gesta lo que hoy identificamos como un boom de las rimas feministas, en el que cientos de femcees descubren su poder y deciden pasar a la acción, reclamando su papel de sujetos activos dentro de una cultura que las había desplazado durante años.[5]

The extreme violence of Latin America's social realities has meant that hip hop took hold and continues to exist as an important youth expression of social realities. Outside of reggaeton, which is commercially popular but mainly Caribbean-based music,[6] hip hop continues to remain an underground sub-culture of anti-establishment expression. This does not mean, however, that the male dominated aspects of the genre, nor machista aspects of Latin American culture do not combine to marginalize women in hip hop as well. Rather this is what binds the women together both as femcees (female MCs) and as women in the region. Hip hop developed in Latin America as a common youth language of societal ills; women in Latin America adapted that language to develop regional feminism and form new female networks (Álvarez 2013).[7]

Significantly, this is not the first album of its kind. A collaboration of thirteen femcees "Femcees, Flow Feminista" was produced in 2014 and financed through crowdfunding with the purpose to support "grupos y redes de mujeres feministas y defensoras de los Derechos Humanos del Estado español, Latinoamérica y el Caribe" (Álvarez 2013).[8] MCs on this album included the following from Spain: BKC, Efecto Doppler, La Furia, Inessa, Mai, La Omega, Phussyon, BOCAdeBABA, Shuga Wuga and Larah Fémina; Krudas Cubensi from Cuba, Mare Advertencia Lirika from Mexico, Ana Tijoux from Chile, Rebeca Lane from Guatemala and Caye Cayejera from Ecuador. These MCs from Latin America, not surprisingly are also the only femcees to have garnered scholarly attention (either in the US or Latin America).

As Carmen Díez Salvatierra outlines, very little research exists on the topic of Latin American femcees, but instead research is mainly limited to pieces on US black feminist rap (2016: 41).

As such, McRobbie and Garber's questions from the 1970s British context—"Are girls, in fact, for reasons which we could discover, really not active or present in youth sub-cultures? Or has something in the way this kind of research is done rendered them invisible?" (1975: 209)—though still relevant in a US hip hop context, are particularly incisive here. Twenty years of US hip hop feminist studies have developed alternative methods of critical engagement to address questions of representation, forms of feminist consciousness, embodied experience, creative aesthetics, and more generally, the political prerogatives of hip hop culture (Durham et al. 2013: 722). While indebted to this body of hip hop feminist scholarship, I hope to broaden the field to be more inclusive of voices south of the border. The context of hip hop is critical to answering these questions about the perceived absence of women; however, the analysis has almost entirely been one concerned "with the ways the conservative backlash of the 1980s and 1990s, deindustrialization, the slashing of the welfare state, and the attendant gutting of social programs and affirmative action, along the increasing racial wealth gap, have affected the life worlds and worldviews of the hip-hop generation" (Durham et al. 2013: 722–3). It is also one which tends to employ black studies as an obvious, unchallenged background, which in the case of Latin America may or may not be valid, as well one that does not account for the way blackness is treated very differently in Latin America.[9]

For example, one of the few female MCs from outside the US to gain US scholarly attention, Las Krudas Cubensi have been analyzed for the way they problematize misrepresentations of blackness and sexuality in Cuba. Here their "afrofeminismo" is one which links contemporary black feminist cultural production in the African diaspora, but also must be understood within a particular context of Cuban racisms and homophobia (Acosta 2013; Álvarez Ramírez in Castillo-Garsow and Jason Nichols 2016). Of course, Krudas Cubensi are not the first Latin American women breaking gender barriers as they search for success as hip-hop artists. Puerto Rican rapper Lisa M, "The Queen of Spanish Rap" was one of the first Latina rappers to garner mainstream visibility with her 1988 and 1990 solo albums, while Chilean rapper Ana Tijoux's socially conscious rhymes earned her a Sony Music Entertainment record deal with Makiza in 1999. Still, this not only represents very limited attention and even less research, but also does not demonstrate the vibrant and diverse field of female MCs outside of the US. Although many have argued that "women have always been a critical part of the foundation of hip-hop culture as well as of its present success" this is not represented in a scholarly context and much less so when one considers scholarship on Latin America (Peoples 2008: 21).[10]

"My rap isn't feminine, but feminist": Individual feministas, collective feminism

What binds together the women of Somos Mujeres Somos Hip Hop, according to Mexican MC Audry Funk is that "We all come from a very machista culture" (Rigby 2015). This is a reference both to cultural upbringings as well as to the male-dominated culture of hip hop, for which women are often relegated to audience members at best and sexual objects at worst. Ignored by journalism and scholarship alike, they are very rarely appreciated as performers, or respected for their rapping skills. As Aisha Durham Brittney C. Cooper and Susana M. Morris argue, "It is hip-hop feminism that is uniquely able to move women from the sidelines of the stages we built, and from the cheering section of audiences that our public pedagogies have made space for, to claim an unapologetic place at the center as knowledge makers and culture creators" (2013: 734). For Latin American women, the combination of societal and hip hop marginalizations are more than just questions of economic equality, but of life and death.

Somos Mujeres Somos Hip Hop

Femicide reaches frightening levels in Latin America, which contains half of the 25 countries with the highest rates internationally (Rigby 2015). Thus, when Audry Funk met MC Roja, one half of Rima Roja en Venus, during a concert held in New York by the Brooklyn hip-hop-and-tattoo crew, Har'd Life Ink, they recognized kindred spirits. Later that year, when Roja organized the first Somos Mujeres Somos Hip Hop festival in Quito, along with Venus Castillo, the other half of Rima Roja en Venus, they invited Funk to come and take part. Consequently, within this overlaying context of Latin America gender inequality and hip hop machismo, I propose an examination of how feminist theory is practiced in the everyday life of Latin American femcees.

Audry Funk is no stranger to collective feminism within a hip hop context. By collective feminism I mean a demand for gender equality that is founded and directed by women with the intention of creating a group of women who work individually and have individual beliefs but also come together for collaborative action. For example, in 2009, Funk helped to found Mujeres Trabajando ("Women at Work"), a group of Mexican hip hop artists dedicated to music that promotes positive messages of women. Eight years later, Audry Funk continues to be a member of the group, formed by women who practice everything from break dance, graffiti, visual arts, photography, and other media forms in addition to rapping. As Funk explains, this type of project is important not just to promote women in hip hop but to support them in their personal lives as wives, mothers, daughters, border crossers, etc. so that they can continue to be hip hoppers as well. (RD Staff 2016). With members now from all over Mexico from Puebla to Juárez, they continue to put on shows while expanding into other areas such as a clothing line called Funky Beast.[11] As such, "Mujeres Trabajando" makes an important statement about valuing the labor of women in hip hop, but also helping to support all the other labor women often must shoulder due to gender roles and expectations so that continuing to do hip hop is possible.

Audry Funk is one of the best-known female MCs from Mexico, having performed in national and international venues including Chile, Bolivia, El Salvador, the Dominican Republic, Ecuador, and New York. Her personal musical style is a unique mix of hip hop with reggae, soul and funk over which she raps in her powerful and deep vocals about the nuances of life as a Mexican woman, with themes from love to discrimination to defying expectations. One of these is about standards of Mexican female beauty. According to Funk:

> I really want to dignify the beauty of women. Here in Mexico on the television you just can't only see blonde girls and skinny girls. In Mexico we are not all blonde and we are not all skinny. So why do the systems want to make you feel bad about your size, your color of the skin, the color of your eyes. Like me, I'm not a skinny girl. I'm a big mama. So I always say I'm a big sexy mama and what? Why do I have to feel bad about that.
>
> _(Funk 2015)_

This stance is particularly clear in her song "Máscaras," her contribution to _Latinoamérica Unida_ in which she also defies listeners' expectations of her. Unlike many of her videos in which bright clothes and city backdrops encourage movement and positive energy, "Máscaras" has a sobering, edgy, anti-discrimination message. Shot in black and white, the video features a stripped down Audry Funk in a hoodie and dark, thick eyeliner. In it she powerfully describes the cages of societal views that limit women. And while domestic violence is one aspect of this cage, gender violence runs much deeper, with roots that extend and oppress in many ways.

Perhaps for this reason, in her bars on the final track she both encourages female strength and unity while also pointing out systems of gender oppression:

Y nos juntamos todas las guerreas	And we unite all the (female) warriors
Disolvemos fronteras	Disolving borders
Qusieron separarnos	They wanted to separate us
Acusarnos de chiseras	They accusing us of being gossipers
Consignar en el olvido	To consign to oblivion
A las que dan vida a las esfera	Those that give life to the planet

Guerreras is an important way of conceptualizing their form of feminism. Not only are female warriors a recognizable symbol of female power, it is one that does not diminish women's importance as the gender that also literally carries and gives life to the future. It is one that reaffirms women's place as mothers while also questioning gender roles that diminish women as weak followers rather than strong leaders.

For this reason, it should come as no surprise that Funk is a member of multiple hip hop collectives such as Somos Mujeres Somos Hip Hop and Mujeres Trabajando, collectives which see one women's success as in no way threatening to others, but rather essential to advancing the calls of all femcees. As such Audry Funk, is also a member of Somos Guerreras (We are Warriors), a feminist hip hop tour organized by another Somos Mujeres Somos Hip Hop MC, Rebeca Lane. Profoundly, as the Guatemalan Lane explains, it is a space where the term feminist, like guerrera, is a source of pride. According to Lane,

> De una forma más profunda me parece que todas tenemos bien puesta la camiseta de guerreras, todas nos calificamos como feministas y me parece que somos una fuerza grande, la guerra para mí sería en contra de los roles de género y en contra de aquella mala idea donde dicen que dos mujeres juntas ni difuntas podemos trabajar y colaborar en santa paz para hacer proyecto grandes y fuertes.[12]

Here Lane makes an important connection between feminism and femicide as well as the ways in which women working together are both seen as dangerous and easily dismissible.[13] Somos Guerreras is a tour Lane and other female artists are taking through Central America. In addition to concerts, the objective behind the tour is to shoot a documentary about women in hip hop as well as give workshops that help facilitate further female networks among a new and younger generation of women. Moreover, for Lane an important reason for women to write graffiti, DJ, rap, breakdance, MC or beatbox, is to prevent violence in their community through female visibility.

Rebeca Lane's concern for femicide is personal. Born in Guatemala City amidst civil war, she was named after an aunt who was kidnaped and disappeared by the military government in 1981 because of her political involvement in the guerrilla movement. As such her music is infused with feminism, social justice and history, in particular as connected to the cause of indigenous land rights (Estevez 2016). Originally a poet and actress, both theater and poetry still form part of her hip hop practice, not just as an individual artist but in the ways she works to create youth spaces of artistic expression in marginalized regions of the city.[14] Poetry led her to spoken-word and as a collaborator in Da-Radio (A Hip Hop online radio) a part of Última Dosis, a Hip Hop collective in 2012 when she started to record as a rapper. In October 2013, her album "Canto" was released and she started to tour Central America and Mexico. Since then she's been a part of numerous music festivals and seminars in Central America regarding human rights and feminism (Gondouin 2017).

Like Funk, in her bars in the final collaborative track she proudly takes up the mantel of "guerrera":

Heredera de guerrera	Heir of a (female) warrior
Que ponen en el vientre	that put in the belly
Como fuente de poder	as the source of power
No somos inocentes	we are not innocent
Somos fuente del potente	we are the source of the powerful
Grito que el continente	Shout that the continent
Lanza al través del rap	spreads by rap
Y aun es suficiente	and it's enough
HH nos inspira	HH inspires us
Y por eso que unidas	and that's why united
Hemos decidido consagrar la vida	we have decided to dedicate our lives
Con la búsqueda de la sabiduría	with the search for wisdom
Nuestra guía	our guide
La necesidad de poner en palabras rebeldía	The need to put our rebellion into words

Like Funk, and the Somos Mujeres Somos Hip Hop concept, Lane draws a direct line between the power of one women to support other women more broadly. Rather than competition, they promote female collective empowerment as a way to change their societies. But as in her statements about "Somos Guerreras," hip hop is key to this feminist guerrera charge.

As Lane describes, during the civil war in Guatemala, art was discouraged. As such hip hop was only really able to emerge post war once peace agreements were signed in 1996 (Lane 2016). Yet, as she points out, the end of artistic oppression in Guatemala has not meant the end to the oppression of women or indigenous people, which she sees as almost a modern-day war for which warriors are needed. According to Lane,

> Guatemala is one of the countries with the highest rates of femicides as a result of domestic violence against women. We are being killed. There are also too many teenage pregnancies as a result of rapes, often within their own family. Also the rape rates are way too high. It is almost as if there is a war in Guatemala.
>
> *(Lane 2016)*

For Lane, hip hop is an opportunity to publicize this violence as a way to stop it. By communicating with other women about these issues, Lane argues that women will stop accepting these types of violent situations and contexts as the norm or acceptable. For this reason, in her individual track "Manos Arriba" she connects poetically visual images of poverty, discrimination and underemployment with hip hop bravado:

Cuando subo a la tárima	When I get up on the stage
yo me siento una reina	I feel like a queen
Y quiero ver a todas	I want to see everyone (female)
(Con la mano para arriba)	with hands in the air
Si te gusta lo que miras	If you like what you see

y lo que mi boca rima	And what my mouth rhymes
Quiero ver a todos	I want to see everyone (gender neutral)
(Con la mano para arriba)	with hands in the air
Si la tira te las tira	If you throw it to you throw it
y en la esquina la esquivas	and in the corner you duck
Quiero ver a todas	I want to see everyone (female)
(Con la mano para arriba)	with hands in the air
La tierra, la campesina,	The land, the peasant
el poder a la vecina	The power of the neighbor (female)
Quiero ver a todos (whaa)	I want to see everyone

In spite of hardships, she unabashedly claims the stage of hip hop while projecting an important message of inclusivity. The rhymes and upbeat rhythm moreover add a layer of musical enjoyment and positivity.

This inclusivity is important because notwithstanding their overarching concern for gender equality, what equality looks like is not dictated. For example, while Audry Funk and Rebeca Lane are in favor of the right to an abortion, MC Roja is unequivocally against it, in all cases except for rape. In fact, part of the collective's significance is the way it accommodates diverse views as well as diverse forms of being women. Rebeca Lane identifies as a lesbian, a feminist, and a "trans-anarchist rapper," but few of the other women in Somos Mujeres are as vocally feminist in their individual practice. It is a hip hop that does not exclude men, but still unapologetically makes women the main event and gender equality the central issue. For Rima Roja en Venus, a rap duo composed of MC Roja and MC Venus of Ecuador, this is key because women don't often work together. According to Roja this is not because women MCs are better, but because they have not as often had a place on the stage,

> Una cosa es la comunidad hip hop, que ha existido desde hace muchos años atrás. Este colectivo no por excluir a los hombres, porque si ves, todos nuestros colaboradores son hombres, pero sí para que se evidencie el trabajo de mujeres que muchos no habían escuchado lo suficiente y las están escuchando ahora.
>
> *("El Hip Hop")*

Somos Mujeres Somos Hip Hop is a powerful statement not just that feminism exists in Latin American hip hop or that femcees exist in these countries, but that hip hop can be a powerful tool for women in contexts of extreme violence and gender inequalities.

Se transmite como plaga	It spreads like a plague
Transciende fronteras	It transends borders
Bajo una sola bandera	Underneath a single flag
Se contagie el entusiasmo	The enthusiasm is contageous
hombro a hombro se trabaja	shoulder by shoulder we work
y la resistencia Latinoamericana se levanta	and the Latin American resistance rises
suenan	They resound
las voces de los barrios libres	the voices of free neighborhoods
hombres y mujeres sin prejuicios	men and women without prejudices
que dividen	that divide
sin géneros ni razas	without genders or races

The overall discourse of Somos Mujeres Somos Hip Hop, like that of Audry Funk, Rebeca Lane and Rima Roja en Venus, is a feminist non-conformist perspective that refuses to adhere to gender norms. This perspective is not just personal, but the basis of their collective work which also affirms an identification with a community-based and collective feminism.

Latinoamérica Unida is more than just a ground-breaking album. Somos Mujeres Somos Hip Hop represents the significance of a feminist hip hop practice in Latin America, based on women working together and on collaborative artistic partice. As such they support a significant challenge to narrow conceptualizations of the hip hop subject as Black and male, and ask us to think carefully about how hip hop feminists and scholars based outside the US incorporate the lived experiences of women south of the border.

Notes

1 All translations are mine and meant to be as literal as possible. As such, in terms of song lyrics they do not approach or attempt to approach the rhythmic, rhyming or other sonic qualities of the music.
2 As I wrote in *La Verdad*, "One excellent example of this is Mexican poet, rap artist, scholar, cultural ambassador, and founder of the Quilomboarte Collective, Bocafloja, who authored an important piece for this edition. One of the most revered icons in Spanish-speaking hip hop communities, Bocafloja travels widely and collaborates with numerous US. Latino artists, encouraging and spreading his redefined version of Hip Hop's four elements,""Decolonize, self- manage, transgress, emancipate" (Castillo-Garsow and Jason Nichols 2016: 8).
3 Notable exceptions include Christopher Dennis's *Afro-Colombian Hip-Hop: Globalization, Transcultural Music, and Ethnic Identities* and the volume *La Verdad* (2016).
4 See Castillo-Garsow and Jason Nichols (2016).
5 ' As in the USA, Latin (American) rap worked as an amplifier of concrete social realities, so it is not surprising that it was permeable to historical wounds (military regimes, feminicide, deep economic gaps) that the Latin American map experienced for a long time. In this way, along with the most playful expressions of the genre, a focus on resistance was developed from which rap was restored as a combat tool. It is on these margins that we find what we today identify as a boom of feminist rhymes, in which hundreds of females discover their power and decide to take action, claiming their role as active subjects within a culture that had displaced them for years."
6 For more about Reggaeton's development and popularity see Raquel Rivera et al. *Reggaeton* (2009) and Petra Rivera-Rideau's *Remixing Reggaeton* (2015).
7 For more on the complex histories of feminism in Latin America see Gargallo (2007), Lugones (2000, 2008), Matos and Paradis (2013), and Restrepo.
8 "…groups and networks of feminist women and defenders of Human Rights in Spain, Latin American and the Caribbean."
9 Tricia Rose's *Black Noise: Rap Music and Black Culture in Contemporary America* (1994) continues to be studied and held up as the landmark it is in hip hop studies. Nevertheless, following this basis, the study of hip hop which now spans over two decades generally limits itself to Black popular culture as a backdrop. For example, more recently P. Khallil Saucier and Tyrone P. Woods, in their unfortunately titled article, "Hip Hop Studies in Black," make an argument to "reintroduce hip hop studies to black studies" which they define as "the political project emanating from the context of black revolution in the 1960s. … It melds the rich archive of black letters back to the slave narratives with the Black Power generation's unwavering response to the structural impossibility of blackness" (2014: 271). Although this does not necessarily exclude Afro-Latina/os who participated in these movements, the article's emphasis on blackness does exclude the diversity of Latina/os who participated in and identify with hip hop as an identity. This continues to be the trend even in a global hip hop context, as titles like *The Vinyl Ain't Final: Hip Hop and the Globalization of Black Popular Culture* (Basu and Lemelle 2006) demonstrate. Following Rose, scholars in black/ African American studies including Michael Eric Dyson, Cornel West, Anthony B. Pinn, Nelson George, Bakari Kitwana, and Murray Forman were among some of the first scholars to give hip hop legitimacy in academia. See Chang (2005); Dyson (1996); Forman (2002); George (2005); Kitwana (2005); Rose (1994). More recent areas of study are gender/ feminism (see Morgan, 1999 and 2006; Morgan J., 2009;

Perry, 2004; Pough, 2004 and 2007; Rabaka 2011 and 2012), regional trends (see Faniel, 2012; Miller, 2012; Schelling et al., 2010), and commercialization/ mainstreaming (Asante, 2008; Rose, 2008; McWhorter, 2008; Watkins, 2005). A few scholars have focused on West Indian influences (Seyfu Hinds, 2002; Hebdige, 1987).

10 Several chapters in *La Verdad* (Castillo-Garsow and Jason Nichols 2016) focus on women in Latin America, in particular see "Daring to be 'mujeres libres, lindas, locas': An Interview with the Ladies Destroying Crew of Nicaragua and Costa Rica" by Jessica N. Pabón"'Conscious Cuban rap': Krudas Cubensi and Supercrónica Obsesión" by Sandra Abd'Allah-Álvarez Ramírez. There are also a few articles and dissertations, see: Álvarez (2013); Chacón (2013); Da Silva et. al (2014); Díez Salvatierra (2016); Dowman (2013); Gondouin (2017); Navarro (2011); Pulgar (2010); Saunders (2009); Silva Londoño (2017); Weller (2005); Zanetti (2009).

11 For more on this project visit her website: www.audryfunk.com/funky-beast.html

12 "In a deeper way, it seems to me that we all firmly wear the warrior shirt, we all identify as feminists and I think we are a big force, the war for me would be against gender roles and against that bad idea where they say that not even dead can two women work together or and collaborate in peace to make big and strong projects."

13 Lane elaborates, "I think it's very important for women to let go of the idea that other women are our enemies, which is what we learn in this heteropatriarchy. I think it's very brave for women to stop thinking that and trying to understand that we are all sisters and that we've all been through the same things and we have to help each other" (Estevez 2016).

14 For example, Lane formed "La Eskina" in 2014, a theater and hip hop crew to combat violence against youth via graffiti, rap, breakdance, deejaying and parkour.

Works cited

Acosta, Kiley Jeanelle Guyton. "Afro-Cuban Counterpoint: Re-envisioning Race, Representation and Resistance in the Hip-Hop Feminist Imaginary." *JENdA: A Journal of Culture and African Women Studies* 22 (2013): n.p.

Álvarez, Sandra. "Krudas Cubensi: rap desde las trompas de Falopio." *Revista Pikara Magazine,* 1 December 2013. Accessed 22 July 2017. www.pikaramagazine.com/2013/05/krudas-cubensi-rap-desde-lastrompas-de-falopio

Basu, Dipannita and Sidney J. Lemelle, eds. *The Vinyl Ain't Final: Hip Hop and the Globalization of Black Popular Culture.* London: Pluto Press, 2006.

Brown R. N. *Black Girlhood Celebration: Toward a Hip Hop Feminist Pedagogy.* New York: Peter Lang, 2008.

Castillo-Garsow, Melissa and Jason Nichols eds. *La Verdad: The International Reader of Hip Hop Latinidades.* Columbus, OH: Ohio State University Press, 2016.

Chacón, Carmen. "Arcoisis frente al mar: Feminismo, racialidad y emancipación en las raperas cubanas." *Afromodernidades* 12 June 2013. Accessed 22 July 2017. https://afromodernidades.wordpress.com/2011/08/12/arco-iris-frente-al-mar-feminismo-racialidad-y-emancipacion-en-las-raperas-cubanas

Chang, Jeff. *Can't Stop, Won't Stop: A History of the Hip-Hop Generation.* New York: St. Martin's Press, 2005.

Charnas, Dan. *The Big Payback: The History of the Business of Hip-Hop.* New York: New American Library, 2010.

Crenshaw, Kimberlé. "Mapping the Margins: Intersectionality, Identity Politics, and Violence Against Women of Color." *Stanford Law Review* 43 (1991): 1241–1299.

Da Silva, Viviane Santiago and Cory J. LaFevers. "Projecto Yabas: Reflections on Hip Hop and Black Women's Self-Making in Brazil." *alternativas* 2 (2014): 1–31.

Díez Salvatierra, Carmen. "Feminismos activistas en el rap latinoamericano: Mare (Advertencia Lírika) y Caye Cayejera. *Ambigua, Revista de Investigaciones sobre Género y Estudios Culturales* 3 (2016): 39–57.

Dowman, Sarah Rose. "Mapeando La Cultura Kruda: Hip-Hop, Punk Rock y Performances Queer Latino Contemporáneo." *Thesis.* Bowling Green, KY: Bowling Green State University, 2013.

Durham, Aisha, Brittney C. Cooper and Susana M. Morris. "The Stage Hip-Hop Feminism Built: A New Directions Essay." *Signs: Journal of Women in Culture and Society* 38.3 (2013): 721–737.

Dyson, Michael Eric. *Between God and Gangsta Rap: Bearing Witness to Black Culture.* New York: Oxford University Press, 1996.

Estevez, Geraldine. "How This Guatemalan Rapper is Using Hip-Hop for Her Feminist Activism." *Latina* 6 April 2016. Web. 27 July 2017. www.latina.com/lifestyle/our-issues/guatemalan-rapper-feminist-activism

Faniel, Maco. *Hip-Hop in Houston: The Origin and the Legacy.* Charleston, SC: History Press, 2012.

Flores, Anel. "'En el rap encontré la identidad que no había encontrado': Mare Advertencia Lirika, pionera del rap en Oaxaca." *Oaxaca Weekly*, 25 June 2012. Accessed 22 July 2017. www.oaxaca.media/cultura/en-el-rap-encontre-la-realidad-que-no-habia-encontrado-mare-advertencia-lirika-pionera-del-rap-en-oaxaca-3/

Forman, Murray. *The 'Hood Comes First: Race, Space, and Place in Rap and Hip-Hop.* Middletown, CT: Wesleyan University Press, 2002.

Funk, Audre. "In Mexico we are not all blonde and skinny." *Global Beats.* BBC World. 4 December 2015. Accessed 22 July 2017. www.bbc.co.uk/programmes/p03b2ck4

Gargallo, Francesa. "Feminismo Latinoamericano." *Revista Venezolana de Estudios de la Mujer* 12.8 (2007): 17–34.

George, Nelson. *Hip Hop America.* New York: Viking, 1998.

Gondouin, Sandra. "Rebeca Lane: 'libre, atrevida y loca', la liberación del cuerpo por una rapera feminist de Guatemala." *Amerika: Mémoires, identités, territoires* 16 (2017). DOI:10.4000/amerika.8132.

Hebdige, Dick. *Cut 'N' Mix: Culture, Identity, and Caribbean Music.* London: Methuen and Company, 1987.

Kitwana, Bakari. *Why White Kids Love Hip Hop: Wankstas, Wiggers, Wannabes, and the New Reality of Race in America.* New York: Basic Civitas Books, 2005.

Lane, Rebeca. "Hip Hop Feministas." *Global Beats.* BBC World. 3 December 2015. Accessed 22 July 2017. www.bbc.co.uk/programmes/p03b0bzl

Lane, Rebeca. "Interview// Rebeca Lane." *Madame Rap* 1 June 2016. Accessed 22 July 2017. https://madamerap.com/2016/01/01/interview-rebecca-lane-for-madame-rap/

Lugones, María. "Pureza, impureza y separación." *Feminismos literarios.* Eds. Neus Carbonell and Meri Torras. Madrid: Arco Libros, 2000: 235–264.

Lugones, María. "Colonialidad y género." *Revista Tabula Rasa* 9 (2008): 73–101.

Mackey, Danielle Marie. "The Women Hip-Hop Justice Warriors of Latin America." *The Establishment.* 8 April 2016. Accessed 22 July 2017. https://theestablishment.co/the-women-hip-hop-justice-warriors-of-latin-america-fa57ffc7817d

Matos, Marlise and Clarisa Paradis. "Los feminimos latinoamericanos y su compleja relación con el Estado: debates actuals." *Iconos. Revista de Ciencias Sociales* 45 (2013): 91–107.

McRobbie Angela and Jenny Garber. "Girls and Subcultures." *Resistance Through Rituals. Youth Subcultures in Post-War Britain."* Eds. Stuart Hall and Tony Jefferson. Birmingham: The Center of Contemporary Cultural Studies from the University of Birmingham, 1975. 209–222.

McWhorter, John H. *All About the Beat: Why Hip-Hop Can't Save Black America.* New York: Gotham Books, 2008.

Miller, Matt. *Bounce: Rap Music and Local Identity in New Orleans.* Amherst, MA: University of Massachusetts Press, 2012.

Molina, Oscar. "Mujeres que hacen feminismo con beats y rimas rápidas." *Hoy.com* 28 April 2014. Accessed 22 July 2017. http://politicasociedad.blogspot.com/2014/04/mujeres-que-hacen-feminismo-con-beats-y.html

Morgan, Joan. *When Chickenheads Come Home to Roost: My Life as a Hip-Hop Feminist.* New York: Simon & Schuster, 1999.

Morgan, Joan. "Hip-Hop Feminism." *The Women's Movement Today: An Encyclopedia of Third-Wave Feminism.* Ed. Leslie Heywood, 172–75. Westport: Greenwood, 2006.

Navarro, Jenell Rae. "Battling Imperialism: Revolutionary Hip Hop in the Americas." *Dissertation.* Claremont, CA: Claremont Graduate University, 2011.

Peoples, Whitney A. "Under Consruction: Identifying Foundations of Hip Hop Feminism and Exploring Bridges between Black Second-Wave and Hip Hop Feminism." *Meridians: Feminism, Race, Transnationalism* 8.1 (2008): 19–52.

Perry, Imani. *Prophets of the Hood: Politics and Poetics in Hip Hop.* Durham, NC: Duke University Press, 2004.

Pillai, Shanti. "Hip-Hop Guayaquil: Culturas Viajeras e Identidades Locales." *Bull. Inst. Fr. Études andines* 28.3 (1999): 485–499.

Pough, Gwendolyn. *Check It While I Wreck It: Black Womanhood, Hip Hop Culture, and the Public Sphere.* Boston, MA: Northeastern University Press, 2004.

Pough, Gwndolyn et al., Eds. *Home Girls Make Some Noise: Hip Hop Feminism Anthology.* Mira Loma, CA: Parker Publishing, 2007.

Pulgar Cáceres, Carla. "Representaciones Sociales de Mujeres que Participan en la Tribu Urbana del Hip Hop." *Thesis.* Santiago: Universidad Academia de Humanismo Cristiano, 2010.

Rabaka, Reiland. *Hip Hop's Amnesia: From Blues and the Black Women's Club Movement to Rap and the Hip Hop Movement.* Lanham, MD: Lexington, 2012.

Rabaka, Reiland. *Hip Hop's Inheritance: From the Harlem Renaissance to the Hip Hop Feminist Movement.* Lanham, MD: Lexington, 2011.

Rabaka, Reiland. *The Hip Hop Movement: From R&B and the Civil Rights Movement to Rap and the Hip Hop Generation.* Lanham: Lexington Books, 2013.

RD Staff. "Entrevista: Audry Funk – Sobre El Proyecto Con Mujeres Trabajando." *Hip Hop RD,* 11 May 2016. Accessed 27 July 2017. www.hiphoprd.com/2016/05/11/entrevista-audry-funk-sobre-el-proyecto-con-mujeres-trabajando/

Restrepo, Alejandra. "Feminismo y discurso de género: reflecciones preliminares para un studio sobre feminism latinoamericano." *Polis. Revista Latinoamericana* 3.9 (2004): np.

Rigby, Claire. "How Latin American Women are Changing Hip Hop." *The Guardian,* 9 August 2015. Accessed 22 July 2017. www.theguardian.com/music/2015/aug/09/how-latin-american-women-are-changing-hip-hip

Rima Roja en Venus. "Who are 'Somos Mujeres, Somos Hip Hop'?" *Global Beats.* BBC World. 4 December 2015. Accessed 22 July 2017. www.bbc.co.uk/programmes/p03b2gnv

Rima Roja en Venus. Interview by Sayle Lemos. Wambra Radio. 26 February 2014. Accessed 22 July 2017. https://wambraradio.com/2014/02/26/rima-roja-en-venus-transmitir-lo-que-uno-vive-es-importante-para-quienes-hacemos-rap/

Rivera Raquel. New York Ricans from the Hip Hop Zone. New York: Palgrave Macmillan, 2003.

Rivera, Raquel, Wayne Marshall and Deborah Pacini Hernandez. *Reggaeton.* Durham, NC: Duke University Press, 2009.

Rivera-Rideau, Petra. *Remixing Reggaetón: The Cultural Politics of Race in Puerto Rico.* Durham, NC: Duke University Press, 2015.

Robles, GA. "El Hip Hop es arma para el poder femenino.' *Radio COCOA,* 20 December 2013. Accessed 22 July 2016. http://radiococoa.com/RC/el-hip-hop-es-arma-para-el-poder-femenino/

Rose, Tricia. *Black Noise: Rap Music and Black Culture in Contemporary America.* Hanover, CT: Wesleyan University Press, 1994.

Saucier, P. Khalil and Tyron P. Woods. "Hip Hop Studies in Black." *Journal of Popular Music Studies* 26.2–26.3 (June 2014): 268–294. doi:10.1111/jpms.12077

Saunders, Tanya. "La Lucha mujerista: Krudas Cubensi and Black Feminist Sexual Politics in Cuba." *Caribbean Review of Gender Studies* 3 (2009):1–20.

Seyfu Hinds, Selwyn. *Gunshots in My Cook-up: Bits and Bites from a Hip Hop Caribbean Life.* New York: Atria Books, 2002.

Schmelling, Michael, Kelefa Sanneh, and Will Welch. 2010. *Atlanta: Hip Hop and the South.* San Francisco, CA: Chronicle Books, 2010.

Sharpley-Whiting, T. D. *Pimps Up, Ho's Down: Hip Hop's Hold on Young Black Women.* New York: New York University Press, 2008.

Silva Londoño, Diana Alejandro. "Somos la viavas de Juárez": hip-hop feminine en Ciudad Juárez. *Revista Mexicana de Sociología* 79.1 (Jan–March 2017): 147–174.

"Somos Guerreras Tour: Esfuerzo colectivo para romper esquemas." *E-Consulta.com,* 6512 January 2016. Accessed 11 July 2017. http://www.e-consulta.com/nota/2016-01-12/espectaculos/somos-guerreras-tour-esfuerzo-colectivo-para-romper-esquemas

Tarifa, Ariana. "Hip Hop as Empowerment: Voices in El Alto, Bolivia." *International Journal of Qualitative Studies in Education* 25.4 (2012): 397–415. http://dx.doi.org/10.1080/09518398.2012.673030

Vargas Tamayac, Rebeca Eunice. "Culturas juveniles y tribus urbanas." *Analistas Independientes Guatemala,* 23 June 2016. Accessed 11 July 2017. www.analistasindependientes.org/2012/06/culturas-juveniles-y-tribus-urbanas-en.html

Vargas Tamayac, Rebeca Eunice. "Identificación nacional en el rap guatemalteco." *Academia.edu,* n.d. Accessed 11 July 2016. www.academia.edu/2301362/Identificación_nacional_en_el_rap_guatemalteco

Watkins, S. Craig. *Hip Hop Matters: Politics, Pop Culture, and the Struggle for the Soul of a Movement.* Boston, MA: Beacon Press, 2005.

Weller, Wivian. "A presença feminine nas (sub)culturas juvenis: a arte de se tornar visível." *Revista Estudos Feministas* 13.1 (2005): 107–126.

Wooldridge, Talia. "¡Escuche Las Krudas!: Raw, Feminist Rap Music from Havana, Cuba." *Canadian Women Studies/ Les Cahiers de la Femme.* 27.1 (2009): 74–81.

Zanetti, Julia and Patricia Lanes. "Jóvenes en el feminism y el hip hop en busca de reconocimiento." *Jóvenes Feministas Presentes.* Eds Fundação Friederich Ebert. Brazil: UNIFEM, 2009. 104–113.

29
WEIRDED SOUNDSCAPES IN CONTEMPORARY CHILEAN NARRATIVE

J. Andrew Brown

In 2008, the Chilean novelist Patricio Jara wrote an article for the *El Sábado* insert of *El Mercurio* titled "Freak Power" (2008) in which he introduced Chile to a group of writers whose first novels challenged the traditional themes and strategies of Chilean literature. The construction of the group as iconoclastic occurs on two levels, the first with a presentation of a view of "traditional" Chilean literature, ironically the kind of literature focused on memory, identity and trauma that began as an attempt to disrupt official versions of Chilean culture and identity supported by the Pinochet dictatorship. By 2008, this literature had, according to the version propagated by "Freak Power," become the official version of Chilean literature, at least as considered by academics and popular critics. Dichotomies are lousy at describing what's really going on, but they do make for good marketing and in the case of the selling of these writers, it has served remarkably well.

These writers, Jorge Baradit, Álvaro Bisama, Francisco Ortega and Mike Wilson, forged an identity based on concepts of the weird in which the novels they published between 2006 and 2012 suggested visions of reality in general and Chile in particular as odd, as invested with the kinds of strangeness and peculiarity usually associated with science fiction and horror. They led a vindication of popular culture fandom, filling their work with references to comic books, music, film and other forms of expression associated with popular culture rather than "serious" literature even as the expressions they selected tended toward underground sources, emphasizing musical genres that, while a part of global popular culture, were certainly not a part of the mainstream. The pinnacle of the phenomenon centered on 2010 with an academic conference on the weird in Latin America in which all four authors participated that pointed toward serious study of the developing genre as well as the publication of a collection of alternative histories of Chile edited by the four called *CHIL3, Relación del Reyno* in which some 30 contributors imagined everything from a global Mapuche empire to Godzilla attacks on Santiago to unpublished poems by Gabriela Mistral that were, in fact, translated lyrics from The Smiths.[1]

The four have gone on in various directions, with especially notable commercial success on the part of Baradit and Ortega and equally notable critical success in the case of Wilson and Bisama, but the four continue to occupy an important place in the development of contemporary Chilean narrative. This, especially as it concerns the ways in which engagement with popular, and especially underground culture, contributes to the construct of identities based on the shared consumption of that culture. In this article, we'll look at work by Wilson and Bisama, examining specifically the ways in which these writers incorporate music and musical reference in the construction of countercultural bodies to effect a kind of weirding of Chilean and global popular culture.

As an American-Argentine writer raised in the US, Paraguay and Argentina and who now lives and publishes in Chile, Mike Wilson has continually produced work that questions the various boundaries that operate in contemporary global culture. From his sf apocalypse *El púgil* about a washed-up boxer wandering through a decayed Buenos Aires accompanied by his sentient refrigerator and encountering a clone of Orson Welles and cyborged escapees from Donnie Darko and AI to his more recent novel *Leñador*, a non-narrative meditation on wood cutting and solitude in the Yukon, Wilson has challenged assumptions about what "makes" what and the categories that contribute to that making.[2]

In his 2011 novel, *Rockabilly*, Wilson explores the strange reality of the suburban United States through the lens of four characters united in the unexplained meteor crash in the back-yard of the main character, Rockabilly, a devotee of the music and culture who has a pinup tattoo on his back that has gained mystical powers. He is watched obsessively by Suicide Girl, an adolescent whose left breast has begun to mysteriously lactate. She is watched by BabyFace, a forty-something man who suffers from a disease that has infantilized his body and left his face looking like the Gerber baby. All three are observed by Bones, a dog who knows them best by the smell of their posteriors. The narrative takes the reader on a tour of the strange-ness of suburban America focusing in particular on the bodies of the odd participants in the narrative. In this paper, I examine the ways in which Wilson engages the weird in his exploration of corporeal expressions of counter culture and the strange, especially as it relates to recent theorizations of the weird and debates about the new weird. I also undertake an understanding of the ways Wilson uses popular music and music subculture as a way to think the "weirded" body.

The characters, aside from Bones, have their names from the various subcultures they adopt either as a conscious choice or because they are obliged. Rockabilly is Rockabilly because of the way he channels the various characteristics of Rockabilly culture. His physical description evokes the standard look of rockabilly culture. His obsession with cars, his work as a mechanic further strengthen the way in which he has modeled his look and his life on the set of prefer-ences associated with the subculture. Significantly, it is when he decides to make the perma-nent gesture towards joining his subcultural tribe that the controlling principle of the novel is unleashed, that is, the supernatural tattoo of the pin up girl on his back that controls him, tempts Suicide Girl, provokes BabyFace and whispers to Bones.

Wilson carefully constructs Rockabilly from his surrounding, both in terms of the space he inhabits as well as the text in which the character operates. The novel begins with an epigraph from Roy Orbison's classic, "Only the Lonely," repeating the chorus of the song that is both a comment on the isolated lives that inhabit the novel as well as a musical invocation of the title of the novel, Orbison's hit a classic of Rockabilly culture. The structure of the novel, with each chapter named after the protagonist whose focus the section is, creates a kind of Rockabilly beat with the repetition of the name. That is, the first word of the novel proper is Rockabilly, following immediately the title of the chapter, also Rockabilly. In that sense, we see the Roy Orbison epigraph bracketed by Rockabilly, reinforcing the connection between Rockabilly the novel, Rockabilly the subculture and Rockabilly the character and overlaying the presentation of Rockabilly as subject with the heavily coded cultural aspects of the underground expression of Rockabilly.[3]

Wilson follows that rather poetic unveiling of the character with a description of the fall of the possible meteorite with a description of Rockabilly's home, a rented house that has been overtaken with his obsession with car repair and restoration. In fact, the meteor falls just as Rockabilly is scrubbing his hands clean from the oil and dirt that are so closely associated with that activity. This presentation again invokes Rockabilly culture, moving from the music to the fascination with vintage automobiles and describing Rockabilly as a body permeated by the dirt that serves as a synecdoche of the cars that are so important to rockabilly identity. (One should note that a falling meteorite is also likely a sly wink at the psychobilly group The Meteors-more on that later). Rockabilly's decision to dig for the meteorite in the hopes of recovering something that can be sold (for millions of dollars, he dreams) further situates Rockabilly within the middle American context that Wilson uses as the backdrop of the novel, the character an American male stagnating in surroundings filling up with junk and where dreams of unlikely wealth motivate what action there is.

The presentation of the other characters work along similar lines, with an emphasis on identity as a conjunction of space, underground culture and body. Significantly, though, the other characters' chapters all work in first person narrative, where Rockabilly's are exclusively in third person. Suicide Girl draws her name from a pornographic website/community that situates itself as "Redefining Beauty Since 2001- We are the daughters of Bettie Page. We're a collection of over 2,500 pin-up girls who are devoted to changing your idea about what makes a woman beautiful...and we're naked." In other descriptions, they present themselves as "pin-up models with tattoos." For the purpose of the novel, the important phrase is "We are the daughters of Bettie Page," a picture of whom graces the cover of Wilson's novel. The character's identification as a suicide girl (it should be noted that there is no mention made of her participation in the website or the community, her name appears to be the only connection) evokes the embrace of a culture of tattoos, pinups and Bettie Page that is an integral part of Rockabilly culture in its depiction of female beauty as that of 1950s pinup models queered by the tattoos worn by those models.

In the novel, we meet Suicide Girl as she gazes at herself in the mirror, dealing with the "asco" that she feels as she examines her features while knowing that the boys in her school find her attractive. From those thoughts, we move to her application of makeup as a part of purposeful process in which the adolescent girl tries to make herself look like "her" (Wilson 2011: 15). The "her" is left ambiguous, and yet from the following description, we see that she is channeling the ideas of beauty as presented by the Suicide Girls website. The novel describes this process as "Me pinto, quiero parecerme a ella, me amarro el pelo, tomo el delineador, me dibujo un lunar en la mejilla y un tatuaje en el brazo, es la silueta de una mujer, me la imagino posando en un traje de baño como los de antes. Así me veo mejor" (15). The drawing of the tattoo is especially evocative as Suicide Girl is, in effect, creating two versions of this "her" both as she applies makeup to her face and then as she draws this new version of herself on her arm. It is at this point that the light Rockabilly is using as he digs for the meteorite shines through Suicide Girl's window and we realize that she is also using Rockabilly's own tattoo as a referent for her makeover. Wilson describes this fascination as occurring on a corporeal level "Estoy a punto de apartarme de mi reflejo cuando un resplandor llena mi dormitorio. Siento la luz, la siento pesada, como si me golpeara, me penetra la carne, me traspasa, me transforma" (15). Just as she had doubled up on her identity with her makeup tattoo, Wilson presents a body continually in flux, in which Suicide Girl is remaking on a variety of levels in the first page of her introduction. The rest of the chapter establishes her obsession with Rockabilly, with the sense that her own adoption of the Suicide Girl persona comes from the desire to situate herself within Rockabilly's own mode of cultural expression. It also presents Chuck, her lizard and the fact that she, despite still being a virgin, is lactating from one breast.

The final human character is Babyface. Wilson again emphasizes the character as corporeal presence in his initial presentation, in this case, with reference to the odd illness Babyface suffers and while the passage is a bit long, it bears including

> La cabeza me pesa, me cuesta abrir los ojos, mi cuerpo yace inmóvil sobre el sillón lay-z-boy, mis manos no responden, lonjas de plomo, logro entreabrir los párpados, veo sombras desdibujadas. Consigo despegar un brazo y palparme el rostro, abarcar mi cráneo ciclópeo. De a poco voy redescubriendo la extensión de mi cabeza. Enorme, redonda, suave. Me paso los dedos por la pelusa sedosa que apenas cubre la cresta de mi cuero cabelludo. Respiro hondo, un par de veces, intentando oxigenarme. Tanteo mi muslo hasta encontrar el catéter, jalo de la sonda, siento como se desprende de mi vejiga y como arde al deslizarse de mi pene. Me mojo un poco. Tengo la lengua seca, se me olvidó sacarme la dentadura, las encías me duelen. Vuelvo a aspirar, cierro los ojos, busco la palanca del sillón y me enderezo. Dejo que la gravedad se encargue de evacuar los fluidos acumulados en mi cabeza.
>
> *(Wilson 2011: 19)*

Babyface presents himself as a monstrous, incontinent body; marked by a continuous flow of liquid that pools and escapes as he tries to move. The character continues within the pattern of the novel by leading with the body and with bodily experience, Babyface's leakiness also establishing a connection with Suicide Girl's miraculous lactation. Even so, Babyface is distinguished by the fact that this body seems to appear separate from Rockabilly culture and indeed, from any type of identity that springs from any kind of popular or underground culture. And yet, we find that his name comes from his disease (ICF, Infantilismo cráneo facial) and the fact that "Los chicos de la otra cuadra tienen razón, soy un Gerber grotesco, un asco" (Wilson 2011: 20). The tools that Wilson provides for thinking Babyface (as well as the tools that Babyface himself uses to think his body) stem from another queering of the infant's face on the jars of the well-known baby food.

In all three instances, then, the characters and their bodies are continually mediated by the popular and underground cultures that surround them. Indeed, traditional identities as signaled by names are completely subsumed by the subcultures chosen by some as in the case of Rockabilly and Suicide Girl and imposed by disease in the case of Babyface. Wilson continues this approach to body and identity throughout the novel, focusing especially on music as a means for determining identity. As the novel proceeds back and forth through flashbacks to the moment in which Rockabilly received her supernatural tattoo mixed with a trip to Walmart by Suicide Girl and Babyface and the subsequent discovery of the death of Suicide Girl's lizard Chuck, we see soundtracks develop that strengthen the ties between characters, subcultures and cultural stereotypes.

Rockabilly's tattoo stretches over several chapters, intercutting the odd messages that she delivers in the present to the other three characters as she undulates on Rockabilly's back while he digs with the story of her making. In the application, Wilson creates a background soundtrack of Johnny Cash and Roy Orbison, mentioning the music at various moments and by so doing accompanying imbuing the character with the music that provides his name. As the tattooing begins, the description of the music is especially engaging,

> Rockabilly se desnudó la espalda, un tema de Johnny Cash navegaba por los espacios de la casa. Ella mascaba chicle. Encendió la pistola de tatuajes, el aparato zumbaba mientras acercaba la aguja oscilante a su piel.
>
> *(Wilson 2011: 30)*

Weirded soundscapes in contemporary Chilean narrative

Wilson creates a doubling of the sound, matching the winding nature of the Johnny Cash song with the spinning thrum of the tattoo needle, creating a setting in which both ink and music are inscribed on Rockabilly's skin. In subsequent chapters, Wilson relates with great detail the inking of the skin, careful to accompany these descriptions with music, this time by Roy Orbison (49). Over and over again, we appreciate the pairing of the penetration of skin, of body with the accompaniment of music as the character Rockabilly becomes a Rockabilly and as his tattoo appears to gain life through a series of acts that invoke a series of procreative acts.

The music is not limited to Rockabilly and his formation, Suicide Girl and Babyface visit Walmart and are accosted by Barry Manilow's Copacabana, making the visit to the fluorescently illuminated store all the more depressing (Wilson 2011: 41). A more momentous usage occurs as Suicide Girl finds a mangled Chuck, blames her mother and begins to plot her death:

> Al desplomarme sobre la cama, se me desdibuja la pieza en una penumbra rosada. Creo escuchar la pala de Rockabilly... o el rasqueteo de Chuck. No estoy segura. Cierro los ojos y Ella se materializa detrás de mis párpados, su tinta se mece, su baile me mantiene en trance mientras tararea una melodía furiosa. Burn She-Devil, Burn.
>
> *(59)*

The "she" referred to is Rockabilly's tattoo, the song she is dancing to as she hypnotizes Suicide Girl is "Burn She-Devil, Burn" by the psychobilly band The Cramps. This song becomes the soundtrack to the insanity (or greater insanity) that develops from this point on as Suicide Girl murders her mother in revenge for Chuck's death and Babyface kills Rockabilly with a shovel. In the above cited passage, we can appreciate how Wilson continues the narrative strategy of linking identity, body and music and couches them in penetrative acts. As Suicide Girl lies on her bed, overcome by her discovery of a mangled Chuck, she hears first a beat that is either Rockabilly's shoveling or Chuck's dying scratches. In both cases, we see sound made as subjects disturb surfaces and penetrate facades. This act of aural penetration exercises a direct effect on Suicide Girl, introducing the tattoo as a living force inside her consciousness, with her appearing inside SG's eyelids. At the moment of this psychic penetration begins the song by The Cramps further strengthening the connection between cultural identity, body and music (and at this point the reader should listen to the song, easily available on YouTube or through streaming).

In a book examining sexuality and popular culture in Latin America, one might wonder at the selection of a book that takes place in the United States, that uses quintessentially (north) American music like rockabilly and that, in fact, contains not a single reference to Latin America. To understand that connection, we need to appreciate the double positioning of the novel. That is, while the novel does explore the quiet desperation of the US suburban landscape, it does so from Chile. The book has yet to be translated to English and, aside from outlets like Amazon, was not sold outside of Chile. Neither was it read outside of Chile, aside from a scattering of academics and students suffering through one of my classes. We need to appreciate, then, the ways in which the novel constructs a way of engaging culture and the body in which US underground culture is used as an instrument for thinking more universal human conditions. At the same time, it offers itself as a mirror that engages certain aspects of contemporary Chile where Santiago has begun to map itself on US geographies, with newly organized suburbs of the city following the Mc Mansions that dot the US landscape. The suburban insanity that runs through the novel becomes a way to think about these new suburbs. The marketing of the novel in 2011 further situated the reading of the novel within a Chilean context as Alfaguara harnessed the boom in tattoos Santiago has experienced in recent years. Publicity photos included the author in front of the tattoo parlors found in the caracol shopping centers in Providencia. The body transformations and mystical tattoo of the novel serve as further mirrors of contemporary Chilean culture even as it sets its action in the US.

Wilson's contemporary Álvaro Bisama uses underground music and culture in similar ways, though with a much more explicit grounding in Chile. Bisama has built a literary career as an academic, a novelist and as a journalist, writing chronicles, reviews, long and short fiction and extensive essays. His contribution to the 2008 phenomenon was *Caja negra* (2007) an undefinable collection of underground culture that the narrator peruses as the chapters count down to the end of the world. His more recent fiction has bridged the gap between weird fiction and narratives of trauma and memory, taking moments and themes from the events surrounding the Pinochet dictatorship and mixing them with meditations on the roles of underground culture and music in surviving those times. We'll consider his story "Death Metal" from his collection *Los muertos* (2014) and include some notes on the novel *Ruido* (2012) that he wrote at the same time as the collection.

"Death Metal" first appeared in a collection of stories also named *Death Metal* that was published in Lima. Due to the success of the Peruvian edition, it was included in an expanded anthology in Santiago under the title *Los muertos*. The stories incorporate Bisama's particular take on an urban weird, horror stories that verge on the fantastic, but that ground themselves in a strangeness that remains on the other side of the supernatural. There are stories of urban cannibals, serial killers, and Nazi fetishists that populate the underside of a neoliberal Santiago. In "Death Metal," we find the reflections of an enthusiast of the genre, remembering his youth in Valparaiso. As he remembers their musical adventures, he tries to make sense of the decision of a friend who died as a suicide bomber. Throughout the story, we see music, and in this case, death metal as an organizing principle of identity and memory in dictatorship and post dictatorship Chile.

As the story begins, we see the narrator depend on music as a way to order his narrative,

> A él lo conocíamos de esa época, de cuando escuchábamos a Kreator. Era más bien pavo, huevoncito. Pendejo. En la universidad cambió. Eso pasa cuando algunos se van del pueblo. Se convierten en otras personas. … Otra vez nos llevaron presos unos pacos de civil. Soñamos. Nos pasamos la noche. Él era chico. Tenía a lo más quince. Siempre andaba con una pollera de Iron Maiden. Hablaba de los cuentos de Lovecraft.
>
> (Bisama 2014: 47)

The band references here serve a variety of functions. Kreator marks an era and gives a specific referent to the genre invoked by the story's title. Indeed, without giving a date, it situates the time remembered in the late 80s when the German thrash metal band began to gain international popularity. With that, Bisama sets these memories at the end of the Pinochet dictatorship without mentioning the dictatorship explicitly, though the reference to the "pacos" combines the repression of the period with the adolescent acts of rebellion. Even so, Kreator is the bond that unites and defines them, the touchstone for memory that sets the stage for the rest of the memories that the narrators relate. As we begin to learn more of the "él," his Iron Maiden t-shirt again combines music, identity and memory and acts as a way to situate the 15-year-old boy within the Chilean milieu.

As the story continues, we see how Bisama links music and Lovecraft in the construction of adolescent identity, the narrator continues:

> Yo le dije que conocía a un tipo que tenía el Necronomicón fotocopiado. Se lo había vendido un librero de Valparaíso. Estaba en inglés. Nadie leía inglés. Lo leímos igual.

Weirded soundscapes in contemporary Chilean narrative

Fingimos que lo leíamos, pero nadie lo entendía. Lo leímos igual. Fingimos que lo leíamos, pero nadie lo entendía. Las bandas del pueblo escribían sus canciones satánicas con un diccionario de inglés-español en la mano. Nadie se preocupaba de la gramática.

(2014: 148)

The combination of horror literature and music provides here a delightful image of cultural appropriation and creative engagement in a global context. The act of reading the Necronomicon in English without being able to read English makes the act a kind of ritual designed to build credibility (an act made all the more fun by the fact that the Necronomicon does not, in fact, exist). This ritual of reading without reading, reading as ritual leads to creation of death metal music as an act of translation, wherein the Spanish English dictionary replaces the Necronomicon as a source of the words of death and Satanism that the youth invest in their music. Bisama reinforces this dynamic a little further on in the story, "Imagínatelo leyendo ese Necronomicon e intentando entender cosas de ahí y luego largándose al Brutal Party mientras todos sacudían la cabeza con esas letras y escuchaban covers de Venom" (2014: 148). Bisama again positions Lovecraft as preparatory to musical expression, a "Brutal Party" referring to death metal concerts and inserting the band Venom into the ongoing musical discussion. Note that they are banging their heads not to Venom, but to the covers that these local bands play even as they write original music fueled by the readings of fake Lovecraft and Spanish/English dictionaries.

The story concludes in the present as the narrator tries to come to terms with his acquaintance's suicidal act. In a series of questions, the narrator tries to draw a line from their adolescent adventures in their identities as "metaleros" to the final act:

¿A quién se le ocurre ir a poner una bomba en bicicleta? ¿A quién se le ocurre leer el Necronomicon fotocopiado? ¿A quién se le ocurre quemar una cabeza de chancho en la punta del cerro? ¿A quién se le ocurre irse del pueblo a la universidad y dejar la universidad? ¿A quién se le ocurre comer tallarines con carne de soya? ¿A quién se le ocurre querer destruir al Estado? ¿A quién se le ocurre vivir en una casa okupa? ¿A quién se le ocurre quedarse en cuclillas en la oscuridad mientras explica en qué se convirtió su vida? ¿A quién se ocurre armar una bomba en la calle? ¿A quién se le ocurre pedalear con una mochila llena de explosivos en medio de la sombras? No lo sé.

(Bisama 2014: 149–50)

The narrator ends the story, refusing to attend the funeral in Santiago, preferring to stay in his little town, reading his photocopy of the *Necronomicon*. The thread he follows from the pig's head sacrifice and the photocopy that were emblems of their teenage identity to the friend's social activism to his act of terrorism repeats the kinds of public hysteria that built up around heavy metal during the 1980s where accusations of devil worship accompanied censorship throughout the world and only fueled adolescent interest in the music. Bisama uses the story to first lean into the critique, emphasizing their attempts to engage in devil worship. And yet, when the friend moves from metal fandom into terrorism, the narrator can't quite understand the link, especially given that the rest of the friends grew up to rather unremarkable lives. Ending the story with a rereading of the old photocopy, a repetition of the old ritual that endowed their musical identities with death metal credibility, becomes an act by which the narrator recognizes its role in the construction of identity and appreciates the promise of understanding the roots of his friend's suicide.

In *Ruido*, a novel Bisama wrote at the same time he was writing the story, he recounts more stories about this group of friends living in on the outskirts of Valparaiso during the 1980s, listening to death metal and wondering at a Chile full of dictatorship and glue-sniffing seers. An analysis of that novel deserves its own article, but the point he makes there about the youth's musical interests is that the horror of the dictatorship impelled them to seek a mirror for that horror, a way to return that horror back. Death metal music provided just such a mirror. In any case, the story and the novel served as literary companions to a surge in writing about the importance of metal in contemporary Chilean culture that Bisama and Patricio Jara have spearheaded, with fiction, books of musical chronicles and musical biographies.[4]

Wilson and Bisama together provide ways in which to think about the identity as constructed by music—specifically, popular, albeit underground, culture and its role in contributing to countercultural identity. What we see in both *Rockabilly* and "Death Metal" are descriptions of the ways in which these countercultural bodies use musical expressions as ways to position themselves within majority cultures and, at the same time, provide mirrors of the decay of various societies. Moreover, the narratives provide tools for Bisama and Wilson readers. That is, with both pieces appearing at the height of the Nueva Narrativa Weird phenomenon in Chilean literature, Wilson and Bisama are not only providing narratives of characters who construct identity through an engagement with varieties of popular culture, they are providing handbooks to the fans that read these novels, suggesting soundtracks that will accompany the readings, with Johnny Cash, Roy Orbison and The Cramps playing during readings of *Rockabilly* and Kreator, Iron Maiden and Venom accompanying the Bisama story. Along those lines, what we see in the weirding of Chilean literature and the weirding of popular musical interest is a series of tools that construct alternative identities and bodies even as they reflect that construction in their narratives.

Notes

1 For a good review of the weird as a genre, both in its classic form as well as the "new weird," see Noys and Murphy (2016). I have also written recently on the use of Lovecraft by these writers, see Brown (2017).
2 For criticism on Wilson's other work, see Bolling (2016), Laraway (2012) and Brown (2010 and 2014).
3 For a good introduction to Rockabilly culture, see Morrison (1998). The Wikipedia page does a nice job as well if you're in a hurry.
4 See Jara (2012).

Works cited

Bisama, Álvaro. *Los muertos.* Santiago: Ediciones B, 2014.
Bisama, Álvaro. *Ruido.* Santiago: Alfaguara, 2012.
Bolling, Becky. "The Walking Dead: *Zombie's* Celluloid Community." *Hispanet Journal.* 5 (2012): 1–25. Accessed 25 March 2016.
Brown, J. Andrew. "Reading Lovecraft at the End of the World." *Paradoxa.* 28 (2016): 177–91.
Brown, J. Andrew. "El oficio del ciborg: Nuevas direcciones para una identidad poshumana en América latina." Heridas abiertas: Bíopolítica y representación en América latina. Ed. Mabel Moraña e Ignacio Sánchez Prado. Madrid: Iberoamericana Verveurt, 2014. 247–58.
Brown. J. Andrew. "Estéticas digitales en *El Púgil* de Mike Wilson Reginato." *Arizona Journal of Hispanic Cultural Studies* 14 (December, 2010): 235–45.
Jara, Patricio. "La nueva literatura fantástica chilena. Freak power." Revista *El Sábado. El Mercurio.* 13 December 2008.
Jara, Patricio. *Pájaros negros: Crónica del heavy metal chileno.* Santiago: Ediciones B. 2012.
Laraway, David. "Teenage Zombie Wasteland: Suburbia After the Apocalypse in Mike Wilson's *Zombie* and Edmundo Paz Soldán's *Los vivos y los muertos.*" In *Latin American Science Fiction: Theory and Practice,* ed. M. Elizabeth Ginway, J. Andrew Brown. New York: Palgrave Macmillan, 2012: 133–54.
Morrison, Craig. *Go Cat Go!: Rockabilly Music and its Makers.* Urbana IL: University of Illinois Press. 1998.

Noys, Benjamin and Timothy Murphy. "Introduction: Old and New Weird." *Genre*. 49.2 (July 2016): 117–30.

Noys, Benjamin. "Morbid Symptoms: An Interview with China Mieville." *Genre*. 49.2 (July 2016): 199–211.

Vandermeer, Jeff. "Introduction." *The New Weird*. Ed. Ann and Jeff Vandermeer. San Francisco, CA: Tachyon. 2008. Ix–xviii.

Wilson, Mike. *Rockabilly*. Santiago: Alfaguara, 2011.

30

DANCE AS MEDICINE

Healing bodies in Nicaragua from the colonial period to the present

John Petrus and Jessica Rutherford

In this chapter, we explore continuity and change in Nicaraguan dance rituals from the colonial period to the present. We focus on the way in which ritual movement, as a visual mode of communication, operates as a site for knowledge transmission (as well as for the preservation of historical memory) for indigenous cultures in the region. At the time of colonial contact in sixteenth-century Nicaragua, for example, these dances served indigenous communities as part of larger healing rituals and ceremonial cycles, which incorporated symbolic postures as well as elements from the natural world in an effort to maintain equilibrium between the gods and humans on earth. The maintenance of this sacred equilibrium via ritual practices such as dance is key to understanding the "multiple therapy" that is characteristic of indigenous medicine, emphasizing the interconnectedness between spiritual and physical aspects of health and wellness.[1] As Guillermo Bonfil Batalla concludes in *México Profundo*, this concept of "multiple therapy" is predicated upon a merging of spirituality and physicality that ultimately blurs the boundaries between them. In his analysis, "What we call religion and what we call medicine are intertwined in many ways, so the distinction in erased" (1996: 35). This intertwining of religion and healing in ritual practices is key to understanding the ways in which dance in the colonial period functions as a form of indigenous medicine, i.e. a healing mechanism that operates in and through spiritual, physical and cultural modes.

We begin this study with an overview of contact-era dance rituals and their role in indigenous medicine in Nicaragua, as depicted in González Fernández de Oviedo's *Historia general y natural de las Indias* [*General and Natural History of the Indies*] (1535).[2] Although written through a Eurocentric lens that has historically denigrated native traditions, this perspective provides insight into the indigenous roots from which many Nicaraguan rites and performative practices stem. To illustrate this point, we trace continuity and change in Nicaraguan dance rituals from the colonial period, considering both their textual and performative aspects, as they first appear in Oviedo's historiographical accounts and then in a well-known national comedy-ballet, *The Güegüense* (also known as *The Macho Ratón*).[3] This seminal piece of Nicaraguan theater serves as an example of the durability of dance rituals, given that we can still find traces of indigenous rites that continue in present-day performances. We find that, beyond its function as a living archive, this dance, in particular, works to complicate gender binaries related to sex and sexuality that still operate today. Finally, we conclude that dance in Nicaragua continues to serve as a site of healing for many Nicaraguan communities.

Dance as medicine

In the early colonial period, European colonists and missionaries worked fervently to eradicate indigenous rites and traditions (and often bodies) in an effort to dominate and exploit Amerindian lands and peoples. Historically, western narratives of the period have denied indigenous people agency to represent the violence that they experienced at the hands of European colonization.[4] However, as scholars such as Inga Clendinnen (2010), Diana Taylor (2003), Lisa Voigt (2016), and others have shown, indigenous festive practices, such as dance, were often tolerated under the auspices of Christianized forms of indigenous rites and practices.[5] For this reason, dance represents a significant site of power and healing for indigenous communities because of its capacity to serve as an alternative archive for marginalized knowledge and experiences. While our genealogy of indigenous dance in Nicaragua is in no way exhaustive, these ancient movements are significant in and of themselves as sites of collective history and of healing.

It is useful here to remember Taylor and Joseph Roach's work on performance art, both of which highlight the epistemological politics of the archive versus the repertoire. Taylor famously critiqued the rift between the privileging of archival documents (considered history) as objective and enduring, while the repertoire (ephemeral social practices, undocumented happenings) is deemed subjective and unreliable, given its innate connection to memory and the body. In this study, we adopt Taylor's position that performance and dance are a "vital act of transfer" in the transmission of social knowledge, cultural memory, and identities in the Americas (2003: 2). Just as histories are transmitted via words on paper, ritual practices utilize the body as a space through which to record history and share information. Roach argues that, "performance genealogies draw on the idea of expressive movements as mnemonic reserves, including patterned movements made and remembered by bodies, residual movements retained implicit in images or words (or in the silences between them)" (in Taylor 2003: 5). While Taylor and Roach focus on performance in general, Judith Lynee Hanna's study *To Dance is Human: A Theory of Nonverbal Communication* (1987) provides an overview of the way in which different disciplines have approached studies in dance specifically. From a cultural studies perspective, Hanna's theory is significant in that it asserts that dance is a cognitive process that operates through a web of signification that is language-like.

Hanna finds that, "Dance is a conceptual natural language with intrinsic and extrinsic meanings, a system of physical movements, and interrelated rules guiding performance in different social situations" (1987: 5). In this sense, and for our purposes, we can read Nicaraguan dance rituals as a text encoded with meanings via its movements, music, and performative paraphernalia. We consider these dance practices to be what Paloma Martinez-Cruz refers to as "centrifugal acts of knowledge transmission" (i.e. ways in which the transmission of knowledge serves the empowerment of a community rather than individual truth claims), a central premise in her work that traces the dismissal and marginalization of feminine knowledge in Mesoamerica from the colonial period to the present, especially that related to healing (2011: 2).[6] By approaching our study of native dance rituals in this way, we recognize their significance as part of a larger counter-narrative to dominant Eurocentric history and epistemology, although we must contend with the limits of the colonial archive in that we only have access to written documentation of ephemeral acts. For this reason, we read Oviedo's history and *The Güegüense* with a critical eye turned to the verbal imagery that their texts provide of these performances.

Taking a (post) colonial studies perspective, we argue that dance in Nicaragua, a territory on the margins of the trade-based network of Anáhuac,[7] serves as a significant site for the transmission of collective cultural memory that contributes to present-day identity constructions in the region.[8] While dance had the potential to serve indigenous populations as a counter discourse to conquest and colonization at the time of contact with Europeans, our reading of the continued practice of the *Güegüense* (the national dance of Nicaragua), and its transformation into a comedy-ballet, indicates that various marginalized groups continue to use dance as a significant site of representation and agency for their communities. In what follows, we look at Nicaraguan dance rituals (referred to interchangeably as *bailes, danzas, areitos,* or *mitotes* in Spanish) to understand the significance of dance in indigenous traditions and histories, serving as a healing mechanism (physically, spiritually, and culturally) to combat the social dis-ease that stems from European efforts at colonization in Nicaragua. While critical readings of colonial documents related to indigenous rites and practices often present an overwhelming depiction of destruction and expropriation, these writings can also offer evidence of cultural survival and continuity.

Spanish cosmographer González Fernández de Oviedo's *Historia general y natural de las Indias* (1535, reprinted in 1959), for example, describes Nicaraguan dance rituals called *areitos* (also referred to as *mitotes* in the text) in which he references three primary categories of native dances that are part of larger rituals, such as those dedicated to agricultural cycles, ritual war dances, and funerary rites. Ostensibly, Oviedo documents these rites in detail despite the fact that he views them as a direct display of the Amerindians reverence and dedication to their "idols," i.e. sacred deities (1959: 413–21). Oviedo justifies his documentation of "idolatrous" indigenous traditions (generally frowned upon by inquisitorial censorship of the period) given that, as Charles V's royal cosmographer of the West Indies, it was his duty to provide an eyewitness account of all that he saw and experienced in the New World.[9] Oviedo's text represents a unique opportunity to garner insight into contact-era practices (albeit biased and incomplete), given that Christian writers often glossed over many indigenous rites and customs in their general and natural histories, as they were hesitant to record information that might help to write these "devilish" rituals into perpetuity.

As we see in Oviedo's description of native dance in colonial Nicaragua, depending on the undertone of the ceremony at hand, the complexity of the ritual repertoire—variations in song, choreography, and the consumption of mind-altering plants—would serve different ritual ends, designed to achieve the spiritual equilibrium necessary to maintain the overall health and wellness of the individual as well as the community. We see this, for example, in one particular *areito* witnessed by Oviedo in colonial Nicaragua, which was part of a larger agricultural rite dedicated to the god of cacao. The Central American pantheon of deities is both complicated and diverse. Typically, individual groups elected a primary god—supplemented with others from the main pantheon—based on the needs and values of their particular community. Oviedo writes that, "Tienen diversos dioses, e así en el tiempo de su cosecha del maíz, o del cacao o del algodón o fésoles, con día señalado, y en diferentes días, les hacen señaladas e particulares e diferentes fiestas, e sus areitos e cantares al propósito del aquel ídolo e recogimiento del pan o fructo que han alcanzado" [They have diverse gods, and like this, in the time of their corn harvest, or the (harvest) of cacao or cotton or beans, with a signaled day, and in different days, they (perform) for (their gods) signaled and particular and different festivals, and their dances and songs (were performed) for the purpose of that idol and (the) harvest of bread and fruit that they have achieved] (1959: 364–5).[10] Central to this particular ritual is the god of *caccguat* or cacao, who they honored in ritual exchange for a good harvest of one of the region's most prized agricultural products.[11]

Oviedo witnessed this fall festival firsthand, which took place in native temples in the kingdom of Tecoatega in the sixteenth century.[12] Oviedo writes that, under the rule of the cacique Agateite, "hacían fiestas e sacrificios, haciendo placer a sí mesmos, e honra a sus dioses" [they used to have festivals and sacrifices, providing pleasure for themselves, and honor to their gods] (1959: 413). Oviedo goes on to provide a detailed description of the movement and aesthetics that guided its performers:

Dance as medicine

Algunos llevaban máscaras de gestos de aves; e aquel contrapás[13] andábanlo alrededor de la plaza e de dos en dos, e desviados a tres o cuatro pasos. Y en medio de la plaza estaba un palo alto, hincado de más de ochenta palmos, y encima, en la punta del palo, estaba un ídolo asentado e muy pintado, que dicen que es el dios del *cacaguat* o cacao. E había cuatro palos en cuadro puestos en torno del palo, e revuelto a eso, una cuerda de bejuco tan gruesa como dos dedos (o de cabuya), e a los cabos de ella, atados dos muchachos de cada siete u ocho años, el uno con un arco en la mano, y en la otra un manojo de flechas; y el otro tenía en la mano un moscador lindo de plumas, y en la otra un espejo.

(413–4)

Some wore bird-like masks; and they walked it [that series of dances] around the plaza […] two by two, and separated by two or three steps. And a tall post was in the middle of the plaza, stuck in the ground more than eighty inches,[14] and on top, at the point of the stick, the idol was seated and very decorated, which they say is the god of *cacaguat* or cacao. And there were four sticks put in a square around the [main] stick, and wrapped around this, a cord of liana as thick as two inches (or [made] of agave cord), and at the tail end of it, two boys [were] attached, each [one] 7 or 8 years old, one with an arch in [one] hand, and with a handful of arrows in the [other] hand; and the other had a beautiful tail of feathers in [one] hand and in the other a mirror.

Beyond the physical movements encoded within the dance itself as well as ritual plant use—as Samuel Martí and Gertrude Prokosch Kurath suggest,[15] and as Oviedo's narrative indicates—musical production also served as a fundamental component for ritual dance: wind and percussion instruments, for example, would be used alongside gourds symbolizing female fertility and the *chicahuaztli* (the rattle-stick), a phallic symbol for rain (1964: 84). As we will see, significant elements of indigenous dance and iconography—such as the bird-like masks, the basic choreography, the *chicahuaztli*, as well as indigenous feather work—continue to form part of the larger cultural repertoire that informs performances of the *Güegüense* in Nicaragua, even today.

In the early colonial period, Oviedo's descriptions of contact-era native dance rites indicate that, for Amerindian traditions, dance (along with its ritual accompaniments in the form of song, music, dress, and ritual plant use) serves as both spiritual and physical medicine in that it formed part of religious rituals that maintained their sacred connection with their gods (in this case, with the deity of cacao). Nicaraguan dance as medicine takes on new significance following European encounter as native communities faced the social dis-ease produced by settler colonialism throughout the Americas. Moreover, post conquest, the preservation of native dance rituals represent important sites of power and knowledge for indigenous peoples who continue to assert their agency and transmit ancestral knowledge. We see this in the continuity and change of the elements of indigenous dance rituals that appear in *The Güegüense*, which has been consistently performed in Nicaragua since the colonial period.

The Güegüense is a comedy-ballet that uses irony, wordplay, satire, and physical comedy to comment on colonial power relations. It is one of the earliest plays transcribed in Nicaragua,[16] certainly the most performed, and perhaps one of the most studied pieces of Nicaraguan literature. The way that this comedy-ballet has survived in both text and in performance allows us to analyze its connections to contact-era indigenous dances. In addition, the continuities and changes to *The Güegüense* over time offer insights into how this ritualistic dance performance has morphed to fit the needs of Nicaraguans at different historical moments. We know, for example, that *The Güegüense* was performed by and for indigenous audiences, and has later come to be performed by and for mestizo audiences. Instead of considering—as the American anthropologist Richard Adams did in 1957—that "Nicaragua was no longer inhabited by groups who could 'legitimately' be called 'Indians,'" we argue that it is necessary to understand both continuity and change with respect to the native legacy of this cultural text, evinced in its reliance on traditional dress, dance, and indigenous languages like Mangue (Field 1999: 29).[17] Indeed, it would not be productive to question whether or not the comedy is purely indigenous or mestizo. While the comedy has often been considered a representation of tensions between mestizos and indigenous peoples, we choose to read it as a broader commentary on subverting power relations while simultaneously preserving movement and sounds sacred to these communities.

Scholars still actively debate exactly when the dialogue of *The Güegüense* was first written down, in what language, and by whose hand. The written history of the comedy-ballet begins with Juan Eligio de la Rocha, a lawyer born in Granada, Nicaragua in 1815. According to anthropologist Les W. Field, in his extensive study of how *The Güegüense* circulated and was interpreted among Nicaraguan and US intellectuals, de la Rocha reported hand copying two manuscripts that he found in the region of Masaya after 1840 while doing research on Mangue, the native language in which the comedy was performed (1999: 47). Later, an amateur German linguist, Karl Hermann Berendt, who was living in Masaya in 1874, "discovered" de la Rocha's work and expanded upon it (Ibid.). Berendt's informants reported that the spoken parts of *The Güegüense* were translated from Mangue to "pure" Náhuatl, the language of commerce for the Nahua and Nicarao populations in pre-contact Nicaragua. Later, *The Güegüense* was performed and transcribed in a dialect/patois that combined Náhuatl and Spanish, the language of catechism and the preferred language of government in the 1600s (Field 1999: 50). This is the same language that Daniel G. Brinton used to transcribe the *Güegüense* from performance to text in the nineteenth century. Subsequently, the English translation (published in 1883) was based on this version. In the translations and interpretations that have followed, Nicaraguan and US intellectuals widely use Brinton's transcription.

It is significant to note that there are no longer any living speakers of Mangue nor the Náhuatl-Spanish dialect that Brinton used to transcribe the *Güegüense*.[18] We see traces of this transcultural dialect, however, when, in order for dialogue to begin in the performance, the Governor must first cry out (code switching between Spanish and Náhuatl): "simocagüe campamento Señores principales, sones, mudanzas, velancicos necana y paltechúa linar mo Cabildo Real" [suspend in the quarters of the leading men the music, dances, songs, ballets, and such pleasant matters of amusement to the Royal Court] (Brinton 1883: 6–7). Moreover, the ritualistic language used by the characters to greet one another harks to prayers used before the imposition of Spanish. For instance, at the beginning of the play, the same greeting/prayer is used three times in a row, separated by bouts of dancing, "Matateco Dio mispiales...Matateco Dio miscuales quilis" [I pray God to protect you...I pray God to prosper you" (6–7). The Spanish word *diós* (god) here becomes *dio*, a generic replacement for specific deities that would have been named in pre-Colombian rituals. We claim that this salute—given that it is repeated ritualistically, with no connection to the plot—is further evidence of the preservation of native ritual healing in that it honors their gods, an essential aspect of health and wellness within indigenous medicine.

As mentioned before, the overarching cosmovision native to Central American required ritual in order to preserve natural order. It is not a stretch, then, that these rituals could be hidden in plain view in the form of comedic street theater, where performances of *The Güegüense* often take place. This point becomes even more salient as we juxtapose elements of *The Güegüense* with Oviedo's descriptions of contact-era *areitos*, which demonstrate that ritual dance movements represent a potential performative outlet, opening up a space to (pre)serve indigenous religious practices and memory for its participants (dancers and their audience). Despite the loss of native speakers that used the Mangue-influenced patois specific to this text, *The Güegüense*'s plot is well known and it continues to be performed, either with or without the original dialogue. The question remains, then, as to why such a performance, including dialogue from a dead language, continues to be performed to the present day. In order to contextualize the cultural significance of the comedy-ballet (and its import as a site for the preservation of indigenous dance rituals), a brief summary of the larger narrative in which the dance is inscribed sheds light on these aspects of the text.

The Güegüense's plot revolves around the use of cunning, trickery, and feigned ignorance as tools for increased social mobility. The main character for which the piece is named, Güegüense,[19] is a travelling merchant with his two sons attempting to make a living by whatever means necessary. The main conflict of the piece revolves around Güegüense's permission (*licencia*) to trade in the Governor's territory and his attempts to prove the quality of his goods and skills as well as those of his sons. The antagonist of the piece is the Governor Tastuanes, the representation of royal authority in the land. As Güegüense engages with the royal authority, we begin to see the social hierarchies that largely determined power and prestige in colonial society, as well as how Güegüense's role functions to subvert these structures. Specifically, the Governor Tastuanes[20] meets with his subordinate, the Alguacil Mayor,[21] and orders him to apprehend Güegüense to extort him. Güegüense overhears the order to bring him in, but uses feigned ignorance as a tool to subvert the Alguacil's authority, pretending to mistake him for a woman.[22] Despite his gendered slight to the Alguacil, Güegüense tentatively accepts the Alguacil's authority, who, in turn, offers to teach Güegüense how to appear before the Governor, performing for him the official words to greet the Governor along with the required movements.[23] Later, Güegüense and his sons present a variety of dances to please the Governor, including the masquerade of the *machos* (mules) filled with bawdy sexual humor. Güegüense then negotiates a marriage between his son, Don Forcico, and the daughter of the Governor, Suche Malinche, a strategic maneuver to secure upward social mobility for the family. The goods for the marriage are loaded on the mules and Güegüense leaves, addressing each character individually.

What is striking about the structure of the performance of *The Güegüense* is that movement frames each plot. Although the specific choreography is not described in the text, its visual manifestation allows us to see that, between every few lines of text, there is a richness of movement and music, which is absent in the archive (the written text) but very much a part of the repertoire (the performance). While the *machos* play a miniscule role in the written play, they are the most prominent figures in the visual performance. At different points in the piece they perform footwork that recalls indigenous choreography, and, saluting the cardinal directions, they dance two by two in parallel lines, forming a spiral that moves in concentric circles. While we cannot trace a direct line between these movements and the *areitos* that Oviedo describes, there are certainly striking similarities. Regarding the specific movement patterns that determine different dance rituals in the early colonial period, for example, we know that these might vary in symbolic gestures and tempo (Martí and Kurath 1964: 84).[24] However, the parallel lines, dancing two by two, and saluting the cardinal directions are foundational elements of traditional indigenous movements that underscore the many variations of native dance rituals in the region.

Another way that *The Güegüense* contributes to the repertoire of indigenous memory is through the costumes and dress used specifically for the comedy-ballet. The participants' costumes are elaborate, colorful, and detailed.[25] All of the characters wear handmade, wooden or screen masks, something that anthropologist Francisco Pérez Estrada considers a central part of indigenous ceremonies and rituals, which colonial authorities often banned because of their ties to the pre-Colombian past (Field 1999: 57). While we cannot ascertain the exact significance of the detailed dress of the performers, we can understand the continued use of these symbols as part of the visual repertoire that preserves indigenous iconography, as Oviedo's general history confirms. In addition, in *The Güegüense,* the figures of authority (the Governor and the Alguacil Mayor) wear headpieces adorned with feathers and flowers as opposed to the gold and silver coins of Güegüense and his sons. These non-European symbols of authority are sites of memory preservation, representing an alternative iconography of power and status that continued well into the colonial period. Finally, the *machos,* or mules, wear elaborate black masks with European blue eyes, although their long braids of multicolor cloth and ribbons gesture toward indigenous aesthetic values. Each mule carries a rattle (*chischiles*), an instrumental accompaniment to the dance that provides percussion for the piece. This instrument is not of European origin and its use can be traced back to indigenous ceremonial gourd rattles, another instance of the broader connections that can be traced between indigenous rituals and how they adapted during and through the colonial period.[26]

Beyond the incorporation of ritual paraphernalia native to Nicaragua into the visual repertoire of the *The Güegüense,* we find that the comedy-ballet also complicates colonial notions of sex and sexuality. With respect to the preservation and the subversion of indigenous notions of sexuality, we suggest that the highly sexual content of the play may be seen as a connection between indigenous beliefs and attitudes towards sex and sexuality before the imposition of what María Lugones (2007) calls the colonial-modern gender system.[27] For example, when Güengüense is negotiating a price with the Alguacil Mayor for having taught him how to properly greet the Governor, he makes a quip about how the Alguacil, once he puts his hands out for payment, has fine nails (on his fingers). The Alguacil responds by saying, "Para tu cuerpo" [For your body], which Brinton translates as "May it burn your body," and later comments that, when he consulted an informant, he described the saying as "an extremely filthy expression" (1883: 40, 41, 80). According to Erick Blandón, the expression is a threat of anal sex, something that Brinton and his informant were too scandalized to mention (2003: 161).

A more radical example of the blatant sexuality present in the comedy is at the end of the play when it is alluded that Güegüense's son, Don Forcico, has sex with a man to procure the wine for his own wedding with the Governor's daughter, Suche Malinche: certainly prohibited by the colonial regime, given that Güegüense asks his son to keep it quiet that he taught him how to prostitute himself in this way.[28] As previous scholarship demonstrates, the inclusion of sexuality within indigenous rituals is well known.[29] Many have tentatively claimed that the jokes and references may be related to indigenous attitudes toward sex and sexuality. However, Blandón's study complicates this matter: since these jokes privilege the masculine and/or penetrating perspective, they may also reflect how European heterocentrism altered the pre-Colombian concepts of sex and sexuality (2003: 169). In any case, the sexual humor in *The Güegüense* subverts the heteronormative moral landscape of the period in its open display of (homo)sexual transgression—a clear performative resistance to the restrictive binary of sexuality prescribed by the colonial-modern gender system, as understood by Lugones.

Finally, with respect to the continued practice of contact-era *areitos* used for healing, there is strong evidence that *The Güegüense* has been performed as part of a spiritual or religious practice. In this sense, remembering the indigenous "multiple therapy" that combined notions of spiritual and physical health and wellness (as is true of native *areitos*), the ritual movement and music represent the power to manifest healing. In the nineteenth century, Brinton writes that,

> Within the memory of those now living, this Baile has occasionally been acted
> in fulfillment of a religious vow pronounced in some emergency of life or affairs.

Dance as medicine

> The period selected for its performance is, usually, at the festival of St. Jerome, September 30th. The preparations for it are elaborate and expensive.
>
> *(1883: xlii)*

In this way, we can see that *The Güegüense* clearly had a ritualistic and spiritual meaning for the people of Masaya. It is important to note that the festival of St. Jerome, also called Tata Chombo[30] by local residents, has been central to interpretations of Nicaragua's folklore, an expression of indigeneity, and religious syncretism.[31] It is a common pilgrimage destination for many Nicaraguans, and it has particular significance for those that seek healing from Tata Chombo, or St. Jerome, often referred to as "the doctor that cures without medicine."[32] In addition, *The Güegüense* continues to be performed in Diriamba, Nicaragua every year for the feast of Saint Sebastian. In this way, we can see how indigenous dance rituals continue to exist within and alongside officially sanctioned rituals by the Catholic Church (including the embedded critiques of colonial power structures mentioned above).

While there have certainly been changes made to these healing rituals over the past five centuries, we wish to signal the importance of the continuity and preservation of indigenous repertoires in the face of colonization and coloniality. It is clear that, even though the *areitos* and the languages they were performed in are not found intact in present-day Nicaragua, there is a rich repertoire of indigenous iconography; movement, rhythm, and music that contribute to a living memory that continue to heal the traumas of colonization. In the summer of 2013, for example, we travelled to Diriamba for a street festival and happened upon a performance of *The Güegüense* in the town's main square. Even though the performance lacked dialogue, the dancers acted out the main plot points, accompanied by lively music, as well as the choreographed movements traditional to the piece.

A large crowd formed around the performance and, as the dance went on, we noticed inquisitive children pointing and asking their elders about different aspects of the spectacle. In response, the elders either explained to the best of their ability, or asked their neighbors—generating community dialogue. This exchange exemplifies what Paloma Martinez-Cruz refers to as "centrifugal acts of knowledge transmission" (2011: 2). In the case of the ritual dance of *The Güegüense*, this allows for the repertoire of indigenous movements, costumes, and music to be both performed and interpreted, transmitting embodied knowledge in a variety of ways (via narrative, spectatorship, interpretation, etc.). That is to say, we do not assert that there is a unilateral truth, message, or purpose that is transmitted by the ritual. Rather, we understand that it is a site where various truths, messages, and purposes are exchanged and fulfilled. In our case, we took in the ephemeral nature of the performance: the unison of the *chischiles*, the bright colors of the costumes, and the set expressions of the masked faces that recall the dance's native past. For some, the dance may have been an affirmation of local identity. For others still, it could be the fulfillment of a religious vow. While we are in no position to ascribe meaning to individual experiences, what is certain is that these dances, rooted in native tradition, continue as significant sites of representation with the capacity to transmit marginalized knowledges.

The healing aspect of the ritual may not serve the primary purpose as it once was for the contact-era *areitos* that Oviedo describes in his general and natural history of the Indies; however, we argue that ritual dance continues to heal, given that that it serves as a site for historical memory and the transmission of non-western knowledge. To be certain, the legacy of European colonization has plagued marginalized populations in Nicaragua; however, there is a profound healing power in the movements and aesthetics that have survived and transformed over the past five hundred years. In this regard, while these rituals have changed drastically in meaning, they continue to heal the imbalance between marginalized repertoires and the hegemonic archive. To protect these ephemeral sources, *The Güegüense* is recognized by UNESCO as a "Masterpiece of the Oral and Intangible Heritage of Humanity," which, as we have shown, helps to preserve indigenous ritual paraphernalia and dance from the contact-era of the colonial period, complicate prescriptive notions of sex and sexuality imposed by the colonial-modern gender system, and support a traditional healing ritual for many communities in Nicaragua today.

Notes

1 Although his study focuses on Mexico, Guillermo Bonfil Batalla (1996) has shown that Amerindian culture, generally speaking, frames healthcare as a "multiple therapy" that addresses both the physical and spiritual equilibrium of the patient. This is central to the premise of our chapter in which we demonstrate the way in which dance (a form of indigenous medicine) serves as a healing mechanism in a spiritual, physical, and cultural sense.

2 Oviedo (1478–1557) is well known for his historiographical works on the New World, being one of the first Spanish cosmographers (under Hapsburg King, Charles V) to travel to the Americas and document local people, plants, and practices. He is best known for his *Sumario de historia natural* (1526) and his *magnus opus*, the *Historia general y natural de las Indias*: first published in 1535, followed by an expanded print edition in 1552, and finally the Spanish Academy of History published the entirety of the collection 1851–5.

3 *The Güegüense* refers to a performative piece, transcribed in the nineteenth century but purportedly performed at least since the seventeenth century in Nicaragua. Within Central American scholarship, there is debate on the date of origin of the first written record of the piece; see Les W. Field, *The Grimace of Macho Ratón* (1999).

4 In his discussion of colonial historiography, José Rabasa (*Writing Violence of the Northern Frontier*, 2000) makes this point, arguing that: "Spain's colonial project inaugurated a form of modern imperialism that constituted Western civilization as a paradigm to be imposed on the rest of the world. These political corollaries reveal power relations that were first exerted in the sixteenth century but are still in full force today. They imply a postcolonial perspective that allows us to critique the culture of conquest informing developmentalist policies and their implementations through military force—these, obviously, always under the guise of love and truth or, in the lingo of today, as advancing democracy" (95). The epistemic violence that colonial writings enact against indigenous peoples that Rabasa notes here is the lynchpin of early modern European writings.

5 As Taylor (*The Archive and the Repertoire*) argues (and Oviedo's text evinces), "Religion proved a vital conduit of social (as well as religious) behavior. The transfers occurred not just in the uneasy tensions between religious systems but within the religious systems themselves" (2003: 44). For this reason, the Christian acceptance of the native dance rituals was not without controversy. Clendinnen cites the first Mexican council of bishops in 1539 (who were also responsible for colonial settlements in Nicaragua), which explicitly restricted: the consumption of alcohol (Castilian wine); the production of traditional music; the burning of ritual incense, such as copal, as well as ritual fires (2010: 115). However, as Clendinnen's research shows, "The effort failed. The Church continued to suffer a population explosion of musicians and singers, and a doubtfully holy cacophony of trumpets and drum and other unsuitable instruments. The Indians persisted in making a song and dance of their religion, in time with the de facto tolerance of their spiritual leaders" (2010: 115). Voigt's research on colonial festivals is among the most recent scholarship on the matter; for a general overview of the research to date on colonial festivals, see her introduction to *Spectacular Wealth* (2016: 1–18).

6 On the continuation of Mesoamerican medicine, see Martinez-Cruz, "Survivor Woman," *Women and Knowledge in Mesoamerica* (2011: 72–95).

7 Anáhuac is the name used by the Mexica to describe the extent of their empire. This area included present-day Mexico, parts of the southwest in United States, and most of the Central American isthmus (present-day Guatemala, El Salvador, Nicaragua, and Costa Rica).

8 This is to say that dance rituals incorporated and transmitted various different cultural influences. There is particular evidence of Nahua influence because it was more prevalent among the Nicarao on the Pacific coast, where most of Nicaragua's population and cities are located. However, there are certainly other cultures at play given the diversity of indigenous groups in Nicaragua.

Dance as medicine

9 On the visual epistemology in Oviedo's work, see Kathleen A. Myers, "The Representation of New World Phenomena" (1993). For a more comprehensive study on Oviedo and his historical writings, also see Myers, *Fernández de Oviedo's Chronicle of America* (2007).

10 All translations from Spanish to English are our own.

11 Cacao is one of many sacred/medicinal plants within the native repertoire that are honored throughout the ceremonial cycle. For a general history of cacao (and tobacco), see Marcy Norton, *Sacred Gifts, Profane Pleasures* (2008).

12 While it is difficult to determine the exact geographical space that the kingdom of Tecoatega (ruled by the cacique Agateite) encompassed in sixteenth-century Nicaragua, Oviedo places the territory alongside several other primary leaders in the region, such as the cacique Mistega, as well as different (nameless) leaders from Nicaragua and Nicoya, in addition to several other principal caciques that, despite his elision of their specific names, Oviedo reports to have commanded a significant number of "vassals" in their own right (1959: 365).

13 *Contrapás* is a reference to a popular dance from Cataluña, an autonomous community in Spain: as we see here, European observers often likened indigenous rites, customs, and nature to familiar practices from home, evinced in Oviedo's analogy of Catalan traditions to those of the Amerindians that he came into contact with in Nicaragua.

14 In early modern Spanish, the word *palmos* represents a measurement of distance, which we can roughly translate as inches.

15 While, in this particular agricultural rite, Oviedo only explicitly references cacao (one example of intoxication), we can assume that this was part of a larger plant repertoire, true of Amerindian groups throughout the hemisphere, as many studies have shown. For example, Martí and Kurath's research demonstrates that ritual dance in Anáhuac was closely tied to the ingestion of intoxicating plants, which served to open a channel between humans and the spirit world (1964).

16 The first mention in the archival record of a transcription comes from the 19th century, but it is likely that earlier transcriptions existed given the series of translations that the play underwent as explained below.

17 When drawing comparisons between the *areitos* of the early colonial period and the dances and festivities performed in the nineteenth century and beyond, we are careful not to draw a direct line under the (tenuous) umbrella term "indigenous."

18 Scholars agree that through the various translations and transcriptions of the *Güegüense,* much of the original wordplay, double-meanings, homophones between Mangue and Náhuatl, etc. is no longer understood. Brinton writes, "Dr. C. H. Berendt … states, positively, that the Náhuatl parts are not understood by the natives themselves at the present day" (1883: xli).

19 Güegüense's name is dialect for Náhuatl *huehuentzin,* "the honored elder" or "the dear old man" (Brinton 1883: xlv). This is ironic because the Güegüense is not honored or respected by the authority figures and is of dubious moral character. However, we are expected to identify with his cunning and wit as he makes profit from trickery.

20 It is unclear in the piece whether or not the Governor is indigenous, mestizo, or European. Indeed, some have argued that we can interpret the piece as a reinterpretation of an older commentary on Nahua authority in the same region of Nicaragua, given that Tastuanes corresponds to *tlatuani* in Náhuatl, meaning "he who speaks well," i.e. the local authority figure or "chief/cacique."

21 According the historian Rodolfo Cardenal, the Alguacil was one of the lowest titles of authority in the colonial period (1996: 78). However, we can see by Güegüense's dialogue that women had less authority, even if they served the Governor.

22 This includes insinuations that he is a sexual servant of the governor, missing the rod that denotes his authority, a clear phallic reference.

23 As explored below, these official words and greetings are highly ritual in nature.

24 Most importantly, as signaled by Martí and Kurath, "Horizontal and vertical space designs had symbolic significance. Offerings and circuits were guided by the cardinal points, that is the rain gods of the four directions and the corresponding positions of the sun. Priests offered sunwise libations, to the east at dawn, the south at noon, the west at sunset, the north at midnight" (1964: 87).

25 Brinton describes the Güegüense's dress in the following manner, "the Güegüence wore the most magnificent apparel of any of the actors. Chains of gold, strings of silver coins, and ornaments of steel draped his person. Indeed, all the participants vied with each other in extravagant costumes. Their garments were fantastically adorned with feathers and flowers, and set off with sashes and handkerchiefs of brilliant colors" (1883: xlvi). This description from the nineteenth century is strikingly similar to

the description given by The Nicaraguan government, which worked to standardize the dress for the characters in 2009 after consulting performers and anthropologists for cultural patrimony ("Así debe vestir el Güegüense").

26 The *chischiles* represent a present-day incarnation of the ceremonial rattle (sometimes made of medal or out of a (more traditional) gourd). Martí and Kurath point out the centrality of this instrument (the *chicahuaztli*, a phallic symbol for rain) in their book *Dances of Anáhuac* (1964: 84).

27 Lugones expands on the concept of the coloniality of power (developed by Aníbal Quijano) in order to offer an intersectional analysis that describes the formation of a colonial/modern system. Specifically, she proposes that the categorization of gender is a colonial imposition, given the existence of societies that did not conceive of gender as an organizing principle. Furthermore, she argues that the colonial/ modern gender system is not an imposition of the European gender system, but rather a system that creates hierarchical expectations based on racialized categories ("Heterosexualism and the Colonial/ Modern Gender System," 2007).

28 The dialogue is the following: *Güe:* Calla, muchacho, que dirá la gente que yo te enseño á hacer amigo? (62) *D. Ambrosio.:* Y pues no es verdad que enseñas á malas mañas á tu hijo? (64). [*Güe.* Shut up, boy. What will the folks say [if they hear] that I taught you to make a friend? (63) *Don Am.* And is it not true that you teach your son evil ways? (65). Brinton later comments in a footnote: "*Hacer amigo*, to make a friend. This is the phrase which is used by courtesans with reference to securing a male patron to pay their expenses, and for that reason Güegüence affects to be shocked by the employment of it by Don Forcico" (1883: 81).

29 See Pete Sigal, *The Flower and the Scorpion: Sexuality and Ritual in Early Nahua Culture* (2011).

30 "Tata" means "Father," but Chombo is a word particular to Masaya used in reference to Saint Jerome, the patron of Masaya. We can assume that this word comes from an indigenous language and once referred to another deity. The festivities for St. Jerome are an example of religious syncretism, mixing indigenous and catholic traditions.

31 See Katherine Borland's book *Unmasking Class, Gender, and Sexuality in Nicaraguan Festival* (2006) for a detailed account of Masaya's festivals and their shifting significance through political movements.

32 See Florence Jaugey's film *El que todo lo puede* (1997) for more about the healing rituals of the festival.

Works cited

"Así Debe Vestir El Güegüense." *El Nuevo Diario*, 5 July 2009. www.elnuevodiario.com.ni/variedades/51686-debe-vestir-gueguense/. Accessed 7 June 2017.

Blandón Guevara, Erick. *Barroco descalzo: Colonialidad, sexualidad, género y raza en la construcción de la hegemonía cultural en Nicaragua*. Managua, Nicaragua: URACCAN, 2003.

Bonfil Batalla, Guillermo. *México Profundo: Reclaiming a Civilization*. Ed. Philip Adams Dennis. Austin, TX: University of Texas Press, 1996.

Borland, Katherine. *Unmasking Class, Gender, and Sexuality in Nicaraguan Festival*. Tucson, AZ: University of Arizona Press, 2006.

Cardenal Chamorro, Rodolfo José. *Manual de historia de Centroamérica*. San Salvador, El Salvador: UCA Editores, 1996.

Clendinnen, Inga. "Ways to the Sacred: Reconstructing "Religion" in Sixteenth Century Mexico." *History and Anthropology*. 5.1, 2010, 105–141.

El que todo lo puede. Dir. Florence Jaugey. Camila Films, 1997. Accessed on Vimeo.com, March 2014.

Fernández de Oviedo y Valdés, Gonzalo, and Pérez de Tudela y Bueso, Juan. *Historia general y natural de Las Indias*. t.117–121 Vol. Madrid: Ediciones Atlas, 1959.

Field, Les W. *The Grimace of Macho Ratón: Artisans, Identity, and Nation in Late-Twentieth Century Western Nicaragua*. Durham, NC: Duke University Press, 1999.

Garrison Brinton, Daniel, ed. *The Güegüence: A Comedy Ballet in the Nahuatl-Spanish Dialect of Nicaragua*. Philadelphia, PA: D. G. Brinton, 1883.

Hanna, Judith Lynne. *To Dance is Human: A Theory of Nonverbal Communication*. Chicago, IL: University of Chicago Press, 1987.

Lugones, María. "Heterosexualism and the Colonial/Modern Gender System". *Hypatia*. 22.1, 2007, 186–219.

Martí, Samuel. *Dances of Anáhuac; the Choreography and Music of Precortesian Dances*. Ed. Gertrude Prokosch Kurath. New York: Wenner-Gren Foundation for Anthropological Research, 1964.

Dance as medicine

Martinez-Cruz, Paloma. *Women and Knowledge in Mesoamerica: From East L.A. to Anahuac*. Tucson, AZ: University of Arizona Press, 2011.

Myers, Kathleen Ann. *Fernández de Oviedo's Chronicle of America: A New History for a New World*. Austin, TX: The University of Texas Press, 2007.

Myers, Kathleen Ann. "The Representation of New World Phenomena: Visual Epistemology and Gonzalo de Oviedo's Illustrations." *Early Images of the Americas: Transfer and Invention*. Eds. Jerry M. Williams and Robert E. Lewis. Tuscon, AZ: University of Arizona Press, 1993.

Norton, Marcy. *Sacred Gifts, Profane Pleasures: A History of Tobacco and Chocolate in the Atlantic World*. Ithaca, NY: Cornell University Press, 2008.

Rabasa, José. *Writing as Violence: The Historiography of Sixteenth-Century New Mexico and Florida and the Legacy of Conquest*. Durham, NC: Duke University Press, 2000.

Roach, Joseph R. *Cities of the Dead: Circum-Atlantic Performance*. New York: Columbia University Press, 1996.

Sigal, Pete. *The Flower and the Scorpion: Sexuality and Ritual in Early Nahua Culture*. Durham, NC, and London: Duke University Press, 2011.

Taylor, Diana. *The Archive and the Repertoire: Performing Cultural Memory in the Americas*. Durham, NC: Duke University Press, 2003.

Voigt, Lisa. *Spectacular Wealth: The Festivals of Colonial South American Minding Towns*. Austin: University of Texas Press, 2016.

31

GENDER PERFORMATIVITY AND INDIGENOUS CONCEPTIONS OF DUALITY IN THE INTI RAYMI–JATUN PUNCHA FESTIVALS OF COTACACHI, ECUADOR

Michelle Wibbelsman

Every year, beginning on June 24 and again on June 29, dancers from indigenous communities in northern Ecuador descend upon the main square of the highland city of Cotacachi. The *sanjuanes*, as the male dancers are known in honor of Saint John the Baptist, take the church *plaza* by force during the Inti Raymi festivals celebrated throughout the Andes, showing their aggression by dancing vigorously, pounding their boots against the pavement, waving *aciales* (whips) in a threatening gesture, and whistling collectively. They wear goatskin chaps (*zamarros*) and broad, black cardboard hats, taking the symbols of hacienda power into their own hands. Some are completely outfitted in olive camouflage—a reference to the military as a symbol of power and authority. They dance like this for days at a time chanting "*jari, jari, jarikuna… churay, churay, carajo!*" (men, men, we are men… put it there, put it there, *carajo!*), asserting their masculinity and their strength. For the duration of the festival, the indigenous dancers dominate the town square, effectively displacing the mestizo residents from this public space and driving them either to observe this exhibition of indigenous power and virility from balconies surrounding the plaza or leave town altogether.

The Inti Raymi or Festival of the Sun, known locally as *Jatun Puncha*, the Great Day, is noticeably dominated by a masculine aesthetic expressed in the vigor of the dance, the symbolism of power, authority, and masculinity reflected in the festival attire, and the violent act of taking the square which effectively enacts a spatial-political counter-conquest, as I explain in greater detail elsewhere (Wibbelsman 2009). Nonetheless, within the multilayered, syncretic, topsy-turvy festival environment, we find that different conceptualizations of masculinity coexist, and competing gender symbolisms play out in distinct ways. Drawing on ethnographic research between 1995 and 2017, in this chapter I focus on gender performativity during the Inti Raymi–Jatun Puncha, specifically hypermasculine performances by indigenous men but also women, that challenge conventional notions of gender fixity and provide insight into Andean conceptualizations of gender duality.

On the most apparent level, the festival exposes a colonial legacy of generalized suppression and subordination of indigenous peoples and cultures in the area. In this historical context, the

Gender performativity and indigenous conceptions of duality

taking of the central plaza, the site of political power *par excellence* according to Chantal Caillavet (2000, 392), constitutes a ritual reversal of the socio-political order and a symbolic inversion of the colonial racialized geography. The Inti Raymi–Jatun Puncha dances constitute a concerted act of reclaiming indigenous sovereignty and authority, largely dismissed under colonial and later state hegemonies, and the dancers' presence in the city is a statement against the marginalization of indigenous identities and epistemologies. The hyperperformance of masculinity during the Inti Raymi points to a historical formula for undercutting indigenous self-determination, namely the emasculation of indigenous male identities (and, by the same hegemonic gesture, the defeminizing of indigenous women). During the festival, male dancers reclaim their repressed masculinity and assert their sexuality as an integral part of their individual and indigenous collective identity. Although in reference to a different social context, Richard N. Pitt and George Sanders (2010, 43) suggest that the performance of hypermasculinity among minority populations can, in fact, be understood as a response to marginalized masculinities.

While Pitt and Sanders's assessment is apt for interpreting the performance of hypermasculinity during the Inti Raymi in the context of racialized colonial and postcolonial regimes, their analysis is necessarily limited in addressing the significance of the dances at an autochthonous level. From a purely indigenous perspective, expressions of hypermasculinity during the Inti Raymi–Jatun Puncha signal a climax of male energy that culminates in a ritual battle known as *tinkuy*, where festival dancers confront each other in violent intra-ethnic clashes. According to dancers, these violent confrontations between members of upper and lower moiety communities are necessary for restoring universal equilibrium since during the days of the festival, sacred waterfalls and springs become acutely energized and the doors of communication with other time-spaces or *pachas* open temporarily, unleashing male forces that brim over in excess and need to be controlled. "This is why," Enrique "Katsa" Cachiguango, native anthropologist and *yachaq* (literally, one who knows; shaman) of the community of Kotama in the Otavalo area of Ecuador, explains, "*runakuna* (indigenous people) have to confront each other, except it is actually the *ayas*, the spirits of the sacred water sites, who are fighting" (Cachiguango interview 2000).

"*Yo soy producto del Inti Raymi; el Inti Raymi me ha enseñado*" ("I am a product of the Inti Raymi; the Inti Raymi has taught me"), asserts Cachiguango, attributing his profound understanding of Andean knowledge and conceptualization of the universe not to his academic degrees, but to his lived experience of the festival (Cachiguango, personal communication June, 2017). Central to the knowledge encoded in the Inti Raymi–Jatun Puncha is a conceptualization of time and space in gendered terms that divides the year into more or less masculine time-space, corresponding to the period between March 21 and September 21 with the height of masculine expression on June 21, the summer solstice, and more or less feminine time-space, corresponding to the season between September 21 and March 21 with the peak of feminine energy on December 21, the winter solstice (Cachiguango personal communication 2017). Various authors have pointed to notions of binary complementarity explicit throughout the Andes and reiterated in gendered terms at all scales (see Harrison 1989, 49; Platt 1986, 245; Estermann 1998, 156; Cachiguango 1999 as examples). Within this worldview, all aspects of nature including mountains, water, plants, animals, rocks, wind, and time-spaces or *pachas*, as well as manmade things such as musical instruments and musical melodies, have feminine and masculine attributes and are considered to be animate beings. The imposing Mount Imbabura that overlooks the Awakening Valley, for instance, is *Taita Imbabura* (Father Imbabura) or *Yayitu Imbabura* (Little Grandfather Imbabura), a living ancestor with masculine qualities and desires. Directly across, on the other side of the Otavalo-Cotacachi Valley, active volcano Cotacachi is *Mama Cotacachi* or *Rasu Warmi* (Mother Cotacachi or Snow Woman, also known by her Christian name, María Isabel Cotacachi de las Nieves).

Similarly, water is not just an essential resource, but rather *Yaku Mama* (Water Mother), referred to not only in gendered terms but also respectfully by her proper title *Mama*, which implies a familial proximity with people and a relationship of mutual nurturing. There is also male water with specific qualities that appeal to different crops such as potatoes, corn, and beans, which are also male and female.

Luz María De la Torre (2010, 8), native scholar from the Otavalo area, points out that in the non-Andean world there has been a tendency to conceive of these gender binaries as bounded or closed categories, pitted against each other in a dynamic of opposition. The pervasive influence of Western Cartesian philosophy has admittedly led to either/or formulations such as masculine/feminine, culture/nature, mind/body, intellect/emotion… As people in Andean communities point out repeatedly, however, from their perspective, binary complementarities do not imply difference, conflict, fixity, strict contrast, or opposition. Instead, the ruling principle is balance obtained through mutual help and influence—a delicate social and cosmic equilibrium that, moreover, needs to be maintained and periodically reestablished through human effort. De la Torre (2010, 6) corroborates these Andean popular perceptions, underscoring the fact that Andean concepts distance themselves from any type of rigidity or polarization, unfolding instead in terms of great variety, movement, and flexibility. She goes on to state that in Andean worldview and Quichua language there are no strict comparative categories. Instead, there are subtle comings and goings of degrees of expression of one human quality or another (De la Torre 2010, 6).

Beyond pairs or binary oppositions, as Cachiguango explains, within Andean logic everything operates more specifically in terms of duality. Every individual, moreover, embodies this duality. People express this in the common saying, "*jari-warmi yanantin kanchik*" ("*somos dualidad masculino-femenina;* We are male-female duality") (Cachiguango personal communication 2017). As a key structuring principle in the Andes, *yanantin* (duality) conveys a relationship of interdependence, often conceived of in gendered terms, necessary for the balance and harmony of the whole (see Platt 1986). More than a state of being, it implies a dynamic process toward an ideal. Within this process, people (as well as natural beings) can embody varying degrees of duality at different times of their lives. De la Torre (2010, 6) provides us with a nuanced vocabulary that captures this progression based on the use of Quichua suffixes that qualify the root words *warmi* (woman) and *jari* or *kari* (man). Women can be *karishina, karilla, kari-kari, karipacha, karimana* (like a man, somewhat masculine, a little bit more than manly, thoroughly masculine, a negation of femininity). Similarly, men can be described as *warmilla, warmilla-warmilla, warmillapacha, warmillamana.* De la Torre (7) explains that these terms reflect behaviors, responsibilities, and personal attributes rather than sexualities or gender identities. *Warmilla* connotes a human condition of orderliness, planned work, dedication, concentration, personal commitment, good will, solidarity. De la Torre (7) characterizes *warmilla* as "creative veracity… the expression of spontaneity… toward the achievement of a master work." On the other hand, she defines *karilla* as an expression of energy, extraordinary strength, positivity, optimism, and resolve in the face of challenges, stating that a person can experience any one of these dispositions in impermanent ways at any given point in his or her life. These characterizations decenter strict gender expectations to the point where it is no longer tenable to speak concretely of gender roles or gender identities, but only of gendered human attributes.

The women's participation during the Inti Raymi–Jatun Puncha provides an ethnographic illustration of these Andean approaches to duality. While the Inti Raymi–Jatun Puncha celebrations take place at the pinnacle of masculine time-space and exude a public male dominance and aesthetic, women also participate and, in fact, play a crucial role in the festival. Emilia Ferraro (2000, 179) points out that the role of women in the attentive preparation of food, beverages,

Gender performativity and indigenous conceptions of duality

and festival costumes is essential for ensuring the success of the event. Although women play a much more public role in nearby communities such as Zuleta and Cayambe, dancing and singing alongside the men throughout the festival, in Cotacachi, the women's participation is publically understated, but no less important. During the taking of the *plaza* itself, women walk alongside their husbands while the men dance, carrying food and drink in their bundles (*kepis*) to sustain the male dancers over the course of the day. The women also regularly carry a *doble acial*, a back-up whip, should their spouses need it to defend themselves in the fights. Groups of women, often with babies strapped to their backs in carrying cloths, walk between the groups of *sanjuanes* as a human buffer to avert the fights. On the days of the festival, there is significant military and police presence at every corner of the *plaza* to break up the fights with tear gas should skirmishes break out. Next to every cluster of law enforcement officers stands a clique of women from both upper and lower moiety communities who make it their duty to inform non-indigenous and non-local police about which coalitions of dancers are likely to collide. They perform a key role in educating police about the dynamics of the festival in order to prevent use of indiscriminate military or police force. Finally, women have spearheaded community discussions on festival violence and, in some cases, been effective in tempering the fighting tradition of the *tinkuy*.

The overtly public participation of the women in the festival in Cotacachi is reserved for July 1, known as the *warmi puncha* or *el día de las mujeres* (the women's day), when the women themselves take the main square. Curiously, on this day, the women dress as men or otherwise dance around the plaza with manifestations of physical strength, endurance, and vigor. They emulate the emphatic male dance step, carry threatening *aciales,* and play musical instruments—the twin flutes in particular, which generally correspond to a domain of male activity. They shout "¡*Churay! ¡Churay!*" ("Put it there!" an expression that calls people to dance harder but also carries a connotation of sexual penetration) and "¡*Kashnamari! ¡Kashnamari!*" ("This is how we are "). The women's performance underscores exertion, endurance, and perseverance not only as male qualities, but as more encompassing ethnic identity markers that contrast with non-indigenous dispositions characterized as weak and incapable of sustaining vigorous activity, signaling an ethnically inscribed moral and social subtext. Elderly indigenous women dance alongside women of younger generations for hours without stopping, demonstrating their hardiness even at an advanced age. On the other end of the age spectrum, children, both boys and girls as young as toddlers, dance with their mothers and are encouraged to resist until the very end. As María Guzmán-Gallegos (2015, 126) writes, "physical strengthening is closely entwined with spiritual strengthening" and the socialization of children through participatory and convivial practices is understood as a production of *runakuna*, sentient persons or fully human beings.

In the meantime, in the context of the women's day, men play a supporting role. They walk alongside their wives while the women dance, providing food and drink, and tending to the younger children. Young men and teenagers integrate into the dance with support in the form of musical accompaniment.

The women dance in revolving spirals first in one direction and then the other at each corner of the square around the group of young musicians. They then move forward in moiety coalitions in counterclockwise direction to the next corner of the plaza with the aim of displacing another group and asserting their control of the church square. They whistle in unison as they advance, aggressively waving switches and *aciales* in a hypermasculine display.

Generally, on the *warmi puncha* the emphasis is on dancing and enjoying the festivities with a performance of strength and exuberance, but without the looming threat of violence. Nonetheless, on one occasion in 2000 I did witness a mock battle between women dancers. In lieu of rocks (as the men use), they were throwing oranges at each other. While the danger of injury was still present, there was much laughter and hilarity surrounding the event, both on the part of the women dancers and the observing public. The women's mock battle was an artful parody of the *tinkuy*. This satirical rendition occurred during a year when festival violence in the previous days of the men's dancing had degenerated from fist fights and rock pelting to knife attacks and use of firearms that had resulted in three gunshot injuries. Humor during the women's day provided some relief for the palpable tension in the air. But beyond that, the women's impromptu parody produced a juxtaposition and arguably a "momentary shift in awareness," which Thomas Clifton (1976, 165) describes as a sudden strengthening of self-consciousness that occurs in moments of performative contrast, surprise or interval.

Humor is integral to conflict management and resolution in the Andes. And the practice of shocking the body, the mind, and the senses into altered states of perception or sensitivity by way of contrasts is a common means to wellbeing. For instance, healers often use contrasts of hot and cold or smooth and coarse substances on the body to restore a patient's health. Along similar lines, comical games played at funerals are intended to lighten the mood and provoke unexpected laughter, momentarily interrupting the mourners' sadness and leading them back toward an emotional equilibrium. By way of their satirical festival performance the women produced such a shift and prompted a self-conscious public reflection on festival violence. After the 2000 festival and for the duration of an entire year, UNORCAC (Union of Indigenous and Peasant Organizations of Cotacachi), a second-tier indigenous organization that represents 43 communities in the canton of Cotacachi, followed through with a series of community-based discussions and workshops on the topic of festival violence with a nuanced reflection that differentiated requisite ritual violence from the gratuitous escalation of aggression during the festival.

Another aspect of the women's day that similarly causes amusement (as well as potential contemplation from a different viewpoint) is the presence of men who in order to continue dancing on the third day of the festival dress as women. They exaggerate breast size and depict large buttocks in their costumes, further highlighting these features in their overstated movements. Some of them have dolls strapped to their backs in carrying cloths to represent their *wawas*, infant children. In their gestures and their costumes, they personify women attempting to dance like men during the Inti Raymi, swaying their hips and at the same time stomping on the ground as they enact what can only be described as a male performance of hyperfemininity performing hypermasculinity.

While the raucous throng of dancers revolved around the plaza during the *warmi puncha* in 2017, in the center of the park, a street comedian drew a large crowd. His slapstick humor overcame generational, linguistic, and racial differences among his audience as indigenous, mestizo, foreign, young, and old onlookers laughed uproariously. As I approached he was commanding a few children selected at random from the crowd to stand up straight and state their names firmly. "¡Niños, griten duro! ¡A ver, como macho, m'ijo!" (Children, yell loudly! Come on, like a man, son!"). Eventually he pitted a tiny child against a tall one and encouraged them to fight, yelling "¡Mata, Calera, mata!" (Kill, Calera, kill!) on behalf of one contestant, and for the other, "¡Topo, Topo, Topo, Topo!" referring to the fiercest upper and lower moiety communities of the Inti Raymi—La Calera and Topo Chico. The audience was delighted to see their local tradition featured in the comedic act and laughed hysterically at the absurdity of the fight. Later on, the comedian selected an unsuspecting young man from the crowd. He sculpted the young man's posture, positioning one of his hands on his hips, and instructing him to wave the other hand loosely above his head. Then he set his masterpiece in motion ordering the young man to walk around swaying his hips and shouting, "¡Sal maricón! ¡Sal maricón!" (Come out, fag! Come on out!). The crowd hooted in amusement. My sense is that laughter at different registers reflected a range of audience dispositions, including nervousness, embarrassment, apprehension, social

Gender performativity and indigenous conceptions of duality

distancing, rejection, recognition, identification, and possibly acceptance. As the afternoon wore on, gender echoed throughout the performance as the central theme with particular jabs at masculinity. The comedian skillfully navigated a fine line between typically off-limits subjects and the familiar, playing on a sense of individual and shared recognition of the "other," and bringing the unmentionable to the surface of public awareness and collective commentary.

The Inti Raymi is a season of excess in all respects, an annual occasion for pushing the boundaries of acceptable behavior and status quo ideals. Festival participants drink to excess; there is an overabundance of food; during the *víspera* or eve of the festival, people dance all night and then all day during the festival days. Masked dances in the area aim for the most sacrilegious and offensive themes, depicting pregnant nuns and cannibalistic, fat-sucking Catholic priests. Other costumes mock the familiar—local vendors, municipal and national authorities, or members of different ethnic communities in the area. Costumes representing Arabs and Mexicans exaggerate stereotypical features of foreign and "exotic" cultures. In the carnivalesque world of topsy-turvy where anything goes and where expectations are regularly overturned, the costumed dances function as a "hidden transcript," to borrow James Scott's (1990) phrase—a vehicle for social criticism and collective reflection veiled in humor and merrymaking. It is also apparent that while stereotyping tends to create distance and perpetuate misunderstandings, embodying "the other" in nuanced and detailed ways during the festival allows people to draw the foreign, the unfamiliar, or the objectionable into a closer experiential understanding. In other words, by way of performing "the other" people gain some level of understanding of "the other."

While the exploration of alterity and playful rapprochement with the other is certainly one dynamic within the festival, the structuring concept of *yanantin* alerts us to another possibility: by eliciting a range of human behaviors and dispositions, festival participants are not only attempting to understand the other, but endeavoring to *become* us–them, male–female duality. Luz María De la Torre (6) notes that in the fluidity between gendered pairs, manifested in particularly emphatic ways in heightened contexts such as annual festivals, male and female binaries, in fact, conflate and merge, leading to the disappearance of identifiably masculine and feminine figures. De la Torre's insistence on this point elicited my reflection on Mary Douglas's (2007, 2,6,7) analysis of chiastic poetic structures in ring compositions that follow an AB C BA pattern wherein the meaning is packed in the middle, even when the middle is absent but implied (as in AB BA). This pattern can be discerned in Andean poetic traditions as well as textile designs, ritual dance patterns, and melodic compositions. It is prevalent in the Andes and reiterated at all scales. As Douglas (6) indicates, this organizing strategy expresses a form of parallelism with an important difference: "it depends on the 'crossing over' or change of direction of the movement at the middle point." The emphasis on movement, change of direction, crossing over, and especially the importance assigned to the middle resonates with *yanantin* as a point of dynamic equilibrium where distinct AB BA parallelisms meld into C.

One individual in Cotacachi perhaps epitomizes *yanantin* as a concerted effort toward this perfect duality, and not only during the Inti Raymi festivities, but beyond the festival context throughout the year. During the 2000 Inti Raymi–Jatun Puncha celebrations, I saw him dancing in the plaza with a group of *sanjuanes* in a full expression of masculinity, extraordinary energy, and vigor. On a different occasion a friend from the area had pointed this individual out to me. "See that old lady over there?" he asked, "she's not actually old, and, in fact, she's not a woman, but actually a man." During my extended stay in the area, I would occasionally spot this individual in Cotacachi. At times, he was participating in the Inti Raymi–Jatun Puncha dances with the men; at other times, he was outfitted as a policeman directing traffic; and once, I saw him dressed as a *viudita*, a widow, begging for alms at the exit of the church. In each context, this person seemed to be accepted, respected even. The male dancers integrated him into the spiraling

Inti Raymi dances; drivers obeyed his directions as a traffic cop even when they recognized him as a local; and the other widows at the church sat with her side by side and shared food. This acceptance of the fluidity of expression of this individual, which morphed from one day to the next, stands in sharp contrast to the general ostracizing of crossdressers, homosexuals, and third gender individuals in mainstream Ecuadorian society. At minimum, it points to indigenous understandings of gendered expression in terms of degrees and range of human qualities in contrast to non-indigenous conceptualizations of gender identities as clearly delimited and relatively unchanging. More importantly, it underscores Luz María De la Torre's (2010, 18) suggestion that indigenous alternative worldviews and practices uphold diversity as a form of capital in the construction of *pluridiversidad* (pluridiversity), a key criterion in a new stage of social, cultural, and political *convivencia* (communal experience and solidarity).

Works cited

Cachiguango, Luis Enrique. (1999). "Yaku Mama: El baño y las peleas rituales del Inti Raymi en Cotama, Otavalo." In *Inti Raymipak Kaway Sapi: La sabiduría andina del Inti Raymi en la visión de los Kichwa Kayampi-Otavalo*. Serie Intercultural Imba Sapi. (pp. 23–40). Ibarra: Centro de Estudios Pluriculturales CEPCU, Instituto Para el Estudio de la Cultura y Tecnología Andina IECTA-AYA UMA, Programa de Voluntarios de las Naciones Unidas VNU.

Caillavet, Chantal. (2000). *Etnias del Norte: Ethnohistoria e Historia de Ecuador*. Madrid: Casa de Velásquez, Lima: IFEA (Instituto Francés de Estudios Andinos), and Quito: Ediciones Abya Yala.

Clifton, Thomas. (1976). "The Poetics of Musical Silence." In *Musical Quarterly* 62 (2): 163–181.

De la Torre, Luz María. (2010). "¿Qué dignifica ser mujer indígena en la contemporaneidad?" In *MESTER*, vol. XXXIX (pp. 1–24).

Douglas, Mary. (2007). *Thinking in Circles: An Essay on Ring Composition*. New Haven, CT: Yale University Press.

Estermann, Josef. (1998). *Filosofía Andina: Estudio Intercultural de la Sabiduría Autóctona Andina*. Quito: Abya-Yala.

Ferraro, Emilia. (2000). "El costo de la vida: deuda e identidad en los Andes ecuatorianos. La fiesta de San Juan en Pesillo." In Andrés Guerrero (Ed.), *Etnicidades*. (pp. 147–200). Quito: FLACSO.

Guzmán-Gallegos, María. (2015). "Amazonian Kichwa Leadership: The Circulation of Wealth and the Ambiguities of Mediation." In Fernando Santos-Granero (Ed.), *Images of Public Wealth or the Anatomy of Well-Being in Indigenous Amazonia*. (pp. 117–138). Tucson, AZ: The University of Arizona Press.

Harrison, Regina. (1989). *Signs, Songs, and Memory in the Andes: Translating Quechua Language and Culture*. Austin, TX: University of Texas Press.

Pitt, Richard N., and George Sanders. 2010 "Revisiting Hypermasculinity: Shorthand for Marginalized Masculinities?" In Whitney Harris and Ronald Ferguson (Eds.), *What's up with the Brothers? Essays and Studies on African American Masculinities*. pp. 33–51. Harriman, TN: Men's Studies Press.

Platt, T. (1986). "Mirrors and Maize: The Concept of Yanantin Among the Macha of Bolivia". In J.V. Murra, N. Wachtel, and J. Revel (Eds.), *Anthropological History of Andean Polities*. (pp. 228–259). Cambridge, UK: Cambridge University Press.

Scott, James. (1990). *Domination and the Arts of Resistance: Hidden Transcripts*. New Haven, CT: Yale University Press.

Wibbelsman, Michelle. (2009). *Ritual Encounters: Otavalan Modern and Mythic Community*. Urbana and Chicago, IL: University of Illinois Press.

PART VII

Staging nuevo hemispheric identities

32

BESIDE MOTHERHOOD

Staging women's lives in Latin American Theatre of the Real

Julie Ann Ward

After her triumphant 2002 production of the Spanish classic *La casa de Bernarda Alba* (*The House of Bernarda Alba*) in Buenos Aires' celebrated Teatro San Martín, Argentine director Vivi Tellas set out to do something different. From the pinnacle of theatrical tradition, staging her experimental version of Federico García Lorca's mythical play about mothers and daughters in a national theatre, she set out to explore the limits of the genre with her *Proyecto Archivos* (*Archives Project*, 2003–12). Following Bernarda Alba's scripted cruelty, which belongs comfortably to the tradition of theatrical mothers like Medea and Mother Courage, Tellas proposed a new dramatic reflection on maternal relationships with her first *Archivo*, *Mi mamá y mi tía* (*My Mother and My Aunt*, 2003), in which she stages her own real-life mother and aunt. The wave of biographical plays that followed in Latin America, particularly those that focus on playwrights' and actors' mothers, proposes a rewriting of motherhood, in which the mother is not 'other,' but a subject with a life story beyond maternity.

The mother as a feminist subject

In this chapter I will briefly trace the theme of motherhood through contemporary works of what Carol Martin (2013) calls theatre of the real from Argentina and Mexico and consider how the elements of biography and theatre of the real contribute to a more integrated view of the figure of the mother. Following Karen Bamford and Sheila Rabillard's (2016) proposal for a return to the mother as a feminist subject in theatre scholarship,[1] I examine Tellas' *Mi mamá y mi tía* and her 2012 *Archivo, La bruja y su hija* (*The Witch and Her Daughter*), in addition to Lola Arias' *Mi vida después* (*My Life After*, 2009) and Mexican troupe Lagartijas Tirada al Sol's *El rumor del incendio* (*The Rumor of the Fire*, 2009) and *Montserrat* (2012). I argue that these plays revise the role of the mother in Latin American drama, by explicitly demonstrating how "mother" is created and staged by her own children.

By pushing back against an archetypal "mother" figure whose function is purely (re)productive, the plays I examine here insist on the child's role in producing (and directing and playing) the mother. The introduction of documentary evidence in some cases resists the child's version of the mother, providing proof that the figure known as "mamá" is complex and goes by other names. This significant shift from an essentialist view of the feminine to a complex, humanizing perspective is a political one.

In this chapter I will provide a brief review of feminist conversations on maternity and motherhood, with particular attention to Julia Kristeva's (2002) concept of the *enceinte* woman and Marianne Hirsch's proposals in *The Mother/Daughter Plot* (1989), and Alison Stone (2012) and Elaine Aston's (2007) calls for more expansive visions of motherhood in feminist psycho-analytical theory. I then analyze examples of portrayals of mothers in Latin American theatre of the real from Vivi Tellas' *Archivos* (2010), Lola Arias' *Mi vida después*, and Lagartijas Tiradas al Sol's *El rumor del incendio* and *Montserrat*. Each of these contributions exemplifies multiple subjectivities for mothers, expanding the concept of the mother beyond the mere functional idea of vessel and recognizing her status as an independent subject. The space of the theatre becomes a forum for celebrating and exemplifying a multifaceted view of the woman.

The topic of artistic representations of motherhood has inspired much debate and creativity in feminist circles. In *Desire in Language*, Julia Kristeva theorizes the maternal body and the impossibility of accounting for it in scientific or religious terms. Rather, through art or through giving birth, one can reach the "limit, this requisite of sociality" (2002: 306) where an enclosed or "*enceinte*" woman exists in a state of equalization, the pre-symbolic. Kristeva proposes that "the language of art [. . .] follows [. . .] the sublimation taking place at the very moment of primal repression within the mother's body, arising perhaps unwittingly out of her marginal position. At the intersection of sign and rhythm, of representation and light, of the symbolic and the semiotic, the artist speaks from a place where she is not, where she knows not" (2002: 308). In this account, then, the mother is set apart from the rest of society like a work of art and, in the gaze of the male artist, merely an object. Marianne Hirsch, in *The Mother/Daughter Plot*, problematizes the collapse of all categories of woman into the catch-all condition of "mother,"

> by distinguishing between female positions—childless woman and mother, mother and daughter—challenges the notion of woman as a singular, unified, transparent category. The multiplicity of "women" is nowhere more obvious than for the figure of the mother, who is always both mother and daughter. Her representation is controlled by her object status, but her discourse, when it is voiced, moves her from object to subject. But, as long as she speaks as mother, she must always remain the object in her child's process of subject-formation; she is never fully a subject.
>
> *(1989: 12)*

In Hirsch's account, the category of mother always supersedes any other possible subject position for a woman. Even if one does move past being Kristeva's *enceinte* woman, the artist's object, she is still her own child's object.

Whereas Kristeva's mother inhabits a liminal space apart from society, and Hirsch's is always in opposition to the subjects that objectify her, Alison Stone (2012) proposes a position of in-between for re-examining Kristeva's matricidal drive. In "Against Matricide" Stone argues for a "maternal third term" rather than the traditional psychoanalytical paternal figure that stands in opposition to the mother-child dyad. She proposes a

> relational space that inherits the features of the maternal body as the young child (according to Kristeva) imagines it. Consequently the developing child becomes situated in a maternal space, which simultaneously enables mothers to emerge as subjects in their own right, distinct from this imaginary space.
>
> I then suggest that potential-maternal space expands into language so that language intrinsically allows the possibility of a speaking position of connection with the mother. Entrance into language need not in itself entail separation or matricide.

Beside motherhood

The problem is not language *per se* but the particular way that speech and logos have been defined under patriarchy. Language as maternal space has the potential to support an alternative, non-matricidal, mode of subject-formation—but a potential unrealized under patriarchy.

(Stone 2012: 119)

This third space, rather than trapping the mother in abject objectification, allows for what Hirsch (1989) identifies as the "multiplicity of 'women'" to emerge into communication. By redefining language within a maternal realm rather than a patriarchal one, the mother continues to exist apart from and in relation to her child and her own maternal status. These theories of maternity almost always define motherhood in spatial terms, whether *enceinte*, as a series of female positions, or a relational space.

In "A Critical Step to the Side," Elaine Aston proposes that three solo performances of the loss of the mother by the daughter "[charge] readers with a [. . .] (political) step to the side of those maternal attachments in order to help us, as Sedgwick would argue, to think 'otherwise'" (2007: 132). This step to the side allows audience members to "[get] to know 'other' psychic, social and cultural geographies of the maternal, rather than the mother that is taken, mistaken, for 'our' (selfish) own" (Aston 2007: 140). Aston bases her proposal on Eve Kosofsky Sedgwick's call to explore "beside" rather than "beneath" or "behind": "*Beside* permits a spacious agnosticism about several of the linear logics that enforce dualistic thinking: non-contradiction or the law of the excluded middle, cause versus effect, subject versus object" (Sedgwick 2003: 8). This attention to spatial detail, and the openness to a logic of *beside*, is especially apt for discussions of the theatre, a space where bodies exist simultaneously alongside one another, partaking in ritual together.

While the plays examined here have not previously been treated together through the lens of gender and sexuality, Margo Milleret demonstrates that their challenge to the traditional Latin American "glorification of motherhood" (2004: 86) has precursors in the theatre of the 1980s and 90s, by "problematiz[ing] mother-daughter relationships as difficult and conflictive" and staging "the negotiations between mother and daughter that can contribute to the formation of an independent self" (87). In his book *Remembering Maternal Bodies*, Benigno Trigo argues that Latina and Latin American women writers "interrogate, interpret, elaborate and rewrite a patriarchal maternal imaginary that results in a symbolic, discursive, and phantasmatic matricide" (Trigo 2006: 3–4). The plays I examine here undertake a similar endeavor, to re-present motherhood in a shared space of multiple subjectivities.

Staging the mother: Vivi Tellas

Vivi Tellas has a long history in the alternative art scene, having formed the rock group Bay Biscuits in 1981 and founded the Teatro Malo (Bad Theatre) festival, an event celebrating anonymous, poorly-written theatre texts. She also has directed public theatrical institutions, such as the Centro de Experimentación Teatral (Center for Theatrical Experimentation) at the Universidad de Buenos Aires (1990–2002), and Buenos Aires' Sarmiento Theatre, the experimental center of the city's Theatre Complex. In her role as institutional director, she has also sparked international theatrical tendencies by convening cycles of various projects involving important theatre practitioners from Argentina and beyond. The first, her *Proyecto Museos* (*Museums Project*, 1994–2001), involved staging productions inspired by museums. The next, the *Proyecto Biodrama* (*Biodrama Project*, 2002–09), asked playwrights to create plays based on the lives of real, living Argentines. It is in the context of this trajectory that she developed her personal project, the *Archivos*. Closely

379

linked to biodrama, the *Archivos* view people as breathing archives, and seek to find theatricality in their everyday lives.

Tellas treats embodied experience as an archive, undoing what Carol Martin calls the "ways in which the West has traditionally conceived of a document as a material artefact, such as an item of writing, photograph, video, etc. that can be placed in an archive" (Martin 2011: 82). By accepting the person as a living archive, the concept of the document expands to include memory, knowledge, and relationship. The titles of the *Archivos* generally refer to the interpreters' (as Tellas calls the non-actors) professions or, in the case of *Mi mamá y mi tía* and *La bruja y su hija*, their position within a family. Tellas' focus on individual family members rather than the family as a collective proposes a new way of looking at the family. Rather than asking for maternal sacrifice, these plays elevate the maternal, placing the individual women portrayed on a pedestal and, simultaneously, under a microscope. At the same time, by reminding us that motherhood, sisterhood, and daughterhood are performances, roles to be played, Tellas' *Archivos* hint at the infinite number of roles that the multi-faceted performers may choose from, beyond their family relationships.

The first of the *Archivos*, *Mi mamá y mi tía*, is an excellent example of the entangled biographies present in Tellas' work. The play stars Graciela and Luisa Ninio, Tellas' mother and aunt, respectively, and ran from 2003–04.[2] Tellas is the implicit "I" in the title, the possessor indicated by "*mi*" (my). Graciela and Luisa are merely objects of the phrase. The title suggests more a memoir than a live-action play, and the Ninio sisters play themselves as characters populating Tellas' memories. Indeed, the moments in which Tellas physically moves her mother and her aunt into position are reminiscent of a window dresser arranging a mannequin, or the early stages of blocking in rehearsals for a play. She is the author of her family, organizing their physical presence before the audience.[3] While *Mi mamá y mi tía* portrays the daughter as the artistic creator of the mother and aunt, *La bruja y su hija* posits a relationship of authorship between mother and daughter. During an obscure interlude where Carmen, *la bruja*, explains her deal with the devil, who agreed to give her a child, she implies that maternity is a sort of black magic. She claims that she asked the Devil for a daughter, but then says she doesn't know whether it was her desire. I read this expression of doubt as a subtle challenge to the Devil's power. She doesn't know whether it was the Devil or her desire that created the child, a double message that supplants the Devil's mastery and proposes Bárbara, *la bruja*, as the creator. In Tellas' *Archivos*, maternity is a corporeal, creative force. The mother is positioned both as the central subject, similar to the theatrical director, and as her child's creation.

Lola Arias

In 2002, Tellas, as director of the Teatro Sarmiento, convoked her biodrama cycle. In 2009, Lola Arias' response to the call premiered to wide acclaim, the last installment of the critically and commercially successful biodrama cycle. *Mi vida después* stages seven actors, six of whom vary between playing themselves and playing one or both of their parents. The seventh, Moreno, is the son of one of these actors. In the play, the actors wear their parents' clothing, display and interpret photographs of their families and use other objects (books written by one actor's father, cassette recordings of another's voice, and a live turtle,) to evoke the stories of their parents' lives. Their parents all lived during, if not through, Argentina's military dictatorship. An especially interesting feature is the way that the play has evolved over its three-year run to include updates on legal cases, DNA test results, and new discoveries. The play, which features professional actors and their own, real-life stories, is a thought-provoking study of the limits of the self, authority and authorship, and the role of theatre in society.[4]

Beside motherhood

At one point in the play, Carla Crespo, playing herself, reconstructs the last years of her father's life. He died before she was born, after having joined the Ejército Revolucionario del Pueblo (People's Revolutionary Army), the armed wing of the Partido Revolucionario de los Trabajadores (Worker's Revolutionary Party). Crespo explains:

> CARLA. I never met my father. He died at the age of 26, four months before I was born. When I turned 27 I thought, "Now I'm older than my father. Now I'm going to live all the things he couldn't live. I'm going to be his future life."
>
> *(Translation in Arias 2009: 37)*[5]

This idea, that the daughter would take the father's place in the world, was presciently mirrored in the last letter he wrote to his wife before his death, a letter that was hidden inside of a doll for twenty years, until Crespo and her aunt tore apart all the dolls in the house to find it. The image of the father's words being secreted inside of a doll reflects that of his future self being placed in his daughter's body. This image became even more poignant when Crespo was pregnant, her maternal body an onstage, living representation of the doll pregnant with the letter.[6]

Crespo's doll, ripped apart to find the word of the father, contains the traces of the psychoanalytical models that Kristeva pushes back against. The idea of woman as mere vessel—in this case a disposable doll carrying the father's message—is a violent and outrageous one. Crespo's body, however, present onstage, having outlived even her father's young ghost, provides another version of the multiple possibilities of women that Hirsch proposes. In particular, while she was pregnant, Crespo's body was the living evidence of the maternal subject. Even as the play consists of casting the adult actors as "children of," and Crespo's monologue focuses on her father's life, the mere fact of her life and presence casts her as a person with potential, beyond daughterhood. She tells herself that she will be her father's "future life," but implicit in this declaration is the fact that she will be writing his future biography. By displaying the multiple subjectivities in which Crespo finds herself—daughter, mother, and stand-in for her father—motherhood is presented as one of many overlapping possibilities in a woman's life. Crespo's spoken language, in contrast to her father's hidden, written language, is a constructive proposition for building a future, an example of Stone's maternal, relational space.

Lagartijas Tiradas al Sol

In Mexico, the troupe Lagartijas Tiradas al Sol focuses on representing the absence of the maternal figure in their documentary plays *El rumor del incendio* and *Montserrat*. In the case of *El rumor del incendio*, the mother in question is Margarita Urías Hermosillo, an anthropologist who participated in teachers' and student movements in the 1960s and 70s in Mexico.[7] She is also the late mother of Luisa Pardo, who, along with Gabino Rodríguez, founded Lagartijas Tiradas al Sol. The play biographies "Comandante Margarita," played by Pardo. At the end of the play Pardo breaks character, introducing herself as Luisa Pardo and revealing her identity as Margarita's real-life daughter. In *Montserrat* it is Rodríguez' mother, Montserrat, who is biographied.[8] The play is structured like a detective story in which Rodríguez learns that his mother, who he believed had died when he was a small child, is actually still alive and in hiding in Costa Rica. As in *El rumor del incendio*, Rodríguez presents documentary evidence for his claims, including photos and letters. He also claims to have found Montserrat, but in this case the photographs to prove the fact of their reunion are glaringly devoid of human subjects.

In the last lines of the play he admits that the reunion is his only memory of his mother, and that he isn't sure whether he dreamed it.

In each play the mother at the center is absent, and the children, left behind, must reconstruct her life. They get to know her as journalists or historians would research their subject, interviewing acquaintances, reading diaries and letters, and examining photographs. In the case of *El rumor del incendio*, Margarita's motherhood is not even mentioned until the very end of the play. Rather, she is presented as a multi-faceted historical figure with various important familial, amorous, and professional relationships. Her contributions to the guerrilla resistance are highlighted as well as her role in founding the Centro de Estudios Históricos at the Universidad Veracruzana in Xalapa, Mexico. The revelation that she is Pardo's mother, then, comes as a surprise. In *Montserrat*, on the other hand, the titular character is always presented as the lost mother of the protagonist, Rodríguez. While maternity is the defining characteristic of Montserrat throughout the play, the fact that she was not present in Rodríguez' life, and the possibility that she might have chosen to abscond the maternal throne to live an alternate life, resist the traditional motherhood her virginal name suggests. Margarita's and Montserrat's absences onstage defy the conception of mother as defined by the needs of her children and their subject-formation.

Lagartijas Tiradas al Sol offer paradoxical representations of the absent mother, documentary plays where the main character is unavailable for comment or intervention. While it could be argued that this robs the biographied mothers of their voice, I read their absence as evidence of their status as subjects apart from their maternity. In *El rumor del incendio* Margarita is presented as a multi-faceted subject with political agency, professional ambitions, and deeply emotional relationships. Margarita's relationship with Pardo, her daughter and the actor who plays her, is a mere epilogue to her epic life story. Because Margarita is deceased and therefore absent from the play, her life is reconstructed from the objective mode of the documentarian. The choice to research Margarita's life rather than to perform a daughter's memories of her mother is a powerful vision of the "'other' psychic, social and cultural geographies of the maternal," as Aston says, "rather than the mother that is taken, mistaken, for 'our' (selfish) own" (2007: 140). With *Montserrat*, on the other hand, it is the child's selfishness that is displayed. The detective adventure Rodríguez leads his audience on is invented; the documentary evidence he supplies is falsified; and much of the text comes from fictional literary sources. The subtle revelation at the play's conclusion of this fact, that the discovery of Montserrat's secret life is an invention, demonstrates that the mother we imagine is a completely separate figure from the woman who is our mother.

In the case of Vivi Tellas' staging of real mothers and daughters, including herself and her own mother and aunt, the hierarchical family order of generations is thrown into disarray. The child invents the mother in *Mi mamá y mi tía*, while the mother begets a child on the force of sheer desire in *La bruja y su hija*. In Lola Arias' work, *Mi vida después*, the idea of mother as vessel is undone and replaced with a mother who is also a daughter, who will take the place of her father. Finally, in Lagartijas Tiradas al Sol's works, the mother is absent and therefore unknowable as a maternal figure. *El rumor del incendio* presents Margarita Urías Hermosillo as first a daughter, a revolutionary, a sister, a prisoner, and a student. Her motherhood is an epilogue to her life story. In *Montserrat* the mother as a figment of her child's desire is shown to be a myth.

In each of the works briefly described here, the figure of the mother is represented onstage in the guise of reality. Through the use of documentary evidence and extratheatrical materials, every play insists that what is being staged is real. The implications of this position are that the audience must think critically about the theatre in general. The space of the spectator is no longer one of entertainment or passivity. Because audiences must grapple with the dramatized content in the context of the real world, the implications of the feminist proposal each play presents with respect to the mother also exist beyond the dark space of the theatre. Spectators may feel encouraged to reflect on or research their mothers' lives, considering them as subjects beyond their own selfish and childish needs. Women who are mothers, and those who are not, may feel encouraged by the possibility of being considered as independent agents beyond their maternal condition, whether potential or realized. This important shift in Latin American theatre offers an alternative way of thinking about motherhood as one among many possible—though not necessary—roles for a person to take on.

Though the representation of motherhood has not been considered a common feature of Latin American theatre of the real, a focus on plays that do stage "real" mothers reveals a coherent feminist proposal to consider women beyond maternity, and mothers as subjects. The theatrical staging of mothers reveals family relationships like motherhood and daughterhood as performances. At the same time, the insistence on the reality of the plays' contents reveals that this complex way of understanding women can—and should—have corresponding effects outside of the theatre. Work remains to be done to carry out this proposal in society. Whether by increasing access to safe birth control and abortions, allowing for women to choose motherhood or not; respecting the decisions of trans men and women to become mothers or not; and increasing gender equality in the workplace, the political sphere, and in the home—these are the outcomes that the works of Tellas, Arias, Lagartijas Tiradas al Sol and others imagine. It is up to the audience to make it so.

Notes

1 Bamford and Rabillard cite "the medium of representation, the performer's body, [which] allows for complex interrogations of concepts of maternity" and "the dialogic structure of the dramatic text as well as the interplay of actor with actor, and players with audience, [which] suggest that drama provides a stage where playwrights can take up Cavarero's invitation to see who mothers are, and in relation to whom" (2016: 134).

2 For a detailed description of the experience of seeing the play, see Sosa (2004). For a reading of Jewish themes in *Mi mamá y mi tía* see Ansaldo. For an overview of the *Archivos* and their productive tension between biography and autobiography see Brownell (2012).

3 Pamela Brownell explains that Tellas herself provides the perspective that provokes the confession, while the viewing public gives meaning to the entire performance (2013: 780).

4 Many critics have examined *Mi vida después* through the lens of Hirsch's postmemory, as Mariana Eva Pérez (2013) points out. Paola Hernández (2011) likens the play's narrative connections between personal and national history to the mediated, imagined memories of those generations that come after a collective trauma, which Hirsch posits (2012: 123). Brenda Werth, meanwhile, points out how the play's emphasis on the past also emphasizes its relationship to the present and future (2010: 193–94). Cecilia Sosa argues that rather than frame the performers' generation as victims, the play offers a potential "for producing an alternative future" (2014: 113), as I show in the example of Carla Crespo here.

5 CARLA. Yo nunca conocí a mi padre. Él murió a los veintiséis años, cuatro meses antes de que yo naciera. Cuando yo cumplí los veintisiete pensé: "ahora soy más vieja que mi padre, ahora voy a vivir lo que él no pudo vivir, voy a ser su vida futura." (Arias 2009: 37)

6 In a 2012 interview, Crespo affirms that her pregnancy changed her relationship with the play, then in its fourth year:

¿Y esas cosas que cambiaron en sus vidas cómo las fueron introduciendo en la obra? ¿Fue igual de difícil que al comienzo o lo sintieron más natural?

Carla: Fue más natural porque ya sabíamos que la obra lo requería. Y a la vez, en mi caso, la confirmación del lugar donde está enterrado mi viejo me renovó la conexión con ese

material. Como ahora mi embarazo renueva un poco la conexión más perturbadora que para
mí tenía en un principio la carta. Van apareciendo elementos que te hacen reconectar con el
material.

(Casullo et al. 2011: n.p.)

7 I analyze the use of auto/biography and documentary modes in the play in "Staging Postmemory"
(Ward 2014).
8 I examine the use of documentary to present fiction in *Montserrat* in "Suspect Texts" (Ward 2017).

Works cited

Ansaldo, Paula. "Temáticas judías en dos biodramas de Vivi Tellas: a propósito de Mi mamá y mi tía (2003) y
Rabbi Rabino (2011)." *Karpa* 7 (2014): n. pag. http://www.calstatela.edu/misc/karpa/Karpa7/Site%20
Folder/ansaldo1.html.
Arias, Lola. *Mi vida después (My Life after)*. Translated Ivana Gamarnik and Andrew Haley. Buenos Aires: Lola
Arias, 2009.
Aston, Elaine. "A Critical Step to the Side: Performing the Loss of the Mother." *Theatre Research International*
32.2 (2007): 130–42.
Bamford, Karen, and Sheila Rabillard. "Introduction to Part II: Special Section. Rethinking the Maternal."
Theatre History Studies 35 (2016): 125–42.
Brownell, Pamela. "La escenificación de una mirada y el testimonio de los cuerpos en el teatro documental
de Vivi Tellas." *Revista Brasileira de Estudos da Presença* 3.3 (2013): 770–88.
Brownell, Pamela. "*Proyecto Archivos*: El teatro documental según Vivi Tellas." *E-misférica* 9.1–2 (2012): n.p.
Casullo, Liza, Carla Crespo, and Vanina Falco. "Mi vida después." Interview by Diego Sánchez and Federico
Scigliano. *Ni a Palos*. 2 October 2012. Accessed 25 July 2017.
Hernández, Paola. "Biografías escénicas: *Mi vida después* de Lola Arias." *Latin American Theatre Review* 45.1
(2011): 115–28.
Hirsch, Marianne. *The Generation of Postmemory*. New York: Columbia University Press, 2012.
Hirsch, Marianne. *The Mother/Daughter Plot: Narrative, Psychoanalysis, Feminism*. Bloomington and
Indianapolis, IN: Indiana University Press, 1989.
Kristeva, Julia. *The Portable Kristeva*. Updated Edition. Ed. Kelly Oliver. New York: Columbia University
Press, 2002.
Martin, Carol. "Theatre of the Real." *Studies in International Performance*. Eds. Janelle Reinelt and Brian
Singleton. New York: Palgrave Macmillan, 2013.
Martin, Carol. "The Use of Media in Documentary." *Get Real: Documentary Theatre Past and Present*.
Performance Interventions. Eds. Alison Forsyth and Chris Megson. Basingstoke, UK: Palgrave
Macmillan, 2011.
Milleret, Margo. *Latin American Women on/in Stages*. SUNY Series in Latin American and Iberian Thought
and Culture. Eds. Jorge J. E. Gracia and Rosemary Geisdorfer Feal. Albany, NY: State University of New
York Press, 2004.
Pérez, Mariana Eva. "*Their Lives After*: Theatre as Testimony and the So-Called 'Second Generation' in
Post-Dictatorship Argentina." *Journal of Romance Studies* 13.3 (2013): 6–16.
Sedgwick, Eve Kosofsky. *Touching Feeling: Affect, Pedagogy, Performativity*. Durham, NC, and London: Duke
University Press, 2003.
Sosa, Cecilia. "The Attire of (Post-)Memory: *Mi vida después*." *Queering Acts of Mourning in the Aftermath of
Argentina's Dictatorship. The Performances of Blood*. Suffolk, UK: Boydell & Brewer, 2014. 105–28.
Sosa, Cecilia. "Cuéntame Tu Vida." *Página* 12 October 17, 2004: sec. Radar.
Stone, Alison. "Against Matricide: Rethinking Subjectivity and the Maternal Body." *Hypatia* 27.1 (2012):
118–38.
Tellas, Vivi. *La bruja y su hija*. 2012. Video by Pamela Brownell.
Tellas, Vivi. *Mi mamá y mi tía*. 2003. Video by Pamela Brownell.
Tellas, Vivi. "Proyecto Archivos." www.archivotellas.com.ar/ 2010. Accessed 12 February 2016.
Trigo, Benigno. "Remembering Maternal Bodies: Melancholy in Latina and Latin American Women's
Writing." *New Concepts in Latino American Cultures*. Eds. Licia Fiol-Matta and José Quiroga. New York:
Palgrave Macmillan, 2006.

Ward, Julie Ann. "Staging Postmemory: Self-Representation and Parental Biographying in Lagartijas Tiradas Al Sol's *El rumor del incendio.* " *Latin American Theatre Review* 47.2 (2014): 25–43.

Ward, Julie Ann. "Suspect Texts: The Mexican Documentary Theatre Tradition, 1968–2013." *Theatre Journal* 69.2 (2017): 197–211.

Werth, Brenda. "Intergenerational Memory and Performative Acts of Recovery." *Theatre, Performance, and Memory Politics in Argentina.* New York and Basingstoke: Palgrave Macmillan, 2010. 173–96.

33

CAN *SARAUS* SPEAK TO GENDER AND MIGRANT POLITICS IN SÃO PAULO?

Derek Pardue

Journalist and political activist living in São Paulo since 2012, Christo Kamanda, asserts in an oral presentation to Brazilian journalists: "The Congolese woman's body has become a primary war zone in the conflict that rages on in Congo (DRC), my home country." He does so to reflect on the atrocities occurring in his native country due to the exploitation of cobalt, used primarily in the manufacturing of lithium batteries. A transgression of bodies. Militarized violence. Rape. These transgressions are stark points of gender definition and individual awareness of masculinity and femininity. A recognition through trauma. The *sarau*, a type of open microphone event, amplifies the individual to the collective and demands the legitimacy of personal experience.

Displacement, violence, bodies, storytelling, time, place and audience expectations are often part of representation when African immigrants step on stage in São Paulo, Brazil. The push and pull of employment and geo-politics produce a precarity that situates immigrants in São Paulo in a complex web of dependency on others for recognition. The seemingly stark differences between roots and routes dissipate and one realizes that a brief insight into the lives of immigrants potentially allows for a sustained reflection on the spatiality of identity.

In this chapter, I describe and interpret two saraus that highlight recent immigration, Sarau dos Imigrantes (immigrant sarau) and Sarau dos Refugiados (refugee sarau). I have chosen two performances in particular, an acapella presentation by a Congolese male trio and a poem recital by a Haitian man. In both cases, there is an attempt to approximate immigrant and Brazilian populations. I selectively apply theories from feminist geography and cultural studies to address the following questions: how do we identify with place through cultural performance and, in a complementary fashion, what do such expressions tell us about local dynamics of race, gender and nativism? Before discussing the particularities of these two saraus I contextualize briefly the topic in terms of cultural politics in São Paulo as well as review critically the scholarship on saraus in Brazil and recent immigration to the country.

Context

This chapter investigates a convergence, and it should be noted that its occurrence continues to be rare. Recent African and Haitian immigrants and Brazilian sarau participants do not meet often. Since saraus focus on rhetorical performance, language is an obstacle for most immigrants to participate effectively. However, as immigrants gain linguistic and cultural fluency and saraus exercise greater flexibility in structural formats, immigrant/sarau crossovers have increased.

Saraus are distinct in that they represent one of the few venues of cultural performance where immigrants can reach directly "popular" audiences, in the Latin American sense of the term "el pueblo" or "o povo," meaning "of the people." Saraus, thus, produce a cultural geography that includes the struggling, marginalized poet and excludes the outsider to Brazilian ways of conviviality. The sarau is then both an antithesis and ally, hostile and complementary to the stranger. Ultimately, I suggest that this contradictory relationship between periphery, popular saraus and African immigration remains unresolved and exists as a challenge for meaningful intercultural dialogue, especially with regard to race and gender. Given the empirical circumstances mentioned above, my conclusions are particularly provisional.

I base this chapter on notes and reflections from previous fieldwork conducted on saraus in 2010 and 2014 in addition to nine months of fieldwork in 2016 and 2017 focused on new immigration presence and activities in the city of São Paulo. I conducted semi-structured interviews with performers, event organizers, members of local NGOs and activist organizations dedicated to immigrant politics in the city. In addition, beyond attending the saraus themselves, I participated in two public events as part of the series "Brechas Urbanas," loosely translated as City Cracks. The connotation refers to the gaps in the urban landscape that require exploration, debate and, ideally, rearticulation in order to construct a more just, inclusive and progressive São Paulo. The Brazilian Bank corporation Itaú sponsored these events throughout 2017 via its cultural wing, Instituto Cultural Itaú. I conducted a brief subsequent interview with one black feminist urban planner after a particularly provocative debate on the gendering of São Paulo in June of 2017.

Background

Since 2010 Brazil has reemerged as a destination for migrants and refugees. The major populations include individuals and families from Haiti, Syria, Colombia, Venezuela, Bolivia and a host of West African countries including Senegal, Democratic Republic of Congo, Mali, Nigeria and Angola. The diversity and intensity of this migration boom is most visible in Brazil's largest city of São Paulo.[1] Numerically, this uptick of migrants is minuscule compared to that of the United States, Germany or, of course, Lebanon or Turkey.[2] Despite the overall small expression of immigration in the Brazilian body politic, it is difficult not to notice a new black presence in certain areas of the city, such as São Paulo's commercial downtown areas even with its intense human traffic and sprawling, improvised architecture-scapes.

During the same period the sarau has become increasingly the dominant venue for urban periphery cultural performance in São Paulo. What differentiates the sarau from previous urban pop is its relatively democratic and open inclusion across normally rigid boundaries of gender, sexuality and age (Coughi and Mouammar 2014; Oliveira 2016; Silva 2012; Smith 2015). For its part, migration of so-called "Africanos", a racialized category including Haitians, has been understood primarily in gendered terms of masculine and feminine spaces of employment and cultural expression (Mejía and Cazarotti 2017).

Broadly speaking, this chapter contributes to an understanding of the city in terms of cultural politics. While I focus my interpretations on the first part of this concept, i.e., "the cultural," it is essential to understand the political milieu of the city at the time of composing this text. After roughly a decade of relatively progressive politics at the national level throughout Latin America, especially in the Southern Cone, the traditional large land-owning elite along with upstart evangelical social conservative entrepreneurs have struck back. This right-wing whiplash has taken place also at the municipal level. São Paulo has been a conservative city since the 1980s and the so-called *abertura,* the period of transition away from a military dictatorship to a representational democracy with formalized political parties (Boito 2016).

Few left-leaning politicians have been able to penetrate the mayor's office and those who have succeeded were quickly brushed aside after one term. Fernando Haddad, a former economics professor and Secretary of Education, was no exception. However, his embrace of urban sustainability, squatter rights, immigrants and refugees, sexual diversity and identity politics, in general, deserves mention. In particular, Haddad's administration was a pioneer in establishing governmental agencies specifically directed towards immigrants in terms of documentation, initial housing (approximately six months) and expedited basic health insurance coverage. In addition, Haddad provided more autonomy and financial backing to public policy for women and racial equality. *Políticas para mulheres* and *políticas para igualdade racial* became full-fledged "secretarias" with their own budgets. This translated into heightened visibility through a series of public events, campaigns, hearings, debates and artistic exhibits.

Despite all of its conservative history, São Paulo became more than just the home of the largest gay pride parade in the world. The city entered in real dialogue with the diverse populations that have always inhabited the area. The difference is that under Haddad the interface between diverse identities and urban material became much more productive and expanded beyond just a relationship of conflict, rebellion and oppression. Any minimally sentient person can observe a vibrant, confidence of people simply being themselves, as one walks through downtown areas, the financial and cultural districts of Paulista Avenue, Jardins and Faria Lima as well as the sprawling periphery areas of Campo Limpo, Jardim Ângela and Capão Redondo, the birthplace of marginal literature and the sarau movement.

The widespread popularity of saraus since 2012 is, in part, a manifestation of a cultural opening facilitated by a visionary mayor. He, too, was ousted in late 2016 through the election of a candidate who has made it clear that São Paulo must wipe the slate clean and return to a fast-paced platform of wild speculation and violent hygenization (Melo 2017). The timid but visible advances of critical feminism, for example, as they relate to not only diversity in identification but also right and use of the city, are currently under attack.

Clearing space: Saraus in Brazil

"The sarau is for who doesn't exist, not for who exists".[3] With these words, Sérgio Vaz, the founder of *Cooperifa* (Cooperative for Culture of the Periphery), and one of the leading voices of the sarau community, established a motto and ideological base for the contemporary open microphone, grassroots movement led by the disenfranchised in urban Brazil. Vaz used this phrase several times in a workshop I attended in 2010 with the implication that it had already become a stock phrase: a simple opening salve for those unaware that the sarau is a critical performance targeting issues of social status and rights to the city.

I was reminded of Vaz's catch phrase during a recent public debate under the auspices of the "Brechas Urbanas" event mentioned in the introduction. Joice Berth, an Afro-Brazilian urban planner and invited guest, remarked that, indeed, cities are gendered, but to conceptualize the city in this manner one must understand gender as performance. Likewise, buildings, public parks and so on are as discursive as they are material iterations. Directing her comments to São Paulo, she described the city as predominantly masculinist, structures intended as unyielding and supposedly certain in their function and meaning. Berth highlighted a few hopeful spaces, such as the MASP (Modern Art Museum of São Paulo), which, in its very structure, allows dynamic gatherings that are potentially diverse and thus representative of the city's inhabitants.[4]

Can saraus *speak to gender and migrant politics in São Paulo?*

Saraus are not only attempts to transform literature and society ideologically by bringing otherwise marginalized communities to the center of attention but also a project to transform the city spatially. The simple message that women, for example, who normally "do not exist", are recognized as poets, activists, artists, is loud and clear at any sarau. They, in effect, normalize the legitimacy of female occupation of public space and stretch the conventions of spatial expectations. In short, saraus play a role in gendering the city of São Paulo.[5] And, while saraus do not act as an "equalizer" in empirical terms for women artists and activists, they are most certainly an important venue for feminist affirmation and basic expressions that link identity politics to social movements (Franchini and França 2011).

The *sarau* as a poetic, and at times political, speech genre has a history in Brazil, which reveals important markers of nation-building and socio-economic class by distinctively connecting speakers and texts to Western Europe and bourgeoisie notions of culture and art (Medeiros 2002). It has frequently represented tension, a dissonant note of critique, which in its current iteration has become a fundamental component of its existence. The contemporary sarau runs through the urban peripheries gathering growing numbers of practitioners and greater attention from state agencies of culture and education. As Nascimento (2006, 2009), Silva (2011) and Tennina (2013) demonstrate, the saraus have been essential in the expansion of so-called "marginal literature" in that they give visibility and foster increased publication, practice and consumption of literature produced *in* and *by* the working-class urban periphery.

However, while academic and activist communities have been quick to discuss the ideological significance of the contemporary sarau in terms of empowerment and literary importance, little has been said about the spatial contours of the movement. Saraus offer an insightful case study towards a more general theory of cities, which highlights spatiality, intended here as a set of social practices that involve the existential knowledge and social networking gained from mobility, rather than a conventional notion of networks based on static indices of geography and cultural presence.

The work of dozens of sarau activists,[6] as well as scholars like Nascimento (2014), Silva and Tennina (2011), Pardue (2012, 2014), Ingrid Hapke (2012) and Christen Smith (2015), demonstrate cross-culturally that poetry contributes to individual and collective desire for change. Recently, Leonora Souza Paula (2016) analyzed the ways in which the movement of marginal literature and saraus renders a social vision of the world in which the periphery is understood and represented no longer as a stigmatized culturally impoverished space, but as a legitimate site of enunciation for representing locally lived experiences. In this sense, saraus seem to stoke the drive to survive this world and imagine another one, what the inspiring US black, feminist, lesbian writer Audre Lorde (1985: 36) once articulated as "what we [black women] feel within and dare make real."

As I have argued elsewhere (Pardue and Amaral, forthcoming), the empowering rhetoric of local actors and social movements complement that of urban theorists and cultural geographers. The geography of city is essentially social. Saraus demonstrate one set of working-class, subaltern, migrant identifications, which has emerged not simply through local community empowerment but also through circuits, social relations and mobility.

Immigration and cultural representation

The increase in relocation in São Paulo is not a new migatory trend, but one that follows generations of intense African slave trade[7] and later Southern European and East Asian migration (Lesser 2013). During the Portuguese colonial period (1500–1822) and the subsequent monarchy (1822–1889), Brazil was the most popular destination for African slaves in the Americas. São Paulo's recent rise in immigration is due initially to growing economic opportunities throughout Brazil and favorable foreign political relations (Cowie 2014) established during the first decade of the 21st century. The documentation process is relatively quick and cheap, and in São Paulo there is a growing infrastructure of institutional support.[8] São Paulo's pull factors combine with a series of push factors, ranging from violent wars (Congo, Nigeria, Syria) to political turmoil (Angola) to natural disasters (Haiti) to widespread economic downturns (Senegal and most of West Africa).

The increased visibility of immigrants in the city, especially new "Africans" including Haitians, has not only turned the heads of self-assuming "native" *Paulistanos* (residents born in São Paulo) but also gained the attention of Brazilian researchers and pools of current graduate students in the social sciences and humanities. Scholars have published scores of reports on a number of essential characteristics and political debates concerning the new wave of immigration to Brazil. These include: immigration and kinship practices (Machado 2011; Mejía and Cazarotto 2017), labor and remittance strategies (Magalhães and Baeninger 2016), cultural comparisons of immigration law (Machado 2012), religiosity and diaspora (Coutinho and Marcelino 2016; Gallo 2011), as well as attempts to explain levels of integration via language acquisition (Soares, Trevisan and Flain 2017). A common thread in this scholarship, albeit implicit, is that migrancy is a complex epistemology and, as such, elements such as language and kinship are not simply about communication and social ties but carry qualitative dimensions of identification. The level of Portuguese proficiency, for example, effects a Haitian's capacity to imagine, recognize and identify with Brazilian styles or ways of being through extra-linguistic forms such as music and cinema.

Inspired by a growing number and heightened visibility of activist immigrants,[9] issues such as racism, xenophobia and gender oppression are gaining traction in public and academic spheres. Such identity issues are experienced spatially; they shape and are significantly influenced by location. I seek to extend the descriptive analysis of migrant spaces and mobility into a comprehensive theory of identification. Scholars such as Rosana Baeninger (2013, 2016) and Bela Feldman (2009, 2016) have given critical attention to the precarious migration trajectories many Africans and Haitians (as well as Bolivians and Colombians) have used to arrive in southern Brazilian cities for employment and family reunification. The common trajectory of, for example, Haiti, Panama, Ecuador, Peru, and then crossing the Brazilian border at Assis Brasil in the state of Acre, on to Brasileia, utilized from 2011 to 2014 by tens of thousands of Haitians, obliges migrants to navigate a series of recruitment camps and "coyote" extortionists. Along the way and during the long periods of waiting for documentation, migrants have reported a number of incidents of racism, physical violence and rape.

For some Africans, these experiences were unexpected and resulted in a racial consciousness, which they then cultivated and incorporated in cultural performances in São Paulo. It is clear that immigrants from Haiti and Islamic francophone Africa experience culture shock and certain tensions in values. To process such encounters takes time and requires venues for expression. While a number of NGOs have organized festivals, fairs, language classes and other cultural events in the name of integration and understanding, the sarau potentially offers a more meaningful opportunity to co-create urban space with Brazilians and contribute to the production of contemporary São Paulo. The sarau thus potentially stands alongside the relatively autonomously managed commercial, residential and religious spaces as part of a new black, immigrant presence.

The saraus: Immigrants and refugees

In June of 2017 the Congolese group "Os Escolhidos" (The Chosen Ones) took the stage and seemed unprepared, wandering around as if looking for a key to unlock the microphones in

Can saraus *speak to gender and migrant politics in São Paulo?*

front of them. Suddenly, the three young men looked forward into the audience and locked into a tight three-part harmony.

The individual singers exchanged melodic leads seamlessly: "These are simple songs. They are about cultivating crops in the fields. We grew up with these songs. Our fathers and uncles passed them down to us. There are hundreds of them. They are a small piece of everyday life from rural Congo that we present here in this big city. We just enjoy singing them when we can." The flow, pitch range and overall melismatic contours reminded me, as an American (as well as many of the Brazilians in the audience), of gospel music from the black, Southern Baptist traditions in the US. When asked about this possible influence or dialogue between the two musical styles, Leon, the singer smiled, respectfully deflected my question and repeated that this was a simple Congolese tradition.

Later, in a follow-up interview we discussed the predominance of Congolese men in the various kinds of political and cultural events in São Paulo. Having passed through Angola on his way to the Americas, member Apolinário was more fluent in Portuguese and affirmed that such absence is a cultural issue. For the most part, he explained, Congolese women make their presence felt at home, in spaces of child-rearing and religion.

In early 2017 Irajá, a middle-aged white Brazilian man, music educator and former live musician in São Paulo alternative rock scene of the 1980s, and two friends saw Yannick Delass, a talented, charismatic Congolese singer and musician perform at an event hosted by Visto Permanente, a local organization that promotes films, music and art by immigrants. They were so impressed with Yannick's performance that they began to brainstorm about the idea of promoting such musical talent. Celso, a member of the organizational trio, explained that his interest stemmed from previous experience mapping German immigration and resettlement in the state of São Paulo. Over the past several years he and neighborhood community leaders in Brooklin, a middle-class district located in between two nouveau riche areas of Moema and Avenida Berrini, have organized a version of Oktoberfest[10] inviting families and artists from the German diaspora to come to the big city and show their stuff.

Saraus, understood as both spatial and political interventions, recast or resignify spaces into new places of meaning. In the urban periphery the corner bar becomes a library and bookstore. In the case of Sarau dos Imigrantes, Roosevelt Plaza (Praça Roosevelt), a public, centrally located plaza, is a multi-faceted field of symbols and expressive culture. The sarau takes place alongside dozens of skateboarders and hipster theater crowds and in its first months of existence has transformed the plaza into a point of immigrant emplacement. The project has taken off and the city government invited the sarau to participate in the Virada Cultural, a massive 24-hour cultural event held in São Paulo with live acts providing free shows in various locales in the city. In addition, they received an invitation to hold weekly events in more than 40 public libraries scattered across the city from June until October of 2017.

There is no doubt that the Sarau dos Imigrantes' expansions has facilitated cultural occupations of various parts of the city. Based on event observation and semi-structured interviews with performers and sarau organizers, questions, however, still remain regarding agency on several levels. Many well-intentioned Brazilians continue to misrecognize some immigrants' terse attitude as personal, when, in fact, the issue is "ownership" of event. Many immigrants seek control. Moreover, the categorization of the sarau is itself a point of debate among those in the already existing sarau circuit. Irajá explained to me that he simply wanted to convey a level of informality with the label "sarau" and that, pragmatically speaking, the artists are invited. It is not an "open" microphone affair in this sense. The mode of presentation is strictly music and there is little opportunity for immigrants to tell a story, scream a manifesto, or reflect on any experiences other than via music. The result, while often pleasing to the ear and provocative to the audience who are unaccustomed to many of the musical traditions performed, is dangerously close to an orientalist exposition. It is then not surprising that performers, such as the Chosen Ones, would perform a relatively traditionalist masculinity on stage. The few women who have participated in the sarau, such as the white Angolan Jessica Areias, tend to identify as part of global culture, in which femininity is conciliatory rather than critical. I develop these initial comments further at the end of the text.

Sarau dos Refugiados

A section of Haitian poet and author Marc Pierre's poem "'A Nagô dream…" reads: In an unhemmed dress, I hear the individual drops of a light rain,/ Hand-in-hand with early morning/ The earth's aroma offers a serenade,/A breath of the divine ancestry/ Paints our chests, our walls with the song of freedom/ *Batucadas*, life and dance!

The poem signifies a continual activity towards freedom. "Nagô," a term referring to Yoruba-speaking West Africans from the "Slave Coast" including Nigeria, Togo and Benin, loosely used here, stands in for Africanity. Curiously, he uses the figure of the dress (*saia*), as an endless (unhemmed), mysterious reality. The dress is the setting of the dream. According to his own reflections, the dress is also a symbol for women and femininity, apparently an unknown but grounded entity, which is ultimately necessary for the impending revolution. Freedom is as inevitable as the rain that ushers in a new day.

Marc Pierre is a charmer, a 21st century dandy, who draws attention from young men and women, intellectuals and local politicians. He often dons a stylish beret complemented by a light scarf. Marc Pierre is remarkably articulate in Portuguese and displays a visible charisma when speaking in Kreyol and French. Observing from the side, I watch Marc Pierre manage his time giving focused attention to his girlfriend, a light-skinned Afro-Brazilian, paying his dues to event organizers as they pass by and assuring that he is noticed by all.

After a recent sarau I took advantage of a rare opportunity when Marc Pierre was alone and we discussed his poem recitation. Despite (or perhaps due to) the burdensome stigma, environmental tragedies and political-economic isolation of Haiti, most Haitians possess a pride of distinction. Such strong sentiment of belonging is not at odds with the existential condition of diaspora. As Joseph Handerson has described, the term "diaspora" is both quotidian and identifying, to the point that individuals are addressed as "hey, y'all, diaspora has arrived" (see Handerson 2015: 56). For Marc Pierre and other Haitians, this distinction emerges from a paradoxical national historicity, a sentiment that sees Haitian history as one of unprecedented black liberation and of isolation from "Latin America," from the Caribbean and from "civilization" (Trouillot 1995). Marc Pierre uses the sarau to profess the importance of Haiti in the global history of black struggle. Particularities arise in the magical properties of gourds, the moringa plant and the Haitian readers of such signs to look into the future and see the entire trajectory of the Nagô dream. In interview, he summarized the poem this way "Haiti, just as individuals like me in a sarau, are voices. We are *tambores* (percussive instruments) that speak. This poem is about the ongoing struggle to speak. That is liberation."

Marc Pierre moves audiences. His reflections on his words are profound and, yet he has remarkably little to say about the curious use of the dress and the gendered division of labor or women's significance in the Nagô dream of liberation. When asked about a more empirical question, the unequal balance of men and women on stage in the refugee saraus, Marc Pierre's response was conventional. Echoing the "Chosen Ones," he gave initially the response that there are simply more Haitian men in the diaspora. As Mejía and Simon (2015) among other scholars have discussed, one of the main reasons that there are more Haitian men in Brazil (and the diaspora overall) is the gendered dynamic of the Haitian family, which includes polygamy or the normalization of polyamorous relationships. My conversation with Marc Pierre quickly came to a close, as he referred me to a Colombian woman activist and sifted back into the crowd.

The "refugee sarau" differs from the "immigrant sarau" in one significant way. The former is more diverse including poetry, theater and music. Moreover, the refugees ranging from Haiti,[11] Syria, Colombia, Angola and the DRC have more control over the presentation and organization of the event. The similarities are also important as one begins to parse the ethnographic data and return to the intersecting issues of agency, identification and place. In both cases, there is a state subsidy. This is more plain and transparent in the refugee sarau, as SESC (Social Service of State Commerce), an agency of the state of São Paulo, offers its infrastructure and statewide network to the group of performers.

As mentioned above, a recurrent theme in conversation with immigrants, and one that plays a role in both saraus, is dependence / autonomy. Whether the topic is housing, employment or cultural activities, immigrants often depend on Brazilians, either as individuals, NGOs or state agencies, to get anything done (Pardue 2017). Pitchou Luamba, lawyer, activist and entrepreneur, recognizes this dependence and has attempted to transform it into an opportunity. "I see the DRC and Brazil in the following way. I am here, my public is mostly Brazilian. Other Congolese and other immigrants are not my clients; they are potential collaborators. I am not selling to them. So, I need to bridge the gap. I depend on Brazilians but I use this to make new culinary creations. A mix between the DRC and Brazilian tastes." While in the realm of food, such "crossover" elements consist of certain ingredients and manners of presentation, in the world of music, theater and other expressive culture, immigrant artists deploy globally recognized images, such as cel phones, and ideologies, such as racism, to convey, for example, the urgency of the violence in the DRC to a generally uninformed audience.

Ethnomusicologist Rose Hikiji has argued that immigrant actors, like Congolese performance artist Shambuyi Wetu, have been effective in cultivating a following by creating "chimeras", i.e., signs that simultaneously signify multiple connotations (Chalcraft, Segarra and Hikiji 2017). For example, Wetu's literal pasting of bloodied cellular phones on his costume convey the banal globalization of communication technologies and the localized violence in Congo linked to the control of cobalt mines. Returning to Marc Pierre's use of the dress within the early morning rain scene, one might follow the chimera of ongoing black struggle and tempestuous weather, nature and rooted accoutrements, and one can appreciate the contestation of agency and its implied connections to mundane objects and everyday places. Yet, one might also wonder what sorts of limitations are operating in these performances.

Immigrant and refugee saraus as a promising but precarious convergence

"Despite all this concrete, the city is really a pile of mud." Maitê Schneider, a popular transsexual activist and successful cultural entrepreneur, captured the spirit of the "City Cracks" (Brechas Urbanas) event perfectly. Her articulate reflections show that the city is a place to mold and, in so doing, inhabitants make themselves. With this in mind, I conclude this preliminary exploration into a new convergence of cultural politics and demographic realities in São Paulo. In the present climate, an ongoing development resulting from a "judicial coup" that seeks to reverse any real democratic gains of the last 15 years, there is both an undercurrent of fear and a burning desire to speak in Brazil. As feminist and cultural critics, in general, have rightly intervened, who can speak, in the name of resistance and transformation, is always a gendered question.

The significance of the sarau encounter is more than an opportunity for artists to exchange ideas, beats and stories. It forces participants and observers to recognize the relationship between performance, occupation and legitimacy. Moreover, the ongoing attempts by Sarau dos Imigrantes and Sarau dos Refugiados to bring together heretofore separate publics of periphery saraus and wary immigrant performers addresses the ever-increasing debate regarding migration, identification and the city. In my provisional analysis of the current scene in São Paulo I suggest that scholars and activists interested in migration should pay attention to regularly scheduled cultural events, such as the sarau, not only to appreciate the spectacle of cultural performance but also to gauge the potential of black feminist interventions into urban geography.

Of course, black feminism does not simply refer to quantitative evidence. More black African and Haitian women on stage will not necessarily result in the kind of critical intersectionality required in São Paulo and desired by many of its politically conscious inhabitants. The fact is that many immigrants in São Paulo understand that one's gender is a determining factor in physical violence in Brazil, ranked fifth in the world in femicide. There are tens of thousands of Brazilians and immigrant activists, who occupy city space and speak in one way or another to these issues.

Saraus have been very successful in creating a venue for progressive articulations on gender and class, race and class and general empowerment for those "who don't exist." However, the link to migrancy and "strangers" is currently missing. The two saraus discussed in this chapter ultimately do not bridge the gap and continue to exist as conciliatory, cultural expositions. Part of the reason for this is their structure. While I do not advocate an orthodox approach to cultural semantics, in this case with regard to "sarau," I do think that the lack of spontaneity, openness and dialogue with established saraus in the São Paulo periphery, have limited the efficacy of the "immigrant" and "refugee" saraus. While such saraus organizers may not be aware of or are not interested in the fact that a peripherization of immigrant demographics has taken place over the past couple of years, this change is crucial to recognize, if one is interested in immigrant empowerment. Expressive culture, such as spoken word, music and street theater, can cultivate a decolonialization of race, gender and belonging, but only if organizers adopt a critical, feminist geography.

Notes

1 São Paulo is the most populous city in the Southern Hemisphere and has been also the primary destination for Southern European, East Asian, especially Japanese, and Middle Eastern migration since the late 19th century. According to the Federal Police, the responsible regulatory governmental agency for immigration, from 2010 to 2015 the number of petitions for refugee status, number of immigrants officially processed, and number of African countries represented rose dramatically.

2 According to statistics from ACNUR or UNHCR (United Nations High Commission for Refugees), updated to 2016, the Brazilian State recognizes approximately 10,000 refugees, the great majority of whom are Venezuelan (33%). Of interest to this chapter, Angola (13%), the DRC (4%), Nigeria (3%), Senegal (2%) and Haiti (6%) comprise significant populations (www.acnur.org/portugues/recursos/estatisticas/dados-sobre-refugio-no-brasil/). It is important to note that the majority of Haitians are not categorized as refugees but enter Brazil via a humanitarian visa, which was put into effect shortly after the 2010 earthquake. In general, immigrants represent a relatively small percentage, approximately 1%, of the population or 2 million residents.

3 The phrase works better in Portuguese: "*O sarau é para quem não é, não para quem é.*"

4 Joice Berth and Andreia Moussab have launched a project to uncover feminist geographies and geographers in Brazil. More details, in English and Portuguese, can be found here: www.catarse.me/arquiteta-sinvisiveis

5 See Newcomb (2006), Fischer (2010), volume 10 of the journal *City and Society* (1998) dedicated to "Gendering the City," as well as Miranne and Young (2000), Doan (2010) and Parker (2011) for

394

examples of anthropologists and geographers who employ theories of presence to explain urban transformations in both identification and institutional terms.

6 For example, the volume, *Polifonias Marginais,* an important work edited by Mario Augusto M. da Silva, Lucía Tennina, Érica P. do Nascimento, and Ingrid Hapke (2015), brings together interviews with writers and activists from the marginal and black literary movements as well as *saraus* community. Collaborators include: Allan da Rosa, Alessandro Buzo, Binho, Dugueto Shabazz, Elizandra Souzam Esmeralda Ribeiro, Ferréz, Raquel Almeida, Sacolinha, Sergio Vaz, Sonia Regina Bischain and Zinho Trindade.

7 For more detailed information, consult http://slavevoyages.org/

8 Former mayor Haddad initiated almost all of this infrastructure. The journalistic platform, Migramundo, is one of the most important sources for current news with regard to immigration issues in São Paulo and in Brazil, more generally. Their reporting highlights the changes made in São Paulo since 2013. For more information, access http://migramundo.com/tag/crai/

9 Examples include Congolinaria, a vegan food business started by a Congolese activist, and MIM (Immigrant Mission), a cultural and political group started by immigrants with the objective of transforming Brazilian society into a more just place.

10 As a Southern hemisphere country, Brazil's seasons are inverted from Germany. Hence, Celso and the organization committee call the event *Maifest,* as the month of May loosely corresponds to October. Of course, in a sub-tropical climate like that of São Paulo, such climatic comparisons are somewhat arbitrary and almost meaningless.

11 In fact, Haitians do not hold refugee status in Brazil. Thousands entered the country under a special category of a "Humanitarian Visa" authorized in the months following the 2010 earthquake. Marc Pierre explained that in reality everyone in whatever distress situation who arrives in Brazil claims to be a "refugee," even though s/he knows that his/her case does not qualify. The reason for this is simply that such a claim facilitates the acquisition of some documents and protocols that allow one to establish the basics of everyday life in Brazil including employment, some types of residency, health care, etc.

Works cited

Baeninger, Rosana and Alberto Augusto Eichman Jakob. 2013. "A migração internacional na Amazônia Legal brasileira e na metrópole de São Paulo." *AGIR—Revista Interdisciplinar de Ciências Sociais e Humanas,* v. 1: 71–109.

Baeninger, Rosana and R.B. Mesquita. 2016. "Integração regional e fronteiras: Desafios para a governança das migrações internacionais na América Latina." *Revista Transporte y Territorio,* v. 14: 14.

Boito, Armando. 2016. "A crise política do neodesenvolvimentismo e a instabilidade da democracia." *Crítica Marxista,* 42: 155–163.

Buzo, Alessandro. 2010. *Hip-hop: Dentro do Movimento.* Rio de Janeiro: Aeroplano.

Chalcraft, Jasper, Josef Juan Segarra and Rose Satiko Gitirana Hikiji. 2017. "Bagagem Desfeita: A Experiência da Imigração por artistas Congoleses." *GIS (Gesto, Imagem e Som),* 2(1): 302–308.

Coutinho, Suzana Ramos and Bernadete Alves de Medeiros Marcelino. 2016. "Migração, religião e políticas públicas: o caso dos haitianos." *Reflexão* 41(2): 225–233.

Cowie, Sam. 2014. "Brazil: Destination of choice for Africans." *Aljazeera* www.aljazeera.com/indepth/features/2014/09/brazil-destination-choice-africans-201493113721757775.html. Accessed March 1, 2016.

Cuoghi, Mariana Campeti and Christiane Carrijo Eckhardt Mouammar. 2014. "Atendimento psicoterapêutico para crianças vítimas de violência sexual: projeto Sarauzinho." *Revista Ciência em Extensão,* 10(3): 210–218.

Doan, Petra L. 2010. "The tyranny of gendered spaces: reflections from beyond the gender dichotomy." *Gender, Place and Culture,* 17: 635–654.

Feldman-Bianco, Bela. 2009. "Reinventando a Localidade: Globalização Heterogênea, Escala da Cidade e a Incorporaçao Desigual de Migrantes Transnacionais." *Horizontes Antropológicos,* v. 31: 19–50.

Feldman-Bianco, Bela, et al. 2013. "The free movement of people around the world would be Utopian: IUAES World Congress 2013: Evolving Humanity, Emerging Worlds, 5–10 August 2013." *Identities: Global Studies in Culture and Power,* 1: 1–30.

Fisher, Melissa Suzanne. 2010. "Wall Street Women: Engendering Global Finance in the Manhattan Landscape." *City and Society,* 22(2): 262–285.

Franchini, Regina and Isadora Lins França (orgs.). 2011. Dossier Feminismos Jovens. Cadernos Pagu 36.

Gallo, Fernanda Bianca Gonçalves. 2011. *Refugiados Congoleses em São Paulo: Sentidose Significados na Igreja Boa Nova Mensagem*. Master's Thesis. Federal University of Bahia, Ethnic Studies Department.

Handerson, Joseph. 2015. *As dinâmicas da mobilidade haitiana no Brasil, no Suriname e na Guiana Francesa*. Tese de doutorado. Rio de Janeiro: UFRJ/Museu Nacional.

Handerson, Joseph. 2015. "Diaspora: Sentidos sociais e mobilidades haitianas." *Horizontes Antropológicos*, 21(43): 51–78.

Hapke, Ingrid. 2012. "Literatura marginal como literatura de testimonio: más allá de lo impreso." *No-Retornable*, v. 11.

Hapke, Ingrid, et al. (orgs.). 2015. *Polifonias Marginais*. vol. 1. Rio de Janeiro: Aeroplano Editora.

Lesser, Jeffrey. 2013. *Immigration, Ethnicity and National Identity in Brazil*. New York: Cambridge University Press.

Lorde, Audre. 1985. "Poetry is Not a Luxury." In *Sister Outsider: Essays and Speeches*. Trumansburg, NY: Crossing Press.

Machado, Igor Renó. 2011. "Kinship and Differentialities: Alternatives to Identity and to Ethnic Frontiers in The Study of Migrations." *Vibrant*, 8: 220–235.

Machado, Igor Renó. 2012. "The Management of Difference: Reflections on Policies Concerning Immigration and the Control of Foreigners in Portugal and Brazil. *Vibrant*, 9: 313–332.

Magalhães, Luís Felipe Aires and Rosana Baeninger. 2016. "Imigração haitiana no Estado de Santa Catarina: Fases do fluxo e contradições da inserção laboral." *Blucher Social Sciences Proceedings*, 2(2): 219–237.

Mejía, Margarita Rosa Gaviria and Rosmari Terezina Cazarotto. 2015. "The Role of Immigrant Women in the Transnational Family which Mobilizes Haitian Migration in Brazil." *Repocs*, 14(27): 171–190.

Mejía, Margarita Rose Gaviria and R. Simon. 2015. *Sonhos que mobilizam o imigrante haitiano: biografia de Renel Simon*. Lajeado-RS: Univates.

Melo, Débora. 2017. "Crítico da 'doutrinação,' Doria distribuirá livros de Mises a escolas." Carta Capital. www.cartacapital.com.br/sociedade/critico-da-doutrinacao-doria-quer-livros-de-livre-mercado-nas-escolas. Accessed 1 July 2017.

Miranne, Kristine B. and Alma H. Young (eds.). 2000. *Gendering the City: Women, Boundaries and Visions of Urban Life*. Rowman and Littlefield Publishers.

Nascimento, Érica Peçanha do. 2006. *"Literatura marginal": os escritores da periferia entram em cena*. Dissertação de mestrado. Programa de Pós-Graduação em Antropologia Social, USP.

Nascimento, Érica Peçanha do. 2009. *Vozes Marginais na Literatura*. Rio de Janeiro: Aeroplano.

Nascimento, Érica Peçanha do. 2014. "Vozes negras e periféricas na literatura: pode o Estado amplificá-las?" In Silva, Cidinha (org.). *Africanidades e relações raciais*. Brasília: Ministério da Cultura & Fundação Palmares, 290–300.

Newcomb, Rachel. 2006. "Gendering the City, Gendering the Nation: Contesting Urban Space in Fes, Morocco." *City and Society* 18(2): 288–311.

Oliveira, Lucas Amaral. 2016. "Speaking for Themselves: Observations on a 'marginal' tradition in Brazilian Literature." *Brasiliana: Journal for Brazilian Studies*, 5: 441–471.

Pardue, Derek. 2012. "Reversal of Fortunes? São Paulo Youth Redirect Urban Development." *Tomo*, n. 21.

Pardue, Derek. 2014. "Pop Speculation: Tracing Geography, Investment, and Identity in Sao Paulo's Hip Hop and Open Mic Scenes." *Alternativas*, vol. 2, 1–23.

Pardue, Derek. 2017. "Cities as Migrant Emplacement." *Anthropology News*. April 5.

Pardue, Derek and Lucas Oliveira. Forthcoming. "City as Mobility: The Contribution of Brazilian *Saraus* to Urban Theory." *Vibrant*.

Parker, Brenda. 2011. "Material Matters: Gender and the City." *Geography Compass*, 433–447.

Paula, Leonora Souza. 2016. "Literatura Periférica: Challenging São Paulo's Cultural Segregation." *The International Journal of the Constructed Environment*, 7(2): 13–24.

Pimentel, M.L. and G.C. Cotinguiba. 2012. "Apontamentos sobre o processo de inserção social dos haitianos em Porto Velho." *Travessia*, 70: 99–106.

Silva, José Carlos Gomes da. 2012. "Juventude e periferia em cena: dramas e dramatizações da vida urbana nos saraus literários da zona sul de São Paulo." Paper presented 28 Reunião Brasileira de Antropologia.

Silva, Simone and Lucía Tennina. 2011. "Literatura Marginal de las regiones suburbanas de la Ciudad de San Pablo: el nomadismo de la voz." *Ipotesi*, Juiz de Fora, v. 15, n.2.

Smith, Christen A. 2015. "A Escrita 'Uterina Preta' de Mjiba: Elizandra Souza and the New Black Female Poets of Brazil." *Journal of Latin American Cultural Studies*, 24(3): 405–415.

Soares, Laura, Caroline Trevisan and Angela Flain. 2017. "Curso de português para imigrantes haitianos: desenvolvimento cronológico, mudanças e reflexões." *Mandinga - Revista de Estudos Linguísticos*, 1(1): 89–101.

Tennina, Lucía. 2011. "Paratextos y 'saraus' de poesia." *Darandina*, Juiz de Fora, vol. 3, n.2.

Tennina, Lucía. 2013. "Saraus das perfierias de São Paulo: poesia entre tragos, silêncios e aplausos." *Estudos de Literatura Brasileira Contemporânea*, vol. 42, 11–28.

Trouillot, Rolph. 1995. *Silencing the Past*. Boston, MA: Beacon Press.

Vez, Sérgio. 2008. *Cooperifa: Antropofagia Periférica*. Rio de Janeiro: Aeroplano.

34

TRANSFEMINISM AND FAKE MUSTACHIOS

Sayak Valencia's decolonial critique at the U.S.–Mexico border

Ignacio Corona

What is transfeminism? The concept denotes a plurality of proposals to rethink the "isms" that encompass the politics of gender, transitional identities and, clearly, the ideologies of feminism, their subject, and their conceptual boundaries. A commitment to the systematic critique and deconstruction of the binary structures that organize gender, as a "naturalized artifice,"[1] and its derived social order may be considered an element common to them. Many transfeminist theorists, however, reject a closed definition of the term and opt to focus instead on what it does, what it proposes, and how it relates to other concepts, such as feminism, queer, trans-sexual, masculinity, post-identity, intersectionality, post-porno, and trans. Its proactive character derives from an emancipatory discourse based on the decentering of the category of gender and its conceptual limits. In that sense, and narrowing on the particular case of Spanish America, the link between gender and politics, from the micropolitical level upwards, appears at the center of an interdisciplinary agenda and as the main focus for the activism and "artivism"[2] of many groups, collectives, and organizations. For the Spanish theorist Paul B. (ex-Beatriz) Preciado, transfeminism "no existe sino como un conjunto de prácticas de resistencia, desborda la denominación queer" (Grupo 2015). This has been echoed by the contributors of the critical anthology *Transfeminismos…* (Solá and Urko: 2016), for whom the concept is "a way to understand gender as a system of oppression and heterosexuality as a political regime" (Marea Negra 2016: 7).[3]

Such a critical stance combines Judith Butler's proposal to "undo restrictively normative conceptions of sexual and gendered life" (2004: 1) and Preciado's views of gender as a "living political fiction" (Tucker 2013). Alluding to Lacan's reformulation of identity as identification, for the latter transfeminism's key strategy is not "identificación sino la des-identificación" (Grupo 2015). Transfeminism is then an open invitation to deconstruct the foundations, intellectual underpinnings, and reproductive mechanisms of gender-based social oppression and patriarchal hegemony, while imagining and implementing subversive and freedom-oriented strategies at the "glocal" level. While transfeminist thinkers are reluctant to provide a closed definition of the term or even to define themselves as a unified critical movement, they do not reject systemic thinking. In that regard, the analogy between gender and political economy, and how this one organizes the social order, is an apt one for transfeminism, as gender itself is "an organizing principle of the current political economy" (Valencia 2013: 109).[4] And questioning the normativity of gender, as transfeminism does, constitutes a political act with the most profound social consequences. Clearly, no social, political, cultural, and economic aspect of society may remain uninvolved: gender underlies and connects them all.

One of the most visible figures of transfeminism in the Latin American context is the Mexican philosopher, poet and performer Sayak Valencia (Margarita Valencia Triana). Born in Tijuana, Valencia is currently a researcher at the local Colegio de la Frontera Norte, appointed to the department of cultural studies. Beyond academic and feminist circles in Mexico and Spain, her occasionally bewhiskered and bearded face probably first called the attention of a national public in the culture section of Mexico City's newspaper *El Universal*, following an academic presentation and performance at the Universidad Autónoma Metropolitana-Xochimilco in the Fall of 2011. The newspaper article published months later was not a review of her presentation *per se*. The hybrid of chronicle and biographical essay was mostly based on an interview with Valencia with the purpose of introducing a wide readership to the philosopher's "provocations" (Villegas 2012). To make visually explicit this point, the text was accompanied by a full-length portrait of Valencia leaning against a lamp post near the colonial building known as Casa de los Azulejos in Mexico City taken by Mexicali's photojournalist Grace Navarro. The philosopher wears a cocktail dress and high heels and appears to be blowing a kiss. She sports long mustachios that evoke those of fellow U.S.–Mexico border performer Guillermo Gómez Peña, of whom her critical work on gender identity, language, decolonial thinking and geopolitics might also be reminiscent. Her gesture, however, is only half-playful. It may well exemplify transfeminism's use of the ludic and humor as powerful political tools in the subversion of monolithic discourses (Sentamans 2016: 33). In fact, the semiotics of Valencia's non-verbal behavior aligns with similar interventions and signifiers of gender deconstruction in public by many queer and postfeminist activists, including the aforementioned Paul B. Preciado. For bystanders familiar with the long tradition of Mexican *performanceras*, who for decades have defied gender stereotypes and advanced a critical discourse against patriarchy through art and performance, Valencia represented a dazzling connection. Under the surface, her choice of self-presentation involved a frontal attack on the Cartesian split of mind and body that still dominates many a disciplinary practice and behavioral regime in order to connect the significant with the signified, the voice with the letter, the theory of transfeminism with its practice. It could even be considered as belying a historical tradition of transcendental philosophy or perhaps of philosophy misunderstood as a purely rational and disembodied practice. As it became evident to her surprised public at UAM, such a self-presentation also involves a visual deconstruction of the stereotype of the philosopher as an older white male to compel, in turn, a complementary imaginative operation: Marx, Nietzsche, Heidegger or Derrida in drag.

Valencia is a prolific author and her publications, including the book derived from her doctoral dissertation (*Capitalismo gore*, 2010) and awarded the 2010 Premio *Estado crítico* in Spain, in the essay category, amply surpass the impact of her "public or urban interventions." As one of the signers of the *Manifiesto por una insurrección transfeminista* (2010) collectively authored by the Red PutaBolloNegraTransFeminista, Valencia demands a radical intervention on the binomial sex/gender through diverse artistic, civil, and political actions:

> Llamamos a la insurrección, a la ocupación de las calles, a los blogs, a la desobediencia, a no pedir permiso, a generar alianzas y estructuras propias; no nos defendamos, ¡hagamos que nos teman! Somos una realidad, operamos en diferentes ciudades y contextos, estamos conectadxs, tenemos objetivos comunes y ya no nos calláis. El feminismo será transfronterizo, transformador transgénero o no será, el feminismo será TransFeminista o no será... [We call to the insurrection, to occupy the streets, the blogs, to public disobedience, to refuse to ask permission, to generate alliances and our own social

structures; let's not defend ourselves, but make them fear us! We are a reality, we are active in different cities and contexts, we are connected, we share common objectives and they will not shut us up. Feminism will be transborder, transformer, transgender or it will not be, feminism will be TransFeminist or it will not be...]

(Red 2010)

Such actions complement the analytical work of revealing power structures and the hierarchies on which they are imposed on everyone. This particular take on insurrectional politics greatly contrasts with the traditional ideas of revolutionary thinking among the Latin American Left. What used to be formulated as an "asexual" political discourse for most part of the 20th century, actually concealing a patriarchal or masculinist perspective, the "Neo-Marx-chismo"[5] a point in case, is then radically transformed with the incorporation of a politics of the sexual and of gender as fundamental facets of the revolutionary inasmuch as a lived practice. The emancipatory stance of feminism is so re-dimensioned by transfeminism by questioning its fundamental binary structure as much as the social, sexual, and psychological practices that sustain it. Something also highlighted by its association with anarcofeminism and its critique of those religious, State and economic discourses that comprise dominant systems of oppression. This could be best symbolized by Ana María Portugals' demolishing cry: "ni dios, ni patrón, ni marido" [nor god, nor boss, nor husband].[6]

Valencia's intervention in the field of feminism is also founded on a "glocalized" position, being more interested in how *transfeminismo* has been used in Spain and Latin America, given its rich manifestation in artistic and performance events, academic fora, and public demonstrations in the last decade, than adding her voice to the controversy between historical feminism and transfeminism in other contexts. For her, transfeminism constitutes an actualization of feminism and asks to focus on the very semantics of the prefix "trans": "hace referencia a algo que atraviesa lo que nombra. Lo vertebra y lo transmuta" ["trans" makes reference to something that goes through what it names. It supports it and transmutes it] (2016: 92). It is then not a matter of surpassing feminism, but of opening social spaces and discursive fields coming from minority subjects, who had not been considered by "white and institutional feminism,"[7] as in the case of the seminal collection of writings by women of color or third-world feminism in Cherríe Moraga and Gloria Anzaldúa's *This Bridge Called my Back* (1981).

Valencia's expansive theoretical framework is therefore a complex agglomeration of critical perspectives that includes transnational, post-marxist, deconstructive, intersectional, and decolonial perspectives geared towards a counter-hegemonic set of ideas and practices. She engages with – appropriates critically and/or "accentuates" – the ideas of Michel Foucault, Judith Butler, Achille Mbembe, Beatriz Preciado, Gloria Anzaldúa, Chela Sandoval, Franz Fanon, Gilles Deleuze, Felix Guattari, Slavoj Žižek, Walter Mignolo, among many others to produce an overarching critique of heteropatriarchy, neoliberalism and coloniality from the glocal South or, more specifically, from the margins of the U.S.–Mexico border. This specific locus of enunciation is a critical point of departure for a situated knowledge that responds to some of the most pressing issues in this region and the country as a whole. From the many facets of her activism and scholarly writing, I would like to refer to the following interrelated themes, which are crucial to a critique of Mexico's present: deconstruction of gender and critique of patriarchalism; gender violence and the necro-economy of neoliberalism; decolonial critique of coloniality and endogamic racism.

Heteropatriarchal hegemony and the political uses of language

According to Carlos Monsiváis, Mexico's indispensable cultural critic of the late 20th century, "diversidad" is "el vocablo de más consecuencias en la América Latina de principios del siglo

XXI" [the most consequential term in LatinAmerica at the start of the XXI century], and as such "le abre un gran espacio a los modos de vida y los productos culturales alternativos" [it opens a great space for alternative ways of life and cultural products] (Monsiváis 2008). For someone who never publicly admitted to his gay sexuality, his subsequent comment that: "si algo se ha combatido es la diversidad. Y se olvida que sin lo diverso no existe lo homogéneo" [if anything has been battled against, it is diversity. And it is forgotten that without the diverse the homogeneous does not exist] bears the weight of a double history of repression, that of the institutions and society as well as that of the own individual. By comparison, Valencia appears as a one of many more visible critics and theorists carrying the torch of diversity in the country. In fact, transfeminism as a practice is much about visibility and irruption in the public sphere as a first step towards a more progressive transformation of society. As in the case of their urban interventions, such a transfeminist practice involves a pedagogy of the unsuspected participants towards questioning their own perceptions, understanding, and system of values. The spontaneous interactions that occurred when she was being photographed by Navarro at the heart of the Capital city may exemplify this. In response to the question posed by a bystander who wanted to know if Valencia was a man or a woman, she commented that she was interested in compelling the curious spectators to actually ask themselves the key questions: What is a man? What is a woman? (Villegas 2012). The practical purpose of these interventions is to introduce "the trans" in the imaginary *quotidian*. They actually derive from forms of "creative dissidence,"[8] which link many movements and organizations in their manifestation in the public space. In effect, they are:

> puentes entre los lenguajes de la *mass media*, la television, las redes sociales [...] y conceptos que vienen de las luchas sociales situadas en siglos pasados y que siguen siendo pertinentes, [luchas] que entienden o están en proceso de entender que el género, la raza, la disidencia sexual y la diversidad funcional no son meros epifenómenos, sino que construyen encarnaciones interseccionales. [...bridges among the languages of the mass media, television, social media ... and concepts that originate in the social struggles from previous centuries and which continue to be pertinent, which understand or are in the process of understanding that gender, race, sexual dissidence and functional diversity are not mere epiphenomena, but which construct intersectional embodiments.][9]

Now, framing the concept of diversity as a fixed or ready-made category may also be problematic as it might be instructive with regards to some interpretations of multiculturalism in the U.S. context. While its incorporation has productively involved a politics of recognition, representation, and identity, even in some cases restitution, at times it has also appeared as somewhat mystified and dependent upon established structures, both in discourse and in social praxis. That is why such a view or application of diversity may invite a critique similar to that of worldview-shaping keywords of disciplinary regimes whether epistemic or legal, such as naturalness and normalcy, which Butler's and Foucault's respective *oeuvre* have contributed to dismantling. Beyond its properly representational aspect, diversity should generate other non-normative sexual practices so as to escape from falling back into hegemonic binarisms. This is the position assumed by Valencia, operating along post-identitary parameters, in her advocacy for a "functional diversity."[10] This one is a loosely defined term that nonetheless confronts head on the binary logic by which gender has been constructed by the discourses of modernity/coloniality.

Such a view coincides with heuristic propositions in other fields and geopolitical contexts, for instance in what has been called citizenship studies in the U.S., in the understanding that citizenship (whether political or cultural) is itself an important object of analysis and critical site of negotiation (Brandzel 2016: 6). According to its main argument, the modern notion of citizenship results of the reification of its underlying or manifest violence and exclusionary mechanisms against (an)Other – the noncitizen – and against "nonnormative others" (5–6). Similar critiques of citizenship also apply in the Latin American context in general, and Mexican context in particular, for exactly the same reasons. Throughout the Spanish-speaking world, such a defense of diversity and the nonnormative corresponds with a general strategy implemented by many groups towards producing non-binary discourses and, in legal terms, a "despatologización" [depatologization] of alternative sexualities in society. Despite setbacks and legislative oppositions in different countries, the latter remains an attainable goal that may unify diverse groups from civil society in their particular struggles. The importance of such "despatologización" of functional diversity is undeniable. In the long term, it would impact the entire social fabric in the generation of new subjectivities and even, at the largest scale, "the social forces that administer capitalism." In reference to this possibility, Valencia follows closely Guattari and Rolnick's argument that "the production of subjectivity is perhaps the most important type of production, more essential than oil and energy" (2006: 40).

This attention to the production of subjectivity adds in her writing to the emphasis she places on language and its constructivist importance in that very process. In producing a discourse of recognition of such a functional diversity in society, and likewise producing agency through a recodification of meaning from an alternative position, she appropriates Deleuze and Guattari's concept of minor language. And from a minor position, she focuses on activating "una política de desobediencia epistémica y lingüística" (Valencia 2013: 106). Ultimately, the goal of this political work with language is to produce other constructive and interpretive possibilities of subjectivity beyond the rigid dichotomic structures of gender, sex and colonial discourse (Valencia 2014: 84). Other concepts are introduced reflecting an innovative use among the communities that resist a heteropatriarcal and violent system. These everyday insurrections are related "to the subversive use of: gender, language, sexuality, racism, functional diversity, pauperization, ecology, etc." (2015: 36). Therefore, there is an incessant reworking of language to resignify social reality and reappropriate terminologies in the name of oppressed communities. In this sense, even insults become useful elements of a situated discourse to make possible a dialogue with dominant discourses from historical memory and from a (trans)feminist and decolonial perspectives (2013: 98). Valencia proposes paying particular attention to what she calls "disfemismos," as opposed to euphemisms, in their enunciative potentiality, which congregates a series of social trajectories. Such a linguistic playfulness is part of an intervention in the structures of language and a critique of the social and political world it "represents." The writing of terms such as $udacas with a money sign to signify the economic precarity of the young unemployed, who, like their €uracas and norteca$ counterparts in the First World, have undergone the nefarious consequences of the repeated crisis of an economic system that has practically dismantled the welfare State in most parts of the world (Valencias 2013: 94–95).

Her combative writing style achieves a certain performative quality and it could be considered part of a subversive practice in the everyday. In contrast with the typical dryness of philosophical writing, hers is a richly metaphorical and tropic style more in line with the Latin American cultural essay tradition. She produces a kind of *messtiza écriture* to put it in those terms, which conflates the lofty expectations of French feminists regarding a revolutionary practice through writing, and Valencia's own neologism of "mess-tizx." Mess-tizx is a symbolical mess for a racial politics based on supposed ethnic purity. It makes visible at the level of the signifier the populations erased from the Anglo-American and European epistemic and linguistic maps. But her inflection also introduces a contrast with the purported goal of personifying social harmony in the idealized *mestizo* figure in the cultural politics of

Transfeminism and fake mustachios

post-revolutionary Mexico. Similar neologisms emerge incessantly in her writing, terms distort or destabilize meanings, fuse in new hybrid units in a linguistic practice that often operates at a metacritical level, rhetorically owing much to poetry, but politically, to a geopolitical positioning from the peripheries. The proliferation of neologisms in Valencia's work is not so much intended to designate new phenomena or even destabilize meaning for deconstruction's sake, but to contribute to opening new analytical perspectives and introducing new horizons of meaning in order to make it possible to intervene in them.

As part of her methodology, she is interested in the genealogy of concepts – indebted perhaps to venerable philological and philosophical traditions – and in how they travel, are appropriated, and potentially resignified in other historical or geopolitical contexts. Resorting to the formalist concept of "ostranienie," following Viktor Shklovsky, she suggests with it a geopolitical and epistemic sense rather than forms of unrecognition or de-familiarization. This dissident practice with language through a critique of the hegemonic and the colonial possibility in concepts coined as well as in theories developed in the First World is an important aspect of her decolonial criticism. The same goes for a rereading and/or reappropriation of concepts. The question for Valencia, as for many other thinkers and scholars confronting the local realities of postcolonial Latin America, is, precisely, "not reproducing coloniality through emancipative theory." Such a turn is decisive, for instance, in opting for the term *cuir*, as it has been increasingly used in the Spanish-speaking South. As Valencia explains, it introduces a critical variation of *queer* at the same time that it conveys an awareness of its respective history in the Anglo-Saxon context (2014: 68). The most fundamental aspect of such a critical linguistic practice of "survival and alliance" is the fact of making visible "los trans/border/messtiz★/marica/lesbian/vestida/put★/tullid★" (Valencia 2015: 34).

The free social space created by a cuir subjectivity is that of a "cuiradanía" that reflects the fictions of identity and rethink and reactivate agencies from a minority and decolonial perspective (Valencia 2014: 84). Key terms in her theoretical formulation from gore capitalism to endriago subjectivity involve that poetic inventiveness that transmutes reality and creates a new horizon of meaning and sense. Linking such a film genre with capitalism does not only convey an association with the prevalence of certain optic regimes in contemporary capitalism, but also with the cultural pervasiveness of violence and its commodification, in a way that supposedly more neutral terms (i.e., advance capitalism) or merely temporal terms (i.e., late capitalism) do not convey. *Capitalismo gore* is that systemic intermingling of economy, violence, and death, and in which necro-empowering is prevalent among the *sujetos endriagos* (Valencia 2014: 74). The endriago subject is trapped in a neoliberal quandary *par excellence* – that is, between the precariousness characteristic of largest sectors of the population and the abundance and proliferation of goods as a fatal temptation. Disenchanted by the scarce opportunities of mobility, such a subject is interpellated by both economic and gender (masculinist) demands and resorts to crime and violence as tools of necro-empowering and fast acquisition of capital (Valencia 2014: 75). The term is posthuman and postrational in reference to the reliance on primordial aggression in order to extract economic surplus through the "industry of crime." The use of the medieval figure of the endriago (a fabulous monster with a human face and body of hydra and dragon) stands for that human being whose rationality and sociality are greatly conflicted or undermined by destructive impulses that attempt against social cohesion and human life, including their own. Beyond designating a sort of new reality, such a metaphor condenses a social analysis of the fact that the traditional concept of social class, as an organizing principle of social phenomena and social structure, does not explain the transversality of the endriago subjectivity, which has become a sort of economic engine in today's society: the criminal class (Valencia 2014: 71).

Fascinating violence and necro-empowering in Mexico's cruel modernity[11]

One of Valencia's main contributions to scholarship on the border region and Mexico's troubles and tribulations at the current juncture is providing insights into neoliberalism's devastating effects, its underlying "necro" and narco-economy, and its linkages to heteropatriarchy. Hers is a view on neoliberal biopolitics and necropolitics from the underside of globalization, taking her cues from a re-reading of Foucault (2008), Žižek (2008) and other theorists through an anti-colonial and transfeminist lens. By constructing violence as an object of analysis, in its systemic and symbolic aspects, she is part of a small group of local "violentólogos," whose academic work aims at providing epistemic tools, frameworks, and strategies helpful to understand and confront the causes and multifarious manifestations of what, for not few authorities and public officials, seems like an unfathomable phenomenon. Such a scholarly work acquires an even greater sense of urgency considering the lack of institutional support for investigative reportage on the drug war and its considerable role in the general deterioration of public security, and the refusal of a sector of the Mexican media to bring those same issues to the public for fear of retaliation.

Valencia's critical intervention in what could now be called violence studies has also been marked geopolitically from within and from without. In fact, it is impossible to disassociate her "organic" reflections on the postmodern cartographies of violence from the recent history of her U.S.–Mexico border locus of enunciation. Not surprisingly the philosopher is contempo-rary to the documented records maintained by women's organizations on the feminicides along the border since the early 1990s. These liminal territories have epitomized for many the spatial manifestation of the neoliberal necro-economy regimes and its toll on human life (i.e., narco-executions, feminicides, death of migrants, etc.). It is such spacialization of violent death that Valencia refers to when she claims that: "es prioritariamente en el Tercer Mundo y sus fronteras donde los efectos del capitalismo gore son más evidentes y brutales" [it is primarily in the Third World and its borders where the effects of gore capitalism are more evident and brutal] (Valencia 2010: 27). Like in other narratives about the border, this one appears imagined, then, as a dys-topian scenario in which the trajectories of globalized legal and illegal economic regimes con-verge, intersect, compete, intensify, and/or collide at full force with its consequent social impact. She has explained that in the gore capitalism, the explicit and unjustified bloodshed (as the price to pay by the "third-worldized" populations the world over, who insist on following the ever more demanding logics of capitalism as a form of progress and legitimacy) [….] frequently merges with the economy of crime (Valencia 2016: 89).

Concerning the specificity of gender-based violence, Valencia understands that gender is at the center of the national social order, among other reasons because its post-revolutionary con-struction became intimately related to the construction of the modern Mexican State (2014: 72). A model of violent masculinity (the prototypical macho) inscribed in the discourse of the national becomes hegemonic and, therefore, reproduced at the micro level (i.e., the family) and macro or institutional level (the State, the cultural industries, etc.). And hegemony is "necro-heteropatriarcal/clasista/racista" (Valencia and Sepúlveda 2016: 85; Valencia 2014: 69). The neo-liberal economic regime operates within that hegemony as evidenced by the production of aestheticized forms of perception that convert violence into an iconic merchandise to be com-modified and capitalized (Valencia and Sepúlveda 2016: 76). The notorious feminicides of Juárez are a point in case of that economic logic behind the commodification of violence (i.e., film series, TV series, magazine articles, scant news reports[12]) and the vicious circle that connects its representation and consumption with further generation of spectacular violence in the gore Market. If the past century was that of violence, in the present century that violence through neoliberalism has acquired a *gore* quality (2010: 26).

Transfeminism and fake mustachios

Valencia proposes to investigate how violence itself seduces and is commodified, for example in necro-neoliberal Mexico, considering in a Marxist way that violence itself has become an economic power (Valencia and Sepúlveda 2016:83). In a recently published article,[13] she explains how violence and death are not only crucial to neoliberalism's necro-economy, but how they also fascinate consumers. Precisely, the reactivation of the capital fluxes by the consumption of violent images, and the imposition of its necroheteropatriarchal and ethnic values by the anesthetization of death as a spectacle in the cultural marketplace, places this spectacle at the center while it hides its economic logic. The figures representing those values appear as desirable, the criminal as powerful:

> la fascinación que se ejerce sobre los sujetos espectadores consumidores de los productos culturales y la información derivada de las violencias, vinculadas a esta estetización de la muerte y del poder, se sirve del régimen necropolítico (y de su trabajo de muerte) y también del regimen psicopolítico para apropiarse de la subjetividad y expandir su control. [the fascination exerted on the subjects as spectators and consumers of cultural products and the information derived from violences, linked to this aesthetization of death and power, it makes use of the necropolitical regime (and its death work) and also of psychopolitic regime to take over subjectivity and expand its control.]
>
> *(Valencia and Sepúlveda 2016: 79)*

Central to the neoliberal "psico/necro/biopolítico" regime is the phenomenon of "fascinating violence," as a process of exhaltation and euphoria that glamourizes violence (84). Departing from insights on scopic regimes by Michel Foucault, Christian Metz and Martin Jays, Valencia defines that fascinating violence in representation as a:

> tecnología de seducción visual que se apropia de los afectos y apela a los códigos de emotividad e identificación, en la medida que crea un simulacro de comunidad extensa enraizada en los valores del capitalismo gore y su culto a la violencia, como herramienta de control, de trabajo y de filiación social. [technology of visual seduction that takes over the affects and appeals to the codes of emotivity and identification, inasmuch as it creates a simulacrum of a vast community rooted in the values of gore capitalism and its cult to violence as a tool for control, work and social affiliation.]
>
> *(Valencia and Sepúlveda 2016: 84)*

The latter part of her conceptualization refers to the aforementioned phenomenon of "necro-empowering," which powerfully "seduces" those who may come from contexts of precariousness and see in extreme violence a form of gaining power and achieving mobility:

> Denominamos necroempoderamiento a los procesos que transforman contextos y/o situaciones de vulnerabilidad y/o subalternidad en posibilidad de acción y autopoder, pero que los reconfiguran desde prácticas distópicas y autoafirmación perversa lograda por medio de prácticas violentas. [We call necroempowering the processes that transform contexts and/or situations of vulnerability and/or subalternity into the possibility of action and autopower, but which reconfigure them since dystopian practices and the perverse auto-affirmation achieved by means of violent practices.]
>
> *(Valencia 2016: 89)*

The other seduction of fascinating violence, its stylized mediatic representation, abounds in the transnational offer of popular culture. As an example, Valencia mentions the TV series *El Señor de los Cielos*, *Breaking Bad*, *La Reina del Sur* and/or *Sense 8*, which acquire particular relevance for her because of their connection to the U.S.–Mexico border and the world of narco-trafficking, one of the key business sectors of the informal neoliberal economy (Valencia and Sepúlveda 2016: 85). These series,

> conforman algunos códigos visuales y estéticos de la fascinante violencia; los cuales construyen modos de percibir a través de narrativas que utilizan y combinan sistemas de vigilancia, de espectacularización, de simulación, con altas dosis de pulsión de muerte y de excitación sexual. [comprise some of the visual and aesthetic codes of the fascinating violence; which construct modes of perception through narratives which use and combine systems of surveillance, spectacle-making, simulation, with high amounts of death drive and sexual arousal.]
>
> *(Valencia and Sepúlveda 2016: 85)*

Valencia is correct in her assessment that these cultural products:

> [T]ienen un impacto a escala global no sólo en cuanto a producción de imaginarios culturales y estandarización de la subjetividad, sino también de flujos de capital. Más aún, estas series en sus disparidades muestran una cartografía relacionada con el imaginario del narco mundo y su relación con variables como la raza, la clase, el género y la geopolítica que reafirman estereotipos ya existentes en torno a estas variantes, pero además re-combinan, re-apropian y edulcoran las lógicas de la violencia económica producida por el neoliberalismo. [(They) have an impact at global scale not only in terms of a production of cultural imaginaries and standardization of subjectivity, but also of capital fluxes. Moreover, in their disparities these series show a cartography related to the imaginary of the narcoworld and its relationship with variables such as race, class, gender and the geopolitics that reaffirm already existing stereotypes around those variants, but which also re-combine, re-appropriate and sweeten the logics of the economic violence produced by neoliberalism.]
>
> *(Valencia and Sepúlveda 2016: 85)*

These popular culture products contribute to dissemination of a visual regime that naturalizes organized crime and its values. Such a situation is not an "ominosa excepción a la regla de los mercados capitalistas contemporáneos, sino que está en concordancia con el proyecto glotaritario" [an ominous exception to the rule of the contemporary capitalist markets, but it also corresponds with the glotaritary project] (Valencia and Sepúlveda 2016: 89). With this neologism she means a global totalitarian regime, alluding to both totalitarian regimes of any political inclination and to the specific spectacularity and technological obsession that characterized fascism, as abundantly analyzed throughout the 20th century. More importantly, this hybrid term calls attention to the disturbing presence of those very same tendencies in the present time and foreseeable future.

Transfeminism and decolonial thinking in the reconstruction of the social fabric

In the double articulation of a transfeminist perspective and decolonial criticism in Valencia's analysis of Mexico's "glocal" realities, the key questions to ask regarding the crucial issues that

Transfeminism and fake mustachios

she raises are what to do and how to confront the specificity of the violence and oppression that patriarchy, heteronormativity, and the dynamics of the gore capitalism generate. Valencia is committed to a reconstruction of the social fabric in the country so immensely damaged by the endriago subjectivity characteristic of gore capitalism (2014: 78). Her activism and artivism are a complement to her cultural and philosophical analysis, which does not limit itself to the contemplation of that epochal turn from a nation-state to a narco-state (2014: 74). The adoption of transfeminist methodologies aims at articulating *resistencias* from a critical and localized point of view to confront the endriago subjectivity and subvert the heteropatriarcal use of the categories of gender, sexuality, ethnicity and race, functional diversity, the ecology, the economy and politics (2014: 78). Her scholarly writings contain urgent calls to deconstruct extreme violence as a tool of necro-empowering and its perverse application in misogynistic, homophobic, and (endo)racist form. Such a prophylactic of transfeminism requires a theoretical and practical framework, along with a decolonial decentering by which a new political subjectivity, new conceptual configurations and new cultural and social conditions may emerge in order to confront old and new oppressions, based on gender, social class, race and sexuality. In this analysis what she calls "endoracism" clearly appears as the most perdurable form of coloniality in the country. It is necessary to continue deconstructing from institutional and non-institutional perspectives.

In her decolonial critique, Valencia regards gender-based oppression as inescapably constructed within the entrapments of colonialism and racism in Mexican culture. A transfeminist intervention passes through the elaboration and wide dissemination of a critical discourse of masculinity that supersedes hegemonic masculinity (machista, racist, patriarchal). A deconstruction of machismo, or of the hegemonic heteropatriarchal figure, is urgent as in relation to the aforementioned problem of narco-trafficking and extreme violence, as tools of necro-empowering at the service of the demands of both hegemonic masculinity and global capitalism. This is part of the task of decentering the category of masculinity that echoes, for instance, Miriam Solá's emphasis on working through the subjective or symbolical economy:

> De ahí la importancia que adquiere la producción de imágenes, el juego de representaciones, la guerrilla de la comunicación, las interrelaciones entre arte y política, el ciberfeminismo como posibilidad de reinventar las identidades a través de las nyueva tecnologías, y todas las estrategias relacionadas con el plano simbólico (campañas gráficas, vídeos, fotografías, relatos ficticios, performances, diseño de webs, blogs), anudadas con el deseo de construer nuevas representaciones propiasde la realidad. [Hence the importance of the production of images, the play of representations, the warfare of communication, the interrelationships between art and politics, cyberfeminism as a possibility of reinvention of identities through new technologies, and all the strategies related with the symbolic plane (graphic campaigns, videos, pictures, stories, performances, web design, blogs) knotted with the desire of constructing new representations of reality]
>
> *(2016: 17–18)*

Such a decentering and production of new identities would have a decisive impact on all social relations at all scales (Valencia 2014: 85). What transfeminism produces is then a sort of pharmacopeia to free from disciplinary norms that produce violence and frustration. From the imposition of those norms that privilege some subjects over others precisely derives gender violence (Valencia 2014: 72). In consequence, it is essential to imagine counter-hegemonic practices. But this project necessarily involves intersectional alliances that cross national borders beyond the supposed guarantees and social protection of a nation-state, which often turns out to be that voracious and structurally inequitable system (2013: 108). Finally, it also involves new form of political praxis for the constructions of "commons," as opposed to generating further spaces to govern the others and perpetuate a notion of politics linked to the hierarchical imposition of a certain biopolitics and necropower.[14] This decolonial call to action in Valencia's writings remains as one of its most distinctive traits as much as her conviction on the capacity of language to mediate the theoretical and philosophical with the practices. And whenever language seems not to suffice to bridge realities and discourses, the performative is always there to help to reinforce and/or complement the intended sense and meaning.

Notes

1 Tatiana Sentamans, "Redes transfeministas y nuevas políticas de representación sexual (II). Estrategas de producción," *Transfeminismos. Epistemes, fricciones y flujos*, edited by Miriam Solá and Elena Urko. Marea Negra, 2016, p. 33.
2 Sayak Valencia, "Del queer al cuir: ostranénie geopolítica y epistémica desde el sur glocal," *Queer & Cuir. Políticas de lo irreal*, edited by Fernando R. Lanuza and Raúl M. Carrasco. Universidad Autónoma de Querétaro, Fotamara, 2015, p. 35.
3 In reference to the Spanish context, Miriam Solá has argued that the term was first used in two papers, "El vestido nuevo de la emperatriz" by Grup de Lesbianes Feministes de Barcelona and "¿Mujer o trans? La inserción de las transexuales en el movimiento feminista" by Kim Perez, presented at the Jornadas Feministas Estatales in Córdoba, Spain, in 2000 (Solá 2016: 16).
4 All translations are mine.
5 Ileana Rodriguez, "Desde LASA." *Debate Feminista* vol. 48, 2013, p. 183.
6 Mujeres anarquistas www.nodo50.org/mujerescreativas/mujeres_anarquistas.htm.
7 Sayak Valencia, "Teoría transfeminista para el análisis de la violencia machista y la reconstrucción no-violenta del tejido social en el México contemporáneo," *Universitas Humanística* vol. 78, 2014, 68.
8 Sayak Valencia, "$udacas, €uracas, norteca$ y otras metáforas del capitalismo gore," *Debate Feminista* vol. 48, 2013, p. 108.
9 p. 109.
10 Sayak Valencia, "Teoría transfeminista para el análisis de la violencia machista y la reconstrucción no-violenta del tejido social en el México contemporáneo," *Universitas Humanística* p. 71.
11 Jean Franco, *Cruel Modernity*, Duke University Press, 2013.
12 Corona, Ignacio. "Over Their Dead Corpse: Reading the Newspapers on Gender Violence," in *Gender Violence at the U.S.–Mexico Border. Media Representation and Public Response*, edited by Héctor Domínguez-Ruvalcaba and Ignacio Corona. University of Arizona Press, 2011, p. 121.
13 Sayak Valencia and Katia Sepúlveda. "Del fascinante fascismo a la fascinante violencia: Psico/bio/necro/política y mercado gore," *Mitologías hoy* vol. 14, December 2016.
14 Sayak Valencia, "Teoría transfeminista para el análisis de la violencia machista y la reconstrucción no-violenta del tejido social en el México contemporáneo," Universitas Humanística, vol. 78, 2014, 84–85.

Works cited

Brandzel, Amy L. *Against Citizenship. The Violence of the Normative*. University of Illinois Press, 2016.
Butler, Judith. *Undoing Gender*. Routledge, 2004.
Carlsen, Laura. "Latin America's Women-led Movements and New Feminisms," *CounterPunch* vol. 24, no. 2, 2017, pp. 10–12. https://issuu.com/counterpunch/docs/vol_24_no_2_/10. Accessed April 20, 2017.
Corona, Ignacio. "Over Their Dead Corpse: Reading the Newspapers on Gender Violence." *Gender Violence at the U.S.–Mexico Border. Media Representation and Public Response*, edited by Héctor Domínguez-Ruvalcaba and Ignacio Corona. University of Arizona Press, 2011, pp. 104–127.
Foucault, Michel. *The Birth of Biopolitics: Lectures at the Collège de France, 1978–79*. Palgrave Macmillan, 2008.
Franco, Jean. *Cruel Modernity*. Duke University Press, 2013.
Grupo de Lecturas críticas en Feminismo y Filosofía (Grupo). "Tanto puede nombre de varón," *Revista Anfibia*, 2015. www.revistaanfibia.com/ensayo/tanto-puede-un-nombre-de-varon/. Accessed June 23, 2017.

Transfeminism and fake mustachios

Guattari, Félix and Suely Rolnik. *Micropolítica. Cartografías del deseo.* Traficantes de Sueños, 2006.
Halberstam, Judith. *Female Masculinity.* Duke University Press, 1998.
Marea Negra. "Presentación." *Transfeminismos. Epistemes, fricciones y flujos*, edited by Miriam Solá and Elena Urko. Marea Negra, 2016, pp. 89–96.
Monsiváis, Carlos. "Tres aproximaciones a la cultura (si ésta se deja)," *Nexos* February 1, 2008. www.nexos.com.mx/?p=12484. Accessed May 14, 2014.
Moraga, Cherríe and Gloria Anzaldúa, eds. *This Bridge Called My Back.* Persephone Press, 1981.
Preciado, Beatriz. "Decimos revolución." *Transfeminismos. Epistemes, fricciones y flujos*, edited by Miriam Solá and Elena Urko. Marea Negra, 2016, pp. 9–12.
Preciado, Paul B. *Testo Junkie: Sex, Drugs, and Biopolitics in the Pharmacopornographic Era.* The Feminist Press, 2008.
Red PutaBolloNegraTransFeminista (Red). "Manifiesto para la insurrección transfeminista," January 1, 2010. http://estrangulaelvacio.blogspot.com/2009/12/manifiesto-para-la-insurreccion_31.html. Accessed June 23, 2017.
Rodriguez, Ileana. "Desde LASA." *Debate Feminista* vol. 48, 2013, pp. 179–186.
Sentamans, Tatiana. "Redes transfeministas y nuevas políticas de representación sexual (II). Estrategas de producción." *Transfeminismos. Epistemes, fricciones y flujos*, edited by Miriam Solá and Elena Urko. Marea Negra, 2016, pp. 147–160.
Solá, Miriam and Elena Urko, eds. *Transfeminismos. Epistemes, fricciones y flujos.* Marea Negra, 2016.
Solá, Miriam. "Pre-textos, con-textos y textos." *Transfeminismos. Epistemes, fricciones y flujos*, edited by Miriam Solá and Elena Urko. Marea Negra, 2016, pp. 15–30.
Tucker, Ricky. "Pharmacopornography: An Interview with Beatriz Preciado." *The Paris Review*, December 4, 2013. www.theparisreview.org/blog/2013/12/04/pharmacopornography-an-interview-with-beatriz-preciado/. Accessed June 23, 2017.
Valencia, Sayak. *Capitalismo gore.* Editorial Melusina, 2010.
Valencia, Sayak. "Del *queer* al *cuir*: ostranénie geopolítica y epistémica desde el sur glocal." *Queer & Cuir. Políticas de lo irreal*, edited by Fernando R. Lanuza and Raúl M. Carrasco. Universidad Autónoma de Querétaro, Fotamara, 2015, pp. 19–38.
Valencia, Sayak. "$udacas, €uracas, norteca$ y otras metáforas del capitalismo gore." *Debate Feminista* vol. 48, 2013, pp. 94–111.
Valencia, Sayak. "Teoría transfeminista para el análisis de la violencia machista y la reconstrucción no-violenta del tejido social en el México contemporáneo." *Universitas Humanística* vol. 78, 2014, 66–88. http://revistas.javeriana.edu.co. Accessed March 15, 2017.
Valencia, Sayak. "Transfeminismo(s) y capitalismo gore." *Transfeminismos. Epistemes, fricciones y flujos*, edited by Miriam Solá and Elena Urko. Marea Negra, 2016, pp. 89–96.
Valencia, Sayak and Katia Sepúlveda. "Del fascinante fascismo a la fascinante violencia: Psico/bio/necro/política y mercado gore." *Mitologías hoy* vol. 14, 2016, 75–91. http://dx.doi.org/10.5565/rev/mitologias.395. Accessed December 18, 2016.
Villegas, Daniela. "Las provocaciones de la filósofa transfeminista." *El Universal.* April 22, 2012. http://sayak.blogspot.com/2012/04/domingo-siplemento-del-periodico.html. Accessed April 22, 2012.
Žižek, Slavoj. *Violence: Six Sideways Reflections.* Picador, 2008.

35

PROUD SINVERGÜENZA OR FOOLISH MARICÓN?

Manu NNa's challenge to Mexican homonormativity

Doug Bush

Manu NNa's stage entrance immediately catches the eye: his black outfit contrasts against a shaggy brown overcoat, and he sports thick rimmed glasses, a long, thick necklace, and unruly blue hair. His comedy set almost immediately turns focus toward a favorite topic: his love life. "I met a man," he confesses. "You know those questions that come up at first—what do you like to do? How big are you? So I ask him, hey, what do you do? He says: "I'm a farmer." I said farmer? I said "You fuck cows, so surely you won't have any problem fucking me, right?"[1] (Manu NNa, "Rodrigo" n.d.). Later he recounts going to a family reunion, yet again without a boyfriend, only to have his uncle be thankful that that means they will be able to continue their sexual relationship. He tells the audience: "The truth is that I'm a big whore. I'm such a whore that I buy the morning after pill at Costco." The audience roars with laughter, breaking into applause. In his 12-minute set, the comedian talks about scary movies, his habit of sleeping with his cousins, riffs on Mexico's annual telethon, and recounts seeing via Facebook that an ex is now engaged. He confesses that he misses the relationship, or at least part of it: "I miss sleeping with him the most. Because when we were fucking and he came he would punch me, so I miss him a lot."[2]

There is no room for interpretation in his act—Manu NNa is gay and never shies away from it. His audience loves it. He is a prime example of the *sinvergüenza* that La Fountain-Stokes describes in his 2011 essay, and, as a consequence, also challenges the homonormativity that has progressively encroached upon Mexico's LGBTTTI community.[3] Since the 1980s, neoliberal and modernizing forces have engaged in an increasing deradicalization of the queer community, forcing into the private sphere what was once fought to be made public—the sexual freedom exemplified in Manu NNa's act—in trade-off for increased political representation and rights. Homonormativity as a matter of course shuns radical discourse, instead appealing to more broadly palatable rhetoric in its appeal for acceptance from society at large.

Although Manu NNa's profile has steadily risen in recent years, 2017 may prove to be a watershed for the 27-year-old comedian. In January, Comedy Central Latinoamérica premiered *Se busca comediante* (*Comedians Wanted*), an 11-episode reality series in which he and three other comics travel across Mexico to seek out new talent, and in May, Netflix released *Simplemente Manu NNa*, an hour-long showcase of his talents, part of the company's efforts to not only expand its market in Latin America, but also to become a destination for both stand-up comedic talent and their audiences (McCarthy 2017). Nevertheless, for those looking for a fix of the rising star, the two shows prove to be very different viewing experiences. The reason lies in homonormativity itself. As we saw in the introduction to this chapter, when Manu NNa controls the narrative, as he does in his stand-up, he is able to "pull back the curtain" on a queer discourse increasingly privatized by the homonormative impulse and, in the process, claims a proud sinvergüenza status. Nevertheless, when he loses control of the narrative as occurs in *Se busca comediante,* he is punished for his transgressions against homonormativity, being recast as foolish maricón[4]—one who is not only dangerous to himself, but also to those who associate with him.

As I will demonstrate in this chapter, Manu NNa's control of the narrative is intrinsically tied to the venue in which he performs: his stand-up represents a "bottom-up" cultural experience consisting of a carefully curated set of jokes by the artist himself in service to his unique comedic voice, while *Se busca,* produced by Comedy Central Latinoamérica and owned by multi-national media conglomerate Viacom, imposes a "top-down" storyline on the performer, one that ultimately disenfranchises his artistic queer Mexican subjectivity.

Homonormativity and the *sinvergüenza*

Sexuality has historically been a complex subject in Mexico where orientation is seen as defined by sexual role more so than as a clear identity. De la Dehesa provides an extensive bibliography of research on Latin American sexualities, concluding that there is a "coexistence of multiple systems organizing sexual desires, practices, and self-understandings within the same society, particularly locating differences across class, regional, ethnic and racial lines" (2010: 15), while in his literary-based study, Foster has claimed that many places in Latin America lack a "gay identity" even if same-sex relationships do exist (1997: 3). Nevertheless, all of the comics that I will reference in this chapter are open about their sexuality in a way that is identifiable to my own North American experience, and I believe that this is tied to their origins. All are based in Mexico City, a cosmopolitan metropolis that has hosted a gay pride parade since 1979, with estimated attendance of 200,000 in 2016 (Hernández). For the many queer Mexicans who come to the capital to live open lives—"outness" has become "an available and affordable option," as Butler would note (1993: 19), particularly for those in the middle class and higher. In this context, I believe we can draw more clearly defined parallels between some Mexican queer identities and those in United States, where the bulk of academic queer research has been performed.

Despite whatever divergences in specific queer identities, Mexico's LGBTTTI movement as a whole has seemed to follow a similar trajectory to those in other western nations. While Marzullo provides a history of the nation's LGBTTTI movement and how identity categories differ in the country (2015: 697–698), McGee and Kampwirth outline how this movement, sparked by both the 1968 Tlatelolco massacre in Mexico City and the 1969 Stonewall Riots in New York, has been co-opted and deradicalized since the AIDS crisis "as an unintended result of [participants] efforts to seek help from powerful outsiders, the state, and international donors" (2015: 52). Neoliberalism's steady creep into the Mexican economy and state since the 1980s has served to further incentivize this deradicalization; the authors explain the rhetoric of the global LGBTTTI movement over the past 30 years has been "that of an individual rights movement that serves to reinforce neoliberal idealizations of the atomized consumer-individual" (McGee and Kampwirth 2015: 61). Furthermore, the incorporation of the LGBTTTI community into the apparatus of the state has become a marker of neoliberal modernity and progress (McGee and Kampwirth 2015: 61),[5] which can clearly be observed in the case of Mexico. The Partido de la Revolución Democrática has long supported LGBTTTI rights, while in 2016, President Enrique Peña Nieto of the Partido de la Revolución Institucional announced his intention to amend the constitution to legalize gay marriage nationwide, a move which ultimately failed and produced strong backlash (Agren 2016).

The deradicalization of the queer community has become a global pattern wherein, as Duggan explains, "democratic diversity of proliferating forms of sexual dissidence is rejected in favor of the naturalized variation of a fixed minority arrayed around a state-endorsed heterosexual primacy and prestige" (2002: 190). In short, it becomes easier to argue for "rights" if they fit into pre-defined heteronormative molds such as marriage and adoption, while discourse that it is not palatable to the wider public must be neutered and people who do not acquiesce hidden away or denigrated as "not representative."[6] The result, I believe, is a stratified queer discourse—a public queer rhetoric that follows homonormative molds, and a continuing private one not "fit" for heterosexual consumption. Halperin and Traub see evidence of this in the most ubiquitous of LGBTTTI events, the gay pride parade. While these events have been critical in terms of visibility and, as, pursuing the goal of the "complete destigmatization of homosexuality" (2009: 3), they have faced backlash within the queer community itself, particularly for their heavy commercialization and their homonormative influence. Halperin and Traub see these events as a site for "gay policemen, lesbian mothers, business leaders, corporate employees, religious devotees, athletes and politicians," leaving out those who do not fit in this homonormative mold, including sex workers, drag queens, people of color, sadomasochists, among others (2009: 9). This has led to the gay shame movement, which aims to listen to those voices that no longer have a place in homonormative neoliberal discourse—those who have been forced into the private realm.

La Fountain-Stokes argues that Latinos do not need pride (or shame) because of the category of the sinvergüenza, explaining that it represents "hav[ing] no shame: to disobey, break the law, disrespect authority (the family, the church, the state), and in a perverse and curious way to be proud of one's transgression, or at the very least lack a feeling of guilt" (2011: 72). While I find this formulation extremely useful as an ontological category, particularly in the case of Manu NNa and his "pulling back the curtain" on privatized queer discourse, his analysis seems grounded in the context of the United States and the struggle that queer persons of color face in having their voices heard within the broader LGBTTTI movement. Thus, while I do employ the term sinvergüenza, I do so as a general term and cognizant of the extensive work by De la Dehesa (2010) and McGee and Kampwirth (2015) who show that LGBTTTI discourse in Mexico has taken cues from and undergone similar shifts as in other parts of the world, at least in urban, middle class and higher sectors of society.

Before looking at Manu NNa's act, I want to explore comedy sets from his queer Mexican contemporaries—primarily Kikis, Nicho Peña, Raul Meneses and Hugo Blanquet—to determine if this "pulling back the curtain" is exclusive to him. While all of these comics do "come out" to their audience in sets available from both Comedy Central Latinoamérica and YouTube, for the most part they do demonstrate a neutered queer discourse. Kikis, for example, jokes about the benefits of a lesbian relationship, such as never running out of tampons (La Kikis 2016), while Meneses riffs on his feminine sounding voice (Meneses 2017), hardly topics that are lightning rods for controversy or off-putting to a wider audience. Peña, meanwhile, makes only occasional references to his sexuality, instead preferring to focus on his portliness (Peña 2016). Blanquet presents the most interesting case; although he does not offer explicit details, he does make numerous references to his sexual life in his Comedy Central set (Blanquet 2016). Nevertheless, sets done for other venues prove to be far more aggressive: one grainy YouTube video shows a performance as his alter drag-ego Diamond Leblanc Luzon at the Maximiliano gay bar in Queretaro, Mexico (Blanquet 2014), while in another clip he jokes about how there is no shame in being the passive sexual partner (Blanquet 2013).[7] Here we must keep in mind that every comedian has a different style and may not be comfortable being explicit about their sexual adventures, but in Blanquet that I believe that we see a conscious choice to neuter his act while performing in front of a broader audience, clipping those bits not fit for heterosexual consumption.

Balancing acts

This, of course, is not Manu NNa's style, and indeed, parts of his Netflix special are raunchier than anything from his earlier stand-up, whether done for Comedy Central or other venues. Nevertheless, the idea of "pulling back the curtain" is critical here: rather than barrage the audience with a constant stream of private queer discourse, he instead does so only at opportune times, negotiating sinvergüenza status through a carefully curated set of jokes designed to engage but not turn off a broader audience. As evidenced when he surveys attendees at various points in *Simplemente Manu NNa*, we must keep in mind that his audience is not exclusively LGBTTTI and thus an entire set of queer-themed jokes, particularly sexual ones, would likely limit his reach. His personal style notwithstanding, a good deal of Manu NNa's Netflix routine could be performed by any comic, particularly when he talks about the perils of going to the gym, his addiction to telenovelas and how they have guided his life, or the bizarre and overextended bit where he questions female members of the audience on whether they had a caesarian section or natural birth.

The beginning of the set serves to ease the audience into his style—in his first bits he talks about how he sleeps with a lot of men and how he has always wanted to be a maid and have sexual relations with the boss. I do not count this as revealing private queer discourse—off-handedly joking about having lots of sexual partners is not particularly risqué, given that many heterosexual comedians engage in the same sort of comedy. His first truly shocking joke lands at the six-minute mark: after revealing that he has lost 25 kilograms, he explains: "I don't know if it was the diet or AIDS ... AIDS doesn't knock, right? But, while I keep losing weight, I won't take antiretrovirals until I reach my ideal weight." There is certainly a distasteful element to this joke, but to whom? Although HIV/AIDS has been used to marginalize gay men for more than 30 years, it is now generally taboo to openly make this association, particularly in the heterosexual community, thanks to years of programs aimed at reducing stigma.[8] Manu NNa's certainly liberal, urban audience would likely not *openly* consider AIDS to be a "gay disease," which is why the joke carries so much weight—he forcefully plays into stereotypes and no-longer acceptable beliefs that the audience may privately hold. At the same time, Manu NNa takes the private and makes it public—HIV/AIDS remains an omnipresent subject in the queer community, and it has used humor at times to lighten the black cloud of the disease—see John Greyson's 1993 musical *Zero Patience*, the comedy of the late Steve Moore, or Christiansen and Hanson's study of HIV/AIDS activist organization ACT UP's rhetoric in the United States. Manu NNa's bit results in extended applause and laughter from the audience, although the comic does clarify that he does not have AIDS, knocking on wood so that he "doesn't get it again."

As we saw earlier, Manu NNa's bread and butter is frank talk about sex, and *Simplemente* does not deviate from that formula. What is fascinating about his approach to these topics is how they are not the center of the story, but rather off-handed comments or punchlines to more mainstream bits—again, a careful negotiation designed to engage but not repel a wider audience. Later in the set, after a discussion of his gym adventures—he sticks to the elliptical machine but frequently reverts to just watching people—he describes keeping an eye on a particular patron who was making noises that seemed more sexual in nature. He recounts:

I was like, "What's up?" ... And I say "I have headphones, what's up? I'm listening. So I go to the manager and say "That guy is working out his sphincter." I know it's an ugly word, sphincter. There's ugly words like sphincter, axilla, groin, and my mouth waters with those three words.

This is just one of many sexual jokes Manu NNa makes during the set, making what is private queer discourse—overtly intimate details that may be unpalatable to a society now expecting a polite, neutered homonormativity—public. Later, after being sick for three days, the comic explains that he decided to go to church to pray:

The bowl guy said "Eat half a cookie," and I said. (exaggerated) "What?" The same "What?" that one says when you hear "Your credit card has been declined." And you say "What?" ... or when they tell you "I came inside." That "What?"

He later explains that he still believes that true gentlemen exist because one of his partners once asked him if they could ejaculate inside. Manu NNa did not think it was problematic, and told his partner not to worry because he wears an IUD, a line delivered to wild audience applause.

Manu NNa also pulls back the curtain on disclosing his sexuality to his parents, a painful right-of-passage for members of the queer community. While the rhetoric of coming out has been increasingly epitomized on placards that read "Love is love," or Lady Gaga's anthem "Born This Way," the comedian flips audience expectations to find the levity in the situation. After talking extensively about how much he loves melodrama, he recounts:

I'll tell you here, face to face, man to man. "Father, I love cock" ... When you come out to your father, your father always thinks, "I hope he's not the bottom" ... My dad said, "Gay?" "Yes, dad, gay." "You aren't a normal gay," he said. "OK, do something gay." What does my father want, a blow job?

Here the comedian effectively identifies the sexual implications of coming out—those frequently neutered by a homonormative public discourse of love, support, and even triumph—and reveals them to a public now widely trained to believe that being homosexual is not just about sexual desire.

You can't say that on TV

Manu NNa is able to cast himself as a proud sinvergüenza in his stand-up specials precisely because he controls the narrative, moving private discourse into the public sphere without much concern for who may be offended. While he is still bound by what the market will support, demand for his daring style must exist given his growing celebrity profile. Taking into consideration his unique voice and the extensive work that he has done for Comedy Central Latinoamérica, including the Mexican version of *Drunk History*, it is little surprise that the network included him on *Se busca comediante*. Nevertheless the show can prove to be a jarring viewing experience because he loses control of the narrative; while the comedian continues to cast himself the same proud sinvergüenza seen in his stand-up, he is frequently recast as foolish maricón by the production itself, one who is not only a potential danger to himself, but also to those around him.

He shares *Se busca* with three other comedians: Alexis de Anda, Bert-Oh, who produces YouTube videos, and El Diablito who appears to be the most well-known of the quartet at

Proud sinvergüenza or foolish maricón?

the time of filming. Being unscripted as far as the audience is aware, the series features the comedians interacting with each other and reacting to ridiculous situations and guests as they travel from city to city in their Comedy Central van. The concept of controlling the narrative is critical in terms of the production itself; while Manu NNa determines what is presented to his stand-up audience through a careful curation of jokes, in *Se Busca* he cedes control of his image to a certain extent through editing and the confessional shot, typically a post-scene interview injected into the narrative to capture reflections about the on-screen action. Editing and confessionals are a topic of frequent discussion amongst reality show audiences who are aware that producers and directors edit raw footage in certain ways to produce certain narratives; Skeggs and Woods, for example, look at how close-ups are edited to elicit judgement and incredulity from the audience in their empirical study (2012: 127).

During first-episode introductions, the narrator casts Manu NNa as a "comedian, actor and diva and, despite looking like he's just stepped out of Pokémon Go, he's the king, um, queen of glamor, Manu NNa." If the audience was not aware that Manu NNa is gay, the show goes to great lengths to make it clear; throughout the first episode (and indeed, the entire series), barbs are thrown at Manu NNa for both his sexuality and his effeminacy. The other comedians snicker when he reveals that his father does not know that he is gay; in a confessional, Bert-Oh observes, incredulous: "He has green hair, he wears more jewelry than an old woman. He's a homosexual piñata" ("Episodio 1" 2017). Manu NNa explains that he does not dress as boldly around his father, but is unable to hide other markers of his homosexuality. "I have a faggy voice, right?" he asks, a question to which Alexis and El Diablito both respond affirmatively. Despite the barbs, Manu NNa never shies away from his sinvergüenza status: throughout the 11-episode run, he continually refers to himself with female adjectives,[9] wears loud outfits, and performs other bits that one would generally expect from his stand-up act should they be familiar with it. Those familiar with his act would also expect his trademark re-radicalization of queer discourse, again, taking what has been increasingly privatized by the homonormative impulse and making it public. In terms of the overt sexual references that we saw in his Netflix special, Manu NNa certainly delivers. These instances are even more fascinating to watch on *Se busca* because they are not merely a theoretical discourse—he interacts with real people *as* his stand-up persona. Nevertheless, this is also where *Se busca* becomes problematic for Manu NNa and a recasting as foolish maricón occurs precisely because of the top-down nature of the production. Although the series contains numerous examples, I will focus on the episodes shot in Monterrey where this recasting is on full display.

Before arriving in the city, the quartet decides to make a stop at a biker bar, an obvious set-up by producers given its status as a place that a sinvergüenza like Manu NNa clearly does not belong. Nevertheless, in a confessional, the comedian seems to take that as a challenge: "I have a condom for whatever may come up … I want them to take me even if it is just to smack me around" ("Episodio 3" 2017). Ironically, the other comedians use Manu NNa as a shield—El Diablito admits that he is scared and Alexis adds, in a confessional: "If they don't kill Manu NNa … then they won't kill me!" Manu NNa, on the other hand, does not cower; after rifling through his handbag, he announces: "I'm a man. I know I look like an overwhelmingly sensual woman, but … I am a man." A biker responds: "But inside of you." Without skipping a beat, Manu NNa counters: "I want a man inside of me." The biker laughs, showing the levity of the conversation, but in an immediate cut to a confessional Bert-Oh responds: "Manu NNa has already started with his joterías,[10] when it's obvious that these guys don't like that stuff. These guys are too crude to put up with those kinds of jokes." As they sit and share a drink over the next few minutes of screen time, Manu NNa continues to push his sinvergüenza status. He dares one of the bikers to grab his hand, but the biker refuses, reassuring that he "respects gender diversity."

415

In a confessional, Alexa notes that, in Manu NNa's case, homosexuality might be contagious. When the biker finally relents, El Diablito jumps up from the table and declares "You touched him, fag!" Although the bikers show no sign of offense or disgust during the extended scene, El Diablito says, in a confessional: "Manu NNa with his jokes, the truth is that it worries me that he will end up like Fabiruchis," a reference to supposedly gay television and radio personality Fabián Lavalle who was found naked and beaten in Mexico City's Colonia Roma in 2007 (Lagunas 2007). The scene concludes with Manu NNa riding the rest of the way to Monterrey on the back of a motorcycle, tightly gripping one of the presumed homophobic bikers.

The idea of losing control of the narrative resonates strongly in this three-minute sequence. For those who know Manu NNa's act, he remains completely in character—his proud sinvergüenza does not waiver even in an environment where that very openness may very well put him in danger.[11] Nevertheless, when he loses control of the narrative—mostly in the confessionals by his co-hosts—he is swiftly recast as the foolish maricón. They dismiss Manu NNa's attempts to connect with the bikers as pushing his "joterías," giving the audience an excuse to laugh *at* the comic, while his "foolishness" becomes a potential physical danger to both himself and others because he does not know that a biker bar is not the time and place to be acting like a sinvergüenza. Another interesting facet of the Monterrey-centric episodes ("Episodio 3" 2017 and "Episodio 4" 2017) is that, while the comics repeatedly warn the audience that the city is extremely homophobic and misogynistic—and we do see this exemplified in some of the comics who audition—it is primarily Bert-Oh and El Diablito that aim a steadily stream of both overt and subtle venom toward Manu NNa. When the quartet visits a ranch in episode 4, in a confessional Bert-Oh shares: "We arrived at the ranch, everybody was decked out in big hats, and boots and surely they're armed. We have to be careful, and hopefully Manu NNa won't start with his joterías." Manu NNa manages to ride a horse without incident, but is again framed as the foolish maricón who puts everybody in danger because he does not know when to stop with his "act."

Another area where Manu NNa's loss of narrative control are apparent are in the use of post-production on-screen graphics, particularly the animated butterfly wings that paint him as a mariposa, a derogatory term for homosexual in Mexico. In episode 5, upon returning to Mexico City and recharging in Alexis's apartment, she decides to change into her geisha outfit, to which Manu NNa declares "This bitch is going to get changed. I will not be left behind." In the next scene, Manu NNa emerges in a rather tame light blue suit and multi-colored shirt, and although his choice of wardrobe is certainly less daring than we have seen him sport in the past, post-production imposes flapping butterfly wings on his back. El Diablito notes that he looks like a cafeteria worker from the 1950s, and in a confessional, Manu NNa responds: "Better dead than simple" ("Episodio 5" 2017). Manu NNa clearly takes pride in his wardrobe choices as a proud sinvergüenza, but producers effectively give the audience permission to laugh at the foolish maricón for daring to be different. These wings also inexplicably appear on his back in Guadalajara as he drunkenly stumbles towards the van ("Episodio 2" 2017), a blatantly homophobic representation given that there is nothing "queer" about this scene other than Manu NNa's mere presence in it.

Due to the nature of the production itself, we are not privileged to Manu NNa's reaction to the confessionals, where some of the strongest foolish maricón rhetoric is produced. Homophobic comments from El Diablito and Bert-Oh in particular come off as jarring because we know that Manu NNa is never in any real danger—these comedians are followed by cameras and have the backing of multi-national media conglomerate Viacom, owner of Comedy Central Latinoamérica. Nevertheless, given what we see on-screen, Manu NNa almost never takes offence to homophobic comments and often plays into them—after all, *Se busca* is a comedy show that strongly promotes "anything goes" attitude."[12] What makes Manu NNa's rhetoric so powerful is that he never appears embarrassed or makes any attempt to tone down his act—he fully owns the character that he has created.

Given that confessional shots, the narrator voice and graphics are all added post-production, the recasting of Manu NNa as foolish maricón thus becomes a purposefully produced top-down storyline that may resonant with the audience even if it is a very easy shot to take—Manu NNa is unmistakably gay, so why not mock that? This disenfranchising of his queer artistic subjectivity also gives the audience, likely younger, urban and liberal, permission to laugh at the comedian because it takes his strength—a proud sinvergüencería that he has worked diligently to cultivate—and turns it into a running joke. This is particularly troubling because, while all of the comedians take their lumps from each other, none come close to the personal, visceral "jokes" directed at Manu NNa.

Is there room in Mexico's increasingly homonormalized queer discourse for a Manu NNa, a comedian who takes the potentially distasteful private and makes it public? I believe that the answer is yes, and we see proof of that in his growing celebrity stature and the fact that Netflix chose him for such a high-profile comedy special. Nevertheless, his recasting as foolish maricón on *Se busca* also shows that there is a strong undercurrent that will punish him for such transgressions. This aspect of the show did not garner mentions in online articles and commentary, suggesting that the viewing public did not see it as problematic or notable. For as far as Mexico has come in the area of legal LGBTTTI rights, personal attitudes and what is deemed "acceptable" seem far slower to evolve.

Notes

1 All translations of Comedy Central and YouTube comedy sets and dialogue from *Se busca comediante* are mine. I rely on Netflix's English subtitles in the case of *Simplemente Manu NNa*.
2 This is both a reference to violence against Mexico's LGBTTTI community and fluidity in sexual identification where those who take the active role in sexual encounters are not necessary considered "gay," as I will discuss later in this chapter. Manu NNa's sexual partner engages in a homosexual encounter, then reverts to violence against the passive partner once the encounter is over, likely out of self-loathing.
3 As Marzullo observes, LGBTTTI is common parlance in Mexico for LGBT, and stands for "lesbianas (lesbians), gays, bisexuales (bisexuals), transgeneros (transgender), transexuales (transsexuals), travesties (cross-dressers), and intersexuales (intersexuals)" (2015: 698).
4 I have debated how to label Manu NNa's framing in *Se busca*, ultimately deciding to employ more widely understandable terms given that it is a reality show meant for a general public. I chose maricón—a highly derogatory Mexican slang for *fag*—because of the extensive use of such words on the show.
5 From the perspective of Mexican LGBTTTI activists, de la Dehesa explains that this shift manifested itself as "a greater prioritization of state-directed efforts and a narrowing of their agendas from transforming broader relations of power in society and gaining social acceptance to an emphasis on legally enforced tolerance" (2010: 5).
6 Many bemoan homonormativity as trading sexual freedom for societal acceptance and political rights—Warner offers an oft-cited example in *The Trouble With Normal* (1999)—but we also must be cognizant of our privilege in doing so given that millions of queers worldwide live under governments that actively persecute them, including the death penalty in some jurisdictions.
7 There is no indication of where this set was performed; given that the stage looks make-shift and the audience's wild reaction, I would assume a queer venue, perhaps a bar.
8 See Arrellano (9–20) for a history of HIV/AIDS in Mexico, particularly the rise and fall of stigma and its association with gay men.
9 This is far easier to accomplish in Spanish than in English, given that adjectives are marked by gender in the former. For example, in one confessional, Manu NNa proclaims "Estoy hart*a*!" instead of hart*o*, the "a" representing female and the "o" male.

417

10 I have chosen to leave "joterías" in its Spanish form as it does not have a perfect English translation and the term has been increasingly reclaimed for use in Queer Latinx Studies. Roughly translated, joterías in this *specific* context could mean "queer stuff/queer crap."

11 Theoretically; given that the comedians are followed by a camera crew and drive a van clearly branded with the well-known Comedy Central logo, it is unlikely that any violence would befall them. We could even question the presence of the bikers themselves—they seem eager to be shown on camera, leading me to believe that were most likely cast beforehand.

12 Perhaps this attitude only applies to banter between the hosts; both Alexis and Manu NNa become visibly irritated with a rancher in Monterrey who makes both homophobic and misogynistic jokes—see "Episodio 3" (2017).

Works cited

Agren, David. "Mexico's gay couples fight backlash against same-sex marriage." *The Guardian*, 19 December 2016, www.theguardian.com/world/2016/dec/19/mexico-same-sex-marriage-backlash-gay.

Arrellano, Luis Manuel. "Estigma y discriminación a personas con VIH." *CONAPRED* 28 July 2008, www.conapred.org.mx/documentos_cedoc/C-05-A.pdf.

Blanquet, Hugo. "Hugo Blanquet." *YouTube*, uploaded by Maximiliano Gay Bar, 27 October 2014, www.youtube.com/watch?v=E8i0GS4XwRo&t=430s.

Blanquet, Hugo. "No es pena ser pasivo." *YouTube*, uploaded by Hugo Blanquet, 8 March 2013, www.youtube.com/watch?v=2wlRMwouy5M.

Blanquet, Hugo. "Stand Up, Hugo Blanquet – Como cambian los tiempos, mi generación." *YouTube*, uploaded by Hugo Blanquet, 7 September 2016, www.youtube.com/watch?v=QF3Ib5OzZrQ.

Butler, Judith. "Critically Queer." *GLQ: A Journal of Lesbian and Gay Studies*, vol. 1, no. 1, 1993, pp. 17–32.

Christiansen, Adrienne E., and Jeremy J. Hanson. "Comedy as Cure for Tragedy: ACT UP and the Rhetoric of AIDS." *Quarterly Journal of Speech*, vol. 82, no. 2, 1996, pp. 157–170.

de la Dehesa, Raphael. *Queering the Public Sphere in Mexico and Brazil: Sexual Rights Movements in Emerging Democracies*. Duke University Press, 2010.

Duggan, Lisa. "The New Homonormativity: The Sexual Politics of Neoliberalism." *Materializing Democracy: Toward a Revitalized Cultural Politics*, edited by Dana D. Nelson and Russ Castronovo. Duke University Press, 2002, pp. 175–194.

"Episodio 1." *Se busca comediante*. Comedy Central Latinoamérica, 30 Jan. 2017.

"Episodio 2." *Se busca comediante*. Comedy Central Latinoamérica, 6 Feb. 2017.

"Episodio 3." *Se busca comediante*. Comedy Central Latinoamérica, 13 Feb. 2017.

"Episodio 4." *Se busca comediante*. Comedy Central Latinoamérica, 20 Feb. 2017.

"Episodio 5." *Se busca comediante*. Comedy Central Latinoamérica, 27 Feb. 2017.

Foster, David William. *Sexual Textualities*. University of Texas Press, 1997.

Halperin, David M. and Valerie Traub. "Beyond Gay Pride." *Gay Shame*, edited by David M. Halperin and Valerie Traub. Chicago University Press, 2009, pp. 3–40.

Hernández, Eduardo. "Reportan asistencia de 200 mil personas en marcha gay de CDMX." *El Universal*, 25 June 2016, www.eluniversal.com.mx/articulo/metropoli/cdmx/2016/06/25/reportan-asistencia-de-200-mil-personas-en-marcha-gay-de-cdmx.

La Fountain-Stokes, Lawrence. "Gay Shame, Latina- and Latino-Style: A Critique of White Queer Performativity." *Gay Latino Studies*, edited by Michael Hames Garcia and Ernesto Martinez. Duke University Press, 2011, pp. 55–80.

Lagunas, Icela. "Encuentran golpeado a Fabián Lavalle en un hotel." *El Universal*, 31 October 2007, http://archivo.eluniversal.com.mx/notas/458327.html.

La Kikis. "La Kikis – 2da Presentacion – Stand Up." *YouTube*, uploaded by Stand Up Special, 14 December 2016, www.youtube.com/watch?v=LdmweqDDyJo.

McCarthy, Sean L. "Netflix's Stand-Up Comedy Domination Is Being Led By Lisa Nishimura and Robbie Praw." *Decider*, 16 May 2017. http://decider.com/2017/05/16/netflix-comedy-lisa-nishimura-robbie-praw.

McGee, Marcus J., and Karen Kampwirth. "The Co-optation of LGBT Movements in Mexico Nicaragua: Modernizing Clientelism?" *Latin American Politics and Society*, vol. 57, no. 4, 2015, pp. 51–73.

Manu NNa. "Rodrigo Aedo – Manu NNa." *Stand-Up México*, season 4, episode 38, Comedy Central Latin America, http://play.comedycentral.la/CC-Stand-up/stand-up-mexico.

Manu NNa. *Simplemente Manu NNa*. 2017. Netflix, www.netflix.com/watch/80124727

Marzullo, Michelle A. "Lgbt/queer Sexuality, History of, North America." *The International Encyclopedia of Human Sexuality*, edited by Patricia Whelehan and Anne Bolin. Wiley, 2015, pp. 693–698.

Meneses, Raúl. "Raúl Meneses | @ #StandupEnComedy." *YouTube*, uploaded by Comedy Central Latinoamérica, 10 January 2017, www.youtube.com/watch?v=9m3LDhIN4YI.

Peña, Nicho. "Nicho Peña – Stand Up." *YouTube*, uploaded by Stand Up Special, 30 November 2016, www.youtube.com/watch?v=H4cxU7r1fTs.

Skeggs, Beverley, and Helen Wood. *Reacting to Reality Television: Performance, Audience and Value*. Routledge, 2012.

Warner, Michael. *The Trouble with Normal: Sex, Politics and the Ethics of Queer Life*. Free Press, 1999.

36

THE CUBAN MISSILE CRISIS OF WHITE MASCULINITY

Tito Bonito and the burlesque butt

Kristie Soares

Named one of 2016's "Most Fascinating People" (*LA Weekly* 2016) and 2017's "Most Comedic Performer" (Burlesque Hall of Fame 2017), Tito Bonito is a 5'10, light-skinned, dark haired Cuban from Miami. He is reminiscent of Desi Arnaz, a likeness that Tito plays up when hosting burlesque shows, often in tuxedos and hats like those Arnaz himself used to wear. Tito's charm and old-fashioned aesthetic make him a perfect choice to gently initiate a crowd of burlesque virgins into the art form on the Monday I see him perform in the Bootleg Bombshells show at a downtown L.A. sports bar. Tito welcomes the crowd—which is largely queer, of color, and/or female—while making clear the erotic and political potential that burlesque has always encapsulated.[1] Although he identifies personally as gay, and makes no secret of it on stage, he tells me after that show that audiences always wonder about his true sexuality. He finds this funny, particularly since throughout the course of this particular night he will give a man a lap dance and spank another, and given that it is not unusual for him to deep throat a microphone between acts. Something about his presentation of self makes his sexuality unintelligible to people, however, likely because his gender presentation is so fluid. On this evening he will start in a suit, but by the end of this night we will see him in a thong, nipple tassles, and—the signature of his act—"assles," tassles glued to the butt cheeks. Tito's intersectional identity as a queer Latino is represented in his costuming by the "assles." Because of their prominent placement on his queer Cuban butt, the "assles" gesture toward the gender performativity and xenophobia that structure the history of burlesque into which Tito inserts himself.

The kind of gender and sexual play that Tito engages in is characteristic of burlesque. The form entered into the U.S. landscape in the late 19th century, and was quickly adopted and shaped by American vaudeville. Scholars such as Mara Dauphin have written that there is significant evidence for "including bodies not sexed as female in the historical archive of femininity," particularly within the vaudeville world "in which femininity was always imitated and rarely tied to biology or nature" (260, 259). Although most burlesque performers have been historically female, and the vast majority of neo-burlesque performers today are also gendered female, there is a long tradition of biologically male bodies performing femininity in vaudeville to which Tito belongs.

There is also a significant tradition of non-white and immigrant bodies performing within burlesque and vaudeville, although their inclusion has been more troublesome. Historically, the non-white and immigrant integration into burlesque has centered around the "cooch

The Cuban Missile Crisis of white masculinity

dance"—originally a version of belly dancing, and eventually expanded to include any kind of "exotic" or non-Western dance. The cooch dance was titillating to American audiences upon its debut at the 1893 Chicago World's Fair, but xenophobic discourses quickly surrounded the world of cooch dancing. The infamous "Night at Minsky's" that marked the beginning of large-scale raids of burlesque clubs in New York, which would eventually lead to the downfall of burlesque in the mid-20th century, was supposedly triggered because one of the cooch dancers went too far—exposing her breasts to the, not incidentally, largely immigrant audience.

Tito's on-stage persona, which in his words ranges from "ratchet, gay club" *Cubanidad* to "Desi Arnaz 1950s," exposes mostly non-Cuban L.A. audiences to Cuban culture.[2] The history of gender play and ethnic othering in burlesque, however, locates his performances within a historical narrative that hints at gender as performative, while simultaneously warning that ethnic otherness, though sexy, is potentially too sexy. Tito's work as the "Cuban Missile Crisis of Burlesque" both confirms and disrupts this narrative, as he performs both his gender and his *Cubanidad* through the figure of what Frances Negrón-Muntaner has called "el culo al aire" [literally: ass in the air; colloquially: being caught with one's pants down] (1997: 191). In using his butt as a visual marker of both his sexuality and his ethnicity, Tito pushes audiences to simultaneously "normalize sexuality" while confronting what he calls "the fear of immigration in America" (Personal Interview).

Epistemology of the butt

Tito began performing burlesque in 2010 after being introduced to it by friends while in theatre school in Chicago. He explains to me that he had always identified as a "pervert"—first having the slur thrown at him as a young man growing up in a Cuban household in Miami, and later embracing his queerness and sexual desire as an adult and burlesque performer. Burlesque, he says, allowed him to make a career of what he had always been inclined to do—take his pants off and dance. His mother, who is supportive of his career, christened him "Tito Bonito" and the "The Cuban Missile Crisis" soon after he began burlesque, and he has made a career of performing as the provocative Cuban persona "Tito" ever since.

Tito's insistence on being called "The Cuban Missile Crisis of Burlesque" gestures toward the fact that his "missile" is attempting to replace the military missiles that have characterized Cuban exile masculinity since the 1960s. His "missile" causes a crisis in the sexuality of some individual audience members, and in the collective appeal to hetero-masculinity held by the Cuban exile community. Tito's relationship to the categories of "*Cubanidad,*" "Americanness," "masculinity," and "femininity" are the result of not only his personal upbringing, but also the larger context of Cuban-American relations in the 20th and 21st centuries. The second half of the 20th and the early 21st centuries have been characterized by a masculinist standoff between anti-Castro Cuban Republicans and Fidel Castro. For Cuban-American queers, particularly those coming of age in Miami, the relationship to both masculinity and femininity is complicated by the hegemonic control that both pro-Castro and anti-Castro forces seem to have over gender expression.[3] Tito's branding as the "Cuban Missile Crisis of Burlesque" references a specific moment of crisis—the infamous nuclear showdown that followed the failed Bay of Pigs invasion—as well as the more general gender crisis faced by Cuban-American queers wishing to separate themselves from the normative gender and sexuality mandated by both their Cuban and American heritages. The question, then, is not so much whether one is pro- or anti-Castro, but rather how one can use gender expression to critique both Castro's dictatorial masculinity *and* the right wing Cuban exile masculinity that opposes it.

The "missile" that both enacts this political critique and stirs up queer desire in Tito's acts is not necessarily, as one might think, his penis. The crisis in the audience actually comes about when Tito turns around. As Frances Negrón-Muntaner writes of Puerto Rican butts in the diaspora:

> In the diaspora, the sexual epistemology of the butt gets even more complicated. Gay men may carry the bottom's fetishism to bed as a nostalgia for Condado fucks: nationalistic lesbians use their culometros to distinguish the boricuas from other too-close-to-call ethnicities: and many Puerto Rican women, who have and admire their Chacon bodies for their power over men and circumstances, roar as they are subjected to the everyday indignities of being told that they are fat, should get on a diet, or should sign up for the gym. Migrant life, with its characteristic economic and emotional instability, ultimately becomes a struggle to avoid ending up with el culo al aire (our butts exposed).
>
> *(1997: 191)*

Negrón-Muntaner argues for an "epistemology of the butt," which understands the Puerto Rican butt (here expanded by me to include the Cuban American butt) as a defining way of understanding cultural identity within the community. To be caught with your "culo al aire" means literally to have your butt in the air, but colloquially it means to be caught with one's pants down. For Negrón-Muntaner, the epistemology of the butt functions so that one identifies ethnically through the butt, while being careful not to expose oneself (or one's butt) to the point of drawing ridicule from non-Puerto Rican people.

Burlesque is an interesting avenue through which to address the politics of the butt, including its larger implications for gender, sexuality, and ethnicity when that butt is attached to a gay Cuban man. Neo-burlesque, which refers to the resurgence of burlesque since the 1990s, "is an attempt to recover the subversive elements of burlesque in order to wrest the act of stripping from more patriarchal interests through a re-focalization on humour, sexual agency and pleasure" (Klein 2014: 250). In this way burlesque, with its reliance on irony and satire, has historically commented upon the gender and sexual norms of Victorian bourgeois society, early 20th century American upper-class society, and since the 1990s U.S.-based norms of beauty, particularly as they relate to body shape. Its commentary on racial and ethnic norms has historically been less clear, however. Well-known Black performers like Josephine Baker have had a long history in burlesque, even as the form has generally had a complicated relationship with racial and ethnic otherness. The cooch dancer figure in late 19th-century burlesque, for instance, "was representative of an exotic foreign culture, demonstrating her native customs for the enlightenment of burlesque's ethnographically-minded audiences" (Allen 1991: 264). The cooch dance was included in the World's Fair, in fact, as a part of a celebration of "the quadricentennial anniversary of Columbus's discovery of the New World and as a showcase for American technological and cultural progress" (Allen 1991: 225). The cooch dancer's body was understood as spectacle in a tradition that could be traced back to the freak show culture surrounding Sarah Baartman, the so-called "Hottentot Venus."[4]

Following the presentation of the first cooch dance by a dancer named Little Egypt, the burlesque world began to adopt cooch dance and the Orientalizing clothing, music, and back stories that accompanied it (Schwartz 2005). Most scholars argue that the irony that otherwise characterized burlesque was missing from most cooch dance, making cooch dance exotic and enticing, but not necessarily critical. Viewers of cooch dance believed themselves to be learning something about another culture, which stripped away the ironic component

The Cuban Missile Crisis of white masculinity

of other burlesque dance. Many scholars posit cooch dance as a turning point in American burlesque, with its departure away from comedy and toward exotic sexuality actually helping bring about the end of the golden age of burlesque.[5] There is an underlying critique of cooch dancers and women of color implicit in these narratives, which suggests that their excessive sexuality is both dangerous and un-ironic. This critique is itself ironic, given that by the time of its full-scale adoption into burlesque, cooch dances were no longer primarily performed by women from other cultures, but were rather fanciful interpretations of these dances by American white women (Deagon 2007).[6] Distancing burlesque from the ethnic other is a rhetorical device often used to scapegoat women of color, rather than acknowledge that the end of the golden age of burlesque was brought about by anti-obscenity laws and the rise of the film industry. For instance, the Minsky Brothers—three Russian brothers that owned the most prominent chain of burlesque houses in mid-20th-century New York—tried to defend against the crackdown on burlesque by distancing themselves from ethnic otherness. When the Minsky brothers would have to testify in congress in 1937, they appealed to the national culture of xenophobia in order to defend their show. Herbert Minsky was quoted as saying that there were: "100–150 burlesque theatres in this country doing their part employing vaudeville performers. We pledge ourselves not to employ foreign strip-tease artists in our cradle of American burlesque" (quoted in Zemeckis 2013).

The inclination to set burlesque apart from ethnic otherness may indirectly have something to do with the "culo al aire," as Negrón-Muntaner reminds us: "A big culo does not only upset hegemonic (white) notions of beauty and good taste, it is a sign for the dark, incomprehensible excess of "Latino" and other African diaspora cultures. Excess of food (unrestrained), excess of shitting (dirty), and excess of sex (heathen) are its three vital signs" (1997: 189). Returning to Tito Bonito, the artist's use of the clearly ethnicized body, and particularly the butt, to do the work of commenting on both the U.S. fear of sexuality and of immigration, represents both a continuity and a departure from burlesque tradition. He relies upon burlesque's historical use of humor and irony to comment on gender and sexuality, even while he departs from tradition by relying on the ethnicized markers of his body—the butt—to force the audience to engage with him not as a spectacle, but as an interlocutor putting the too muchness of the ethnic other literally in their faces.

This is most evident in Tito's signature act, "Cuba Libre," which begins with an audio mash-up of "Hail to the Chief," Desi Arnaz's "Babalú," and an excerpt of President Kennedy's Cuban Missile Crisis speech. Tito emerges furtively from the dark, playing a tiny bongo and holding a small American flag. He wears a white *guayabera*, khaki pants, and flip flops—identifiable as typical Cuban male gear. Around his waist is a blue inflatable raft that clearly reads as a children's pool toy. With an exaggerated masculinity communicated by his chest thumping and stern facial expressions, Tito begins to sing along as Desi Arnaz. The sternness of his face as he sings juxtaposes against the playfulness of this tiny bongo, flag, and pool raft. Suddenly, in a theatrical arm sweep, Tito throws the American flag to the floor. He feigns a single tear dripping down his face, and—almost instantly—begins to take off his clothes, flip flops first.

This first portion of Tito's act is characterized by business as usual in Cuban exile politics—i.e. Cuban alpha male retells the maddening and tragic story of exile, aided by a literal raft around his waist and the most recognizable Cuban-American audio of the 1950s and 60s booming behind him. The shedding of the American flag marks a turning point, however—a moment that unleashes the queerness of Tito's character. If Tito is angry holding the American flag, then non-flag holding Tito is not just happy, he is gay.

Moments after the flag hits the ground Tito's face softens as his character appears to discover the bongo, here a proxy for his own penis. He looks young and curious now, as he begins to furiously hit the bongo, eventually lowering it to his crotch so that this action looks like masturbation. At the moment of ejaculation, Tito's juvenile persona stops his feverish drumming and flops over onto his side, only to be energized again by the opening to Celia Cruz's "La Vida es un Carnaval." The trajectory here is one of masculinization in reverse—Tito's character goes from alpha male, to adolescent boy discovering his sexuality, to, finally, Celia Cruz.

Dance scholar Sherrill Dodds makes a "claim for the capacity of faces in motion to act as a site of meaning-production" (Dodds 2014: 52). For Dodds, the face is as important a tool as the body to convey meaning in dance performances. Indeed, Tito's message becomes clear when we understand the throwing of the flag against his expressions. For Tito's character, the American flag functions as a form of repression—keeping him from both smiling and experiencing sexual desire. It is only when he sheds the flag that Tito's face displays pleasure, the zenith of which is accompanied by an explosion of music by queer icon Celia Cruz.[7]

Tito is also displaying here what Reisa Klein refers to as "bodily humor" in neo-burlesque, "which encompasses various embodied performances through exaggerated gestures, costumes, a focus on pleasure and playfulness, coupled with striptease and the other attributes of traditional burlesque (2014: 247). Although he is still wearing his clothes, minus the flip flops, Tito satirizes Cuban maleness through his exaggerated portrayal of both his austerity—indicated by his thumping his fist against his chest—and his sexual curiosity—indicated by the frenzied masturbation choreography.

In this third and final part of the performance, Tito rises up from the ground to the sounds of Celia Cruz's music. As he stands, he makes eye contact with the audience as he licks his lips in pleasure. If the adolescent Tito was marked by surprise at his sexuality, this final Tito is marked by visceral delight. Tito engages here in what Sherrill Dodds refers to as the "choreography of facial commentary"—that is, the facial expressions that the burlesque performer choreographs into their act to signal to the audience their opinions or underlying intentions (2013: 80). In this case the underlying commentary is pleasure, which Tito communicates with a knowing smile and raise of his eyebrows. With this pleasure comes the entrance of the butt. He slowly and deliberately removes his clothing while swiveling his hips eventually gyrating them enough to seemingly compel a woman in a black dress, before waiting off stage, to dance with him. The two dance 32 counts of salsa together, but although Tito is performing the traditionally less flashy role of the leader, the brightness of his blue pool raft, his white undershirt, and the movement of his bottom half make him the obvious focus of the pairing. The woman eventually sneaks off of the stage, while Tito proceeds to rip his undershirt off in a fit of sexual ecstasy. He sensually strips off his blue pool raft, now metaphorically free of the masculinist struggle it represented in the first part of the performance.

The raftless Tito dances around the stage topless, drawing the focus now to his crotch and butt as he prepares for his final declaration: dropping his pants to reveal his Cuban-flag covered butt. As he turns around to bow, the audience discovers that this whole time Tito has been wearing a black thong with a Cuban flag tucked into the back. The truth of his identity has been there inside his pants all along; he is indeed a Cuban man, but his sexuality and gender performance are queered by where he keeps his Cubanness—on his butt. He lifts the flag so that the audience can applaud his bare butt cheeks, which he gyrates enticingly before bending down to pick up just two props for his stage exit—his bright blue raft and the tiny American flag which he waves with a comic enthusiasm as he backs off of the stage, indicating the fragility of both U.S.-based and Cuban masculinities.

Terrie Waddell characterizes burlesque as "a *lived* experience, energized by the pleasure involved in its development and sustenance, performer-audience camaraderie, and the need

The Cuban Missile Crisis of white masculinity

for burlesque to be preserved as an art form that pokes fun at gender stereotypes" (2013: 99). Waddell links the last characteristic of poking fun of gender stereotypes to burlesque's trickster quality, which seeks to destabilize an audience's assumptions without clearly telling them what assumptions they should replace them with. This is the case in Tito's performance of "Cuba Libre." We know the answer is on the "culo," but what is the "culo" trying to tell us? Tito describes his Cuba Libre act on his website as "a political commentary on the Cuban immigration into the United States during the 1960s." It does seem to make some sort of commentary on Cuban immigration—from the voiceover recordings of President Kennedy's Cuban Missile Crisis speech to the excerpts of Desi Arnaz's "Babalú"—and yet the exact political messaging is not clear. While a right-wing Cuban exile reading might construe the act as a critique of Castro's communism, Tito's satirical portrayal of Cuban exile masculinity in the first third of the act suggests that he does not intend to uphold a stereotypical notion of Cuban machismo or heteronormativity. Rather, the subtitle to this act on Tito's webpage gives us a hint. It reads, simply, "La Mentirita" (the little lie). Again, a right-wing exile reading might suggest that the "lie" is contained in the name of the act, namely the suggestion that Cuba is "libre" [free]. I would suggest a counter-reading, which is that the *mentirita* the subtitle references is literally revealed at the end of this act, when Tito turns around, drops his pants, and exposes his Cuban-flag covered butt. Tito's butt is a symbol of the *mentirita* that is the concept of a stable Cuban exile masculinity, which was itself unraveled by the simulated masturbation that gave way to the queerness of his salsa dancing and his thong. Tito's act makes clear that if Cuban exile masculinity of the variety of Desi Arnaz and Brigade 2506 (the paramilitary group that the CIA backed and then failed to back during the Cuban Missile Crisis) has ever existed, then it is long dead now. Replaced instead by adolescents jacking off and *cuming* into consciousness—quite literally—as queer Celia Cruz impersonators.

There is also another *mentirita*, however, which Tito hints at through his treatment of the American flag. Tito has been exposed with his *culo al aire*, in the literal sense of having his butt exposed, but he has not been exposed with his *culo al aire* in the colloquial sense of the phrase. That is, he has not been caught with his pants down in front of a U.S.-based audience made up almost entirely of non-Cubans. Yes, Tito critiques Cuban masculinity, but he also critiques American perceptions of Cuban men when he throws the flag to the ground at a key moment in the act. If non-Cuban audience members believe they understand Tito as he inhabits the most stereotypical markers of Cuban masculinity in the first third of the act, they are forced into a rude awakening when he comes into consciousness midway through. Where the first version of Tito was vulgar in his movements and facial expressions, the second and third Titos demonstrate what Maria Elena Buszek might call an "awarishness" that posits him as subject rather than object. Buszek uses the term to refer to the self-conscious wink or nod that 19th-century burlesque performers used to let audience members know that the performers knew exactly what they were doing. This awarishness "called into question the legitimacy of defining female sexuality according to a binary structure, but also marked as desirable the spectrum of unstable and taboo identities as imaged between these poles" (Buszek 1999: 142). In the case of Tito, he is calling into question both heteromasculinity and pre-determined notions of the immigrant as un-nuanced savage. Far from the cooch dancers that American audiences ogled and exoticized, Tito forces this U.S.-based audience to confront whether their ideas of exotic otherness as indicated by Desi Arnaz's babalú and the conga drum. In doing so, Tito places himself on the "monster/beauty" continuum, inhabiting monstrosity and beauty at the same time (Sally 2009: 7). He is the "monster" immigrant of which many are so afraid, and the queer "beauty" that no one in the audience can take their eyes off of.

The labor of the butt

When I arrive to see Tito perform at the sports bar, I am immediately harassed by a drunk straight white man at the door. He wants to buy me a drink, gets mad when I won't let him, tries to buy my wife a drink, and then gets a little too close. This is the environment in which Tito must work. Although the room will gradually fill with queers, people of color, and cisgender white women as show time approaches, the environment does not, on its surface, look like a safe place for a queer Latino man to take his pants off onstage. Because most neo-burlesque is performed in bars and cabarets without a formal stage, performers generally move around the crowd, often in very close physical proximity to people that may be drunk, inclined to touch performers, or both. There is a strict rule in burlesque against audience members touching performers, but this rule must be explained and enforced by someone.

Because Tito hosts as well as performs, the task of establishing the norms of conduct often falls to him. In an interview he tells me that as a young boy he was never taught the concept of consent: "I was taught you could just touch whatever you want." Today, as a self-proclaimed "faggot feminist," he makes consent one of the cornerstones of his hosting by articulating when an audience member does or does not have consent to touch him. As a cisgender man, Tito acknowledges that he knows he "won't always be welcome" in all spaces in this predominantly female art form, and this understanding of his male privilege makes him particularly skilled at controlling male audience members. One evening when I attend his show, I note a young Latino man that appears to be in his 20s and is clearly intoxicated. He speaks out of turn, flirting with Tito loudly, mostly in Spanish and occasionally in accented English. Because Tito positions himself as Latino early in his hosting, not just by virtue of his name but also by the use of Spanish words and jokes, he is able to control this audience member using both an insider and an outsider dynamic. As an insider, Tito appears to care for the audience member, good naturedly chiding him at several points throughout the night. This joking often centers on the audience member's Latinidad, with Tito often making reference to the current political situation by referencing Trump and whether the audience member, and presumably Tito himself, will be allowed to stay in the country. The audience member seems in on these jokes, laughing along and often talking back. When he goes too far, however, Tito disciplines him through jokes that are more cutting or, in the case of when he interrupts Tito's act to throw dollar bills in his face, through rolling his eyes and turning away from him for the entirety of the rest of the night. When I ask Tito about this later, he says he tries "to be disrespectful to put him in his place but still nice because at the end of the day he is throwing $20 bills at us."

This mode of navigating money and audience behavior is common in professions in which affective labor and physical labor are rewarded by tips. In the case of this particular show, performers are paid a fee but can also make more money off of audience tips. Tito's *culo* takes on another dimension here, as it is both a cornerstone of his social commentary and the cornerstone of his economic potential. Burlesque is notorious for paying very little, with performers often noting that one goes into burlesque for the love of it, and into striptease for the money. Sherrill Dodds notes that the "economic stability and intellectual capital" required to perform burlesque consistently "constitutes a position of class privilege" (2013: 84). In the case of Tito Bonito, he readily recognizes that his own ability to survive primarily from his burlesque income is a result of his masculine privilege. He refers to his gender presentation as "faggot butch," and recognizes that his rarity as a male performer makes him more marketable, and that his masculine gender presentation is also a source of social capital among male performers.

Tito uses his classically masculine gender presentation—particularly when he hosts shows in suit and tie—to gain audience trust. In his words: "The men in the audience fall in love with me as a friend […] and then all of a sudden you're blind-sided." In part because of his seemingly-normative

The Cuban Missile Crisis of white masculinity

gender presentation, he is able to make his ethnic identity very clear from the start, sometimes opening a show in Spanish by shouting "Sábado Gigante! Don Francisco aquí"—a reference to the long-running Spanish-language variety show hosted by the Chilean Don Francisco ("Cuban Missile Series"). Likewise, Tito does not shy away from making jokes that reference political situations that are relevant to the Cuban exile community, for instance joking that "my government name if you wanna look me up on Facebook is Elian González Ruiz de Bustamante Acosta Hurtado de los Santos"—a reference to Elian González, the young boy who was the subject of an international custody battle between Cuba and the United States in 2000 ("Mini Missile-Sizzling"). He will also occasionally perform as Fidevil, a queer version of Fidel Castro performed with a beard, military cap, thong, and red devil horns—here a reference not only to anti-Castro sentiment among Miami Cuban exiles, but also to the masculinist image that Castro sought to portray.

During a show that I attended, he is the last performer of the night. Because he is the only male performer in the Bootleg Bombshells show, it is possible that new audience members may not be aware that he will eventually perform. He transitions from hosting to performing casually, handing his microphone to a fellow performer, and then fixing eyes sexily with an audience member. Tito dances to slow R&B music, removing his suit jacket and sequined red suspenders. Like the acts by female dancers before him, he works the crowd, eventually removing his shirt to show his bare chest covered by just two red nipple tassles. Where most of the female dancers rely on the removal of their tops as an act closer, referred to colloquially as the "big reveal," Tito tends to remove his shirt in the middle of his act. Nipple tassles highlight his nipples as erogenous zones that we, the audience, are not allowed to see. The key moment comes when Tito removes his pants to reveal a silver thong, his buttocks also sporting two black "assles" that he twirls seductively as he writhes on the floor. On all fours, Tito positions himself over a pile of money and begins to toss it over his shoulder at his own butt, reminding the audience that when the "culo" is "al aire," the right thing to do is throw money.

★

In a photoshoot taken on a train car by photographer Kriss Abigail, which appears on Tito's website, we see Tito dressed from the waist up in a black collar shirt with a striped black and white tie. Tito holds on to the railings between two train cars, peering out between them as though her were a harried businessman on the way to work. Below the waist Tito wears black brief underwear, however, and black dress socks held up by a sock garter. Tito twists one leg over the other, as though he is a Rockette about to perform her signature kick. The juxtaposition between Tito's top half and his bottom half in this photo tells of the interplay between two frameworks. On the top half, a heteronormative framework—a young man going to work. On the bottom half, the epistemology of the butt, and in this case the Cuban butt. If the businessman is the emblem of all that is normative in U.S.-based masculinity (Cuban-American or otherwise), then Tito's version of the Cuban-American working man is an indication of how gender, sexuality, and ethnicity can be queered in the world of burlesque. By forcing audiences to confront their fears of sex and immigration through the figure of the "culo al aire," Tito inserts himself into a historical narrative of burlesque that performs not just gender and sexuality, but also *Cubanidad*, in a way that is both sexy and political.

Notes

1 Tito's audience composition is indicative of the typical audience in neo-burlesque, which is largely queer and female (Ferreday 2008).
2 For a further theorization of the concept of "ratchet," a slur generally referring to a combination of raunchiness and low-class aesthetics, see Hernández's "Carnal Teachings" (2014).

Kristie Soares

3 The relationship is complicated also by the imperialist power that the U.S. has exerted over Cuba historically. For instance, the 1901 Platt Amendment that made Cuba a "sovereign" state allowed the U.S. to lease Guantanamo Bay and to intervene in Cuban foreign affairs.
4 For more on Sarah Baartman, an African woman whose buttocks was exhibited in 19th-century European freak shows, see Strother (1999).
5 One night in particular is often cited in histories detailing the decline of burlesque—the night they raided Minsky's in 1925 (Pullen 2002). This event may actually have never occurred, as Kirsten Pullen argues in her investigation of public record, but its rhetorical importance remains as a crucial moment in the story of the persecution of burlesque.
6 Of note here is also burlesque's historic ties to minstrelsy, with American burlesque performers sometimes adopting blackface as part of parody (Mahar 1999: 342) and female minstrel companies pairing minstrelsy with burlesque (see Moody 1944).

Works cited

Abigail, Kriss. "Photograph of Tito Bonito." Titobonito.com. Accessed 28 June 2017.
Allen, Robert G. *Horrible Prettiness: Burlesque and American Culture.* University of North Carolina Press, 1991.
Bonito, Tito. "Tito Bonito at the 2013 BURLYPICKS; Most Comedic." *YouTube*, uploaded by Burlesque B, 24 November 2013, www.youtube.com/watch?v=K-xk6zVF3tw.
Bonito, Tito. "Cuban Missile Series," Season 2 Episode 3. *YouTube*, uploaded by Tito Bonito, 26 November 2014. www.youtube.com/watch?v=fEj60YTh11Q.
Bonito, Tito. "#MiniMissile – Sizzling Circus Sirens." *YouTube*, uploaded by Tito Bonito, 2 August 2015, www.youtube.com/watch?v=Cgzd2XlYNWM.
Bonito, Tito. "Bootleg Bombshells" Performance. Down & Out, Los Angeles. 13 March 2017.
Bonito, Tito. Personal Interview. 26 June 2017.
"Burlesque Hall of Fame Announces 27th Annual Tournament of Tease Winners." Burlesque Hall of Fame. bhofweekend.com/press/2017-winners/burlesque-hall-of-fame-weekend- tournament-of-tease-2017/
Buszek, Maria Elena. "Representing 'Awarishness': Burlesque, Feminist Transgression, and the 19th-Century Pin-up." *The Drama Review*, vol. 43, no. 4, 1999, pp. 141–162.
Cushman, Ellen. "Face, Skins, and the Identity Politics of Rereading Race." *Rhetoric Review*, vol. 24 no. 4, 2005, pp. 389–395.
Dauphin, Mara. "The Trouble With Tim: Historicizing the Male Body in Female Celebrity." *Celebrity Studies*, vol. 6 no. 2, 2014, pp. 258–260.
Deagon, Andrea. "Almée or Salomé?: Hybrid Dances of the East, 1890–1930.*" Congress on Research in Dance Conference Proceedings*, vol. 39, 2007, pp. 36–46.
Dodds, Sherril. "Embodied Transformations in Neo-Burlesque Striptease." *Dance Research Journal*, vol. 45, no. 3, 2013, pp. 75–90.
Dodds, Sherril. "The Choreographic Interface: Dancing Facial Expression in Hip-Hop and Neo-Burlesque Striptease." *DRJ*, vol. 46, no. 2, 2014, pp. 38–56.
Ferreday, Debra. "'Showing the girl': The new burlesque." *Feminist Theory*, vol. 9, no. 1, 2008, pp. 47–65.
Hernandez, Jillian. 2014. "Carnal teachings: Raunch aesthetics as queer feminist pedagogies in Yo! Majesty's hip hop practice." *Women and Performance*, vol. 24, no. 1, 2014, pp. 88–106.
Klein, Reisa. "Laughing It Off: Neo-Burlesque Striptease and the Case of the Sexual Overtones as a Theatre of Resistance." *IC-Revista Científica de Información y Comunicación*, vol. 11, 2014, pp. 245–265.
LA Weekly. "People 2016." http://features.laweekly.com/people-2016/
Mahar, William John. *Behind the Burnt Cork Mask: Early Blackface Minstrelsy and Antebellum American Popular Culture.* University of Illinois Press, 1999.
Moody, Richard. "Negro Minstrelsy." *Quarterly Journal of Speech*, vol. 30, no. 3, 1944, pp. 321-328.
Negrón-Muntaner, Frances. "Jennifer's Butt." *Aztlán*, vol. 22, no. 2, 1997, pp. 181–194.
Platt Amendment. *Ourdocuments.gov.* www.ourdocuments.gov/doc.php?flash=true&doc=55. Accessed 10 Jul 2017.
Pullen, Kirsten. "They Never Raided Minsky's: Popular Memory and the Performance of History." *Performance Research*, vol. 7, no. 4, 2002, pp. 116–120.
Sally, Lynn. "'It Is the Ugly That Is So Beautiful': Performing the Monster/Beauty Continuum in American Neo-Burlesque." *Journal of American Drama and Theatre*, vol. 21, no. 3, 2009, pp. 5–23.

The Cuban Missile Crisis of white masculinity

Schwartz, Michael. "Spectacles in Terpsichorean Disrobing: Antecedents and Ideologies of the Striptease." *Text and Presentation 2004*. Edited by Stratos E. Constantinidis. McFarland & Company, 2005.

SH Photography. "Cuba Libre Photograph 1." TitoBonito.com. Accessed 28 June 2017.

SH Photography. "Cuba Libre Photograph 2." Titobonito.com. Accessed 28 June 2017.

Strother, Z. S. "Display of the Body Hottentot." *Africans on Stage: Studies in Ethnological Show Business*. Edited by Bernth Lindfors, Indiana University Press, 1999.

Waddell, Terrie. "Trickster-Infused Burlesque: Gender Play In the Betwixt and Between." *Australasian Drama Studies*, vol. 63, 2013, pp. 96–110.

Zemeckis, Leslie. *Behind the Burly Q: The Story of Burlesque in America*. Skyhorse Publishing, 2013.

INDEX

abject 225, 379
Africa; African 2, 3, 5, 13, 57, 60, 80, 197, 208, 305, 338, 386–387, 389–390, 423
African American 77
Afro-Brazilian 179, 300, 302–303, 305, 307–308, 388, 392
Afro-Caribbean 79
Afrofuturism 87
Afro-Honduran 219
Afro-Latina; Afro-Latino 72, 75, 76, 78, 80, 219
AIDS 412–413
Alcaraz, Lalo 10, 57, 64–65
Alfaro Siqueiros, David 246
alien 130–134
Amazon 23
American Dream 68
Américas 1, 9, 12, 13, 14; Americas 91, 207, 220, 336, 359
Amerindian 262, 264–266, 268–269, 358
analog era 35
Anarcofeminism 400
Anglo privilege; white privilege 5
Angola 387
anti-colonial 78, 79
anxiety 115–116, 170, 260
Anzaldúa, Gloria 61, 67–68, 400
Arabs 373
Arenas, Reinaldo 4
Argentina; Argentine; Argentinian 48, 91, 129, 198, 201, 211, 294, 301, 335, 348, 377, 379
Arias, Lola 378, 380, 382–383
Arnaz, Desi 420–421, 423, 425
asexual 400
Assassin's Creed IV: Black Flag 31–32, 35, 39–43
Aston, Elaine 378–379
authorized culture; official culture 139, 150

autoeroticism 291
avatars 31
Aztec 89, 263

Baartman, Sarah 422
Balderston, Daniel 5
Baradit, Jorge 6
baseball 12, 72, 74–78, 310, 320, 323–330
bathrooms; public bathrooms 246, 293, 296
Beezley, William H. 2
Belausteguigoitia, Marisa 4
Bergmann, Emilie 5
Bermudez, Silvia 2–3
Beverly, John 2
black feminism; black feminist rap 337, 389
blackness; black identity 300–302, 304–305, 307–308, 338, 343, 389–392
black women 73, 179, 336, 389
bloggers; blogs 27, 103
Bogotá 246
Bolivia; Bolivians 335, 339, 387, 390
Bollywood 197
Bonito, Tito 420–427
border; borders; borderlands; US-Mexican border 51, 224, 228, 233, 238, 250, 343, 390, 398, 400, 404, 406–407
Borderlands/La Frontera 61
border wall 250
Boricua; Borinqueña 71, 78, 79, 80
Borinsky, Alicia 6
boxing 310–314, 316, 318, 320, 348
Brazil; Brazilian 3–4, 12, 129, 177–181, 184, 213, 228, 253, 273–274, 276–278, 279, 280, 300–303, 306–308, 386–388, 390–391
Brown, Bill 107
Brown, J. Andrew 6

Index

Bueno, Eva P. 2–3
burlesque 420–426
Butler, Judith 223, 288, 398, 400–401

Cáceres, Martín 6
Cadava, Eduardo L. 7
Caesar, Terry 2, 3
camp 106–109, 113
Campbell, Bruce 6
Campos, Brenda 7
Cánepa Koch, Gisela 7
capitalism 107, 154, 170, 188–189, 191, 213, 264,
313, 403–404, 406
Caribbean 3, 325–327, 337, 392
Carpentier, Alejo 5
cartoon 3, 35–37, 42, 64, 84, 315, 320
Cash, Johnny 350, 354
Castagnet, Martin Felipe 6
Castañeda, Mari 7
Castillo, Debra 4
Castro, Fidel 324, 326–330, 421
Castro, Verónica 197
Castro-Klarén 4
Catholic Church 4, 60, 296, 363
Central America 1, 57–58, 86, 315, 319, 340–341,
358, 360
Chaviano, Daína 6
Chile; Chilean 12–13, 83, 152, 155–161, 163,
252–253, 255, 257–258, 262, 265, 335, 339,
347–348, 351–352, 354, 427
China 197
Chinese 148
cholo; chola 264–266, 270
cinemasturbation; cinematic masturbation 267
city; cityscape 31–32, 34–37, 40–41, 43
Cleger, Osvaldo 19
Clinton, Hillary 64–65, 69
collective memory; cultural memory; memory;
remembering 139–141, 143, 145–147, 149–150,
153–154, 159, 326, 357
Colombia 23, 50, 63, 152, 217, 246, 256, 335–336,
387, 390, 393
colonialism 14, 71, 73, 75, 77–78, 81, 179, 220,
246, 248, 254, 320, 356–359, 362–363, 368–369,
400–401, 407
colonization 5, 13, 57
comics; comic books 10, 72, 74, 78–81, 83–90
commodity; commodification 83, 157, 188, 236,
325, 328, 336, 340, 349, 356, 358–359
community; *comunidad* 252, 257, 265–266, 268,
270, 368, 371–372, 389,
410, 412
cooch dance 421–423
Cornejo, Inés 2
Costa Rica 318, 335
Coulter, Ann 220
Crenshaw, Kimberlé 73, 336
Cruz, Celia 424–425

Cuba; Cuban 92, 129, 310, 324, 326–330, 338,
420–422, 424, 427
Cuban Missile Crisis 420–423
cultural performance 386–387
Curcio-Nagy, Linda A. 2
cybernetic material 20
cyborg 84 87, 348
Cypess, Sandra 4

dance; dance medicine 356–359, 361, 363–364,
368–369, 371, 373–374
De Beauvoir, Simon 314
De la Cruz Castro Ricalde, María 8
De la Luz Casas Pérez, María 7
De la Mora, Sergio 8
Del Rio, Dolores 8
Democratic Republic of Congo 387; Congolese
391–393
diaspora 72, 73, 74, 78, 81, 390–392, 423
digital age 35
digital native 20
Disney 3
Dominican; Dominican Republic 328, 339
Donoso, Jose 5
Dorfman, Ariel 3
Doty, Alexander 5
dramatic irony 130–132
drug war 404
duality 368, 370
dystopia 85

Ecuador; Ecuadorean 13; 59, 328, 335–336, 339,
342, 368
El Salvador; Salvadoran 51, 59, 83, 339
empowerment 252
epistemology of the butt 420–424
Ericka-Beckman 2
Esquivel, Laura 19
Esteban Muñoz, José 5
Estevam, Carlos 3
Etsy 23, 58
eugenics 134, 136
exotic Other 212–213, 215–216, 218, 226, 373,
421, 423

Facebook 23, 27, 58, 65, 246, 410, 427
fangirls 22
Felipe, Liliana 4
femicide; feminicide 174, 339–340, 394, 404
femininity 105–106, 122, 125, 172–173, 179, 190,
217, 223, 225, 227, 277, 302, 314, 338, 369–370,
372–373, 386–387, 392, 420–421
feminism; feminist 4, 12–13, 61–62, 65, 88,
158, 252, 335–343, 377–378, 382, 387–388,
393–394, 398, 402, 406
feminist arts pedagogy 252–255, 257, 259, 262
Fernández, Bernardo 6
first world 3, 402–403

432

Index

flâneur; virtual, authors; readers 31–34, 36, 38–41
fluidity 59, 87–88, 182, 184, 246, 373–374, 420
Foster, David William 5–6, 8, 12, 273, 288
Foucault, Michel 111–112, 293, 400–401, 404–405
Franco, Jean 2, 4
Fraser Delgado, Celeste 5
Freire, Paulo 255
Frydlewsky, Silvina 7
futurism 87

Gallo, Rubén 2
GamerGate 53
García Bernal, Gael 8, 290
García Canclini, Néstor 2–3
García, Enrique 6
Get the Gringo: How I Spent My Summer Vacation 233–234, 236, 238
Gibson, Mel 231–233, 235, 237–238
Golden Age cinema 3, 8, 169–170, 172, 198–200, 310
Golden Age of Piracy 40
González, Elena 4
González, Reynaldo 2
Gorodischer, Angélica 6
GPS 20, 26, 33
graffiti; *grafiteros* 245–251, 340
Graffiti School *Comunidad*; GSC 252, 254–258, 260
Grand Theft Auto 40–48
graphic narrative 83, 90
graphic novel 74–75, 78, 83, 87–88
gringos; gringo savior 11, 57, 231, 233–238, 316, 325
Guadalupe, Virgen 66, 225, 289
Guatemala; Guatemalan 59, 61, 262, 267, 335–336, 341
Gutiérrez Mouat, Ricardo 2
Guy, Donna 5

Haiti; Haitian 386–387, 390, 392–393
Hands of Stone 315–316, 318–320
Hartman Ortiz, Angélica María 197–201
Havana 32, 35, 40, 42, 250, 327
Hayek, Salma 8, 172, 197
Hayles, N. Katherine 24
hegemonic masculinity 287, 313, 407
hegemony 117, 169–170, 178, 181, 198, 254, 273, 277–278, 300, 313, 364, 400, 404
Heinrich, Annemarie 7
hemisexual 207–208, 219–220
hero; heroes; heroism; hero narratives 71, 72, 74, 75, 76, 78, 80, 81, 89–90, 232–233, 235, 287, 290–291, 297, 311, 316, 318, 320
heroines; countercultural 187, 190
heteronormativity 57, 60, 66, 69, 104, 112, 126, 188, 190, 207, 212, 217, 223, 291, 297, 406, 421, 427
heteropatriarchal; heteropatriarchy 328, 400–401, 404–407

heterosexism; heterosexuality 290, 293, 295, 297
heterosexuality 119, 124, 217–218, 225, 228, 297, 398, 412–413
Hinds, Harold 6
hip-hop; hip hop 13, 267, 335–338, 341–343
Hirsch, Marianne 378–379
historical fiction 71
Hollywood 66, 187, 196–201, 203, 206–209, 213, 215–217, 219–220, 222, 227, 232, 234, 310, 312
home; house 106, 109–111, 178, 180, 209
homoaffectivity 274, 277, 287, 292–293, 297
homoeroticism 103–104, 111, 157, 274, 291, 294, 297
homonormativity 410–412, 414, 417
homophobia 254, 288, 290–291, 416
homosexual; homosexuality 104, 111–112, 156–157, 217, 222–225, 227–229, 232, 297, 374, 412, 414, 416
homosocial; homosociality 273–274, 277, 287–290, 292–293, 296
horror 6, 8, 51, 84, 131, 136, 347, 352–354
Hottentot Venus 422
Howe, Robert 4
hybrid 3, 9–10, 19–25, 66, 72–73, 86, 88, 249, 300, 302, 305, 307–308, 399, 403, 406
hypersexualized bodies 8, 47, 89, 226

identification; identity 46, 52, 54, 68, 72–75, 77–78, 81, 88, 91, 94–95, 98, 104, 106, 111, 113, 115–116, 118, 126, 131, 156, 170, 220, 223, 227, 229, 249, 265, 278, 294, 300, 302, 347, 349, 352–354, 357, 369–371, 386, 388, 390, 399, 407, 411, 420
imaginaries; Amerindian 263, 266, 268
imperialism 2–3, 12, 57, 62, 67–68, 84, 318, 320, 324
India 169
Indian 5, 360
indigeneity 5, 363
indigenous; *indígena* 2, 3, 7, 13, 57, 60, 62, 76–79, 87, 89, 170, 201, 208, 245, 258, 261, 264–266, 270, 307, 336, 356–361, 363, 368–369, 371–372, 374
indigenous futurism 87
Instagram 23, 246
interactive media 31, 35–36
interior design 103–106, 110, 112
intermediality 91, 94
Internet; Web 19–22, 24, 28, 246
Internet trolls 22
internment camps 140–141
intersectionality 57, 69, 71–75, 79–81, 253, 262–263, 336
Irwin, Robert 5
Italian; Italian-American 201, 208
Iturbide, Graciela 7

Japan; Japanese 86, 143–146, 148–149, 197
Japanese Peruvian 140–141

Jesus 129–130, 132–134, 231
Julian Smith, Paul 5

Kantaris, Geoffrey 2
King, Edward 6
Korean 148
Kosofsky Sedgwick, Eve 379
Kristeva, Julia 378, 381
Kummels, Ingrid 7

La Fountain Stokes, Lawrence 5
Lamas, Marta 4
La Sirena 62–63, 66, 69
Latinidad 59
Latin lover 206–209, 211, 213, 215–220, 225–227, 236, 325
League of Legends 48
Lemebel, Pedro 4
lesbian 62, 69, 342, 403
LGBTQ 4, 7–10, 11, 14, 46, 53–54, 64, 202, 206, 222–223
LGBTTTI 410–413, 417
López, Alma 10
López, Ana 7, 8
López, Jennifer 197
López Nieves, Luis 71
Lorde, Audre 159, 389
lotería 10, 57–62, 64–69, 87
Lotería: A Novel 66, 68–69
L'Hoeste, Héctor, 6
Luna, Ilana 8

Machete; *Machete Kills* 237–238
machismo 62, 124–126, 246, 313–314, 316–317, 319–320, 324, 329, 335, 339, 407
machista 336
macho 7, 86, 156, 212, 222–229, 232, 287, 289–291, 293–294, 297, 316–317, 319, 361–362, 372
magical realism 86
male gaze 31, 36, 41, 47, 198, 254, 280, 295
Mali 387
Malinche 224, 289, 361–362
man cave 103–105, 109
Manu NNa 412–417
maricón 410–411, 416–417
Martín-Barbero, Jesús 2
masculatinidad 327
masculinity 14, 46, 72, 85–86, 103–105, 110, 112, 125–126, 206, 209, 212, 218, 220, 222–227, 232–234, 273–274, 276–280, 287–297, 301, 313–316, 319, 323–327, 329–330, 368–370, 372–373, 386–388, 392, 407, 421, 424–426
Masiello, Francine 4
mass culture 9, 19, 21–25, 28, 87
mass media 153–154, 157, 162–163, 196–197, 199, 203, 311, 401
Mastrini, Guillermo 2

Mattelart, Armand 3
Maya; Mayan 263, 266
media landscape 197
melodrama 115–122, 124–127, 414
memory 347, 352, 362, 381, 401; *see also* collective memory
Merino, Ana 6
Mesoamerica; Mesoamerican 66, 88–89
mestiza; mestizaje; mestizo 5, 61, 172, 187–188, 190, 203, 215, 238, 264–266, 270, 300, 360, 368, 371, 401–402
MeToo movement 232
metropolis; metropolitan 81, 177–178, 193, 246–249, 276, 411
Mexico; Mexican; Mexicanidad 3–4, 7–9, 11–14, 48–52, 57–68, 85–86, 91–94, 129, 169–174, 187–190, 192, 196–203, 206, 212–213, 220, 222–238, 250, 254, 264, 267–269, 287–288, 290–292, 296, 310, 314, 316, 318, 335, 339–340, 373, 377, 381–382, 399, 403–407, 410–411, 416–417
Mexican-American 57, 63, 67, 310
millennial 61–62
Mistral, Gabriela 4
Molloy, Sylvia 4–5
Monsiváis, Carlos 3
Moraga, Cherríe 400
Morrison, Toni 238
motherhood 377–383
multiculturalism 401
Mulvey, Laura 291
Muriel, Josefina 4

narrative contract 38–39
Nazi 246, 276, 352
neoliberalism 8, 14, 158–159, 163, 169–172, 177, 192, 400, 403–406, 411
Nicaragua; Nicaraguan 13, 310, 328, 356, 358, 360, 363–364
Niebylski, Dianna 8
Nigeria 387
non-binary 46–47, 50–54, 217, 261
North America 1, 8, 11, 21, 48–49, 71, 233, 235, 411
Nouzeilles, Gabriela 7
Novo López, Salvador 4
Nuyoricans 73

objects; objectivity; objectification 7, 107–112, 116, 118, 120–121, 124–125, 127, 162–163, 191–192, 198, 265, 319, 379
Ohio State University, The 257–258, 261
oral history 139–143
Orozco, Clemente 246
Ortega, Eliana 4
Ortiz, Fernando 2, 3
Ortiz, Renato 2

434

Index

othering 1–3; *see also* exotic Other
O'Bryen, Rory 2
O'Connor, Patrick 8

Pacaembu Stadium 275–280
Panama; Panamanian 315–317, 320
Paraguay 348
Paz, Octavio 5, 224–225, 227, 254
Paz Soldán, Edmundo 6
Pearl Harbor 142
Performativity 13, 223, 368, 407, 420
Perlongher, Néstor 4
personhood 255
Perú 328, 335
Peruvian 144, 148, 270
Piglia, Ricardo 6
pigmentocracies 169–170
Podalsky, Laura 8
Poniatowska, Elena 4
Portuguese 390
post-apocalyptic 83–84, 87, 90
postfeminism 399
post-human 83–88, 90, 403
Prado, Eugenia 6
Pratt, Mary L. 4
Praxis; Feminist art 253, 256, 258
praxis; social 401
Premat, Adriana 6
print culture 19, 22, 200
Prison 199, 233–235, 246, 317
privacy 107
proletarianization 153, 157, 161
Puerto Rican 10
Puerto Rico; Puerto Rican 71–81, 248,
    250, 310
pugilism 311–313
Puig, Manuel 5–6, 10, 115, 118, 156–157
Pulse Nightclub shooting 229

queer; queerness; queering 5, 8, 10, 14, 57, 62,
    88, 90, 152, 158, 170, 207, 222–228, 291, 297,
    350, 398–399, 403, 410–413, 417, 420–421,
    423–427
Quiroga, Horacio 6
Quiroga, José 5

Rama, Angel 2
refugees 390, 393
Richard, Nelly 4
Rios, Diana 7
Rivera, Diego 246
Rockabilly; Rockabilly culture 348–351, 354
Rodriguez, Ileana 2
Rodríguez, Jesusa 4
Rodríguez, Lito 222–223, 225–229
Rossell, Daniela 7
Rowe, William 2–3

Sabato, Ernesto 6
Sáinz Castro, Verónica Judith 200–201
Sánchez Gómez, José Miguel 6
Sánchez Prado, Ignacio 8
Sandoval, Chela 400
Sanz, Joanna Page 6
São Paulo 177–184, 222, 227–228, 273, 275–276,
    279, 300, 386–394
Sarduy, Severo 5
Savage 425
savage hybridity 301–302, 305, 308
Schelling, Vivian 2–3
Schweblein, Samanta 6
science fiction; sci-fi 6, 9–10, 83–84, 86–87, 90,
    129–133, 347–348
Senegal 387
Sense8 11, 206, 222–229
Sesame Street 7
Seva 71, 72
Shakira 197
Sifuentes-Jáuregui, Ben 5
Snapchat 20, 246
social media 23, 28, 46, 48, 53–54, 223, 246, 401
Somos Mujeres Somos Hip Hop 335–343
sound 2, 5, 7, 13, 20, 23, 26–28, 34, 40, 51, 91,
    95–96, 159, 180–181, 187–193, 211, 215, 218,
    231, 233, 236, 310, 312, 314, 316, 318, 335, 347,
    350–351, 354, 360, 412, 424
soundscapes 347
South America 1, 86, 92, 177, 197, 216, 301
space; public space 103, 106–107, 109–111, 130,
    133, 177, 191, 197, 220, 253–256, 259, 261,
    273–274, 336, 368, 379, 389, 401, 403
spectacle 12, 41, 159–160, 323, 325–330, 422
speculative fiction 83–84, 86, 90
Spedding, Alison 6
spirituality 79
Stavans, Ilan 8, 58–59, 75, 245
Steele, Cynthia 4
stereotype 14, 32, 47, 67, 94, 179, 206, 208, 213,
    215–217, 220, 223–224, 227–229, 264, 311, 314,
    319, 323, 325, 330, 350, 373, 399, 413, 425
Stern, Grete 7
Stone, Alison 378
storytelling 6, 10–11, 23, 39, 74, 84, 143, 209, 266,
    311, 386
street art 12
subjectivity 72, 74, 81, 87–88, 116, 118, 125, 163,
    170, 193, 262, 265, 377, 379, 381–382, 401, 403

Tate, Julia 7
Tatum, Charles 6
Taylor, Diana 2
Tellas, Vivi 378–380, 382–383
theatre 377, 379–380, 382–383
things; thing theory 106–107
third world 3

Tiradas al Sol, Lagartijas 378, 381–383
Torres San Martín, Patricia 8
trans; transgender 52, 229, 319, 401, 403
transfeminism; *transfeminismo* 398–401, 407
trauma 13, 66, 72, 81, 347, 352, 363, 386
Treaty of Guadalupe Hidalgo 62
Trevi, Gloria 197, 201–202
Trump, Donald 64–65, 216, 220, 232–233, 236–238, 246, 250, 316
Twitter 20, 23–24, 28, 64, 246

undocumented 47, 52
United States 51–53, 58–60, 66–69, 73, 76, 77, 78, 85–86, 92, 196, 222, 237–238, 253, 276, 292, 310, 324–325, 329–330, 337, 348, 351, 391, 412–413, 422, 427
Uruguay 301

Valencia, Sayak 398–399, 403–407
Valencia Triana, Margarita 398–399, 403–407
vaudeville 420, 423
Venezuela; Venezuelan 323–324, 326, 328, 335, 387
Venkatesh, Vinodh 8
video games; video game player 9–10, 31–32, 35, 39–40, 43, 46–49, 51–54

violence 61
virgin; virginity 124, 202, 349
voyeurism 291

whiteness 324, 329, 420
white privilege 65, 232, 238, 324
white savior 235
Williams, Gareth 2
women 2, 4, 6–7, 11–12, 14, 22, 27, 32, 42, 46, 49–51, 54, 59, 65, 87–88, 90, 98, 103, 105, 106, 115–116, 121–123, 126, 129–130, 169–173, 179–180, 183–184, 190–193, 203, 234, 274, 277, 287, 289, 296, 300–301, 308, 314–315, 318, 336, 338–339, 341–342, 368, 370–372, 377–378, 380, 382–383, 386, 388, 392, 423

xenophobia 390, 420, 423

Youtube 19, 23, 26, 103, 198, 267, 328–329, 351, 412, 414

Zambrano, Mario Alberto 10, 57, 66, 69
Zapata, Luis 4–5
zombie 84